Children's Literature Review

volume 2

Children's Literature Review

Excerpts from Reviews,
Criticism, and Commentary
on Books for Children
and Young People

Carolyn Riley

Editor

Gale Research Company
Book Tower
Detroit, Michigan 48226

Carolyn Riley, *Editor*
Phyllis Carmel Mendelson, *Managing Editor*
Susan Johnson and Gerard J. Senick, *Assistant Editors*

L. E. Wisniewski, *Permissions Assistant*

Arthur Chartow, *Cover Design*

Preface

As publishers of the established reference series *Something About the Author, Contemporary Authors, Contemporary Literary Criticism,* and *Book Review Index*—all reference tools for schools and libraries—we recognize a need for a digest of comment concerning children's literature. Accordingly, we now offer a new reference series, *Children's Literature Review,* in which excerpts of recent reviews of both fiction and nonfiction for children and young people are arranged in a useful collection for teachers, librarians, and researchers in this field.

Children's Literature Review presents significant passages from current published criticism of both contemporary and older works for children. Most of the content of *CLR* is devoted to reviews and criticism of the works of today's authors. Current criticism of the works of authors of an earlier period is excerpted for *CLR,* however, if it is directed to a contemporary audience.

Therefore, no arbitrary time limits are applied to the selection of authors for *CLR.* Rather, the criterion for selection of material is, "Will today's student, teacher, or critic find this pertinent to today's needs?"

As serious students of children's literature know, the very nature of criticism in this field is now being debated widely and fervently. As a result, the criticism of children's literature is itself an emerging discipline. One of the most valuable aspects of the new series is that, by bringing together *all kinds* of critical approaches, *CLR* enables students to evaluate the debate itself.

Each semiannual volume of *CLR* presents criticism of about fory authors and includes excerpts from more than forty-five books and various issues of about thirty-five periodicals. Each excerpt is fully identified for the convenience of readers who may wish to consult the entire chapter, article, or review excerpted.

A short paragraph preceding each author-listing identifies the author by nationality, principal genre, and, where appropriate, major awards received. Also in this section, cross-references are made to *Contemporary Authors* and *Something about the Author*—two of Gale's established bio-bibliographical reference series.

Children's Literature Review listings consist of three parts: general commentary, which deals with whole canons or major themes; excerpts pertaining to individual titles, arranged chronologically under those titles; and locator or index citations for material which, although not excerpted for *CLR,* might be of interest to students or researchers.

Three cumulative indexes appear in each volume of *Children's Literature Review.* In addition to the author and critic indexes familiar to users of *Contemporary Literary Criticism, CLR* includes a title index listing in alphabetical order all works used in the text as subheadings for critical excerpts concerning those particular titles.

CLR Is An On-Going Series

Since *Children's Literature Review* is to be a multi-volume work of indefinite but considerable size, neither this volume nor any *one* subsequent volume should be judged apart from the concept that a single volume is but a part of a larger and more comprehensive whole. In addition to the important writers already covered in Volumes 1 and 2, listings for many other authors, 140 of whom are listed on page vi, are being prepared for future volumes.

If readers wish to suggest authors they would like to have covered in coming volumes, or if they have other suggestions or comments, they are cordially invited to write the editor.

Authors to Appear in
Coming Volumes of *CLR*

Adams, Richard
Alexander, Martha
Andersen, Hans Christian
Ardizzone, Edward
Asimov, Isaac
Bacon, Martha
Baker, Betty
Banner, Angela
Barrie, Sir James M.
Baum, L. Frank
Behn, Harry
Bierhorst, John
Boston, L. M.
Bova, Ben
Chönz, Selena
Christopher, John
Clark, Ann Nolan
Clifton, Lucille
Cohen, Daniel
Collier, James Lincoln
Conford, Ellen
Cooper, Susan
Cormier, Robert
D'Aulaire, Edgar and Ingri
de Brunhoff, Jean
de la Mare, Walter
de Paola, Tomi
Dickinson, Peter
Donovan, John
Eager, Edward
Eckert, Allan W.
Ellis, Ella T.
Enright, Elizabeth
Fall, Thomas
Farmer, Penelope
Feelings, Muriel
Forbes, Esther
Forman, James
Gág, Wanda
Garfield, Leon
Garner, Alan
Gobhai, Mehli
Godden, Rumer
Goffstein, M. B.
Goodall, John S.
Gorey, Edward

Grahame, Kenneth
Harris, Christie
Haskins, James
Haugaard, Erik Christian
Henry, Marguerite
Hinton, S. E.
Hoban, Russell
Houston, James
Hunter, Kristin
Hunter, Mollie
Ipcar, Dahlov
Ishmole, Jack
Iwasaki, Chihiro
Jarrell, Randall
Jeshke, Susan
Juster, Norman
Kellogg, Stephen
Kettlekamp, Larry
Kerr, M. E.
Kjelgaard, Jim
Krumgold, Joseph
Krüss, James
Kuskin, Karla
Latham, Frank
Lavine, Sigmund
Lee, Dennis
Lenski, Lois
Levitin, Sonia
Lewis, C. S.
Liston, Robert
Lofting, Hugh
Macaulay, David
Manley, Seon
Mann, Peggy
Marshall, James
Mayne, William
Mathis, Sharon Bell
McCord, David
McCloskey, Robert
Nesbit, E.
Neville, Emily Cheney
North, Sterling
Norton, Andre
Norton, Mary
Oakley, Graham
Ormondroyd, Edward

Pace, Mildred
Pearce, Philippa
Peck, Robert Newton
Peyton, K. M.
Pinkwater, Manus
Price, Christine
Poole, Josephine
Quackenbush, Robert
Ransome, Arthur
Rau, Margaret
Rey, H. A.
Reeves, James
Richler, Mordecai
Rodgers, Mary
Sasek, Miroslav
Scarry, Richard
Schwartz, Alvin
Selden, George
Sharp, Margery
Snyder, Zilpha Keatley
Stolz, Mary
Taylor, Theodore
Terris, Susan
Thiele, Colin
Trease, Geoffrey
Ungerer, Tomi
Uttley, Alison
Verney, John
Villicana, Eugenio
Viorst, Judith
Waber, Bernard
Wahl, Jan
Watson, Clyde
Wells, Harriet
Wersba, Barbara
White, Robb
Wibberley, Leonard
Yashima, Taro
Yep, Laurence
Yolen, Jane
Zaffo, George
Zimnik, Reiner
Zindel, Paul
Zion, Gene

A

ANNO, Mitsumasa 1926-

A Japanese author and illustrator, Anno is well known for his visual puzzles, which are "pictures to stretch the imagination." (See also *Contemporary Authors,* **Vols. 49-52, and** *Something About the Author,* **Vol. 5.)**

ANNO'S ALPHABET: AN ADVENTURE IN IMAGINATION (1975)

[*Anno's Alphabet* is a] stunning illustrator's showcase but an unreliable alphabet teaching tool. Although by format (8¾″ x 9¾″) and by custom this is intended for pre-readers, it would best be used in junior and senior high school level graphic design courses. . . . Although the draftsmanship is dazzling, youngest children (particularly those with left/right reversal tendencies) will only have their letter confusion reinforced.

> *Lillian N. Gerhardt, in* School Library Journal *(reprinted from* School Library Journal, *January, 1975, published by R. R. Bowker Co., a Xerox company; copyright* © *1975 by Xerox Corporation), January, 1975, pp. 36-7.*

The apt subtitle doesn't do full justice to the ingenuity with which Anno has crafted his solid oak capital letters with their optical illusion effects; or to the richly original object representing a word beginning with the letter on the opposite page; or to the borders, delicately insinuated with plants, creatures, and other things beginning with the same letter. The organic continuity of the art work, predicted in a wordless introduction featuring a tree becoming a book, is sustained in touches like the E's bottom board dropping off to lie uselessly in the border of the F page. The concluding guide to some of the things appearing on each page will clear up any confusion over properly naming some of the less obvious objects. [This is a] clean, subtle ABC worth the long look that will indelibly imprint each letter.

> The Booklist *(reprinted by permission of the American Library Association; copyright 1975 by the American Library Association), January 15, 1975, p. 505.*

Taking a format that is ages old Mr. Anno has used artistry and imagination, his personal tools, to create an alphabet book that is truly his own. . . .

This is an unusually handsome book. The paintings have been done with humor and great skill. The color is rich, restrained and beautifully printed. But Anno doesn't just paint lovely pages, he visualizes ideas. Like J, a jester juggling jacks (Is the jester small? Are the jacks big?) he is full of tricks. There are constant surprises in the drawing that make the eye stop. Where did that line begin? How did it get over there? . . .

This ABC will entertain the very young although it has subtleties they may miss at first. In time they will also appreciate the more complicated of the graphic acrobatics and the mind behind them. And if you already have an ABC never mind. This is not just another one. It is Anno's. It should be yours.

> *Karla Kuskin, in* The New York Times Book Review (© *1975 by The New York Times Company; reprinted by permission), March 9, 1975, p. 8.*

Presumably alphabet books are for children learning the first tool of reading, but [*Anno's Alphabet*] . . . is for anyone who enjoys a beautiful creation. The letters are shown as solid pieces of rough, grained wood; the facing pages show objects beginning with each letter (no words), and each page has a different frame of flowers and animal forms, delicately drawn in black and white. The letters and facing objects are in strong but muted colors, and they are varied and distinctive: an exquisitely scrolled lock, an old map, an odd nutcracker, a tube of orange paint on an easel, a meticulously detailed pen point. Nice to have a child's first alphabet be an introduction to art.

> *Zena Sutherland, in* Bulletin of the Center for Children's Books (© *1975 by the University of Chicago; all rights reserved), April, 1975, pp. 125-26.*

OTHER CITATIONS

Kirkus Reviews, *January 1, 1975, p. 17.*

The Junior Bookshelf, *February, 1975, p. 17.*

Ethel L. Heins, in The Horn Book Magazine, *April, 1975, pp. 134-35.*

Publishers' Weekly, *April 7, 1975, p. 82.*

DR. ANNO'S MAGICAL MIDNIGHT CIRCUS (1972)

After one unnecessary page of unattractively designed text, the witty and inventive creator of *Topsy-Turvies* and *Upside-Downers* introduces a series of unique circus acts.... [Anno] invests each of his doublespread scenes with marvelously inventive details, as, for example, instrumentalists playing familiar household items. The drawings, which use attractive watercolors for figures and backgrounds, are humorous and have a pleasing rhythm.

> *Virginia Haviland, in* The Horn Book Magazine *(copyright © 1973 by The Horn Book, Inc., Boston), February, 1973, p. 36.*

[*Dr. Anno's Magical Midnight Circus* is a splendidly] imaginative picture book which, by a series of visual conjuring tricks, transforms various items left on the kitchen table overnight into the materials for a performance presented in the best flamboyant tradition of circus showmanship. There is no text after the introductory spiel, but the pictures are worth prolonged investigation.

> The Times Literary Supplement *(© Times Newspapers Ltd., 1973), April 6, 1973, p. 389.*

OTHER CITATIONS

Publishers' Weekly, *August 7, 1972, p. 50.*

Carole Hotelling, in School Library Journal, *February, 1973, pp. 55-6.*

TOPSY-TURVIES: PICTURES TO STRETCH THE IMAGINATION (1970)

[*Topsy-Turvies* is an] ingenious, insidious invitation to [look] ... at the apparently impossible—here accomplished by inscrutable little men on page after wordless page.... In a few cases the substantiating details will be more intelligible to Japanese children (for whom this was created) but optical illusions are universal currency and the man in the bottle cap paddling toward the floating bottle on the high seas is equally an enigma everywhere. Chancy ... but worth it for the few who may be highly susceptible.

> Kirkus Reviews *(copyright © 1970 The Kirkus Service, Inc.), March 15, 1970, p. 315.*

Topsy-Turvies skips past the predictable into the boundless world of the improbable; by supplying unusual material for minds to stretch on, it is a ... stimulating, successful book.... [This is] a unique looking book that plays visual tricks on the laws of gravity and perspective.... Some of the incongruities and puzzles will escape young children who also may not have concentration spans long enough to get them through the whole book at one sitting. But these difficulties won't limit the book's use since the pictures—so varied, attractive and curious—also can be appreciated just on the sensory level, or as they were intended but in small quantities, a few at a time.

> *Marilyn R. Singer, in* School Library Journal *(reprinted from* School Library Journal, *April, 1970, published by R. R. Bowker Co., a Xerox company; copyright © 1970 by Xerox Corporation), April, 1970, p. 107.*

[In *Topsy-Turvies*, Anno] takes all the known laws of perspective and neatly twists them—just a little—to form a compilation of intricately detailed visual puzzles.... In a constant flow of motion ..., the elves march or run or dive —may even rest—but are never static figures. Both in their faces and in their bodies they express individual and very human moods; tired, mischievous, or speculative, they are always alive. Although younger children may not be able to discover the "real" solutions to the puzzles the elves demonstrate, they will be captivated by the little figures as they progress through their elaborately conceived world of building blocks, bottles, and playing cards. Older children, too, will be fascinated by the sophisticated perspective puzzles presented in sharply detailed line and watercolor drawings subtly vibrant with color.

> *Sheryl B. Andrews, in* The Horn Book Magazine *(copyright © 1970 by The Horn Book, Inc., Boston), August, 1970, p. 376.*

In *Topsy-Turvies*, which is totally wordless, the gnomish fellows occupy a series of strange landscapes, many scaled by artifacts of our world such as paint tubes and toy cars. The scenes are presented with artful ambiguities of perspective and a duplication of viewpoint and of gravity. Stairs go forever up—or is it down? Ceilings are also floors, and ramps hesitate. The watercolors are nearly all quite beautiful and rich in detail.

> *Philip and Phylis Morrison, in* Scientific American *(copyright © 1971 by Scientific American, Inc.; all rights reserved), December, 1971, p. 110.*

OTHER CITATIONS

Publishers' Weekly, *February 16, 1970, p. 74.*

Jane Yolen, in Book World, *May 17, 1970 (Part 2), p. 4.*

The Booklist, *June 15, 1970, p. 1275.*

Zena Sutherland, in Bulletin of the Center for Children's Books, *December, 1970, p. 53.*

UPSIDE-DOWNERS: MORE PICTURES TO STRETCH THE IMAGINATION (1971)

[In *Upside-Downers*] the illustrations follow the same pattern [as in *Topsy-Turvies*], but there is a text, with the characters (playing cards) arguing about which way is up, and the words printed both in normal fashion and upside down.... The illustrations are, with a few exceptions, just slightly less imaginative than were those of the earlier book, and the text adds little to what is primarily an amusing visual exercise.

> *Zena Sutherland, in* Bulletin of the Center for Children's Books *(© 1972 by The University of Chicago; all rights reserved), January, 1972, p. 70.*

In [this] companion volume to *Topsy-Turvies*, [Mitsumasa Anno] performs further feats of optical ingenuity with the same joyous dexterity that characterized the earlier book. The laws of perspective are still flagrantly defied; and to the inventive pictures, words have been added.... The verbal riddles add another dimension to the visual puzzles;

for the words are printed both upside-down and downside-up so that two people facing each other can read the book as a dialogue. A kind of mad logic runs through the book. . . .

> *Ethel L. Heins, in* The Horn Book Magazine *(copyright © 1972 by The Horn Book, Inc., Boston), February, 1972, p. 39.*

OTHER CITATIONS

Publishers' Weekly, *September 27, 1971, p. 67.*

Kirkus Reviews, *October 15, 1971, p. 1111.*

Philip and Phylis Morrison, in Scientific American, *December, 1971, p. 110.*

The Booklist, *April 1, 1972, p. 670.*

B

BABBITT, Natalie 1932-

Natalie Babbitt is an American author, illustrator, and poet. (See also *Contemporary Authors,* **Vols. 49-52, and** *Something About the Author,* **Vol. 6.)**

THE DEVIL'S STORYBOOK (1974)

[In *The Devil's Storybook*] Natalie Babbitt eschews fire and brimstone and dramatic villainy to portray a petty, proprietary sort of devil, often conniving but frequently outsmarted (even a goat named Walpurgis almost gets the best of him), with a very middle class concern for his image.... Natalie Babbitt's traditional themes abound in elegant twists, and she polishes even the straightest to a pleasing, most un-Angelic perfection.

> Kirkus Reviews *(copyright © 1974 The Kirkus Service, Inc.), July 1, 1974, p. 679.*

A masterful Devil's advocate, Natalie Babbitt presents ten brief testimonials to Satan's unflagging gusto for dirty tricks.... Most of his schemes end on a note of "Curses, foiled again!" but occasionally the Devil does score a well-won point.... There are a couple of clinkers—an overly long wild goose chase for "The Harps of Heaven" and a sappy story about "A Very Pretty Lady" who relinquishes her looks for love—but these are minor transgressions. Neatly framed pen sketches of beefy peasants and roguish inmates of Hell add folktale flavor and provide further proof of this Devil's fallibility (whether he's disguised as a fairy godmother, a bearded elder, or a mouse, his forked tail always gives him away).

> *Jane Abramson, in* School Library Journal *(reprinted from* School Library Journal, *October, 1974, published by R. R. Bowker Co., a Xerox company; copyright © 1974 by Xerox Corporation), October, 1974, p. 102.*

[*The Devil's Storybook* contains ten] comic stories about the machinations of the Devil to increase the population of his realm. He is not always successful and, despite his clever ruses, meets frustration as often as his intended victims do.... The stories are delightful in their narrative fluency, full of surprises, and frequently spiced with dashes of Saki-like mischief. A suitably wicked but hilarious black-and-white drawing centered in a circle accompanies each tale.

> *Paul Heins, in* The Horn Book Magazine *(copyright © 1974 by The Horn Book, Inc., Boston), October, 1974, p. 134.*

Ten short stories about a middle-aged, vain, and rather paunchy devil are imaginative, varied, and engagingly illustrated. There's some variation in the solidity of the plots, but the quiet humor and vitality of the writing style are ubiquitous.

> *Zena Sutherland, in* Bulletin of the Center for Children's Books *(© 1974 by the University of Chicago; all rights reserved), December, 1974, p. 58.*

OTHER CITATIONS

Publishers' Weekly, *July 1, 1974, p. 82.*

DICK FOOTE AND THE SHARK (1967)

The credibility gap is somewhat strained in this old-fashioned narrative poem.... Wilder and funnier samples of [the] verses than we are given would enhance the book.... However, the story is told in jaunty quatrains with lots of bouncing inner rhymes that are good to read aloud, and the pictures—in black and white with a wash of bayberry green—are trim, neat, seaworthy.

> *Eve Merriam, in* The New York Times Book Review *(© 1967 by The New York Times Company; reprinted by permission), July 2, 1967, p. 16.*

There isn't enough nonsense [in *Dick Foote and the Shark*] to spread out over the 46 monotonous stanzas of galumphing verse it takes to tell the simple story. The illustrations are more successful than the verse; sharp ink drawings set against a wash of green sea subtly poke fun at the inhabitants of 19th-century Cape Cod.

> *Elinor Cullen, in* School Library Journal *(reprinted from* School Library Journal, *September, 1967, published by R. R. Bowker Co., a Xerox company; copyright © 1967 by Xerox Corporation), September, 1967, p. 159.*

OTHER CITATIONS

Kirkus Service, *June 1, 1967, p. 639.*

Zena Sutherland, in Bulletin of the Center for Children's Books, *October, 1967, pp. 21-2.*

GOODY HALL (1971)

[Natalie Babbitt] has concocted a juvenile Gothic that is less a take-off than an affectionate dalliance with the convention. All the traditional ingredients are here: a young hero hired as tutor in an isolated, imposing house; servants from the village who provide a gossipy commentary on the goings-on; an empty tomb, a seance, and a hollow statue filled with stolen jewels; a double glimpsed in a night garden; and a bang-up Victorian happy ending replete with laughter, tears, reunited family and neat resolutions. The preposterous coincidences of the plot occur here in the ludicrous parallels between the adventures of Hercules and those of the hero, an unimpressive, "baggy" young man who misquotes Shakespeare and wryly endures the name of Hercules Feltwright. Another *Delicious* blend of style, wit and adventure.

> Kirkus Reviews *(copyright © 1971 The Kirkus Service, Inc.), April 15, 1971, p. 431.*

The whole story has a dreamlike, allegorical quality that perfectly matches the setting, yet it is not without humor, and the mystery of Midas Goody's disappearance, when finally revealed, is entirely plausible.... [When] legend and disguises are put aside at last, the solution is warm and satisfying. An imaginative story for discriminating readers.

> *Sarah Law Kennerly, in* School Library Journal *(reprinted from* School Library Journal, *May, 1971, published by R. R. Bowker Co., a Xerox company; copyright © 1971 by Xerox Corporation), May, 1971, p. 82.*

Natalie Babbitt spins a web for her story ["Goody Hall"]. She sets us down in a delicious English countryside, shows us a frosted sugarcake of a house (suggesting dark secrets), introduces a gypsy, a baggy-panted tutor . . ., a poor little rich boy . . . and his strange mother. . . . Of course, we're caught in Mrs. Babbitt's web and we expect to be lost and bewildered and perhaps a little scared before she sees fit to release us.

But it doesn't work out that way. Mrs. Babbitt stops her spinning to give a long explanation of how Hercules got his name and how, like the mythological hero, he performed his labors. She tells us stories about Mott Snave, master thief and terror of the countryside, who unfortunately played his big scenes before the book opened. Meanwhile, we are in Mrs. Babbitt's web, and it's a pretty web; but in the end we feel the way the Goodys did about their house. Prettiness isn't everything.

> *Jean Fritz, in* The New York Times Book Review *(© 1971 by The New York Times Company; reprinted by permission), May 2, 1971 (Part 2), p. 18.*

OTHER CITATIONS

Publishers' Weekly, *April 19, 1971, pp. 47-8.*

Selma G. Lanes, in Book World, *May 9, 1971 (Part 2), p. 4.*

The Booklist, *July 15, 1971, p. 954.*

Virginia Haviland, in The Horn Book Magazine, *August, 1971, pp. 380-81.*

Zena Sutherland, in Saturday Review, *September 18, 1971, p. 49.*

Jean Stafford, in The New Yorker, *December 4, 1971, p. 199.*

KNEEKNOCK RISE (1970)

["Kneeknock Rise"] is thoughtfully written and written to provoke thought. To an extent it will succeed. It does not, however, touch the feelings very deeply, beyond arousing uneasiness. There's a coldness about the treatment of the characters, who are not an altogether reassuring company to begin with. They represent attitudes. Egan is given more warmth and more reality than the others. . . . The child reader will be aware that in the long run the Megrimum is symbolic. The story is about the mysterious, but more than that it's about belief in the mysterious. Do we believe in the Megrimum, or don't we? By placing the burden of final judgment on the child reader, the author may be wiser than she thinks. Children do know well some things that we have forgotten.

The drawings by the author are a good deal more serene than her story. Their gentle, flowing line has created lovely animals in particular; beside them, the human beings look curiously static.

> *Eudora Welty, in* The New York Times Book Review *(© 1970 by The New York Times Company; reprinted by permission), May 24, 1970 (Part 2), p. 45.*

[*Kneeknock Rise* is] a wonderfully fluent fable about man's need to have something to believe in. . . . [It] is simple and its meaning precise enough: Science cannot or will not explain all. The strength of this tale is in Natalie Babbitt's clean, modern, very confident telling. For children, especially, this is fine writing: there are no distracting posturings in her style, yet she does show style indeed.

> *Jean C. Thomson, in* School Library Journal *(reprinted from* School Library Journal, *September, 1970, published by R. R. Bowker Co., a Xerox company; copyright © 1970 by Xerox Corporation), September, 1970, p. 156.*

[In *Kneeknock Rise*] the Insteppers refused to give up their mythical Megrimum, and Egan had learned a lesson about people: don't confuse them by presenting facts; they prefer their fancies. The pithy message, the moments of humor, and the freshness of the story are made more enjoyable by a smooth and lively writing style.

> *Zena Sutherland, in* Bulletin of the Center for Children's Books *(© 1970 by the University of Chicago; all rights reserved), December, 1970, p. 54.*

OTHER CITATIONS

Kirkus Reviews, *May 15, 1970, p. 551.*

Ruth Hill Viguers, in The Horn Book Magazine, *June, 1970, p. 295.*

The Booklist, *September 15, 1970, p. 99.*

The New York Times Book Review, *February 10, 1974, p. 30.*

PHOEBE'S REVOLT (1968)

Against a backdrop of 1904 New York and Edith Wharton gentility, Phoebe does her thing with style and wit. Girls who've balked at bows will sympathize; parents who spot the Gibson girl-gaslight details will have the first and last laugh.

> Kirkus Service *(copyright © 1968 The Kirkus Service, Inc.), June 15, 1968, p. 641.*

The story [of *Phoebe's Revolt*] is told in cheerful verse, with a note of mock Victorian floridity that is delightfully in accord with the illustrations. Dripping with decorated and decorous ladies, the pictures are full of nostalgia-evoking details—pier glasses, leaded windows, gas jets, overhead flush tanks, wicker doll carriages, and an incredibly elegant toilet bowl.

> *Zena Sutherland, in* Saturday Review *(copyright © 1968 by Saturday Review, Inc.; reprinted with permission), November 9, 1968, p. 68.*

OTHER CITATIONS

Zena Sutherland, in Bulletin of the Center for Children's Books, *March, 1969, p. 106.*

THE SEARCH FOR DELICIOUS (1969)

The definition of this well-constructed story, combining fine imagery, humor, strong characterizations, legend, and an unobtrusive theme of good versus evil is: a good book for children hungry for light entertainment.

> *Doris Solomon, in* School Library Journal *(reprinted from* School Library Journal, *May, 1969, published by R. R. Bowker Co., a Xerox company; copyright © 1969 by Xerox Corporation), May, 1969, p. 8.*

This is a lovely story with an orphan boy and a king, a prime minister, and a mermaid missing her magic whistle. There's also a woldweller (who lives in a tree), dwarfs—and a happy ending. You know from the very beginning this is a happy book; so it must have a happy ending. The suspense is how *that* is going to happen in the face of all the obstacles young Gaylen meets. . . .

Gaylen's feats are adventures of the spirit as well as of the flesh, which must succeed because we do not doubt them. The telling . . . is spirited and humorous, sensitive without ever being sad—in the key of the minstrel's song, "Be gay and sing! You may as well."

> *John Lawson, in* The New York Times

Book Review *(© 1969 by The New York Times Company; reprinted by permission), May 4, 1969 (Part 2), p. 34.*

[This] allegorical story points up the foolishness of a petty argument that leads to a full-scale conflict. . . . The writing is distinguished by an immediate clarity and true poetry—with the metaphoric descriptions, appropriate names for characters (Hemlock, the arch-villain brother of the queen; Whimsey Mildew, the housewife), and interpolated songs in the manner of some of the great fantasies. Touches of spoofing fun and the homeliness of everyday existence lighten the succession of dramatic incidents. A wholly delightful story.

> *Virginia Haviland, in* The Horn Book Magazine *(copyright © 1969 by The Horn Book, Inc., Boston), August, 1969, p. 407.*

[*The Search for Delicious* is a] fanciful tale of a quest and a kingdom, of age-old dwarves and a child mermaid, and particularly of the efforts of a boy courier to save his country. . . . The style is light and pleasant, the humor minimal; the fantasy and romance are smoothly blended, but the tale moves slowly; although some of the discussion about the search for Delicious occurs throughout the story, most of it is concentrated at the beginning and the end, so that it seems merely an amusing idea that serves as a rather contrived framework for the romantic fantasy.

> *Zena Sutherland, in* Bulletin of the Center for Children's Books *(© 1969 by the University of Chicago; all rights reserved), October, 1969, p. 21.*

This is a fairytale in modern style; the Prologue, however, belongs to ancient myth. There are many traditional features of the Quest, but the subject of the search is disappointingly trivial, amid all the authentic trappings, and the author's delightful delicate decorations. . . . The combination of plot-level and styles succeeds on the whole, because of the crisp humorous writing and the beauty of vivid poetic phrases and descriptions.

> The Junior Bookshelf, *June, 1975, pp. 191-92.*

The Search for Delicious is a neo-fairy-tale, with a touch of Thurber in the way wit and irony persuade one to take a fresh look at chivalry and magic. . . . For Gaylen, the Prime Minister's Special Assistant, the ride through the kingdom collecting opinions looks like being a holiday and proves an exciting and rewarding adventure: for Hemlock, the Queen's disaffected and ambitious brother, it provides the chance to foment rebellion. The intellectually-conceived mixture of politics and magic, the juxtaposition of gossiping peasants, mysterious woldweller, friendly minstrel and unhappy mermaid, make a captivating story told in a style that is wittily apt and attractively lilting in tone. The book is elegantly produced and each chapter is signalled by a decorative initial letter incorporated in a tiny, delicate and expressive drawing.

> *Margery Fisher, in her* Growing Point, *September, 1975, pp. 2686-87.*

OTHER CITATIONS

Pamela T. Cleaver, in Children's Book Review, *Summer, 1975, p. 64.*

THE SOMETHING (1970)

There's sly amusement here—and perhaps a message? That just as we are afraid of nameless fears, so too, are nameless fears, in their dreams, afraid of us. Or maybe we're being told something about the dawning of the Age of Aquarius—and love? . . . Anyway, whatever the point, the story represents another unique Babbitt creation. It's got "something."

> *George A. Woods, in* The New York Times Book Review *(© 1970 by The New York Times Company; reprinted by permission), October 25, 1970, p. 38.*

Throughout [*The Something*], the pictures provide most of the fun—e.g., the one showing Mylo's mom, all humpbacked, toothy, gorilla-armed, and pansy-hatted, going shopping for him. But the book as a whole is a pleasure, with every line in picture and prose showing the author's great understanding of the nature of Things and of fears concerning them.

> *Jean C. Thomson, in* School Library Journal *(reprinted from* School Library Journal, *January, 1971, published by R. R. Bowker Co., a Xerox company; copyright © 1971 by Xerox Corporation), January, 1971, p. 39.*

Illustrated with drawings that endow the grotesque Mylo and his mother with endearing charm and printed on soft yellow pages except for the dream sequence which appears on gray pages, the clever, ironic story interprets common childhood fears of the dark in a way that should prove highly amusing to many small children.

> The Booklist *(reprinted by permission of the American Library Association; copyright 1971 by the American Library Association), January 1, 1971, p. 370.*

OTHER CITATIONS

Publishers' Weekly, *October 12, 1970, p. 55.*

Kirkus Reviews, *October 15, 1970, p. 1137.*

Zena Sutherland, in Saturday Review, *January 23, 1971, p. 70.*

TUCK EVERLASTING (1975)

At a time when death has become an acceptable, even voguish subject in children's fiction, Natalie Babbitt comes through with a stylistic gem about living forever. . . . Though the mood is delicate, there is no lack of action, with the Tucks (previously suspected of witchcraft) now pursued for kidnapping Winnie. . . . Though Babbit makes the family a sad one, most of their reasons for discontent are circumstantial and there isn't a great deal of wisdom to be gleaned from their fate or Winnie's decision not to share it. However the compelling fitness of theme and event and the apt but unexpected imagery (the opening sentences compare the first week in August when this takes place to "the highest seat of a Ferris wheel when it pauses in its

turning") help to justify the extravagant early assertion that had the secret about to be revealed been known at the time of the action, the very earth "would have trembled on its axis like a beetle on a pin."

> Kirkus Reviews *(copyright © 1975 The Kirkus Service, Inc.), October 15, 1975, p. 1181.*

Immortality has been a divine right, a promise of bliss, a punishment. In Natalie Babbitt's "Tuck Everlasting" it is just an accident. Waters of eternal life have been bubbling up and seeping away, unpolluted and undiscovered in a primeval wood outside the village of Treegap. At the end of the 18th century a pioneering family called Tuck (and their horse) drank of the waters. They appear to have been the only ones ever. They are nice people; their unshakable niceness is perhaps the only really unlikely part of the story, and the condition of its being a story for children. . . .

It's not what happens but what happens as a result *of* what happens that makes it a good story. . . .

The story is macabre and moral, exciting and excellently written. It has no absolute end, because Time hasn't. Not so very long ago the Tucks revisiting Treegap, found that the wood had been bulldozed through; the spring had vanished. And Winnie Foster? The younger Tuck son, forever aged 17 had wanted her to wait until the same age, then drink the springwater and be eternally his sweetheart. But the Tucks find her tombstone: she grew up and married and had children and died in 1948.

"Good girl," said Pa Tuck.

> *Phillippa Pearce, in* The New York Times Book Review *(© 1975 by The New York Times Company; reprinted by permission), November 16, 1975, p. 32.*

With great care Babbitt crafts words into places, people, and events that seem to have emerged from an untrampled imagination. She catches the whole nature of a thing with one deft twist—"a herd of cows who were, to say the least, relaxed." . . . With its serious intentions and light touch the story [of *Tuck Everlasting*] is, like the Tucks, timeless.

> *Betsy Hearne, in* The Booklist *(reprinted by permission of the American Library Association; copyright 1975 by the American Library Association), December 1, 1975, p. 510.*

*   *   *

BAWDEN, Nina (pseudonym of Nina Mary Mabey Kark) 1925-

Nina Bawden is an Englishwoman who writes for both children and adults. (See also *Contemporary Authors*, Vols. 17-18, and *Something About the Author*, Vol. 4.)

GENERAL COMMENTARY

[Nina Bawden] is especially good at intermingling children of divergent cultures and social groups; and she is sensitive to the plight of the underprivileged. And one feels that her stories, containing varying mixtures of intrigue and suspense, as well as interestingly defined characters, could be made into exciting films for children.

Ethel L. Heins, in The Horn Book Magazine *(copyright © 1971 by The Horn Book, Inc., Boston), October, 1971, p. 482.*

We see a real world in Nina Bawden's books, stretching from junk yards to prim, over-immaculate front parlours. Yet it would be facile to place this author in any simple 'social realist' category, since at the same time she is also taken up with the theme of fantasy, both in her characters' lives and in the stories themselves as she writes them. The result, then, is neither fantasy nor realism, but the tension between them. It could be argued that this type of tension runs through all fiction, but it is particularly evident in the works of Nina Bawden and one reason, I would suggest, why they are so particularly relevant for a young audience. (p. 35)

[All] Nina Bawden's books end with a more or less satisfying round-up—the 'Day of Judgement' Chesterton once demanded for the final chapter of good children's literature, where obvious villains are despatched and the good regroup their forces, free now from danger. These are not necessarily the pat happy endings of romantic fiction—characters may be more suitably rewarded here by a change of attitude rather than fortune—but even so, Nina Bawden stays within a conventional framework when it comes to finishing a story. . . . But most children are not quite ready for the implications of a truly amoral universe, where natural justice can seem so very scant; they need sustaining myths as well as glimpses of the truth, and so often Nina Bawden achieves this balance with great skill, for her books are both wise and immensely entertaining. (pp. 37-8)

Happy endings apart, which I think can be justified when writing for a younger audience, there is otherwise very little tolerance of sloppy, unreal thinking in Nina Bawden's books. . . . [Her] characters are constantly made to recognize that most things don't work out easily 'like something in a book'—a comment she can get away with because her books have that quality of the real, so that readers forget that this, after all, is a story too. . . . If Nina Bawden's young characters get into trouble with the police, however noble their motives, there is no twinkle-eyed Inspector to bail them out and promise to come to tea next day. Instead, it's the real works: police station, worried parents and horrible embarrassment. When a crook is caught, it's usually a messy unheroic business, leaving you feeling sick in the stomach. (pp. 38-9)

Telling the truth to children, or at least some of it, could sound rather a severe brief for any writer, and yet Nina Bawden's books could never be described as finger-wagging morality tales. At the same time, she also tells the truth about children too, and so the characters we get could never themselves fit easily into any tidy moral parable. Instead, they are as rumbustious, romantic, coarse, funny, bad-tempered, and long-suffering as the real thing. (p. 39)

[Nina Bawden's] understanding of children and perception of some of their typical predicaments are based not on theory or any particular educational premise, but on her honesty, her skills as a writer and an overall feeling for childhood that is unsentimental and observant. In her writing, children may indeed recognize some of their own dilemmas, but much else besides that has nothing to do with psychology at all: the joy at producing your own artificial belches, the irritation with adults who put on bright, insincere voices for you, the boredom of school or much of childhood. . . . (pp. 40-1)

If she has one flaw for adult readers, it could be that some of Nina Bawden's characterizations are a little repetitive. One moody, unpredictable character tends to be balanced, in book after book, by another more sober child who may also make mistakes but on the whole sees reason, and eventually makes everyone else recognize it too. But I don't think this is a fault children would be worried by; if a writer has as one aim to explain some important things to readers, the writing may have to become very explicit at times, with the sober character acting as commentator and judge. In the same way, underlying emotions are sometimes signified as clearly as if by semaphore: people scowl, turn pink, or their eyes suddenly brighten. . . . But if we don't get some of the silences of half spoken sentiments of, say, a William Mayne novel, there are quite as many compensations: a bright, comprehensible world, full of dialogue and details that immediately hit home, and odd anecdotes casually thrown in that another writer might have saved for a whole chapter:

> Simon said, 'My Uncle Horace had his car struck by lightning once. He said everything went blue, and smelt of seaweed.'

> There's a place I know in Ireland where they simply build the wall across the road: when a car wants to go through, they knock the wall down and build it up again.

All Nina Bawden's books have a definite quality: the humour is abundant and never forced, and there are always moments of great pace and excitement. It would be quite wrong, though, to give the impression that her writing is simply and breezily extrovert. Her characters are convincing, complex people; although each story resolves itself, there are also some less tangible losses: the end of childhood, in *The White Horse Gang,* or the coming to terms with what you can't have, in *The Runaway Summer.* Although some things are explained, others remain mysterious: Perdita's strange powers, in *The Witch's Daughter,* or the vision Abe saw—or imagined—on his ride through Gibbet Wood in *The White Horse Gang.* (pp. 42-3)

[*Carrie's War* is] probably her best [book for children]. Of her earlier work, *The Secret Passage* [published in America as *The House of Secrets*] and *On the Run* [published in America as *Three on the Run*] sometimes suffer slightly through being too full of incident, so that the climax becomes an almost breathless tying together of loose ends. *The Witch's Daughter,* although so good in many ways, need never have got caught up with unconvincing jewel thieves, and perhaps the escaped wolf in *The White Horse Gang* is a little too strong for an otherwise perceptive and understated story of children just around adolescence. In her later books, however, the drama has tended to come as much from the personalities of the characters themselves, and the way they relate to each other; there are still exciting plots, but perhaps not so determinedly adventurous as before. It is the brooding presence of Mr Evans the grocer in *Carrie's War,* bullying his sister and the evacuees yet also lonely and excluded from their happiness, that supplies the greatest drama and excitement, despite the slightly spooky sub plot. The only moment this fine novel falters is when it does start to approach some of the business of melodrama, with missing wills and suspicions of underhand dealings. The ending is sad but somehow right, and after the last page has finished clearly a great deal more has still got to happen—no tidy resolutions here, but the promise that things might settle themselves. (p. 44)

> *Nicholas Tucker, "Getting Used to Things as They Are: Nina Bawden as a Children's Novelist," in* Children's Literature in Education *(© 1974, APS Publications, Inc., New York; reprinted by permission of the publisher), No. 13, 1974, pp. 35-44.*

CARRIE'S WAR (1973)

The murky atmosphere of the eccentric country household and the nitpicking routines dictated by Mr. Evans' compulsive thrift are adroitly contrasted [in *Carrie's War*], but the real reward is Carrie's insight into the loneliness of an unsympathetic old man. The realities of chilblains and fried bread in a Welsh mining town and the mysteries of that remembered "dark green, silent place" in the valley overgrown by yew trees are fused into a story of hushed suspense and emotional complexity.

> Kirkus Reviews *(copyright © 1973 The Kirkus Service, Inc.), May 1, 1973, p. 514.*

By deft handling of the story-within-a-story, [Nina Bawden] has produced a sophisticated blend of diverse elements without sacrificing the credibility of the young heroine [in *Carrie's War*]. The homely but frustrating details of everyday life during wartime—life relatively unthreatened by immediate danger but affected by political events—add another element to the developing body of literature dealing with childhood experiences during World War II.

> *Mary M. Burns, in* The Horn Book Magazine *(copyright © 1973 by The Horn Book, Inc., Boston), June, 1973, p. 275.*

Seven years ago I remarked in these pages that "Nina Bawden writes about childhood as though she had never left it. As though, indeed, she were still exploring its terrain —scraping her knees and forgetting to blow her nose." I feel that those words are still true, but the tenor of children's books has changed so radically in the past decade that "Carrie's War" left me oddly disappointed—as though a promise had not been kept.

The promise I think, is in the nature of Miss Bawden's talent—which is huge—and the disappointment comes from the fact that this talent does not seem to have grown. Children's books, for good or ill, are now so wide-open in their approach to life that anything can happen between their pages—and usually does. Miss Bawden, meanwhile, is still writing a particular kind of English mystery in which the reader is scared, but not too scared, in which people are evil, but not too evil, and in which happy endings abound. Perhaps it is unkind to criticize her for conventionality, but one knows that she is better than this and longs for something wilder, more daring, more personal.

Her characterizations are indeed well done, and the reader is genuinely moved by Carrie and Nick—a brother and sister who have been evacuated to Wales during the World War II bombing of London. And if the children are real, even more convincing are Mr. Evans and his sister Auntie Lou, who take the youngsters in and offer them a home. Mr. Evans is so mean that he forbids Carrie and Nick to go upstairs more than twice a day (lest they wear out the carpet) and he is so fanatically "Chapel" that an air of leaden religion hangs over the house. But he is a villain with a troubled heart and by far the most interesting person in the book.

As to the mystery, it concerns the children's involvement with Mr. Evans's other sister, Mrs. Gotobed, who is an invalid and lives in a haunted house along with a kindly witch and a simpleton. This latter character, Mister Johnny, might have walked directly out of a Truman Capote short story and fascinated me no end. Alas, there is not enough of him or of anyone else, since all these figures take second place to the plot. How one wishes that Miss Bawden would forget about plot and step through the looking glass of herself—where the real mysteries wait.

> *Barbara Wersba, in* The New York Times Book Review *(© 1973 by The New York Times Company; reprinted by permission), June 3, 1973, p. 8.*

Carrie's War is not much about the War itself. The evacuation of Carrie and Nick from London is little more than a device to get them into the different, not just the safer, environment of Wales. From that point their encounters with other people, normal or eccentric, could have occurred at any time and anywhere; the War raises its head mainly through the sporadic contacts with their mother who has evacuated herself to Scotland. The real story is sandwiched between Carrie's initial visit to Wales and her return thirty years later, and an entertaining story it is, full of incidents and characters whose sense of humour, though at times disguised, makes all concerned human. The Welsh background is skilfully used, though in convincing moderation, and Faith Jaques' illustrations have just the right flavour of old-fashionedness which makes them authentic for readers of another generation.

> The Junior Bookshelf, *August, 1973, pp. 262-63.*

When someone takes time to count, Nina Bawden's body of work will be seen as the remarkable achievement it is. We are already conditioned to its excellence by the strong plot and dialogue combination. [*Carrie's War*] is one of her best. . . . (Read Hester Burton's *In Time of Trial* alongside it to see where the different preoccupations lie.) The children in the story are drawn with the vividness we have come to expect; the 'special' this time is an inarticulate boy. There is also Councillor Evans, Carrie's host who has one sister who has risen in the world and the other who keeps his house. Mrs. Bawden's gift is the transformation of recognizable adult and child stereotypes (the dotty old lady, the frightened spinster, the intelligent unathletic boy) that children need into memorable characters. The added dimension is the special sense of locale, enhanced by Faith Jaques's fine drawings. One feels the small-timeness of the surroundings pressing in on the children while the war seems a distant adult preoccupation. The moods vary from the comic to the intensely sad. The reader is brought close to the action because the writer is close to Carrie. [*Carrie's War* is] excellent.

> *Margaret Meek, in* The School Librarian, *September, 1973, pp. 259-60.*

The narrative [in *Carrie's War*] is slight, but the characters are so alive and real that all interest is in them; the excitement is in the people rather than the events, and in the dialogue, which is sharply witty. Nina Bawden's great achievement is to handle these extraordinary characters, and to reach a grand promise of hope in the ending, without sentimentality or melodrama. The only disappointing feature is Albert, . . . a lively enough character but too much of a stereotype. A mature book, this, concerned with doubt and certainty, insight and sympathy. . . .

> *M. H. Miller, in* Children's Book Review *(© 1973 Five Owls Press Ltd.; all rights reserved), September, 1973, p. 111.*

A story of two children, evacuated from London during the Blitz and sent to a small Welsh town, is told with consummate skill and deft characterization. . . . Not until she visited, years later, with her own children, did Carrie learn all the intricacies of that unhappy time. The story is taut in construction, notable for its cast, compassionate in its treatment of the harsh Mr. Evans as it is of the gentle retarded man who lived at the farm.

> *Zena Sutherland, in* Bulletin of the Center for Children's Books *(© 1973 by the University of Chicago; all rights reserved), September, 1973, p. 3.*

[Nina Bawden uses a] clean, uncluttered but well-sculptured style that carries [*Carrie's War*] along easily. . . . [It] takes young readers into an area too often side-stepped in books for them: the warring, irrational relationships adults are prone to fall into, and the shameful way children are used by them to fight their emotionally damaging battles. . . . [That's] an adventure it takes a writer of the rare gifts of Nina Bawden to tell to children with the kind of child-appealing drama that will keep them not just reading with unalloyed pleasure, but with awakened understanding as well.

> *Aidan Chambers, in* The Horn Book Magazine *(copyright © 1974 by The Horn Book, Inc., Boston), June, 1974, pp. 266, 268.*

Carrie's War (1973) is Miss Bawden's best book for children up to the time of its appearance. . . . The web of relationships among Carrie, her younger brother Nick, and the people in whose lives they become involved, is skilfully and finely spun; and the book is technically excellent in the way it brings this (to children) distant past into contact with the present, and leaves the way unobtrusively open for the reader to supply a happy ending if so minded.

> *John Rowe Townsend, in his* Written for Children: An Outline of English-Language Children's Literature *(copyright © 1965, 1974 by John Rowe Townsend; reprinted by permission of J. B. Lippincott Company), revised edition, Lippincott, 1974, p. 269.*

Nina Bawden gives her characters reality not by describing them but by letting us see what they think of one another and how much they understand. We learn about Nick by noticing from his remarks, to Mr Evans particularly, that he has a shrewd, detached way of knowing what people are like because he is not old enough to be confused by their inconsistencies, whereas Carrie, although she dislikes Mr Evans for his meanness and his bullying manner and sympathizes with Auntie Lou, can despise the one for her passive resistance and can feel sorry for the other because he is tired and despondent and over-worked. We learn what Albert Sandwich, that erudite schoolboy, is like by the way he teases Carrie for her romantic guesses about people and their motives, and by the way Hepzibah teases him. There is a continual shift of focus in the story as its complex plot is carried along by way of conversations and unspoken words and thoughts; the book has an extraordinarily close texture and gives a remarkable illusion of reality.

> *Margery Fisher, in her* Who's Who in Children's Books: A Treasury of the Familiar Characters of Childhood *(copyright © 1975 by Margery Fisher; reprinted by permission of Holt, Rinehart and Winston), Holt, Rinehart and Winston, 1975, p. 63.*

OTHER CITATIONS

Publishers' Weekly, *May 28, 1973, p. 40.*

The Booklist, *June 15, 1973, p. 987.*

Sister Avila, in School Library Journal, *September, 1973, p. 138.*

Ann Thwaite, in Children's Literature in Education, *No. 14, 1974, p. 20.*

A HANDFUL OF THIEVES (1967)

The five children [in *A Handful of Thieves*] are well differentiated and their problems with the adult world are subtly suggested; they are likable, lively and entirely credible throughout. Only the thief is caricatured—and quite entertainingly—for amongst its other virtues the book portrays lower class people and scenes without the tone of patronage which mars most books attempting to show how the "other half" lives. This is not about some "other half", but about people. The dialogue and Fred's terms of reference ring true throughout, the background is the shabbier section of an industrial town but there is none of the consciousness of slumming shown by many authors now struggling to depict the proletariat who never shared their own world of nannies and pony clubs. Like a good adult mystery, this succeeds as light entertainment and leaves the reader with several new ideas to think over as well.

> The Junior Bookshelf, *October, 1967, p. 318.*

[*A Handful of Thieves* contains excellent] characterization, a thorough-going mystery, fast action, enough suspense . . ., and convincing dialogue. . . . Miss Bawden rightly makes no concessions toward the argument that it is all right to do to others what they did to you, while she keeps an even balance between tough-minded independence and family warmth and security. She can, when necessary, even invoke sentiment without being embarrassing.

Patience M. Daltry, in The Christian Science Monitor *(reprinted by permission from* The Christian Science Monitor; © 1967 The Christian Science Publishing Society; all rights reserved), November 2, 1967, p. B15.

[*A Handful of Thieves* portrays] a most distinctive gang, with each child a different person to his parents and to his peers. The story bounces along, so flexible is the prose, so deliberate the telling. Young readers will enjoy the energy of the characters and adults admire the craftsmanship which conveys the quizzical self-regard of the story-teller, who varies between being totally engrossed in his narrative and humorously portraying his friends. A considerable achievement.

The Times Literary Supplement *(© Times Newspapers Ltd., 1967), November 30, 1967, p. 1151.*

[In *A Handful of Thieves*] Nina Bawden does manage to give a convincing illusion of reality to a story of kids living in a city. Because this is fiction and not real life, play gets mixed up with the sternest facts to produce a story with its share of tension and drama. Its interest lies, however, mostly in its picture of a youthful gang and their relations with the adult world. . . .

What puts life into [a] faded formula is Nina Bawden's skill in drawing recognizable children and her restraint in requiring of them no more than they can reasonably perform. . . . The social manners of the story are impeccable; all the children have the right instincts, and the frontier between them and the adult world is clearly demarcated. *A Handful of Thieves* comes dangerously near to being a model children's novel, and such rarely prove to be working models. It is saved by the robust commonsense shared by the characters and their creator.

Marcus Crouch, in his The Nesbit Tradition: The Children's Novel in England 1945-1970 *(© Marcus Crouch 1972), Ernest Benn, 1972, pp. 46-7.*

OTHER CITATIONS

Jean C. Thomson, in School Library Journal, *September, 1967, pp. 114-15.*

The Booklist and Subscription Books Bulletin, *October 15, 1967, p. 272.*

Robin Gottlieb, in Book World, *November 5, 1967 (Part 2), p. 16.*

Zena Sutherland, in Bulletin of the Center for Children's Books, *February, 1968, p. 90.*

THE HOUSE OF SECRETS (1964)

Much of [*The House of Secrets*, published in Great Britain as *The Secret Passage*,] will appear at first sight to be markedly "old hat" to the experienced reader; the motherless family dumped on the apparently unsympathetic aunt, the half-crazed old lady lodger with the cache of sovereigns; the local girl who pretends to be someone else; and the good-natured but feckless sculptor who turns out to "have something" after all. Not to mention the stolen de-

lights of another house enjoyed via the secret passage. Nevertheless, Miss Bawden's sense of humour and fluent style, the neatness of her narrative structure, have added something to the old recipe which gives the book a flavour worth savouring at least once.

The Junior Bookshelf, *January, 1964, p. 41.*

OTHER CITATIONS

Zena Sutherland, in Bulletin of the Center for Children's Books, *September, 1964, pp. 2-3.*

THE PEPPERMINT PIG (1975)

[*The Peppermint Pig*] focuses on uprooted children in strange surroundings. . . . Bawden possesses the enviable knack of turning stock situations—Poll's bout with scarlet fever; Theo's petty feuding with a schoolmate—into absorbing events and recasting familiar types into fresh characterizations, e.g., a prim spinster who complains about adjoining outhouses where people must sit "back to back—and NO RELATION" is both ridiculous and touchingly human. Written with the polish and perception that readers have come to expect from Bawden, this is an uncommonly good family album whose portraits stand out in remarkably sharp focus and are free of fussy nostalgic frills.

Jane Abramson, in School Library Journal *(reprinted from* School Library Journal, *February, 1975, published by R. R. Bowker Co., a Xerox company; copyright © 1975 by Xerox Corporation), February, 1975, p. 43.*

[*The Peppermint Pig*] is essentially a looking backward story—less structured than *Carrie's War* but crammed with sharp, truthful moments and the collective family legends that are almost, but not quite, the same thing.

Kirkus Reviews *(copyright © 1975 The Kirkus Service, Inc.) March 1, 1975, p. 244.*

Nina Bawden, in *The Peppermint Pig*, has provided the children with what many young readers are seeking—a setting in another time and place, and has added her trademark, suspense. After an encouraging beginning, Bawden diminishes the impact of her work by dealing with too many confrontations in a limited amount of time. Poll experiences more critical situations than the reader can absorb. . . . The swift movement of events may have been designed to hold the readers's interest; however it seems disjointed and contrived.

Neglected in *The Peppermint Pig* is an opportunity to let the reader fully explore an exciting historical period. This failure is really the child's loss. Bawden is at her best with her descriptive passages such as "her face was like thin, crumpled paper under the spread sails of her hat." With this talent for description, she could easily have done a better job in verbally illustrating Victorian England.

Martha Unickel, in Pacific Sun Literary Quarterly, *2nd quarter, May 14, 1975, p. 24.*

[In "The Peppermint Pig"] Nina Bawden is a master at capturing the taste of growing up. The loving that can turn so quickly into hating. The ridicule that can give way to compassion. The sudden, sad insight into a brother who for all his cleverness will always be lonely. The surprises that even an enemy can contain. The miracle of morning after a long siege of illness.

The story is webbed with a delicate network of inter-personal complications, and it is this network, with Poll at the center, that gives the book its emotional texture, far more important than the events themselves.

> *Jean Fritz, in* The New York Times Book Review (© *1975 by The New York Times Company; reprinted by permission), May 18, 1975, p. 8.*

For all its considerable merits, I found [*The Peppermint Pig*] a thin read. Among a plethora of characters, several important ones are left very sketchy, only just removed from stereotype, and there is little room for any to develop. The pig itself, a charming creature, cannot bear its burden of symbolism adequately. Certain episodes, e.g. "the most frightening journey", the visit to the slums, are sadly tame. It seems that Nina Bawden, in the hugely successful *Carrie's War,* said all she has to say in this vein. Hence, in *The Peppermint Pig,* the constant striving for effect, from the very opening, in the choice of episodes and in the writing itself. A good read . . . but not likely to linger in the memory.

> *The Junior Bookshelf, June, 1975, pp. 192-93.*

Representing a departure for the author, [*The Peppermint Pig*] is historical rather than contemporary, subtle rather than mysterious; and its plot is more relaxed than suspenseful. Time and setting come sharply through the writing, which is typically graceful, witty, clear, and fluid. But the distinction of the book rests solidly upon the luminous characterizations and the crisscrossing of their intense relationships: the four children, the neighbors, the aunts, and the mother—a mettlesome, loving woman accustomed "to speaking her mind and not mincing her words to make them digestible."

> *Ethel L. Heins, in* The Horn Book Magazine *(copyright © 1975 by the Horn Book, Inc., Boston), June, 1975, p. 265.*

Time and relationships are all-important in this story. It opens with irresistible drama, "Old Granny Greengrass had her finger chopped off in the butcher's when she was buying half a leg of lamb". It is one of those anecdotes enshrined and embroidered in families. It is told by an unnamed and invisible narrator who is child to one of the old lady's great-grandchildren—Poll, at a cautious guess. Certainly Poll is the centre of the story; even Theo's sufferings at the hand of nasty Noah Bugg are seen through the eyes of his observant little sister, who realises but never fully understands the tortuous way his mind works. But Poll is no isolated child. She is the centre of a family, members past and present, of a world of people all endowed with individuality through Nina Bawden's vigorous, particularised narrative and dialogue. Substantial in background, unerring in its reflection of the social patterns of the turn of this century, this is a fine example of the work of a novelist who has never reserved a particle of her skill when writing for the young.

> *Margery Fisher, in her* Growing Point, *September, 1975, p. 2692.*

OTHER CITATIONS

The Booklist, *February 15, 1975, pp. 615, 617.*

Publishers' Weekly, *March 3, 1975, p. 70.*

SQUIB (1971)

At first it seems that in [*Squib*] Nina Bawden is resisting the temptation to write another exciting adventure story. She appears to be in quieter, more subtle territory. The drowned brother miraculously restored and the rich man's son kidnapped and held to ransom are only in the imaginations of two of her characters: Kate and Robin. But Squib's own story turns out to be just as romantic and just as unlikely; it is unlikely not because it couldn't happen but because it is insufficiently explained and motivated.

Nina Bawden has always had room in her books for the underprivileged and the problem children. Squib is a classic case. . . . But he does not come to life. There is never a moment when the reader would feel about Squib as the woman Flora Thompson recorded who had read *Froggy's Little Brother:* "Poor little mite. If we could have got him here he could have slept with our young Sammy and this air'd have set him up in no time." Squib remains a case. Perhaps we do not want our children harrowed. Certainly Nina Bawden is as good as she has ever been—and that is very good indeed—on domestic details, class differences and points of contact, and the way people talk.

> *The Times Literary Supplement (© Times Newspapers Ltd., 1971), July 2, 1971, p. 775.*

Each of four children [in *Squib*] responds in terms of his own frame of reference to the odd presence and still odder sudden absence of the bruised and lonely little boy in the park who has no name but Squib. Gently fixing (not fixating—and she's on top of the difference) on his ineffable yet palpable sadness, Mrs. Bawden makes him the pivot of an unaffected, unencumbered story that settles in nicely and sits comfortably. . . . [The] finale illumines quite a bit more than just Squib's identity as the characters sharpen into personalities through a roundly natural give and take.

> *Kirkus Reviews (copyright © 1971 The Kirkus Service, Inc.), July 15, 1971, pp. 738-39.*

In *Squib* [Nina Bawden] has gathered together the many strands of her talents and woven them into a story which would, given the opportunity, gladden the heart of many a reader well beyond the age-group for which it was written. . . . [She] has an unerring ear and eye for the subtleties in relationships between children in a group—each one is a detailed portrait of a living, breathing human being, freckles an' all. Hers is not merely a children's world though; adults are present in fair proportion and are *shown* as adult—in other words, preoccupied, generous, harassed, loving and illogical—their lives interweaving with, and influencing, those of the children.

The story races along apace, but there is time along the

way to enjoy the wonderful dialogue which in itself, without the aid of any descriptive passages, would crystallise each character in the mind's eye.

Shirley Hughes's line drawings capture the atmosphere of the story which has qualities in abundance.

> *Margot Petts, in* Children's Book Review *(© 1971 by Five Owls Press Ltd.; all rights reserved), September, 1971, pp. 121-22.*

The interest of [*Squib*] to a grown-up reader is in the wholly believable resolution of Kate's troubles through the care of an ill-treated waif; to a child, in the adventures that lead to the waif's rescue. The story is solidly grounded in England —the plain England of council schools, old people's homes, and gangs on motorbikes—and in a firm social morality.

> *Janet Adam Smith, in* The New York Review of Books *(reprinted with permission from* The New York Review of Books; *copyright © 1971 NYREV, Inc.), December 2, 1971, p. 26.*

The children's attempt to rescue Squib from a situation they don't quite understand but know is wrong, somehow, provides a dramatic and satisfying ending. The relationships among the children, and the family situation of each, are drawn with perception and warmth, and the story is written with just-bearable suspense.

> *Zena Sutherland, in* Bulletin of the Center for Children's Books *(© 1972 by the University of Chicago; all rights reserved), July-August, 1972, p. 165.*

OTHER CITATIONS

Catherine Storr, in New Statesman, *June 4, 1971, p. 778.*

The Junior Bookshelf, *August, 1971, pp. 233-34.*

The Booklist, *November 15, 1971, p. 290.*

Sarah Law Kennerly, in School Library Journal, *December, 1971, p. 72.*

THREE ON THE RUN (1965)

An account of children escaping from adults—wicked or merely obtuse—inevitably has strong appeal. Here the differences represented by the three escapees add to the interest: Ben, an English country boy visiting his widower father in London; Lil, a sly, unschooled city child alone while her mother is in the hospital; and Thomas, son of Chief Okapi, the prime minister of an East African country, and a pawn in a political conspiracy. The story verges on fantasy, but the children are real; the naturalness with which each sees the others as friends, accepting without question their different backgrounds and cultures, is child-like and convincing.

> *Ruth Hill Viguers, in* The Horn Book Magazine *(copyright © 1965, by The Horn Book, Inc., Boston), August, 1965, pp. 385-86.*

[*Three on the Run* is] an adventure story with some weak aspects and some very strong. The small print and the vocabulary level make the book fairly difficult for a reader

who would be interested in children as young as the three protagonists seem to be; the characters are well-defined, but several of them hint of stereotype. The relationships are good, and the story has pace and some suspense, but the plot is contrived, and it needn't have been.

> *Zena Sutherland, in* Bulletin of the Center for Children's Books *(copyright 1966 by the University of Chicago; all rights reserved), June, 1966, pp. 157-58.*

OTHER CITATIONS

Alice Dalgliesh and Frances Foster, in Saturday Review, *May 15, 1965, p. 46.*

Johanna Hurwitz, in School Library Journal, *September, 1965, p. 193.*

THE WHITE HORSE GANG (1966)

There is nothing very startling about this story, set in a small, out-of-the-way English town, nor is there a great deal of point to it, but unobtrusively it offers some very pleasant moments with its precise and often humorous indications of the three young characters who formed the White Horse Gang. . . . The three involve themselves in some stock situations, but they seem refreshing and genuine.

> Virginia Kirkus' Service *(copyright © 1966 Virginia Kirkus' Service, Inc.), February 15, 1966, p. 181.*

This is a fairly conventional story and the characters run true to type. But is this type true to life? Would a nine year-old boy behave in this way? It would rather seem to be the way adult writers of children's books expect, or think, children behave. The book is well written, but the plot is too loose. It should be suitable for 9-11 year-olds, but many of them will find it rather heavy. To become a child again and see life through his eyes is something only very few writers achieve.

> The Junior Bookshelf, *June, 1966, p. 176.*

Nina Bawden writes about childhood as though she had never left it. As though, indeed, she were still exploring its terrain—scraping her knees and forgetting to blow her nose. This, coupled with the fact that she writes well, makes "The White Horse Gang" a more important book than its title indicates. Ostensibly a mystery, it is really the study of three English children in a small town. . . . Understanding that [these children] are at once amoral and upright, cold-blooded and sensitive, she presents them with marvelous candor; and if a few threads of plot remain untied at the end, it hardly matters. Her story rings true.

> *Barbara Wersba, in* The New York Times Book Review *(© 1966 by The New York Times Company; reprinted by permission), June 22, 1966, p. 26.*

[*The White Horse Gang* is] a story that has a country setting, touches of sophistication and humor, and a nicely unified plot. There are, in the plot and in some of the characterizations, tendencies to broad exaggeration that weaken the story somewhat. . . . There is a contrived last dramatic touch when a wolf escapes from a local circus and endangers the boys, but the book ends with a rather touching scene. . . .

> *Zena Sutherland, in* Bulletin of the Center for Children's Books *(copyright 1966 by the University of Chicago; all rights reserved), July-August, 1966, p. 174.*

OTHER CITATIONS

Mabel Berry, in School Library Journal, *April, 1966, p. 89.*

The Times Literary Supplement, *May 19, 1966, p. 432.*

Virginia Haviland, in The Horn Book Magazine, *June, 1966, p. 310.*

The Booklist and Subscription Books Bulletin, *June 15, 1966, p. 998.*

THE WITCH'S DAUGHTER (1966)

It's too bad Nina Bawden hasn't written as exceptionally for children as she has about them in her adult novels. Perhaps the transatlantic transition has something to do with it —the vocabulary outstrips the interest level of this age; and there are certain elements in this wistful half world, somewhere just between reality and fantasy, to which American readers are less attuned. . . . Girls will respond more than boys to the story [*The Witch's Daughter*] in which the adventure is subsidiary to the gently sentimental appeal.

> Virginia Kirkus' Service *(copyright © 1966 Virginia Kirkus' Service, Inc.), July 1, 1966, p. 624.*

Nina Bawden, author of other equally exciting adventure novels, has written a credible suspense story, with a likeable and resourceful cast. A plausible plot, superior dialogue, and an appropriate setting also work into a dramatization as gripping as the story of Tom and Huck hiding from Injun Joe. "The Witch's Daughter" should delight all children who have ever dreamed of searching for buried treasure.

> *Diane Wagner, in* The New York Times Book Review *(© 1966 by The New York Times Company; reprinted by permission), November 6, 1966, p. 44.*

The Witch's Daughter is very good in parts, much less as a whole. The author, Nina Bawden, is almost defeated by her determination to tell a thrilling yarn. In her book are the materials for a wonderful story—an island, a half-wild little girl, a blind child, natural hazards of cliff and cave— without the need to call in the worn-out devices of thieves and hidden treasure. However, Miss Bawden is a professional, and she makes a good, competent job of her absurd plot. Her sinister, toffee-sucking thug is well enough drawn, though only the most naive of young readers will take him and his soft-hearted colleague seriously. The central character, Perdita, the witch's daughter, running free over the hills and bogs of her island home, is to be taken entirely seriously. So is Janey, who is blind and who saves the others in a nightmare journey in the dark through a deep cave. These are the products of a mature imagination, which has also created for them an attractive and detailed

setting. If the rest were of this quality, *The Witch's Daughter* would be a story of the first order, instead of merely giving occasional promises of high excellence.

> The Times Literary Supplement *(© The Times Publishing Company Ltd. 1966), November 24, 1966, p. 1070.*

The plot [of *The Witch's Daughter*] moves fairly predictably, but the book, like the author's earlier ones, is memorable for its depth of aim. The heightened mental senses of Perdita are contrasted with Janey's heightened physical senses, both of which save lives. There is a sympathetic yet realistic picture of the selfishness of the handicapped child and the vanity of the child who is "different." Perdita has to face the waning of her powers as she learns to mix with others, and as in real life, black and white are not sharply defined: Mr. Smith's nemesis is tragedy for Perdita, to whom he was kindness and security. The end is very moving.

> The Junior Bookshelf, *December, 1966, p. 376.*

OTHER CITATIONS

Patricia Dahl, in School Library Journal, *September, 1966, p. 174.*

Elizabeth Enright, in Book Week, *October 30, 1966 (Part 2), p. 26.*

*   *   *

BLUME, Judy   1938-

An American author, Judy Blume is noted for her candid and humorous stories about the problems of suburban adolescents. (See also *Contemporary Authors*, Vols. 29-32, and *Something About the Author*, Vol. 2.)

ARE YOU THERE, GOD? IT'S ME, MARGARET. (1970)

The comical longings of little girls who want to be big girls —exercising to the chant of "We must—we must—increase our bust!"—and the wistful longing of Margaret, who talks comfortably to God, for a religion, come together as her anxiety to be normal, which is natural enough in sixth grade. And if that's what we want to tell kids, this is a fresh, unclinical case in point: Mrs. Blume . . . has an easy way with words and some choice ones when the occasion arises. But there's danger in the preoccupation with the physical signs of puberty . . . [for] the effect is to confirm common anxieties instead of allaying them. (And countertrends notwithstanding, much is made of that first bra, that first dab of lipstick.) More promising is Margaret's pursuit of religion: to decide for herself (earlier than her 'liberal' parents intended), she goes to temple with a grandmother, to church with a friend; but neither makes any sense to her —"Twelve is very late to learn." Fortunately, after a disillusioning sectarian dispute, she resumes talking to God . . . to thank him for that telltale sign of womanhood. Which raises the last question: of a satirical stance in lieu of a perspective.

> Kirkus Reviews *(copyright © 1970 The Kirkus Service, Inc.), October 1, 1970, p. 1093.*

[A] good book by any terms is "Are You There God? It's Me, Margaret" by Judy Blume. . . . Margaret is a real pre-teen with stirrings of desire unencumbered by narrow-focused sex. That is to say, she is becoming aware of her own body without yet thinking of it in relationship to another's. . . .

Grandmother Simon, who is viewed by Margaret's parents as a potentially bad influence upon her, is a welcome relief from the Jewish mother-cum-chicken-soup. Few males of any age will be interested in Margaret's growing up. But for feminine readers this is a funny, warm and loving book, one that captures the essence of beginning adolescence.

> *Dorothy Broderick, in* The New York Times Book Review *(© 1970 by The New York Times Company; reprinted by permission), November 8, 1970, p. 14.*

Are You There God? will appeal to a rather limited age range, but it will be the right book for many girls awaiting the menstrual cycle. . . . The writing is not as polished as in stories with similar contemporary suburban settings by Elaine Konigsburg, but the content is important, the dialogue (humorous and serious) is realistic and the feelings come through with sincerity.

> *Jeanette Daane, in* School Library Journal *(reprinted from* School Library Journal, *December, 1970, published by R. R. Bowker Co., a Xerox company; copyright © 1970 by Xerox Corporation), December, 1970, p. 42.*

Pre-teen girls' concern with breast development and menstruation and their burgeoning interest in boys are treated with honesty and humor in a tender, funny first-person story narrated by an almost twelve-year-old girl who discusses her private hopes and anxieties in candid conversations with God. The preoccupation with bodily changes which Margaret and three of her classmates share is realistically portrayed within the framework of typical pre-teen school, home, and social activities. . . . Family and peer relationships and dialog ring true.

> *The Booklist (reprinted by permission of the American Library Association; copyright 1971 by the American Library Association), January 15, 1971, p. 418.*

OTHER CITATIONS

Publishers' Weekly, *January 11, 1971, pp. 62-3.*

Zena Sutherland, in Bulletin of the Center for Children's Books, *February, 1971, p. 87.*

John Rowe Townsend, in his Written for Children: An Outline of English-Language Children's Literature, *revised edition, Lippincott, 1974, p. 279.*

BLUBBER (1974)

Judy Blume presents the scenes of viciousness (the girls forcing a chocolate ant down Linda's throat or making her show the boys her underpants) without commentary and young readers will be appalled long before Jill exhibits any qualms—while enjoying, as usual, those indelicacies like farts and nose picking which only strengthen their general conviction that this author writes directly to them.

> Kirkus Reviews *(copyright © 1974 The Kirkus Service, Inc.), October 1, 1974, p. 1059.*

More contrived than some of [Blume's] other work, [*Blubber*] is an inside look at how obnoxious some well-to-do, suburban, fifth-grade children can be to each other and to adults. Blubber is the nickname given to a class victim by the class leader, who is possessed of a meanness with which all the others go along, including the story's narrator, Jill Brenner. Jill never learns that it's wrong to persecute someone; she simply finds out that when the tables are turned, it hurts, and that one has to think fast to ward off tormenters. The book's serious weaknesses—a narrow focus on the characters' unkindness that doesn't show them as real people with mixed qualities, plus a suspiciously sudden and total class reversal—will probably not deter fans of *Are You There, God? It's Me, Margaret* . . . from enjoying the glib dialog and familiar details of classroom coexistence.

> *The Booklist (reprinted by permission of the American Library Association; copyright 1975 by the American Library Association), January 1, 1975, pp. 459-60.*

Realistically, no miracles happen [in *Blubber*]. The social relationships settle down, but Linda is still an outsider and Wendy still arrogant. The change is in Jill, whose sense of values shifts to include the compassion that understanding another's position brings. The plot is nicely balanced by Jill's friendship with reliable Tracy Wu, her support and sympathy from understanding parents, her relationship with an erudite younger brother, a Hallowe'en escapade, etc. A good family story as well as a school story, this [has] good characterization and dialogue, a vigorous first-person writing style, and—Judy Blume demonstrates again—a respectful and perceptive understanding of the anguished concerns of the pre-teen years.

> *Zena Sutherland, in* Bulletin of the Center for Children's Books *(© 1975 by The University of Chicago; all rights reserved), May, 1975, p. 142.*

OTHER CITATIONS

Jane Abramson, in School Library Journal, *November, 1974, p. 54.*

DEENIE (1973)

Judy Blume seems to be growing impatient with fictional considerations and more preoccupied with her bibliotherapeutic themes—which is not to deny that this could hit a responsive nerve with her body-centered early adolescent readers. At the beginning Deenie is an ordinary seventh grader preoccupied with making the cheerleading squad, disgusted by hunchbacks and cripples and a classmate with eczema, and plagued by a stereotypically insensitive mother determined to make a professional model of her pretty daughter. Then the gym teacher suspects and doctors confirm that Deenie has scoliosis, "a structural curvature of the spine which has a strong tendency to progress rapidly during the adolescent growth spurt." The rest of her story—about half of which seems to take place in doctors' offices, where we are exposed to all the processes involved in making a brace mold, deals with her adjustment to the brace that she will wear for four years in order to grow up straight. Instead of giving Deenie any personality or independent existence beyond her malady, the author throws in the subtopic of masturbation—Deenie likes to touch her "special place" to get "that good feeling," and is relieved when the gym teacher tells the class it's okay—which only makes the story's hygienic slant more pronounced.

> *Kirkus Reviews (copyright © 1973 The Kirkus Service, Inc.), September 1, 1973, p. 965.*

Deenie's own reactions as well as those of her family, friends, teachers, and strangers are always believable, from the most selfish to the most sympathetic. Blume's tangential discussion of female masturbation is also well-handled. . . . Although the story concerns middle-class suburban New Jerseyites, all children will recognize and react to the complicated network of feelings that Deenie experiences. [This is a] compelling book which reads fast without stinting on content or characterization.

> *Melinda Schroeder, in* School Library Journal *(reprinted from* School Library Journal, *May, 1974, published by R. R. Bowker Co., a Xerox company; copyright © 1974 by Xerox Corporation), May, 1974, p. 53.*

Blume is a skilled writer and the book is well-motivated. But *Deenie* smacks of the Victorian didactic fiction that was supposed to set children's feet on the proper path. Blume's heavy-handed "problem" approach gives the novel the feel of an orthopedist's guide for patients.

> *Elizabeth Hall, in* Psychology Today *(reprinted by permission; copyright © 1974 by Ziff-Davis Publishing Company; all rights reserved), September, 1974, p. 134.*

OTHER CITATIONS

Publishers' Weekly, *October 8, 1973, p. 97.*

Zena Sutherland, in Bulletin of the Center for Children's Books, *April, 1974, pp. 123-24.*

FOREVER (1975)

Increasingly Judy Blume's books center on single topics and the topic here, as pronounced in the first sentence, is getting laid. . . . As usual with this immensely popular author, *Forever* has a lot of easy, empathic verity and very little heft. Cath, like Blume's other heroines, is deliberately ordinary, which means here (despite friends, nice family, etc.) that outside of the love affair she's pretty much a blank. In fact this could be a real magnet for all those girls who took to *Are You There God It's Me Margaret* just a few years ago and haven't changed all that much since. Another way of looking at *Forever* is as an updated *Seventeenth Summer.*

> *Kirkus Reviews (copyright © 1975 The Kirkus Service, Inc.), October 1, 1975, pp. 1136-37.*

Actually, both kids [in *Forever*] are so kind and considerate, so understanding, so everything, that readers may wonder what's wrong with them. Finally, [Cath] realizes that first love isn't always *Forever,* that she is growing and accepting changes. Sniff, sniff. Obviously it's not a quality book, but that fact won't bother the many girls who will read it, identify, cry happily, and recommend it to their friends. Librarians buying for junior high schools should be aware that the sexual scenes, while not at all explicit compared to the run of adult novels, may be more than parents of young teens bargain for.

> *Regina Minudri, in* School Library Journal *(reprinted from* School Library Journal, *November, 1975, published by R. R. Bowker Co., a Xerox company; copyright © 1975 by Xerox Corporation), November, 1975, p. 95.*

IGGIE'S HOUSE (1970)

["Iggie's House"] is written almost entirely from Winnie's point of view—emotional, righteous, bewildered. In these self-conscious times it will certainly find a home on background reading lists for youngsters who are interested in studying human relations.

> *Susan Rowe, in* The New York Times Book Review *(© 1970 by The New York Times Company; reprinted by permission), May 24, 1970 (Part 2), p. 22.*

Featherweight tomboys have made adequate reading for tomboys before; featherweight sociology will not do, however, and the message of this simplistic novel (which presents the problem of block-busting) deteriorates as it is expanded. . . . [The] book ends happily; however, since real life is often a nastier proposition, it's no favor to present children, especially middle-class children, with the notion that it's this easy to cope with integration.

> *Jean C. Thomson, in* School Library Journal *(reprinted from* School Library Journal, *September, 1970, published by R. R. Bowker Co., a Xerox company; copyright © 1970 by Xerox Corporation), September, 1970, p. 98.*

The ending is expectable, the purpose worthy, and the most perceptive aspect of [*Iggie's House*] is in the interpretation of the reactions of the black family. The theme and treatment are not unusual, and the story is weakened by some not-quite-believable dialogue. . . .

> *Zena Sutherland, in* Bulletin of the Center for Children's Books *(© 1970 by the University of Chicago; all rights reserved), October, 1970, p. 22.*

OTHER CITATIONS

Kirkus Reviews, *April 1, 1970, p. 380.*

IT'S NOT THE END OF THE WORLD (1972)

["It's not the end of the world,"] though for a while it seems that way to 12-year-old Karen Newman whose parents are in the process of getting a divorce. . . . [The story] is told in the first person without solemnity or forced comfort, and Ms. Blume's sharp sketches of 12-year-old quirks and concerns will hold even those who don't share Karen's problem.

> Kirkus Reviews *(copyright © 1972 The Kirkus Service, Inc.), April 15, 1972, p. 476.*

Blending awareness of adolescent emotions with a sense of contemporary mores, [Judy Blume]—in a brisk, first-person narrative—believably delineates the bewilderment and anxiety afflicting the children of about-to-be-divorced parents. . . . [*It's Not the End of the World* is an] honest, but not depressing, problem novel which explores with precision and sympathy the distinctive personality of a twelve-year-old.

> *Mary M. Burns, in* The Horn Book Magazine *(copyright © 1972 by The Horn Book, Inc., Boston), October, 1972, p. 466.*

In this slow-paced story of adjustment, 12-year-old Karen Newman eventually decides that her parents' divorce is not the ultimate disaster. . . . Although drawn out and repetitive, the believable portrayals of Karen, her parents, and her suburban New Jersey surroundings make the book an adequate addition to junior fiction collections.

> *Margaret A. Dorsey, in* School Library Journal *(reprinted from* School Library Journal, *October, 1972, published by R. R. Bowker Co., a Xerox company; copyright © 1972 by Xerox Corporation), October, 1972, p. 109.*

OTHER CITATIONS

Lael Scott, in The New York Times Book Review, *September 3, 1972, p. 8.*

Zena Sutherland, in Bulletin of the Center for Children's Books, *October, 1972, p. 23.*

The Booklist, *October 1, 1972, p. 147.*

OTHERWISE KNOWN AS SHEILA THE GREAT (1972)

Judy Blume is a careful student of such childhood customs as slumber parties, playing "cooties" and eating Oreo cookies from the inside out, and Sheila's ongoing crisis of image ("Other kids get Home Free. Why not me?") is as easy to identify with as it is to laugh at.

> Kirkus Reviews *(copyright © 1972 The Kirkus Service, Inc.), September 1, 1972, p. 1025.*

Due to Blume's vague characterization of her heroine, readers will wonder if "Sheila the Great" is a fearful, insecure child (she's afraid of dogs, the dark, learning to swim, and, most of all, admitting to her shortcomings), a spoiled brat who lies constantly, or simply a normal young girl with typical growing pains. . . . Her rationalizations fall flat, and her continual telling of white lies to her friends, her family, and herself becomes more annoying than amusing. Although the author's style is smooth, youngsters who have been waiting for Blume's next book will find Sheila's vacation an unrewarding experience.

> *Linda Johnson, in* School Library Journal *(reprinted from* School Library Journal, *May, 1973, published by R. R. Bowker Co., a Xerox company; copyright © 1973 by Xerox Corporation), May, 1973 p. 69.*

OTHER CITATIONS

Publishers' Weekly, *August 14, 1972, p. 46.*

The Booklist, *November 15, 1972, p. 298.*

TALES OF A FOURTH GRADE NOTHING (1972)

Fudge's antics are standard toddler attention-getters . . . , but Peter's jaundiced observations [in *Tales of a Fourth Grade Nothing*] exploit their risibility to the fullest. Yet the absence of any palpable jealousy or anger in Peter's reportage causes it to degenerate into a series of momentarily amusing anecdotes, and, if not exactly a nothing, Peter is considerably less than might have been expected from the author of *Then Again, Maybe I Won't* (1971).

> Kirkus Reviews *(copyright © 1971 The Kirkus Service, Inc.), February 1, 1972, p. 134.*

In this light, humorous, episodic story, nine-year-old Peter Hatcher tells of his problems with his little brother Fudge, a two-and-a-half-year-old attention-stealer. . . . Fudge is too exaggerated to be very believable, but Peter's difficulties with him will be readily understood by children with younger brothers and sisters.

> The Booklist *(reprinted by permission of the American Library Association; copyright 1972 by the American Library Association), July 1, 1972, p. 941.*

Each chapter in this amusing book records another Awful Incident in the life of Peter Hatcher (as told by Peter) whose greatest trial is his brother Fudge, age two. . . . [*Tales of a Fourth Grade Nothing*] isn't as solid as other books by Judy Blume, but it's fun, it has a mildly therapeutic effect, and it's written and illustrated [by Roy Doty] with a light touch.

> *Zena Sutherland, in* Bulletin of the Center for Children's Books *(© 1972 by the University of Chicago; all rights reserved), July-August, 1972, p. 166.*

OTHER CITATIONS

Publishers' Weekly, *February 14, 1972, pp. 69-70.*

Nan Pavey Kurtz, in School Library Journal, *May, 1972, p. 74.*

Zena Sutherland, in Saturday Review, *May 20, 1972, p. 81.*

THEN AGAIN, MAYBE I WON'T (1971)

Whether she is writing about female or male sexual awakening, and whatever other adolescent problems, Judy Blume is on target. Her understanding of young people is sympathetic and psychologically sound; her skill engages the reader in human drama without ever resorting to melodrama. "Then Again, Maybe I Won't" is the story of 13-year-old Tony Miglione's adjustments to his own growing sexuality and to the difficulties of being a member of an upwardly mobile family.... Judy Blume weaves each piece [of the plot] together with a master craftsman's touch, [and] the result is a valid portrait of life as it is lived by all too many of us.

> *Dorothy M. Broderick in* The New York Times Book Review *(© 1972 by The New York Times Company; reprinted by permission), January 16, 1972, p. 8.*

Deftly handled, Tony's dilemma [in *Then Again, Maybe I Won't*] is really that he has become mature enough to see the conflicts and imperfections in his own life and in those around him, and he is sensitive enough to accept compromise. Although there are developments in the story, the book has no strong plot line. It is, however, impressive for its realistic and sympathetic identification with a boy's viewpoint.

> *Zena Sutherland, in* Bulletin of the Center for Children's Books *(© 1972 by the University of Chicago; all rights reserved), February, 1972, p. 87.*

OTHER CITATIONS

Zena Sutherland, in Saturday Review, *September 18, 1971, p. 49*

Kirkus Reviews, *November 1, 1971, p. 1155.*

Publishers' Weekly, *December 13, 1971, p. 42.*

The Booklist, *February 1, 1972, p. 465.*

Sarah M. Thrash, in School Library Journal, *April, 1972, p. 142.*

                    *   *   *

BURNFORD, Sheila   1918-

A Scottish-born Canadian, Sheila Burnford is best known for her animal story, *The Incredible Journey,* **which received the 1963 Canadian Book of the Year for Children medal and a 1971 Lewis Carroll Shelf Award. (See also** *Contemporary Authors,* **Vols. 1-4, rev. ed., and** *Something About the Author,* **Vol. 3.)**

THE INCREDIBLE JOURNEY (1961)

Incredible the journey may have been, but the adventures the animals had, their instinctive devotion to each other, their suffering and all-but-miraculous survival are so completely credible it is difficult to believe that this is fiction. The animals have distinct personalities which are emphasized under the stresses and crises of their ordeal but which remain true to their kind, and there is no humanizing. There is not one false note. There are humans in the story, and even those only briefly glimpsed are sharply defined; but the concentration of interest never deviates from the animals, not even in the final joyous reunion.

This is not merely a story for animal lovers. It is for all who enjoy the drama of a single purpose achieved with suffering but without complaint, and disciplined writing which evokes the rugged beauty of the Canadian wilderness as

well as the excitement of the journey.... From the youngest child (only old enough to sit quietly on someone's lap) to the oldest grownup, there is something here for everyone. It is dramatically illustrated by Carl Burger.

> *Ruth Hill Viguers, in* The Horn Book Magazine *(copyright, 1961, by the Horn Book, Inc., Boston), June, 1961, p. 253.*

[This is a] beautifully written book. Three house pets, staying with a friend of the family while their owners were abroad, disappeared into the Canadian wilderness, and in completely credible and powerful detail the author describes their long trek toward their old home. An old bull terrier, a young Labrador retriever, and a Siamese cat are in alliance against all the dangers of the wilds, against all the human obstacles, against any threat to one of the three in their migration. Each of the animals is indelibly real, and the reunion with the family that thought them lost is deeply moving. The writing style is remarkable, the action suspenseful.

> *Zena Sutherland, in* Bulletin of the Center for Children's Books *(copyright 1962 by the University of Chicago; all rights reserved), March, 1962, p. 107.*

[Sheila Burnford] writes so convincingly about animal habits and of life in the Canadian north country that readers might feel that [*The Incredible Journey*] is a true story rather than a work of fiction....

Through this story of three remarkable animals, the author has illustrated many admirable qualities: devotion to a cause, courage to face great difficulties, and the bonds of fidelity which can exist between animal and man.

> *John Gillespie and Diana Lembo, in their* Juniorplots: A Book Talk Manual for Teachers and Librarians *(copyright © 1967 by the R. R. Bowker Co.), Bowker, 1967, pp. 155, 157.*

The year 1961 saw the publication of [this] remarkable animal story [which presents] a detailed account of three heroic animals who travel through two hundred and fifty miles of Canadian wilderness to the place and people that mean home and love to them.... The reunion with the human beings they love is an unforgettable scene, written with restraint and integrity. The animals are never humanized or sentimentalized, and this beautifully written saga of three gallant animals is a superb story to read aloud either in the home or classroom.

> *May Hill Arbuthnot and Zena Sutherland, in their* Children and Books *(copyright © 1947, 1957, 1964, 1972 by Scott, Foresman and Co.), 4th edition, Scott, Foresman, 1972, pp. 413-14.*

[*The Incredible Journey*] represents almost all the virtues and failings characteristic of popular films: a simple plot, a strong emphasis on characterization, a large measure of sentimentality, and a compelling vividness, pace, and charm....

The journey is imaginary, but the animals are modelled after the author's own pets and are given all the human attributes that pet-lovers are apt to ascribe to their charges. Thus the Labrador is represented as following not instinct, but consistent, logical thought. . . .

So, too, the cat exhibits such motivations as selflessness (it attacks a bear cub and even a bear on behalf of the bulldog) and generosity (continually hunting food to give to the older dog). And there is not a moment's altercation among the three animals; they treat each other with complete sweetness throughout a long and difficult journey when their own survival was hourly at stake.

All this Mrs Burnford relates so graphically and even poetically that it very nearly convinces. But not quite. The journey remains incredible and, despite its undoubted emotional impact, the book is not entirely honest. . . . *The Incredible Journey* will be read and remembered, but not as a true exemplar of the realistic animal story. It should be considered rather as the heir of *Black Beauty* and *Beautiful Joe,* in which there is a deliberate attempt to use animals as the vehicles for human emotions.

> *Sheila Egoff, in her* The Republic of Childhood: A Critical Guide to Canadian Children's Literature in English *(© Oxford University Press, Canadian Branch, 1967, 1975), 2nd edition, Oxford University Press, 1975, pp. 125-26.*

OTHER CITATIONS

Virginia Kirkus' Service, *December 1, 1960, p. 1007.*

The Junior Bookshelf, *July, 1961, p. 161.*

Constantine Georgiou, in his Children and Their Literature, *Prentice-Hall, 1969, pp. 395-96.*

MR. NOAH AND THE SECOND FLOOD (1973)

The text [of *Mr. Noah and the Second Flood*] is too long and has too many subtleties to appeal to the young children for whom it might appear by the format that the book was intended. An adult would appreciate its wry humour more than children, although it is described as a "fable" on the

dustjacket. The black and white illustrations [by Michael Foreman] are sophisticated and effective.

> The Junior Bookshelf, *June, 1973, p. 195.*

[This] cautionary fable about man's destroying the world through pollution is written in a deceptively bland style and with moments of wry humor. . . . The theme has been used in other, recent variations, but the treatment is new and the writing style is graceful; the action of the story bogs down a bit in the long process of animal-gathering and food preparation (ten years) but it picks up at the end, and the story closes with some decisions made and the future a question mark.

> *Zena Sutherland, in Bulletin of the Center for Children's Books (© 1973 by the University of Chicago; all rights reserved), December, 1973, p. 59.*

"Mr. Noah and the Second Flood" . . . is a highly satisfactory and subtle interpretation of the legend [of Noah's Ark] in contemporary terms. . . .

[Sheila Burnford] involves us in imagining what it would be like to stock, realistically, such an ark-archeological wonder today, e.g. coping with an anteater's diet of 15,000 termites at a time. Mrs. Noah is an important figure here; she copes. There are poignant moments, particularly when Noah calls the roll of the "P's," and no pandas, pangolins or polar bears show up. To tell more of this "cautionary fable" would ruin its impact. The story has bite and meaning for ecology-minded readers from 10-up. The line drawings by Michael Foreman complement the text without intruding.

> *Judy Noyes, in* The New York Times Book Review *(© 1973 by The New York Times Company; reprinted by permission), December 16, 1973, p. 8.*

OTHER CITATIONS

Kirkus Reviews, *July 15, 1973, p. 753.*

Publishers' Weekly, *August 27, 1973, p. 280.*

C

CARROLL, Lewis (pseudonym of Charles Lutwidge Dodgson) 1832-1898

A mathematician, ordained deacon, amateur draftsman, and photographer who wrote serious verse and mathematical books, Lewis Carroll wrote nonsense poems and the two celebrated stories about Alice.

GENERAL COMMENTARY

A good deal of the piquancy of the Alice books is due to their merciless irreverence: in Alice's dreaming mind, the bottoms dismayingly drop out of the didactic little poems by Dr. Watts and Jane Taylor which Victorian children were made to learn, and their simple and trite images are replaced by grotesque and silly ones, which have rushed in like goblins to take possession. And in the White Knight's song about the aged man a-sitting . . . on a gate, a parody of Wordsworth's *Leech-Gatherer,* Lewis Carroll, in his subterranean fashion, ridiculed the stuffed-shirt side of Wordsworth as savagely as Byron had ever done. Wordsworth was a great admiration of Dodgson's; yet as soon as he enters his world of dreams, Lewis Carroll is moved to stick pins in him. . . .

The poetry and the logic in Dodgson were closely bound up together. It has often been pointed out that only a mind primarily logical could have invented the jokes of the Alice books, of which the author is always conscious that they are examples of faulty syllogisms. But it also worked the other way: his eccentric imagination invaded his scholarly work. His *Symbolic Logic* . . . contains syllogisms with terms as absurd as any in the Alice books:

> A prudent man shuns hyenas;
> No banker is imprudent.
> No banker fails to shun hyenas.

Dodgson's *Euclid and His Modern Rivals* had nothing to do with non-Euclidean geometry, but in the section called *A New Theory of Parallels* of his *Curiosa Mathematica* he grazed one of the conceptions of relativist theory; and is there not a touch of Einstein in the scenes in which the Red Queen has to keep running in order to remain in the same place and in which the White Queen gives a scream of pain before she has pricked her finger?

In literature, Lewis Carroll went deeper than his contemporaries realized and than he usually gets credit for even today. As studies in dream psychology, the Alice books are most remarkable: they do not suffer by comparison with the best serious performances in this field—with Strindberg or Joyce or Flaubert's *Tentation de Saint Antoine.* One of Alice's recent editors says that the heroine's personality is kept simple in order to throw into relief the eccentrics and monsters she meets. But the creatures that she meets, the whole dream, *are* Alice's personality and her waking life. They are the world of teachers, family and pets, as it appears to a little girl, and also the little girl who is looking at this world. The creatures are always snapping at her and chiding her, saying brusque and rude and blighting things (as if their creator himself were snapping back at the authorities and pieties he served); and she in turn has a child's primitive cruelty. . . .But though Alice is sometimes brutal, she is always well-bred; and, though she wanders in a world full of mysteries and of sometimes disagreeable surprises, she is always a sensible and self-possessed little upper-class English girl, who never fails in the last resort to face down the outlandish creatures that plague her: she can always bring the dream to an end by telling the King and Queen and the Court that they're nothing but a pack of cards or by picking up the Red Queen and shaking her. She can also be sympathetic and sometimes—for example, with the White King—exhibits a maternal instinct, but always in a sensible and practical way. Lewis Carroll is never sentimental about Alice. . . .

I do not, however, agree . . . that the Alice that grown-ups read is really a different work from the Alice that is read by children. The grown-ups understand it better, but the prime source of the interest is the same. Why is it that very young children listen so attentively to Alice, remember it all so well and ask to hear it again, when many other stories seem to leave little impression? It is . . . surely the psychological truth of these books that lays its hold on us all. Lewis Carroll is in touch with the real mind of childhood and hence with the more primitive elements of the mind of maturity, too—unlike certain other writers who merely exploit for grown-ups an artificial child-mind of convention which is in reality neither child-like nor adult. The shiftings and the transformations, the mishaps and the triumphs of Alice's dream, the mysteries and the riddles, the gibberish that conveys unmistakable meanings, are all based upon relationships that contradict the assumptions of our conscious lives but that are lurking not far behind them. In the "straight" parts of *Sylvie and Bruno*, Lewis Carroll was mawkishly Victorian to the point of unintentional parody (having produced in *The Two Voices* a masterpiece of intentional parody!), but in the Alice books he quite got away from the upholstery and the gloomy institutions of the nineteenth-century world. I believe that they are likely to survive when a good deal of the more monumental work of that world—the productions of the Carlyles and the Ruskins, the Spencers and the George Eliots—shall have sunk with the middleclass ideals of which they were the champions as well as the critics. Charles Dodgson who, in morals and religion, in his attitude toward social institutions, was professedly and as he himself believed, more conventional than any of these, had over them the curious advantage of working at once with the abstract materials of mathematical and logical conceptions and with the irrationalities of dreams. His art has a purity that is almost unique in a period so cluttered and cumbered, in which even the preachers of doom to the reign of materialism bore the stamp and the stain of the industrial system in the hard insistence of their sentences and in the turbidity of their belchings of rhetoric. They have shrunk now, but Alice still stands.

> *Edmund Wilson, "C. L. Dodgson: The Poet Logician" (originally published in* The New Republic, *May 18, 1932), in his* The Shores of Light *(reprinted with the permission of Farrar, Straus & Giroux, Inc.; copyright 1932, 1952 by Edmund Wilson), Farrar, Straus, 1952.*

[A] marvel is that *Wonderland* should have been followed by so consummate a sequel as *Through the Looking-Glass.* They are twin stars on whose *relative* radiance alone literary astronomers may be left to disagree.

Both stories have a structural framework—in the one playing-cards, in the other a game of chess, the moves in which Dodgson only to some extent attempted to justify. These no doubt suggested a few of his chief characters, or rather their social status; but what other tale-teller could have made Carroll's use of them? All that he owed to the device of the looking-glass, except that it is one which has perplexed and delighted child, philosopher and savage alike, is that the hand-writing in the story is the wrong way round, and that when Alice wished to go forwards she had to walk backwards—a method of progression that is sometimes of service even in life itself. Both stories, too—and this is a more questionable contrivance, particularly as it introduces a rather sententious elder sister—turn out to be dreams. (p. 214)

All this however affects the imaginative reality—the supreme illusion—of the *Alices* no more than its intricate chronology and knowledge of the law affect that of *Wuthering Heights,* and these have been proved to be unassailable. In reading the Carroll stories, that is, we scarcely notice, however consistent and admirable it may be, their ingenious design. And that is true also of *As You Like It.* Quite apart from any such design, at any rate, they would still remain in essence perhaps the most *original* books in the world. Indeed the genius in Carroll seems to have worked more subtly than the mind which it was possessed by realized. (pp. 214-15)

The intellectual thread, none the less, which runs through

the *Alices* is the reverse of being negligible. It is on this that their translucent beads of phantasy are strung, and it is the more effective for being so consistent and artfully concealed. As in the actual writing of poetry the critical faculties of the poet are in a supreme and constant activity, so with the *Alices.* Their 'characters', for example, in all their rich diversity are in exquisite keeping with one another. It may too have been due not to design but to happy accident . . . that though both books were written for children, the only child in them, apart from an occasional infant, is Alice herself. (p. 215)

[Alice] might indeed have been a miniature model of all the Victorian virtues and still have fallen . . . short if it were not for her freedom from silliness and her saving good sense—a good sense that never bespangles itself by becoming merely clever. However tart and touchy, however queer and querulous and quarrelsome her 'retinue' in Wonderland and in Looking-Glass Land may be, and she all but always gets the worst of every argument, it is this sagacity of mind and heart that keeps her talk from being merely 'childish' and theirs from seeming grown-uppish, and, in one word, prevents the hazardous situation from falling into the non-nonsensical. She wends serenely on like a quiet moon in a chequered sky. Apart, too, from an occasional Carrollian comment, the sole medium of the stories is *her* pellucid consciousness: an ideal preached by Henry James himself, and practised—in how different a setting—in [his] *What Maisie Knew.*

It is this rational poise in a topsy-turvy world . . . that gives the two tales their exquisite balance. For though laws there certainly are in the realm of Nonsense, they are all of them unwritten laws. Its subjects obey them unaware of any restrictions. Anything may happen there except only what can't happen *there.* . . . And though 'morals' pepper their pages—'Everything's got a moral if only you can find it'—the stories themselves have none. 'In fact', as Carroll said himself, 'they do not teach anything at all'.

Instead, they stealthily instil into us a unique state of mind. Their jam—wild strawberry—*is* the powder—virgin gold-dust—though we may never be conscious of its cathartic effects. Although, too, Carroll's Nonsense in itself, in Dryden's words, may be such that it 'never can be understood', there is no need to understand it. It is self-evident: and indeed may vanish away if we try to do so. Precisely the converse is true of the sober-sided order of nonsense. The longer we ponder on that the more hollowly the tub resounds, the drabber grows the day. The *Alices* lighten our beings like sunshine, like that divine rainbow in the skies beneath which the living things of the world went out into radiance and freedom from the narrow . . . darkness of the Ark. And any mind in their influence is freed the while from all its cares. Carroll's Wonderland indeed is a (queer little) universe of the mind resembling Einstein's in that it is a finite infinity endlessly explorable though never to be explored. How blue are its heavens, how grass-green its grass —its fauna and flora being more curiously reviving company not only than any but the pick of *this* world's but than those of almost any other book I know. And even for variety and precision, from the Mad Hatter down to Bill the Lizard, that company is rivalled only by the novelists who are as generous as they are skilled—an astonishing feat, since Carroll's creations are not only of his own species but of his own genus. (pp. 215-17)

The *Alices* indeed have the timelessness, the placelessness, and an atmosphere resembling in their own odd fashion not only those of the *Songs of Innocence* and Traherne's . . . *Meditations,* but of the medieval descriptions of paradise and many of the gem-like Italian pictures of the fifteenth century. This atmosphere is conveyed, as it could alone be conveyed, in a prose of limpid simplicity, as frictionless as the unfolding of the petals of an evening primrose in the cool of twilight; a prose, too, that could be the work only of a writer who like John Ruskin had from his earliest years examined every word he used with a scrupulous attention. . . . (p. 219)

What relation any such region of the world of dreams has to the world of our actual, who can say? Our modern oneiro-mantics have their science, but the lover of the *Alices* is in no need of it. What relation any such dream-world has to some other state of being seen only in glimpses here and now might be a more valuable but is an even less answer-able question. In any case, and even though there are other delights in them which only many years' experience of life can fully reveal, it is the child that is left in us who tastes the sweetest honey and laves its imagination in the clearest waters to be found in the *Alices*. (pp. 220-21)

> *Walter de la Mare, "Lewis Carroll's Dream Vision" (1932; reprinted by permission of The Literary Trustees of Walter de la Mare and The Society of Authors as their repre-sentative), in* Alice's Adventures in Wonder-land: A Critical Handbook, *edited by Donald Rackin, Wadsworth Publishing Co., 1969, pp. 213-21.*

Alice, an undeniably Sexagesimal and yet ageless product, was more than a flare of genius. It was the spiritual volcano of children's books, as the activities of John Newbery had been their commercial volcano. There had preceded it emi-nently, in the unconscious struggle for natural liberty, *The Butterfly's Ball, Holiday House* and Lear's *Nonsense.* But Roscoe produced only a temporary levity; Catherine Sin-clair was not a little in awe of her tall surroundings; Lear "loved to see little folks merry", and lay on his back kicking his heels in an ecstasy; whereas Lewis Carroll . . . was whole-heartedly forthright, straightforward, plain—any adjective that defines the negative of *arrière-pensée.* Ex-cept in the tiniest details of customary manners—the adjur-ation to curtsey, for instance, or Alice's compact vision of lessons as she fell down the rabbithole—there is not a back-hidden thought, an ulterior motive, in the *Alices* from be-ginning to end. The logic, the metaphysics, as well as the inhibitions, prohibitions, or what not, are in the text, it may be, but only if you happen to know, as a critic and rather tiresome historian, the facts of Charles Lutwidge Dodg-son's academic career. . . .

Yet [the *Alice* books] fell then and still fall into the category of "fairy-tales"; and as Dodgson himself once thought of calling the Wonderland book *Alice's Hour in Elfland,* that is perhaps justifiable, though neither fairy nor elf appears from one end to the other. There is simply magic, and even that is treated as just an extension of the natural—"curi-ouser and curiouser". The essence of the story in the trans-lation of the ordinary into the extraordinary in a plausible way—not as a conjuring trick (a white rabbit out of a mad-man's hat, so to speak), but as an almost logical extension

of properties inherent in this or that person or animal. The lizard, the dormouse, the caterpillar, the cat (grin or no grin)—they behave as they ought to behave if our simple faith could give them human speech and mien; and the in-ventions, the story-book or nursery-rhyme folk, are just as inevitable, once you grant them anthropoid life. The fault of the many imitators of Lewis Carroll—who are to this day a permanent plague to all editors and publishers of literature for children—is that they force the transition from one na-ture to the other; they invent, but they have not the logic.

> *F. J. Harvey Darton, in his* Children's Books in England: Five Centuries of Social Life, *Cambridge University Press, 2nd edi-tion, 1958, pp. 267-69.*

Though nearly all the Americans I know personally loved Lewis Carroll as children, they may not be representative of American taste in general. Certainly, in every American book read by children—from "Huckleberry Finn" to the "Oz" books—which I have come across, nothing could be more remote from their worlds than the world of Alice.

The American child-hero—are there any American child-heroines?—is a Noble Savage, an anarchist and, even when he reflects, predominantly concerned with movement and action. He may do almost anything except sit still. His he-roic virtue—that is to say, his superiority to adults—lies in his freedom from conventional ways of thinking and acting: *all* social habits, from manners to creeds, are regarded as false or hypocritical or both. All Emperors are really naked. Alice, surely, must come to the average American as a shock. (p. 15)

What is most likely to bewilder an American child . . . is not Alice's class-consciousness, which is easy to miss, but the peculiar relation of children and grown-ups to law and social manners. It is the child-heroine Alice who is invari-ably reasonable, self-controlled and polite, while all the other inhabitants, human or animal, of Wonderland and the Looking-Glass are unsocial eccentrics—at the mercy of their passions and extremely bad-mannered, like the Queen of Hearts, the Duchess, the Hatter and Humpty Dumpty, or grotesquely incompetent, like the White Queen and the White Knight.

What Alice finds so extraordinary about the people and events in these worlds is the anarchy which she is forever trying to make sense and order out of. In both books, games play an important role. The whole structure of "Alice Through the Looking-Glass" is based on chess, and the Queen of Hearts' favorite pastime is croquet—both of them games which Alice knows how to play. To play a game, it is essential that the players know and obey its rules, and are skillful enough to do the right or reasonable thing at least half the time. Anarchy and incompetence are incompatible with play.

Croquet played with hedge-hogs, flamingos and soldiers instead of the conventional balls, mallets and hoops is con-ceivable, provided that they are willing to imitate the be-havior of these inanimate objects, but, in Wonderland, they behave as they choose and the game is impossible to play.

In the Looking-Glass world, the problem is different. It is not, like Wonderland, a place of complete anarchy where everybody says and does whatever comes into his head, but a completely determined world without choice. Tweedledum and Tweedledee, the Lion and the Unicorn, the Red Knight and the White, must fight at regular intervals, irrespective of their feelings. In Wonderland, Alice has to adjust herself to a life without laws; in Looking-Glass Land, to one governed by laws to which she is unaccustomed. She has to learn, for example, to walk away from a place in order to reach it, or to run fast in order to remain where she is. In Wonderland, she is the only person with self-control; in Looking-Glass Land, the only competent one. But for the way she plays a pawn, one feels that the game of chess would never be completed.

In both worlds, one of the most important and powerful characters is not a person but the English language. Alice, who had hitherto supposed that words were passive objects, discovers that they have a life and will of their own. When she tries to remember poems she has learned, new lines come into her head unbidden and, when she thinks she knows what a word means, it turns out to mean something else. . . .

Nothing, surely, could be more remote from the American image of the pioneering, hunting, pre-political hero than this preoccupation with language. It is the concern of the solitary thinker, for language is the mother of thought, and of the politician—in the Greek sense—for speech is the medium by which we disclose ourselves to others. The American hero is neither. (p. 17)

Wonderland and Looking-Glass Land are fun to visit but no places to live in. Even when she is there, Alice can ask herself with some nostalgia "if anything would ever happen in a natural way again," and by "natural" she means the opposite of what Rousseau would mean. She means peaceful civilized society. (p. 19)

> *W. H. Auden, "Today's 'Wonder World' Needs Alice," in* The New York Times Magazine *(© 1962 by The New York Times Company; reprinted by permission), July 1, 1962, pp. 15-19.*

My own view is—though it arouses some Carrollians to a pitch of frenzy—that *Alice* is no longer a children's book. I do not deny that here and there a few unusual children, more in England than here, are still capable of enjoying it, but I believe their number is steadily diminishing. Like *Gulliver's Travels, Robinson Crusoe,* and *Huckleberry Finn, Alice* has joined that curious list of books that librarians call 'children's classics' but which are read and relished mostly by grownups. . . .

The truth is that, from a modern child's point of view, the Alice books are plotless, pointless, unfunny, and more frightening than a monster movie. (p. 18)

For intelligent children over fifteen and adults who . . . are not bored by fantasy, the Alice books are rich in subtle humour, social satire, and philosophical depth. Both books, especially the second [*Through the Looking Glass*], are crammed with paradoxical nonsense of exactly the sort that mathematicians and logicians revel in. It is no accident that you are likely to find more references to *Alice* in a book by a modern philosopher of science than in a book by a literary critic. . . . Alice dreams about the Red King but the Red King, too, is dreaming, and Alice is only a 'thing' in *his* dream. This double regress of Alices and kings, into infinitely more dreamlike levels nested in the skulls of each, is

a delicious thought to philosophers concerned with separating reality from illusion. But if a small child understands it at all, he is more likely to be upset than amused.

Moreover, *Alice* swarms with jokes that no American child will catch (e.g., the Ugly Duchess's clever double pun on the proverb 'Take care of the pence and the pounds will take care of themselves'). And there are jokes not even an English child today can understand (e.g., the parodies on poems, now forgotten, that Victorian children memorized). There are even jokes that a child in Carroll's time would not understand unless he was part of the Oxford community (e.g., the three Liddell-little puns in the first verse of the prefatory poem. The last name of Henry Liddell, dean of Christ Church and the father of Alice, rhymed with 'middle'.) It is all this, from the obscure word plays to the philosophical and mathematical paradoxes, that keep the *Alice* books alive among adults long after they have ceased to delight the average child. (pp. 18-19)

> *Martin Gardner, "A Child's Garden of Bewilderment" in* Saturday Review *(copyright © 1965 by Saturday Review Inc.; reprinted with permission), July 17, 1965, pp. 18-19.*

Alice, "Child of the pure unclouded brow," with her eager, expressive face, her long, straight hair, and her pinafore that adapts to so many sizes, is the eternal ingénue who combines Miranda's reaction to the wonders of a brave new world with Daisy Miller's resolve not to miss the tourist attractions. No novelist has identified more intimately with the point of view of his heroine [than Lewis Carroll]. Except for parenthetical comments, which occur less and less frequently, the empathy is complete. . . . Since Alice is in the habit of talking to herself, there can be a good deal of monologue. When she falls silent the narrator, like a good contemporary of Flaubert, can employ *le style indirect libre:* "Down, down, down. Would the fall *never* come to an end? 'I wonder how many miles I've fallen by this time?' she said aloud." (p. 595)

As for the pictorial presentation, it is an integral part of the author's design. He started with his own sketches, chose his illustrator with the utmost concern, and worked with Tenniel in the most indelible of collaborations. Consequently, there is little description in Dodgson's prose. It is all the more convincing because he simply assumes that the sights are there, and that we visualize them through the eyes of his beholder. Instead of describing the Gryphon, he enjoins us parenthetically: "If you don't know what a Gryphon is, look at the picture." Picture and text join forces to align the reader's awareness with that of Alice. Her inherent responsiveness is controlled by the consistent gravity of demeanor imposed upon her by the inhabitants of Wonderland. After the aimless competition of the Caucus-Race, when she is compelled to supply the prizes for everybody, including herself: "Alice thought the whole thing very absurd, but they all looked so grave that she did not dare to laugh; and, as she could not think of anything to say, she simply bowed, and took the thimble, looking as solemn as she could." So it is that children learn to suppress their native instinct for laughter in the company of adults. "He talks just as if it was a game!" says Alice of the Red King. But, though it may be a game for her, he is in dead earnest.

Alice soon gets used to the tone of desperate seriousness in which she is greeted by all the creatures she meets, with the exception of the Cheshire Cat, and we get used to the plethora of exclamation points. She is sustained through their dead-pan dialogues by the sense of wonder, the sort of curiosity that animates great poets and scientists. (p. 596)

One of the most touching episodes, and possibly the profoundest, takes place in the wood where things have no name. This is truly that *selva oscura* where the straight way is lost, that forest of symbols whose meanings have been forgotten, that limbo of silence which prompts a cosmic shudder. Less traditionally, since Dodgson was among the pioneers of symbolic logic, it could represent—in W. V. Quine's phrase—"the gulf between meaning and naming." There Alice comes across an unfrightened fawn, who momentarily allows itself to be stroked. Happily they co-exist for a time, undivided by identities or classifications. But the moment of self-recognition introduces a shock of alienation. . . .

A universe where the self has no labels or signposts to go by, in Dodgson's account, seems less estranging than a familiar environment which casts us in suspicious and hostile roles. Just as Hawthorne's faunlike protagonist regains the language of the birds and beasts when he returns to the countryside, so childhood has the faculty of communicating with nature spontaneously. Adulthood, on the other hand, superimposes its artifice, and Alice's experiences run increasingly counter to nature. (pp. 598-99)

The stuff of dreams is as illusory as those scented rushes which lose their fragrance and beauty when Alice picks them. Yet Dodgson catches the cinematographic movement of dreams when the grocery shop, after changing into the boat from which she gathers the dream-rushes, changes back into the shop which is identifiable as an Oxford landmark. . . . The narration, with its corkscrew twists, carefully observes the postulate that Dodgson formulated in his seriocomic treatise, "Dynamics of a Particle": "Let it be granted that a speaker may digress from any one point to any other point." Alice proceeds by digression through Wonderland, since it does not really matter which way she goes. In the Looking-Glass Land, which is regulated by a stricter set of ground rules, she is forced to move backward from time to time. Dodgson had given himself his *donnée* by sending her down the rabbit-hole "without the least idea what was to happen afterwards." What extemporaneously followed seemed to consist, as he subsequently recounted it, "almost wholly of fits and scraps, single ideas which came of themselves." Though it may have been obsession which gave them a thematic unity, it was artistry which devised their literary form.

Symmetrically, each of the two books comprises twelve chapters. Both of them conflate the dream vision with the genre known as the *voyage imaginaire;* in effect, they merge the fairy tale with science fiction. The journey, in either case, is not a quest like "The Hunting of the Snark" —or that log-book it almost seems to parody, *Moby-Dick.* Rather, it is an exploration—underground, in the first instance, and so originally entitled *Alice's Adventures Under Ground.* This relates it to a wealth of symbols for the claustral limits of the human condition, from Plato to Dostoevsky. Falling can betoken many things: above all, the precondition of knowledge. Subterranean descent can land in an underworld, be it Hell or Elysium or the other side of

the earth, the Antipodes, which Alice malapropistically calls "the Antipathies"—not so exact an opposite to our side as the Looking-Glass Country, but a topsy-turvydom of sorts like Butler's *Erewhon.* As we approach it, it seems to be a juvenile utopia, what with its solemn games and half-remembered lessons and ritualized performances of nursery rhymes. Before we leave it, it becomes an unconscious *Bildungsroman,* projecting and resisting the girlish drama of physical and psychological development. "What do you suppose is the use of a child without any meaning? [fumes the Red Queen.] Even a joke should have some meaning—and a child's more important than a joke, I hope." (pp. 604-05)

For [Carroll], *Alice's Adventures in Wonderland* had been a discovery, an improvisation, a series of serendipities; whereas *Through the Looking-Glass,* seven years later, was faced with the usual difficulty of sequels. It made up in systematic elaboration for what it lost in spontaneous flow. If it is less organically imagined, it is replete with brilliant paradoxes, some of which do anticipate modern science. (p. 606)

Inasmuch as surprise is of the essence, there is little recurrence from book to book. We hardly recognize the Hare and the Hatter of Wonderland when they are metamorphosed into the messengers Haigha and Hatta of the Looking-Glass. . . . Alice has been impelled underground by a swift train of circumstances; she dissolves the looking-glass, for herself and her kitten, with the hypnotic formula: "Let's pretend." She is more self-conscious on her first trip, and we are more interested in what happens to her. On her second, we tend to accept her and to look around with her, as if we were accompanying her through Disneyland or the World's Fair. The shift from identity to duality is a transference from self to otherness. The presiding figures from the game of cards are as remote as epic deities until the end of Part I. Their counterparts from chess are more regularly present throughout Part II, which is framed by a chess problem—not a very deliberative one. Alice becomes a pawn, replacing the Queen's daughter Lily, and looks ahead to being queened; whereas—except for her disappointed wish to arrive at the garden—her earlier wanderings, through cavernous passages and quasi-Elysian fields, had no set destination.

The excursion shifts from time to space, from an impressionistic continuum to a more static outlook, as she crosses the chessboard landscape. Above its checkered topography looms the presence of the geometrician who laid it out and manipulates the chessmen. What is happening has happened before and will happen again, at predictable intervals as long as folklore persists. Tweedledum and Tweedledee will fight; the Lion and the Unicorn will be drummed out of town; Humpty Dumpty will fall from his wall and, though not reconstructed by all the King's horses or men, will somehow be enabled to re-enact the performance. Now, all fairylands, utopias, paradises, and other imagined worlds— whatever improvements they may have to offer—are bound to draw their inspiration from the one world that their imaginer knows at first hand. It would be unlikely if Dodgson's creations were not liberally sprinkled with local and topical allusions. Sir John Tenniel, who was mainly a political caricaturist, occasionally injected an overt touch: in his drawing of the Lion and Unicorn we discern the features of rival candidates, the Earl of Derby and Disraeli. The latter also seems to have posed for the traveler dressed in white paper, peculiarly appropriate for a Prime Minister, who sits opposite Alice in the railway carriage. (pp. 606-07)

The poem that both illustrates and demonstrates the enigma [of Lewis Carroll's poetry] for us is bound to be "Jabberwocky," which—as its title obscurely hints—seems to be a heroic lay about language. Alice has discovered it in a book, at the outset of her second expedition, and it has filled her head with ideas; but she does not comprehend them until the midpoint, when she encounters Humpty Dumpty, whose onomatopoetic name fulfils his linguistic theories and asserts his cavalier nominalism. "The question is," as he expounds it to Alice, "which is to be master— that's all." The ancient nursery rhyme from which he derives his being was once a riddle rhymed in many languages. The answer is a symbol with many meanings, from the egg that germinates life to the fall that shatters it.

Hence he is fully qualified to be Dodgson's philosopher and philogist; from the precarious eminence of his hybris, he dominates the problems of interpretation; and, after his lecture to Alice on semantics, he sets forth an exegesis of "Jabberwocky" which is a model for higher and newer criticism . . . Humpty Dumpty puts on a dazzling exhibition of his mastery over words, in glossing the unfamiliar nouns and verbs and adjectives. Some of these are no more than archaisms; others, which interest us more, are neologisms; and the most interesting, among the latter, are those composites which Dodgson invented and patented as portmanteau words for the diction of dreams. (pp. 612-13)

"Jabberwocky," despite the double talk of its somnambulistic vocabulary, conforms to all the conventions of balladry. Childe Roland to the dark tower comes; Jack ends by killing the Giant; and, if the Snark proves a Boojum, it is not permitted to vanish away. Grappling with the nameless terrors that menace us all, Dodgson might have boasted, like his insomniac Baker:

> I engage with the Snark—every night after dark—
> In a dreamy delirious fight. . . .

The White King is similarly obsessed with Bandersnatches, who can never be caught or stopped, but who would seem to be lesser evils than the Jabberwock. The slaying of that dread apparition marks a rite of passage for the beamish boy, whoever he may be. (p. 614)

[The White Knight] is the kindliest of [Alice's] guides and advisers, indeed the truest hero of her story; and it is their encounter, we are told, that she will always remember most clearly. . . . Their farewell is as poignant as Dante's from Vergil at the upper boundaries of Purgatory. But the Knight has a closer precedent in Don Quixote, whom he emulates with his uncertain horsemanship and his headful of chimerical plans. His memorable song, which functions as a kind of cadenza to the work as a whole, parodies Wordsworth's "Resolution and Independence," where the dejected poet is revivified by the example of the old leech-gatherer plying his humble trade on the lonely moor. An earlier version of Dodgson's burlesque had been separately published, and he drew the character of the Knight to suit the speaker in it. Therefore it is a portrait within a portrait. (p. 615)

The image reflected from the one to the other ad infinitum is thus a self-caricature: Dodgson as Lewis Carroll as the White Knight as the speaker of the poem as its interloc-

utor. . . . No doubt many voices in the two stories are primarily his own: the grumpiness of the Caterpillar, the amusement of the Cheshire Cat, the pedagogy of Humpty Dumpty. In the amiable eccentric who sings the song—and even more in the useless ingenuities, the woolgathering projects, and the endearing crotchets of its quixotic protagonist—Dodgson has offered us his *apologia pro vita sua*. Virginia Woolf discerned that he had preserved a child within him intact; meanwhile his outer self had become a pedant, who measured everyone's words with a literalness which exposed the contradictions by which they lived; yet, in the dialogue between the incongruous pair, childhood took the measure of pedantry. Understandably the White Knight is disappointed when Alice sheds no tears at his recital. But the game is virtually over. Alice has only to leap across the brook, be crowned, and wake up to a less adventurous actuality. The storyteller, folding his chessboard and putting away the pieces, can voice the satisfaction of a demiurge who has populated a cosmos and set it in motion, with the White Knight's vaunt: "It's my own invention!" (pp. 615-16)

Harry Levin, "Wonderland Revisited," in The Kenyon Review *(copyright 1965 by Kenyon College), Autumn, 1965, pp. 591-616.*

The moral of *Alice* is . . . the first clear, simple and definite demonstration that childhood is and should be a golden age to be enjoyed and explored to the full: treasured in actuality while it is present and in memory when it is past, but with no suggestion of trying to prolong it or of escaping into it from the responsibilities of later life. Extrovert Alice expresses this philosophy in every word and action throughout her adventures; she is the absolute antithesis of introvert Peter Pan with his: 'I want always to be a little boy and to have fun.'

Roger Lancelyn Green, in his Tellers of Tales: British Authors of Children's Books from 1800 to 1964 *(copyright 1946, © 1965 by Edmund Ward, Publishers, Ltd.; reprinted courtesy of Kaye & Ward Ltd.), revised edition, Kaye & Ward Ltd., 1965, p. 58.*

The revolutionary quality of [*Alice's Adventures in Wonderland* and *Through the Looking Glass*] lies in the fact that they were written purely to give pleasure to children; moreover they were written purely for pleasure on the part of the author, too, for thus is a masterpiece made. Here, then, for the first time we find a story designed for children without a trace of a lesson or moral. In a sense the Alice story is childhood itself, with its wonder and its wisdom; with the grave little heroine, curious but never prying, anxious to please but never afraid, moving with the gentle grace of unspoiled childhood through all the extraordinary events and among the extraordinary characters of Wonderland and the Looking-Glass World.

Anne Thaxter Eaton, in A Critical History of Children's Literature, *by Cornelia Meigs, Anne Thaxter Eaton, Elizabeth Nesbitt, and Ruth Hill Viguers, edited by Cornelia Meigs (copyright © 1969 by Macmillan Publishing Co., Inc.), revised edition, Macmillan, 1969, pp. 194-95.*

There are very few incidents in Lewis Carroll's work that do not inject meanings that touch us by the element of truth they possess, and children capable of grasping the ideas behind the symbols and allegories will find themselves viewing life from another angle and so becoming more and more conscious of their own world while still enjoying the vibrant storyland of Alice. . . .

Alice stands as a supreme example of literary art. Its dream world offers a new view of reality and gives young readers a sense of expansion from the imaginative experience, which, in the end, is the test of any good fantasy.

> *Constantine Georgiou, in his* Children and Their Literature *(© 1969; reprinted by permission of Prentice-Hall, Inc., Englewood Cliffs, New Jersey), Prentice-Hall, 1969, p. 275.*

With these twin masterpieces the work of fantasy for children reached a pinnacle never surpassed. They exhibit an astonishing rightness in every word and situation. Adults delight in the cleverness, the hidden logic, the wise nonsense, the quotable phrases, yet to a child they have a fascination which has little to do with such refinements. For him the appeal lies in the story, where strange and amusing things happen, and all kinds of funny and fascinating creatures behave with the most convincing oddity. Wonderland becomes a real place—as vivid as dreamland. What gives the tales such perfect balance and certainty is the character of Alice herself, who never changes in her nature however large or small she may grow, or however queerly the verses she knows by heart are changed in the speaking. Sensible, good-natured, charmingly gentle and lovable, she personifies the best traits of Victorian childhood.

> *Mary F. Thwaite, in her* From Primer to Pleasure in Reading: An Introduction to the History of Children's Books in England from the Invention of Printing to 1914 with an Outline of Some Developments in Other Countries *(copyright © 1963 by M. F. Thwaite), 2nd edition, The Library Association, 1972, p. 116.*

For many of us Lewis Caroll's two *Alice* books may have provided the first glimpse into Victorian England. With their curious blend of literal-mindedness and dream, formal etiquette and the logic of insanity, they tell the adult reader a great deal about the Victorian mind. Alice herself, prim and earnest in pinafore and pumps, confronting a world out of control by looking for the rules and murmuring her lessons, stands as one image of the Victorian middle-class child. She sits in Tenniel's first illustration to *Through the Looking-Glass and What Alice Found There* in a snug, semi-foetal position, encircled by a protective armchair and encircling a plump kitten and a ball of yarn. She seems to be a beautiful child, but the position of her head makes her look as though she had no face. She muses dreamily on the snowstorm raging outside, part of a series of circles within circles, enclosures within enclosures, suggesting the self-containment of innocence and eternity.

Behind the purity of this design lie two Victorian domestic myths: Wordsworth's "seer blessed," the child fresh from the Imperial Palace and still washed by his continuing contact with "that immortal sea," and the pure woman Alice

will become, preserving an oasis for God and order in a dim and tangled world. Even Victorians who did not share Lewis Carroll's phobia about the ugliness and uncleanliness of little boys saw little girls as the purest members of a species of questionable origin, combining as they did the inherent spirituality of child and woman. Carroll's Alice seems sister to such famous figures as Dickens' Little Nell and George Eliot's Eppie, who embody the poise of original innocence in a fallen, sooty world. (pp. 31-2)

Lewis Carroll remembered what Charles Dodgson and many later commentators did not, that while *Looking-Glass* may have been the dream of the Red King, *Wonderland* is Alice's dream. Despite critical attempts to psychoanalyze Charles Dodgson through the writings of Lewis Carroll, the author of *Alice's Adventures in Wonderland* was too precise a logician and too controlled an artist to confuse his own dream with that of his character. The question "who dreamed it?" underlies all Carroll's dream tales, part of a pervasive Victorian quest for the origins of the self that culminates in the controlled regression of Freudian analysis. There is no equivocation in Carroll's first *Alice* book: the dainty child carries the threatening kingdom of Wonderland within her. A closer look at the character of Alice may reveal new complexities in the sentimentalized and attenuated Wordsworthianism many critics have assumed she represents, and may deepen through examination of a single example our vision of that "fabulous monster," the Victorian child.

Lewis Carroll once wrote to a child that while he forgot the story of *Alice,* "I think it was about 'malice.'" Some Freudian critics would have us believe it was about phallus. Alice herself seems aware of the implications of her shifting name when at the beginning of her adventures she asks herself the question that will weave through her story:

> I wonder if I've been changed in the night? Let me think: *was* I the same when I got up this morning? I almost think I can remember feeling a little different. But if I'm not the same, the next question is, 'Who in the world am I?' Ah, *that's* the great puzzle!

Other little girls traveling through fantastic countries, such as George Macdonald's Princess Irene and L. Frank Baum's Dorothy Gale, ask repeatedly "*where* am I?" rather than "*who* am I?" Only Alice turns her eyes inward from the beginning, sensing that the mystery of her surroundings is the mystery of her identity.

Even the above-ground Alice speaks in two voices, like many Victorians other than Dodgson-Carroll:

> She generally gave herself very good advice, (though she very seldom followed it), and sometimes she scolded herself so severely as to bring tears into her eyes; and once she remembered trying to box her own ears for having cheated herself in a game of croquet she was playing against herself, for this curious child was very fond of pretending to be two people.

The pun on "curious" defines Alice's fluctuating personality. Her eagerness to know and to be right, her compulsive reciting of her lessons ("I'm sure I can't be Mabel, for I know all sorts of things") turn inside out into the bizarre anarchy of her dream country, as the lessons themselves turn inside out into strange and savage tales of animals eating each other. In both senses of the word, Alice becomes "curiouser and curiouser" as she moves more deeply into Wonderland; she is both the croquet game without rules and its violent arbiter, the Queen of Hearts. The sea that almost drowns her is composed of her own tears, and the dream that nearly obliterates her is composed of fragments of her own personality. (pp. 32-4)

The demure propriety of Tenniel's Alice may have led readers to see her role in *Alice's Adventures in Wonderland* as more passive than it is. Although her size changes seem arbitrary and terrifying, she in fact directs them; only in the final courtroom scene does she change size without first wishing to, and there, her sudden growth gives her the power to break out of a dream that has become too dangerous. Most of Wonderland's savage songs come from Alice: the Caterpillar, Gryphon and Mock Turtle know that her cruel parodies of contemporary moralistic doggerel are "wrong from beginning to end." She is almost always threatening to the animals of Wonderland. As the mouse and birds almost drown in her pool of tears, she eyes them with a strange hunger which suggests that of the *Looking-Glass* Walrus who weeps at the Oysters while devouring them behind his handkerchief. Her persistent allusions to her predatory cat Dinah and to a "nice little dog, near our house," who "kills all the rats" finally drive the animals away, leaving Alice to wonder forlornly—and disingenuously—why nobody in Wonderland likes Dinah.

Dinah is a strange figure. She is the only above-ground character whom Alice mentions repeatedly, almost always in terms of her eating some smaller animal. She seems finally to function as a personification of Alice's own subtly cannibalistic hunger, as Fury in the Mouse's tale is personified as a dog. . . . While Dinah is always in a predatory attitude, most of the Wonderland animals are lugubrious victims; together, they encompass the two sides of animal nature that are in Alice as well. (pp. 35-6)

Even when Dinah is not mentioned, Alice's attitude toward the animals she encounters is often one of casual cruelty. . . . The more sinister and Darwinian aspects of animal nature are introduced into Wonderland by the gentle Alice, in part through projections of her hunger onto Dinah and the "nice little dog" (she meets a "dear little puppy" after she has grown small and is afraid he will eat her up) and in part through the semi-cannibalistic appetite her songs express. With the exception of the powerful Cheshire Cat . . . most of the Wonderland animals stand in some danger of being exploited or eaten. The Dormouse is their prototype: he is fussy and cantankerous, with the nastiness of a self-aware victim, and he is stuffed into a teapot as the Mock Turtle, sobbing out his own elegy, will be stuffed into a tureen. (p. 37)

[All] the human or quasi-human characters . . . develop aspects of Alice that exist only under the surface of her dialogue. The Duchess' household also turns inside out the domesticated Wordsworthian ideal: with baby and pepper flung about indiscriminately, pastoral tranquillity is inverted into a whirlwind of savage sexuality. The furious Cook embodies the equation between eating and killing that underlies Alice's apparently innocent remarks about Dinah. The violent Duchess' unctuous search for "the moral" of things echoes Alice's own violence and search for "the

rules." At the Mad Tea Party, the Hatter extends Alice's "great interest in questions of eating and drinking" into an insane *modus vivendi*; like Alice, the Hatter and the Duchess sing savage songs about eating that embody the underside of Victorian literary treacle. The Queen's croquet game magnifies Alice's own desire to cheat at croquet and to punish herself violently for doing so. Its use of live animals may be a subtler extension of Alice's own desire to twist the animal kingdom to the absurd rules of civilization, which seem to revolve largely around eating and being eaten. Alice is able to appreciate the Queen's savagery so quickly because her size changes have made her increasingly aware of who she, herself, is from the point of view of a Caterpillar, a Mouse, a Pigeon, and, especially, a Cheshire Cat.

The Cheshire Cat . . . is the only figure other than Alice who encompasses all the others. . . . [There is a] spiritual kinship between Alice and the Cat, the only creature in Wonderland whom she calls her "friend." . . . The Cat shares Alice's equivocal placidity: "The Cat only grinned when it saw Alice. It looked good-natured, she thought: still it had *very* long claws and a great many teeth, so she felt it ought to be treated with respect". . . . The Cat is the only creature to make explicit the identification between Alice and the madness of Wonderland: "'. . . we're all mad here. I'm mad. You're mad.' 'How do you know I'm mad?' said Alice. 'You must be,' said the Cat, 'or you wouldn't have come here.' Alice didn't think that proved it at all. . . .'" . . . Although Alice cannot accept it and closes into silence, the Cat's remark may be the answer she has been groping toward in her incessant question, "who am I?" As an alter ego, the Cat is wiser than Alice—and safer—because he is the only character in the book who is aware of his own madness. In his serene acceptance of the fury within and without, his total control over his appearance and disappearance, he almost suggests a post-analytic version of the puzzled Alice.

As Alice dissolves increasingly into Wonderland, so the Cat dissolves into his own head, and finally into his own grinning mouth. The core of Alice's nature, too, seems to lie in her mouth: the eating and drinking that direct her size changes and motivate much of her behavior, the songs and verses that pop out of her inadvertently, are all involved with things entering and leaving her mouth. . . . Walter de la Mare associates Alice with "a quiet moon" which is by implication a full moon. I think it is more appropriate to associate her with the grinning crescent that seems to follow her throughout her adventures, choosing to become visible only at particular moments, and teaching her the one lesson she must learn in order to arrive at a definition of who she is. (pp. 38-9)

Presented from the point of view of her older sister's sentimental pietism, the world to which Alice awakens seems far more dream-like and hazy than the sharp contours of Wonderland. Alice's lesson about her own identity has never been stated explicitly, for the stammerer Dodgson was able to talk freely only in his private language of puns and nonsense. . . .

[An] important technique in learning to read Carroll is our ability to interpret his private system of symbols and signals and to appreciate the many meanings of silence. . . . Only in *Alice's Adventures in Wonderland* was Carroll able to fall all the way through the rabbit hole to the point where top and bottom become one, bats and cats melt into each other, and the vessel of innocence and purity is also the source of inescapable corruption. (p. 41)

Throughout the books, the schism between Blacks (later Reds) and Whites is developed. Alice's greater innocence and passivity [in *Through the Looking Glass*] are stressed by her identification with Lily, the white pawn. The dominant metaphor of a chess game whose movements are determined by invisible players spreads her sense of helplessness and predestination over the book. The nursery rhymes of which most of the characters form a part also make their movements seem predestined; the characters in *Wonderland* tend more to create their own nursery rhymes. The question that weaves through the book is no longer "who am I?" but "which dreamed it?" If the story is the dream of the Red King (the sleeping embodiment of passion and masculinity), then Alice, the White Pawn (or pure female child) is exonerated from its violence, although in another sense, as she herself perceives, she is also in greater danger of extinction. Her increasing sweetness and innocence in the second book make her more ghost-like as well, and it is appropriate that more death jokes surround her in the second *Alice* book than in the first. (p. 42)

Carroll's Alice . . . explodes out of Wonderland hungry and unregenerate. By a subtle dramatization of Alice's attitude toward animals and toward the animal in herself, by his final resting on the symbol of her mouth, Carroll probed in all its complexity the underground world within the little girl's pinafore. The ambiguity of the concluding trial finally, and wisely, waives questions of original guilt or innocence. The ultimate effect of Alice's adventures implicates her, female child though she is, in the troubled human condition; most Victorians refused to grant women and children this respect. The sympathetic delicacy and precision with which Carroll traced the chaos of a little girl's psyche seems equalled and surpassed only later in such explorations as D. H. Lawrence's of the young Ursula Brangwen in *The Rainbow*, the chaos of whose growth encompasses her hunger for violence, sexuality, liberty, and beatitude. In the imaginative literature of its century, *Alice's Adventures in Wonderland* stands alone. (pp. 46-7)

> *Nina Auerbach, "Alice and Wonderland: A Curious Child," in* Victorian Studies (© *The Trustees of Indiana University 1972), September, 1973, pp. 31-47.*

No one at this date is going to deny the greatness of Lewis Carroll's genius: his marvellous gift for perverted logic, for parody, for contriving impossible juxtapositions: 'They roused him with muffins, they roused him with ice.' He is only rivalled by Edward Lear to whom he bears little resemblance. He was the Shakespeare of absurdity and if there had been no Lewis Carroll (and there nearly was not, for Charles Dodgson was a wholly different person) our world would be much poorer and unlike the one we have. . . .

All poets, including the greatest, write some bad poetry . . ., and all Lewis Carroll's serious poems are extremely bad. His style in them was a good example of what Ronald Knox used to call 'slosh', a useful portmanteau word combining 'slop' and 'tosh'. . . .

Nor is all his purely comic verse of a high order. Some of

it, such as *Melancholetta*, is utterly unworthy of the masterly parodist of Wordsworth in *The Three Voices*, and some of his great things are spoilt by the introduction of comic ideas that do not come off. The lace-making beaver in *The Hunting of the Snark* always seems to me a blot on a masterpiece. *Phantasmagoria* may be described as Carroll's most sustained failure, and *Poeta Fit, non Nascitur* strikes me as a dismally missed opportunity. Nevertheless his comic verse is rarely without any interest. . . .

Criticising Lewis Carroll is really a waste of time. What is great about him is so great that even if it represented only a minute proportion of the whole of his output, it would place him on the heights of Parnassus. To denigrate him is like making faces at Homer.

> *Christopher Sykes, in* Books and Bookmen *(© copyright Christopher Sykes), October, 1973, p. 36.*

Uniquely, Dodgson discovered an intellectual legitimacy in the childish viewpoint, making it available to both childish and adult intelligences. . . .

The Alices are eccentric performances about the child's need to deal with an eccentric world, and an ideal of courtesy is at their center. . . .

[They] are admittedly minor works and eccentric in their appeal to convention, but there is nothing weak-minded about the fun they poke at grown-up usages. The collusion with childhood is almost totally without intellectual condescension; this fact is remarkable enough in itself to justify the courtesy of criticism. (p. 606)

In the conventional fairy tale, the talking animals usually side with the child or offer it refuge from the oppressive adult world. Dodgson has adapted the convention by putting the creatures in place of the adults and making them intensely argumentative rather than physically menacing; the joke is partly at the child's expense that the familiar creatures of nursery fiction would function in this way and prove so incomprehensible. But their incomprehensibility is not a matter of sheer nonsense when measured by logical standards . . . and their impatience with Alice, which mirrors the chronic impatience of elders with their juniors, if rather more intense, has somewhere behind it the notion that language is perfectly adequate to the business of transmitting culture from one generation to the next. The child can speak and therefore should be able to take in the meaning of what is said; her inability is treated as refusal, as if she could perfectly well understand if she only *wanted* to badly enough. Her confusion is taken as a sign of moral weakness or—worse—outright viciousness of temper. Like the baby who sneezes when peppered by the cook, she does it to annoy, because she knows it teases. (pp. 607-08)

Powerless in the real world, the dreaming child loses her authority over the familiar creatures of play—pets, cards, figures from nursery rhymes, chessmen—by a further diminution of size; this produces a feeling of defenselessness that occasionally makes Alice cry but is not finally terrifying. ("What fun!" chuckles the Gryphon. "It's all her fancy that: they never executes anybody, you know.") Whatever its aspect of bluster, the adult world in the books clearly means her no harm, and even submits at times to her management. What produces the appearance of authority is Alice's eagerness to learn—always happy, as

Dodgson says of her, to find out some new sort of rule—and the dreamlike failure of her usual rituals for asserting herself when urged by the creatures to "remember who she is" (a pun collapsing personal identity and social status). The hint is clear that the condition will pass away with the dream, the way grown-up authority over her will pass away in real life when she gets to full size. (p. 611)

Alice is put through her paces on command . . . and it is appropriate to the dream-mechanism that she remain unaware, as her younger readers do not, of the power her superior sort of nonsense has in putting grown-ups in their place; the child may be spellbound in the dream of grown-up authority, but it is her dream, after all, and the creatures have only the life she gives them, so real coerciveness is out of the question; there is simply no point in making an uncomfortable sort of issue about it. . . . [The] creatures are so thoroughly the victims of their own absurdity that Alice can move among them with the evenhanded curiosity of a visitor to a foreign land, submissive to local ordinances but largely uninvolved in what she sees. (pp. 612-13)

The Knight, with his gentle face and mild eyes, his self-imposed duty to go no further than the edge of maturity, and his need for only passing sympathy as he turns back into the shadows of the forest, makes an ideal figure of the grown-up as Dodgson conceives it. He is intellectually childish, because adults know nothing to distinguish them from children, but emotionally he is without either the petulance or the complacency that leads most of the other creatures to bully or exploit the child. At the other extreme, I would put the creatures at the Mad Tea Party. They begin by trying to deny the child any place at the table, are more impatient at her interruptions than anyone else in the book, mock her interest in riddles, and hint at the presence of real mysteries to which the childish intelligence is unsuitable. (p. 617)

[Alice] functions as the critical intelligence in the book, and the Hatter and Hare find it necessary to put her down. . . . The tea that the creatures are forced to be at forever is not High Tea, which was just coming in, but the child's supper; everyone is secretly condemned to remain in some way at the childish level, but the churlishness that the creatures show the child here finds it appropriate punishment in their having to live forever in the mess of the child's mealtime, while taking no pleasure in the conversation at table. (p. 618)

Because she is the most even-tempered, the least self-concerned, the child is the most sensibly behaved person in the books; for the same reasons she has the best manners. . . . [If] the Alices present a desperately incomplete image of childhood, the same can be said for any literary presentation of character; the deliberate enabling of attitudes and responses where they are implausible is simply part of the conventions of fiction. The real question is the use to which the conventions are put, which is here to shed an ironic light on the projects of maturity; the child's complacency, born of the dream, is a touchstone of disinterested curiosity, not a model for imitation. (pp. 618-19)

The Alice of the books is an ideal figure, but not in the sense that Wordsworth's pygmy darlings are ideals. (p. 619)

[She] is not meant to solace anyone, quite the reverse, in fact (although she is permitted to give the Wordsworthian figure of the White Knight a little encouragement), and the opposition between her and the grown-ups cannot be figured in terms of sensibility versus intellect. . . .

The simple fact about Alice is that she has not lived long enough to worry about things adding up, and her curiosity (an intellectual quality, not a matter of sensibility) carries her lightly along on the current of time. She thinks like adults but without their anxieties, and the idealization lies not in its mythic qualities but in its resolute one-sidedness, which ignores the darker, ambitious motives that shade the intellectual character of children in reality. Her qualities are most deliberately on view in the Wool-and-Water Shop, which is Oxford, the higher learning, and civilization, all rolled into one. Things flow about, but the grown-up intellect has to pretend that they can be valued and ticketed, although what you are looking for is always on the next shelf above the one you are looking at, and will even go through the ceiling "as if it were quite used to it." The child, too, sees only by glimpses but is undismayed by this, unlike adults, because she is temperamentally attuned to the fact that nothing stands still. This is not to say that she is somehow closer to nature. (p. 621)

The mad world of the books is the world of culture, with its radical discontinuities; anyone who enters it has lost the community of nature, although the common possession of speech makes one imagine otherwise. Alice can recognize its oddities because in her own way she knows what the ability to speak presupposes—namely, how to distinguish consistency from inconsistency by attending to context in the use of terms. But the common possession of this ability, and the logical sense that goes with it, is not enough to establish common sense in the world of culture. The grown-up figures in the books fail to realize this and act as if the child can perfectly well understand if she wants to. If they are mocked, it is not because they are madder than she, but because they get so intensely logical about the normative character of their eccentricities. (p. 622)

If there is a virtue about childhood for Dodgson, it lies . . . in the child's intellectual good manners, her unflagging, disinterested curiosity, her willingness to entertain the paradoxes of grown-ups without belaboring them in the name of her own. If the real world recognizes it as politeness to let eccentricity sometimes pass unnoticed, sociability is quite basically founded in the books upon accepting the wholesale equivocation of all conduct. The famous "Jabberwocky" that opens [*Through the Looking Glass*] points the moral of this: the normal words in the poem furnish something like the fictive equivalent to the logical structure of an argument, in relation to which the neologisms are left free to take on whatever meanings their associations suggest to any reader. Here again the child shows decent humility of spirit: "Somehow it seems to fill my head with ideas—only I don't know exactly what they are!" It is no wonder that Alice became a patron saint of surrealism. (p. 623)

Perhaps we can admit this much of innocence to the child: endlessly curious, she continues to hope that the moral imagination will say something sensible. (p. 629)

Alvin C. Kibel, "Logic and Satire in Alice in Wonderland," in The American Scholar *(copyright © 1974 by the United Chapters of Phi Beta Kappa; reprinted by permission of the publishers), Vol. 43, No. 4, Autumn, 1974, pp. 605-29.*

Superficially [*Alice's Adventures in Wonderland* and *Through the Looking Glass*] resemble each other closely. In each, Alice meets a succession of fantastic characters, and each ends with a big set-piece: the trial scene in *Wonderland* and the banquet in *Looking-Glass*. But the striking difference is that for better or worse *Looking-Glass* is much more contrived than *Wonderland*. The earlier book was based on actual stories told to children; the later one was written at leisure to please the author himself. The machinery used to begin *Wonderland* is very simple and casual; Alice follows the White Rabbit down a rabbit-hole and the story is under way. *Looking-Glass* begins more elaborately with Alice's climbing through the mirror and with the reversal of normal processes at the other side of the glass, which is worked out in considerable detail. *Wonderland* has no obvious formal structure; its incidents follow each other quite casually, like a dream sequence. *Looking-Glass* is based on the very tight pattern of a game of chess.

> *John Rowe Townsend, in his* Written for Children: An Outline of English-Language Children's Literature *(copyright © 1965, 1974 by John Rowe Townsend; reprinted by permission of J. B. Lippincott Company), revised edition, Lippincott, 1974, p. 96.*

The personality of the dreamer is not as a rule important in a dream, but Alice's personality is shown clearly, in her rambling soliloquies with their fragments of past lessons and adult injunctions, her careful selection of a suitable mode of address for a Queen, a nursery-rhyme character, a sobbing Mock Turtle. The whimsical simplification called *The Nursery Alice* has almost no conversation; as a result, it reads like a blue-print for Alice's first dream and she becomes a mere mechanical pretext for it. . . .

Children who read the books when they are too young are often frightened by them, especially by the nightmarish changes of size and the persecution of Bill the Lizard; they are not ready to appreciate the core of self-command in Alice herself. They respond to the safer parts of the humour in the stories, while leaving to adults the pleasure of identifying parodies, playing the chess game, enjoying Carroll's erudition and logic and, sometimes, guessing at his secret longings and aberrations. *Alice in Wonderland* and *Through the Looking Glass* were the first celebrations of nonsense in children's literature; they have become a shibboleth of the English-speaking intellectual world and a favourite playground for supererudite research. In the view of many they are not in fact suitable books for children: at least they are unmistakably stories of a child's world.

> *Margery Fisher, in her* Who's Who in Children's Books: A Treasury of the Familiar Characters of Childhood *(copyright © 1975 by Margery Fisher; reprinted by permission of Holt, Rinehart and Winston), Holt, Rinehart and Winston, 1975, p. 17.*

ALICE'S ADVENTURES IN WONDERLAND (1865)

When we analyze *Alice in Wonderland* we see that it is not, as *Pilgrim's Progress* or *Gulliver's Travels*, a thinly disguised allegory or a satire on life. It depends on other qualities for its unity. Lewis Carroll builds up striking patterns of language and idea, each part held in subtle relation to the others. The unity of the book is not in the design alone, but also in the consistent point of view. The story is Alice's dream as Alice dreamed it; the point of view is invariably that of the rational child in an irrational dream. The language is the language of nonsense, but at the same time we are sensible of the essence of truth it contains. . . .

In [the *Alice* books] the illusion created by Lewis Carroll is so complete that we lose sight of the complicated and ingenious pattern of their structure. The books are undeniably written on two planes, that of the child and that of the adult. Perhaps it would be truer to say that the writing is a language to which the heart of childhood has the little golden key, while the implications of the ideas reveal themselves more and more with the added experience of life. As we ponder them we cannot wonder that *Alice in Wonderland* is to so many an inexhaustible source of pleasure in its crisp fresh humor, its rich and subtle symbolism, and the infinite speculation it leads to.

> *Lillian H. Smith, in her* The Unreluctant Years: A Critical Approach to Children's Literature *(reprinted by permission; copyright 1953 by the American Library Association), American Library Association, 1953, pp. 154, 156-57.*

Nothing could be more specifically English than the humor [in *Alice in Wonderland*]. Humor, being always a contradiction between what one says and what one seems to say, is often a serious way of expressing amusing things, but it can also be an amusing way of expressing serious things. I appeal to all those who have ever given themselves up to that infernal pastime called croquet. Every croquet match resembles that of the Queen's, either for the furies that it arouses if one takes it tragically (Off with his head!) or for the indescribable tumult which usually interrupts the game. And so the description that one finds of it in *Alice in Wonderland* has its share of resemblance and truth. Likewise, nobody will claim that the conversations held around a cup of tea are substantial; and anyone, who, for ten, twenty or thirty years of his life, has devoted two hours a day to such a practice, runs a great risk of resembling the Dormouse or the Hatter. Or again, read the last part of the story, the trial of the Knave of Hearts who had stolen the tarts, as a bit of the *Nursery Rhymes* we have quoted tells us; and among the diverse depositions of the witnesses, each one more extravagant than the others, remember that of Alice. . . .

It is nonsense. But it is not pure invention: there are trials conducted in this way. We laugh for some profound reason of which we are hardly conscious, but which takes shape in our mind. The idea is caricatural, but is not completely false. On the contrary, it touches us by the element of truth that it contains.

The English are a calm and cold people. But let them relax, for a single day, that compulsion for self-control which governs them and they will show a capacity for boisterous unrestraint that is surprising. Let them, for a single day, allow their imagination full swing and they will experiment to the very limits of their repressed curiosity. It is the same with laughter. When they enjoy looking at the universe on its fantastic side, distorting it with deforming mirrors, there is no stopping them. They have their own kind of laughter, rather simple, apparently, but in reality rich with a very complicated content, skillfully mixed with humor. A foreigner can try to understand *Alice in Wonderland;* but to appreciate fully this marvelous story one must be English.

Paul Hazard, in his Books, Children and Men, *translated by Marguerite Mitchell (copyright © The Horn Book, Inc.; all rights reserved; reprinted with permission), 4th edition, Horn Book, 1960, p. 139, 140.*

[*Alice's Adventures in Wonderland*] is, quite simply and categorically, an exceptionally good book on every count; many books which are quite good, even very good, have been neglected and have often gone out of print but anything as astonishingly good as Alice is sure to attract a succession of readers of many types and not merely adults. It has an atmosphere of its own which can be sensed fairly young, it is continuously entertaining and apparently inexhaustible; it never stales and seems better at each repetition. It is quite possible that a child who does enjoy Alice has a higher appreciation of some of its aspects than an adult whose experience makes him more conscious of its technical perfection and its application to almost any situation encountered in life. (pp. 265-66)

It seems so natural it might almost have sprung up like a flower or a sun and although there was much in Carroll which explains its virtues there was quite as much again which would seem to interfere with its perfection. Even he said it had come of itself and each re-reading shows how marvellously well it managed the job, with practically every scene and every dialogue—certainly every character— memorable from almost the first meeting. Perhaps no other book will ever be quite so all-of-a-piece, so individual and unique, and if its flavour comes across reasonably well even in a middling translation its impact in English can hardly be lost on anyone really sensitive to the language. Since children are still finding their way around our words and their meaning and are often extremely sensitive to the language they often are more intrigued with this aspect of the book than they realise themselves, for they are usually led to believe that the story is the most important part of any book. (pp. 266-67)

J. H. Dohm, "Alice in America," in The Junior Bookshelf, *October, 1965, pp. 261-67.*

Alice's Adventures in Wonderland comes within the decade of *Eric, or Little by Little* (1858), *The Water Babies* (1863), and *Jessica's First Prayer* (1867), but the pious, the moralistic, and the didactic are as much absent from its pages as if they had never existed at all in children's literature. For some children the charm of the Alice books may rest on the sheer fantasy—Alice's extraordinary changes of size, the Cheshire Cat's grin, the pig baby; for others on the relentless logic with which Carroll works out his ideas, so that in Looking-Glass Country, where everything works backwards, Alice has to walk in the opposite direction to the place she wants to reach in order to arrive there, is given a dry biscuit by the Red Queen to quench her thirst after running, and learns to pass a cake round first and cut it up afterwards. Another amusing ingredient is the clever use of words—the puns of the Gnat, the Mock Turtle's verbal confusions, like the four branches of Arithmetic—Ambition, Distraction, Uglification, and Derision; or the use, in comparisons by the White Knight, of adjectives in the

wrong sense—wind "as strong as soup", or, of himself stuck upside down in his helmet, "as fast as lightning". But possibly the most refreshing thing of all about these books is the way the nonsense is set in sparkling contrast against a background of dull, everyday, schoolroom life.

Gillian Avery, in her Nineteenth Century Children: Heroes and Heroines in English Children's Stories 1780-1900 *(copyright © 1965 by Gillian Avery), Hodder and Stoughton Ltd, 1965, p. 129.*

It [is] time . . . that *Alice* be treated for what it most certainly is—a book of major and permanent importance in the tradition of English fiction, a work that still pertains directly to the experience of the unspecialized reader, and one that exemplifies the profound questioning of reality which characterizes the mainstream of nineteenth-century English literature.

The fact that Carroll's first version of *Alice's Adventures in Wonderland* was called *Alice's Adventures under Ground* is surprisingly prophetic. Perhaps even the final version would be more appropriately entitled *Alice's Adventures under Ground,* since, above all else, it embodies a comic horror-vision of the chaotic land beneath the man-made groundwork of Western thought and convention. . . .

Merely to list the reverses Alice encounters in Wonderland is to survey at a glance an almost total destruction of the fabric of our so-called logical, orderly, and coherent approach to the world. Practically all pattern, save the consistency of chaos, is annihilated. First, there are the usual modes of thought—ordinary mathematics and logic: in Wonderland they possess absolutely no meaning. Next are the even more basic social and linguistic conventions: these too lose all validity. Finally, the fundamental framework of conscious prediction—orderly Time and Space—appears nowhere except in the confused memory . . . of the befuddled but obstinate visitor from above ground. Alice, therefore, becomes the reader's surrogate on a frightful journey into meaningless night. The only difference between Alice and the reader—and this is significant—is that she soberly, tenaciously, childishly refuses to accept chaos completely for what it is, while the adult reader almost invariably responds with the only defense left open to him in the face of unquestionable chaos—he laughs. Naturally he laughs for other reasons, too. But the essence of Alice's adventures beneath commonly accepted ground is the grimmest comedy conceivable, the comedy of man's absurd condition in an apparently meaningless world. . . .

[Alice] deals with the impossible as if it had to conform to the regular causal operations of her old world above ground. But the adult reader knows better: in addition to recognizing the fallacies of Alice's reasoning in terms of traditional above-ground logic, the reader also realizes that in an underground world where "impossibility" is, as it were, the rule, Alice has no right to assume that the old logic itself still applies. . . .

Not only is Alice's previous identity meaningless in Wonderland; the very concept of permanent identity is invalid. A pack of cards can be a group of people, a child can turn into a pig, a cat's grin can exist without a cat. Even inanimate objects like stones lack simple consistency. . . .

From the very beginning of the underground adventures,

another worldly convention—that verbal communication is potentially logical and unambiguous—has been surreptitiously assailed. Finally, when Alice and the strange animals emerge soaking from her pool of tears, linguistic order dissolves completely, appropriately in a dramatized pun. The Mouse announces in all seriousness that he will dry them: his method is to recite a passage from a history textbook, the "driest thing" he knows. . . . Here Wonderland, through the comic agency of the Mouse and his "dry" history lesson, subverts a fundamental principle of everyday language. His confusion of symbol and object has far-reaching metaphysical significance, but all we need note here is that this confusion is one more contribution to the clear pattern of destruction running through all of Alice's adventures. . . .

By demanding that language be consistently sequential, Wonderland, so to speak, destroys the false logic of language with logic itself. This new strategy demonstrates one more weapon in Wonderland's comic arsenal: whenever the world above ground claims to be strictly consistent—as in Space, size, or mathematics—Wonderland is, by its very operations, maddeningly . . . inconsistent. But whenever the world above ground is admittedly inconsistent—as in grammar—then Wonderland strenuously demands complete consistency. Such an oblique attack forces the reader to remember what he always knew—one cannot expect ordinary language to be unambiguous like mathematics. However, the urgent, rude insistence of Wonderland creatures . . . neatly satirizes the common world's illogicality; and so, in the midst of all the fun, one more conventional prop of order begins to crumble. . . .

The rudeness of the Caterpillar contributes to the continuing antipathy between Alice and the creatures of Wonderland. Generally, she is met with condescension or mistrust, and most of the creatures she encounters are quick to contradict her. No doubt there is an element of fear in their authoritarian rudeness: they probably suspect that Alice, somewhat like an adult with children, holds the power of life and death over them. . . .

In Chapter vi an important aspect of the chaos is that the creatures here, like the clairvoyant Caterpillar, rarely consider their environment or their actions as anything but normal. To them there is certainly nothing wonderful about Wonderland. . . .

Is it because Alice is a child that she fails after all this to see Wonderland for what it is? Is it her youthful ignorance that makes her miss the dangerous significance of a grin without a cat—an attribute without a subject? All she can think at this point is: "Well! I've often seen a cat without a grin, . . . but a grin without a cat! It's the most curious thing I ever saw in all my life!" . . . But this represents the response of most adults, too. . . .

Immediately after the highly subversive Mad Tea Party, Alice meets in Chapter viii a whole new set of creatures—playing cards that are alive, so alive, in fact, that one has become one of the most well-known "persons" in English literature, the furious Queen of Hearts. Carroll's method of making these cards appear human is an example of his technical ability throughout *Alice*. . . .

In this way another above-ground principle—that there is a distinct cleavage between the animate and inanimate worlds—is humorously overthrown. One thing, however, remains constant: these card-creatures are just as irrational and chaotic as all the previous animal inhabitants of the insane underground. Indeed, the chaos is compounded, when these inanimate-objects-turned-human treat the normally live creatures of Alice's former existence as inanimate artifacts. Wonderland has again turned the tables, hereby using live animals like hedgehogs and flamingoes for croquet balls and mallets. . . .

Since Alice rarely relinquishes her notions of order without some struggle, it is fitting that in "The Queen's Croquet-Ground" she should try to remind herself of the above-ground distinction between live and inanimate entities. When the Queen of Hearts rudely demands, as so many other creatures have demanded, that Alice identify herself, Alice "very politely" says: "My name is Alice, so please your Majesty," but adds to herself, "Why, they're only a pack of cards, after all. I needn't be afraid of them!" At this point, Alice . . . is falling back on those now inoperative above-ground principles which, illusory or not, can preserve her sanity and her very existence. . . .

A more important reason for Alice's drift toward rebellion is that she has begun to sense that her quest for unambiguous meaning and immortal order is fruitless. Haphazard as her trip may at first seem, Alice has nevertheless been moving towards the grounds of Wonderland which correspond to the grounds of her old world. The rulers of Wonderland (the King and Queen of Hearts) and their "beautiful garden" have been Alice's spiritual goal almost from the beginning, and it is appropriate that the rulers and court of Wonderland should hold the secret of their realm's meaning and be the ultimate source of its order. The fact that they are court cards and hearts emphasizes their central, vital position, as does the fact that they are introduced with names written all in capital letters, a device stressed by Carroll in his revisions. Ironically, Alice is for once correct in judging Wonderland on the basis of her previous "in-the-world" experience. But what do these repositories of meaning and order turn out to be? Mere abstract, manufactured, and arbitrary symbols—just a pack of cards, pictures of kings and queens, men and women. Their grounds of meaning turn out to be croquet-grounds and their principles the rules of an insane, topsy-turvy *game*. . . .

It must be remembered that *Alice's Adventures in Wonderland* is not a piece of formal philosophy; it is, instead, a comic myth of man's insoluble problem of meaning in a meaningless world. Thus, the fact that Alice herself is unaware of the significance of her journey to the end of night and unaware of her reasons for finally denying the validity of her vision is by no means a flaw in the book. Alice, as the mythical representative of all her fellows above ground, acts appropriately and appropriately is unaware of the meaning of her actions. . . .

Some may argue that *Alice* would be better classified as a "nightmare-vision" [than a dream-vision] because a nightmare is an unsuccessful dream, while a dream is a method whereby the dreamer successfully works out and solves in dramatic form a deep-seated problem, often a problem whose existence the conscious faculties will not allow themselves even to admit. Certainly *Alice* does deal with and dramatize what is by nature and definition outside the awareness of the everyday conscious intellect; and some readers assume that Alice's dream does not come to any satisfying conclusion, that the problem of the disorder beneath man-made order is left unsolved; but I have argued here that this is not so, that *Alice's Adventures in Wonderland* solves the problem by a kind of alogical dreamwork affirmation of man's artificially constructed universe.

> *Donald Rackin, "Alice's Journey to the End of Night," in* PMLA, *81 (copyright © 1966 by the Modern Language Association of America; reprinted by permission of the Modern Language Association of America), October, 1966, pp. 313-26.*

There can be no question that the course of the action [in *Alice's Adventures in Wonderland*] with all its attendant dangers fascinates children. But what gives the book its wisdom and its charm, but at the same time makes it to a great extent incomprehensible to non-English children, is its many conversations and monologues. . . .

The suspension of accepted relationships where size and values and events are concerned has made the book a storehouse for psychologists, surrealists, and men of letters. But you have only to look at the face of Lewis Carroll, you have only to consult his diaries or the letters he wrote to his young friends to realize that there is nothing more to this story than an attempt to think up an amusing tale for a child of whom he was very fond. Since the whole thing was improvised he perhaps followed more closely than is the case with other children's authors the suggestions of his subconscious, allowing every action to follow on from previous ones without a lot of careful thought. The conversations, too, are written entirely in the tone of voice which the little girl would use in talking to her friends. What makes the story so lively and so extraordinarily well-fitted for reading aloud is this naturalness of speech which has come from the author's fondness for children.

> *Bettina Hürlimann, in her* Three Centuries of Children's Books in Europe, *translated and edited by Brian W. Alderson (English translation © Oxford University Press 1967), Oxford University Press, 1967, pp. 67-8.*

Alas! poor Alice. Her encounter with that sly old fantasy-monger and clown prince of surrealism, Salvador Dali, is certainly the most vulgar adventure that has yet befallen her. . . .

[This 1969 Maecenas Press—Random House edition of "Alice's Adventures in Wonderland"] consists of a handsomely printed text (the only good thing about this dubious venture) on expensive paper gathered in unbound folios, the whole lavishly presented in a linen-and-leather case. The text includes an "original" Dali etching, used as a frontispiece, plus 12 "original mixed-media" illustrations.

Dali's part in this trumpery is an esthetic fiasco. . . . To illustrate [Alice's] inspired fantasy, still fresh and funny after more than a century, he has produced a suite of "dream" clichés that heavily mine the early Dali lode (as well as that of late Chagall)—even including the famous limp watch, used here to evoke the puns about time in the Mad Tea Party scene. Beside this wishy-washy ephemera the crisp farcical drawings of Sir John Tenniel, the Punch cartoonist who served as "Alice's" first illustrator, stand out as masterpieces.

> *Grace Glueck, in* The New York Times Book Review *(© 1969 by The New York Times Company; reprinted by permission), December 7, 1969, p. 72.*

Carroll was essentially sexless, but unlike Henry James, who was also sexless, he did not shrivel up into an inner psychological fairy tale world, but stayed right up front with his fairy tales—provoking, contradicting, challenging, and confounding reality through the ingenious use of fantasy and allegory. And he was no sophisticated "modern," calculating, degenerate in the sense of Humbert Humbert in *Lolita*, but was rather astonishingly innocent and open about his sexual strangeness. He knew he was weird, but in his weirdness he was able to remain the quintessential child, who in the end knew that the world was a whole lot nuttier than even he was. This viewpoint is the charm, and the truth, of *Alice in Wonderland*. It is something all children know—and gradually forget as they grow up and somehow "adjust" to adult madness and irrationality. The genius of *Alice in Wonderland* as a children's book is that it reminds both children and grownups of that.

> *Warren Hinckle, in* City of San Francisco *(© by City Publishing Co., Inc.), October 21, 1975, p. 17.*

THE HUNTING OF THE SNARK: AN AGONY IN EIGHT FITS (1876)

[*The Hunting of the Snark*] is the only example of a long Nonsense poem, perfect from start to finish . . . without Lear's underlying touch of mysticism, but far beyond him on the intellectual and constructive level: delightful to children as a simple Nonsense narrative, but beyond them in the deeper subtleties of humour and paradoxical logic—the additional stratum which makes both it and the *Alice* books so outstandingly attractive to adult readers.

> *Roger Lancelyn Green, in his* Tellers of Tales: British Authors of Children's Books from 1800 to 1964 *(copyright 1946, © 1965 by Edmund Ward, Publishers, Ltd.; reprinted courtesy of Kaye & Ward Ltd.), revised edition, Kaye & Ward Ltd., 1965, p. 60.*

Lewis Carroll fans will be pleased with this [1966 Pantheon] picturebook version of an old favorite. The illustrations [by Kelly Oechsli] are full of humorous detail and are most appropriate to the nonsensical text.

> School Library Journal *(reprinted from* School Library Journal, *May, 1966, published by R. R. Bowker Co., a Xerox company; copyright © 1966 by Xerox Corporation), May, 1966, p. 178.*

Helen Oxenbury's detailed, droll drawings, some in color, enhance the nonsensical, macabre aspects of [*The Hunting of the Snark*, Watts, 1966]. . . . [This is a] parody of heroic ballads that will delight admirers of Lewis Carroll and anyone who enjoys nonsense verse.

> *Eleanor Glaser, in* School Library Journal *(reprinted from* School Library Journal, *Sep-*

tember, 1971, published by R. R. Bowker Co., a Xerox company; copyright © 1971 by Xerox Corporation), September, 1971, p. 113.

OTHER CITATIONS

Helen B. Crawshaw, in The Horn Book Magazine, *June, 1966, p. 301.*

The Booklist and Subscription Books Bulletin, *October 1, 1966, p. 189.*

Publishers' Weekly, *June 14, 1971, p. 54.*

THE NURSERY "ALICE" (1890)

This is McGraw-Hill's [1966] hardcover edition of a Dover paperback reprint of the 1890 *Nursery Alice*. Written by Lewis Carroll as an adaptation of *Alice in Wonderland* for, according to his own preface, the "illiterate, ungrammatical, dimpled Darlings," the children "aged from Nought to Five." It is a sugary adaptation in large print with Tenniel pictures very possibly colored by the author.... Admirers of *Alice in Wonderland* will wish the *Nursery Alice* had never been written and will prefer to introduce *Alice* to children when they are old enough to appreciate it....

> *Aileen O'Brien Murphy, in* School Library Journal *(reprinted from* School Library Journal, *February, 1967, published by R. R. Bowker Co., a Xerox company; copyright © 1967 by Xerox Corporation), February, 1967, p. 57.*

Dover Books, following their facsimile volume of *Alice's Adventures Under Ground,* now offer another Carroll facsimile rarity, the *Nursery Alice* of 1890, with its twenty pictures in colour. From a connoisseur's view this is an extremely interesting piece of publishing; it is also, however, a very odd work, and needs a little explaining. When Carroll set about making an easy "Alice" for "Children aged from Nought to Five" (to ten or so if they came from "the lower orders") a quarter of a century had passed since what one might call the Authorized Version had appeared. These years had not been kind to Carroll's strong qualities of wit and astringency; both had been largely dissolved away in a pious, sentimental, melancholy flux....

[The] story is about a quarter of the original length; most of the verses are gone; there are one or two small additions. The notable feature, however, is the manner of presentation. A hint of its voice (at once intimate yet coy) already sounds in Carroll's preface. He is speaking of his recent wish, to be read by the youngest children of all:

> To be read? Nay, not so! Say rather to be thumbed, to be cooed over, to be dog's-eared, to be rumpled, to be kissed, by the illiterate, ungrammatical, dimpled Darlings....

> Poor little Bill! Don't you pity him very much? How frightened he must have been. Wasn't *that* a curious sort of present to give her? Mr. Tenniel says the screaming bird is a *Storkling* (of course you know what *that* is?) and the little white head is a *Mouseling.* Isn't it a little *darling?*

So the text continually runs. The odd thing is that—though "lower orders" of 10 should *not* be shown the volume—pram-aged listeners might well be lulled by familiar adult-to-infant cadences caught with an awful exactness in the kind explanations of the former splendid lunacies of the tale.

> The Times Literary Supplement *(© The Times Publishing Company Ltd. 1966), May 25, 1967, p. 445.*

THE PIG-TALE (1889)

"The Pig-Tale," taken from *Sylvie and Bruno,* describes in fourteen polished, mock-solemn stanzas, a fat pig's ultimately fatal campaign to learn how to jump; this is bracketed and interrupted with verses representing Carroll's most discombobulating waggery.... The far-out note struck in the verses is echoed in [Leonard] Lubin's ingenious illustrations [in the 1975 edition] where the absurdities of the rhymes are visualized literally, and the sepia tones, fine precision of line (resembling the 19th century camera lucida productions) and even the styles of dress and decor give the effect of elegant parody.

> Kirkus Reviews *(copyright © 1975 The Kirkus Service, Inc.), April 1, 1975, p. 378.*

Leonard Lubin's masterful sepia illustrations, ornate initial letters and elegant frames around each page extend the sly wit of Lewis Carroll's poem "The Pig-Tale" ... Lubin's intricate line drawings reflect even the subtlest nuances of the characters' expressions. Since the pig ends up "still as a stone and could not stir a stump," some faint-hearted readers might be upset. If the verses are read aloud, the rollicking cadences of Carroll's rhymes will erase any momentary grief over the pig's tragic fate.

> *Alice Bach, in* The New York Times Book Review *(© 1975 by The New York Times Company; reprinted by permission), May 4, 1975, p. 42.*

[*The Pig-Tale*] is accompanied by other nonsense rhymes about little birds who do unlikely things ... all of which lack the wit and liveliness of Carroll's better-known verse. Despite the excellent illustrations, this [book] will appeal to few children.

> *Esther Manes, in* School Library Journal *(reprinted from* School Library Journal, *September, 1975, published by R. R. Bowker Co., a Xerox company; copyright © 1975 by Xerox Corporation), September, 1975, pp. 77-8.*

POEMS OF LEWIS CARROLL (1974)

In an incisive introduction, [Myra Cohn] Livingston presents a well-rounded portrait of Lewis Carroll which will spur readers to delve into his poetry. The carefully chosen assortment offers familiar poems from *Alice in Wonderland* ..., lesser-known compositions from *Sylvie and Bruno,* acrostic poems, puzzle poems, and finally, the ever-popular "Hunting of the Snark." Complexities of language and content (for example, the targets of each parody) are explained in a helpful section, "Notes on the Poems." Illustrated with artwork from the original editions, this is a commendable Carroll sampler.

> *Daisy Kouzel, in* School Library Journal *(reprinted from* School Library Journal, *April, 1974, published by R. R. Bowker Co., a Xerox company; copyright © 1974 by Xerox Corporation), April, 1974, p. 68.*

[This] collection of forty-four verses testifies that Lewis Carroll's satiric skills outweighed his poetic skills; for as poetry, the verse is often lame, but the biting humor seldom falters. With great vitality, Carroll delivered barbed and inventive parodies. . . . The compiler [Myra Cohn Livingston] has wisely chosen to leave out Carroll's most sentimental poetic endeavors; containing the best and the maddest of his poetry, [*Poems of Lewis Carroll*] attractively combines parodies, puzzles, and acrostics; material from the two Alice books and the two Bruno and Sylvie books; *The Hunting of the Snark;* and reproductions of illustrations by [John Tenniel, Harry Furniss, Henry Holiday, Arthur B. Frost, and Lewis Carroll].

> *Anita Silvey, in* The Horn Book Magazine *(copyright © 1974 by The Horn Book, Inc., Boston), April, 1974, pp. 157-58.*

How nice to have so much of Carroll's delightful daftness in one volume, with poems from Wonderland, ciphers and riddle-poems, the famous "Hiawatha" parody, odd bits of humorous verse, and the saga of the Snark. [Myra Cohn Livingston's] biographical introduction and notes on the poems make the book all the more interesting and useful to Carroll buffs.

> *Zena Sutherland, in* Bulletin of the Center for Children's Books *(© 1974 by the University of Chicago; all rights reserved), June, 1974, p. 154.*

SYLVIE AND BRUNO (1889)

Sylvie and Bruno, at once fairies and human children, move easily in and out of the two worlds manipulated by Lewis Carroll. One is the world of comic fairy tale in which an incipient palace revolution reflects, distantly, late Victorian social conditions. In this world Sylvie and Bruno are the children of the banished Warden and wander at will through the landscapes in the narrator's mind. In his day to day reality they appear now and then in an earl's gardens or drawing room to assuage the pangs of love suffered by Lady Muriel, with whom the narrator is involved as an elderly, much-loved friend—supposedly, Carroll himself.

Into this 'real' world the children carry characters already evident in the fairy world. Sylvie, a pretty little girl with curly brown hair and a loving disposition, is the typical elder sister who, in the absence of a mother, watches over Bruno with anxious responsibility. Bruno displays the characteristics of the typical small boy of nineteenth-century nursery fiction. . . . To twentieth-century eyes Bruno—spoilt, a little greedy, rebellious but loving in his better moments—is hardly an attractive character; perhaps the readers of the last century found it easier to accept the baby-talk which hardly seems to suit a fairy ('Can't oo

make out *nuffin* wizout I 'splain it?'). It must also be conceded that Bruno's peculiarly childish logic, and Sylvie's gentle exasperation when confronted with it, are suited to their ages (presumably five and eight or thereabouts) at any period and in any society. There is more than a touch of Alice's robust good sense in Sylvie and of Looking-Glass logic in Bruno—enough to make it possible for adult readers to tackle this loose bundle of reflections on religion, society and personal relationships which has only the barest claim to be considered as a two-part book for children.

> *Margery Fisher, in her* Who's Who in Children's Books: A Treasury of the Familiar Characters of Childhood *(copyright © 1975 by Margery Fisher; reprinted by permission of Holt, Rinehart and Winston), Holt, Rinehart and Winston, 1975, p. 337.*

THROUGH THE LOOKING GLASS AND WHAT ALICE FOUND THERE (1871)

The Centenary Edition of *Through the Looking-Glass*, prepared by The Committee of the Lewis Carroll Society, is an excuse to display the peculiar talents of [illustrator] Ralph Steadman. . . . His style, with all its spattered ink and whirlpool eyes, suggests a Rorschach test discovering outright madness, and despite Alice's appropriation by the drug crowd it runs counter to the spirit of Lewis Carroll every wobbly step of the way. Steadman's Alice looks like a constipated Bea Lillie (on occasion she also bears a remarkable resemblance to Dame Edith Sitwell), and the total effect of the illustrations is schizophrenic: either the reader can follow the admittedly striking work of Mr. Steadman or he can read Mr. Carroll. To do both is simply to invite the prospect of a long bad trip.

> *Joseph Kanon, in* Saturday Review of the Arts *(copyright © 1973 by Saturday Review, Inc.; reprinted with permission), February 3, 1973, p. 68.*

Because John Tenniel's drawings for the Alice books are inextricably tied to our memories of Lewis Carroll's texts, it would seem foolish for another artist to undertake them again, yet the unique combination of madness and logic, wit and menace is a sore temptation. Arthur Rackham and Walt Disney failed, but Ralph Steadman has succeeded. His Alice is older than she should be, and not as pretty as Tenniel's—her nose and hair are longer—but the pen-and-ink drawings that accompany [The Centenary Edition] not only work, they are spectacular. They are large, often double-page spreads, and vigorous. Large areas of black and white are arranged for dramatic contrast, as are bold and sweeping lines with minute attention to witty detail. . . . Steadman stresses the themes of chessboards and reflections, and leans heavily on the absurd: his Jabberwocky is no winged serpent but a whiffling, burbling Mongoloid, with a Union Jack for a tongue.

> *Peter S. Prescott, in* Newsweek *(copyright 1973 by Newsweek, Inc.; all rights reserved; reprinted by permission), February 26, 1973, p. 87.*

The chess puzzle underlying *Through the Looking-Glass* is an apt figure for embodying what were probably Dodgson's views about the continuities underlying cultural life. As A. L. Taylor has observed, the model for what happens on the board is not a chess problem at all, but a chess lesson, in which one side is given a license to willfulness in order to provide illustrations of the rules and the other side is generously allowed to win. The various powers of the pieces are translated into aspects of character whose animating motives have nothing to do with the intelligibility of the action as a whole. As the creatures fulfill the nursery rhymes, so they accomplish the purpose of the lesson; the moves confronting the child seem perfectly episodic, while those of the pawn, obversely, display mechanical adherence to the simplest of all rules. (p. 627)

The hope of the child in learning the rules is not to imitate the hectoring aggressiveness or fuddled eccentricity of the creatures, but to enact the possibilities latent in both for a genuine rule-observant strategy, a move in a real game. But the hope is inevitably defrauded, for the circumstances of the lesson ensure that a coherent move, one that is neither willfully eccentric nor compulsively obedient to rule never gets made. (p. 628)

> *Alvin C. Kibel, "Logic and Satire in Alice in Wonderland," in* The American Scholar *(copyright © 1974 by the United Chapters of Phi Beta Kappa; reprinted by permission of the publishers), Vol. 43, No. 4, Autumn, 1974, pp. 605-29.*

*   *   *

CHRISTOPHER, John (pseudonym)   1922-

John Christopher is an English novelist who has written several science fiction books for children.

GENERAL COMMENTARY

One begins to wonder whether John Christopher's worlds are not *conditioned* a little too much. Pessimism is justified in our century, of all times, yet somehow Christopher's pessimism is too facile—few of the characters, apart from the heroes, are more than sketched in, and except for the Aunt in *The Prince in Waiting* and Mrs. Gifford in *The Guardians* we rarely encounter any presentation of genuine personal suffering powerful enough to lend conviction to the starkness of Christopher's view of things. (pp. 78-9)

It is our feeling that critics of children's literature have tended to overrate Christopher for the same reason that they have been so keen to claim that he is not 'really' writing SF. If science fiction is thought of in terms of lurid pulp then anything that is well written, reasonably convincing and serious in its preoccupations must be not SF but something else—'fascinating prediction', 'allegorical history' or whatever. Alternatively, if such a book is reluctantly admitted within the SF pale, then it is called 'outstanding' simply because it surpasses the abysmal stuff some SF writers churn out for children. . . . But if one adopts a more informed approach, and views Christopher in relation to the vast amount of good, bad and indifferent SF writing for both adults and children, then one cannot but feel that his place is a more modest one. True, he gets some thought-provoking themes across via a compelling narrative, and he is likely to be read for years to come for excitement alone, but he lacks the depth that would make him either an original user of SF conventions or a first-rate novelist. (p. 79)

> *Hugh Crago and Maureen Crago, "John Christopher: An Assessment with Reservations," in* Children's Book Review *(© 1971 by Five Owls Press Ltd.; all rights reserved), June, 1971, pp. 77-9.*

The common thread of [John Christopher's] novels is a preoccupation with the question of freedom and authority: painful freedom and comfortable submission to authority. While the author (like Aldous Huxley in *Brave New World* and George Orwell in *1984*) is clearly on the side of freedom, he never presents it as an unthought-about, self-evident good. Sharp and disconcerting, the thought recurs—most notably at the end of *The Lotus Caves*—that the acceptance of authority can, in some ways, be enviable. The case for freedom is not that freedom is nice, but that it demands more from us—demands the qualities that make us human. John Christopher is at grips with a fundamental question, and this gives weight to his novels; his own talents give them distinction. (p. 52)

> *John Rowe Townsend, "John Christopher," in his* A Sense of Story: Essays on Contemporary Writers for Children *(copyright © 1971 by John Rowe Townsend; reprinted by permission of J. B. Lippincott Company), Lippincott, 1971, pp. 48-55.*

The differences between the Christopher books for adults and for children are not great. The children's books are at least as well written, demand as much intelligence from the reader, and are likely to stimulate equal thought, but they do not require an adult background of experience. Behind John Christopher the stylist and storyteller is a Christopher who is deeply questioning about human nature and, one suspects, inclined to pessimism.

> *John Rowe Townsend, in his* Written for Children: An Outline of English-Language Children's Literature *(copyright © 1965, 1974 by John Rowe Townsend; reprinted by permission of J. B. Lippincott Company), revised edition, Lippincott, 1974, p. 216.*

BEYOND THE BURNING LANDS (1971)

Despite his undoubted success one must question John Christopher's wisdom in trying to revive the three-decker. It is not that interest cannot be sustained over so extended a story; it is waiting for the next volume that is so intolerably irksome.

In the three-decker, the middle volume presents the greatest difficulties. *The Prince in Waiting* [the first volume of the trilogy] was fine; writer and reader alike were keyed up for a new experience, a new scene and new characters. *Beyond the Burning Lands* [the second volume] makes demands on the memory, and the discreet hints which Mr Christopher drops are not enough to help those readers who missed the first volume. . . .

It is not easy to follow the thought behind this story—which no doubt the next volume will in time make plain—but there can be no question of Mr. Christopher's mastery of his scene or his skill in devising episodes of high adventure.

The Times Literary Supplement (© *Times Newspapers Ltd., 1971), July 2, 1971, p. 767.*

Never more than the bare bones of a book, full of Christopher's simple, tough sentences and his uncompromising denial of any higher destiny for mankind, *Beyond the Burning Lands* nevertheless avoids both the elementary adventure-story gratifications of the *Tripods* trilogy, and the fatalism of *The Guardians.* The theme of technology triumphant, which seemed the logical sequel to the events of *The Prince in Waiting,* retreats into the background (and here I stand corrected); instead, the author develops the more human aspects of the earlier book, and Luke now emerges as the most fully rounded and likeable of Christopher's heroes to date. The strength of this book is, in fact, in its characters rather than in its action. The actual crossing of the Burning Lands is a tame affair, and it might be argued that Luke's sojourn in the palace of King Cymru really offers little challenge to the reader's imagination—though it does show Luke in a new light. The slaying of the Bayemot (a creature straight out of pulp SF, and unexpected in this more mature context) is curiously convincing, but the perfunctory Sky People episode seems introduced solely for variety. Imaginative conviction has never been Christopher's strong point, of course; now that he is writing so much better of *people,* the weaknesses of his invention matter less. Whether his readers will stay with him in the more complex, less gratifying world of the current trilogy is another matter. Perhaps his sheer terseness will hold them.

> *Hugh Crago, in* Children's Book Review (© *1971 by Five Owls Press Ltd.; all rights reserved), September, 1971, pp. 122-23.*

With *The Prince in Waiting,* [Christopher] began another series comparable in action and pace to the White Mountain trilogy. *Beyond the Burning Lands,* the second book is —unfortunately—an interim book.... [The] seeds for a future book ... have all been skillfully intertwined in a vividly depicted adventure story; yet one could wish for a more satisfying conclusion to a book meant to stand on its own. At the end, Luke kills his brother Peter—now half-mad—in single combat, and assumes the throne, thinking "of the unalterable past—and all my dead."

> *Sheryl B. Andrews, in* The Horn Book Magazine (copyright © 1971 by The Horn Book, Inc., Boston), December, 1971, p. 619.*

[*Beyond the Burning Lands*] continues the story of Luke, who is destined to become ruler of a city-state in an England returned to feudalism and abjuring all technology.... The setting is wholly-conceived, the story well paced and full of action, and the book is given depth by the subtle— and at times not so subtle—ways in which Christopher mocks the frailties of our own society.

> *Zena Sutherland, in* Bulletin of the Center for Children's Books (© 1972 by the University of Chicago; all rights reserved), February, 1972, p. 88.*

OTHER CITATIONS

Kirkus Reviews, *July 1, 1971, p. 681.*

The Junior Bookshelf, *October, 1971, pp. 315-16.*

Elizabeth Haynes, in School Library Journal, *December, 1971, p. 62.*

The Booklist, *December 1, 1971, p. 333.*

THE CITY OF GOLD AND LEAD (1967)

Though [*The City of Gold and Lead*] and its forerunner [*The White Mountains*] are full of tension, mystery, and moral message, the package appears to be merely competent science fiction. There is, nevertheless, a need for such at this age level, and the fans will enjoy it.

> *Jean C. Thomson, in* School Library Journal *(reprinted from* School Library Journal, *September, 1967, published by R. R. Bowker Co., a Xerox company; copyright © 1967 by Xerox Corporation), September, 1967, p. 116.*

As read after *The White Mountains,* this is a suitable extension of a harrowingly convincing supposition; as read on its own, it is superbly written science fiction—to catch the complex undertones, it is necessary to read the two in sequence.

> Kirkus Service (copyright © 1967 Virginia Kirkus Service, Inc.), September 15, 1967, p. 1143.

[This] story is exciting enough, but all the original concepts —of the "Capped" humans whose thoughts and reactions are controlled electronically by their masters and of a future society returned to medieval feudalism and chivalry—were introduced in [*The White Mountain*] and no surprises are left.

> The Times Literary Supplement, (© *Times Newspapers Ltd., 1967), November 30, 1967, p. 1160.*

[Christopher] succeeds notably in developing a strong atmosphere [in *The City of Gold and Lead*]: one feels the green light, the enervating heat, the stifling controls. The boy heroes are not superhuman; their very frailties only increase the tension of the tale.

> *Virginia Haviland, in* The Horn Book Magazine (copyright © 1967 by The Horn Book, Inc., Boston), December, 1967, p. 757.*

[*The City of Gold and Lead*] is just as effective as ... *The White Mountains....* The concept of the world of the Masters is beautifully developed, a whole alien culture grafted onto the submissive remnants of mankind in the world of the future; the story is kept within a tight framework, and the suspense is masterfully maintained.

> *Zena Sutherland, in* Bulletin of the Center for Children's Books (copyright 1968 by The University of Chicago; all rights reserved), January, 1968, p. 76.*

[In *The City of Gold and Lead,* Christopher] conveys a wonderful sense of the Tripods, immense, silent, dominating the landscape as men go about their daily work.... The concept of the real Masters and their triangular world is beautifully worked out, though their odd form of life is described rather than explained—perhaps because this will be clarified in a sequel. There are disturbing features, however. Inevitably, the Masters are given human characteristics, which include deliberate sadism. There is the unpleasant idea of the Pyramid of Beauty, where Will finds Eloise of the earlier book, with all other girls in the City, preserved in rows like dead butterflies for the aesthetic enjoyment of the Masters. A measure of the book's success is that one is impatient for the obviously intended sequel. . . .

> The Junior Bookshelf, *February, 1968, p. 59.*

OTHER CITATIONS

The Booklist and Subscription Books Bulletin, *January 1, 1968, p. 542.*

Digby B. Whitman, in Book World, *March 17, 1968, p. 12.*

Peter J. Henniker-Heaton, in The Christian Science Monitor, *May 2, 1968, p. B8.*

Jonathan Segal, in The New York Times Book Review, *May 5, 1968 (Part 2), p. 16.*

DOM AND VA (1973)

Postulating an encounter between two kinds of early man in Africa, Christopher brings about a synthesis in the persons of Dom, a boy from a wandering savage tribe of hunters and fighters ("killers by nature") and Va, a girl from a matriarchal village of gentle planters and cattle herders. . . . Christopher's telescoping of the dawn of civilization into a year in the life of one young couple makes for unconvincing fiction, and his plodding reiteration of each episode so that everything can be experienced from both points of view (but with no new perspectives for the reader the second time around) makes it boring as well. As for all those intriguing questions that the situation might seem to raise—about sex-linked aggression or culture patterns or the limits of non-violence or the delicate balance of civilized survival or whatever—not only are they unresolved by Christopher's specious compromise but they have never been examined or defined.

> Kirkus Reviews *(copyright © 1973 The Kirkus Service, Inc.), March 15, 1973, p. 324.*

In contrasting the cultural patterns of the nomad tribe and Va's more civilized people, and in showing how Dom gradually acquires some of Va's mores, Christopher gives an introduction to the theory of cultural diffusion, but its achievement as shown is not quite convincing. The writing style is not as well sustained as in his earlier books, perhaps because of his attempt to show Dom's and Va's attitudes and reactions in repetitive episodes. They are, however, convincing as characters, and the book has enough action to sustain interest.

> *Zena Sutherland, in* Bulletin of the Center for Children's Books *(© 1973 by the University of Chicago; all rights reserved), July-August, 1973, p. 168.*

[*Dom and Va*] is a thoughtful and thought-provoking story

and it demonstrates that the old taboos on sex are disappearing in young people's literature as elsewhere. When Dom and Va begin to found a tribe of their own (combining the better qualities of each?) their first son's conception is dealt with in a couple of matter-of-fact, unemotional sentences and his birth in little more.

> *George van Schaick, in* New Statesman *(© The Statesman & Nation Publishing Co. Ltd. 1973), November 9, 1973, p. 702.*

Mr. Christopher bases his cruel and uncompromising story of 500,000 years ago on bones and other relics in the Olduvai Gorge. . . . [Dom and Va's] meeting and mating are completely lacking in tenderness although the onlooker senses a certain poignancy in their ceaseless self-assertion which ends frequently in bouts of violence reminiscent of every cartoon ever reproduced concerning cave-man technique with cave-woman. There is, naturally, no conventional happy ending but the book is a seriously intended reconstruction of a feasible social and individual situation in prehistoric times.

> The Junior Bookshelf, *December, 1973, p. 402.*

[*Dom and Va*] is an attempt to fictionalise the idea, made popular by Ardrey (among many others) that civilisation in primitive times began when meat-eating hunters met tool-using farmers, and their cultures gradually blended. This is not so much a love story, more an episode of the mating season. . . .

The author perceptively suggests in both dialogue and narration the way in which the primitive men must have made their decisions, by instinct and tradition. When the hunters come across a herd of domesticated animals they slaughter them all as if they were wild; the farmers, on the other hand, do not kill an animal without asking its pardon. Dom, however, is capable of adapting: he prefers Va to the women of his own tribe because of her talents and love of beauty, and when beating has no effect he turns to kindness. Va, too, prefers his strength to the passiveness of the men of her tribe. The writer's messages are clear: not only is it essential to adapt to changes, but without strength to defend it, civilisation cannot expect to survive. This is a very satisfying book which makes its points about human nature in a more skilful and subtle way than the writer had previously achieved in his tales of the future, and its simple style should make it accessible to more than a minority of readers.

> *Jessica Kemball-Cook, in* Children's Book Review *(© 1973 Five Owls Press Ltd.; all rights reserved), December, 1973, pp. 176-77.*

OTHER CITATIONS

Paul Heins, in The Horn Book Magazine, *August, 1973, pp. 385-86.*

The Booklist, *September 15, 1973, p. 115.*

THE GUARDIANS (1970)

Set in a well-conceived Orwellian England, this routine

adventure is of interest chiefly because the protagonist, 13-year-old Rob Randall, is, realistically enough, blind to the evils around him until nearly the last page. . . . The characterizations, plot and pace are adequate to interest most young readers as Mr. Christopher makes his point that a society of contented individuals is not necessarily a free one.

> *Margaret A. Dorsey, in* School Library Journal *(reprinted from* School Library Journal, *April, 1970, published by R. R. Bowker Co., a Xerox company; copyright © 1970 by Xerox Corporation), April, 1970, p. 129.*

The world of *The Guardians* has a Huxleyan tidiness. Men are conditioned to their estate, and even if, by an error of genetics, someone is out of line the answer is a simple surgical operation for the removal of initiative. . . .

It is an ugly picture and an uncomfortably convincing one. Without calling upon any of the apparatus of science fiction, Mr. Christopher creates a recognizable future, in which the delicate artificial balance of society is maintained by "a special group of dedicated men who will act as guardians over the rest." It is a more likely, and a much more scaring, prospect than all the world disasters and Lords of the Galaxy dreamed up by S.F. writers of the main stream.

> The Times Literary Supplement *(© Times Newspapers Ltd., 1970), April 16, 1970, p. 417.*

What emerges from *The Guardians* is a sober, ironic, and well developed presentation of a theme that runs through all of Christopher's work—that man *does* live by bread alone, that to be happy he does not really need the burdens and responsibilities genuine freedom entails. It is in *The Guardians* that this theme is most clearly expounded, for in the *Tripods* trilogy the Masters intend the eventual destruction of mankind and there is no alternative but to oppose them. It is (until the end, at least) a black and white universe. . . . But *The Guardians*, like *The Lotus Caves*, is less simplified. Rob's decision to continue the struggle against the Guardians at the end of the book is somehow a decision of despair. (p. 78)

> *Hugh Crago and Maureen Crago, "John Christopher: An Assessment with Reservations," in* Children's Book Review *(© 1971 by Five Owls Press Ltd.; all rights reserved), June, 1971, pp. 77-9.*

Society is at the heart of John Christopher's most consistently successful novel for young readers, *The Guardians*. . . . It is a story somewhere between *Brave New World* and *1984* and in concept not less horrifying than either. Except that the hero is young, this is not especially a story for children, but in its disillusionment and its revolt alike it speaks the contemporary language of adolescence. Christopher is not greatly interested in personalities, and this keeps his books out of the first rank as novels. As an exciting and relevant social document *The Guardians* has not been equalled in recent years.

> *Marcus Crouch, in his* The Nesbit Tradition: The Children's Novel in England 1945-1970 *(© Marcus Crouch 1972), Ernest Benn, 1972, pp. 51-2.*

OTHER CITATIONS

Kirkus Reviews, *January 5, 1970, p. 58.*

The Booklist, *April 15, 1970, p. 1042.*

Zena Sutherland, in Saturday Review, *May 9, 1970, pp. 47, 69.*

The Junior Bookshelf, *June, 1970, p. 160.*

Zena Sutherland, in Bulletin of the Center for Children's Books, *July-August, 1970, p. 173.*

Lisa Hammel, in The New York Times Book Review, *September 20, 1970, pp. 46-7.*

THE LOTUS CAVES **(1969)**

In describing the life of the [future] colonists [of the moon] —who live in an atmosphere of sterility in spite of attempts to re-create the conditions on the earth—the author is highly convincing and logical. . . . The explanation of the "god-Plant" from another galaxy is good science fiction, and the boys' escape is fairly exciting. But the characters are not well developed, and the story lacks the impact and significance of the author's previous books.

> *Sidney D. Long, in* The Horn Book Magazine *(copyright © 1969 by The Horn Book, Inc., Boston), December, 1969, pp. 673, 675.*

The Lotus Caves . . . begins unpromisingly: the dialogue is trite and slick, and there is a . . . refusal to penetrate the human aspects of the situation beyond a blanket denunciation of the restrictions imposed by life in the Bubble. But once the two boys get away from all this and encounter the Plant the quality of the writing and of the ideas improves markedly. In contrast to the hectic onrushing pace of the *Tripods* books [or, as it is also called, *The White Mountains* trilogy], Christopher permits himself here to pause and reflect, and the theme of the Plant's ambiguous allure develops gradually with full scope for mystery and speculation—qualities which could have made the *Tripods* books more memorable (the potentialities were there, all right) had they not been stifled by Christopher's desire to push the story onwards at all costs. (p. 78)

> *Hugh Crago and Maureen Crago, "John Christopher: An Assessment with Reservations," in* Children's Book Review *(© 1971 by Five Owls Press Ltd.; all rights reserved), June, 1971, pp. 77-9.*

There are elements [in *The Lotus Caves*] of Arcadia, of Eden, of Shangri-La, as well as of the Odyssey, from which the title and theme in part are drawn. It is a strange and memorable story, perhaps as much fantasy as science fiction, yet raising issues which are easily translated into practical terms. A demanding benevolence is by no means unknown in human relationships. On a second reading one notes what could easily be missed the first time round—a subtle change in the relationship between the two boys. Steve is the loner, the odd-boy-out, but it is Marty who can better resist the Plant and who assumes the leadership. The author has avoided the too-easy assumption that the nonconformist has necessarily more inner strength. (p. 51)

John Rowe Townsend, "John Christopher," in his A Sense of Story: Essays on Contemporary Writing for Children (copyright © 1971 by John Rowe Townsend; reprinted by permission of J. B. Lippincott Company), Lippincott, 1971, pp. 48-55.

THE POOL OF FIRE (1968)

[The Pool of Fire is a] rather mediocre conclusion to the science-fiction trilogy whose previous books were The White Mountains and The City of Gold and Lead. Although narrator Will manages to put in a good performance, the series of minimal climaxes that form the thread of the plot are like disturbing obstructions on the tightrope he must walk to the finish of the story. . . . Fritz and Will take men into the city of their earlier confinement, managing finally to blow it apart. Even this, the most interesting part of the book, suffers from the sketchy characterizations of Fritz's and Will's accomplices. . . . Some of the moralizing on international cooperation is good, but the Masters never seem more than a distant threat, and the big bang-up ending that readers were promised by the first two books is a fizzle-out.

> Jean C. Thomson, in School Library Journal (reprinted from School Library Journal, September, 1968, published by R. R. Bowker Co., a Xerox company; copyright © 1968 by Xerox Corporation), September, 1968, p. 131.

The race against time [in "The Pool of Fire"] enables Mr. Christopher to keep suspense at a high pitch, a quality lacking in the other volumes [of this trilogy]. He concludes on a realistic but depressing note: after men have worked together to defeat a common enemy, they are again fragmenting into nationalistic groups.

> F. W. Foley, in The New York Times Book Review (© 1968 by The New York Times Company; reprinted by permission), October 13, 1968, p. 26.

[The Pool of Fire ends on] a depressing if realistic note, somehow less satisfying in a book of science fantasy than it would be were the book simply a story of the future. This volume does not have the same pace as did the first two [in the trilogy], nor the same cohesion; the style is good, the action is plentiful, and the whole concept is durably imaginative, however.

> Zena Sutherland, in Bulletin of the Center for Children's Books (copyright 1968 by The University of Chicago; all rights reserved), November, 1968, p. 40.

OTHER CITATIONS

Kirkus Service, August 1, 1968, pp. 823-24.

Jane Hollowood, in Punch, September 4, 1968, p. 347.

THE PRINCE IN WAITING (1970)

Mr. Christopher tells a very good tale [in The Prince in Waiting]. The high points of his story are firmly managed. There is a powerful description of the tourney in which Luke wins honour as a fighter, by a mixture of cunning and courage, in a contest organized on medieval lines. Scenes of battle, of hunting and of tragedy are presented with equal force. All the book lacks is compulsion. One reads with excitement and deep interest but without personal involvement. Luke is a brave and sensitive lad and a fairly clever one, but one does not seriously share his predicament.

> The Times Literary Supplement (© Times Newspapers Ltd., 1970), December 11, 1970, p. 1460.

[In The Prince in Waiting, Christopher] recreates a world with a medieval (or even earlier) flavour in which exist a kind of chivalry and certainly a retrogressive condition of bitter local rivalries and small-time rulers whose permanence depends on acquisition by conquest. To a certain extent this reflects current thinking about the trend of survival after the hypothetical nuclear holocaust but it suggests a political or social structure which would seem likely to develop eventually in the same channels as that of the last five centuries. The tension of the first three chapters does not seem to be maintained thereafter; the work deteriorates (perhaps too strong a word) into petty squabbles in which Luke, the Prince in Waiting, certainly plays too much of a waiting part on the sidelines of the action, neither gaining in prestige nor developing as a personality—a consequence which lowers one's sense of drama in the successive events.

> The Junior Bookshelf, February, 1971, pp. 51-2.

In [The Lotus Caves], Christopher wrote his best book to date by concentrating heavily on a single poetic and suggestive idea. But the first volume of his new trilogy returns to the themes and characters of the Tripods series. . . . [In The Prince in Waiting] characters and emotions are perceptibly less simplified, and though the ideas presented are still commonplaces of adult SF, the worst excesses of the Tripods trilogy (like the cliché-ridden depiction of the alien Masters) are replaced by a credible picture of the purely human power struggles that lead to the young hero's sudden rise and fall. Less gripping than the early novels, this story still holds one's interest easily.

Alas, by explaining away in the final pages almost all the mysteries so subtly introduced earlier, Christopher wholly forfeits the ironic tension between what the reader knows and what the characters know—a tension basic to the success of this kind of SF. What is left for the final volumes but an all-too-predictable victory for technology? Christopher fans will read The Prince in Waiting anyway, but I hope they will then read [Walter M. Miller, Jr.'s] A Canticle for Leibowitz, which covers the same ground much more memorably.

> Hugh Crago, in Children's Book Review (© 1971 by Five Owls Press Ltd.; all rights reserved), February, 1971, pp. 18-19.

[In The Prince in Waiting, John Christopher's] style is forceful, almost blunt at times, and the characters are strong and individualistic. The events, related with emotional intensity, are never overshadowed by the reminiscences of the highly complex and mechanical age before the Disaster. Actually, most of this science-fiction story has a medieval flavor, but the rationalistic explanations of the Seers at the end of the book tend to mar the tonality so successfully suggested up to this point, even though the explanations may be intended as a transition to the second part of a new trilogy.

> *Paul Heins, in* The Horn Book Magazine *(copyright © 1971 by The Horn Book, Inc., Boston), February, 1971, p. 54.*

The author of the *Tripods* trilogy writes books of no mean order and his most recent is as intriguing as the rest. At some time in the future England has become a land of medieval encampment towns in which the inhabitants include druidical seers and superstitious feudal lords. Curious reappearances from the old order of things begin to upset the new structures. Luke, the 'Prince in Waiting', discovers the existence of secrets from a technological past. The intrigue builds up to a climax which the next book must resolve.

I have only one doubt about this ingenious plot. The narrative of the past-in-the-future has all the external trappings of a historical novel, but because this genre is now so well established in its own right, this version isn't entirely convincing. Perhaps it was not meant to be; but apart from the hero and his mother the characters have a two-dimensional quality. The second half of the book is better than the first, once the story proper takes over from the machinery of the telling.

> *Margaret Meek, in* The School Librarian, *June, 1971, p. 155.*

The setting of small, warring kingdoms, tournaments, a feudal society, primitive weapons and machines, seems at first archaic, but [*The Prince in Waiting*] is, in fact, set in the future and this gives Mr. Christopher the opportunity to present, through the fast-moving and exciting plot, some of the moral problems which he raised in . . . *The Guardians* —the question of the extent of free will, of the rights of the individual, particularly of the responsibility of the individual who can stand outside the system and evaluate it, if necessary defying the supreme authorities.

> *Catherine Storr, in* New Statesman *(© The Statesman & Nation Publishing Co. Ltd. 1971), June 4, 1971, p. 777.*

OTHER CITATIONS

Kirkus Reviews, *October 15, 1970, pp. 1160-61.*

Elizabeth Haynes, in School Library Journal, *November, 1970, p. 115.*

The Booklist, *December 1, 1970, p. 306.*

Zena Sutherland, in Saturday Review, *January 23, 1971, p. 71.*

THE SWORD OF THE SPIRITS (1972)

Once again, since Luke's static and unsympathetic personality inhibits emotional involvement, it's the exotic backgrounds (mixing castles and cinema screens, kings and polymufs) and the game of figuring out what the author is trying to say about Science that must be relied upon to hold the reader's interest.

> Kirkus Reviews *(copyright © 1972 The Kirkus Service, Inc.), February 1, 1972, p. 143.*

[This is a] thought-provoking conclusion to Christopher's second science fiction trilogy. . . . *Sword of the Spirits* can be read as a fast-paced adventure, but it is also a serious consideration of the meanings of technology, honor, peace, freedom and love.

> *Joanne Nykiel, in* School Library Journal *(reprinted from* School Library Journal, *April, 1972, published by R. R. Bowker Co., a Xerox company; copyright © 1972 by Xerox Corporation), April, 1972, pp. 143-44.*

[*The Sword of the Spirits* is heavy] with the feudal atmosphere of horror and love, pride and fate. . . . More psychologically oriented than the adventure-crammed narratives of the first two books, the last volume of the trilogy ends on a note of bitterness and loss, and misses being either high tragedy or completely satisfying science fiction.

> *Sheryl B. Andrews, in* The Horn Book Magazine *(copyright © 1972 by The Horn Book, Inc., Boston), August, 1972, pp. 374-75.*

One closes the final volume of John Christopher's 'Prince' trilogy [*The Prince in Waiting, Beyond the Burning Lands,* and *The Sword of the Spirits*] with a feeling of puzzlement. Once again, the author has constructed a fable notable for directness rather than subtlety—yet this time the fable takes second place to a human tragedy. Once again, the story is set in a future world that has reverted to the medieval in its technology and social customs, a world that is drawn fully enough to sustain credence, but with little invention to spare. . . . Certainly the closing chapters of *The Sword of the Spirits* recall some of Christopher's earlier novels in the haste with which they push events forward, and this is in marked contrast to the careful detail with which the portrayal of Luke has been built up over 480 pages. As a consequence, the Prince of Winchester towers over the forced plot and inadequately realised romantic complications like the hero of an early Shakespearian tragedy, completed with the Bradleian 'fatal flaw'—pride. The task of integrating him fully into the fable seems to have defeated the author; perhaps the two should never have been associated. The trilogy is a work of dignity, but not of full conviction. It is probably Christopher's best work to date, but I suspect that the fable form can carry him no further.

> *Hugh Crago, in* Children's Book Review *(© 1972 by Five Owls Press Ltd.; all rights reserved), September, 1972, p. 113.*

OTHER CITATIONS

The Booklist, *May 15, 1972, p. 818.*

The Junior Bookshelf, *June, 1972, p. 173.*

Catherine Storr, in New Statesman, *June 2, 1972, p. 759.*

Zena Sutherland, Bulletin of the Center for Children's Books, *July-August, 1972, pp. 166-67.*

THE WHITE MOUNTAINS (1967)

John Christopher's *The White Mountains* is a first-rate tale of flight and pursuit. Youngsters who have doubts about becoming members of the adult world will find 13-year-old Will Parker's story absorbing. . . .

Christopher's novel is the first in a planned series about the Tripods and their overthrow. If the subsequent novels are as exciting and as psychologically sound as *The White Mountains,* young readers have much to look forward to.

> *Alan L. Madsen, in* Book Week (© The Washington Post), *July 2, 1967, p. 12.*

Is it reading too much into this book to suggest that it is built on one of today's key problems? Apart from the moral decisions young Will has to make at the Castle of the Red Tower, there is, not too deeply hidden in the plot, the realisation that man may be overwhelmed by machines and his freedom destroyed. The final paragraphs look forward to liberty and hope—and the end of the Tripods.

> The Junior Bookshelf, *August, 1967, p. 248.*

[Planned] as a first story about the Tripods, [*The White Mountains*] is slightly weak in having an inconclusive ending, but the writing is imaginative enough to more than compensate for this. The plot develops with sustained pace, as three boys of the future world make their hazardous way to the White Mountains—Switzerland—wherein exists the only colony of men who are free of the dreaded Tripods, the machines that rule the world by emplanting steel controls on men's brains.

> *Zena Sutherland, in* Bulletin of the Center for Children's Books *(copyright 1967 by the University of Chicago; all rights reserved), December, 1967, p. 57.*

OTHER CITATIONS

Patience M. Daltry, in The Christian Science Monitor, *August 3, 1967, p. 11.*

Peter J. Henniker-Heaton, in The Christian Science Monitor, *November 7, 1968, p. 137.*

THE WHITE MOUNTAINS TRILOGY:
The White Mountains; The City of Gold and Lead; The Pool of Fire

The themes of the *Tripods* trilogy [also known as *The White Mountains* trilogy] are similar to those of many, many SF novels of the past. An alien race has reduced mankind to servitude, yet (because of the capping process) it is a happy servitude. The struggle for freedom succeeds, but the new world government breaks down in its own inner conflicts. So far, so predictable. The aliens themselves—green, reptilian, tentacled—are not just SF commonplaces, but SF clichés. To describe the books as 'original', as several reviewers did, is simply to admit a lack of knowledge of SF. Throughout his books, in fact, Christopher's use of the SF formulae is pretty standard. . . . But . . . one way of appraising a novelist who uses SF mechanisms, as Christopher does, is to examine the conviction with which he employs those mechanisms.

Here it becomes apparent that Christopher lacks that con-

viction. Once you start to think beyond the surface excitement of the *Tripods* series, doubts about the imaginative basis on which it is built begin to creep in. The amazing revival of technology in the White Mountain rebel community is described in so summary a way as to raise questions about its probability. (pp. 77-8)

It is hard to escape the idea that Christopher is applying these concepts in a rather slapdash way, relying on his compelling storytelling to sweep the reader over weaknesses in the imaginative structure. One could object that Christopher is not trying to write the sort of SF novel that explores ideas in depth, yet time and time again ideas creep in—only to be treated in a perfunctory manner. The speedy breakdown of world government after the Masters' overthrow provides, perhaps, an ironic corrective to the optimistic 'technology conquers all' of the rest of the *Tripods* series, but it is so oversimplified in presentation as to seem merely thrown in to give the books a moral. . . . [As] simple, strong adventure stories with a thriller's skimping of depth and subtlety, they are very acceptable. But their excellence goes no further. (p. 78)

> *Hugh Crago and Maureen Crago, "John Christopher: An Assessment with Reservations," in* Children's Book Review *(© 1971 by Five Owls Press Ltd.; all rights reserved), June, 1971, pp. 77-9.*

John Christopher succeeds admirably in *The White Mountains* [trilogy] in establishing the believability of his twenty-first-century world. . . . The ending is sober and realistic, a reminder that vigilance against tyranny must be constant. The whole concept of the trilogy is developed with pace and skill, the pitting of good against evil, in a world where few can see the evil, adding suspense to the well-structured action. . . .

All of Christopher's books are concerned with serious problems of mankind and man's environment; his gift as a science-fiction writer is his ability to treat these problems seriously without making a tract out of an absorbing adventure story.

> *May Hill Arbuthnot and Zena Sutherland, in their* Children and Books *(copyright © 1947, 1957, 1964, 1972 by Scott, Foresman and Co.), 4th edition, Scott, Foresman, 1972, p. 260.*

Some of the ideas [in the 'White Mountains' trilogy] are familiar; but the cool, clean style, the controlled intelligence with which the plot is unfolded, and the touches of true imagination on large or small scale, together with a strong professional command of story-telling, made the trilogy an immediate success both with children and critics.

> *John Rowe Townsend, in his* Written for Children: An Outline of English-Language Children's Literature *(copyright © 1965, 1974 by John Rowe Townsend; reprinted by permission of J. B. Lippincott Company), revised edition, Lippincott, 1974, p. 215.*

WILD JACK (1974)

The details of twenty-third century life are too sparse and

commonplace to make [*Wild Jack*] convincing as science fiction, the ideas and motifs too clichéd to bring any revelations, and the twists and turns of plot too often arbitrary to make the story at all believable. But, as usual, the author's ability to tell a rattling fine tale—full of moments of conflict, narrow escapes, tests of courage, and dangerous missions—keeps the reader transfixed through all the improbabilities.

> *Anita Silvey, in* The Horn Book Magazine *(copyright © 1974 by The Horn Book, Inc., Boston), August, 1974, p. 375.*

Once again John Christopher has created a world with a clean simplistic dichotomy. . . . Neither the plot nor the range of Clive's personal choices [in *Wild Jack*] . . . would strain the most lackadaisical reader but Christopher, an economical and indeed parsimonious writer, draws the battle lines with a clarity that makes it difficult to opt out. Surely, we haven't seen the last of Wild Jack and his continued escapades ought to rival the journey to the *White Mountains* in popularity.

> Kirkus Reviews *(copyright © 1974 The Kirkus Service, Inc.), August 1, 1974, pp. 803-04.*

[The] picture [presented in *Wild Jack*] is too simplified and leaves questions unanswered. Surely the Outlaws, too, are an elitist group, though chosen by different criteria [than the establishment group]. Their way of life could not support large numbers or there would not be an unlimited supply of fresh food. There are no women in the tribe except Wild Jack's daughter—and how could she possibly fancy our ineffectual, naive hero? Why don't the City police know more about the Outlaws? Wild Jack's aims are never made clear and one is left wondering whether he is content just to live independently of the Cities or whether he wants to overthrow them.

This is a sketchy book, resembling Christopher's others in theme, but not as good.

> *Jessica Kemball-Cook, in* Children's Book Review *(© 1975 Five Owls Press Ltd.; all rights reserved), Winter, 1974-75, p. 150.*

The plotting [in *Wild Jack*] is sound until Clive and two comrades find a buried boat on the island. Thereafter the author shamelessly manipulates the story. The boat drifts just where he wants, for instance, and for no other reason. There is no character development because there are no live characters. The ending with a suggestion of romance is the sort of cliché that Hollywood grew out of many years ago.

The story has its moments, especially the episode in which the boys are caught and tested by the Savages. The basic trouble is that John Christopher seems to have assumed that his material is interesting for its own sake. The result is an undemanding, unsatisfying novel, disappointing from the author of *The Guardians*.

> The Junior Bookshelf, *February, 1975, p. 58.*

Bows against the Barons [by Geoffrey Trease] belongs to the political climate of the 1930s; the fears of the 70s lie behind another Robin Hood figure, John Christopher's Wild Jack. . . . A bogyman to children, a constant source of anxiety to the Councillors, he is a kind of Robin Hood, teaching those who flock to him that one day they will rise and fight for their rights. The tall man with his black beard and hooked nose saves the life and the reason of three boys who have escaped from one of the dread punishment islands; his intelligence, his simple forest weapons and customs, his strength and compassion are realized through them. His crusade against the Councillors and their evil domination suggests both Trease's Robin Hood and the romantic hero of legend.

> *Margery Fisher, in her* Who's Who in Children's Books: A Treasury of the Familiar Characters of Childhood *(copyright © 1975 by Margery Fisher; reprinted by permission of Holt, Rinehart and Winston), Holt, Rinehart and Winston, 1975, pp. 306, 309.*

OTHER CITATIONS

Jack Forman, in School Library Journal, *October, 1974, p. 110.*

Zena Sutherland, in Bulletin of the Center for Children's Books, *February, 1975, pp. 90-1.*

*　　　*　　　*

CLEARY, Beverly　1916-

Beverly Cleary, formerly a children's librarian, is an American author well known for her humorous stories about Henry Huggins and his friends. She received the 1975 Laura Ingalls Wilder Award. (See also *Contemporary Authors*, Vols. 1-4, rev. ed., and *Something About the Author*, Vol. 2.)

GENERAL COMMENTARY

[Beverly Cleary makes a consistent effort to reach all standards of quality in each of her books]: (1) she . . . always writes with integrity and respect for her readers, (2) her characters and plots are believable and lively—though sometimes the plots seem slight in holding together a series of episodes or happenings, (3) she has accuracy and authenticity of background or setting, (4) she has a special style of writing—and it might be added she has an ear for the natural vocabulary of her reader, and (5) she attempts to give the reader something to wonder and think about—as well as a good story to enjoy and laugh about.

Simplicity of style and manner is almost deceptive in Beverly Cleary's stories. She seems to be a natural storyteller with an ear for the language of the contemporary child and an intuitive understanding of the unique personality of the child and his world. While Mrs. Cleary must have called upon many places, people and incidents from her own experience, her stories are not remembrances of things past. Beverly Cleary's stories are about the contemporary, average American child or teenager and most often the time of the story is today. The adults—parents, neighbors, teachers—seem average too. The joys and sadness, the successes and failures, the frustrations, the problems in relationships seem to be the ones that are expected in childhood and adolescence. But there is a need in children's literature for all sides of childhood to be presented. Mrs. Cleary may be called the Boswell of the average child. (p. 81)

Margaret Novinger, "Beverly Cleary: A Favorite Author of Children" (originally published in Southeastern Librarian, *Fall, 1968), in* Authors and Illustrators of Children's Books: Writings on Their Lives and Works, *edited by Miriam Hoffman and Eva Samuels (copyright © 1972 by Xerox Corp.), Bowker, 1972, pp. 70-83.*

With the third-grader *Henry Huggins* (1950) Beverly Cleary began a long succession of books that have been much enjoyed by children between seven and ten.... Rarely in easily read books are family relationships so well handled as they are in Mrs. Cleary's stories. She has an acute ear for children's dialogue, a strong sense of humor, and skill in translating children's actions and predicaments to the printed page that make all her books amusing, some of them very funny.

Ruth Hill Viguers, in A Critical History of Children's Literature, *by Cornelia Meigs, Anne Thaxter Eaton, Elizabeth Nesbitt, and Ruth Hill Viguers, edited by Cornelia Meigs (copyright © 1953, 1969 by Macmillan Publishing Co., Inc.), revised edition, Macmillan, 1969, p. 577.*

Pure Americana, from supermarkets to backyard barbecues, the stories [about Henry Huggins and his friends] are delightfully humorous.... These books may not all be gems of literary style, but the characters are real boys and girls, convincingly alive.

May Hill Arbuthnot and Zena Sutherland, in their Children and Books *(copyright © 1947, 1957, 1964, 1972 by Scott, Foresman and Co.), 4th edition, Scott, Foresman, 1972, pp. 442-43.*

BEEZUS AND RAMONA (1955)

Beezus, in case somebody doesn't know, is Beatrice Quimby, neighbor and stanch friend of Henry Huggins. She is also caretaker and victim of 4-year-old Ramona, the most exasperating little sister we've encountered since Tarkington created Jane Baxter....

In resolving Beezus' struggles with her conscience Mrs. Cleary adds a grace-note of tenderness to her deft comedy and at the same time gives hope to other harried older sisters.

Ellen Lewis Buell, in The New York Times Book Review *(© 1955 by The New York Times Company; reprinted by permission), September 25, 1955, p. 34.*

Ramona's misdemeanors added spice to the earlier books, but when taken in a large dose such as this one they almost cease to be funny, and many readers will find themselves sympathizing with Beezus in her moments of acute dislike of Ramona rather than being amused by Ramona's antics. For girls with younger sisters, the book has value showing that disagreements and even times of dislike among brothers and sisters are not unusual and are not necessarily bad. The book has its humorous spots and will undoubtedly appeal to Cleary fans.

Bulletin of the Center for Children's Books *(published by the University of Chicago), October, 1955, p. 21.*

Ramona Quimby, the strong-willed four-year-old who has spiced previous episodes of this gay series, now has a whole book in which to try the patience of well-behaved big sister Beezus.... This is a very funny book; its situations are credible, and it has a perceptive handling of family relationships that is unfortunately rare in easily read books.

Heloise P. Mailloux, in The Horn Book Magazine *(copyright, 1955, by The Horn Book, Inc., Boston), October, 1955, p. 364.*

OTHER CITATIONS

Virginia Kirkus' Service, *July 1, 1955, p. 418.*

ELLEN TEBBITS (1951)

Ellen Tebbits is a typical fourth grader whose life is made miserable by long underwear and happy by being allowed to clean erasers. Like Henry Huggins, Ellen's problems are those of all fourth graders and they are told with a sympathy and humor that makes them fun to read. This lacks some of the spontaneity of *Henry Huggins* but it is pleasant reading.

Bulletin of the Center for Children's Books *(published by the University of Chicago), September, 1951, p. 2.*

Mrs. Cleary writes from a sure knowledge of the third-grader's world. Her humor [in "Ellen Tebbits"] isn't always so uproarious as it is in "Henry Huggins," but there is plenty of it, pointed up by Louis Darling's clever drawings.... There are poignant moments, too, when the inevitable falling out occurs between best friends. It all rings true.

Ellen Lewis Buell, in The New York Times Book Review *(© 1951 by The New York Times Company; reprinted by permission), September 23, 1951, p. 36.*

OTHER CITATIONS

Virginia Kirkus' Bookshop Service, *July 1, 1951, p. 319.*

Jennie D. Lindquist and Siri M. Andrews, in The Horn Book Magazine, *December, 1951, p. 408.*

EMILY'S RUNAWAY IMAGINATION (1961)

[*Emily's Runaway Imagination* is a] truly delightful book about a lively child living in a rural community in 1920. Emily is vividly real, and the various incidents of her life are believable, humorous, and endearing. Emily and her mother are the moving spirits in the drive to start a town library, and the moderate success they have is satisfying because it is treated with realism. The period details lend color without being obtrusive, and the relationships and attitudes of the small town are described with a gentle affection. [This is a] pleasant story for girls, written in the artfully artless style that marks true craftsmanship.

Zena Sutherland, in Bulletin of the Center for Children's Books *(copyright 1961 by the University of Chicago; all rights reserved), November, 1961, p. 40.*

More conventional, quieter in its humor than the crisply funny yet poignant "Ellen Tebbits" this story of a little girl growing up in rural Oregon in the early Nineteen Twenties has its own charm of place and character. . . . Friendly but shy, bumbling but sentient, [Emily] is a child other little girls will be glad to know.

Ellen Lewis Buell, in The New York Times Book Review *(© 1961 by The New York Times Company; reprinted by permission), November 26, 1961, p. 50.*

OTHER CITATIONS

Alice Dalgliesh, in Saturday Review, *October 28, 1961, pp. 35-6.*

Palmer Price Clark, in School Library Journal, *November, 1961, p. 50.*

Charlotte Jackson, in The Atlantic Monthly, *December, 1961, p. 119.*

FIFTEEN (1956)

[*Fifteen* is] a book about a girl and her first boy friend that is funny and grand because it doesn't pretend to be anything other than what it is. In it there are no high ideals, no strong minded plans for the future—just boy plus girl and all that goes with it. . . . It is very amusing, perceptive writing that tells much about being fifteen and should make marvellous reading for any girl who finds herself left out of things and normally irritated by the rest of the world.

Virginia Kirkus' Service, *July 1, 1956, p. 442.*

[This] story has some of the same humor, and an understanding of teen-agers comparable to the author's understanding of eight-year-olds as shown in the stories of Henry Huggins and his friends. Sandra seems a bit over-drawn, but the other characters are well-defined, and the book makes pleasant, light reading.

Bulletin of the Center for Children's Books *(published by the University of Chicago), December, 1956, p. 48.*

[In *Fifteen*] Mrs. Cleary has produced a frank story about the difficult years of adolescence. The main characters, Jane and Stan, are likeable, sincere youngsters with whom young adults will identify. Although the character development is somewhat superficial, the growth in the heroine's insight makes this popular story worth reading. . . .

The growth of mutual self-confidence and insight that comes through this experience [of first romance] is competently shown. In addition, the warm attachment between Jane and Julie is shown in proper perspective.

John Gillespie and Diana Lembo, in their Juniorplots: A Book Talk Manual for Teachers and Librarians *(copyright © 1967 by the R. R. Bowker Co), Bowker, 1967, pp. 111, 113.*

In Beverly Cleary's novel *Fifteen* many of the first pains of growing up are delicately set down. But essentially the book shows the great value of family stability during the difficult period of adolescence. Frequently reference is made to parental attitudes to teenage behaviour and to the teenager's reaction to parental guidance and control, and there is always an underlying feeling that here is a basically secure family which can offer a wealth of service to the growing child.

B. W. Cooper, in The School Librarian, *June, 1971, p. 118.*

A first date, finding out about each other, doubts about parental approval (and parental behaviour), jealousy, worries about dress and deportment—all the agonies of a girl moving into a new phase of life are described in the social context of almost twenty years ago [in *Fifteen*]. All the same, the book is still read. [Jane Purdy's] feelings are still those of the 'teens, for all the assumed maturity of our times, just as her self-doubt and self-communings belong to any period.

Margery Fisher, in her Who's Who in Children's Books: A Treasury of the Familiar Characters of Childhood *(copyright © 1975 by Margery Fisher; reprinted by permission of Holt, Rinehart and Winston), Holt, Rinehart and Winston, 1975, p. 153.*

OTHER CITATIONS

Ellen Lewis Buell, in The New York Times Book Review, *September 15, 1956, p. 38.*

HENRY AND RIBSY (1954)

Beverly Cleary's book *Henry and Ribsy* is [a] good example of a story that expresses humor appropriate to the age level for which it is intended, in this case the nine through eleven year olds. . . . All the situations show Henry and Ribsy bested for the moment but carrying the complete sympathy and support of the author and the reader. Nearly all the situations are dependent upon Henry's devotion to his dog, Ribsy, and his family's love and acceptance of the two in spite of their occasional and very human annoyance at the steady round of small troubles that Henry and Ribsy bring them.

The world Miss Cleary creates for Henry and Ribsy is the very world in which the nine-year-old boy is most actively involved, his school, his home, his friends, and neighbors, and his dog if he has one. The fact that in spite of all that happens to Henry he is still able to maintain a certain degree of aplomb is also an accurate portrayal of the level of objectivity that children of this age have generally reached. This is not to say that Henry is not upset over the predicaments that Ribsy generates for him; but his unhappiness has a maturity to it that prevents him from going into tantrums or losing hope. This is in keeping with the general developmental level and optimism of the child at this age. . . .

The form of humor dominant here, that of comic predicaments arising out of someone's misfortune and inability to handle situations that may seem simple to the uninvolved, is one of the forms of humor especially appreciated by children of this age. In every respect the humor of this story is appropriate to the age level for which it is intended.

> *Katharine H. Kappas, in* A Critical Approach to Children's Literature: The Thirty-first Annual Conference of the Graduate Library School August 1-3, 1966, *edited by Sara Innis Fenwick (© 1967 by The University of Chicago), University of Chicago Press, 1967, pp. 76-7.*

OTHER CITATIONS

Virginia Kirkus' Bookshop Service, *July 15, 1954, p. 435.*

Bulletin of the Center for Children's Books, *December, 1954, p. 28.*

HENRY AND THE PAPER ROUTE (1957)

Henry Huggins is that middle-sized boy who lives on Klickitat Street, somewhere in Oregon, and who is as typical of the present younger generation as Penrod was of his. In three previous books he has given readers so many laughs that it seems almost churlish to note that Henry has slacked up a little in his tempo.

To be sure, he is very natural and unconsciously appealing as he struggles to land a paper route, is played for a sucker by an older boy who exploits his eagerness, and runs afoul of a near-genius who also wants that route. It is part of Henry's charm that his experiences are just those that might happen to any boy you know. The near-catastrophes that hitherto always boiled up around Henry when he went into action are, however, few in this new book and so the comedy is muted. Still there is Ramona, the neighboring 4-year-old tormentor, whom readers love for her very orneriness. When, finally, Ramona takes over she is as wildly funny as ever.

> *Ellen Lewis Buell, in* The New York Times Book Review *(© 1957 by The New York Times Company; reprinted by permission), September 22, 1957, p. 36.*

OTHER CITATIONS

Zena Sutherland, in Bulletin of the Center for Children's Books, *January, 1958, p. 51.*

HENRY HUGGINS (1950)

Young Henry has a lot in common with the popular hero of "Little Eddie," by Carolyn Haywood. True, Henry hasn't quite Eddie's talent for the unexpected, but still he manages to complicate matters pretty thoroughly for himself and for his remarkably patient parents. . . .

["Henry Huggins"] presents] everyday life as children know it. Maybe Henry is a little luckier than the average boy, but he's not really any funnier. He just seems that way, which is fine.

> *Ellen Lewis Buell, in* The New York Times Book Review *(© 1950 by The New York*

Times Company; reprinted by permission), October 22, 1950, p. 42.

Henry Huggins is one of those busy, conscientious, lively boys perhaps more readily found in fiction than in real life. . . .

Henry is no super-boy. When he gets permission from his mother to keep the stray dog he finds wandering in the town, he encounters difficulties when he smuggles it on a bus in parcel-wrappings. His corner in bubble-gum at school leaves him with an inexplicable deficit. In short, there is enough human inconsistency in Henry's nature and in his exploits to make him a personality of the humorous kind, as well as an acceptable focal point in several books.

> *Margery Fisher, in her* Who's Who in Children's Books: A Treasury of the Familiar Characters of Childhood *(copyright © 1975 by Margery Fisher; reprinted by permission of Holt, Rinehart and Winston), Holt, Rinehart and Winston, 1975, p. 139.*

OTHER CITATIONS

Virginia Kirkus' Bookshop Service, *July 15, 1950, p. 386.*

Bulletin of the Center for Children's Books, *September, 1950, p. 54.*

Jennie D. Lindquist and Siri M. Andrews, in The Horn Book Magazine, *September, 1950, p. 372.*

Constantine Georgiou, in his Children and Their Literature, *Prentice-Hall, 1969, pp. 390-91.*

THE HULLABALOO ABC (1960)

Twenty-six couplets [in *The Hullabaloo ABC*] introduce the young child to the alphabet. In rhymes which are not mechanical but nevertheless easily memorized, he not only is introduced to letters, he becomes familiar in print with recognizable articles and phenomena. Bold illustrations by Earl Thollander in colors which are at once muted and decorative make this a bright incentive to learning.

> Virginia Kirkus' Service, *May 1, 1960, p. 355.*

[*The Hullabaloo ABC* is an] alphabet book that is different. Each letter is the base for a brief bit of rhyme; each rhyme describes some activity; all the activities are those of a small boy and girl on a farm. There is no attempt to use familiar or easy words as a mnemonic device; rather, the author seems to have chosen to write a descriptive phrase that might be remembered. For example: "G is for grunt. That's the pig. Nothing moves him. He's too big."

> *Zena Sutherland, in* Bulletin of the Center for Children's Books *(published by the University of Chicago), June, 1960, p. 159.*

A busy day on the farm where two children create a hullabaloo is the setting for this charming and unusual alphabet book. The colorful illustrations by Earl Thollander carry out the exuberance and action of the verses.

> *Marian Herr, in* Junior Libraries *(reprinted from* Junior Libraries, *September, 1960,*

published by R. R. Bowker Co., a Xerox company; copyright 1960 by Xerox Corporation), September, 1960, p. 90.

JEAN AND JOHNNY (1959)

[Jean's] formation from a drab little girl to a poised young lady, her trial and error struggle to adapt herself to a feminine role, set against a mid-western small town background, are treated in a refreshing manner [in *Jean and Johnny*]. . . . [Beverly Cleary's] is a revealing looking glass for the many readers who will instinctively identify themselves with Jean.

> *Virginia Kirkus' Service, June 15, 1959, pp. 404-05.*

With less high comedy than usual but with her usual understanding and common sense, Beverly Cleary illuminates a situation which a good many young girls will find almost embarrassingly true to life. . . . Mrs. Cleary is a deft and knowledgeable delineator of the high school scene, and of the home front, too. One of the nicest parts of the book is the portrayal of Jean and her family making do, sometimes a bit ruefully but without complaining, on a very small income.

> *Ellen Lewis Buell, in* The New York Times Book Review *(© 1959 by The New York Times Company; reprinted by permission), September 20, 1959, p. 52.*

OTHER CITATIONS

Zena Sutherland, in Bulletin of the Center for Children's Books, *September, 1959, p. 5.*

THE LUCKIEST GIRL (1958)

Beverly Cleary writes so deftly and amusingly [in "The Luckiest Girl"] that Shelley's mistakes don't seem quite so agonizing as they might have been. But she does make clear Shelley's realization that the tug of war between a girl growing up and a devoted mother is an almost universal experience—one to be met with understanding on both sides. For this point alone the story ought to be required reading for teen-age daughters *and* their mothers. And both groups will have a lot of fun with it.

> *Ellen Lewis Buell, in* The New York Times Book Review *(© 1958 by The New York Times Company; reprinted by permission), September 14, 1958, p. 32.*

[*The Luckiest Girl* is a] moving and honest story of adolescence, well-rounded and frequently humorous. The relationships between children and adults, and among the children and young people, are portrayed with perception and told with restraint.

> *Zena Sutherland, in* Bulletin of the Center for Children's Books *(published by the University of Chicago), November, 1958, p. 44.*

MITCH AND AMY (1967)

[*Mitch and Amy*] is an idealized portrait of life in a well-

run, middle class household. The plot, alternating in point of view between brother and sister, consists of a series of everyday activities, such as school and scout projects and meeting new friends. Too much homey detail slows the story, making this a book for more patient readers than those devoted to *Henry Huggins* and friends.

> *Elena Fiant, in* School Library Journal *(reprinted from* School Library Journal, *May, 1967, published by R. R. Bowker Co., a Xerox company; copyright © 1967 by Xerox Corporation), May, 1967, pp. 55-6.*

Probably only a parent of twins could create so convincing a pair as nine-year-old Mitch and Amy and could write about them so realistically and so unsentimentally. . . . The twins' major and minor concerns . . . seem as familiar an aspect of American school life as the problems and paraphernalia of the classroom. The author brings to her writing her usual easy humor and sensitivity to the sights and sounds of school children.

> *Ethel L. Heins, in* The Horn Book Magazine *(copyright © 1967, by The Horn Book, Inc., Boston), June, 1967, p. 346.*

In *Mitch and Amy* this sensitive author brings to her writing the usual bright humor that has characterized the Beverly Cleary books. With convincingly real illustrations by George Porter, *Mitch and Amy* focuses on some of the sights and sounds of school life. . . . Here the reader of the same or similar age has plenty of opportunity to identify with children in conflict with the neighborhood bully or to emphathize with Mitch's book-report difficulties and Amy's struggles with arithmetic. Yet, in this true-to-life book the reader is not robbed of a chance to laugh at certain exaggerations that heighten the humor in a superbly written realistic story.

> *Constantine Georgiou, in his* Children and Their Literature *(© 1969; reprinted by permission of Prentice-Hall, Inc., Englewood Cliffs, New Jersey), Prentice-Hall, 1969, pp. 375-76.*

OTHER CITATIONS

Kirkus Service, *February 1, 1967, p. 130.*

Patience M. Daltry, in The Christian Science Monitor, *March 9, 1967, p. 15.*

The Booklist and Subscription Books Bulletin, *March 15, 1967, p. 794.*

THE MOUSE AND THE MOTORCYCLE (1965)

[*The Mouse and the Motorcycle* is] plain clothes fantasy grounded in the everyday—except for the original conceit of a mouse who can talk and ride a motorcycle. . . . The whimsy is slight—the story is not—and both its interest and its vocabulary are for the youngest members of this age group [eight- to eleven-year-olds].

> Virginia Kirkus' Service *(copyright © 1965 Virginia Kirkus' Service, Inc.), September 1, 1965, p. 905.*

Amusing, realistic details worked into an ingenious pattern lend conviction to Beverly Cleary's first work of fantasy.... [*The Mouse and the Motorcycle* is an] honest, unpretentious book, briskly matter-of-fact in style, but imaginative in plot.

> *Ethel L. Heins, in* The Horn Book Magazine *(copyright © 1965, by The Horn Book, Inc., Boston), December, 1965, p. 628.*

This cheerful book concentrates on the mouse's side of the relationship with the boy: the dangers which it encounters when it rides the motorcycle into a pile of laundry, is nearly swept up by the vacuum cleaner, or is pursued by a terrier dog. Keith's role is chiefly to provide food for the mouse. He is repaid when Ralph, knowing the boy is feverish, brings him an aspirin tablet.

Surprisingly, this talking mouse seems more realistic than the same author's kindergarten pupil, Ramona. In a light-hearted story the ability of the mouse to talk to sympathetic humans is handled particularly well.

> *The Junior Bookshelf, February, 1975, p. 33.*

The humanizing of Ralph is carried out in a spirit of gay and practical fancy. The mouse is able to make the motorcycle move because he makes the right noises. The fact that the toy actually moves fast is established so calmly that it is equally easy to accept Ralph's use of it. He is established ... as a personality in human terms partly because of his obvious likeness to Keith. They are not surprised that they can communicate because 'Two creatures who shared a love for motorcycles naturally spoke the same language'; besides, they both want to grow up and are tired of being told to be patient. Ralph is somewhat more than a speed-maniac. For all his impetuous love of excitement, he is sympathetic enough to Keith's illness to face real danger to find him an aspirin, and in the second book [*Runaway Ralph,* 1970] he helps Garf partly for his own ends but partly because he is sorry for such a mixed-up boy. In fact he remains, engagingly, both mouse and boy.

> *Margery Fisher, in her* Who's Who in Children's Books: A Treasury of the Familiar Characters of Childhood *(copyright © 1975 by Margery Fisher; reprinted by permission of Holt, Rinehart and Winston), Holt, Rinehart and Winston, 1975, pp. 299-300.*

OTHER CITATIONS

Alice Dalgliesh, in Saturday Review, *November 13, 1965, p. 58.*

Beatrice M. Adams, in School Library Journal, *December, 1965, p. 72.*

Zena Sutherland, in Bulletin of the Center for Children's Books, *December, 1965, p. 60.*

Margaret Sherwood Libby, in Book Week, *December 5, 1965, p. 50.*

RAMONA THE BRAVE (1975)

Having already weathered similar emotional storms, middle graders will read about Ramona's fear of the dark, first-day-at-school jitters, etc. with a relish that is part sympathy and part superiority. And although Ramona is semi-reformed, Cleary's legions of fans need not worry—she's still naughty enough for readers to start speculating on her second grade shenanigans.

> *Jane Abramson, in* School Library Journal *(reprinted from* School Library Journal, *April, 1975, published by R. R. Bowker Co., a Xerox company; copyright © 1975 by Xerox Corporation), April, 1975, p. 50.*

In her earlier works, Cleary has told tales of suburban middle-class life within the traditional framework of home and family. This time [in *Ramona the Brave*], she has updated to the present day her previous Ramona works to be topically relevant.

In exploring the emotions of Ramona, Miss Cleary seems to have a better understanding of young children than Nina Bawden. Ramona's problems, which include an unsympathetic teacher, a prissy older sister, and her fear of the dark, are limited enough to be dealt with effectively, and universal enough to be understood by all children. The characters respond realistically to each situation.

> *Martha Unickel, in* Pacific Sun Literary Quarterly, *2nd quarter, May 14, 1975, p. 24.*

One of the most endearing protagonists of children's fiction makes her second appearance as the star of her own show. A first grader, Ramona feels the burden of rising maturity and often yearns for the carefree days of kindergarten.... Although Ramona is exhilarated over learning to read, her impetuousness and fierce sense of justice still embroil her in inevitable clashes with the teacher, and she often feels she is "failing at the job of growing up." Once again the author writes with intuitive accuracy of the jumbled feelings of an uncannily real little girl.

> *Ethel L. Heins, in* The Horn Book Magazine *(copyright © 1975 by the Horn Book, Inc., Boston), June, 1975, p. 266.*

[This] book's anecdotal form and Cleary's infallible perceptions of the world from the other side of seven combine to make long-lasting pleasure reading, while [Alan] Tiegreen's line drawings are endearing and rightly unsentimental.

> *The Booklist (reprinted by permission of the American Library Association; copyright 1975 by the American Library Association), June 1, 1975, p. 1010.*

OTHER CITATIONS

Kirkus Reviews, *March 15, 1975, p. 305.*

Publishers' Weekly, *March 31, 1975, p. 50.*

RAMONA THE PEST (1968)

[*Ramona the Pest*] is replete with strikingly accurate details of home and school life as seen through a child's eyes. Children a few years older than Ramona should respond with immediate recognition to her humorous experiences and escapades.

The Booklist and Subscription Books Bulletin *(reprinted by permission of the American Library Association; copyright 1968 by the American Library Association), May 1, 1968, p. 1041.*

Writing a book about a five-year-old that older children will enjoy is an art, and in this story Beverly Cleary has created a comic and endearing character in the irrepressible Ramona, who starts kindergarten with some reluctance, but promptly falls in love with the teacher. Unfortunately, her independent—and occasionally irritating—behavior leads to stern measures. Ramona decides to become a kindergarten dropout, and it takes all her mother's patience and her teacher's wiles to woo her back. Some of the scenes—such as the one in which Ramona makes abortive attempts to be the best rester in the class—are priceless.

> Zena Sutherland, in Saturday Review *(copyright © 1968 by Saturday Review, Inc.; reprinted with permission), May 11, 1968, p. 38.*

Eight- or nine-year-old children who can look back with the superiority of middle age upon their kindergarten days will smile knowingly at Ramona's first encounters with school life. Beverly Cleary readers are well acquainted with the importunate Ramona; inevitably she now stars in a book of her own and proves to be a spirited, resourceful, and determined heroine. Ramona did not submit to the process of education without a struggle, and the skirmishes, vividly described, will remind the young reader of the child he once was (or wished he had dared to be!). The author has a sure instinct for the thought and expression of five-year-olds....

> Ethel L. Heins, in The Horn Book Magazine *(copyright © 1968 by The Horn Book, Inc., Boston), August, 1968, pp. 419-20.*

Ramona is apparently the American counterpart of Dorothy Edwards' "Naughty Little Sister". She appears to us [in England], as American products sometimes do, more brash, noisier, less appealing. Yet this book contains a great deal of acute observation of five-year-old behaviour. The stories turn again and again to the humour of a five-year-old's preoccupation with what the author euphemistically calls "going to the bathroom". I don't find this theme funny, but it is true that visiting the lavatory is an important part of kindergarten routine. It is also true that a five-year-old will probably find nothing offensive in wearing live worms as rings, and will feel a compulsion to test out the springy qualities of ringlets.

Ramona is a credible and realistic presentation of a five-year-old child. Perhaps it is part of that realism that she is not over-endowed with charm.

> The Junior Bookshelf, *April, 1974, p. 92.*

Ramona's exploits ... are centred on a type-character in children's fiction, the lively, naughty child who enjoys the special dispensation of being the youngest.... If Ramona is not a type but an individual, this must be put to the credit of Beverly Cleary, who lightly but firmly sketches the child's relationships with other people and gives her a personal idiom and manner. Above all, she develops Ramona's

character. In ... *Ramona the Pest*, Ramona, dressed as a witch for the school Hallowe'en procession, is suddenly visited by misgivings. Her mask is identical with several others and nobody seems to know who she is. 'What if everyone in the whole world forgot her.' The dawn of thought in a child of five or so has seldom been more comically or tellingly shown.

> Margery Fisher, in her Who's Who in Children's Books: A Treasury of the Familiar Characters of Childhood *(copyright © 1975 by Margery Fisher; reprinted by permission of Holt, Rinehart and Winston), Holt, Rinehart and Winston, 1975, p. 300.*

OTHER CITATIONS

Patience M. Daltry, in The Christian Science Monitor, *May 2, 1968, p. B7.*

Ellen Goodman, in The New York Times Book Review, *May 5, 1968 (Part 2), pp. 32, 34.*

Jessica McDaniel, in School Library Journal, *September, 1968, p. 188.*

THE REAL HOLE (1960)

Small boys will be particularly sympathetic to four-year-old Jimmy in his determination to make a real hole. The resourceful father who provides the tool and then discovers a way to make use of that hole sets a good example to all parents hard pressed to know how to channel such energy.

> Anne Izard, in School Library Journal *(reprinted from* School Library Journal, *September, 1960, published by R. R. Bowker Co., a Xerox company; copyright © 1960 by Xerox Corporation), September, 1960, p. 55.*

[*The Real Hole* is an] enchanting picture book to read aloud. The text has a sincerity and simplicity that are tremendously effective, with humor that is inherent in the situation and the conversation of the very real children.... [Mary Stevens'] illustrations, some in color and others in black and white, have a lively and humorous charm.

> Zena Sutherland, in Bulletin of the Center for Children's Books *(published by the University of Chicago), September, 1960, p. 4.*

OTHER CITATIONS

Virginia Kirkus' Service, *July 1, 1960, p. 494.*

The Booklist and Subscription Books Bulletin, *October 15, 1960, p. 126.*

RIBSY (1964)

[In *Ribsy*] Mrs. Cleary's style is—as always—refreshing; the characters are real, the dialogue is lively, the humor is unquenchable. The emphasis here is on [the dog] Ribsy rather than his owner; the story is therefore episodic, with some sequences that are ridiculous—but hilariously ridiculous.

> Zena Sutherland, in Bulletin of the Center

for Children's Books (*copyright 1964 by the University of Chicago; all rights reserved*), November, 1964, p. 35.

Henry Huggins's lost dog stars in this delightful story that sparkles with naturalness, heart and humor. . . . Exciting, fast-moving, fresh—with funny pictures, too—this story, told from Ribsy's point of view, will please all dog-lovers.

> *Jane Wylie, in* The New York Times Book Review (© *1964 by The New York Times Company; reprinted by permission*), November 1, 1964 (Part 2), pp. 34, 36.

OTHER CITATIONS

Charlotte Jackson, in The Atlantic Monthly, *December, 1964, p. 162.*

SOCKS (1973)

[*Socks*] is funny, easy to read, and a situation easy for independent readers to correlate to their own reactions. . . . [In] the deftest way possible, the author deals with everything the second, third, and fourth grade singleton is likely to encounter with a new baby around the house. . . . Try to get this one past the recognized indifference of middle childhood to cats; the beast is an adult fancy, the book is good fun for children.

> *Lillian N. Gerhardt, in* School Library Journal (*reprinted from* School Library Journal, *September, 1973, published by R. R. Bowker Co., a Xerox company; copyright* © *1973 by Xerox Corporation*), September, 1973, p. 108.

[*Socks* is] a new-baby story told from the cat's viewpoint although not told by the cat. . . . When Socks does finally reclaim his position as a member of the inner circle, he becomes adjusted to the baby in a hilarious true-to-life episode that achieves the Ultimate Goal, a new friend who always wants to play and snuggle. Not being child-centered, this may have a smaller audience than earlier Cleary books, but it is written with the same easy grace, the same felicitous humor and sharply observant eye.

> *Zena Sutherland, in* Bulletin of the Center for Children's Books (© *1973 by the University of Chicago; all rights reserved*), October, 1973, p. 23.

OTHER CITATIONS

Kirkus Reviews, *June 1, 1973, p. 599.*

Publishers' Weekly, *August 27, 1973, p. 282.*

*   *   *

COATSWORTH, Elizabeth   1893-

An American author and poet, Elizabeth Coatsworth received the 1931 Newbery Medal for *The Cat Who Went to Heaven*. (See also *Contemporary Authors*, Vols. 5-8, rev. ed., and *Something About the Author*, Vol. 2.)

GENERAL COMMENTARY

Elizabeth Coatsworth's special contribution to children's

books of our time lies in the never-failing, superior intelligence of her style, and next in her ever-present sense of the poetry of the situation in hand, whether it is expressed in verse or prose; and finally in her choice of interesting subject matter, a worthy challenge to the imaginative reader, young or old. (p. 98)

> *Louise Seaman Bechtel, "From Java to Maine with Elizabeth Coatsworth," in* Newbery Medal Books: 1922-1955, *edited by Bertha Mahoney Miller and Elinor Whitney Field (copyright* © *1955 by The Horn Book, Inc., Boston),* Horn Book, *1968, pp. 94-8.*

In her perceptive descriptions of life in early America and life in other countries [Elizabeth Coatsworth] has presented realistic characters who exhibit integrity, courage, independence, and compassion. . . . A seeing eye, keen memory, a pen skilled in the art of writing, and an understanding heart have combined to create a body of literature for children that does indeed increase the appetite for living. (p. 84)

It is difficult to characterize the style of a writer who is both storyteller and lyricist. Miss Coatsworth's prose and poetry are outstanding for their incisive, detailed description and vivid sensory impressions. (p. 97)

A unique aspect of Coatsworth's style is the inclusion of poetry in works of fiction. . . . [These] poems . . . establish mood, enrich the setting, provide clues for plot or character, present images, or raise questions. In *The Fair American*, for example, a poem described a beggar in the African city. Eventually, the reader will realize that the poem foretold the disguise of Uncle Patterson and his means of escape. . . . The songs of the housekeeper in *The Cat Who Went to Heaven* continue the story and express the deep mystery of life, as in the eighth song,

> *This is too great a mystery*
> *for me to comprehend*
> *The mercy of the Buddha*
> *Has no end.*
> *This is too beautiful a thing*
> *To understand—*
> *His garments touch the furthest*
> *Grain of sand.*   (pp. 98-9)

Miss Coatsworth uses a wide variety of rhyme patterns. Some of her poems jingle with rhythm; many express a stately cadence. Frequently, the lines are long and varied in length. The flowing movement reflects the rhythm of the low hills, and river flowing to the sea. Calm and peace emanate from these lines, evoking life on the farm, in the meadow, or on the sea. (p. 100)

Miss Coatsworth is very skilled in including authentic information unobtrusively. In *Dancing Tom*, store boats and theatre boats are described as aspects of pioneer life. Suspense rises throughout this story of a dancing pig that saved a baby's life. *Down Tumbledown Mountain* utilizes the repetition of a folk song, *The Swapping Song*, and the pattern of the accumulative tale in a story that describes early mountain life. In *The Sod House* the Traubels settle in Kansas with the specific purpose of voting for Kansas as a free state. Through the story of their precarious life on the plain, Miss Coatsworth presents issues of pre-Civil war times.

Not only does Miss Coatsworth's sharp eye and piercing memory record details of a scene; her ear is tuned to the language of the time and setting. Maine and New England speech patterns are evident in the Sally stories. When Sally and her relatives are ready to move, they ask, "How soon do we flit?"

As might be expected of such a prolific writer, the quality has been uneven. Most of her work is very well written; a few books, such as *The Giant Golden Book of Cat Stories*, are slight and do not have the fine quality or substance of *Ronnie and the Chief's Son, Sword of the Wilderness*, or *Door to the North*.

Characters in Miss Coatsworth's books are drawn clearly, as though outlined in crayon. There are few details of motivation and characters seldom change as they interact with events. Action, rather than inner thought or decision, usually takes precedence. The writer places the character in a situation; we see his strengths, and occasional weaknesses, through his action. (p. 102)

Miss Coatsworth's optimism is reflected in her books and poems. Like the Widow Paulssen in *Troll Weather*, many people only see danger in nature; Miss Coatsworth expresses her belief in friendly trolls who live in golden houses. *Troll Weather* is [a] quiet story with a thread of mystery; it is truly an affirmation of joy in a beautiful world.

More recent books have raised the question of man's destiny, whether it is determined by him or another force. . . . Coatsworth's approach to writing seems to express the idea that behavior is foreordained. By taking an incident, a place, a bit of a journal, a newspaper account, an anecdote, a memory, the author creates a story by asking, "Who might be here? What might happen? Why?" She has noted that once created, the characters take over the story. Having created the characters with their strengths and weaknesses and placed them in a time and setting where political events and powers of Nature swirled around them, their behavior was decreed. "Perhaps we follow the god who chooses us and have ourselves no choice in the matter."

Whether the gods chose Elizabeth Coatsworth to write for children or whether she decided to write stories and poems for them, the world is richer for a lifetime of creative effort. From Chimney Farm has come a shelf of books that will continue to enrich the lives of all who encounter the questing spirit of this highly imaginative writer. (p. 104)

> *Doris Young Kuhn, "Elizabeth Coatsworth: Perceptive Impressionist," (originally published in* Elementary English, *December, 1969), in* Authors and Illustrators of Children's Books: Writings on Their Lives and Works, *edited by Miriam Hoffman and Eva Samuels (copyright © 1972 by Xerox Corp.), Bowker, 1972, pp. 84-106.*

[Elizabeth Coatsworth's] first story, *The Cat and the Captain* (1927), gave little indication of her potential craftsmanship as a writer, her creative strength as a storyteller, or the rich sources from which she could draw. Slight though the book was, it was the beginning of her career as a writer for children. Only three years later *The Cat Who Went to Heaven* (1930) was published. . . . [It] glows with the se-

renity of Japan and sympathy for a religion that esteems even the lowly animals. In it Elizabeth Coatsworth's power as a storyteller declared itself. (p. 452)

The least of [her books] are well-constructed, lucidly written, appealing stories. The best are extraordinary literary creations. One of the most beautiful of these is *The Enchanted, an Incredible Tale* (1951). . . . The story has a mysterious magic yet it is entirely natural. The Maine woods and villages are clearly seen, and the atmosphere is pervaded by joy in the simple act of living, in the continuity of the cycle of seasons, and in life itself. The measure of the book's appeal is not by age or background but by the freshness of the reader's imagination. (pp. 452-53)

Elizabeth Coatsworth . . . recaptured for children the enchantment she has long felt for Maine. . . . Her first period story, *Away Goes Sally* (1934), made the most of the entrancing idea of living in a little house on runners, slowly sliding through the snowy New England roads and forests, drawn by twelve strong oxen, to transport its occupants from Massachusetts to a new home in Maine. A great deal of kindly humor is woven throughout the story of Sally and her aunts and uncles and with the many lively events are glimpses of the quiet beauty of the New England winter. Some of Miss Coatsworth's loveliest poetry is to be found between the chapters of this and other books, but her prose, too, is that of a poet, lucent and concise. . . . There is no sacrifice of reality in the more colorful plots and settings of [her] stories. The clarity of style carries conviction, and, with no extra words the reader is kept aware of the excitement in beauty everywhere, the friendly comfort of life on the well-loved Maine farm, the joy of being aboard a trim ship with the salt wind on one's face, the strange magic of North Africa and alien ways. (pp. 513-14)

As a writer who can tell stories without condescension but within the ability of the youngest readers, Elizabeth Coatsworth was a forerunner of the authors who, in the late fifties, promoted more conspicuously radical changes in books for beginning readers. (p. 514)

> *Ruth Hill Viguers, in* A Critical History of Children's Literature, *by Cornelia Meigs, Anne Thaxter Eaton, Elizabeth Nesbitt, and Ruth Hill Viguers, edited by Cornelia Meigs (copyright © 1953, 1969 by Macmillan Publishing Co., Inc.), revised edition, Macmillan, 1969.*

Building a poem around a series of comparisons seems . . . to be a favorite pattern for Elizabeth Coatsworth. It is an exceedingly provocative one for children to study and to try for themselves.

Another aspect of her style is the smooth, flowing lines that fall so gently on the ear. Poem after poem has this quietness. The lyric text of *Under the Green Willow*, a picture book, has a subdued, rhythmic quality. From *Away Goes Sally* read "Hard from the southeast blows the wind," with its description of a gathering storm without and the cozy comfort of an open fire within. Note these lines, for example:

> *And the cat comes to bask herself*
> *In the soft heat,*
> *And Madame Peace draws up her chair*
> *To warm her feet.*

With those concluding lines, you can fairly feel yourself relaxing and stretching a bit. "No leaf is left," "How gray the rain," and "In the forest it is cool" are only a few examples of that quietness with which the poems abound. Although the lines can frolic now and then, slow-moving calmness predominates. For this reason, reading many of the poems at a time is monotonous.

Both in her prose and in her poetry, Elizabeth Coatsworth makes an effective use of words, often rich with associative meaning, such as "Madame Peace" drawing up her chair to the fire to "warm her feet"—not extraordinary words but laden with associations of peace, warmth, and comfort. On the whole these poems are not markedly musical, but they are rich in sensory words.... You can find examples of her use of words which make you see, smell, taste, touch, and hear.

The single lines and phrases already quoted reveal her sensitive response to nature. Her nature poems seem to fall into two classes. Some are straight nature descriptions, and others are brief, lovely descriptions which lead toward, or climax in, a human mood or situation....

These poems linking together nature and human concerns are notable but they may prove a bit subtle for children and may require discussion before the literal minded children catch their implications. But the nature descriptions are understandable to all children....

The poetry of Elizabeth Coatsworth is more ideational than most juvenile verse. It belongs chiefly to older children and will stretch their minds and imaginations.

> *May Hill Arbuthnot and Zena Sutherland, in their* Children and Books *(copyright © 1947, 1957, 1964, 1972 by Scott, Foresman and Co.), 4th edition, Scott, Foresman, 1972, pp. 362-63.*

ALL-OF-A-SUDDEN SUSAN (1974)

[*All-of-a-Sudden Susan*] has some positive values: Susan's courage, a warm relationship between Susan and her older brother, plenty of action and a firm, clean writing style. The element of magic doesn't conflict with the basic realism of the story, but it adds nothing to it, serving only as a device to cheer Susan at a point when even an imaginative child would probably be less susceptible to fanciful play than at ordinary times.

> *Zena Sutherland, in* Bulletin of the Center for Children's Books *(© 1975 by the University of Chicago; all rights reserved), April, 1975, p. 128.*

OTHER CITATIONS

Kirkus Reviews, *December 15, 1974, p. 1303.*

Cathy S. Coyle, in School Library Journal, *March, 1975, p. 86.*

BESS AND THE SPHINX (1967)

Miss Coatsworth is the heroine of this turn-of-the-century story of a trip abroad.... Young girl readers will find Bess much like themselves, however, for the author's real con-

cern is not so much the trip as the ignominy of being small in an adult world. She vividly remembers the fears, the inadequacies, and small tragedies of her childhood.... Bess's mystical moment, when she finds an ancient amulet at the foot of the great silent Sphinx, may be lost on some young readers, but the book as a whole is a pleasant chronology of adventures and attitudes.

> *Marjorie Lewis, in* School Library Journal *(reprinted from* School Library Journal, *October, 1967, published by R. R. Bowker Co., a Xerox company; copyright © 1967 by Xerox Corporation), October, 1967, p. 162.*

Miss Coatsworth has the rare ability to remember objectively. The simple tale of [*Bess and the Sphinx*] is not purely nostalgic. Any girl reading the account or hearing it will be able to put herself in Bess's shoes and experience through Bess's eyes and heart the scenes and events that would be most likely to delight and impress her if she herself were really to travel. The soft drawings [by Bernice Loewenstein] suit the appealing story.

> *Ruth Hill Viguers, in* The Horn Book Magazine *(copyright © 1967, by The Horn Book, Inc., Boston), December, 1967, p. 747.*

[*Bess and the Sphinx*] might have made more impact if it had been told in the first person. Impact is further diminished by the inclusion between chapters of a number of rather feeble and not always relevant verses. But readers will be glad to know that even in 1898 grandmothers were saying: "Children nowadays don't take any care of things, their own or other people's". There are other good bits, as well as some attractive illustrations by Bernice Loewenstein.

> The Times Literary Supplement *(© Times Newspapers Ltd. 1974), July 5, 1974, p. 722.*

Elizabeth Coatsworth's books have a quiet imperturbable quality about them and this story, based on an event in the author's own childhood, makes a particularly serene little book, even though it tells of a journey to Egypt, of the travellers' adventures and the rough journey home. The author's own depth of feeling is translated into an unassuming tale which, although it reaches no great heights, conveys a faithful and sincere picture of character and incident. The author has given us greater work than this, and criticism could be levelled at a certain dullness and frailty of story, but her qualities make themselves evident even in a small way and echo softly her more outstanding achievements.

> The Junior Bookshelf, *August, 1974, p. 208.*

This story is based on the author's own experiences when a small child and is told in the rather stilted and disjointed manner of personal reminiscence and childhood impressions. There is a faint whiff of Laura Ingalls Wilder in the storytelling but where Mrs. Wilder rounded out her stories and gave a full sense of the period, Miss Coatsworth, with her much briefer style, fails to convey this feeling. If it were not for Bernice Loewenstein's clear and simple drawings, it would be difficult to place the period at all. However, apart from the fact that Bess spends so much of her time in tears, there is much in the book that will appeal to small children.

> *Sylvia Mogg, in* Children's Book Review (©
> *1974 Five Owls Press Ltd.; all rights re-*
> *served), Autumn, 1974, p. 117.*

OTHER CITATIONS

Polly Goodwin, in Book World, *October 22, 1967, p. 14.*

Zena Sutherland, in Bulletin of the Center for Children's
Books, *January, 1968, p. 76.*

THE CAT AND THE CAPTAIN (1927)

This [1974] revision of Coatsworth's first children's book
deletes unflattering references to Blacks and contains new
illustrations [by Bernice Loewenstein] but adheres to the
original story. . . . Characterization of humans is minimal—
the retired sea captain who "owns" the cat is not fleshed
out and the housekeeper is a caricature—but the cat's
pranks provide light-hearted fun for independent readers as
well as listening audiences.

> *Margaret M. Bauman, in* School Library
> Journal (*reprinted from* School Library Jour-
> nal, *September, 1974, published by R. R.*
> *Bowker Co., a Xerox company; copyright ©*
> *1974 by Xerox Corporation), September,*
> *1974, p. 56.*

[This] new edition of Elizabeth Coatsworth's first book for
children, originally published in 1927, has tidy little black
and white drawings [by Bernice Loewenstein] that fit the
neat modesty of the story's scope and subject. . . . [This
book doesn't have] a startling plot, but it's adequately carried along by a few amusing incidents; the Cat never ex-
ceeds believable feline behavior, and the writing style is
deft; bland but humorous, lightly affectionate about the
Cat.

> *Zena Sutherland, in* Bulletin of the Center
> for Children's Books (© *1974 by the Univer-*
> *sity of Chicago; all rights reserved), Novem-*
> *ber, 1974, p. 40.*

OTHER CITATIONS

Ethel L. Heins, in The Horn Book Magazine, *August,*
1974, p. 395.

THE CAT WHO WENT TO HEAVEN (1930)

Into her lovely and imaginative story *The Cat Who Went to
Heaven* Elizabeth Coatsworth has put something of the
serenity and beauty of the East and of the gentleness of a
religion that has a place even for the humblest of living
creatures . . .

> *Anne Thaxter Eaton, in her* Reading With
> Children (*copyright 1940 by Anne Thaxter*
> *Eaton; reprinted by permission of The Vi-*
> *king Press, Inc.), Viking, 1940, p. 104.*

Imbued with the delicacy and depth of an ancient oriental
print, this beautiful, poetic story is based on Japanese legends and the spiritual teachings of Buddhism. . . . [The]
miraculous outcome of this tender story helps the young
reader to understand a religion that recognizes and blesses

all living creatures on earth. Illustrations [by Lynd Ward]
reflect the beauty and sensitivity of the tale and seem to
become individual parts of the Japanese artist's temple picture.

> *Constantine Georgiou, in his* Children and
> Their Literature (© *1969; reprinted by per-*
> *mission of Prentice-Hall, Inc., Englewood*
> *Cliffs, New Jersey), Prentice-Hall, 1969, p.*
> *284.*

[*The Cat Who Went to Heaven*] has a delicate, catlike air,
and captures exactly the oriental spirit—at least as we in
the West conceive it to be. Into the narrative are woven,
neatly and intricately, a series of Chinese legends. It is also
interspersed with the 'songs of the housekeeper', which
unfortunately are insipid stuff. They could have been plain
and homely without being as feeble as this:

> Dear Pussy, you are white as milk,
> Your mouth's a blossom, your coat's silk—
> What most distinguished family tree
> Produced so great a rarity?

There is a bathetic echo here of Blake's *Tyger:* 'What
immortal hand or eye Could frame thy fearful symmetry?'

> *John Rowe Townsend, in his* Written for
> Children: An Outline of English-Language
> Children's Literature (*copyright © 1965,*
> *1974 by John Rowe Townsend; reprinted by*
> *permission of J. B. Lippincott Company),*
> *revised edition, Lippincott, 1974, p. 175.*

THE CHILDREN COME RUNNING (1960)

This beautiful book reproduces a generous selection of the
stunning UNICEF Christmas cards of the past nine years.
Quotations, verses, and stories tie the pictures loosely together. Though it may be objected that such a text is bound
to be a little artificial, there is no denying the skill and artistry Elizabeth Coatsworth has brought to her task.

> Saturday Review (*copyright © 1960 by Sat-*
> *urday Review, Inc.; reprinted with permis-*
> *sion), November 12, 1960, p. 98.*

For the benefit of the United Nations Children's Fund, a
collection of cards that have been created by famous artists
are presented with the addition of some text, in prose or
poetry, by Miss Coatsworth. While the writing has been
fashioned to illustrate the paintings, little of it seems contrived. There are, however, some pieces which do so seem:
some of the poetry, and a rather long prose selection, "The
Kite and the Wind," which encompasses several of the illustrations and has a tinge of travelogue about it. Even this
is not mediocre because the writing style has merit.

> *Zena Sutherland, in* Bulletin of the Center
> for Children's Books (*copyright 1960 by the*
> *University of Chicago; all rights reserved),*
> *December, 1960, p. 56.*

DAISY (1973)

[*Daisy* presents] Christmas in Mexico City during horse
and carriage days, as experienced by a timid American girl

who gains in confidence as a result of her adventures. . . . [This] developmental miracle . . . requires as much faith from the reader as the announced healings do of visitors to the cathedral. . . . [Her] sudden blooming is all the less impressive for being a dimmer, South-of-the-border rerun of 1967's *Bess and the Sphinx*.

> *Kirkus Reviews (copyright © 1973 The Kirkus Service, Inc.), January 1, 1973, pp. 4-5.*

Set in Mexico, [*Daisy*] is a quiet story of a young girl who is traveling with her mother, father, and older sister. . . . Interesting facts about Mexican history and customs fall easily into place during the family's visit. Daisy's warm, spontaneous response to her benefactors and her appreciation of their religious traditions convey an unobtrusive message of brotherhood.

> *Mary B. Mason, in* School Library Journal *(reprinted from* School Library Journal, *March, 1973, published by R. R. Bowker Co., a Xerox company; copyright © 1973 by Xerox Corporation), March, 1973, pp. 104-05.*

OTHER CITATIONS

Kirkus Reviews, *January 1, 1973, pp. 4-5.*

Zena Sutherland, *in* Bulletin of the Center for Children's Books, *April, 1973, p. 122.*

DESERT DAN (1960)

Elizabeth Coatsworth's well-known sympathy for, and understanding of, animals has excellent play in a story about old Dan, who roamed the western American desert with three burros, a goat, and a bantam rooster. . . . The story . . . presents the desert in all its beauty and all its harshness, with Dan, who epitomizes love and understanding, winning over some truly spine-tingling odds.

> *Silence Buck Bellows, in* The Christian Science Monitor *(reprinted by permission from* The Christian Science Monitor; *© 1960 The Christian Science Publishing Society; all rights reserved), November 3, 1960, p. 5B.*

[*Desert Dan* is a] gentle story, but [it is] slow-moving and [has] a plot that is of little interest unless the reader likes animal stories; the writing style is good, and the author establishes firmly the personalities of the animals as well as the character of the kindly old man. The illustrations [by Harper Johnson] are realistic and effective in black and white; as in the text, there is an occasional sentimental presentation of the baby burro.

> *Zena Sutherland, in* Bulletin of the Center for Children's Books *(copyright 1961 by the University of Chicago; all rights reserved), April, 1961, p. 125.*

Nothing much happens in this short story but the personality of the gentle old man and the individuality of his animal friends give life and charm to the book. The background of the desert, sometimes so beautiful, at other times

so inimical, is beautifully described. . . . [This book] will appeal to many ages.

> The Junior Bookshelf, *January, 1964, p. 41.*

OTHER CITATIONS

Virginia Kirkus' Service, *July 15, 1960, p. 556.*

DOOR TO THE NORTH (1950)

[In "Door to the North"] Miss Coatsworth uses every surmise and fact about the Scandinavian colonies planted after Leif Ericsson's New World discovery. She fills the gaps in her historical material with reasonable speculation. Then, in an after-chapter, she dissociates fact from fiction with scholarly exactness. Olaf's experiences could well have happened, and under the breathless spell of her storytelling one is quite convinced that they did. And Mr. Chapman's masterly drawings are as notable as the text.

> *Nina Brown Baker, in* The New York Times Book Review *(© 1950 by The New York Times Company; reprinted by permission), November 12, 1950, p. 14.*

Outstanding among books dealing with the history of our own country is *Door to the North, a Saga of Fourteenth Century America* by Elizabeth Coatsworth, illustrated by Frederick T. Chapman. . . . Not only does [Miss Coatsworth] evoke vivid pictures of Norway and Greenland in the time of the Vikings; her characters talk like men of courage and conviction. Familiarity with the Greenland and Icelandic sagas is evident in her characters and their conversation. In an informing Afterword Miss Coatsworth has brought her story close to contemporary Minnesota and has revealed to the attentive reader her discovery of the fascinating mysteries it holds.

> *Anne Carroll Moore, in* The Horn Book Magazine *(copyright, 1951, by The Horn Book, Inc., Boston), January, 1951, p. 26.*

This fresh approach to fourteenth-century exploration in North America is given a strong personal appeal through the experiences of a young member of the party, who had urgent need to prove his courage to the leader. [*Door to the North* is a] well-written, absorbing book for young people.

> *Alice M. Jordan, in* The Horn Book Magazine *(copyright, 1951, by The Horn Book, Inc., Boston), March, 1951, p. 112.*

OTHER CITATIONS

Virginia Kirkus' Bookshop Service, *September 1, 1950, pp. 519-20.*

Bulletin of the Center for Children's Books, *November, 1950, p. 67.*

DOWN HALF THE WORLD (1968)

Down Half the World is an appropriate title for this book of poetry since the collection itself is divided almost in half in terms of both theme and quality. There are historical poems and nature poems; there are excellent poems and poor ones. The historical poems are often sentimental and at times contrived and the young reader may have difficulty in relating to them. They might, however, achieve meaning in a joint English-History program covering as they do such figures as Henry IV, Mary Tudor, Columbus, Thoreau, etc. Unfortunately, introductory notes explaining the historical figures and the situations which inspired the poems have not been included and as a result several lose important levels of meaning. The nature poems also suffer occasionally from sentimentality but they are often moving and are well varied stylistically. In "Hang Fu," for example, the poet has exquisitely captured the stirring simplicity of oriental nature poetry. Although it has fine moments, the lack of cohesion in this collection keeps it from being a truly satisfying work.

> Kirkus Service (copyright © 1968 The Kirkus Service, Inc.), April 15, 1968, p. 470.

Whether capturing a moment in history or some wondrous facet of nature, Miss Coatsworth's poetry displays rare insight and beauty, and [*Down Half the World*] will make a fine addition to the poetry collection of any library. . . . Miss Coatsworth's delight in and facility with words is obvious, but it is her thought which makes the strongest impact.

> *Terry Myers, in* School Library Journal *(reprinted from* School Library Journal, *May, 1968, published by R. R. Bowker Co., a Xerox company; copyright © 1968 by Xerox Corporation), May, 1968, p. 88.*

A book of poems by Elizabeth Coatsworth is a wonderful pageant! So many images pass through the mind. There are scenes: a July storm, a pond reflecting clouds, icicles dripping, spring hail, the view from Cadillac Mountain, the enormous sea rearranging its islands for the night. And creatures: deer, a whale, the Loch Ness monster, the unicorn, Daniel Webster's horses. The poems are not necessarily about them but they are there. Oftener than anything else one sees people, and many of them are people out of history: empresses, an infanta, the women of Syracuse, Mary Tudor, Columbus, Montezuma, Dr. Johnson, Samuel Pepys, Samson, Jeanne d'Albret—not much about any one, but how much the reader learns from the little thrust of light a poem throws. Whether or not the import of a poem is clear on the first reading, a picture is always clear. The varied, beautiful collection will touch the imaginations of older boys and girls and their elders.

> *Ruth Hill Viguers, in* The Horn Book Magazine *(copyright © 1968 by The Horn Book, Inc., Boston), June, 1968, pp. 332-33.*

THE ENCHANTED: AN INCREDIBLE TALE (1951)

In less skillful hands, this might have become a half-baked fairy story sloshed with over-writing. Mrs. Coatsworth knows what she is about—and her book has discipline of form as well as loveliness of style. She drugs the reader into her own acceptance of the strangeness of all nature, and after a few chapters one feels that "The Enchanted" is not only a beautiful book, but one which is essentially believable.

> *Jane Cobb, in* The New York Times Book Review *(© 1951 by The New York Times Company; reprinted by permission), July 1, 1951, p. 14.*

There is an ineradicable magic that defies criticism and analysis and it is this rare quality that gives to *The Enchanted* an atmosphere of pure joy in living, at sixteen or at five times sixteen. I rejoice that the publishers have given it a format which might have been designed in the forest. It is such a book as I would like to send to countries which have no conception that country life in America can still hold romance and reality on terms of equality.

> *Anne Carroll Moore, in* The Horn Book Magazine *(copyright, 1951, by The Horn Book, Inc., Boston), September, 1951, p. 316.*

Because the story [of *The Enchanted*] is rooted in the daily realities of the farmer's life and has a setting which is the natural soil of the Indian legend, it achieves a convincing balance between reality and fantasy. Each character is fully realized and the spare, crystalline prose of this author-poet is literature of a superior quality.

> *Judith C. Ullom, in* School Library Journal *(reprinted from* School Library Journal, *May, 1968, published by R. R. Bowker Co., a Xerox company; copyright © 1968 by Xerox Corporation), May, 1968, p. 85.*

It was dawn and the fire had gone out when I finished the last page of Elizabeth Coatsworth's "The Enchanted, An Incredible Tale". . . . I had not lifted my head for some hours, nor stopped to notice the discreet and accurate illustrations by Mary Frank. I had been under a potent spell, the spell of a masterpiece, for that is what this memorable tale surely is. Written in Elizabeth Coatsworth's transparent style, so good an instrument that one hardly notices it, we are set down in the wilderness of Maine, and it is all so real that almost to the end the reader is unaware that he has been caught up into myth. Who would wish it ever to end? Yet it must before it reveals its secret. . . . I myself was shot through by the arrow of mystery the author looses, and will not be the same again.

> *Mary Sarton, in* The New York Times Book Review *(© 1968 by The New York Times Company; reprinted by permission), May 5, 1968 (Part 2), p. 43.*

OTHER CITATIONS

Virginia Kirkus' Bookshop Service, *May 1, 1951, p. 233.*

FIRST ADVENTURE (1950)

[*First Adventure* is a] charming reconstruction of the true story of the wanderings of little John Billington, son of an unpopular family in the Plymouth colony in 1621. . . . The author has caught the exhilaration of running away, the fear of the unknown terrors of the wilderness, and the fun of being admired and waited upon by strangers (not unlike the glee of pampered "lost" children at the police stations today). There is a brief section explaining the source of the story.

Virginia Kirkus' Bookshop Service, *August 15, 1950, pp. 463-64.*

Based on the first recorded adventure of a white child in New England, Miss Coatsworth's story is as appealing as it is easy to read. . . . The dogged courage of the lost boy is effectively described. The story's chief charm lies, however, in the fact that Johnny is so much like any small boy of today that long-ago Plymouth, as seen through his eyes, seems almost contemporary too.

> *Ellen Lewis Buell, in* The New York Times Book Review (© *1951 by The New York Times Company; reprinted by permission), January 7, 1951, p. 8.*

OTHER CITATIONS

Bulletin of the Center for Children's Books, *February, 1951, p. 19.*

THE FOX FRIEND (1966)

A provocative piece this [is] . . . just a short space in time described and offered up without comment. It concerns an afternoon encounter between an elderly beagle-ish mongrel out of condition through overweight and a lean and powerful fox. . . . The vocabulary is as simple as the incident, direct and clear. The contrasts between the animals, the implied natures of the wild and the tame, the refreshing lack of explanation all make this an interesting book. It suggests itself as a catalyst for thoughtful discussion. The illustrations are sharply pictorial and exact, closely following the events and actions described in the text.

> *Virginia Kirkus' Service (copyright © 1966 Virginia Kirkus' Service, Inc.), January 15, 1966, pp. 54-5.*

Most of the story [of *The Fox Friend*] concerns a process of animals watched by Perky: a chipmunk, a porcupine, a skunk, et cetera. One weakness of the story is that Perky's reactions to the animals are expressed in thoughts at a human level; for example, Perky thinks as she sees the skunk's kittens, "I'd like to go and play with them. But I don't suppose their mother would care for that, and I have an idea that she has a special way of showing she isn't pleased."

> *Zena Sutherland, in* Bulletin of the Center for Children's Books (copyright 1966 by the University of Chicago; all rights reserved), *July-August, 1966, p. 176.*

OTHER CITATIONS

Elsie T. Dobbins, in School Library Journal, *March, 1966, p. 224.*

GEORGE AND RED (1969)

Although the adventures and escapades of George Standish, whose father "ran a successful flour mill," and Red MacDonald, the son of the next-door neighbor, are Tom Sawyer-like in nature, they are rich in historical details. Some of the deftly introduced allusions are local, as in the fear of invasion from Canada at the outbreak of the Civil War or in the ill-fated Fenian expedition to Canada after the war. Others, as the outbreak of hostilities between the North and the South and the assassination of Lincoln are more broadly American. The precise prose of the storytelling is frequently edged with humor, and the atmosphere of a less sophisticated, of a more rural America is caught in the boy-like experiences of George and Red. The double-spread black-and-white drawings [by Paul Giovanopoulos] are in harmony with the time and place of the story.

> *Paul Heins, in* The Horn Book Magazine (copyright © 1969 by The Horn Book, Inc., Boston), *August, 1969, p. 408.*

Friendship is the underlying theme of this pleasant little adventure story of two young boys living in northern New York state in the 1860's. . . . Along with their adventures the boys discover that helping others brings obligations, and so they move believably from little boy pranks into the world of duties and responsibilities. The fine-line illustrations [by Paul Giovanopoulos] are very well done, but stronger than is warranted by the story, which is acceptable but average.

> *Mary Ann Kelly, in* School Library Journal (reprinted from School Library Journal, *September, 1969, published by R. R. Bowker Co., a Xerox company; copyright © 1969 by Xerox Corporation), September, 1969, p. 106.*

[*George and Red* contains three] brief stories about two boys living in a small town on the Canadian border a century ago, handsomely illustrated and competently written; despite the practiced style and the interesting historical background, the tales seem to lack focus and climax.

> *Zena Sutherland, in* Bulletin of the Center for Children's Books (© 1969 by the University of Chicago; all rights reserved), *December, 1969, p. 57.*

THE GIANT GOLDEN BOOK OF CAT STORIES (1953)

"The Giant Golden Book of Cat Stories" contains thirty-five stories, poems and sketches. As in many of the large, economy-sized collections some of the stories are very slight. There is also an exaggerated quaintness—cats in bonnets and shawls—which is odd to find in Miss Coatsworth's work. The poems are charming and certain stories, such as "Bold John" and "The Kitten Everyone Chased," are memorable. Unfortunately this cannot be said for [Feodor] Rojankovsky's lush and lavish illustrations.

> *Ellen Lewis Buell, in* The New York Times Book Review (© 1953 by The New York Times Company; reprinted by permission), *March 15, 1953, p. 24.*

[This is a] collection of short stories, very brief articles, poems, and one song, all of them about cats, except for three articles which are about other animals. The stories are uneven in quality of writing and are generally quite pointless, especially the ones about talking animals. The articles contribute nothing to a child's understanding of cats, and seem to have no real purpose in the book unless it is for padding.

Bulletin of the Center for Children's Books *(published by the University of Chicago), December, 1954, p. 28.*

GRANDMOTHER CAT AND THE HERMIT (1970)

[*Grandmother Cat and the Hermit* is a] pleasant, quiet tale of a summer shared by a boy and his unlovely cat with a hermit living in a hidden canyon. . . . [This is a] contemporary, typically Elizabeth Coatsworth story that compares well with her best books.

Rose Mary Pace, in School Library Journal *(reprinted from* School Library Journal, *May, 1970, published by R. R. Bowker Co., a Xerox company; copyright © 1970 by Xerox Corporation), May, 1970, p. 70.*

By summer's end the hermit [in *Grandmother Cat and the Hermit*] realizes the value of companionship, partly through his friendship with Dave, and deciding to move on, teaches the boy to accept life's changes. The secret outdoor retreat that is the heart of this meaningful story will appeal to children. [Irving] Boker's drawings reflect the quiet tone of [the] narrative.

The Booklist *(reprinted by permission of the American Library Association; copyright 1970 by the American Library Association), July 15, 1970, p. 1406.*

OTHER CITATIONS

Kirkus Reviews, *March 15, 1970, pp. 320-21.*

THE HAND OF APOLLO (1965)

What Elizabeth Coatsworth is driving at in *The Hand of Apollo* is not easy to see. Greece under the Romans is the setting for this somewhat strange work. . . . [The book has good] background and a fine opening situation—both of which swiftly come to naught as plot, character, and even good sense are each in their turn sacrificed to the author's iron determination to Be Poetic. . . . Mood and atmosphere are sometimes well created, and a number of passages have a fanciful charm, but by and large there is a disheartening absence of such items as cohesive, interesting story and believable characters. There are many spiritual effusions; but unfortunately they have a flavor far more Goethe than Greek.

Gerald Gottlieb, in Book Week *(© The Washington Post), November 14, 1965, p. 27.*

Though accurate enough historically and geographically, this book is not primarily concerned with recreating everyday life at the time of the sack of Corinth by the Romans. It is sheer poetry, filled with the light and dappled shade of the Greek islands, sun on white cliffs, the fragrance of wild flowers, the sound of gulls, the smell and thrust of the sea. . . . The book is beautifully constructed and ends with the future assured but not shown.

The Junior Bookshelf, *June, 1967, p. 179.*

Inspired by an incident in history, *The Hand of Apollo* by Elizabeth Coatsworth recreates the splendor and shadow of ancient Greece. . . .

Serenely told, the book shares an ancient vision that becomes splendidly credible. Elizabeth Coatsworth's mastery of the classic period enables her to choose details of dress, speech, terrain, and religion that make the background for the book very vivid. Along with this there is the richness of language, so skillfully used that the rush of events is never impeded. A young reader can become enthralled with a story that shows the power of a boy's conviction which "meant learning to give himself to creation rather than to destruction" even though it involved going against his father's wishes. Dedicated to poetry, the sensitive and fine portrait of an ancient youth stands as a testimony of deep, personal convictions.

Constantine Georgiou, in his Children and Their Literature *(© 1969; reprinted by permission of Prentice-Hall, Inc., Englewood Cliffs, New Jersey), Prentice-Hall, 1969, p. 321.*

OTHER CITATIONS

Kirkus Service, *October 1, 1965, p. 1046.*

Laura F. Seacord, in School Library Journal, *January, 1966, p. 128.*

Marjorie Burger, in The New York Times Book Review, *January 2, 1966, p. 18.*

Zena Sutherland, in Bulletin of the Center for Children's Books, *February, 1966, p. 96.*

HERE I STAY (1938)

This is a gentle story written with deep underlying power as typified by the girl's character. There are some beautiful descriptive passages, for example "Autumn sat on the hills like an Indian sachem, Margaret thought, in brown buckskin and a blanket of scarlet and yellow". Anyone who has seen a Maine Fall will realise just how wonderful this passage is. The book is a study in solitude and courage of the mind and the body; one would hope it would bring peace and gentleness to its teenage readers. For me it is one of the most beautiful, I keep using this word advisedly, books I have ever read about pioneering in any land.

The Junior Bookshelf, *December, 1972, p. 397.*

Here I Stay may well be the sad epitaph of this book if, as seems probable, it is only to be found on the *children's* shelves in libraries and bookshops. Many readers searching the adult shelves for a peaceful, interesting story about 'ordinary' people living good lives would welcome and enjoy this book. Children, because they *are* children and evaluate human qualities through a child's experience, may miss its quality and find it dull. . . . It is written of Margaret Winslow, the heroine of *Here I Stay* '. . . tranquility was the law of her being.' The book is essentially a celebration of the tranquil spirit, a quiet thanksgiving for the inner resources that enable a human being to live in solitude for months at a time without a diminishing of human sympathy and understanding. . . .

The simplicity of her life is enriched by the quality of her perception of her environment; the reader is enriched by Elizabeth Coatsworth's understanding of those who live off the land, in harmony with the changing rhythm of the seasons and at peace with themselves.

> *Nina Danischewsky, in* Children's Book Review (© *1973 Five Owls Press, Ltd.; all rights reserved), December, 1972, pp. 186-87.*

HIDE AND SEEK (1956)

A child's game is carried out to its more imaginative consequences here as Elizabeth Coatsworth's rhymes pursue a little boy hither and yon. . . . [This is a] well worn concept traditionally portrayed, but the enjoyable verses and pictures in green by Genevieve Vaughan-Jackson make a come and come again book.

> Virginia Kirkus' Service, *April 1, 1956, p. 243.*

In rhymed text the author tells of a small boy playing hide and seek with his mother. The content is obscure and the rhymes are often forced. The book becomes too subtle for very young children when the little boy is actually pictured in the places where his mother guesses him to be—in a bird's nest, in a hole in the ground, in an airplane, etc.

> Bulletin of the Center for Children's Books *(published by the University of Chicago), October, 1956, p. 19.*

INDIAN ENCOUNTERS: AN ANTHOLOGY OF STORIES AND POEMS (1960)

Short stories, historical recreations, adventure, human interest bits and poetry provide a full canvas for Miss Coatsworth in this collection of stories related to the American Indian in his many facets. These are drawn from her many books for which, in some capacity or other, the Indian has provided material. . . . Almost always the Indian as interpreted by the white man is revealed against a background of action and mood as a being of many aspects and complexions. It reveals Miss Coatsworth as deeply concerned in her topic.

> Virginia Kirkus' Service, *March 15, 1960, p. 235.*

The stories [included in *Indian Encounters*] have excitement and suspense, reflect many aspects of Indian life and character, and will be excellent for reading aloud. (A good choice for around the camp fire.) Many of them are excerpts from books much too good to be known only by a sampling, and, as young people fascinated by these accounts will inevitably want more, it is a pity that the books from which the stories are taken cannot be more easily identified.

> *Ruth Hill Viguers, in* The Horn Book Magazine *(copyright, 1960, by the Horn Book, Inc., Boston), August, 1960, p. 297.*

This is a collection for older children of short stories and poems about American Indians as the whites saw them from the days of the Vikings to modern times. The fascination which the coloured race exercised over the Europeans pervades the whole book. The incidents are vividly drawn, unusual, unexpected and a good antidote to the monotony of television Westerns.

> The Times Literary Supplement (© *The Times Publishing Company Ltd. 1960), November 25, 1960, p. xxviii.*

OTHER CITATIONS

Marian A. Herr, in Junior Libraries, *September, 1960, p. 80.*

INDIAN MOUND FARM (1969)

To a modern child, life on a farm near the end of the last century would not seem very exciting. In spite of Elizabeth Coatsworth's expressive prose and warm, human characters, this small, slow story will probably bore all but a select group of very sensitive girls. . . . Fermin Rocker's soft drawings complement the delicate prose, and the six poems, written as preludes to the chapters, alone make the book worth having.

> *Muriel Kolb, in* School Library Journal *(reprinted from* School Library Journal, *November, 1969, published by R. R. Bowker Co., a Xerox company; copyright* © *1969 by Xerox Corporation), November, 1969, p. 117.*

[This] account of Pamelia's summer [at her aunt's farm near St. Louis] is deftly written, with an occasional bit of contrivance (the same gypsy shows up at the farm) and with a sedate quality that rather suits the setting but slows the pace of the story. Poems are inserted between chapters, not carrying out the action but pertinent to some aspect of the book.

> *Zena Sutherland, in* Bulletin of the Center for Children's Books (© *1970 by the University of Chicago; all rights reserved), January, 1970, p. 77.*

JOCK'S ISLAND (1963)

The writing [in *Jock's Island*] is quiet and the story is slow paced; the device of having the young man talk to the dog (therefore explaining a great deal that would otherwise seem parenthetical) does not quite come off naturally, so that the story loses impact.

> *Zena Sutherland, in* Bulletin of the Center for Children's Books *(copyright 1964 by the University of Chicago; all rights reserved), April, 1964, p. 123.*

[This] simple story is beautifully written. The menacing volcano, the deserted village, the bewildered animals, are not easily forgotten. The friendship between the dog and the man will appeal to young readers, but it is not sentimentalised. [*Jock's Island* is a] memorable book. . . .

> The Junior Bookshelf, *June, 1965, p. 152.*

OTHER CITATIONS

Saturday Review, *November 9, 1963, pp. 61-2.*

Jane Wylie, in The New York Times Book Review, *November 10, 1963 (Part 2), p. 46.*

LIGHTHOUSE ISLAND (1968)

[*Lighthouse Island* is a] bland book with a growing awareness of nature as its theme. Young Alex, an Ohio boy, is spending the summer on a Maine island with his aunt and uncle who keep the lighthouse there. Alex's initial loneliness and predictable growing appreciation of the natural things around him, including puffins, a white kid, terns, whales, and porpoises, are related simply but boringly. Symeon Shimin's softly shaded blue and pale orange illustrations are pleasant; like the text, however, they lack vitality.

> *Dallas Y. Shaffer, in* School Library Journal *(reprinted from* School Library Journal, *February, 1969, published by R. R. Bowker Co., a Xerox company; copyright © 1969 by Xerox Corporation), February, 1969, p. 74.*

The story has a quiet appeal that is enhanced by the soft but vigorous illustrations; the static quality of the book is compensated for by the vivid creation of the setting and the smooth flow of the writing.

> *Zena Sutherland, in* Bulletin of the Center for Children's Books *(copyright 1969 by The University of Chicago; all rights reserved), February, 1969, p. 91.*

[This] brief, well-told story and the many illustrations envelop the reader in the atmosphere and the rugged beauty of a Maine island and remind children of the automated present that there was a time when lighthouses were operated by keepers with families, when just such an exciting setting as this could be home for a few lucky children. Unfortunately, the type is superimposed on the illustrations, making some of the pages discouraging to read and destroying the flow of the pictures.

> *Ruth Hill Viguers, in* The Horn Book Magazine *(copyright © 1969 by The Horn Book, Inc., Boston), April, 1969, p. 165.*

MARRA'S WORLD (1975)

In *Pure Magic* . . . Coatsworth wrote of a boy who was a fox; here strange, shunned Marra is the daughter of a seal. . . . [As] in *Pure Magic* Coatsworth uses a normal child as realistic ballast and Alison does help keep this on course when the two girls are caught in a fog and Marra's mother, a mournful gray seal named Nerea, leads their boat to shore. It's all very slight and slightly odd but pleasant too, and less self-consciously hushed than *Pure Magic*. And you can ride a long way on that first sentence—"Marra's grandmother hated her and showed it every day of her life."

> Kirkus Reviews *(copyright © 1975, The Kirkus Service, Inc.), October 1, 1975, p. 1129.*

The outcast theme [in *Marra's World*] is occasionally overstated à la folklore instead of fiction, but otherwise Coatsworth . . . has perfectly tuned her rich yet simple prose to a haunting story.

> *Betsy Hearne, in* The Booklist *(reprinted by permission of the American Library Association; copyright 1975 by the American Library Association), November 15, 1975, pp. 450-51.*

OTHER CITATIONS

Publishers' Weekly, *August 4, 1975, pp. 56-7.*

William Cole, in Saturday Review, *November 29, 1975, p. 30.*

THE NOBLE DOLL (1961)

[*The Noble Doll* is a] quiet story, sentimental and rather fragile, about the lovely relationship between a child and an old woman. The scene is Mexico and the time is Christmas, but the scene and time are less important than the two characters. . . . The ending is a bit pat, and the way in which Luisa's mother offers to part with her child may be difficult for our children to understand. The story has wonderful background, good style, and great warmth; the illustrations [by Leo Politi] are enchanting.

> *Zena Sutherland, in* Bulletin of the Center for Children's Books *(copyright 1961 by the University of Chicago; all rights reserved), December, 1961, p. 57.*

OTHER CITATIONS

Virginia Kirkus' Service, *July 15, 1961, p. 608.*

Ruth Hill Viguers, in The Horn Book Magazine, *December, 1961, p. 544.*

Ellen Lewis Buell, in The New York Times Book Review, *December 3, 1961, p. 68.*

Alice Dalgliesh, in Saturday Review, *December 16, 1961, p. 23.*

THE PEACEABLE KINGDOM (1958)

[*The Peaceable Kingdom* contains three] poems on Biblical themes. . . . All the poems reflect a calm faith and a gentle affection for the animal world; they are pleasant rather than outstanding poetry, well-suited to reading aloud.

> *Zena Sutherland, in* Bulletin of the Center for Children's Books *(published by the University of Chicago), December, 1958, p. 61.*

In "The Peaceable Kingdom" Elizabeth Coatsworth has taken Bible themes, appropriate for any sect or religion, and put them in new dress. The idealism and wisdom will appeal to grown-ups and older children while the animals appearing in each story will attract the young ones. The first and longest poem is the best. "Journey" tells of the animals hurrying to the ark (with the baby ones having a hard time keeping up) in a compelling ballad rhythm that reads aloud well. "Rest in Egypt" is a little stiff, but the title poem, "The Peaceable Kingdom," about a young girl safe in the forest, has appropriate beauty. Unfortunately, illustrator Fritz Eichenberg's girl is somewhat witch-like and his animals don't always have sufficient magnificence.

> *Elizabeth Minot Graves, in* The New York Times Book Review *(© 1959 by The New York Times Company; reprinted by permission), January 4, 1959, p. 26.*

THE PLACE (1966)

The Place . . . is the kind of valid, well-written story one might expect of Elizabeth Coatsworth. . . . [It] is full of the exotic land and people and customs, but never too full; it moves in nicely sustained suspense and without ever departing from the logic of the characters. The author also uses as the pivot of her plot an often neglected aspect of the society of the young: the tremendous, solemn oaths children swear that cause and affect important and deadly serious ethical quandaries and occur right along with giggles and wishing for a horse of your own and striving for the approval of parents.

> *Maggie Rennert, in* Book Week *(© The Washington Post), September 4, 1966, p. 15.*

There is unusually vivid Mexican feeling and atmosphere in [this] story of the young daughter of an American archaeologist in Yucatan whose friends—two Indian children—show her a sacred place of the Indians. The characters are alive and appealing, and the child's sensitive awareness of an obligation to keep secret something too great for her own understanding is convincing. Illustrations in pencil and green wash [by Marjorie Auerbach] reflect the setting but lack the strength of the text.

> *Ruth Hill Viguers, in* The Horn Book Magazine *(copyright © 1966, by the Horn Book, Inc., Boston), October, 1966, p. 561.*

OTHER CITATIONS

Irene Davis, in School Library Journal, *June, 1966, p. 245.*

The Booklist and Subscription Books Bulletin, *October 15, 1966, p. 263.*

THE SAILING HATRACK (1972)

[*The Sailing Hatrack* is an] appealing book; and so it should be. It has the advantage of an unusual and interesting setting: life on a store boat around the coast of Maine in the late 1800's. The characters are simple, kindly and sympathetic. The incidents are exciting and the illustrations finely drawn. But—surely an environment so limiting must have produced some slightly harsher characters. If only Cliff Trask, skipper of the store-boat, had shouted at orphan Emily when she allowed two tramp-like clammers to steal his stock and then ran off and hid; if only his wife had been snappy when Ken Philbrook, the young hero, had been lost at sea in a fog and made her fear him dead for twenty-four hours; if only father had been a little sharp when Ken and Emily allowed themselves to be swept seawards on an icefloe and had to be rescued by the thieving clammers. Nevertheless, Elizabeth Coatsworth tells her

story effectively, and perhaps her young readers prefer a world where adults carp less.

> *C.E.J. Smith, in* Children's Book Review *(© 1972 by Five Owls Press Ltd.; all rights reserved), June, 1972, p. 81.*

OTHER CITATIONS

The Junior Bookshelf, *August, 1972, p. 227.*

THE SECRET (1965)

The story of Mark's secret is really a story of time passing: five generations of a family live in a house near the forest, and with each generation the forest and its creatures encroach on the cleared land. . . . [Elizabeth Coatsworth's] text is slow-moving, [Don Bolognese's] illustrations adequate. The theme of the book is appealing, but the execution seems weak and the measuring of time by generations may not be clear to the audience.

> *Zena Sutherland, in* Bulletin of the Center for Children's Books *(copyright 1966 by the University of Chicago; all rights reserved), February, 1966, p. 96.*

Here is a most beautiful short story from one of the world's masters of the children's book. If it reminds one of anything but itself, it is of William Mayne at his best and least self-conscious. It is, like Elizabeth Coatsworth herself, New England American to the very heart.

The Secret is about a homestead in New England, and of the gradual contraction, generation by generation, of its cultivated land as the forests of the north take over. The repetitive text is exquisitely done, with a still simplicity which is deeply moving. Don Bolognese's pictures are not of this quality, but in their own way they reinforce the tender, half-sad mood of the text. This is not an easy book, but to the sensitive child who loves the country it can be a memorable and formative experience.

> The Junior Bookshelf, *December, 1967, p. 376.*

OTHER CITATIONS

Barbara Novak O'Doherty, in The New York Times Book Review, *May 9, 1965 (Part 2), p. 4.*

SILKY: AN INCREDIBLE TALE (1953)

Miss Coatsworth will lead you quietly into the mystery of Silky and take you along her own way. Seldom is a ghostly visitant a force of life rather than of death; a force of love rather than of hate. Silky, through all the strange forebodings and disquietings that accompany the unfolding of this story, emerges as an affirmation of the miracle of rebirth in the human spirit, and of something other as its instrumentality.

As with all Miss Coatsworth's work, "Silky" is a poet's book, mystic, delicate, lovely.

> *Edmund Fuller, in* The New York Times Book Review *(© 1953 by The New York Times Company; reprinted by permission), April 12, 1953, p. 4.*

As in *The Enchanted*, the Maine background [in *Silky*] is authentic and delightful. The long short story is charming, possibly a bit macabre, and specifically for those who like style and imagination.

> *Margaret C. Scoggin, in* The Horn Book Magazine *(copyright, 1953, by The Horn Book, Inc., Boston), June, 1953, p. 229.*

THE SPARROW BUSH (1966)

The author precedes [*The Sparrow Bush*] with a graceful short preface which generalizes about the position of poetry before and after the invention of printing and defines her 53 rhymes here as mostly personal and playful. There is some beauty; the kind that exists within the simple, direct observation about an object or a moment. As for sudden shafts of strangeness, try *The Two Cats,* where two housepets unblinkingly carry a reminder of their special powers and relationship to the wild or *Far Away,* a complete story in eighteen lines, a haunting statement on human memory and devotion to nearly forgotten or lost origins.

> *Virginia Kirkus' Service (copyright © 1965 Virginia Kirkus' Service, Inc.), December, 15, 1965, p. 1226.*

[Elizabeth Coatsworth's verses in *The Sparrow Bush*] have flashes of true insight and beauty as they transmit the moods and perceptions of an observer of nature—the woods and the sea, animals and birds, the seasons and weather—often expressed in a playful humor, in a childlike manner. This is typical and charming Coatsworth, to be added to those choice poems found between the chapters of her early books and in her two previous collections. Wonderfully alive wood engravings [by Stefan Martin] accent the quality of mood or subject.

> *Virginia Haviland, in* The Horn Book Magazine *(copyright © 1966, by The Horn Book, Inc., Boston), April, 1966, p. 208.*

Miss Coatsworth is an experienced versifier, and she writes competently in a variety of forms, but the child's range of curiosity in the poems [in "The Sparrow Bush"] is limited to clouds and flowers and birds and animals. Again, these are perfectly legitimate subjects; yet to the child of 1966 a title like "Shoe the Horse" must seem medieval.

> *Walker Gibson, in* The New York Times Book Review *(© 1966 by The New York Times Company; reprinted by permission), May 8, 1966 (Part 2), p. 36.*

There is a modesty about Elizabeth Coatsworth's rhymes and riddles in her third collection, *The Sparrow Bush,* a reticence which disarms criticism because it has already disarmed itself: nothing is assertive here, nothing shrill or even very loud; it offers instead a certain willingness to be, merely oneself which is the surest evidence that a self is genuinely *there.* At first it seemed to me that these fanciful pieces were too old-fashioned in their decorum:

> Mice danced minuets,
> Squirrels two-stepped gaily,
> And the unmarried cottontails
> Gave tea-parties daily.

But there is a certain tough-minded grasp of rhythm and vocabulary (consider the use of "unmarried" here) which makes these lines stand on their own, without archaism, without being poetical or—ever—silly. It is a gentle book, and the character which speaks out of its preoccupations with animals and energies as a child discovers them in nature is never very dramatic; still, margin is always left for the odd, the ugly, and best of all, the unknown, so that to read through the collection (elegantly illustrated by Stefan Martin) is to confront a particular person, one who can say, quite ominously: "I'm waiting for what's going to happen to me—/ And a big black crow is cawing."

> *Richard Howard, in* Book Week *(© The Washington Post), September 11, 1966, p. 16.*

OTHER CITATIONS

Johanna Hurwitz, in School Library Journal, *March, 1966, p. 232.*

SWORD OF THE WILDERNESS (1967)

Elizabeth Coatsworth's *Sword of the Wilderness* is beautifully printed and superbly illustrated by Roger Payne. It is also, as Elizabeth Coatsworth's many admirers would expect, a novel of great depth and maturity, written fluently yet with meticulous attention to historical accuracy....

American pioneer stories of the best kind, like Mrs Coatsworth's and Laura Ingalls Wilder's, combine family warmth with rip-roaring adventure. *Sword of the Wilderness,* though short, illustrated and easy to read, is in truth an adolescent's book because Seth grows to be aware of adult emotions during his period of captivity [among Indians].

> The Times Literary Supplement *(© Times Newspapers Ltd., 1972), November 3, 1972, p. 1321.*

[*Sword of the Wilderness*] is surely told, with insight into the mind and attitudes of both white men and Indians, and there are vivid pictures of the natural settings and the changing seasons. The generous sweep of Roger Payne's illustrations, with their attractive human faces, adds to the beauty of the story.

> The Junior Bookshelf, *December, 1972, p. 397.*

OTHER CITATIONS

Judith Aldridge, in Children's Book Review, *December, 1972, p. 187.*

TAMAR'S WAGER (1971)

This story of eighteenth century Virginia is nearly forty years old and shows its age. The blurb calls it a tale of high adventure, but for over half the book it is a lushly painted picture of gracious living in one of the large plantation houses, whilst the second half describes the not very adventurous expedition to the valley of the Shenandoah when the half Indian daughter of the house does a rather improbable impersonation of an Indian boy. Not one of the characters comes to life, all with one exception are boringly noble, whilst the negro servants are contented shadows in the background. This last, plus the long descriptive passages, dates the book at once and there is not enough meat in the story to help it to outlive its age. Elderly adults on either side of the Atlantic might consider this to be a charming idyll of colonial times, but the eight to nine-year-olds for whom it is meant are unlikely to be enthusiastic.

> The Junior Bookshelf, *August, 1971, p. 223.*

OTHER CITATIONS

Judith Aldridge, in Children's Book Review, *September, 1971, p. 125.*

THEY WALK IN THE NIGHT (1969)

Poetic writing—in prose and verse—tells an allegorical story set, according to the author, in "an Africa of the mind . . . made up of elements of the real Africa where there are coffee plantations and rivers. . . ." The white child Alida, aiming to surprise her mother with newly picked water lilies for her birthday, leaves the coffee farm before sunrise in a little rowboat without oars, thinking to pull her way back to the dock "by the lily stems." . . . She returns home in the care of the Antelope Man. "Alida, Alida, gentle Alida,/ The voyage you made, we, also,/ must make,/ And meet the antelope, and the clawed/ leopard,/ The owl, and the snake./ Alida, Alida, gentle Alida,/ You left for an hour and/ were gone for a day,/ Or was it a lifetime,/ gentle Alida?/ Who can say?" [Stefan Martin's] wood engravings are as haunting as the text, which can be read on two levels —the literal and the allegorical.

> *Virginia Haviland, in* The Horn Book Magazine *(copyright © 1969 by The Horn Book, Inc., Boston), August, 1969, p. 402.*

["They Walk in the Night"] is not for the faint-hearted, nor for the literal-minded. For all its spare and lovely language, and Stefan Martin's truly beautiful woodcuts, this is a nightmare story, an eerie journey into the unknown by a frightened child. . . . Few small readers will catch the allegorical intent, while many will long remember the loneliness of the river, the thump of the drums, and the painful grip of the leopard man's steel claws on Alida's helpless wrist.

> *Natalie Babbitt, in* The New York Times Book Review *(© 1969 by The New York Times Company; reprinted by permission), September 28, 1969, p. 34.*

Like the dream sequence of Lynd Ward's *Wild Pilgrimage* [Stefan Martin's] stark, dramatic woodcut illustrations [for *They Walk in the Night*] have a quality of fantasy. [Coatsworth's] text, too, has that quality, the prose occasionally giving way to poetry. . . . Whether [Alida's adventure] is real or a dream, it has an unfortunate connotation: the white child threatened by the natives, the hint of the old white-goddess caper in such statements as, ". . . the men stood about, staring in silence at Alida, at her long yellow hair, at her white dress, at the little ring on her hand. They looked at her as though she were something rare and precious . . .".

> *Zena Sutherland, in* Bulletin of the Center

for Children's Books *(© 1970 by the University of Chicago; all rights reserved), February, 1970, p. 94.*

UNDER THE GREEN WILLOW (1971)

[*Under the Green Willow* is a] little book of graphic distinction, which a child will appreciate even if only on a subconscious level. The words have the imagery of a brief poem: "There is a place I know,/ says the sun,/ where ducks/ and ducklings,/ turtles,/ and trout,/ catfish with whiskers,/ and young eels,/ all crowd together in the water/ under a willow tree waiting for crumbs. . . ." On each page [a Janina Domanska] etching, stylized in pattern, conveys an astonishing sense of movement. . . .

> *Virginia Haviland, in* The Horn Book Magazine *(copyright © 1971 by The Horn Book, Inc., Boston), June, 1971, p. 277.*

The text [of *Under the Green Willow*], brief and lyric, describes the darting life in the clear, sunny waters: the wily trout that snatches a crumb before the others can get near, the catfish nipping at the ducks' toes, the confident ducks kicking at the turtles in their way. Not a story, but a small, incisive picture of water life.

> *Zena Sutherland, in* Bulletin of the Center for Children's Books *(© 1971 by the University of Chicago; all rights reserved), June, 1971, p. 155.*

OTHER CITATIONS

Kirkus Reviews, *February 1, 1971, p. 101.*

George A. Woods, in The New York Times Book Review, *March 7, 1971, p. 30.*

The Booklist, *June 1, 1971, p. 833.*

THE WANDERERS (1972)

Miss Coatsworth's message—that an exuberant love of God and His creations elbows out evil or just plain nastiness—pervades but does not inhibit this easy-rolling tale of the miraculous progress of Father Ambrosius through Ireland in the days of raiding Vikings. . . . [*The Wanderers* is essentially] a gentle, lyric tale for children open to its non-sectarian religiosity. Muscular, traditional illustrations by Trina Schart Hyman.

> Kirkus Reviews *(copyright © 1972 The Kirkus Service, Inc.), November 1, 1972, p. 1238.*

[*The Wanderers* is a] dull religious adventure about Father Ambrosius, a medieval Irish wanderer who dedicates his life to God. . . . The characters are flat, the plot meanders, and the tone is sentimental throughout. Hyman's black-and-white drawings add some excitement but are not interesting enough to carry this thin tale.

> *Donald K. Fry, in* School Library Journal *(reprinted from* School Library Journal, *February, 1973, published by R. R. Bowker Co., a Xerox company; copyright © 1973 by Xerox Corporation), February, 1973, p. 66.*

A medieval setting, a deeply devout approach, and a romantic style frame [*The Wanderers,*] a tale that moves slowly and is not quite convincing. . . . Father Ambrosius is revered as a rescuer and healer; his magical wallet is always replenished, and when he and the boys go off to a deserted, rocky isle off the coast of Ireland they withstand even a Viking crew. The writing style is graceful, the plot plodding.

> *Zena Sutherland, in* Bulletin of the Center for Children's Books *(© 1973 by the University of Chicago; all rights reserved), March, 1973, p. 103.*

[*The Wanderers* is a] perfectly wrought heroic-religious tale of ancient Christianized Ireland. . . . The narration has the beauty of old tales, and it is enhanced by the kind of poetic expression the gifted author has often shown before. Humor lightens the story while moments of conflict intensify its narrative line and support the interpolation of the poetic expressions. [Trina Schart Hyman's] drawings . . . clearly [illuminate] the unusual tale.

> *Virginia Haviland, in* The Horn Book Magazine *(copyright © 1973 by The Horn Book, Inc., Boston), April, 1973, p. 141.*

OTHER CITATIONS

The Booklist, *March 15, 1973, p. 712.*

THE WHITE ROOM (1958)

In her fourth "incredible tale" ("The Enchanted," "Silky" and "Mountain Bride" were the others) Elizabeth Coatsworth blends local legend, folk superstition, racial memory and Christian myth with modern psychology in an allegory of disintegration and renewal on a Maine coast farm. In the hands of a less nimble seamstress the result could have been a hopeless crazy quilt, but Miss Coatsworth's discipline is, for the most part, in command. . . .

The successful legend is as much dependent on the manner of telling as on the narrative elements. Here the author's poetic sense and her experience with children's books are of enormous aid. Her language is clear, yet connotative. Her people have the sharp definition peculiar to characters in ancient ballads. Her handling of the "white room" motif is always skillful. If the dénouement is a trifle labored, the flaw detracts only slightly from Miss Coatsworth's faculty for coalescing the known and unknown, fact and fancy, humanity, and nature.

> *David Phillips, in* The New York Times Book Review *(© 1958 by The New York Times Company; reprinted by permission), July 13, 1958, p. 23.*

*   *   *

COBB, Vicki   1938-

An American scientific researcher, science teacher, and creator of television programs, Vicki Cobb is noted for her entertaining approach to science books for children. (See also *Contemporary Authors,* **Vols. 33-36.)**

ARTS AND CRAFTS YOU CAN EAT (1974)

Mrs. Cobb, who used her kitchen as a lab in *Science Ex-*

periments You Can Eat . . ., now turns it into a studio and invites readers to express themselves with chocolate marshmallow scratchboards, molded marzipan and the like. Unfortunately the sequel lacks the inherent cookery education value of its predecessor and one problem is that the projects included here . . . are neither art (despite the introduction's high claims) nor especially appetizing. Another problem is that [Peter] Lippman's casual line drawings, while agreeable enough for most purposes, are unlikely to convince anyone that the visual result will justify the preparation of—for example—mashed potato ("use instant if you wish") and baby food casserole. Still the concept of edible crafts has obvious virtues, Mrs. Cobb has conscientiously explored its myriad possibilities, and kids can find both creative enjoyment and—even if they fail as artists—an earthier kind of satisfaction in making springerlee cookies with "found" molds, icing cakes with homemade equipment, painting cookies with their own edible tempera using egg yolk for an emulsifer, or just playing around with snack food sculpture.

> Kirkus Reviews *(copyright © 1974 The Kirkus Service, Inc.), April 1, 1974, p. 368.*

In "Arts and Crafts You Can Eat," by Vicki Cobb . . ., we read: "Artificial food colors are clear, bright, inexpensive, and easy to use. Although they are artificial food additives, there is no evidence to suggest that they are harmful in any way." A dangerous half-truth. This book offers some amusing rainy-day cutouts kids can make in the kitchen, but many are dubious eating and some, like colored sandwiches and milk drinks, downright nauseating.

> *John L. Hess, in* The New York Times Book Review *(© 1974 by The New York Times Company; reprinted by permission), May 5, 1974, p. 42.*

A companion volume to the already popular *Science Experiments You Can Eat,* [*Arts and Crafts You Can Eat*] describes various projects that will transform a kitchen into an artist's studio. Instructions for drawing and painting, making prints and designs, modeling, molding, and carving are applied to a diverse set of edible materials to create artistic as well as culinary delights. Not all of the projects can be devoured; one chapter presents inventive ways of recycling garbage. . . . The clear and precise directions make failures unlikely but if they occur, the author consoles the readers by reminding them that they can always eat their mistakes.

> *Anita Silvey, in* The Horn Book Magazine *(copyright © 1974 by The Horn Book, Inc., Boston), June, 1974, p. 292.*

OTHER CITATIONS

Publishers' Weekly, *March 11, 1974, p. 49.*

Julie Cummins, *in* School Library Journal, *September, 1974, p. 76.*

CELLS: THE BASIC STRUCTURE OF LIFE (1970)

This is a fair attempt to enrich or to attract the interest of an early elementary pupil to the diversities of the structure and function of cells. The author presents a smattering of an introduction to microscopes, healthy and nonhealthy cells and animal mitosis. Perhaps at the expense of oversimplification few inaccuracies have crept into the pages; yet, on the other hand, one section is introduced with the phrase "As we go up the evolutionary scale, from amoeba to man, we find organisms capable of more and more complicated interaction with environment." The illustrations are excellent. The best introduction to cells are provided by them.

> Science Books (copyright 1970 by the American Association for the Advancement of Science), Vol. 6, No. 3 (December, 1970), p. 227.

OTHER CITATIONS

Pat Barnes, in School Library Journal, November, 1970, p. 106.

GASES (1970)

This book obviously was written by one who has no understanding of the subject. It opens with the notion that air is a substance, despite the fact that air is commonly referred to as a mixture of substances. Unfortunately, the illustrations [by Ellie Haines] are as bad as the text. . . . There are errors of fact and interpretation. "The pressure of the air inside the balloon (partially inflated) is equal to the pressure of the atmosphere pushing on the outside of the balloon." "And the fact that the presence of air does not change the rate at which molecules diffuse is an indication of the enormous space between molecules. The paths of individual molecules do not appear to be changed very often by collisions with air molecules, indicating that there are relatively few such collisions." "He increased the heat of the sun's rays by passing them through a giant lens called a burning glass." The sun's rays were gathered or focused. The heat of the sun's rays was certainly not increased.

> Science Books (copyright 1971 by the American Association for the Advancement of Science), Vol. VII, No. 4 (March, 1971), p. 301.

I was . . . disturbed by some of the inaccuracies in Vicki Cobb's Gases. The most serious slip is on page 25, where Miss Cobb discusses diffusion. She says that ammonia molecules spread across a room from open bottle to nose about as fast as they would in a vacuum and that they must therefore suffer few collisions with other molecules because their paths are not changed very often. A completely wrong statement. . . .

Miss Cobb did well in demonstrating that air and other gases are matter, though her air-weighing experiment on page 5 does not work (Archimedes could have told why). Although she does well with Charles' and Boyle's laws, the book has too many slips in its statements of fact.

> Harry C. Stubbs, in The Horn Book Magazine (copyright © 1971 by The Horn Book, Inc., Boston), April, 1971, p. 187.

For this age group [grades 4-8], this probably is the best book available dealing exclusively with gases. . . . Throughout, a number of simple, home experiments are described.

The illustrations, photographs and reproductions are all excellent, detailing equipment and happily showing many of the scientists in their laboratories instead of in the usual frilled and furbeloved poses.

> Susan Catania, in School Library Journal (reprinted from School Library Journal, September, 1971, published by R. R. Bowker Co., a Xerox Company; copyright © 1971 by Xerox Corporation), September, 1971, p. 158.

HEAT (1973)

Small type, few illustrations, and involved discussions of molecular and kinetic theory preclude consideration of this as a "first book." The discussions of the nature of heat and temperature, ways of measuring and converting heat, and metabolism are informative and useful for older elementary students. However, personification of the workings of an internal combustion engine detracts from the presentation of scientific material, and an experiment involving heating a paper clip on the kitchen stove is potentially dangerous.

> Shirley A. Smith, in School Library Journal (reprinted from School Library Journal, December, 1973, published by R. R. Bowker Co., a Xerox company; copyright © 1973 by Xerox Corporation), December, 1973, pp. 47-8.

"Heat" is hard to define in terms simple enough for a young child to understand, and although this is a "First" book, it is for children in the fourth grade and higher. From the imaginative cover onwards, this book will capture the children's interest. Chapters are clearly defined and headed, and they include accounts of historical work done on heat problems as well as modern theories and applications. . . . Amusing, clear and appropriate illustrations [by Robert Byrd] come with each chapter. There is both a bibliography and an index.

> Science Books (copyright 1974 by the American Association for the Advancement of Science), Vol. X, No. 4 (March, 1974), p. 326.

HOW THE DOCTOR KNOWS YOU'RE FINE (1973)

Cobb preps young patients for a routine check-up, explaining what the doctor looks at and why, and emphasizing —as the title indicates—the assumption that everything will be fine. . . . But the assurance is not evasive, and Cobb admits that shots will "hurt a little," then concentrates on how lucky we are to get the vaccines instead of the diseases they were made to prevent. Because she maintains just the right tone throughout, we hope the doctor knows how to obtain this for his-or-her waiting room.

> Kirkus Reviews (copyright © 1973 The Kirkus Service, Inc.), October 1, 1973, p. 1099.

[This is a] simple and comprehensible description of a child's physical examination. . . . Most of the ordinary aspects of a regular medical check-up are covered, but urine and hearing tests are not mentioned. The illustrations [by Anthony Ravielli] are clear, informative and greatly extend the text, which is more detailed than Robert Froman's useful *Let's Find Out about the Clinic*. . . .

> Isadora Kunitz, in School Library Journal *(reprinted from* School Library Journal, *December, 1973, published by R. R. Bowker Co., a Xerox company; copyright © 1973 by Xerox Corporation), December, 1973, p. 41.*

OTHER CITATIONS

Zena Sutherland, in Bulletin of the Center for Children's Books, *January, 1974, p. 76.*

The Booklist, *January 15, 1974, p. 540.*

THE LONG AND SHORT OF MEASUREMENT (1973)

This beginning treatment of measurement suggests simple methods of comparison and explains the need for standard units. . . . Carol Nicklaus' illustrations are adequate (except for the presentation of thermometers). Where additional books on measurement are needed, the experimental approach here makes this a more useful title than Margaret Friskey's *About Measurement*. . . .

> Sandra Weir, in School Library Journal *(reprinted from* School Library Journal, *September, 1973, published by R. R. Bowker Co., a Xerox company; copyright © 1973 by Xerox Corporation), September, 1973, p. 109.*

Vicki Cobb's *The Long and Short of Measurement* points up the difficulty of measuring with the unaided senses and devotes most of its pages to the usual solution to that problem—comparing the unknowns with accepted standards. . . . Her use of the word *standard* is rather nonstandard—she uses the word for both the foot and the inch, for example; and I was a little disappointed at the brevity of her treatment of the metric system. She does, however, suggest some good activities for primary-grade readers. Math teachers at this level could easily use some of these to steer their students toward appreciating the need for understanding and using fractions.

> Harry C. Stubbs, in The Horn Book Magazine *(copyright © 1974 by The Horn Book, Inc., Boston), October, 1974, p. 155.*

MAKING SENSE OF MONEY (1971)

[*Making Sense of Money* is a] discussion of money as a medium of exchange, of banking procedures, and of earning and spending money. The text is lucid enough in its particulars, but the organization is weak; for example, the first paragraph describes the importance of money, concluding with the sentence, "What is so special about money that makes everyone want to have it?". . . The subject is divided into several areas, each of which is given accurate but not thorough treatment, and there is a certain amount of repetition. A relative index is appended.

> Zena Sutherland, in Bulletin of the Center for Children's Books *(© 1971 by the Univer-*

sity of Chicago; all rights reserved), October, 1971, pp. 23-4.

SCIENCE EXPERIMENTS YOU CAN EAT (1972)

Every kitchen is, among other things, a laboratory, and these lighthearted experiment/recipes prove that a good cook is a good chemist (and vice versa). The introduction of basic concepts such as solutes, suspensions, and precipitates leads to some fairly predictable culinary activities—growing sugar crystals, immersing celery stalks in food coloring and testing for starches—but how many chefs realize that making meringues and baking bread are really a question of denaturing protein, or that mayonnaise is a simple emulsion? A not inconsiderable by-product is a better understanding of foods themselves—the difference between all-purpose and cake flours, the composition of double-acting baking powder and the correct method of cooking spinach. Ms. Cobb's commentary moves easily from the Tyndall effect and the work of Pasteur to hints on unmolding a gelatin dessert; the experiments she presents are undemanding, require little more than the equipment found in most well stocked kitchens and, best of all, they're edible.

> Kirkus Reviews *(copyright © 1972 The Kirkus Service, Inc.), March 15, 1972, p. 327.*

[This] manual of experiments which thrifty scientists may subsequently eat is best suited for knowledgeable science fans. The experiments, involving such fundamentals as the characteristics of solutions and the properties of sugars, carbohydrates, and fats, are clearly described and easy to follow. However, molecules, super-saturated solutions, and calories are never sufficiently defined, and beginning chemists whose experiments do not work for any reason will not learn much from the sketchy explanations.

> Alice Tabari, in School Library Journal *(reprinted from* School Library Journal, *May, 1972, published by R. R. Bowker Co., a Xerox company; copyright © 1972 by Xerox Corporation), May, 1972, p. 84.*

Cooking is a most ancient branch of applied biochemistry. This cheerily casual and inviting book takes full advantage of the kitchen; the experiments are neither wasteful, unpleasant nor dangerous. You can eat them! . . . The most advanced experiment is one that tests the action of the enzyme of a meat tenderizer. Here the effect is titrated by counting the chews before each treated piece of meat was swallowed. (The equipment includes "a hungry friend.") With such a measure careful controls are needed, and randomization of the order of chewing is part of the experiment. (The author stops short of using nonparametric tests of significance.) The book is a first-rate introduction to the sciences of matter for boys and girls old enough to work by themselves, probably around junior high school age.

> Scientific American *(copyright © 1972 by Scientific American, Inc.; all rights reserved), December, 1972, p. 119.*

[*Science Experiments You Can Eat*] contains very good chemistry and is nicely and logically arranged. It is not, however, entirely free of errors: Cream of tartar (page 10) is potassium hydrogen tartrate, not tartaric acid; and beet sugar (page 43) is sucrose, not dextrose. These slips, however, are completely buried in the good points.

> *Harry C. Stubbs, in* The Horn Book Magazine *(copyright © 1973 by The Horn Book, Inc., Boston), October, 1973, p. 489.*

[This book is] an interesting mixture of science and cookery in which various chemical principles are illustrated—like freezing, through the making of ice lollipops; mayonnaise (a stabilised suspension); cooking spinach (colour changes in chlorophyl); yoghourt (how bacteria produce lactic acid). Drawings in caricature style make the points clear and the book should help the young to become intelligent and adventurous cooks, and sensible dieticians into the bargain.

> *Margery Fisher, in her* Growing Point, *September, 1975, p. 2695.*

OTHER CITATIONS

Science Books, *September, 1972, p. 126.*

Jean Stafford, in The New Yorker, *December 2, 1972, p. 191.*

SENSE OF DIRECTION: UP AND DOWN AND ALL AROUND (1972)

This once-over very lightly is no substitute for a Boy Scout manual but as a low-pressure lesson in the need for standardization it might serve to introduce a school unit. Similarly the chapters on maps and globes . . ., with their rather chatty tone and jaunty pictures, might be more palatable than the usual textbook treatment of the same material. But [*Sense of Direction*] is more promising as a teaching tool for stimulating awareness of the subject than impressive for the information it conveys.

> Kirkus Reviews *(copyright © 1972 The Kirkus Service, Inc.), March 15, 1972, p. 327.*

If there are children who need to know more about how to find their way about, geographically speaking, this volume may be of some help. The book must be intended for reading aloud, because children old enough to read the text for themselves will probably already know left from right and up from down. In addition to direction instructions, the book contains sections on compasses, distance measuring, mapping and latitude and longitude. This review did not find much here that is not adequately covered in the first four grades of the elementary school. In addition, the text contains some ambiguities and omissions which lessen its usefulness. Miss Cobb tells us on page 18 that at noon your shadow will point North. She doesn't say that this is true only in the northern hemisphere. Also, on page 36, the author states that ". . . knots means miles per hour." Wouldn't it be better to state that knots can be converted to miles per hour? There is no mention of nautical vs. statute

miles—as there should have been to explain to the reader why conversions are important in the first place. On page 40, the reader is asked to search for a lake in the northwest corner of Illinois—but the lake is in the northeast corner of the map. In short, the book does not display the good "sense of direction" which it seeks to teach.

> Science Books *(copyright 1972 by the American Association for the Advancement of Science), Vol. VIII, No. 3 (December, 1972), pp. 212-13.*

[*Sense of Direction: Up and Down and All Around* is a] somewhat misleading title, since this is a book that includes such topics as measuring distance on land and at sea. The information is useful, the text is clearly written but has occasional jarring remarks like, "If Christopher Columbus and others like him had stayed home, America might never have been discovered." . . . The material is organized to move from immediate locality to wider and wider areas, but it seems unnecessary to explain right and left to the audience that can comprehend longitude and latitude.

> *Zena Sutherland, in* Bulletin of the Center for Children's Books *(© 1973 by the University of Chicago; all rights reserved), January, 1973, p. 73.*

OTHER CITATIONS

Shirley A. Smith, in School Library Journal, *October, 1972, p. 109.*

Harry C. Stubbs, in The Horn Book Magazine, *October, 1972, p. 491.*

SUPERSUITS (1975)

It is good that the author points out that man doesn't really live in a wide variety of environments but that he brings his own environment with him wherever he goes. It is also good to remember that a local environment can change drastically in a short time or within a short distance.

There are a few slips in the book. Not every object hits the ground "above 125 miles an hour" (page 73) when dropped from a great height, although this speed is typical for a human body. I will always disapprove of the implication that spacecraft in which weightlessness is being experienced are "[outside] earth's gravitational field" (page 83). Any craft or other object orbiting the earth is well within that field. I realize that a detailed explanation for weightlessness is beyond the scope of this book, but I still think an accurate phrase could be found.

> *Harry C. Stubbs, in* The Horn Book Magazine *(copyright © 1975 by the Horn Book, Inc., Boston), October, 1975, p. 491.*

OTHER CITATIONS

Publishers' Weekly, *March 24, 1975, p. 48.*

Kirkus Reviews, *May 1, 1975, p. 515.*

E

ENGDAHL, Sylvia Louise 1933-

Sylvia Louise Engdahl is an American author known for her science fiction stories. (See also *Contemporary Authors*, **Vols. 29-32, and** *Something About the Author*, **Vol. 4.)**

BEYOND THE TOMORROW MOUNTAINS (1973)

Noren, whose heresy earned him access to the knowledge controlled by the Scholar caste [in *This Star Shall Abide*], faces another, more subtle crisis [in *Beyond the Tomorrow Mountains*] because of his inability to place his faith in the Mother Star. . . . It's hard to be as sure as Noren is of the necessity for his planet's elaborate self-perpetuating theocracy, and since its justification is the major point of this trilogy so far, this is a serious failure. The fascination of both volumes lies in Engdahl's ability to create a many-layered society with a tragic past and a doubtful future that depends on its ability to cope with a harsh, brutal environment; but Noren's quest seems more and more to lead to preprogrammed answers and the journey *Beyond the Tomorrow Mountains* is powered largely by the momentum of its predecessor.

> Kirkus Reviews (*copyright © 1973 The Kirkus Service, Inc.*), February 15, 1973, p. 193.

[This] sequel does not equal in intensity the dramatic and ironical exposition of the theme of heresy and recantation so powerfully presented in *This Star Shall Abide*. The long-drawn-out conflict in Noren's mind between the claims of reason (or science) and those of faith (or religion) incorporates itself in a series of crucial situations rather than in a series of crucial events; and despite the genuine metaphysical significance of the novel, it is not a compelling story.

> *Paul Heins, in* The Horn Book Magazine (*copyright © 1973 by The Horn Book, Inc., Boston*), June, 1973, p. 276.

A sequel to *This Star Shall Abide*, a science fiction story set in the future, [*Beyond the Tomorrow Mountains*] takes the young protagonist Noren farther along the path of education for leadership. . . . More than most science fiction writers for young people, Engdahl's books are concerned with individual motivation and ethical conduct; the writing style is often heavy and therefore the book moves slowly,

but it offers depth and provocative ideas for the mature reader who wants more than just action.

> *Zena Sutherland, in* Bulletin of the Center for Children's Books (*© 1973 by the University of Chicago; all rights reserved*), June, 1973, p. 153.

OTHER CITATIONS

The Booklist, *June 1, 1973, pp. 946-47.*

Margaret A. Dorsey, in School Library Journal, *September, 1973, pp. 81-2.*

ENCHANTRESS FROM THE STARS (1970)

The multiplex situation established, the conclusion foregone, the questions forgotten, the reader [of *Enchantress from the Stars*] has only the lugubrious romance between Elana and Georyn to tide her (never him) over long stretches of self-examination in three [ascents] . . . until, goal in sight, Elana overturns all. . . . You have to bear with her . . ., and it's an extra trial in a book that's not easy going to begin with. (Start again and the questions are clear if not compelling.)

> Kirkus Reviews (*copyright © 1970 The Kirkus Service, Inc.*), March 15, 1970, p. 329.

The three characters tell their story in very different styles [in *Enchantress from the Stars*], and it may be this device which causes the plot to move somewhat slowly. But three different civilizations at three different levels of development are sensitively shown, and the book raises some questions about the responsibility of a more advanced people for a lesser one, and about the steps the human race must go through in its struggle to raise itself above the basic savagery in human nature.

> *Elizabeth Haynes, in* School Library Journal (*reprinted from* School Library Journal, *May, 1970, published by R. R. Bowker Co., a Xerox company; copyright © 1970 by Xerox Corporation*), May, 1970, p. 82.

["Enchantress from the Stars" presents] an original and

charming exercise of one of fiction's finest prerogatives, getting into other skins and seeing through (literally) alien eyes. The manipulation of "less-advanced" peoples by "higher" civilizations, a stock in trade of Heinleinian science fiction, is basic to the plot, but is not accepted uncritically. The main characters are nice young people, and their relationship is well handled. Lively, elegant drawings by Rodney Shackell are well suited to the story. Girls who like their fantasy realistic, or an aspect of magic to their realism, should enjoy this one.

> *Ursula K. LeGuin, in* The New York Times Book Review *(© 1970 by The New York Times Company; reprinted by permission), May 3, 1970, pp. 22-3.*

Enchantress from the Stars deserves a better title and a less lurid jacket, for it is a serious and thought provoking novel, not SF for the sake of electronic gadgetry.

A story from the past (a quest by a medieval wood-cutter's son to slay a dragon) is intermingled with the future (an attempt by one of the most advanced civilizations in the universe to stop a less mature race—us—from interfering with the natural development of a primitive planet), and both stories have some interesting comments to make about real life, for both "dragon" and our earth-digger are one and the same.

This is not unlike the use of past and future in John Christopher's [White Mountains] trilogy, or Andre Norton's *Forever Foray,* and it is just as successful. Technological progress which may aid mankind enormously is balanced against the damage it causes to ecology and natural growth; writer and, therefore, reader are on the side of the latter. Combined with this is an adolescent love-story that is no romantic nonsense; it is realistic and moving. The story is full of drama and suspense, and is very well written.

> The Times Literary Supplement *(© Times Newspapers Ltd., 1974), September 20, 1974, p. 1006.*

There is a serious attempt [in *Enchantress from the Stars*] to consider problems such as the relationship of colonists, good and bad, with the native, or the nature of loyalty to a small group, or the connection between superstition and psychic powers. There is a lot of rather tedious explanation by Elana about their advanced civilisation, and from her father on the powers of the mind, duty and so forth. The inescapable triviality and lack of dignity of Elana's chatty report to her cousin only emphasises more sharply, however, the style used to convey Georyn's view of events: this has the authentic ring of the Brothers Grimm and, at times, of the *Morte d'Arthur,* but when Georyn and the Enchantress fall in love, a novelettish modernity intrudes on the fairy-tale style, with phrases like "fix them some food". The concept of explaining the "magic" of more primitive peoples as contact with the greater sophistication of other civilisations is admirable, as is the suggestion that progress arises through a questioning intelligence like Georyn's. The author frequently spoils her effects, however, by anticipation and by anticlimax, and the overthrow of the "dragon" through the immediate collapse of the Imperials on seeing Georyn use psychokinesis seems highly improbable. And yet there are so many good things, perhaps particularly the way Georyn surprises his teachers by the

greatness of his faith. All three central characters, in remaining true to the best beliefs of their own civilisations, learn from each other, a nice lesson in worldwide community!

> The Junior Bookshelf, *October, 1974, pp. 294-95.*

OTHER CITATIONS

Ruth Hill Viguers, in The Horn Book Magazine, *April, 1970, pp. 165-66.*

The Booklist, *July 15, 1970, p. 1407.*

C. Stuart Hannabuss, in Children's Book Review, *Winter 1974-75, p. 151.*

THE FAR SIDE OF EVIL (1971)

[*The Far Side of Evil* is] a further development of many of the concepts previously expressed in *Enchantress from the Stars.* . . . While the reader will find the basic plot exciting, the book itself seems too long, and the constant emotional reiteration by Elana of the author's philosophic conjectures can be wearing.

> *Sheryl B. Andrews, in* The Horn Book Magazine *(copyright © 1971 by The Horn Book, Inc., Boston), April, 1971, p. 172.*

OTHER CITATIONS

Kirkus Reviews, *February 1, 1971, pp. 112-13.*

Elizabeth Haynes, in School Library Journal, *April, 1971, p. 116.*

The Booklist, *May 15, 1971, p. 798.*

Publishers' Weekly, *May 31, 1971, p. 135.*

HERITAGE OF THE STAR (1973)

[*Heritage of the Star*] is a re-working of several popular SF themes: the idea of the hidden power-clique; the religious-analogy story which describes false cults of the future based on a misunderstanding of some aspect of our present; and the space-ship emigration theme as in Heinlein's *Orphans of the Sky.* Miss Engdahl does not only combine these themes into a fairly well co-ordinated whole, but adds a good deal of detailed discussion, some of which is padding, about the reasons for the caste system and the fake religion. It's a very wordy book, and although it is set within the framework of children's SF, and the first half is pure adventure, the turgid political discussions tend to slow the pace. For addicts of long science fiction books only, and although quite good of its kind other material should rather be recommended—Asimov's *Foundation,* for example, or Heinlein's *Future History* series, or even E. E. Smith's *Lensman* books.

> *Jessica Kemball-Cook, in* Children's Book Review *(© 1973 Five Owls Press Ltd.; all rights reserved), December, 1973, p. 182.*

JOURNEY BETWEEN WORLDS (1970)

Deftly blending scientific possibility, suspense, and

youthful emotion in the first-person narrative, [Engdahl] has projected a plausible picture of the post-twentieth-century world—a world where pioneers on Mars are envisioned as a continuation of the endless chain of settlers who have been moving to new frontiers ever since the human race began.

> *Mary M. Burns, in* The Horn Book Magazine *(copyright © 1970 by The Horn Book, Inc., Boston), October, 1970, p. 481.*

Told entirely in the first person, this story is long on self-analysis and short on action. Several timely topics are touched upon, including pollution, population control, and the justification for space research, but the characters are one-dimensional—often a little too good to be true. In short, fans won by Engdahl's first novel will most likely be turned off by this one.

> *Elizabeth Haynes, in* School Library Journal *(reprinted from* School Library Journal, *October, 1970, published by R. R. Bowker Co., a Xerox company; copyright © 1970 by Xerox Corporation), October, 1970, p. 138.*

Set in the far future, [*Journey Between Worlds* is] a story about a quiet and conventional adolescent whose pattern is shaken by an unexpected journey. . . . The love story occasionally falters, but the descriptions of the world of the future and of the flight through space are convincing, the characterization is capable if not subtle, and the writing style is competent.

> *Zena Sutherland, in* Bulletin of the Center for Children's Books *(© 1971 by the University of Chicago; all rights reserved), January, 1971, p. 72.*

OTHER CITATIONS

Kirkus Reviews, *August 15, 1970, p. 885.*

Patience M. Canham, in The Christian Science Monitor, *November 12, 1970, p. B4.*

THE PLANET-GIRDED SUNS: MAN'S VIEW OF OTHER SOLAR SYSTEMS (1974)

Sylvia Louise Engdahl turns from science fiction to the history of ideas to prove that the concept of intelligent life outside our solar system is nothing new—in fact, its popular acceptance is traced here all the way back to Giordano Bruno who, more than Copernicus, was responsible for the post-Aristotelian cosmology. . . . Engdahl has marshalled an impressive and fascinating selection of primary sources —including a roster of believers that includes Newton, Ben Franklin, Walt Whitman, and rocket pioneer Robert Goddard; and excerpts from popular hymns, poetry, and 17th century proto-science fiction. . . . Whether or not any of this justifies further efforts to make contact with other life-forms, Engdahl has shown how deep this vein of speculation runs . . . and reminded us that our ancestors entertained a view of the universe that was larger and more imaginative than the history books lead us to believe. Challenging and original.

> Kirkus Reviews *(copyright © 1974 The*

Kirkus Service, Inc.), December 1, 1974, p. 1260.

The Planet-Girded Suns is a beautiful example of what the disciplined imagination can do; it is discipline which puts this book in a category so completely different from that of most books about flying saucers. . . . It is a fine, carefully done history of the ideas about other worlds—nicely balanced in its presentation of the informational and mystical elements of the subject.

> *Harry C. Stubbs, in* The Horn Book Magazine *(copyright © 1975 by the Horn Book, Inc., Boston), February, 1975, p. 74.*

The notion that sentient beings inhabit planets in other solar systems like our own is certainly not new. Engdahl traces the popularity of this idea from early times to the late 19th Century, when it was a generally accepted concept, its fall into disrepute in the early 20th Century, and its present resurgence. Making extensive use of direct quotations from contemporary sources, the author's principal emphasis is on the attitudes of literate people of the time—why they accepted or rejected the idea—and not on the technical case for or against alien beings. . . . Easy to read and on a timely subject approached from an unusual point of view, this also serves as a model to show how an idea is "researched" and documented.

> *Ovide V. Fortier, in* School Library Journal *(reprinted from* School Library Journal, *March, 1975, published by R. R. Bowker Co., a Xerox company; copyright © 1975 by Xerox Corporation), March, 1975, p. 105.*

OTHER CITATIONS

The Booklist, *January 15, 1975, p. 501.*

THIS STAR SHALL ABIDE (1972)

Unlike Noren, the heretic turned repentant, you may not be fully convinced that the elite corps of knowledge-bearers founded by the First Scholar was totally necessary. But the recorded dreams which show Noren how it was for that first generation which escaped the Six Worlds after the Sun turned nova—besides being one of the most elaborate justifications for benevolent dictatorship ever created—present a satisfyingly fantastic post-disaster scenario comparable to John Christopher's *White Mountains* trilogy. . . . The first of a projected two volume series, *This Star* will *Abide* a good deal longer than most here today, gone tomorrow sci-fi.

> Kirkus Reviews *(copyright © 1972 The Kirkus Service, Inc.), March 15, 1972, p. 335.*

[This is superior] future fiction concerning the fate of an idealistic misfit, Noren, who rebels against his highly repressive society. . . . Although there is little overt action, the attention of mature sci fi readers will be held by the skillful writing and excellent plot and character development.

> *Elizabeth Haynes, in* School Library Journal *(reprinted from* School Library Journal,

May, 1972, published by R. R. Bowker Co., a Xerox company; copyright © 1972 by Xerox Corporation), May, 1972, p. 85.

[Sylvia Louise Engdahl] has written an unusual kind of science-fiction novel. She takes for granted man's ability to colonize in space and concentrates on a crucial human situation—youth's questioning of established practices. . . . Despite the slow start of the narrative and sections of unrelieved exposition, [*This Star Shall Abide*] is noteworthy for its dramatization of the crucial meeting of science, man, and the universe. Because of his devotion to the truth, Noren has to accept revelations that had been distasteful to him as true; and in the process of his enlightenment, a flashback into cosmic history explains the coming into being of Noren's world after the sun in our solar system had exploded.

> *Paul Heins, in* The Horn Book Magazine, *(copyright © 1972 by The Horn Book, Inc., Boston), June, 1972, p. 274.*

OTHER CITATIONS

The Booklist, *May 15, 1972, p. 820.*

Zena Sutherland, in Bulletin of the Center for Children's Books, *February, 1973, p. 89.*

*   *   *

ESTES, Eleanor   1906-

Eleanor Estes, formerly a children's librarian, is an American author who received the 1952 Newbery Award for *Ginger Pye*. She is best known for her stories about the Moffats. (See also *Contemporary Authors*, Vols. 1-4, rev. ed., and *Something About the Author*, Vol. 4.)

GENERAL COMMENTARY

Eleanor Estes has many gifts as a writer for children. One of her major gifts is that of immediacy. Her books seem to be the product of some miracle child writing of the contemporary scene and their affairs of childhood with the skill and selectivity of the mature writer. . . .

To this observer it seems that the vitality of Eleanor Estes derives from the fact that she sees childhood whole—its zest, its dilemmas, its cruelties and compassion. She never moves outside that understanding, because she never needs to lean upon the crutch of adult concepts or explanations. Her stories move and have their being in their own complete world, peopled by children. There are wonderful adults in them, to be sure, but they are adults as children see them, smiling or cross, largely divided as children instinctively divide their world into those who are for and those who are against children.

She has an unerring ear for the conversation of children, not only for the way they speak, but for the content of their conversation. There is wit in it, and sharp observation, and it is always completely childlike. (p. 258)

The humor of Eleanor Estes is shot through with an exhilarating absurdity almost akin to Edward Lear. The pompous are made ridiculous, and the inefficient and ill-equipped are inventive and triumphant. (p. 259)

Here is a writer who is not afraid of sorrow in relation to

children. There were always threats to the security of the Moffats, and the doubts that assail the human wayfarer concern the contemplations of Rachel and even of Uncle Bennie. *The Hundred Dresses* is a revelation of a child's suffering. The book transcends all of the labels which have been applied to it in the name of brotherhood, tolerance and intercultural understanding. It is an enduring story of compassion.

Above all, there is in the children of the books that powerful drive toward joy which characterizes childhood itself. Who has not been touched by observing in the most lonely and most lost that quick response to even a whisper of pleasure, a shadow of hope to savor life? It is highly suitable that *The Moffats* in the French translation bears the title *Les Joyeux Moffats*. (pp. 259-60)

> *Frances Clarke Sayers, "The Books of Eleanor Estes," in* The Horn Book Magazine *(copyright, 1952, by The Horn Book, Inc., Boston), August, 1952, pp. 257-60.*

The three books about the four Moffat children are enjoyed by children, especially girls, because of Janey, the middle Moffat. This series is not quite modern times, but the seamstress mother and the small town activities are not too remote to prevent them from being completely understandable. Janey and her small brother, Rufus, are generally trying to achieve some worthy end, but whether it is Janey in the school play getting her bear head on backwards, or Rufus trying to obtain a library card and going completely astray in the big building, their paths are strewn with mishaps that make delightful reading.

> *May Hill Arbuthnot, in her* Children's Reading in the Home *(copyright © 1969 by Scott, Foresman and Co.), Scott, Foresman, 1969, pp. 112-13.*

When [Eleanor Estes] began to write, her native genius, radiant humor, and very special understanding of children were evident. It is difficult to remember when we have not known the Moffats—Jane, Rufus, Sylvie, Joey and their mother—their friends and neighbors on New Dollar Street, and the important inhabitants of the town of Cranbury. The events of the stories themselves are often commonplace, but the turn they take is never ordinary. The children are ingenious and enterprising, but never unrealistically so, the one-track pattern of their minds is the perfect vehicle for the pursuit of a plan to an often surprising conclusion. Mrs. Estes' writing is as inevitably full of surprise as it is of fun, and the characters are completely realized. Throughout the three books, *The Moffats* (1941), *The Middle Moffat* (1942), and *Rufus M.* (1943), each character remains himself, changing with time, of course, but growing in his own pattern.

> *Ruth Hill Viguers, in* A Critical History of Children's Literature, *by Cornelia Meigs, Anne Thaxter Eaton, Elizabeth Nesbitt, and Ruth Hill Viguers, edited by Cornelia Meigs (copyright © 1953, 1969 by Macmillan Co., Inc.), revised edition, Macmillan, 1969, p. 568.*

Within the United States one of the most captivating book families is unquestionably "the Moffats," created by Eleanor Estes. . . .

There is no general theme, no long suspense, and no exciting climax to these books. Each chapter is a complete episode in the life of one of the Moffats. . . .

The ultimate humor in these Moffat situations is touched off by the artist—Louis Slobodkin. The Moffat tales and Mr. Slobodkin's illustrations represent the perfect union of story and pictures—Rufus M. leaping for a deadly catch in a baseball game; Janey viewing the world amiably from an upside-down angle, looking between her own stout legs, head almost on the ground.

> *May Hill Arbuthnot and Zena Sutherland, in their* Children and Books *(copyright © 1947, 1957, 1964, 1972 by Scott, Foresman and Co.), 4th edition, Scott, Foresman, 1972, pp. 439-40.*

The characters of the Moffatts, especially Jane and Rufus, are based on a selective cumulation of episodes familiar to any family. Innumerable small girls, in or out of fiction, have longed for real curls, or suffered the pangs and excitements of moving house; innumerable small boys have dug up seeds to see if they were growing or looked under a railway bridge in ecstatic terror. The Moffatts do all these things and more. They acquire their solidity through the very natural snatches of talk among themselves and with their elders, and from the meticulously drawn background of their home, of Cranbury folk and Cranbury streets and Cranbury customs of half a century ago.

> *Margery Fisher, in her* Who's Who in Children's Books: A Treasury of the Familiar Characters of Childhood *(copyright © 1975 by Margery Fisher; reprinted by permission of Holt, Rinehart and Winston), Holt, Rinehart and Winston, 1975, p. 234.*

THE ALLEY (1964)

[The] plot is of minor importance in this book. The characterizations of the Alley's people are delightful, the relationships and the group structuring in the community of children are superbly drawn, both in exposition and in dialogue; the style is distinctive: easy, warm, and humorous.

> *Zena Sutherland, in* Bulletin of the Center for Children's Books *(copyright 1964 by the University of Chicago; all rights reserved), November, 1964, p. 35.*

Eleanor Estes . . . has a gift for spinning a good story and making young characters come alive in a lively and amusing manner. The children [in "The Alley"] are all true to life in their thoughts, words and actions—be they good or bad. Yet, although one expects children to be bad occasionally, one wonders at the turn of events that has two policemen stealing a pen and ring while investigating a robbery at Connie's house. The author does explain that most policemen are honest, but this incident will not go down well with some parents—and not just in policemen's families.

> *Marjorie Burger, in* The New York Times Book Review *(© 1964 by The New York Times Company; reprinted by permission), November 1, 1964 (Part 2), p. 36.*

OTHER CITATIONS

Elizabeth Enright, in Book Week, *November 1, 1964 (Part 2), p. 16.*

Alice Dalgliesh, in Saturday Review, *November 7, 1964, p. 53.*

The Booklist and Subscription Books Bulletin, *January 1, 1965, p. 435.*

Patience M. Daltry, in The Christian Science Monitor, *June 28, 1965, p. 5.*

THE COAT-HANGER CHRISTMAS TREE (1973)

Marianna's innocent logic and single-track determination [in *The Coat-Hanger Christmas Tree*] has some of the old Estes child's-eye charm and none of the tiresome foolishness of *The Tunnel of Hugsy Goode . . .*, but *The Tunnel's* anachronistic ambience still pervades (for specifics, Allie wears a zip-on maxicoat but Mama says goldurn and "tell that to the Marines"—but it's not just the specifics), and this is strictly a seasonal trimming, to be packed away when the Christmas time nostalgia is past.

> Kirkus Reviews *(copyright © 1973 The Kirkus Service, Inc.), July 15, 1973, p. 755.*

The plot [of *The Coat-Hanger Christmas Tree*] isn't strong, but the characterization is convincing, and the story is appealing in the same way that the books about the Moffats are: gentle, cozy, realistic, achieving a sense of family life and home atmosphere that frame and permeate the small events of the action.

> *Zena Sutherland, in* Bulletin of the Center for Children's Books *(© 1973 by the University of Chicago; all rights reserved), November, 1973, pp. 41-2.*

Although thin and slight by comparison with her early books, [*The Coat-Hanger Christmas Tree*] nonetheless bears evidence of a still-able writer, with its evocative, sharply focused background and its insights into the tenacity of children.

> *Ethel L. Heins, in* The Horn Book Magazine *(copyright © 1973 by The Horn Book, Inc., Boston), December, 1973, p. 583.*

OTHER CITATIONS

Publishers' Weekly, *July 16, 1973, p. 111.*

GINGER PYE (1951)

["Ginger Pye"] is told with a real feeling for childhood—its desperate earnestness, its melodramatic imaginings, its unconscious humor. The mood is right, but the trouble is there is more mood than substance. Rachel's flashbacks of memory, suggestive of a juvenile Proust, may well irritate readers who want to know what happened to Ginger.

> *Ellen Lewis Buell, in* The New York Times Book Review *(© 1951 by The New York Times Company; reprinted by permission), April 22, 1951, p. 30.*

Rachel, Jerry, the ever-goodnatured Uncle Bennie and the dog, Ginger Pye, are the principal characters in a story written with the same sympathy, humor and understanding that have made the Moffats so dearly loved everywhere. An outstanding book.

> *Jennie D. Lindquist and Siri M. Andrews, in* The Horn Book Magazine *(copyright, 1951, by The Horn Book, Inc., Boston), May, 1951, p. 182.*

[*Ginger Pye*] lacks all taste of strangeness. The Pye family buy a puppy, lose it, look for it, and months later they find it again. The story never comes to life although some of the descriptions are well done—the sunlight through stained-glass windows as the children dust pews on a Saturday afternoon and the cold of Thanksgiving Day as they look for the puppy through a flurry of snow. If one already knew the Pyes, had seen them once a week in a television serial, it might be enthralling to hear more about them, but on the evidence of this book the acquaintance hardly seems worthwhile.

> The Times Literary Supplement *(© The Times Publishing Company Ltd. 1961), December 1, 1961, p. xxi.*

OTHER CITATIONS

Bulletin of the Center for Children's Books, *May, 1951, p. 43.*

A LITTLE OVEN (1955)

A play on words, a little international misunderstanding and a tenderness basic to childhood combine to make another Eleanor Estes story.... Artlessly, the narrative creates deeper meanings by what is left unsaid. The author's pastel water colors expand a deceptive simplicity. (Possibly this is directed almost more to mothers than to children.)

> Virginia Kirkus' Service, *May 15, 1955, p. 327.*

Whoever has lived intimately with young children will be grateful to Eleanor Estes for a book which springs from pure joy in childhood and childlike fun. To look upon *A Little Oven* ... as just another picture book in the vast limbo of production for the pre-school child is to miss the subtle and true quality in a record of friendship between two very little girls who come to live in Connecticut....

So perfectly integrated are Mrs. Estes' simple water color scenes with the words of her graphic text as to leave pictures even clearer in the mind than on the pages of a book I would put lower down on the same shelf with *The Hundred Dresses* and *The Moffats*. Helena and Genevieve are real characters and so are their mothers who represent something more than figures of fun or of wishful thinking.

> *Anne Carroll Moore, in* The Horn Book Magazine *(copyright, 1955, by The Horn Book, Inc., Boston), August, 1955, p. 255.*

OTHER CITATIONS

Bulletin of the Center for Children's Books, *December, 1955, p. 44.*

THE LOLLIPOP PRINCESS: A PLAY FOR PAPER DOLLS IN ONE ACT (1967)

Illustrations and script for [this] paper-doll play have a childlike, ingenuous quality which will amuse adults as an example of the kind of spontaneous production that children invent for their own entertainment. However, it does not succeed as a picture book, and is unnecessary for young dramatists who ought to be encouraged to invent their own play-adaptations. The only valid audience for this would seem to be insatiable Moffat fans.

> *Nancy Young Orr, in* School Library Journal *(reprinted from* School Library Journal, *December, 1967, published by R. R. Bowker Co., a Xerox company; copyright © 1967 by Xerox Corporation), December, 1967, p. 60.*

[This] play, originally intended as part of a Moffat book, has the true flavor of children's dialogue and a plot-line based on the most familiar of plots. A princess, ill with despair because she craves new lollipop flavors, is saved by a prince who restores her appetite and wins her hand after other suitors have failed. The author maintains a childlike air without ever being pointedly coy or childish.

> *Zena Sutherland, in* Bulletin of the Center for Children's Books *(copyright 1967 by the University of Chicago; all rights reserved), December, 1967, p. 58.*

OTHER CITATIONS

Kirkus Service, *October 15, 1967, p. 1269.*

Ursula Nordstrom, in Saturday Review, *November 11, 1967, p. 45.*

Ethel L. Heins, in The Horn Book Magazine, *December, 1967, pp. 760-61.*

THE MIDDLE MOFFAT (1942)

[*The Middle Moffat*] is a light, gentle book filled with homey, innocent humor and nostalgia for a period in our history when an automobile ride was a novelty and radios were still considered rarities. The Moffats' ability to "make do" on limited resources might help children appreciate many comforts that they take for granted. The closely-knit family situation and the many unhackneyed, genuinely funny episodes add to the book's charm.

> *John Gillespie and Diana Lembo, in their* Introducing Books: A Guide for the Middle Grades *(copyright © 1970 by Xerox Corp.), Bowker, 1970, p. 10.*

OTHER CITATIONS

The Times Literary Supplement, *May 20, 1960, p. xiii.*

MIRANDA THE GREAT (1967)

Perhaps if a dog had done all the things attributed here to the cat Miranda, there would be less tendency to carp at the idea that a cool cat during the barbarians' sack and burning of Rome adopted over 30 abandoned kittens and took title to the Colosseum. . . . [*Miranda the Great*] is a cat fancier's fantasy—a story of cats as they could be *if* they wanted to be. Excellent illustrations by [Edward] Ardizzone and written with no concessions to limited vocabularies.

> *Lillian N. Gerhardt, in* School Library Journal *(reprinted from* School Library Journal, *March, 1967, published by R. R. Bowker Co., a Xerox company; copyright © 1967 by Xerox Corporation), March, 1967, p. 125.*

The humor [in *Miranda the Great*] is just a bit low-keyed for the middle grades reader, the references occasionally adult. For example, the father of the Roman family groans, "'What senseless destruction! O tempora! O mores!' he said, for he was a learned man." The story will have greatest appeal to animal lovers; it is an imaginatively conceived book, a bit slow-moving, but with the double charms of gentleness and humor, and with expectably charming Ardizzone illustrations.

> *Zena Sutherland, in* Bulletin of the Center for Children's Books *(copyright 1967 by the University of Chicago; all rights reserved), April, 1967, p. 120.*

What a wonderful story to read aloud to young children! The author's rare ability to recognize details most appealing to children and weave them through her storytelling has never been more evident. Suspense and humor are here in abundance to delight grown-ups as well as children, though people of different ages will probably chuckle over different things. The child who knows Miranda and Punka will have a link with ancient and modern Rome more enduring than later acquaintance made through history books.

> *Ruth Hill Viguers, in* The Horn Book Magazine *(copyright © 1967, by The Horn Book, Inc., Boston), April, 1967, p. 201.*

OTHER CITATIONS

Kirkus Service, *February 1, 1967, p. 130.*

THE MOFFATS (1941)

[*The Moffats*] has the actuality, the relevance to the everyday lives of readers in libraries, so commonly lacking in the books of professional writers who derive their material from memory more often than from observation. It would be fair to add that *The Moffats* creaks a little. It has some of the self-consciousness of a book with a purpose. . . .

This, however, is not a gloomy book. The Moffats are not poor in spirit, and they squeeze the last drop of fun and excitement out of every day. Even the awful happenings—Jane's flight from the police, scarlet fever, Joe's performance of the sailor's hornpipe—have a positive awfulness about them. They are dreadful, but they are not dull. Mrs. Estes has an eye for character. The Moffats themselves are drawn in full detail. They have a life independent of the book, and their author was forced to go on writing about them in further stories. [They] live in a community, and it is a particular charm of this book that the reader is allowed to

explore Cranbury thoroughly, to know its topography and its inhabitants.

> *The Times Literary Supplement (© The Times Publishing Company Ltd. 1959), May 29, 1959, p. xvii.*

PINKY PYE (1958)

Pinky Pye has an atmosphere of unsentimental, homely sweetness which is peculiarly American. It has, too, a gallery of memorable portraits, and a landscape, carpeted with poison ivy, described with loving detail. It is a quiet story in which the biggest excitements are scaled down. It captivates by its intense charm and its artful simplicity.

> *The Times Literary Supplement (© The Times Publishing Company Ltd. 1959), May 29, 1959, p. xvii.*

Eleanor Estes brings Pinky to life by adding to the enumeration of her actions and appearance the loving comments of the Pyes as they watch her. Then, too, the author enters into Pinky's thoughts in a lightly whimsical manner that takes proper account of cat behavior. Finally, she includes in the story extracts from the supposed autobiography written, in fact, by Mr. Pye. By moving from one approach to another Eleanor Estes avoids sentimentality and gives the cat the kind of acquired personality which this particular species of domestic pet is apt to have.

> *Margery Fisher, in her* Who's Who in Children's Books: A Treasury of the Familiar Characters of Childhood *(copyright © 1975 by Margery Fisher; reprinted by permission of Holt, Rinehart and Winston), Holt, Rinehart and Winston, 1975, p. 282.*

OTHER CITATIONS

Virginia Kirkus' Service, *April 1, 1958, p. 283.*

Zena Sutherland, *in* Bulletin of the Center for Children's Books, *July-August, 1958, p. 120.*

RUFUS M. (1943)

[*Rufus M.*] is not Eleanor Estes's best. In fact, it is even in parts rather dull—and has one whole chapter about baseball. Nevertheless, some of her quality comes through—warmth, humour, happiness, realism and security; it is sad that, for one reviewer at least, these quite invaluable qualities are always spoilt by her adult's indulgence. But the chapter about Rufus and the cardboard boy lingers in the memory.

> *The Times Literary Supplement (© The Times Publishing Company Ltd. 1960), November 25, 1960, p. vii.*

THE TUNNEL OF HUGSY GOODE (1972)

[In *The Tunnel of Hugsy Goode*, Eleanor Estes] has gone to a great deal of trouble to re-create a contemporary childhood adventure by scrupulously noting the interests, clothes, mores, and pastimes of children in the 1960's. But although her details are precise, her observations apt, and her imagination active, she has created a world where characters move like programmed robots, unable to think or act with spontaneity. . . . Nicholas Carroll (surely one of the least convincing child characters in recent fiction) narrates the story and perforce must bear most of the blame for its failure.

> *Sidney D. Long, in* The Horn Book Magazine *(copyright © 1972 by The Horn Book, Inc., Boston), April, 1972, pp. 143-44.*

Although the elaborate superstructure of boy-girl hostilities [in *The Tunnel of Hugsy Goode*] threatens to swamp the action, there is enough humor and warmth in the story of the investigations of the tunnel to compensate more than amply. The characters are vivid, and the Alley community retains its distinctive charm.

> *Zena Sutherland, in* Bulletin of the Center for Children's Books *(© 1972 by the University of Chicago; all rights reserved), April, 1972, p. 121.*

There are contrivances [in "The Tunnel of Hugsy Goode"] —a key conspicuously planted on a path to a hidden door, a raccoon running off (and more than once!) with a tape recorder, boys who exclaim, "by cricky"; but Eleanor Estes's characters are always likable, and if her style is sometimes anachronistic, it is charming, illuminated by a real insight into childhood.

> *Jean Fritz, in* The New York Times Book Review *(© 1972 by The New York Times Company; reprinted by permission), April 23, 1972, p. 8.*

The Tunnel of Hugsy Goode . . . is a disappointing sequel to Eleanor Estes' *The Alley*. . . . Much of the mystery and humor that distinguished the earlier book is missing here, and the narrator, at once precocious and naive Copin, slows down the action with too many digressions.

> *Willa M. Levy, in* School Library Journal *(reprinted from* School Library Journal, *May, 1972, published by R. R. Bowker Co., a Xerox company; copyright © 1972 by Xerox Corporation), May, 1972, p. 92.*

OTHER CITATIONS

Kirkus Reviews, *December 1, 1971, p. 1256.*

Publishers' Weekly, *January 17, 1972, p. 59.*

Zena Sutherland, in Saturday Review, *March 25, 1972, p. 110.*

THE WITCH FAMILY (1960)

[*The Witch Family*] is a very special book that is certain to give boundless pleasure—at any time of the year—to children who are not afraid of venturing beyond vocabulary levels, who enjoy play with words, and who like their reality and fantasy mixed; and especially if it is read aloud by adults who are able *to give themselves up* to the childlike nonsense and fancy of the story.

> *Ruth Hill Viguers, in* The Horn Book Magazine *(copyright, 1960, by the Horn Book, Inc., Boston), October, 1960, p. 395.*

The sure touch which made real human beings of the Moffats and the Pyes is regrettably lacking in this fantasy about witches who come to life from the crayon drawings of a rather formidable little girl and her meek friend. In spite of a smooth and polished style, the plot seems contrived.

> Saturday Review *(copyright © 1960 by Saturday Review, Inc.; reprinted with permission), November 12, 1960, p. 94.*

To many adults the writing [in *The Witch Family*] may seem self-conscious and the blending of fantasy and reality inept and sometimes confusing, but to those children who move unhesitantly between the real and unreal and are equally at home in both worlds no such shortcomings will be apparent. To them the story with all its delicious witch lore will be pure delight.

> The Booklist and Subscription Books Bulletin *(reprinted by permission of the American Library Association; copyright 1961 by the American Library Association), February 1, 1961, p. 329.*

[*The Witch Family*] rests on a pleasant ingenuity whereby the holiday drawings of two little girls in part control the story in which they and the witches they have created all play parts. . . . [An] engaging character is Malachi, the spelling Bee, who acts as spy and intermediary and mentor all in one. Many of his jokes verge on the corny but still on the restrainedly corny so that the level of humour in the book is upheld. It is not everybody's humour any more than magic of this kind is everybody's magic, but anyone who takes to the book in the first place is assured of many moments of subtle entertainment.

> The Junior Bookshelf, *July, 1962, p. 129.*

In Eleanor Estes's *The Witch Family* we are . . . given the creative play of the protagonists' imagination, the premise here being simply a serene, taken-for-granted faith in its power, and from this premise the logic of the tale is constructed and the boundary lines drawn. The delicacy of implication by which the young reader is made to understand that two small girls' imaginings are creating the witch family, and that though it *is* being created bit by bit by the children it is nonetheless real, is to me quite remarkable. What is so satisfying is precisely the airiness of implication, the complete lack of explanation throughout the subsequent movements back and forth between fantasy and reality.

It is a delight to discover the way in which Eleanor Estes uses words in *The Witch Family*, especially when we realize that its readers must be quite young, for the children in the book are almost seven and then just seven. First there is the play with words, and this play is thoroughly in the spirit of childhood. Amy, who is the chief imaginer, *banquished* the Old Witch, the head witch of all the witches, an act which commences the story, and she explains to Clarissa that she joined *banish* and *vanquish* to create this deeply satisfying word. . . . Then there is *witchiplication*, a very hard and important subject for witches, and as this is a real, right, regular witch book, we find such words as *necromancy, abracadabra, incantations* and *runes*. What a pleasure it is to come across such a sentence as this for young readers, "The little witches, hearing the Head Witches' expert, expressive enunciation, drew back in awe"....

Eleanor Cameron, in her The Green and Burning Tree: On the Writing and Enjoyment of Children's Books *(copyright © 1962, 1964, 1966, 1969 by Eleanor Cameron; reprinted by permission of Little, Brown and Co. in association with The Atlantic Monthly Press), Little, Brown, 1969, pp. 19, 28.*

First published in the United States in 1960 and in England in 1962, [*The Witch Family*] is a book that does not date. Little girls will always be little girls, no matter what anti-sexist writers say, and I don't see American Hallowe'en customs changing yet awhile either. Hallowe'en is the motive force and climax of this perceptive domestic fantasy....

Old Witch is a composite portrait, starting in stories told by Amy's mother which are firmly based on fairy-tale tradition; Amy and Clarissa, satisfying complements to one another, sit together drawing pictures and augmenting the stories at will. Old Witch's desired victims are the Easter rabbits and their painted eggs, her spells are the simple Abracadabra chants of a child's sympathetic magic and her herb cookery is a recognisable translation from a middle-class kitchen....

It is in the skilful merging of magic and everyday that the story excels; the magic is a logical extension of school, meals, friends, childhood in a prosperous Washington suburb. The children have two modes of expression, visual and verbal. As they draw and colour they exercise the literal quality of imagination proper to their age; the description of the field where the Easter rabbits escape from the witch's malice by a familiar folk-tale stratagem is a masterly mixture of shrewd psychology and easy fun. The personalities of the two girls are implied in what they draw and in what they say as they discuss inventive possibilities. Amy, at once tough and soft-hearted, decides to allow Old Witch a companion, Little Witch Girl, and later adds out of her own secret longings a charmingly responsive baby-witch. Clarissa contributes details that show that she is socially more adept and confident than Amy but physically a little less venturesome....

Psychology alone does not make a classic—and I believe this story is a classic. Just as she has unobtrusively woven fancy and domestic reality together, so Eleanor Estes has devised a flexible style, crisp and idiomatic in dialogue, neat and direct in narrative, but broadening now and then into a maturity of language that should commend the book to a wide age-range. Here is a moment in the painting-field, where Old Witch's cat Tom, who knows very well there is one live rabbit among the fake bunnies that have deceived his mistress, does a little stalking:

> So, he came sniffing along, dum-de-dum-dum, slowly, deliberately, across the painting field. He stopped at every rabbit he encountered and smelled it thoughtfully and knowingly, as if measuring the amount of sage, say, in it. Then, leaving it untouched, he cleaned his paw, or his ear, and proceeded to the next one. He had but one worry–that possibly Old Witch would grab up the real rabbit before he got to it. Still the game was so delightful that he was willing to take this risk, and he did not race greedily and ignominiously for Jack. Dignity accompanied his thoughtful progress towards his quarry.

The humour and the insights of the story demand this kind of flexible, mature prose just as the chatter and interchange of ideas of Amy and Clarissa need the light, humorous, completely uncondescending treatment they receive in this incomparable comedy of imaginative childhood.

Margery Fisher, in her Growing Point, *September, 1975, pp. 2684-85.*

As the game develops (the little girls solemnly drawing each scene and discussing it together) their characters grow for the reader.... [Old Witch's] lapses from grace clearly give Amy the chance to escape from the orderly progress of her home life. Because the children come to fear Old Witch a little they invent Malachi, a bee whom a magic spell has enabled—to spell! This beautifully logical idea preserves the balance of mischief and obedience essential to the children, while Malachi's solemn buzzing pronouncements seem to reflect Clarissa's sturdy and amusing affectation of adult behaviour.

As the days pass other characters are invented—the Little Witch Girl Hannah and the baby sister she longed for, a whole school of malicious little witch girls, a mermaid in a glass cavern with a baby sister of her own, the Easter rabbits and their painted eggs; each one stands for some wish or vagary, some remembered fear or joy—for instance, I am sure Clarissa sees herself in Brave Jack the rabbit guard. Amy emerges as a child dependent on affection, her own and that of other people. Her letters to Old Witch always end in her special way: 'I love you and you love me.' After a last mock-scarifying dream adventure on the night of Hallowe'en when she experiments with Hannah's broomstick and is carried up to Old Witch's house, she decides to allow the wicked old woman some grass and flowers for comfort, since she appears to have reformed. But not entirely—for as Amy says, and as Clarissa agrees, 'What is the good of Old Witch if she is good all the time.' Oblique character drawing has seldom been as shrewd or as comical as it is in this American family tale.

Margery Fisher, in her Who's Who in Children's Books: A Treasury of the Familiar Characters of Childhood *(copyright © 1975 by Margery Fisher; reprinted by permission of Holt, Rinehart and Winston), Holt, Rinehart and Winston, 1975, p. 20.*

OTHER CITATIONS

Zena Sutherland, in Bulletin of the Center for Children's Books, *December, 1960, p. 57.*

Silence Buck Bellows, in The Christian Science Monitor, *December 22, 1960, p. 5.*

The Times Literary Supplement, *June 1, 1962, p. 393.*

F

FRITZ, Jean   1915-

An American author born and reared in China, Jean Fritz is noted for her historical novels about famous men of the American Revolution. (See also *Contemporary Authors*, Vols. 1-4, rev. ed., and *Something About the Author*, Vol. 1.)

AND THEN WHAT HAPPENED, PAUL REVERE? (1973)

In "And Then What Happened, Paul Revere?" Jean Fritz tells, in her deceivingly simple and seemingly effortless way, of Paul Revere's early years and, of course, of his famous ride and then continues to relate what happened to him in later life. Her slender story is packed with amusing facts and details and has just the right amount of witty repetition. Its casual and unassuming tone is perfectly delightful. Margot Tomes's many pictures ideally complement the story—what greater tribute can one pay an illustrator? —and are as filled with humor and the atmosphere of those days as the tale they illustrate.

> *Peter Spier, in* The New York Times Book Review (© *1973 by The New York Times Company; reprinted by permission), November 4, 1973 (Part 2), p. 59.*

What Paul Revere did before, between, and after his ride to Lexington lends understanding of him as a person and of the incidents that led up to the Revolutionary War. The fair explanations are furthered by humanizing details. . . . The entertaining presentation of little-known facts, useful for independent reading or coordinating into a history unit, will be enjoyed by primary and middle graders. [Margot Tomes'] illustrations, often funny, accurately portray the era and show many facets of Colonial life.

> *Phyllis Galt, in* School Library Journal *(reprinted from* School Library Journal, *December, 1973, published by R. R. Bowker Co., a Xerox company; copyright* © *1973 by Xerox Corporation), December, 1973, p. 42.*

[*And Then What Happened, Paul Revere?*] is funny, fast-paced, and historically accurate; it is given added interest by the establishment of Revere's character: busy, bustling, versatile, and patriotic, a man who loved people and excitement.

> *Zena Sutherland, in* Bulletin of the Center

for Children's Books (© *1974 by the University of Chicago; all rights reserved), March, 1974, pp. 109-10.*

The boundless energy and zest which were the dynamic forces in the busy life of Paul Revere vitalize [this] brief, simply written biography. . . . The slightly unfamiliar and entertaining version of his "Big Ride" is documented in the informal and readable notes at the end of the book. The light-hearted humor in [Margot Tomes'] illustrations—like that in the writing—proves that historical accuracy need not be solemn.

> *Ethel L. Heins, in* The Horn Book Magazine, (copyright © *1974 by The Horn Book, Inc., Boston), April, 1974, pp. 159-60.*

OTHER CITATIONS

Kirkus Reviews, *October 1, 1973, p. 1100.*

Joyce Alpern, in Book World, *November 11, 1973 (Part 2), p. 5C.*

Publishers' Weekly, *November 12, 1973, p. 37.*

BRADY (1960)

Mrs. Fritz has achieved special success—her greatest—in this story of a boy who grows up because he "discovers something outside of him is bigger than he is." . . . The writing of this story is unhurried and vivid. Brady is entirely believable—both he and his father are drawn with particular skill—and the incidents of controversy centered in Abolitionism and church division are made exciting. The background of farm and family activity has colorful period flavor.

> *Virginia Haviland, in* The Horn Book Magazine (copyright, *1960, by the Horn Book, Inc., Boston), December, 1960, p. 512.*

[*Brady* is a] strong and moving story about a youngster living in the troubled years before the Civil War. . . . This is not only an excellent period story, but a beautifully developed character study. Brady changes gradually in response to other people, to new interests, to time; he is completely believable. Other characterization is good, and the book has good writing style, good values, and smooth pace.

Zena Sutherland, in Bulletin of the Center for Children's Books *(copyright 1961 by the University of Chicago; all rights reserved), March, 1961, p. 109.*

The runaway for whom no motivation is provided is fourteen-year-old Moss in *Brady*. Jean Fritz, the author, is so busy depicting Moss as just an average boy that she neglects to tell us why he ran away. It does not stand to reason that a boy who has been a slave all his life and who chooses to take the risks involved in running away can be without a story to tell—most likely a hair-raising story.

The problem with *Brady* . . . is that it pretends to be dealing with a large, vital issue—slavery—while it is really about how Brady learns to keep his mouth shut and to grow into a man. It expresses, through a multitude of characters, every conceivable view about slavery. But when it comes to the heart of the matter—the slave himself—it glosses over the situation and becomes just another book about growing up with a bit of adventure thrown in. Since the focus is on the white boy's growth, it is extremely doubtful that many young readers would come away from it with any real idea of the degradation slavery inflicted upon those caught in its web.

Dorothy M. Broderick, in her Image of the Black in Children's Fiction *(copyright © 1973 Dorothy M. Broderick), Bowker, 1973, pp. 37-8.*

OTHER CITATIONS

Virginia Kirkus' Service, *August 15, 1960, p. 682.*

Miriam S. Mathes, in School Library Journal, *September, 1960, p. 63.*

The Booklist and Subscription Books Bulletin, *January 15, 1961, p. 300.*

The Junior Bookshelf, *June, 1966, p. 180.*

Constantine Georgiou, in his Children and Their Literature, *Prentice-Hall, 1969, pp. 335-36.*

EARLY THUNDER (1967)

There is a fresh, and adult approach [in "Early Thunder"], and the book stands head and shoulders above the average teen-age tale of Colonial times, but Mrs. Fritz has only partly succeeded. Her boy is too lifeless, too academic. He and his friends talk like no boys ever talked, and their arguments are pedantic and sociological, and indeed each character in the book talks alike, more or less. We never rightly know what the leading characters look like, nor is there very much excitement of pace.

This is a pity, for the idea of the book is interesting and some of the situations in it are most inventive. Mrs. Fritz must be given a good score for a sensible try. Lynd Ward's illustrations, as always, are rewarding and decorative.

Howard Fast, in The New York Times Book Review *(© 1967 by The New York Times Company; reprinted by permission), October 22, 1967, p. 62.*

[*Early Thunder* is a] superior historical novel, focused on the young hero's crisis of conscience. Events rapidly transpiring in Salem, Massachusetts, in 1774-1775 force 14-year-old Daniel West to re-examine his loyalties and, finally, to change from Tory to Whig. The background, language, and events seem accurate. Moreover, the building of suspense and the realistic portrayal of characters and motivations should hold the interest of even those teen-agers reluctant to read anything not placed in the present day. Throughout the book, the author provides the opportunity for subtle comparisons between this historic struggle over conflicting philosophies of government and similar situations today.

Bernice Levine, in School Library Journal *(reprinted from* School Library Journal, *November, 1967, published by R. R. Bowker Co., a Xerox company; copyright © 1967 by Xerox Corporation), November, 1967, p. 76.*

While there are many dramatic incidents in the absorbing story, the greatest significance of the book is in the reality of setting and characters. The reader lives completely in the early American town and knows its people, among whom, as in any period of conflict, there is always a Daniel West, seeing right and wrong on both sides, longing for the consistency that is never possible, and eventually giving himself wholly to the cause in which he has come to believe. The most alive story of the American Revolution that has appeared in many years. The next logical step is [Esther Forbes'] *Johnny Tremain.* . . .

Ruth Hill Viguers, in The Horn Book Magazine *(copyright © 1967, by The Horn Book, Inc., Boston), December, 1967, p. 758.*

OTHER CITATIONS

Kirkus Service, *October 1, 1967, p. 1218.*

Polly Goodwin, in Book World, *October 1, 1967, p. 24.*

Ursula Nordstrom, in Saturday Review, *November 11, 1967, p. 48.*

The Booklist and Subscription Books Bulletin, *December 1, 1967, p. 446.*

FISH HEAD (1954)

This cat adventurer will greatly appeal to children (who want to but often can't do what they like). The tale has movement and action. The plentiful illustrations [by Marc Simont] are vivid and imaginative. And the story skillfully demonstrates that socially acceptable behavior (in cat or child) need entail no loss of excitement.

Shirley Camper, in The New York Times Book Review *(© 1954 by The New York Times Company; reprinted by permission), November 28, 1954, p. 36.*

Fish Head is a fresh and witty tale about a thieving wharf cat, "a raggedy, scraggledy, patched-up, scratched-up cat, with a chewed-up tail." . . . This is a first-rate story for anyone up to the age of seven, told with verve and originality. The illustrations [by Marc Simont] are vivid and vigorous, full of action and splashy colour.

The Times Literary Supplement, *November 23, 1956, p. v.*

OTHER CITATIONS

Virginia Kirkus' Bookshop Service, *October 1, 1954, p. 677.*

Jennie D. Lindquist, *in* The Horn Book Magazine, *December, 1954, p. 428.*

Bulletin of the Center for Children's Books, *July, 1955, p. 100.*

GEORGE WASHINGTON'S BREAKFAST (1969)

[This is a] good story about young George W. Allen, born on February 22, who feels a tremendous rapport with the father of his country. Interesting bits of trivia abound, as the author tells all the tidbits George W. knows about Washington—his dogs, horses, and so on. But George can't find anywhere an account of what Washington ate for breakfast. . . . Paul Galdone's red, white, and blue illustrations don't equal many of his earlier ones, but they are appropriate to the story and, like it, are not overstated. Younger and reluctant readers may enjoy this, as it offers a painless way of picking up information.

> *Leota Wells, in* School Library Journal *(reprinted from* School Library Journal, *March, 1969, published by R. R. Bowker Co., a Xerox company; copyright © 1969 by Xerox Corporation), March, 1969, p. 150.*

The fictional framework [of *George Washington's Breakfast*] is deft, the illustrations [by Paul Galdone] echoing its light humor, and the story gives both a believable picture of a small, determined boy and a good introduction to the vicissitudes of historical research.

> *Zena Sutherland, in* Bulletin of the Center for Children's Books *(© 1969 by the University of Chicago; all rights reserved), May, 1969, p. 142.*

I, ADAM (1963)

Most of [this] story is concerned with Adam's struggles at the farm with the evil doings of Sharkey, who steals the deed and is jailed; this theme gives color and pace to the quiet but more meaningful struggle that Adam is having within himself. The book has fine style, vivid characterizations, and good—but not obtrusive—period details.

> *Zena Sutherland, in* Bulletin of the Center for Children's Books *(copyright 1963 by the University of Chicago; all rights reserved), December, 1963, p. 59.*

Too many books that portray a boy's growth into maturity lack conviction. This brilliant, restrained novel masters the natural development of the hero's consciousness and the 1850 Connecticut setting. . . .

Fundamentally Adam's problems, pleasures and dilemmas are not unlike those of young people today. Readers will discover that to set life's course truly takes both courage and common sense.

William Turner Levy, in The New York Times Book Review *(© 1964 by The New York Times Company; reprinted by permission), January 5, 1964, p. 18.*

Taken at its surface value this is a pleasantly entertaining story, even if the characters rarely come wholly to life, but the author has pretensions to expounding deeper philosophic truths, and at this level she really has very little to say, though this is concealed by an air of great importance.

> The Junior Bookshelf, *June, 1965, pp 154-55.*

The author's moral [in *I, Adam*], earnestly driven home in the last chapters, is "To thine own self be true." The book perhaps could have done without this moral; few adolescents these days lack the courage to state what they wish for themselves. But it is an exciting, well-written story.

> The Times Literary Supplement *(© The Times Publishing Company Ltd. 1965), June 17, 1965, p. 505.*

OTHER CITATIONS

Marion West Stoer, in The Christian Science Monitor, *November 14, 1963, p. B9.*

SAN FRANCISCO (1962)

An unusual glimpse of one of our most fascinating cities, . . . this combines historical anecdote, geography and selective guided tours in a knowledgeable, never dull text. . . . The story of the earthquake and fire and how the city rallied to rebuild ends a most insightful tour whose purpose is to reveal the diversified character of San Francisco. There are black and white illustrations by Emil Weiss, but the ideal accompaniment to this would be [Miroslav] Sasek's *This is San Francisco.* . . .

> Virginia Kirkus' Service, *July 15, 1962, p. 631.*

[This is a] good book about the city [of San Francisco] as it is today, with historical material incorporated throughout the text, so that the volume serves as a guide with background information. . . . Illustrations [by Emil Weiss] are profuse and lively; five maps at the back of the book suggest walks along some of the streets of San Francisco. Although the writing seems occasionally florid, the book is both interesting and useful; a fairly extensive index is appended.

> *Zena Sutherland, in* Bulletin of the Center for Children's Books *(copyright 1962 by the University of Chicago; all rights reserved), December, 1962, p. 57.*

WHERE WAS PATRICK HENRY ON THE 29TH OF MAY? (1975)

[Despite] the gimmicky emphasis on the 29th of May—the day Henry's "bawling out" of King George reached treasonable proportions—this life is far from dull. In fact it conveys a sense of the great orator's character that's absent in more sedate, older biographies. . . . Along the way Fritz introduces some memorable historical asides. . . . Margot Tomes makes the most of Henry's theatrical posturing [in her illustrations] and altogether this spunky, irreverent performance captures the essence of the celebrated "Patrick flash."

> Kirkus Reviews *(copyright © 1975 The Kirkus Service, Inc.), June 15, 1975, p. 664.*

A refreshing change from biographies weighted heavily on the super-hero side, [*Where Was Patrick Henry on the 29th of May?*] stresses both good and bad characteristics of Henry and throws in unusual and often humorous facts. . . . How he became a brilliant lawyer and "the greatest orator who ever lived," according to Jefferson, is both fascinating and amusing. Margot Tomes' droll illustrations are plentiful and add much to this punchy Bicentenniel booster.

> *Maie Wall Clark, in* School Library Journal *(reprinted from* School Library Journal, *September, 1975, published by R. R. Bowker Co., a Xerox company; copyright © 1975 by Xerox Corporation), September, 1975, p. 81.*

Once again author and artist [Margot Tomes] combine their talents to make historical writing comprehensible and inviting to young children. Not that they serve up information in the form of sugar-coated pills—far from it. This is history, with all its humanity but without its solemnity. . . .

> *Ethel L. Heins, in* The Horn Book Magazine *(copyright © 1975 by the Horn Book, Inc., Boston), October, 1975, p. 475.*

Jean Fritz really has an approach to history that is unique; she makes it fun. In this biography of Patrick Henry, the prose sails blithely along almost with the conversational tone of storytelling but all the research is there, not showing up as dry facts but incorporated into the story. [*Where Was Patrick Henry on the 29th of May?* is] a delightful addition to the Bicentennial Year and all the years thereafter.

> *Zena Sutherland, in* Bulletin of the Center for Children's Books *(© 1975 by the University of Chicago; all rights reserved), November, 1975, p. 44.*

OTHER CITATIONS

Nash K. Burger, in The New York Times Book Review, *June 29, 1975, p. 8.*

WHO'S THAT STEPPING ON PLYMOUTH ROCK? (1975)

The skittish saga of Plymouth Rock says more about how we Americans memorialize our heritage than about the heritage itself. . . . We're inclined to agree that the whole business isn't all that earthshaking, and [J. B.] Handelsman's weightless illustrations add to the overall impression of insignificance. Nevertheless, we can imagine lots of children saddled with bicentennial reports and field trips welcoming the chance to cast a stone or two at the mythmakers. And at least Jean Fritz always manages to tell us something we haven't heard before . . . and with such easy informality that even a footnote like this is worth a glance.

> Kirkus Reviews *(copyright © 1975 The Kirkus Service, Inc.), October 15, 1975, p. 1189.*

In her latest light-hearted look at American history Fritz points her incisive, and sometimes irreverent, finger at those who have stepped on Plymouth Rock from 1620 to the present. One of America's most visible patriotic symbols, the Rock has had an unusually checkered history, including lack of attention and even downright mistreatment (not to mention being broken in half). Fritz's subtle humor leads readers to the conclusion that the highest honor for the Rock lies in just being left alone. [*Who's That Stepping on Plymouth Rock?* is highly] interesting, definitely enlightening, undeniably Fritz.

> *Joe Bearden, in* School Library Journal *(reprinted from* School Library Journal, *November, 1975, published by R. R. Bowker Co., a Xerox company; copyright © 1975 by Xerox Corporation), November, 1975, p. 61.*

WHY DON'T YOU GET A HORSE, SAM ADAMS? (1974)

The cheekiness implied in the title [*Why Don't You Get a Horse, Sam Adams?*] is not quite borne out in the text of this story, which exploits the patriot's stubborn reluctance to learn to ride; but [Trina Schart] Hyman's seemingly effortless, deft lines and the engaging drollery reflected in her details amply extend Fritz' bridled humor. An afterword attests to the historical facts behind the amusing perspective, and the novel approach in the same vein as Fritz' earlier *And Then What Happened, Paul Revere?* . . . works well to raise this above the crowd of Bicentennial-related publications.

> The Booklist *(reprinted by permission of the American Library Association; copyright 1974 by the American Library Association), December 15, 1974, p. 425.*

It's hard to picture Sam Adams, preoccupied with the business of fomenting revolution, paying too much attention to the badgering of his conventional cousin and dashing John Hancock who want him to learn to ride horseback like a proper patriot. But the incident is true, even if it seems gimmicky compared to Fritz's more substantial burlesque of Paul Revere's rides. And Hyman's spirited illustrations buttress this slighter story with just the right combination of historical dash and broad humor.

> Kirkus Reviews *(copyright © 1975 The Kirkus Service, Inc.), January 1, 1975, p. 20.*

[*Why Don't You Get a Horse, Sam Adams?* presents] a piece of history far more entertaining and readable than most fiction. . . . As expertly as in *And Then What Happened, Paul Revere?*, [Jean Fritz] has humanized a figure of the Revolution: Adams emerges a marvelously funny and believable man. [Trina Schart Hyman's] illustrations play upon his foibles; they are, in fact, even more outrageously mocking than the text. A tour de force, for both author and illustrator.

> *Anita Silvey, in* The Horn Book Magazine

(copyright © 1975 by the Horn Book, Inc., Boston), February, 1975, p. 59.

OTHER CITATIONS

Leah Deland, in School Library Journal, *December, 1974, p. 36.*

Zena Sutherland, in Bulletin of the Center for Children's Books, *April, 1975, p. 129.*

G

GREENE, Bette   1934-

Bette Greene is an American author. (See also *Something About the Author*, Vol. 8.)

PHILIP HALL LIKES ME. I RECKON MAYBE (1974)

Anyone who has reached the saturation point on hearing songs of young love magnified and electronified and wailed by 8-year-old rock stars in white studded suits may think that the last thing in the world they would want to read would be a book on an 11-year-old's first crush. They'd be wrong. Because "Philip Hall Likes Me. I Reckon Maybe" is charming and fresh enough to waft away all strains of electronic luh-huh-uve and bring first love back to what it is —an intense, joy-despair relationship somewhere between friendship and romance that seems, at the time, eternal. . . .

This is a lighter, less dramatic book than Bette Greene's acclaimed "Summer of My German Soldier" and it leaves the reader with a more positive feeling. The Lambert family is loving and supportive; the father is a gentle tease, the mother, a positive tower of strength. "Life don't always be the way we want it to be," she tells Beth when an allergy makes her give up a beloved puppy, "Life be the way it is."

There are bad guys—a sleazy shopkeeper and a turkey thieving father and son, but mainly this is a book about good ordinary people and the maturation of a girl. The heroine grows during the year of the book, but it is a finely done, subtle growth—none of this, "Suddenly she was aware that . . .''

There is a nice sort of timelessness about the book too, perhaps because the author has caught something unchanging in young people, and I think the book will retain its warm appeal for a long while.

> *Betsy Byars, in* The New York Times Book Review (© *1974 by The New York Times Company; reprinted by permission), December 8, 1974, p. 8.*

[Bette Greene] has caught the warm atmosphere of rural Arkansas and the spunky personality of a black sixth-grade girl possessed by an affection for her class rival Philip Hall. The dialog is too nifty, and there are a number of incidents, such as Beth's solving the mystery of her father's disappearing turkeys, that seem transparently constructed to make the heroine appear clever and the other characters, especially adults, look slapstick-dumb. In spite of these bothersome elements, the light flavor, savory descriptions, and childlike scrapes—episodically strung together through various months of a year—make pleasant reading.

> *The Booklist (reprinted by permission of the American Library Association; copyright 1975 by the American Library Association), March 15, 1975, p. 760.*

[This] book has a curiously old-fashioned flavor—not because of setting but because of substance. The relaxed, humorous story tells of a year in the life of a bright and lively black girl whose only real problems resulted from her infatuation with the boy from the next farm. . . . With little tension or character development, the book is episodic and deals chiefly with Beth's minor trials and triumphs. . . . It must be pointed out that although the first-person narrative appears to contain a hybrid mixture of dialect and Black English, the characters seem black only superficially.

> *Ethel L. Heins, in* The Horn Book Magazine (copyright © *1975 by the Horn Book, Inc., Boston), April, 1975, p. 149.*

The writing style [in *Philip Hall Likes Me. I Reckon Maybe*] is deceptively casual, characterization and dialogue are sound, and the protagonist (who tells the story) a resourceful, lively girl whose charm and vitality come through clearly in [Charles Lilly's] deft, realistic illustrations.

> *Zena Sutherland, in* Bulletin of the Center for Children's Books (© *1975 by the University of Chicago; all rights reserved), April, 1975, p. 130.*

OTHER CITATIONS

Publishers' Weekly, *August 12, 1974, p. 58.*

Kirkus Reviews, *October 15, 1974, p. 1102.*

Susan Cooper, in The Christian Science Monitor, *November 6, 1974, p. 12.*

Rosalind K. Goddard, in School Library Journal, *February, 1975, p. 46.*

SUMMER OF MY GERMAN SOLDIER (1973)

Of course Patty's actions [in *Summer of My German Soldier*] aren't meant to seem that controversial to us, but the German's anglicized background and clear anti-Nazi sympathies (he's portrayed as a genteel idealist who can no longer tolerate confinement even in the safety of the POW camp) make her deed almost boringly unambiguous. And Patty's relationship with the servant Ruth—who loves Patty, teaches her pride, and finally loses her job by defending her—seems so much truer and more important than the thin, escapist fantasies she spins around thin, escapist Anton that Patty's rebellion seems unintentionally pathetic and misdirected. Mr. Bergen, unloving and bitter about not being loved, and Mrs. Bergen, still the spoiled daughter even in middle age, are a good deal more substantial than the usual set of unsympathetic parents, and the mixture of fear, resentment, and regression that their rejection inspires in Patty is accurately measured. If only the German soldier were equally human, his presence in Arkansas might seem less incongruous.

> *Kirkus Reviews (copyright © 1973 The Kirkus Service, Inc.), October 15, 1973, p. 1170.*

In some ways Bette Greene's material [in "Summer of My German Soldier"] is not promising. Her characters could easily have come out of an ordinary movie melodrama. Along with the loving black maid, there's a nasty minister's wife, a hard-boiled girl reporter, a bigoted business man, a town gossip, a spoiled-brat little sister and a chicken-soup grandma. The incidents, the kind of suspense and the tears evoked, all skirt cliché as well; and the author's moral values might too; yet the writing is fresh. . . .

The reason for the book's freshness . . . is its fineness, in the literal sense. The stuff of it is fine, like the texture of Patty herself. The detail is too meaningfully specific, too highly selective to be trite. Armed with earned moral insight, Mrs. Greene sneaks past our conditioned reflexes satisfyingly often.

> *Peter Sourian, in* The New York Times Book Review *(© 1973 by The New York Times Company; reprinted by permission), November 4, 1973, p. 29.*

Because it so consistently maintains a twelve-year-old's perspective, [*Summer of My German Soldier*], unlike much of current, realistic fiction for young people, is more than a mirror of reality. It offers no panaceas for loneliness, no easy solutions for problems; and this verisimilitude extends to the depiction of the minor characters as well. . . . [This is a] moving first novel, unforgettable because of the genuine emotion it evokes.

> *Mary M. Burns, in* The Horn Book Magazine *(copyright © 1974 by the Horn Book, Inc., Boston), February, 1974, p. 56.*

When [the German prisoner-of-war] escapes, Patty and her only friend, the negro servant Ruth, befriend him. But the prisoner is pursued and killed, and neither the sensible Ruth nor a friendly reporter can save Patty from the reformatory. In the same way, the attractive qualities of these two characters are not sufficient to dispel the universally unhappy atmosphere of this book. Patty has many enemies, and suffers much abuse, but unfortunately she fails to become a sympathetic character.

> *The Junior Bookshelf, February, 1975, p. 62.*

It would be an act of sheer ignorance to assert that children's books predicate only a world of escapist fantasy and cosiness. War books, for instance, concentrate too much now on how people really feel for this assertion to hold. The people who get caught up in war are points of focus, and human and moral issues are constantly implied by what they do and how they react. It is a way of making war real and at the same time of making it a subject of comment—most of these books tacitly disapprove of war. The growth of World War Two stories for young people reflects today's concern for the problems spinning off from Vietnam, the Middle East, racism and so on . . . *Summer of my German Soldier* is a courageous but patchy example of how things like this have influenced writing for young people. . . . The story is rather deliberately structured to bring in rather 'staged' conversations, but the issues raised, and the characters who raise them, are proof of the book's integrity.

> *C. S. Hannabuss, in* Children's Book Review *(© 1975 Five Owls Press Ltd.; all rights reserved), Spring, 1975, p. 19.*

OTHER CITATIONS

Publishers' Weekly, *August 27, 1973, p. 280.*

H

HOGROGIAN, Nonny 1932-

Nonny Hogrogian, an American author-illustrator, was awarded the Caldecott Medal in 1966 for *Always Room for One More* and in 1972 for *One Fine Day*. (See also *Contemporary Authors*, Vols. 45-48, and *Something About the Author*, Vol. 7.)

APPLES (1972)

On another truly *Fine Day*, this one enjoyed in an Impressionistic sunlit meadow (it's all done with green and blue and yellow pastelled lines), a wordless cycle of apples begins and ends with a mustached peddler's two-wheeled cart. . . . [*Apples* is a] visual pleasure, and it's worth a thousand wordy ecology lessons.

> Kirkus Reviews *(copyright © 1972 The Kirkus Service, Inc.), May 15, 1972, p. 574.*

The jacket-copy describes this as "the story of life" of an apple orchard, but unfortunately it's a dull story. Full-page, pale crayon drawings minus text merely show how a succession of apple cores cast off by a boy, rabbit, crow, girl, hen, pig, donkey, dog and sheep grow into apple trees. With each new double-page spread the number of trees increases, converting bare ground into a thriving apple orchard. Some of the spreads are unified by showing the previous apple eater disappear off the right-hand page while his or her successor walks along on the left. But this is done inconsistently and, furthermore, the apple trees pictured look like spindly bushes. All in all, *Apples* is bland, unsubstantial fare.

> Diane Gersoni Stavn, in School Library Journal *(reprinted from* School Library Journal, *September, 1972, published by R. R. Bowker Co., a Xerox company; copyright © 1972 by Xerox Corporation), September, 1972, p. 66.*

Told without words, [*Apples*] presents delightful movement and color. The tender greens and blues make a charming background for the steady progression of characters that move with the rhythm of a piece of music. One must not look too closely for a story line because the story is not so important as is the experience of viewing the book. The elements of realism in the portrayal of the characters, of idealism in the setting, and of magic are blended in a harmonious and joyous whole.

> Beryl Robinson, in The Horn Book Magazine *(copyright © 1972 by The Horn Book, Inc., Boston), October, 1972, p. 457.*

[*Apples* is an] attractive picture book without words, the plot slight but clear. . . . There is no indication of seasonal change and time passing; in the end the apple vendor (who was seen at the beginning) is picking apples and filling his cart. He goes off—end of story. Not imposing, but pleasant.

> Zena Sutherland, in Bulletin of the Center for Children's Books *(© 1972 by the University of Chicago; all rights reserved), October, 1972, p. 27.*

OTHER CITATIONS

The Booklist, *October 1, 1972, p. 148.*

BILLY GOAT AND HIS WELL-FED FRIENDS (1972)

Nonny Hogrogian's softly shaded pictures of [*Billy Goat and His Well-Fed Friends*] have undeniable charm (though by now her economically expressive way with eyes and mouths comes as no surprise), but why not take on the Grimms' "Traveling Musicians" and be done with it?

> Kirkus Reviews *(copyright © 1972 The Kirkus Service, Inc.), October 1, 1972, p. 1142.*

[*Billy Goat and His Well-Fed Friends* is an] interesting, entertaining book about animal friends and the way in which they faced up to their dilemma together. . . . This is a simple, repetitive story which the youngest children will just love to read and repeat. The illustrations are both beautiful and clear, and easily understood.

> Sister Agnes McAdam, in Children's Book Review *(© 1974 Five Owls Press Ltd.; all rights reserved), Summer, 1974, p. 60.*

OTHER CITATIONS

Carol Chatfield, in School Library Journal, *December, 1972, p. 70.*

The Booklist, *April 15, 1973, p. 812.*

THE HERMIT AND HARRY AND ME (1972)

The hermit crouches and the unmistakably Hogrogian children (they're becoming a sort of trademark that endures through varying media and methods) frolic in crisp black line sketches that set a few spots of bright color—mainly the girl's yellow dress and Harry's orange shirt—against a neutral background. A pointless, even abortive outing, but scenic as usual.

> Kirkus Reviews *(copyright © 1972 The Kirkus Service, Inc.), October 15, 1972, p. 1185.*

"The Hermit and Harry and Me" . . . [is] a parable about the unaccountability of making friends. . . . Sprightly drawings are highlighted in cheery yellow and orange, with just a pinch of olive drab and brown for the dour hermit's garb. The difficulty is that Miss Hogrogian's message is at once so sophisticated and *sotto voce* a young child is likely to miss the point.

> *Selma Lanes, in* The New York Times Book Review *(© 1972 by The New York Times Company; reprinted by permission), November 5, 1972 (Part 2), p. 44.*

OTHER CITATIONS

Joanne E. Bernstein, in School Library Journal, *January, 1973, p. 61.*

ONE FINE DAY (1971)

Happy . . . is precisely the word that comes to mind when considering artist Nonny Hogrogian's new book, "One Fine Day". . . . Yet, pleasing as it is to contemplate this illustrator's cool competence, there is nary a visual surprise in the familiar folktale of the sly fox who loses his tail to an angry old woman's carving knife. Though we can almost feel the homespun of the old heroine's dress and hear the metallic clang of her emptied milk can, there is no lingering aftertaste that makes us either want to hear or see it all over again. It is simply another competently executed picture book.

> *Selma G. Lanes, in* The New York Times Book Review *(© 1971 by The New York Times Company; reprinted by permission), September 19, 1971, p. 8.*

[This] picture story book based on an Armenian folk tale is illustrated with bold, simple compositions in soft colors, the pictures echoing the humor of the story. Nicely told, the tale uses a familiar cumulative pattern. . . . [*One Fine Day* is a] charming picture book that is just right for reading aloud to small children, the scale of the pictures also appropriate for group use.

> *Zena Sutherland, in* Bulletin of the Center for Children's Books *(© 1971 by the University of Chicago; all rights reserved), November, 1971, pp. 44-5.*

Using her own variant of a familiar theme, the author sends the fox from old woman, to cow, to meadow, to water, to maiden, to peddler, to hen, to miller, and back again [in *One Fine Day*]—a journey singularly uneventful but beautifully illustrated. The pictures are marked by skillful characterizations and a fine sense of design.

> *Sidney D. Long, in* The Horn Book Magazine *(copyright © 1971 by The Horn Book, Inc., Boston), December, 1971, p. 604.*

[*One Fine Day* is a] book that has won golden opinions in America, and comes to [England] with a gold medal stuck on its front to prove it. The story, which is advertised in the blurb as an Armenian folk-tale, is very much on the lines of 'The Old Woman and Her Pig'. . . .

Stories . . ., composed of a succession of brief incidents, are naturally suited to presentation in picturebook form and Nonny Hogrogian has availed herself of the chance to create a series of handsomely designed double-page spreads in clear, warm colours—most of the pictures centring upon the altogether abashed and humbled orange fox.

The attractiveness of these pages, however, is only superficial and closer acquaintance breeds serious doubts about the praise that has been lavished on the book in America. In the first place, the text of the story is very stiff and ungainly, compared with the lively rhythms of its English equivalent. (Just try getting some expression into: 'So the fox dried his tears and went to find the cow. "Dear cow," he begged, "please give me some milk so I can give it to the old woman so she will sew my tail in place." The cow replied, "I'll give you some milk if you bring me some grass."' And so on.)

In the second place, Miss Hogrogian's pictures, for all the care and skill of their composition, neither cumulate with the story nor at any one time bring verve to the plodding words. They are cool, static productions, each planned with thoroughness, but finally adding up to a sum considerably less than the parts.

Miss Hogrogian manages some nice facial expressions, but these do not amount by any means to narrative dynamics and even the subtleties (the fox disappearing off the page at the beginning and end of the book, the pedlar almost pulling his donkey from one page to the next) have a tired air. For all the gilt of its medal, the book is finally a rather beautiful bore.

> *Brian W. Alderson, in* Children's Book Review *(© 1973 Five Owls Press Ltd.; all rights reserved), February, 1973, p. 8.*

OTHER CITATIONS

Publishers' Weekly, *September 27, 1971, p. 67.*

The Booklist, *October 1, 1971, pp. 150, 152.*

David Winder, in The Christian Science Monitor, *November 11, 1971, p. B2.*

ONE I LOVE, TWO I LOVE: AND OTHER LOVING MOTHER GOOSE RHYMES (1972)

If you think that a collection of 17 rhymes about love and related pursuits must be all sweet tenderness, you don't remember your Mother Goose; this wise old bird is well aware that the poetry is more in the chase and the cheating than the happy ever after. . . . Neither the dreams nor the disillusionment, though, are taken with undue sobriety, and the sly and bashful poses of Ms. Hogrogian's beautifully unpretty milkmaids and goose girls and dungareed farm boys are framed in spring-colored country scenes that give even the needles and pins a compensating loveliness.

> Kirkus Reviews *(copyright © 1972 The Kirkus Service, Inc.), May 15, 1972, p. 574.*

Slight, sweet, and sunny, [this is] a small book that comprises over a dozen rhymes that have to do with love, marriage, kissing, courting, etc. Some of the choices ("Daffy-down-dilly" for example) seem only remotely related to the scope indicated by the title and subtitle, but the attractive drawings add appeal to the durable verses, so there seems little for complaint.

> *Zena Sutherland, in* Bulletin of the Center for Children's Books *(© 1972 by the University of Chicago; all rights reserved), July-August, 1972, p. 174.*

OTHER CITATIONS

Ethel L. Heins, in The Horn Book Magazine, *August, 1972, p. 362.*

THE RENOWNED HISTORY OF LITTLE RED RIDING HOOD (1967)

In *The Renowned History of Little Red Riding-Hood*, Nonny Hogrogian has chosen to illustrate, in a Pennsylvania Dutch setting, a sprightly, early rendition of the tale. On the face of it, her little book would seem to be a quaint and benign confection: sweet, singsong rhymes; pages strewn with butterflies and wildflowers; a roguish but non-scary wolf; and a dear, smug waif for heroine. Its closing lines, however, pack a mean wallop: this wolf wolfs down both heroine and grandma with nary a woodsman to raise an axe. Its moral, of course—once the small listener emerges from shock—should put child molesters out of business. ("This story demonstrates that children discreet/ Should never confide in each stranger they meet.") It is stern stuff, however, for effete contemporary children unaccustomed to playing for keeps with storybook wolves.

> *Selma G. Lanes, in* Book World *(© The Washington Post), November 5, 1967 (Part 2), p. 1.*

[Nonny Hogrogian] has chosen to illustrate as a charming tiny picture book an early nineteenth-century rhyming version of the classic nursery tale found in the rare book collection of Elisabeth Ball. Deft pen lines overlaid with clear red, or with pale pink, lavender, and green wash interpret with ample emotion and humor a splendidly wicked wolf and the "poor innocent child". . . . A treasure for the youngest and the oldest of bibliophiles.

> *Virginia Haviland, in* The Horn Book Magazine *(copyright © 1967, by The Horn Book, Inc., Boston), December, 1967, pp. 742-43.*

[Hogrogian's] new illustrations for this miniature book . . .

will enhance its special appeal to children's book fanciers who are likely to make a more receptive audience for it than today's children. The text, taken from a book first published in London in 1808, consists of moralistic rhymes ("There dwelt in a cottage which stood on the green,/As sweet a creature as ever was seen") which spell out "Little Red Riding Hood's tragical fate"—a fate which has, nevertheless, been enlivened with comic elements in the new drawings.

> *Aileen O'Brien Murphy, in* School Library Journal *(reprinted from* School Library Journal, *December, 1967, published by R. R. Bowker Co., a Xerox company; copyright © 1967 by Xerox Corporation), December, 1967, pp. 63-4.*

OTHER CITATIONS

Kirkus Service, *September 1, 1967, p. 1040.*

The Booklist and Subscription Books Bulletin, *February 1, 1968, p. 642.*

Zena Sutherland, in Bulletin of the Center for Children's Books, *April, 1968, p. 128.*

ROOSTER BROTHER (1974)

In design (though the landscape and media differ) the double-page pictures [in *Rooster Brother*] sometimes resemble the scenes in *Apples* (1972) and the supple, smirking figures resemble countless previous Hogrogian peasants, giving the whole a disappointingly familiar look. In themselves though her poppy fields are as pretty as ever, her widow and lad as appealing as they have to be, and those gloating, mustachioed robbers look properly roguish—and properly foolish in the baths after Rooster Brother steals their clothes.

> Kirkus Reviews *(copyright © 1974 The Kirkus Service, Inc.), April 1, 1974, p. 360.*

Rooster Brother is an American folk-tale, told and illustrated with a simplicity and directness which should make it ideal for reading aloud . . . As [Melkon] tricks each [robber] in turn, he leaves a note, 'Brother Rooster was here, He will strike again', and the repetition of this gives a satisfying pattern to the story . . . There is clarity, detail, and a nice sense of humour in the illustrations . . . and they have been integrated with the text to make a very well designed whole.

> *John A. Cunliffe, in* Children's Book Review *(© 1975 Five Owls Press Ltd.; all rights reserved), Spring, 1975, pp. 28-9.*

OTHER CITATIONS

Publishers' Weekly, *April 22, 1974, p. 75.*

Sada Fretz, in Book World, *May 19, 1974, p. 4.*

Margery Fisher, in her Growing Point, *May, 1975, pp. 2647-48.*

THE THIRTEEN DAYS OF YULE (1968)

The Thirteen Days of Yule . . ., a Scottish version of the

"Twelve Days of Christmas" carol, is the slim textual accompaniment to bright, graceful watercolor illustrations by Nonny Hogrogian. . . . No music is included, and the verse won't fit the traditional tune, so there's little point to it all except those happy pictures by a popular illustrator in a book sized (8″ x 8″) for individual lap reading.

> *Margaret A. Dorsey, in* School Library Journal *(reprinted from* School Library Journal, *October, 1968, published by R. R. Bowker Co., a Xerox company; copyright ©* 1968 by Xerox Corporation), *October, 1968, p. 177.*

Everything [in "The Thirteen Days of Yule"] is drawn with restrained delicacy, colorfully and with a kind of tentative merriment. It's very nice but also like some luxuriously impractical gift that one doesn't quite know what to do with.

> *George A. Woods, in* The New York Times Book Review *(© 1968 by The New York Times Company; reprinted by permission), December 1, 1968, p. 74.*

OTHER CITATIONS

Zena Sutherland, in Bulletin of the Center for Children's Books, *December, 1968, p. 60.*

J

JANSSON, Tove 1914-

A Finnish artist, playwright, illustrator, and author for both adults and children, Tove Jansson is best known to children as the creator of the Moomins. She received the 1966 Hans Christian Andersen Award. (See also *Contemporary Authors*, Vols. 17-18, and *Something About the Author*, Vol. 3.)

GENERAL COMMENTARY

Here we have something very subtle, nonsense stories full of melancholy wisdom and terror, neither wholly fantasy nor wholly humour. It is impossible not to compare these stories with the work of Edward Lear and Lewis Carroll. Who would not see cousinly resemblances between the Hattifatteners and the Dong with a Luminous Nose, or between the Moomin parents and Mr and Mrs Discobolos, or between Snufkin and some of Lewis Carroll's touching small animals? The resemblance in each case is not one of feature or idiom; it lies in the mature atmosphere of the stories, the sunny sky of comedy in which there is always drifting a distant cloud of sadness and unease. . . .

Tove Jansson has done as Lewis Carroll and Lear did. She has corkscrewed her way down into a world of childhood where the unlikely is readily accepted, where incongruity seems entirely natural and at the same time can be comic. But she has kept her adult wits about her, so that we are always aware of shape and logic and order in an unusual world. As with *Alice in Wonderland*, these Moomin books are folk lore and fantasy to young children, humour to older boys and girls, and poetry to all. For what binds the elements of nonsense, absurdity, satire and wit together is an underlying note of seriousness, of speculation, an implication of the uncertainty of human wishes and human knowledge.

> *Margery Fisher, in her* Intent Upon Reading: A Critical Appraisal of Modern Fiction for Children *(copyright © 1961 by Margery Fisher), Hodder & Stoughton Children's Books (formerly Brockhampton Press), 1961, pp. 160-62 (published in America by Franklin Watts, 1962).*

Tove Jansson is one of the legend-makers. To impose on the world a new concept, a dimension developed in every detail, is one of the most precious achievements of a writer. In our day Mary Norton has brought it off, and Tove Jansson, and any other? I think not.

This is not to make for Tove Jansson any extravagant claims. Though a master creator of legend, she is a rather muddled story-teller. Though an inventor of memorable types, she seems sometimes to lack the skill, or the will, to explore her characters in depth. Perhaps too for some readers the pervading atmosphere of her writing may seem over-sweet. Writers who have abundantly the qualities she lacks stand nevertheless on the brink of oblivion. The Moomins have a part in the culture of our century. (pp. 353-54)

Tove Jansson's invention is so convincing that her books suffer a little from the muddle of real life. It is all here in glorious bounty, but without the benefit of selectivity. Who is the hero of these stories—Moomintroll? As in real life, there are no heroes, only people. The writer's spotlight wanders about, picking out a Moomin or a Hemulen or a Mymble, and then passes on. Those who like a tidy classification of characters are disappointed. The others are duly grateful for this prodigality of riches. (p. 355)

Snufkin is perhaps the most fully developed of Tove Jansson's creations. He appears first just as a wanderer who avoids ties. . . . He remains consistently in character, but his love of life and difficulty and loneliness becomes deeper and more convincing. . . . In the book of short stories, *Tales from Moomin Valley*, he has a most effective chapter to himself, "The Spring Tune," which is perhaps the finest single piece which Tove Jansson has yet written. . . . (pp. 355-56)

How seriously one takes these essentially comic books. In fact, although there are some exquisitely funny episodes . . . for the most part Tove Jansson's humour is of the kind which produces a warm glow rather than a loud laugh. Part of its secret is incongruity, the association of human situations and emotions with fantastic non-human characters; still more it comes from a comic view of life, a humour not of situation or even of character but of being. (p. 356)

The warm, kindly, generous world of Tove Jansson is a world like our own, yet strange, a world in which exciting things happen, perils are faced bravely, and at the end of every adventure there await Moominhouse and the calm constant loving kindness of Moominmamma. And always there is the promise of another day. (p. 357)

Marcus Crouch, "Moomin-Sagas," in The
Junior Bookshelf, *December, 1966, pp. 353-
57.*

The Moomins are splendid little creatures. . . . But for all
the crazy things they get up to, these merry little fellows
have an inner wholesomeness, and they have greatly enriched the world of fantasy. They distinguish themselves
from the traditional dwarfs of Scandinavian fairy stories,
the trolls, by their origin, which lies neither in reality nor in
tradition but, if I mistake not, is solely the highly successful
product of a young poetess's imagination. Her books are
somewhat less intellectual and witty than English books in
this category, but the Moomins have an appeal to even the
least sophisticated child.

Bettina Hürlimann, in her Three Centuries
of Children's Books in Europe, *translated
and edited by Brian W. Alderson (English
translation © Oxford University Press
1967), Oxford University Press, 1967, p. 381.*

After reading three Moomin books and scanning two others, all I can tell you is that Moomins are small, cheerful,
imaginary creatures who resemble hippos; that their names
are Moominpappa, Moominmamma and Moomintroll; and
that they live in the Moominvalley of Moominland. I can
further relate that the stories for ages 9 to 12 have copious
pictures and seem to be well translated. But after this, reportage fails, for the more one reads about Moomins the
less one knows about them.

As chapter after chapter unfolds (and book after book), the
Moomins wander about their mythical country, meet other
imaginary creatures with names like the Groke, and Mud-
dler and the Snork Maiden, exchange gay little thoughts,
and generally enjoy life—but since we have never learned
what Moomins are in the first place, or where they came
from, or what their purpose is in the vast scheme of things,
our empathy is frail. An added burden is that the stories
have no real beginning or end, so that reading them in sequence is as baffling as reading them out of sequence (or
upside down, for that matter). Some vital links have been
lost, and these seem to be plot, character, theme and
common sense. As a creature says in "The Exploits of
Moominpappa": "I'm often having ideas that I can't explain."

The real trouble, I'm afraid, is that this fantasy-world of
Moomins and Moominlore is so delightful to the author that
she has forgotten to make it clear to the reader. Indeed, she
seems to be inventing her books from page to page and
loving every minute of it. Far be it from me to deny Miss
Jansson this pleasure in Moomins—they are, after all, little
and harmless—but her obvious and lengthy enjoyment of
them has somewhat dampened my own. I might even say
that it has given me a case of Moomincholy.

Barbara Wersba, in The New York Times
Book Review *(© 1968 by The New York
Times Company; reprinted by permission),
May 5, 1968 (Part 2), p. 43.*

Tove Jansson has made [a unique contribution] to children's literature. Thanks to brilliant translators there are no
problems of communication. The [Moomin] books seem
strange but not alien. They speak directly to children—and

not children alone—who come from many different environments. Although they make gentle fun of human follies
and foibles they are not satirical and are unaffected by
fashion. In them Miss Jansson has created one of the most
convincing and most completely realized of imagined
worlds. The reader is impelled into involvement with these
queer creatures and their society, a society which has certain parallels with the world of humans but which is not
merely a distorted image of reality. The strength of the
books is largely in their creativity, their concept of a world
and its inhabitants; it is reinforced by phychological penetration, by the gnomic wisdom of the comment, and by
admirable story-telling. What is more the books are fun.
Miss Jansson clothes the undoubted seriousness of her vision in rich wit and humour.

The Times Literary Supplement *(© Times
Newspapers Ltd., 1971), October 22, 1971,
p. 1315.*

Miss Jansson's instinct is for the episode; indeed some of
her very best work—in *Tales from Moominvalley* (1963)—
is in short-story form, capturing briefly and unforgettably
the essence of such situations as The Case of the Invisible
Child. (The child faded away in face of hostility and indifference, but became visible when angry or amused.) Most
of the books are strings of stories, highly amusing and consistent in sustaining the atmosphere of a strange land, but
not aspiring to the novel's complex structure or evolutionary narrative.

Marcus Crouch, in his The Nesbit Tradition: The Children's Novel in England 1945-
1970 *(© Marcus Crouch 1972), Ernest
Benn, 1972, pp. 136-37.*

In most of the Moomin books, the mainspring of events is
some kind of disaster. The Moomin world is afflicted by
floods, falling rockets, volcanic eruptions, and hurricanes.
But these adversities serve only to heighten what is most
important of all: liberty, friendship, and love. Tove Jansson
writes about relationships to possessions and to a traditional way-of-life, about loneliness, fear, and security. The
Moomin books depict the insecurity of contemporary man;
at the same time, they show a genuine way to live. The
most important thing is to cut loose from acquisitiveness
and to love one's neighbor without expecting anything in
return. Tove Jansson's writing is very much concerned
with social relations and the importance of people coming
to terms with each other. Although she had a predilection
for idyllic family relations in her writing, the idyll is not
hermetically sealed off from the outside world; for there is
always lurking an unidentified menace which can obliterate
everything in the twinkling of an eye. Nothing on this earth
can endure, and inward calm is attainable if one does not
clutch at transient things. Tootick, one of the key figures in
Moominland Midwinter (1957) . . ., says: "Everything is so
uncertain and that is what I find so reassuring."

Mary Orvig, in The Horn Book Magazine
*(copyright © 1973 by The Horn Book, Inc.,
Boston), February, 1973, p. 20.*

(The) Moomins are an expandable family. . . . The hospi-
tality of Moomin-valley comes partly from Moomintroll's
gregarious nature and partly from the warmth and inner cer-

tainty that bring so many lost, lonely or confused individuals to seek reassurance from Moominmamma.

Fantastic and comic as these invented creatures are, they express certain basic ideas about human behaviour—people's responsibility to one another, the right to be private and so on. Behind the original, entrancing world of the Moomins one can also see the shadows of a Scandinavian landscape and folk lore. It seems that the Moomins have evolved from a race of trolls but now, instead of being hairy, nocturnal and hostile, they are tubby, benevolent, sunshine-loving animals, not unlike small hippopotamuses. . . . The friends and neighbours of the Moomins are as diverse and original as they are themselves.

Moomintroll's eager curiosity initiates most of the action in the books. He sets out to find the observatory where he may find out about the comet which threatens danger to the valley; he is lost and found again in a flood which introduces the Moomins to the astonishing world of the theatre; he experiments dangerously with the Hobgoblin's hat; he tries to make friends with the silent Groke, who freezes everything she touches. Meanwhile his father, an erratic and self-absorbed character, writes (and reads aloud) his Memoirs, and tries to find a new life on a lighthouse island where he has to face his own deficiencies. With grace, elegance and wit Tove Jansson carries us through her stories into odd corners of life and makes pertinent comments on humanity. We have it on her own authority that the characters are based on her own family and friends; they are emphatically not human types. Fillyjonk is one particular obsessed housewife, with her wayward view of life; Little My is not just everybody's naughty little sister, but a unique, crabby, critical, deflatory child; the Hemulens are all bureaucratic and bossy, but each in different ways and with different degrees of melancholy; Snufkin is not 'the artist' but an individual whose music is made in solitude but nourished by his unpossessive friendships. Through these characters Tove Jansson has taken a wry, sympathetic and very straight look at the deepest and most personal philosophies of people in a community.

> *Margery Fisher, in her* Who's Who in Children's Books: A Treasury of the Familiar Characters of Childhood *(copyright © 1975 by Margery Fisher; reprinted by permission of Holt, Rinehart and Winston), Holt, Rinehart and Winston, 1975, pp. 234, 238.*

COMET IN MOOMINLAND (1946; translation published in America, 1968)

Moomintroll, Sniff and the Snork Maiden appear again in a story which has fun, excitement and charming fantasy, and in which the drawings are as fresh and delightful as the text.

> The Times Literary Supplement, *November 23, 1951, p. iv.*

The journey [in *Comet in Moominland*] seems pointless (though imaginative in the Jansson manner) especially after the quick letdown end (the comet misses the earth, all goes back to normal) and the ingenuous childishness of the bestiary is beginning to get cute. Moomin addicts won't complain though and this episode is more suited to children than [*Moominpappa at Sea*] was.

> Kirkus Service *(copyright © 1967 Virginia Kirkus' Service, Inc.), December 15, 1967, p. 1472.*

OTHER CITATIONS

Carolyn F. Ruffin, in The Christian Science Monitor, *May 2, 1968, p. B5.*

Zena Sutherland, in Saturday Review, *May 11, 1968, pp. 38-9.*

Digby B. Whitman, in Book World, *June 2, 1968, p. 20.*

THE EXPLOITS OF MOOMINPAPPA (1950; translation published in America, 1966)

Moominpappa's style [in *The Exploits of Moominpappa*] is fresh and agreeably modest, although he is not afraid of fine writing. His adventures are entirely convincing though completely impossible: only the Autocrat's Garden Party and the Island Ghost episodes seem slightly to lack the true Moomin spontaneity. Surely no one person has ever possessed so wide a variety of curious friends, and it was a helpful idea to include a gallery of their portraits as an appendix to the present work.

> The Times Literary Supplement, *November 28, 1952, p. viii.*

The Moomin world has, in its characters, the same sort of set of individualists that are in the [A. A.] Milne books; the plot is more complicated and the writing—especially the dialogue—far more sophisticated. Although older readers may enjoy subtler references that the younger ones miss, there is enough humor even at the simplest level to amuse any age.

> *Zena Sutherland, in* Bulletin of the Center for Children's Books *(copyright 1967 by the University of Chicago; all rights reserved), June, 1967, p. 154.*

OTHER CITATIONS

Virginia Kirkus' Service, *November 15, 1966, p. 1180.*

FINN FAMILY MOOMINTROLL (1949; translation published in America, 1965)

Finn Family Moomintroll [once published in the U.S. as *The Happy Moomins*, 1952] . . . is still the best introduction to this wonderful little world. It establishes the atmosphere of the Moominhouse, a kind of innocent Abbey of Theleme, where everyone does what he likes, and because this is a world of danger but without malice, harms no one else. . . . The narrative in this . . . book is weak and episodic, but what episodes! Through the story drift an assortment of minor characters, all memorable and all liable to reappear, in this or later books, as players of major roles. *Finn Family Moomintroll* introduces . . . the most haunting, and persistent, of the Moomin villains who leaven the prevailing sweetness of the stories. This is the Groke, whom "you felt . . . was terribly evil and would wait for ever." The Groke comes back from time to time throughout the books, casting her spell of dread and freezing the ground where she sits. Yet even the Groke is lonely rather than wicked. . . . (p. 354)

Marcus Crouch, "Moomin-Sagas," in The Junior Bookshelf, December, 1966, pp. 353-57.

OTHER CITATIONS

The Times Literary Supplement, November 17, 1950, p. xii.

Bulletin of the Center for Children's Books, June, 1952, p. 74.

Alison Lurie, in The New York Review of Books, December 9, 1965, p. 38.

MOOMINPAPPA AT SEA (1965; translation published in America, 1967)

The Moomins have grown up: their lighthouse and their island in this episode are the property of adults as well as children.... A psychological drama with an allegorical level, this chapter of the Moomin story cedes Moomin territory to the adults without totally dispossessing the children.

Kirkus Service (copyright © 1967 Virginia Kirkus' Service, Inc.), January 15, 1967, p. 58.

This is a somewhat more somber book than the previous stories about Moomins and their friends, since the isolated setting is forbidding in itself and since it imposes an absence of the daft and cheerful assortment that usually surround the family.... The intricate nonsense and the wholly-created Moomin characters are entertaining as always, but the mood of the setting and the narrow focus on a few characters make the story seem rather slow-moving.

Zena Sutherland, in Bulletin of the Center for Children's Books (copyright 1967 by the University of Chicago; all rights reserved), September, 1967, pp. 9-10.

OTHER CITATIONS

The Junior Bookshelf, June, 1966, pp. 173-74.

Virginia Haviland, in The Horn Book Magazine, June, 1967, pp. 341-42.

Lavinia Marina Learmont, in Books and Bookmen, March, 1974, p. 100.

MOOMINSUMMER MADNESS (1954; translation published in America, 1961)

An entirely new world full of cheery dauntless little creatures whose names slide pleasantly off the tongue has been captured by [Tove] Jansson—though more successfully in her drawings than in her writings. The Moomins look like appealing elephants with tiny bodies, act like naïve human beings.... ["Moominsummer Madness"] badly needs a down-to-earth mortal to measure things by—to do the job Alice did in "Alice in Wonderland" or Dorothy in "The Wizard of Oz." As it is, a bothersome, nightmare quality is never quite dispelled. And in any case, references beyond their experience will probably sap the interest of the 7-year-old readers who might like the idea. This is sad, for in a different setting it could be exhilarating to meet Snufkin [and the other Moomin characters].

Pamela Marsh, in The New York Times Book Review (© 1961 by The New York Times Company; reprinted by permission), May 14, 1961 (Part 2), p. 28.

Moominsummer Madness is rich in those felicities of expression which make the Moomin books seem full of quotations. Its fantasy is presented in a characteristically matter-of-fact fashion and supported by apt, if improbable, circumstantial detail. Snufkin and Miss Jansson know that when sowing Hattifattener seed one scatters sparsely "so that the Hattifatteners wouldn't have their paws entangled when they came up". All the Moomin books have this in common that, however comical and absurd the situation and the action, the author takes them quite seriously and demands no less of her readers. This is not difficult to grant her because in these books tenderness and robust good sense are matched to produce an admirable balanced community.

The Times Literary Supplement (© Times Newspapers Ltd., 1971), October 22, 1971, p. 1316.

MOOMINVALLEY IN NOVEMBER (1970; translation published in America, 1971)

[This] ... Moomin book is the strangest of all and perhaps the least immediately accessible. This is partly a case of Hamlet without the Prince; it is more a matter of plot-manipulation. Where Tove Jansson excels is in the interplay of character. She is a master of funny and eloquent dialogue which advances the action and establishes character. In Moominvalley in November a quarter of the book passes before the company is assembled. This introductory sequence is brilliantly done; the description of Fillyjonk's nearly fatal mishap during her autumn cleaning is detailed and tense. The reader nevertheless may feel that he is kept too long waiting for the purpose of the story to reveal itself. Much of the conflict is of an inner kind; the story is a matter of clashing personalities, not events. It is possibly the cleverest of the Moomin books; for the same reason it may prove to have the narrowest appeal.

The Times Literary Supplement (© Times Newspapers Ltd., 1971), October 22, 1971, p. 1315.

[Moominvalley in November is tightly] threaded to earlier stories of Moominvalley.... Drenched in atmosphere—November rains and lengthening nights, mists and cold, smells and sounds of the sea—the book traces the course of each character and then brings them together at the Moomins' house. The highly subtle narrative is frequently pure poetry, and among the Moominvalley volumes it is perhaps the most reflective and least direct for children.... The author's drawings, on almost every page, contribute their usual droll humor and concreteness to the singular creatures.

Virginia Haviland, in The Horn Book Magazine (copyright © 1972 by The Horn Book, Inc., Boston), February, 1972, pp. 48-9.

Although the engaging Jansson characters [in *Moominvalley in November*] may be more appreciated by established Moomin fans who know their peculiarities, the querulous Fillyjonk and timorous Toft, Snufkin the loner and Mymble the self-satisfied, forgetful old Grandpa-Grumble and the take-charge Hemulen are a delightful sextet as they meet in the vacant Moominvalley home and adjust to the absence of their hosts and to each other. As always, the writing is deft and funny, the imaginary and imaginative creatures endearing.

> *Zena Sutherland, in* Bulletin of the Center for Children's Books (© *1972 by the University of Chicago; all rights reserved), March, 1972, p. 108.*

OTHER CITATIONS

Catherine Storr, in New Statesman, *November 12, 1971, p. 664.*

THE SUMMER BOOK (1975)

[*The Summer Book* is a] memorably vivid, though somewhat philosophical portrait of a small girl and her grandmother.... The prose is musical, filling the mind with many tones and hues of the tiny Finnish island's landscape; wit is balanced with heavy, scattered symbolism derived from the seaside setting, and an aura of mystery is maintained throughout. The two beguiling personalities who move about—sometimes colliding harshly, other times co-existing warmly—are captivating and recognizably universal in their imperfections. As imaginative as the author's invigorating Moomin fantasies, this will find a small, mature, and sensitive audience.

> The Booklist (*reprinted by permission of the American Library Association; copyright 1975 by the American Library Association), February 1, 1975, pp. 570-71.*

Far removed from the author's *Moomin* books, this is a slow-paced, episodic, and sharply observed account of life on a small Scandinavian island as experienced by young Sophia, her grandmother, and her father.... Jansson does present—magnificiently—an elderly woman who snaps and grouses yet lives in the present and sees all around her with acid clarity. But this viewpoint, together with the lack of plot, severly limits the book's appeal to young readers.

> *Margaret A. Dorsey, in* School Library Journal (*reprinted from* School Library Journal, *April, 1975, published by R. R. Bowker Co., a Xerox company; copyright © 1975 by Xerox Corporation), April, 1975, p. 66.*

Translated from the Swedish [by Thomas Teal,] this idyll of an island summer is quite unlike the author's beloved stories of Moominland. Slow-moving and self-contained, the book describes the small events of sun-filled days spent by Sophia and her grandmother, and it is permeated by the love and the rare understanding between them.... Grandmother is a marvelous character, candid and wise and earthy. The writing style has flow and vitality, and while there is no plot and not enough action for some readers, this is a treasure for those who appreciate nuance, depth, and percipience.

> *Zena Sutherland, in* Bulletin of the Center for Children's Books (© *1975 by the University of Chicago; all rights reserved), July-August, 1975, p. 178.*

WHO WILL COMFORT TOFFLE? (1960; translation published in America, 1969)

Who Will Comfort Toffle? is one of the few ... books in which the tale takes precedence over the illustrations. This story, a captivating northern fantasy with Carrollian undertones, has the special advantage of being told in verse: seven-iambic lines ("And Mymble made a daisy chain to decorate her hair") rhyming in couplets. This makes it both agreeable to listen to and inviting to remember. It is in any case a memorable narrative.... The stylized evocative manner of the pictures will be familiar to readers of the author's Moomin books.

> The Times Literary Supplement (© *The Times Publishing Company Ltd. 1961), May 19, 1961, p. xii.*

Maybe the story of how nobody or nothing comforts Toffle until he sets out to comfort Miffle will sound less like piffle to children who already know Hemulen and the Groke, the Fillyjonks and Whompses, Mymble and Snufkin and the other Moomins. Otherwise it's a long, strained, preachy rhyme ("But who will comfort Toffle thus: 'It's useless feeling blue,/ What is the good of shells and stones unless you show them too!'") peopled with curiosities who crowd many of the illustrations too.

> Kirkus Reviews (*copyright © 1969 The Kirkus Service, Inc.), October 1, 1969, p. 1057.*

Some of the characters familiar to readers of the Moomin stories appear in this rhyming read-aloud story of a frightened Toffle.... The message comes across clearly: there is comfort in doing things for others.... [The] oversize pages are crowded with figures, the colors harsh. There is some humor in the story but the characters pop in and out, never acquiring the personality that they have in Moomin-books, so that the story seems slow and cluttered.

> *Zena Sutherland, in* Bulletin of the Center for Children's Books (© *1970 by the University of Chicago; all rights reserved), May, 1970, p. 145.*

K

KLEIN, Norma   1938-

Norma Klein, an American author of novels and short stories for both children and adults, is well known for confronting contemporary, controversial subjects in her writings. (See also *Contemporary Authors,* **Vols. 41-44, and** *Something About the Author,* **Vol. 7.)**

BLUE TREES, RED SKY (1975)

Although the characterization [in *Blue Trees, Red Sky*] is good, the kidding the children do about penises, vaginas, and "peeing" seems forced into the story for effect, and the slender plot does not hold interest. Klein's stories are usually more natural and believable than this offering that hammers young readers with its theme.

> *Lynn Bradley, in* School Library Journal *(reprinted from* School Library Journal, *November, 1975, published by R. R. Bowker Co., a Xerox company; copyright © 1975 by Xerox Corporation), November, 1975, p. 64.*

The 10 present-tense episodes surrounding [the] characters and situations [in *Blue Trees, Red Sky*] can be read separately, and in each Valerie pointedly learns to accept things as they are handed to her.... In conscientious Klein fashion the characters show the obligatory interest in their genitalia. But she zeros in on other common concerns too.

> *Barbara Elleman, in* The Booklist *(reprinted by permission of the American Library Association; copyright 1975 by the American Library Association), December 1, 1975, p. 516.*

OTHER CITATIONS

Kirkus Reviews, *October 1, 1975, p. 1130.*

———————

CONFESSIONS OF AN ONLY CHILD (1974)

As in previous children's books by Norma Klein, the concern [in *Confessions of an Only Child*] is all with grownup matters—this time mother's pregnancy, her loss of the baby, and later her successful delivery of another. Here however the parents' personalities blend into the background and it is nine year-old Toe's ambivalent feelings about the prospective sibling that come to the fore. The episodic story is younger, sweeter and simpler than *Mom the Wolf Man and Me* . . . or even *It's Not What You Expect* . . ., suffering somewhat from the noted blandness of the fictional happy family but honest and likable enough in detailing Toe's everyday thoughts and conversations—about her new Indian tent, Dad's spaghetti, or friend Libby's pesty baby sister—between the obstetrical reports.

> *Kirkus Reviews (copyright © 1974 The Kirkus Service, Inc.), February 1, 1974, p. 110.*

Like the heroine of the author's much-praised "Mom, the Wolf Man and Me," [the 8-year-old girl in "Confessions of an Only Child"] is a with-it kid who lives in a real contemporary world. She plays with Barbie dolls and helps her father put quarters in the washing machine in the basement. Her heroically sensible parents have taught her where babies come from....

It should be good that a children's book can be written so frankly, but after awhile I found myself wishing the parents of this smug little girl had told her it was the stork.

> *Jane Langton, in* The New York Times Book Review *(© 1974 by The New York Times Company; reprinted by permission), May 5, 1974, p. 16.*

In *Confessions of an Only Child,* . . . Norma Klein handles weighty material with a gentle hand.... Sexuality is acknowledged and dealt with head-on in a natural, graceful fashion; Antonia's dog eliminates and the world does not end; her mother's navel disappears in advanced pregnancy and this interesting fact is noticed; death is accepted. Klein's considerable talent and sensitive insights are especially evident in the sections where her small heroine considers death and discovers the painful truth that what we think we want (in her case, to be an only child) is not always sweet upon attainment. . . .

By treating their problems seriously and making the ordinary real, Norma Klein gives children what they must have: a guide to survival. I reserve the hope that once this basic need is met, Klein's talents will focus on making the extraordinary real, giving children something they also should have: heroines who not only keep the spirit alive, but excite it.

Gabrielle Burton, in Book World (© *The Washington Post), May 19, 1974, p. 3.*

What [Norma Klein] achieves in [*Confessions of an Only Child*], as she has in her books for older readers, is a completely convincing picture of real people. The dialogue is natural, the characterization skilled, and the relationships between children and adults particularly deft.

> *Zena Sutherland, in* Bulletin of the Center for Children's Books (© *1974 by the University of Chicago; all rights reserved), June, 1974, p. 159.*

OTHER CITATIONS

Publishers' Weekly, *March 4, 1974, p. 76.*

Pamela D. Pollack, in School Library Journal, *April, 1974, pp. 58, 60.*

GIRLS CAN BE ANYTHING (1973)

Amusing cartoon illustrations [by Roy Doty] show Marina and her friend Adam in imaginative play.... Peace and equality are achieved, and both presidents give a delicious banquet of candy, gum, potato chips, etc. The illustration shows an impressive state banquet, a light touch that is sustained through both the text and the illustrations of a very pleasant story that makes its point in a convincing manner.

> *Zena Sutherland, in* Bulletin of the Center for Children's Books (© *1973 by the University of Chicago; all rights reserved), April, 1973, p. 126.*

[This is a] message book about kindergarten pals Marina and Adam who get along fine until Adam starts dictating the girl's role in their games.... Unfortunately, the average cartoons [by Roy Doty] often reinforce standard stereotypes—e.g., while Father reads the newspaper, Mother sits daintily stitching. However, the book as a whole will entertain kids, and the much-needed message is palatably handled.

> *Diane Gersoni Stavn, in* School Library Journal (*reprinted from* School Library Journal, *May, 1973, published by R. R. Bowker Co., a Xerox company; copyright © 1973 by Xerox Corporation), May, 1973, p. 64.*

OTHER CITATIONS

Kirkus Reviews, *February 1, 1973, p. 109.*

The Booklist, *May 1, 1973, pp. 856, 859.*

Joyce Alpern, in Book World, *May 13, 1973 (Part 2), p. 2.*

Publishers' Weekly, *May 21, 1973, p. 50.*

IF I HAD MY WAY (1974)

Ellie's conclusion [in *If I Had My Way*], that "grownups sure are a lot of work ... but I guess they're worth it," doesn't strike us as much of a message, and we have the feeling that Norma Klein didn't quite know what to do with her upside-down world once she'd put Ellie in it. Still, other members of the newest recognized minority are likely to get a minor kick out of the wish-fulfilling turnabout.

> Kirkus Reviews (*copyright © 1974 The Kirkus Service, Inc.), February 1, 1974, p. 106.*

The people in "If I Had My Way ... look like well drawn plaster casts in "now" attire. The tone of the story is similar. An annoyed child named Ellie imagines, or dreams, it is not very clear which, that she is parent to her parents. The idea could have been funny. Instead the special wisdom comes down to "They [adults] sure are a lot of hard work ... but I guess they're worth it." It is doubtful that many children will find that either incisive or cute.

> *Karla Kuskin, in* The New York Times Book Review (© *1974 by The New York Times Company; reprinted by permission), May 5, 1974, p. 47.*

[In *If I Had My Way*, sweet] dreams of revenge are enjoyed by a small girl suffering from a severe case of dethronment.... [When she wakes, there's] her brother, gurgling in his crib; there's mother urging her to hurry and get dressed. And that's the end of the story, no sweetness and light. It's realistic, it's funny, it's honest, and the illustrations [by Ray Cruz] pick up all the overtones.

> *Zena Sutherland, in* Bulletin of the Center for Children's Books (© *1974 by the University of Chicago; all rights reserved), September, 1974, p. 11.*

OTHER CITATIONS

Publishers' Weekly, *April 8, 1974, p. 83.*

Kristin E. Hammond, in School Library Journal, *May, 1974, p. 48.*

IT'S NOT WHAT YOU EXPECT (1973)

Most immediately this is the story of how fourteen-year-old narrator Carla and her twin brother Oliver, a gourmet cook, conceive and—with a little help from a few young friends—successfully operate a French restaurant during their summer vacation.... It's a little hard to reconcile the restaurant's function as pure daydream fulfillment with the sexual concerns and marital problems that are obviously intended as realistic, just as it's sometimes hard to remember that Klein is writing for children when she describes Carla's mother or Oliver's madeleines ("These are like butter cookies, only better. They are supposed to carry you back to your childhood"). But [Norma Klein] has a way of making it all sound natural and mildly interesting for older children who like their vacation fantasies with a sophisticated contemporary flavor.

> Kirkus Reviews (*copyright © 1973 The Kirkus Service, Inc.), February 15, 1973, p. 194.*

If there were a single word to describe "It's Not What You Expect," it might be "modest." But "modest" only in the very best sense of that word: restrained, unpretentious, calm, clear, unconfused. In the young adult genre, this is a rare set of attributes. Norma Klein . . . is not only singularly adept at delineating fine female characters but knows she shouldn't impose Categorical Imperatives on her young readers. Indeed her novels reveal that life is a mystery and a pretty good one, at that. . . . Through a natural ("modest") blend of comedy and mellowed irony, the story comes across without much fuss. If Carla and Oliver with all their classical music and Gourmet magazine hang-ups seem a bit middle-aged, well, that's the way kids are at 14.

> Carolyn Balducci, in The New York Times Book Review (© 1973 by The New York Times Company; reprinted by permission), June 3, 1973, pp. 8, 10.

As she did in *Mom, the Wolf Man and Me*, Norma Klein adds another dimension to the junior novel by having living, breathing adults as well as adolescents [in *It's Not What You Expect*]. . . . The writing style is lively, the characters vividly drawn, the treatment balanced.

> Zena Sutherland, in Bulletin of the Center for Children's Books (© 1973 by the University of Chicago; all rights reserved), July-August, 1973, p. 172.

The characterizations in general and Carla's close relationship with Oliver are well drawn, as are Carla's moods—the intensity, self-criticism, drive, and idealism that inevitably result in disillusionment for her. Although the sum of adversities seems casually amassed and treated, this is a lively, perceptive story for sophisticated readers.

> The Booklist (reprinted by permission of the American Library Association; copyright 1973 by the American Library Association), September 15, 1973, p. 122.

OTHER CITATIONS

Publishers' Weekly, March 5, 1973, pp. 82-3.

Joseph McLellan, in Book World, May 13, 1973 (Part 2), p. 7.

MOM, THE WOLF MAN, AND ME (1972)

Chiefly, [Norma Klein] uses Brett's cheerful independence as a foil for some not unsympathetic satire on adult foibles —friend Evelyn's mother turns husband hunting into a career, Andrew's father (a rabbi) is suffocatingly authoritarian, mother's old boyfriend Wally is sweet but hopelessly henpecked by his estranged wife. If none of these characters are exactly original, at least Brett's live and let live attitude is a welcome change from some of her self-consciously clever counterparts.

> Kirkus Reviews (copyright © 1972 The Kirkus Service, Inc.), September 1, 1972, p. 1027.

["Mom, the Wolf Man and Me" presents] an extraordinary, dear, funny bunch of almost ordinary people. . . . [Through Brett's] eye of perception, we share the tension of the novel: will Mom and Theo go the way of all flesh— from love to marriage to a baby carriage? Our conditioned reflex demands a happy ending. Our socialized expectation

decrees that a happy ending means getting married. But in this daffy, daring novel the syllogism is no longer automatic —and so we care terribly about Brett's feelings and Mom's decision.

Adult readers (and there should be many) need this book for revivification and a glimpse of what they're calling alternate life styles. Our children need this book to bridge the credibility gap in their sex education. . . . And Norma Klein deserves our thanks for a story that replaces moral labels with real human beings.

> Letty Cottin Pogrebin, in The New York Times Book Review (© 1972 by The New York Times Company; reprinted by permission), September 24, 1972, p. 8.

Here [pre-teens] are treated to a commendably honest view of the way some people choose to live. Though the 11-year-old narrator Brett and her friends are always in the foreground, the grown-ups actually dominate the story. This won't offer any identification problems for young readers, however, because for once the adults are as human as the children (Brett's mother in particular); they are still growing, changing, having problems, trying solutions. . . . If anything, the author makes Brett almost too matter of fact, but it's a good antidote to the controversial issues: if the 11-year-old narrator can be so casual about her mother not being married and having intercourse then there's no reason for readers and librarians to get upset. The only other fault that might be found here is the relative lack of action, a problem common to many first person narratives. Rich characters and dynamic interactions, much humor and warmth are the book's justification. Best of all, the author makes readers aware that their lives will be shaped by the values they have. And it's all done without preaching!

> Marilyn R. Singer, in School Library Journal (reprinted from School Library Journal, December, 1972, published by R. R. Bowker Co., a Xerox company; copyright © 1972 by Xerox Corporation), December, 1972, pp. 60-1.

Focusing on life-styles rather than characters. [*Mom, the Wolf Man and Me*] is written in a lively modern style and is candid and objective in treatment but lacks depth. Children of conventional background are likely to be fascinated by the uninhibited portrayal of contemporary life and the book will have much appeal for them. Because of the controversial nature of the subject matter from the adult point of view, however, it is suggested that librarians should read the book before purchase.

> The Booklist (reprinted by permission of the American Library Association; copyright 1973 by the American Library Association), January 1, 1973, pp. 449-50.

The effect of [*Mom, The Wolf Man and Me*] would be totally different if the tone were strident or smart. But the writing is low-keyed, witty, and honest, accurately echoing the spontaneous expression of contemporary children; and the unorthodox characters are warmly human.

> Ethel L. Heins, in The Horn Book Magazine (copyright © 1973 by The Horn Book, Inc., Boston), February, 1973, p. 57.

This kind of book can easily suffer from the wrong kind of comment. The picture of an unmarried mother who makes a virtue out of her situation could offend those who believe that books of this kind should always classify and computerize good and bad. It would be a pity if such a shrewd, perceptive study of individuals were outlawed or, conversely, if it were praised for a courageous stand against convention. In fact this is an expert example of first-person narrative, in which every detail and every conversation, reported or direct, is properly related to Brett, the speaker throughout. From her comments we can deduce a great deal about the smugly conventional Evelyn, who gets her ideas from *A Child's Guide to Divorce* and is so disastrously unprepared for life; about Grandma, who deplores her daughter's way of life, and Grandpa, who believes in freedom and courage; above all, we can guess at what Brett partly understands, her mother's approach to life. It is a relief to read a book written in a mood so far from the usual lugubrious, sickly or melodramatic tone of novels for the 'teens. Norma Klein's crisp, witty, intelligent style indicates that she is primarily interested in character—in the fascinating differences between one human being and another, the surprising effect they can have on one another. To do this through the words of a girl of eleven—brash, abrupt, unintrospective, sometimes naïve—is a real achievement.

> *Margery Fisher, in her* Who's Who in Children's Books: A Treasury of the Familiar Characters of Childhood *(copyright © 1975 by Margery Fisher; reprinted by permission of Holt, Rinehart and Winston), Holt, Rinehart and Winston, 1975, p. 54.*

OTHER CITATIONS

Publishers' Weekly, *November 13, 1972, p. 46.*

Zena Sutherland, in Bulletin of the Center for Children's Books, *February, 1973, p. 93.*

NAOMI IN THE MIDDLE (1974)

Naomi's adjustment to the idea of a new sibling is effected with remarkable ease, and older sister Bobo's warning about a middle child's woes is promptly counteracted by Daddy's reassurances. All told, it's a rather thin psychological elixir, though as usual, the author tosses in a dose of currently prescribed tonic—anti-sexism in tomboy Bobo's characterization, some frank and natural conversation about how babies are started—and makes it easily palatable with Naomi's views and observations on such everyday happy family doings as a trip to the aquarium with Daddy, Grandma's gratifying reaction to an April fool trick, and Bobo's really quite moderate hassling of her younger sister. Fair to middlin'.

> Kirkus Reviews *(copyright © 1974 The Kirkus Service, Inc.), November 1, 1974, p. 1151.*

["Naomi in the Middle"] is short, realistic and disappointing. . . . The dialogue is short and snappy. Mrs. Klein's ear for the conversations of today's child is accurate, and she has a penchant for the comic scene.

But the book is essentially plotless, actionless, and it does not substitute any real emotion or character development for the missing elements. There are no deep insights, no wrestling with truths. The book is a photograph—no, a snapshot—of a particular urban, white, liberal-minded family. This is accurate reportage, engaging for a moment, easy to forget.

> *Jane Yolen, in* The New York Times Book Review *(© 1974 by The New York Times Company; reprinted by permission), November 3, 1974, p. 48.*

This book is about sex, a mother's pregnancy and sibling rivalry as viewed by Naomi, the seven-year-old second child in a family that is soon to have a third. Within a light, somewhat humorous fictional format, the author tries to handle, forthrightly, subjects usually considered taboo in children's books. . . .

While the author deserves praise for dealing with "bold" subject matter, the parents' responses to the young girls' concerns are somewhat less than satisfactory. In fact, they are superficial and perfunctory, leaving the impression that the children are not to be taken seriously. To Naomi's statement about not wanting sex, her mother replies, "When you're old enough you'll like it." End of discussion. When Naomi laments her status as the second child, her mother says only, "Daddy was a middle child." When Bobo threatens to leave home if the mother has twins, the mother's response is, "I doubt it will be twins." Not much reassurance for children.

The book is also limited by the white, very middle classness of its characters and by its basic assumption of universal heterosexuality.

But *Naomi in the Middle* is one of the few books of its kind, using words like "penis" and "vagina" easily within a fictional framework and projecting a feeling that sex and pregnancy are "healthy" things. The story reads well and fast, and the drawings by Leigh Grant are terrific.

> *Sue Ribner, in* Interracial Books for Children Bulletin *(reprinted by permission of Interracial Books for Children Bulletin, 1841 Broadway, New York, N.Y. 10023), Vol. 6, No. 1, 1975, p. 4.*

This isn't the usual adjustment-to-new-baby story, but a very funny and ingenuous book that catches exactly the innocent shrewdness of a child of seven, and the dethronement theme is nicely balanced by a spectrum of familiar events: shopping for a birthday present, making valentines, playing a trick on April Fool's Day with Grandma holding up her end and being convincingly flabbergasted.

> *Zena Sutherland, in* Bulletin of the Center for Children's Books *(© 1975 by the University of Chicago; all rights reserved), March, 1975, p. 116.*

OTHER CITATIONS

Gail E. Muirhead, in School Library Journal, *November, 1974, p. 57.*

TAKING SIDES (1974)

Whereas Brett, of *Mom, the Wolf Man and Me,* had to

adjust to the marriage of her single mother, Nell, [of *Taking Sides*], faces the prospect of her parents' divorce. . . . [Her] conversations with her parents (both unusually sympathetic, intelligent people) are unconventionally candid and her observations—on love and illusion in *Cries and Whispers*, on Heather's always busy family, on phobia-prone Arden—are acute and original. Nell's awareness of adult problems is certainly precocious, but it does provide an unusual perspective on parents as human beings. And though Nell never reveals as much of herself as she notices in others, she is a warm and insightful companion.

> *Kirkus Reviews (copyright © 1974 The Kirkus Service, Inc), July 1, 1974, p. 688.*

In not exploring this remarkable promise from father to daughter ["Do you promise to live until I'm grown up with my own family?" "I promise."], Norma Klein has packaged a piece of meretricious reassurance, the lying about life, that has signaled the sloppiest of children's fiction since Nancy Drew solved every case just in the nick of time. Admitting to children the uncertainty of life is far more honest than this book, which pretends at reality through the mention of 10-speed bikes, vegetarians and an Afro doll named Caleb. The pain of sickness, the tensions of separation, the fear of death are as deeply felt here as the steamroller that momentarily flattens a cartoon character. Like that feckless creature, Nell skitters away, unaffected, unhurt and seemingly incapable of any residual caring, thought, or emotion.

Since Norma Klein has chosen to act as faithful scribe to trendy teen-age dialogue and scattered teen-age thoughts, she has avoided the writer's essential task—to reflect upon and shape the material of the novel with a special perspective, a vision unique to each writer's imagination. By blunting the writer's sharpest tool, the imaginative use of language, she has denied the reader a sense of place of orientation in the world that the novel purports to create.

> *Alice Bach, in* The New York Times Book Review *(© 1974 by The New York Times Company; reprinted by permission), September 29, 1974, p. 8.*

The flaws, as well as the attributes, of [Nell's] parents and the other characters are matter-of-factly portrayed, and Nell's developing curiosity about sex is also handled naturally. There is no climax or conclusion (which may dissatisfy some junior high readers); rather, Nell's maturation is told in her own words as she copes with the changes in her life.

> *Cathy S. Coyle, in* School Library Journal *(reprinted from* School Library Journal, *October, 1974, published by R. R. Bowker Co., a Xerox company; copyright © 1974 by Xerox Corporation), October, 1974, p. 119.*

[*Taking Sides*] isn't [mild], because Norma Klein sees relationships and describes them with such candor and clarity; here, as in her other books, the adults are neither Proper Parents nor stock types but human beings with faults and virtues. They're real—and so is Nell. And again—as in earlier books—this is written with sophistication. . . .

> *Zena Sutherland, in* Bulletin of the Center for Children's Books *(© 1974 by the University of Chicago; all rights reserved), November, 1974, p. 46.*

WHAT IT'S ALL ABOUT (1975)

This catalogue of contemporary lifestyles, centered around ten-year-old Bern who is half-Jewish, half-Japanese, is peculiarly without passion or life. . . . Everyone is so pleasant and kind, readers may wonder why there was a divorce in the first place. Instead of really dealing with *What It's All About*, Klein treats only the superficial aspects of these separated lives. There are many details, extraneous to the story, which stop the flow instead of building up the characterizations and plot. If there's a story here, it's hidden away in Bern's notebooks over which everybody exclaims and which are never revealed to readers.

> *Leila C. Shapiro, in* School Library Journal *(reprinted from* School Library Journal, *November, 1975, published by R. R. Bowker Co., a Xerox company; copyright © 1975 by Xerox Corporation), November, 1975, p. 79.*

A vegetable soup of problems, this serves up a situation not so uncommon as most people would like to believe, but Klein's casually sophisticated treatment may make it seem remote. . . . As usual Klein's style is slick, the dialog easygoing, and the characters real enough to stick around in a reader's mind for a while.

> *Betsy Hearne, in* The Booklist *(reprinted by permission of the American Library Association; copyright 1975 by the American Library Association), November 1, 1975, p. 369.*

In *What It's All About . . .*, by Norma Klein, a delightfully open-hearted, open-minded book written with a whimsical tolerance for all kinds of human folly in the business of love-and-marriage (and with a belief in children's adaptability to even the most unconventional arrangements), "exceptions to every rule" abound. . . .

It may not be Father Knows Best, or even The Brady Bunch, but it's a "perfectly good, fine family" just the same.

> *Alix Nelson, in* The New York Times Book Review *(© 1975 by The New York Times Company; reprinted by permission), November 16, 1975, p. 50.*

*   *   *

KURELEK, William   1927-

William Kurelek is a Canadian painter.

LUMBERJACK (1974)

Lumberjack doesn't quite have the magic that the vast open spaces and tang of honest nostalgia brought to *Prairie Boy's Winter*. . . . It simply records Kurelek's own memories of his stints in Canadian logging camps back in 1946 and 1951 and somehow makes that since-mechanized milieu so real that one can feel the logger's aching backs and mosquito bites and the warmth of the bunkhouse stove at night. Both the first-person text and naive realism of Kurelek's paintings focus on day-to-day concerns.... Fortunately, Kurelek was there to record it while it lasted, and his anecdotes have an eidetic truth. Kids shouldn't keep this all for themselves—this is a book to share with fathers and grandfathers.

> Kirkus Reviews *(copyright © 1974 The Kirkus Service, Inc.), November 1, 1974, pp. 1155-56.*

Kurelek tells us how the lumberjack's job is done, and adds notes on his clothes, cots and food. Mostly all he does is cut, cut, cut. Yet this is rightly adequate, for Kurelek's book does not pretend nor preach. Readers are not allowed to taste the salt of his sweat or feel the blisters burn on his hands, and yet the satisfying scriptures of hard labor hit home with each bite of iron into poplar.

If this hard book has a soft spot, it is its lack of personality in its people. Jacks are characters. Brawlers, drinkers, gamblers, jokesters. Kurekek's loggers are as wooden as their logs, little more than general store mannequins who pose silently in checkerboard shirts. But I like this book for its homely honesty. Wisely perhaps, all frills of literature have been hacked off by a craftsman who cuts as well with a pen as he trims his timber with an axe. Log by log, each remembrance piles neatly into firewood to warm a reader who is willing enough to lug it. Kurelek is no poet. Still, so earnestly does he wade into his work and revere its sanctity, pleasing images often fall as cones from a white pine. To wit, "I seemed to be alone out there. Just big Mother Nature and little me, fiddling around at her feet." Good phrase. I'll wager I would like the man who wrote it, because first he felt it. He is a boy in the book, but his story is told by manhood in awe of self struggle and mounted peaks. It is unsmooth text, and rough spruce. Tough bark, but blow by blow, the lumberjack author jerks his story from the snow and the pine needles and muskeg moss....

On every page, you will be rewarded by paintings in color, as plain as the prose, drawn with a heavy hand; yet in a compelling and manly style that complements its words, working in concert like a two-man bucksaw. And because the art is so charming, so right ... the song suddenly has a lyric to tap your toe to, even though it is a heavy clog, a plod of boots making lonely tracks, notes written in the snow. Clumsy words, thick and cold and weary with work. You almost have to heft up each one with a woodhook and haul it from the hills by the grit and grunt of your own gut. But if you want my opinion, spit on your hands and do the job.

It's a good book, good chow, good bunkside reading. Lumberjacks, like flapjacks, are plain and yet filling.

> Robert Newton Peck, *in* The New York Times Book Review *(© 1974 by The New York Times Company; reprinted by permission), November 3, 1974, p. 29.*

[In *Lumberjack,* Kurelek] celebrates his memories of two sojourns in Canadian lumber camps; and in the epilogue he tells of and illustrates the mechanical tree harvester that has replaced the lumberjack.... [His] full-color paintings are superb, while [his] text plods along with information and autobiographical detail.... [There] is a varied interplay of darksome forest scenes, lumber-camp interiors, closeups of people, and aerial perspective. The colors are rich, and the elemental simplicity of the human forms suggests the solid, peasant-like figures in the paintings of Bruegel and Diego Rivera. The scenes are quietly composed to capture the tranquility of remembered emotion. [This is] a picture book for readers and viewers of all ages—especially viewers.

> Paul Heins, *in* The Horn Book Magazine *(copyright © 1974 by the Horn Book, Inc., Boston), December, 1974, p. 684.*

In [*Lumberjack*] Kurelek writes with simplicity and deep affection about a way of life and a time that are gone, based on his own memories of being a lumberjack in Canada 25 years ago, when strong men did the work machines now do. His full-color paintings powerfully evoke the daily life of the lumberjacks and the breathtaking beauty of their northern surroundings.

> Eliot Fremont-Smith and Karla Kuskin, *in* New York Magazine *(© 1974 by The NYM Corp.; reprinted with the permission of* New York Magazine, Eliot Fremont-Smith, and Karla Kuskin), December 16, 1974, p. 107.

[In *Lumberjack*], Kurelek has drawn and written his way into the past. After the flapdoodle and sheer flapjackery often associated with lumberjack nostalgia, Kurelek's quiet combined memoir and illustrated how-to book (notching trees, washing socks, grinding axes, dynamiting log jams) is refreshingly simple, grubby and authentic. Some of his paintings have a crabbed look, as if done by a Peter Bruegel with arthritis of the drawing hand, but they open an affecting window on the life and times of lumbermen in the Northern bush.

> Timothy Foote, *in* Time *(reprinted by permission from* Time, The Weekly Newsmagazine; *copyright Time Inc.), December 23, 1974, p. 73.*

Lumberjack is a significant contribution to Canada's social history, mostly because the author recollects a memorable time in his own life. As a college student in 1946 he gets a summer job at a lumber camp in Northern Ontario—and he enters a whole new world. His trek into the unknown is such a departure from his winter life that his recall of it seems not only total but vital and fresh, as he tells us all the homely details that made up "that good life."

In *Lumberjack* Kurelek has freed himself from the constraints now obvious in *A Prairie Boy's Winter*. It was his first book, and for children, and though his evocation of childhood is superb, there is evident in the telling a distance and a diffidence that affected his spontaneity.

But *Lumberjack* tells of a young man going to work in the bush against his father's wishes. Even the spruce scented wind seems to communicate the challenge of freedom and adventure to him. And we relish the young man's exuberance as he starts on his way to "somewhere great."

> Irma McDonough, *in* In Review: Canadian Books for Children, *Winter, 1975, pp. 33-4.*

OTHER CITATIONS

The Booklist, *September 1, 1974, p. 44.*

Publishers' Weekly, *October 7, 1974, pp. 63-4.*

Ruth M. McConnell, in School Library Journal, *January, 1975, p. 47.*

Bulletin of the Center for Children's Books, *April, 1975, p. 132.*

A PRAIRIE BOY'S SUMMER (1975)

A Prairie Boy's Summer somehow contains fewer magical moments and more plain hard work than his [*A Prairie Boy's*] *Winter* did, but Kurekek's naive roughhewn canvases still turn the flat, western landscape into a strange and wonderful place, whether rich with geometrical rows of golden wheat or eerie as the surface of the moon as it is during "the burning of quack grass and harrowing." With his usual candor, Kurelek confesses here that as a child "one of his dreams was of being surrounded by a group of highschool students listening in admiration to his stories of the adventures of a farm boy." And indeed he makes such workaday chores as "making a smudge," "mending pig's fence," and "stooking" seem absorbingly interesting while his memory of the old swimming hole is undimmed by nostalgia—the lurking catfish and the crayfish he feared stepping on are still uppermost in his mind. Kurelek's recollections continue to be both fond and precise, and though his readers may be younger than the highschool boys of his dream they are sure to gather round once again.

> Kirkus Reviews *(copyright © 1975 The Kirkus Service, Inc.), April 15, 1975, p. 462.*

On the left-hand page of "A Prairie Boy's Summer" are the deceptively spare accounts of a Western farm's busy season. On the facing pages, 20 of them, are paintings illustrating the text. It's hard to decide which satisfies more. . . .

[The] book walks the straight furrow between the sentimentality of nostalgia and the brutalizing of sweated labor. A boy too small to tip a fuel drum must patiently siphon the gas, occasionally getting a mouthful of it.

Who are these people whose labor defines them and reaches out to embrace their children? They hardly have time for ethnic identity, though they use a Ukrainian word to describe the small fires set to burn weeds. But we never follow them into the farmhouse—they don't summer there. It's a curious triumph how well we know these people who rarely speak and never go to town.

For the disadvantaged reader who doesn't know where the food on his plate comes from, much is made clear. Not only the sequence of seasonal chores, but sudden sensory impressions: a cow's fly-swatter tail slapping across the back of the milker's neck, the feel of a jolt of lightning that's traveled a mile of barbed-wire fencing.

The style of the illustrations is consciously primitive. Figures looking more like Edward Gorey's than Grant Wood's refuse to rise to the false monumentalism of a WPA mural. They are, like their lives, in perspective. Translated to these Willa Cather steppes, they have prevailed and are beginning to flourish. A timeless message, never more welcome than now.

> *Richard Peck, in* The New York Times Book Review *(© 1975 by The New York Times Company; reprinted by permission), May 4, 1975, p. 38.*

[The] modest narrative [in *A Prairie Boy's Summer*] is replete with small details that will spark sharp recollections for any who have experienced a similar background and will ably convey a sensory ambience to those who haven't. The vignettes' simple unaffectedness matches a feel of earthy simplicity in the artist's paintings. As a whole, however, these do not seem as rich and full-bodied as the art for either *Prairie Boy's Winter* or *Lumberjack* . . ., though some of them rise to his earlier standard.

> The Booklist *(reprinted by permission of the American Library Association; copyright 1975 by the American Library Association), June 1, 1975, p. 1014.*

Since summer is the time that farm children work hardest, [*A Prairie Boy's Summer*] has less about playtime activities than did the author-artist's *A Prairie Boy's Winter*, but it has enough variety to be interesting. . . . It is, of course, the pictures by this distinguished Canadian artist that give the book its distinction; each full-color page glows with life and vigor, and the paintings have both a felicity of small details and a remarkable evocation of the breadth and sweep of the Manitoba prairie.

> *Zena Sutherland, in* Bulletin of the Center for Children's Books *(© 1975 by the University of Chicago; all rights reserved), July-August, 1975, pp. 179-80.*

OTHER CITATIONS

Ruth M. McConnell, in School Library Journal, *September, 1975, p. 106.*

A PRAIRIE BOY'S WINTER (1973)

[This is a] dull, pedestrian narrative about life on a prairie farm in wintertime. The children's activities, ranging from feeding pigs and hauling wood to skating and snowball fights, are vividly depicted in colorful, full-page illustrations which offer interesting perspectives of the prairie landscape. However, the text lacks the charm and vigor of the pictures, and the author's didactic approach and passive recital with little dialogue obscure the excitement of the events.

> *Patricia M. Cuts, in* School Library Journal *(reprinted from* School Library Journal, *October, 1973, published by R. R. Bowker Co., a Xerox company; copyright © 1973 by Xerox Corporation), October, 1973, p. 117.*

Opposite every full-page illustration [in *A Prairie Boy's Winter*] is a page of text, loosely narrated and frankly subservient to the beautiful, evocative art. One might wish, actually, that the text could have established a definite background in time and place: Is the setting north-central U.S.A., or is it Canada? And a casual reference to one of the father's Ukrainian sayings leads to unanswered questions about the family and their neighbors.

Ethel L. Heins, in The Horn Book Magazine *(copyright © 1973 by The Horn Book, Inc., Boston), October, 1973, p. 456.*

At first it's hard to tell whether this is meant to be a mood piece, a documentary of farm life or autobiographical fiction. But it soon becomes evident that William, the Ukrainian-American farm boy, is indeed the artist himself and as Kurelek hits his stride his reminiscences become more idiomatic and more personal. The loosely connected anecdotes about games and chores are vivified by the sort of specifics that are crucial at the time but so easily forgotten. . . . Each story is inspired by one of Kurelek's primitivist paintings (reproduced full page, in a picture book format) showing well bundled figures working and playing against vast snowy expanses and empty blue skies that reflect a child's eye view of the endless, empty prairie. The pictures are not as naive as they seem at first glance; many of the figures could have come straight from a Breughel canvas, but Kurelek makes them just as much at home in the Midwest. These blue-tinted tableaux, in which time and action seem magically frozen, and the homely detail of the text complement and extend each other with remarkable ease.

Kirkus Reviews *(copyright © 1973 The Kirkus Service, Inc.), October 15, 1973, p. 1160.*

[In "A Prairie Boy's Winter"], Kurelek reweaves the fabric of his own childhood winters in Alberta, Canada. With an exactitude born of lingering affection, he paints and writes about games played and farm chores accomplished on frozen seas of remembered prairie snow.

We see and feel the "blizzard's howling whiteness that took his breath away." We are right there as his Ukrainian mother shouts her daily dinner call to the family pigs, "tsyok, tsyok, tsyok, tsyow." Kurelek's 20 full-page paintings combine a child's directness of expression with a technique subtle enough to make absolute distinctions in tone and texture between newly fallen snow and the waterlogged blanket of slush that characterizes the landscape of early spring. He captures the color of cold, the weight of a late autumn sky heavy with pending precipitation.

And he is profligate with fact: telling us that cows go crazy over their daily rations of ensilage (a "finely chopped green corn that has partly fermented under its own weight"); and how, precisely, schoolchildren in his day created their own hockey rinks by pouring water from "the old copper boiler off the school stove" over hard-packed snow. From crow's early November departure to late March return, we are privileged to experience a very particular childhood winter.

Selma G. Lanes, in The New York Times Book Review *(© 1973 by The New York Times Company; reprinted by permission), December 9, 1973, p. 8.*

The evocation of childhood is a nostalgic pursuit, but all of us, including children, find a magnetism in the remembrance of things past. Here Kurelek intensifies his memories by recalling them in both paintings and words. His pictures pleasure the eye immediately and his words underscore the quiet response of this other, younger William to a prairie winter in the 1930's.

Work and play have equal importance in William's life as the autumn turns through winter into spring in the eternal round. The prairie sky follows the seasonal changes depicted in the 20 pictures, from the slate grey of autumn darkened by the departing crows to the brilliant azure pierced by one ebony crow that heralds spring.

Irma McDonough, in In Review: Canadian Books for Children, *Winter, 1974, p. 37.*

A Prairie Boy's Winter is accompanied by a text supplied by the artist, the combination a striking confirmation of the . . . Cutler thesis that a firm visual impression will prompt a narrative which accommodates and amplifies pictorial details. Kurelek's drawings are indeed evocative, virtually demanding some form of verbal participation. The individual prints display themes of wonder in the middle of a wasteland, inventiveness in the face of isolation, and the sportive imagination opposing a wearying monotony of routine. Throughout there are various shapes—circles, triangles, and squares—simultaneously suggestive of no exit and of infinite artistic possibility. The hockey rink and the pinwheel, devised by the children for wintertime delight, symbolize as well the confines of the harsh surroundings. Yet the human spirit endures, perhaps in part as a result of this ceaseless dialogue with the environment, which, however cruel, incessantly demands response. This same kind of dialogue is carried on between the paintings and the text. The first painting, The Coming of Winter, is a suitable example of this interplay. . . .

Here the grayish-blue sky dominates almost three quarters of the canvas. There are no clouds, as the tint by itself suffices to convey an ominous mood. Everywhere the fullness of space imposes itself, dwarfing the nine figures of children who are little more than enclothed stick figures distinguishable for each other only through their relative sizes, their postures, and the color of their clothing. Separating the children from the endless expanse, a line of white poplars bereft of foliage exposes about a dozen deserted crows' nests, while a few splotches of white in the horizon and the overall barrenness reinforce the theme of winter's imminent arrival. Dotting the sky are several score of black wings, apparently in exodus. One child points to the sky, perhaps first articulating the obvious and then lapsing into his commentary. Almost as if to supply this muted voice the narrative commences, at first overlapping with the picture by restating its images, and then breaking out on its own. . . .

The simple text, a polished recollection retrieved from childhood, shows not only expansion of details but also a sense of the dramatic. The crows are not simply symbols of impending winter, but are native denizens chattering in the cornfields, competing with the farmers, and, perhaps as well, suggestive of pesky children whose departure brings at once sighs of relief and tears of desolation. The sameness of the prairie landscape is offset by suggestions of perpetual movement, the motion of the crows southward, of the children schoolward; the inevitable cycle of the seasons with their fierce activity and transformations pulls everything onto a stage whose space cries out to be filled.

Leonard R. Mendelsohn, "Children's Literature in Canada," in Children's Literature: Annual of The Modern Language Association Seminar on Children's Literature and The Children's Literature Association, *Vol.*

4, edited by Francelia Butler (© 1975 by Francelia Butler; all rights reserved), Temple University Press, 1975, pp. 141-42.

OTHER CITATIONS

Publishers' Weekly, *October 1, 1973, p. 82.*

The Booklist, *January 15, 1974, p. 543.*

L

LAWSON, Robert   1892-1957

Recipient of the 1941 Caldecott Medal for *They Were Strong and Good* and the 1945 Newbery Medal for *Rabbit Hill*, Robert Lawson was an American author-illustrator noted for his animal stories as well as for his humorous historical stories "told by" the pets of famous people.

GENERAL COMMENTARY

Mr. Lawson's works demonstrate the fortuitous combination of the use of the language of words and the language of lines and colors to complement each other. The fluidity and unity of text and illustrations in his books would be difficult to achieve if the author and illustrator were not the same person. Yet he also seemed to possess the sensitivity and ability to project another's thoughts because some of his finest work has been done illustrating for another author. Nor was his style set and monotonous. It possessed a wide range of expression. (pp. 265-66)

In the traditional manner of satirists he used animal society as an analogue with which to poke fun at human society. Mr. Lawson's comments were often satirical, but the satire is the warmly loving, affectionately chiding satire of Horace, never the vituperative, shrilly hating satire of Juvenal. In the tradition of Horace one remembers the great eighteenth century caricaturist Daumier. While there is no artistic analogy between Daumier's corpulent bourgeoisie and Lawson's delicately-drawn animals, both are illuminated by a love for life, and for all living things, that takes the barb out of satire. (p. 266)

> *Annette H. Weston, "Robert Lawson: Author and Illustrator" (originally published in* Elementary English, *January, 1970), in* Authors and Illustrators of Children's Books: Writings on Their Lives and Works, *edited by Miriam Hoffman and Eva Samuels (copyright © 1972 by Xerox Corp.), Bowker, 1972, pp. 256-67.*

[Native] elements—the theme of America-the-bountiful, the fabulous nature of American storytelling, the modes of American speech, the use of comic narrators—are motifs which recur in many of [Robert Lawson's] books. And it is the combination of these elements which evokes a recognizable setting against which many of his best realized characters move and speak with credibility. (p. 24)

[It] is in the books he both wrote and illustrated that the scope of Lawson's world may be most clearly defined and his relationship to the mainstream of American cultural tradition most easily discerned. Individually, these books, from *Ben and Me* to *The Great Wheel*, attracted considerable attention at the time of their publication; collectively, and viewed retrospectively, they reflect a particular vision of America, American ideals, and the American national character. For, in his dual role, Lawson not only synthesized the manifestations of the American spirit as revealed in the first half of the twentieth century, he also employed the forms, personae, and techniques of certain American literary conventions in a rare blend of fact and fantasy. An "illustrator in the great tradition," as Helen Dean Fish once described him, he was also a humorist in the American tradition. (pp. 29-30)

Undoubtedly, Lawson's delineation of the homely virtues thought to be particularly American and his exaltation of the humble—animals and humans alike—contributed much to his popularity in the forties and fifties. Like the youngster who commented after seeing an exhibition of his drawings, "He draws them up neat, and you can tell what they mean," those who reviewed Lawson's books could indeed tell what they meant. He mirrored American values and familiar American foibles, although tending to ignore what today's reviewers might call "relevant social issues."

But then, relevant social issues are particular concerns peculiar to a particular time. Lawson's America was largely an internal rather than an external reality, a special inner country of his own. His most successful and probably most enduring books, such as *Ben and Me . . ., Mr. Revere and I . . ., Rabbit Hill . . ., The Tough Winter . . .,* are evocative not provocative, depending more on timelessness of theme than on timeliness of subject for their appeal.

Lawson's America, however, was not unrelated to the reality. Defining "America" and "Americanism" is a puzzle which has perplexed generations of historians. Yet, as amorphous and as multifaceted as the notion of America is, Lawson managed to suggest its diversity, contradictions, and optimism: the class-conscious but casteless social attitudes; the worship of invention contrasted with the distaste for a mechanical society; the adulation of heroes but trust in the common-sense of plain folk; and, over-riding all other factors, the idealistic belief expressed in *Rabbit Hill* that somehow, someway "There is enough for all."

This he accomplished with a humorous juxtaposition of illustration and text, primarily through the medium of fantasy; but his fantasy folk are not ethereal, sentimental creatures. Rather, they are the earthy revivifications of the folk tales. Because he was basically a fabulist, his humans are often stereotyped, two-dimensional. Paradoxically, his animals have more individuality as they assume human characteristics. Indeed, one sometimes senses that he was more at home with his animal than with his human creations. (pp. 30-2)

> *Mary Mehlman Burns, "'There Is Enough for All': Robert Lawson's America" (Part 1), in* The Horn Book Magazine *(copyright © 1972 by The Horn Book, Inc., Boston), February, 1972, pp. 24-32.*

[If] Lawson emphasized American virtues in *They Were Strong and Good, Watchwords of Liberty*, and *The Great Wheel*, he was equally fascinated with American idiosyncrasies as demonstrated by his books which are humorous commentaries upon the American-way-of-life. For virtues and idiosyncrasies are not so different as one might suppose. A virtue carried to an extreme often becomes an idiosyncrasy. Humor is one yardstick for measuring the distance as Lawson demonstrated in *Country Colic . . .*, an alphabetical "Weeder's Digest" for adult suburbanites. (p. 297)

Nor were American industries, institutions, or ambitions any less humorous in Lawson's view than American suburbanites. *Mr. Wilmer* . . . exploded the myth of product endorsements and the art of becoming a Prominent Figure; *Mr. Twigg's Mistake* . . . satirized the nutritional claims of breakfast cereals before Nader's Raiders discovered their insufficiencies; while *The Fabulous Flight* . . . presented several irreverent views of Washington Society. All three stories are fantasies involving animals rather than fantasies about animals. With the exception of *The Fabulous Flight*, their humor lies primarily in a series of comic situations or in the witty, somewhat sophisticated repartee of the hero's friend (as in *Mr. Wilmer*) or of the hero's father (as in *Mr. Twigg's Mistake*). And one suspects that both characters, as well as the gun-collecting Professor in *Smeller Martin* . . ., are really portraits of Lawson himself. (p. 298)

The affinity of humor for its native habitat perhaps explains why *Rabbit Hill* and *Robbut: A Tale of Tails* . . . seem to have found a wider foreign audience than Lawson's historical fantasies. Abroad, Ben Franklin and Paul Revere are historical personages; in America, they are almost legendary. In contrast, the small animals of *Rabbit Hill* evoke sympathy and understanding for small animals everywhere; while *Robbut*—the woeful tale of a young rabbit who coveted by turns the sinuous, slick, or plumed tails of his companions—is basically a long fable, as non-national as Aesop.

Generally speaking, the four historical fantasies—*Ben and Me, I Discover Columbus . . ., Mr. Revere and I*, and *Captain Kidd's Cat . . .*—are talking-beast tales as are *Rabbit Hill, The Tough Winter, Edward, Hoppy and Joe . . .*, and *Robbut*. Specifically, there is a difference between the two groups. The first employs pets in the roles of comic, humble monologists, stock figures in the conventions of American humor. The second concentrates on animal communities and involves human beings primarily as symbols of the man-nature relationship. In *Rabbit Hill* and *The Tough Winter*, the statue of Saint Francis which presides over the Hill is appropriate as an expression of the interdependence of man and nature, for the gentle Saint of Assisi was perhaps the first real ecologist in Western culture.

However universal their themes, the stories of these animal communities have about them a distinctly American atmosphere. If Kenneth Grahame's *Wind in the Willows* owes much to its superb evocation of the English countryside, Lawson's animal communities have their roots firmly planted in New England soil. And his young animals— Little Georgie, Edward, Hoppy, and Robbut—are small boys rather than playboys like Toad.

The sense of place is not, however, conveyed through lengthy, pictorial descriptions but through descriptive dialogue. A skilled raconteur, Lawson had a finely tuned ear for revealing fragments of conversation and characteristic intonations. His texts and pictures are complementary parts of the whole; the characters creating themselves in conversation, the illustrations enlarging and framing those self-portraits. Which perhaps explains why his most popular characters are as memorable for what they say as for what they do, as well as explaining why they are essentially American conceptions. For Lawson was as firmly rooted in America and New England as his characters were. True, the American motif is not a self-conscious element in the most enduring of his books; nor is it the only major element. Like Saint Francis, he had a sincere but not sentimental love for all things. And it is this kindliness which makes him humorous rather than merely witty. (pp. 299-301)

> *Mary Mehlman Burns, "'There Is Enough for All': Robert Lawson's America" (Conclusion), in* The Horn Book Magazine *(copyright © 1972 by The Horn Book, Inc., Boston), June, 1972, pp. 295-305.*

The vigorous drawings of animals which appeared wherever possible in Robert Lawson's early illustrations of fantasy indicated one of the directions his later work would take. His ease with animal symmetry is as evident as his occasional unease with the human form. And like all fabulists he often used animals to comment on human actions. Though he seldom clothed them with anything more than a hat or a stick, the human attributes he gave them sent chills down the spines of market-minded editors, who had been told that children's librarians avoided animals that talked, to say nothing of those that wore pants. . . .

Besides his careful attention to period costume, [Robert Lawson's] historical drawings continually reflect his special interests in structural detail, in tools and old guns, and in the flag. He drew the American flag of Betsy Ross and of Francis Scott Key; the flag below which Jackson toasted the Union and that before which children of his own day pledged the oath of allegiance. If these were symbols of his Americanism, so was his pride in his Confederate father and pioneer mother; so would be his willingness to poke fun at familiar historical figures. . . .

Though Robert Lawson could catch a likeness deftly when he wanted to and though different types of character intrigued him, he did not care especially to do "ordinary modern people." . . . His drawings of women and children most often reflected this disinterest; sometimes they seem little more than patterns. Yet all manner of men live in his illustrations, and he worked hard to make his pictures of them say what he wanted them to. . . . The gap between his *Pilgrim's Progress* [1939] and his *McWhinney's Jaunt* [1947] was bridged with an extraordinary production of fantastic, historical, natural, and humorous drawings. Accompanying this enormous creativity were a narrative sense and a facility with words rarely found in artists. [Robert Lawson] is still the only man who has won both of the highest awards given to children's books in the United States: the Caldecott Medal for *They Were Strong and Good*, and the Newbery Medal for *Rabbit Hill*.

> *Helen L. Jones, in her* Robert Lawson, Illustrator *(copyright © 1972 by Helen L. Jones; all rights reserved), Little, Brown, 1972, pp. 22, 52, 92.*

[Robert Lawson] was a very good craftsman and an excellent depictor of character. . . . He had a strong, almost scientifically-accurate line. His compositions are always traditional. His pictures are full of detail and complete in representation. His wildest fantasies are adequately based on his technical skill.

He was really a 19th-century illustrator, and quintessentially American. Even his earliest work appeared old-fashioned for its time—but this does not detract from its merits. These not only stemmed from his skill but from his ability as a storyteller and the soundness and humor of his conception of the people in the text he was illustrating.

> *Maria Cimino, in* The New York Times Book Review *(© 1973 by The New York Times Company; reprinted by permission), March 18, 1973, p. 10.*

[*Ben and Me, Mr. Revere and I*, and *Captain Kidd's Cat*] are hearty, humorous stories, based on a splendid idea and a sufficiency of research, and they are accompanied by the author's own hearty, humorous drawings. To my mind, they show Robert Lawson at his best; his award-winning *Rabbit Hill* (1944), which tells how the new folk at the big house become benefactors to the local wildlife, has a taste of saccharine about it.

> *John Rowe Townsend, in his* Written for Children: An Outline of English-Language Children's Literature *(copyright © 1965, 1974 by John Rowe Townsend; reprinted by permission of J. B. Lippincott Company), revised edition, Lippincott, 1974, p. 244.*

Georgie is a rabbit to be reckoned with. Popular with the other animals on Rabbit Hill, he has a natural curiosity that stands him in good stead. . . . Georgie is perhaps the most smoothly humanized of [all the characters], the pattern of a nice, wholesome, ordinary, small boy.

These two animal fantasies [*Rabbit Hill*, 1944, and *The Long Winter*, 1954] can be read in several ways. It is tempting to see *Rabbit Hill*, written during the war years, as an allegory suggesting that man might learn to live and share with his fellow man just as the Folks, by their trust and generous provision of food, induce the Little Animals to leave the vegetable garden unplundered. Again, one

might regard the stories as the pipe-dreams of a gardener who knows very well that good crops and a healthy animal community will never go together. But the books belong also to a long and honourable tradition in which animals are given personalities and certain domestic attributes while their specific natures are not distorted. Georgie's mother uses baskets to carry food to her burrow for the winter; Georgie learns from his father the 'checks and doublings' with which he can escape the local dogs. Each animal has his typical and appropriate character, from Porkey the stout and obstinate woodchuck and the dignified Red Buck (who condescends to the 'little fellows') to excitable, ubiquitous Willie Fieldmouse, Phewie the skunk (a connoisseur in garbage) and the Grey Squirrel, who has 'the *most* forgetful memory'. These animal characters need stir nobody's inhibitions about humanized animals; they are recognizably the affectionately delineated and rightful ecological tenants of a piece of Connecticut farmland.

> *Margery Fisher, in her* Who's Who in Children's Books: A Treasury of the Familiar Characters of Childhood *(copyright © 1975 by Margery Fisher; reprinted by permission of Holt, Rinehart and Winston), Holt, Rinehart and Winston, 1975, pp. 116-17.*

CAPTAIN KIDD'S CAT (1956)

This is [the cat] McDermott's own highly flavored account of Kidd's ostensible pirate-hunting expedition in the "Adventure"—a roistering tale, filled with pirate lore, with drama and comedy, related in a dry, straight-faced manner. And, necessarily, there is tragedy, too, for everyone knows what happened to Captain Kidd. McDermott, however, lived and flourished, and stoutly maintained to the end that Kidd was betrayed by his friends and crew. It must have been some comfort to him that, back in 1701, a great many people seem to have agreed with him.

> *Ellen Lewis Buell, in* The New York Times Book Review *(© 1956 by The New York Times Company; reprinted by permission), February 12, 1956, p. 30.*

In the same vein as his *Ben and Me* and *Mr. Revere and I*, Lawson tells the "inside" story of Captain Kidd. . . . As in the earlier books, the story is told with a tongue-in-cheek type of humor whose subtleties may be lost on many readers, and with more than a grain of authenticity.

> Bulletin of the Center for Children's Books *(published by the University of Chicago), June, 1956, p. 115.*

OTHER CITATIONS

Virginia Kirkus' Service, *January 1, 1956, p. 3.*

THE GREAT WHEEL (1957)

From the true story of the Ferris Wheel, the late Robert Lawson has created a charming story and illustrated it with his beautiful black-and-white drawings. He has made the people and situations so real that one cannot tell, nor does one care, where fiction ends and fact begins. It is sad that this is the last story we will have from Mr. Lawson, but it is good that this one should have the same beauty and dignity of his others.

> *Phyllis Fenner, in* The New York Times Book Review (© *1957 by The New York Times Company; reprinted by permission), September 22, 1957, p. 36.*

In some ways this last book by the late Robert Lawson is also his best, combining as it does his superb wit and deft characterizations with a subject that should have wide appeal.

> Bulletin of the Center for Children's Books *(published by the University of Chicago), December, 1957, p. 45.*

[This is a] pleasant, happy story, saved from too great sentimentality by its authentic Irishness. This does not only stem from the Galway village eighteen year-old Conn leaves to "follow the evening star westward till he rides on the greatest wheel in all the world"—as his aunt foretold—but from the continued Irish lilt of the dialogue wisely suggested by structure rather than phoney dialect. The friends Conn makes on his sea-passage, the prosperous New York relations who want him to earn a sure livelihood laying sewers and pavements, and his wild uncle Patrick, foreman to the great engineer Ferris, are all attractive people. If the course of his romance with flaxen-haired Trudy, whom he waits so long to find again, is too inevitable, the book is still worth reading for the good picture of how the Chicago World Fair of 1893 was built, and the engineering details—not too technical to be exciting—of the step-by-step construction of the Great Wheel which everyone but Ferris and his men thought impossible.

> The Junior Bookshelf, *April, 1967, pp. 124-25.*

The narrative [of *The Great Wheel*] is quite pleasant and the pace leisurely; perhaps one of the troubles about this book is that everyone is too nice, the outlines a little woolly, no strong emotions either delineated or aroused.

> The Times Literary Supplement (© *Times Newspapers Ltd., 1967), May 25, 1967, p. 458.*

MR. REVERE AND I (1953)

Following somewhat the same pattern as *Ben and Me*, the author tells of the events leading up to, and including Paul Revere's famous ride.... The story is told with humor and a light touch that makes it fun to read and will, at the same time, give the young reader a vivid picture of the times. Lawson's illustrations are, as usual, filled with action and humor.

> Bulletin of the Center for Children's Books *(published by the University of Chicago), December, 1953, p. 31.*

With many fine drawings that are as vivid and full of fun as the story, [*Mr. Revere and I*] is altogether an original presentation of some great moments in our history. For ageless enjoyment in reading aloud, and for more sophisticated young readers who liked the similarly engaging and hu-

morous story told in *Ben and Me* by Franklin's "Good Mouse Amos."

> *Virginia Haviland, in* The Horn Book Magazine *(copyright, 1953, by The Horn Book, Inc., Boston), December, 1953, p. 464.*

In *Mr. Revere and I...*, Robert Lawson has taken a famous episode in American history for a holiday ride which will inform as well as delight horse lovers who look for the unusual and the readers of history who respect a writer who retains his sense of humor and proportion. Mr. Lawson's clear-cut pictures with their finely interpreted backgrounds, true in every historical detail, and his style have given him a place of his own in American life history.

> *Anne Carroll Moore, in* The Horn Book Magazine *(copyright, 1953, by The Horn Book, Inc., Boston), December, 1953, p. 425.*

[Offensive] stereotyping of Native Americans flaws Robert Lawson's *Mr. Revere and I* (... 1953). This famous account of the beginnings of the American Revolution is, however, memorable for the manner in which historic personages such as Sam Adams and John Hancock come to life vigorously and humorously and thus deserves to keep its place on recommended lists for the Bicentennial.

> *Judith Sloane Hoberman, in* School Library Journal *(reprinted from* School Library Journal, *February, 1975, published by R. R. Bowker Co., a Xerox company; copyright © 1975 by Xerox Corporation), February, 1975, p. 24.*

OTHER CITATIONS

Virginia Kirkus' Bookshop Service, *June 15, 1953, p. 357.*

Marjorie Fischer, in The New York Times Book Review, *November 15, 1953 (Part 2), p. 26.*

RABBIT HILL (1944)

At the heart of Robert Lawson's engaging animal fantasy, *Rabbit Hill*, is love for the animals themselves and the Connecticut countryside that they inhabit. The philosophy of "live and let live" emerges from this kindly tale of a rabbit family and other wildlife creatures surrounding the "Big House" on a hill....

Told with sympathy for even the humblest of small animals, the fantasy is founded on a wide understanding of nature and wildlife creatures. Each creature is given a distinct personality not unlike his own natural one. But the characters are drawn with an artist's eye and a poet's heart so that the animals on Rabbit Hill stand out as perhaps the most humanizing community of wild animals ever to appear in a child's book.

> *Constantine Georgiou, in his* Children and Their Literature (© *1969; reprinted by permission of Prentice-Hall, Inc., Englewood Cliffs, New Jersey), Prentice-Hall, 1969, p. 254.*

Robert Lawson ... told in *Rabbit Hill* ... a tale so spontaneous and natural that it seems to have reached the printed page without effort. Story and illustrations, both by Mr. Lawson, and humorous as well as beautiful, are set against Connecticut meadows, farms, and woods, which the author-illustrator presented with the kind of affection that Beatrix Potter brought to her stories of the English countryside.

> *Ruth Hill Viguers, in* A Critical History of Children's Literature, *by Cornelia Meigs, Anne Thaxter Eaton, Elizabeth Nesbitt, and Ruth Hill Viguers, edited by Cornelia Meigs (copyright © 1953, 1969 by Macmillan Publishing Co., Inc.), revised edition, Macmillan, 1969, p. 469.*

Consideration of the needs of all living things is the most important element in this story. In addition, it stresses respect and tolerance for each other's abilities and weaknesses and suggests that these are keystones toward a peaceful environment.

> *John Gillespie and Diana Lembo, in their* Introducing Books: A Guide for the Middle Grades *(copyright © 1970 by Xerox Corp.), Bowker, 1970, p. 149.*

[*Rabbit Hill*] may not have the superlative literary qualities of *The Wind in the Willows,* but [it is] exceedingly well written and marvelously illustrated. All of the animals, from suspicious Uncle Analdas to worrying Mother Rabbit, are delightfully individualized. Their precarious lives, their small needs, and their many hardships are sympathetically related, and the happy conclusions are not too idealistic, as anyone can testify who has harbored wild creatures. [This story] and [its] illustrations should do more than any lectures to develop in young children a feeling of tenderness and regard for small animals.

> *May Hill Arbuthnot and Zena Sutherland, in their* Children and Books *(copyright © 1947, 1957, 1964, 1972 by Scott, Foresman and Co.), 4th edition, Scott, Foresman, 1972, p. 230.*

SMELLER MARTIN (1950)

Robert Lawson has done it again. Theft, arson, insanity, murder, a mob scene, a questionable attitude toward the Negro, and an undesirable one toward the clergy—everything but sex is in this latest book. The story is built around a young boy's remarkable sense of smell and the use he makes of this ability at home and at school. The love affair of a thirty-five year old aunt also adds an element that should have great (?) appeal for the youngster in grades five to nine. Lawson's illustrations are superior as usual. It is regrettable that he does not confine himself to that medium.

> Bulletin of the Center for Children's Books *(published by the University of Chicago), December, 1950, p. 5.*

OTHER CITATIONS

Siri M. Andrews, in The Horn Book Magazine, *November, 1950, p. 474.*

Irene Smith, in The New York Times Book Review, *November 12, 1950, p. 30.*

THE TOUGH WINTER (1954)

[*The Tough Winter*] takes the characters on The Hill through a humorous if hard three months and still proves [Mr. Lawson] can personalize his animals without being in the least sentimental. . . . [The] reader's reward is Mr. Lawson's matchless description of incident, in words and pictures.

> Virginia Kirkus' Bookshop Service, *July 1, 1954, p. 383.*

In this sequel to his Newbery-Award book, "Rabbit Hill," Robert Lawson presents again the entertaining animal community of a Connecticut countryside. . . .

There is gentle humor in the book's sensitive, beautiful drawings. The prose reflects a love of nature and a feeling of respect for all small beings, in many of whom we can recognize traits of our closest human friends.

> *C. Elta Van Norman, in* The New York Times Book Review *(© 1954 by The New York Times Company; reprinted by permission), November 14, 1954 (Part 2), p. 32.*

The Tough Winter . . . surpasses in the beauty of the drawings and the realization of an idea brought to fulfillment in the text anything Mr. Lawson has done before. To me it is the ultimate reassurance that the artist who remains true to his ideal never lets himself go downhill. He simply gets better and better. . . .

As one who read [this book] independently and vividly recalled the Great Snowstorm at Christmastime in the Forties, I was so thrilled by the beauty and true Christmas spirit of those pages that I put *The Tough Winter* down at the top of my list of Christmas books as well as the most distinguished book published for children this year.

> *Anne Carroll Moore, in* The Horn Book Magazine *(copyright, 1954, by The Horn Book, Inc., Boston), December, 1954, p. 413.*

Robert Lawson continued the adventures of his Rabbit Hill characters in *The Tough Winter*. This story, despite its gentle humor, is a grave picture of what can happen to small animals during long periods of icy, freezing weather. This time there are no kindly human beings on hand to help the animals, and their plight is desperate. If ever there was an effective plea for first aid to winterbound birds and beasts, this book is it.

> *May Hill Arbuthnot, in her* Children's Reading in the Home, *(copyright © 1969 by Scott, Foresman and Co.), Scott, Foresman, 1969, p. 100.*

Uncle Analdas is hardly a comfortable guest for the rabbit family. All the same, there is something admirable about the stupid, obstinate animal. When matters really become desperate in *The Tough Winter*, Uncle Analdas decides the Folks must be fetched home to help. No doubt long privation has made him a little light-headed, but he commands respect as he stumps off down the road, shrinking from car headlights and mumbling 'Too many dingblasted ramifications' as he tries to remember Father Rabbit's description of the bluegrass country. Vain, self-important, tetchy, Uncle Analdas is the most entertaining of a cast of very entertaining animal characters.

> *Margery Fisher, in her* Who's Who in Children's Books: A Treasury of the Familiar Characters of Childhood *(copyright © 1975 by Margery Fisher; reprinted by permission of Holt, Rinehart and Winston), Holt, Rinehart and Winston, 1975, p. 366.*

OTHER CITATIONS

Jennie D. Lindquist, in The Horn Book Magazine, *October, 1954, p. 343.*

Bulletin of the Center for Children's Books, *March, 1955, p. 61.*

*   *   *

LESTER, Julius   1939-

Julius Lester is a Black American critic, editor, musician, and folklorist well-known for his books about Black culture and folklore for both adults and children. (See also *Contemporary Authors*, Vols. 17-18.)

BLACK FOLKTALES (1969)

Although these tales have been told before, in most of them Lester brings a fresh street-talk language to them and thus breathes new life into them. It is a tribute to the universality of these tales—and Lester's ability to see it—that we are thus presented with old truths dressed for today. The author is most successful with the classic "Stagolee." Two of the tales dealing with love, "The Girl With the Large Eyes," and "The Son of Kim-ana-u-eze," are left in simple, straightforward language. This was a wise decision on Lester's part, for they are beautiful enough in original translation, and the Yoruba and Ambundu influences come through clearly. . . .

I have two complaints. The first is that the collection is too short. Second, I wish Lester had included "Shine" and, perhaps, "The Monkey and the Lion." Otherwise "Black Folktales" is a fine collection and adds more laurels to the crown of the author.

> *John A. Williams, in* The New York Times Book Review *(© 1969 by The New York Times Company; reprinted by permission), November 9, 1969, pp. 10, 12.*

There is little question that [Julius Lester] has the cadence and humor of a skilled storyteller; [but] there is little question that [*Black Folktales*] is a vehicle for hostility. . . . There is no story that concerns white people in which they are not pictured as venal or stupid or both.

> *Zena Sutherland, in* Bulletin of the Center for Children's Books *(© 1970 by the University of Chicago; all rights reserved), February, 1970, p. 101.*

Julius Lester has given children's literature its first view from the inside of Afro-American folklore in this powerful, funny, sardonic collection of tales which sing out in their own beautiful idiom. . . . This is folklore serving its primeval function—a testament of living culture.

> *Gertrude B. Herman, in* School Library Journal *(reprinted from* School Library Journal, *September, 1970, published by R. R. Bowker Co., a Xerox company; copyright © 1970 by Xerox Corporation), September, 1970, p. 173.*

―――――――――――

THE KNEE-HIGH MAN, AND OTHER TALES (1972)

[In *The Knee-High Man*] Mr. Rabbit and Mr. Bear achieve a new and welcome dignity beyond their upgraded titles as Julius Lester tells their story with appetizing enthusiasm . . . and an almost total absence of dialect or interpretation. The morals are as straight as the tales are brief. . . . There are six stories in all, drawn from Zora Neale Hurston's *Mules and Men*, Dorson's *American Negro Folktales* and Hughes and Bontemps' *The Book of Negro Folklore*, and looking right at home amid Ralph Pinto's mellow, fully realized rural settings. A small book, but like the Knee-High man, just right for its size.

> Kirkus Reviews *(copyright © 1972 The Kirkus Service, Inc.), August 15, 1972, p. 941.*

To understand most fully the six tales retold here one would need a tremendous comprehension of, and feeling for, the black experience. Most readers today, but especially the non-ghetto reader, lack such knowledge and so will miss the innuendos which glimmer in the tales. . . .

Certainly such subtleties must be a part of the prompting which caused Lester to select these less well-known tales. They reflect the fun of folk wit yet, in at least four instances, powerfully important lessons ride the humor. . . .

Strangely enough, one feels the stories are mild (as opposed to robust) in spirit with the first reading. This vanishes with a second reading and the strength of each narrative emerges. Incidentally, these are excellent for story telling and should be so presented for the greatest impact.

> *Ethel Richard, in* The New York Times Book Review *(© 1973 by The New York Times Company; reprinted by permission), February 4, 1973, p. 8.*

The six [stories] in this collection are told with consummate wit and artistry and should be enjoyed by both adult and child. Brer Rabbit always left me rather embarrassed but here the stories are crystal clear, there is no [cloying] condescension. All are animal tales, although probably they originally reflected the relationship between slave and owner. Today they read as good stories, amusing, sad and instructive. In a note at the end of the book the author explains their origin and symbolism, but understanding of this is not necessary to enjoy the antics of Mr. Rabbit and Mr. Bear or to appreciate this new, for me, explanation of why waves have white caps. The story I enjoyed most was *Why dogs hate cats*, but they are all excellent for reading to any age or for the bright seven year old to read to himself.

Ralph Pinto's illustrations are perfectly in keeping with the narrative, so from every aspect it is a very handsome book.

> The Junior Bookshelf, *February, 1975, p. 43.*

OTHER CITATIONS

Publishers' Weekly, *August 7, 1972, p. 50.*

Virginia Haviland, in The Horn Book Magazine, *October, 1972, p. 463.*

Diane Gersoni Stavn, in School Library Journal, *November, 1972, p. 60.*

The Booklist, *December 15, 1972, p. 405.*

Times Literary Supplement, *July 5, 1974, p. 722.*

LONG JOURNEY HOME: STORIES FROM BLACK HISTORY (1972)

Lester does not feel it necessary to make every black man and woman a superhero. He realizes that there is as much dignity in endurance and survival as in hopeless rebellion. He also sees that it does not detract from the male ego to show women as strong, dignified characters in their own right.... *Long Journey Home* contains six stories from black history, all based on at least some historical fact, and all embellished with historically plausible characters and situations....

Probably the most beautiful story in this thoughtful book is "The Man Who Was a Horse," an account of a black cowboy rounding up a herd of wild mustangs. It is an extended metaphor for the enslavement of free, proud beings.... Pride in the black experience runs throughout the stories and this may well create in a black audience as eagerness to read other historical works to learn the truth of their past (but not necessarily "books for children").

And yet even in this excellent book there is a lapse, trivial enough on the face of it, but important when one stops to consider it. The stories are not arranged in chronological sequence, and the reader therefore gets no sense of one of the most important elements of history—the order in which events took place. He must bring to these stories his own knowledge of the historical sequence and setting.

> *Eric Foner and Naomi Lewis, in* The New York Review of Books *(reprinted with permission from* The New York Review of Books; *copyright © 1972, NYREV, Inc.), April 20, 1972, pp. 41-2.*

More of Julius Lester's recreations of "the history ... made by the many," these stories—several based on such elusive sources as a footnote in a Federal Writers Project publication which referred to a place named Ybo Landing in Georgia or "an occurrence common during the early years of Emancipation"—fall definitely into the category of historical fiction. As such, they are remarkably varied.... [The] title story ... is a sparkling idiomatic storytelling which moves fluently from humor to anger and pathos. Less polemical than Lester's *Black Folk Tales*, [*Long Journey Home*] is both more entertaining and more effective.

> Kirkus Reviews *(copyright © 1972 The Kirkus Service, Inc.), June 1, 1972, p. 629.*

Julius Lester has an eye for capturing the essence of a human experience. He is also an excellent storyteller whose reinterpretations of original source material, from history or legend, boldly proclaim the heritage of Afro-Americans. "Long Journey Home," his third effort for young readers, consists of six stories powerfully recalling the era of slavery and its effects on black men and women....

[This] is a vibrant collection of stories. They recapture the spirit of a past generation of black people authentically—the humor, the wit, the gesture, the innuendo of the vernacular. The stories point the way for young blacks to find their roots, so important to the realization of their identities, as well as offer a stimulating and informative experience for all.

> *Rosalind K. Goddard, in* The New York Times Book Review *(© 1972 by The New York Times Company; reprinted by permission), July 23, 1972, p. 8.*

Julius Lester's *Long Journey Home* ... is about the journey to freedom. Based on actual events in American history, these six stories deal with the restless men who shared a capricious destiny; one which could claim them as slaves one day and declare them free the next....

Author Lester is an engrossing story-teller, with a fine sense for the speech and life-rhythms of his characters. But it is an angry book as well—an anger which, at the sharpest (as in "Ben"), dulls the edge of the story. At its best, as in "Louis" and "The Man Who Was a Horse," "Long Journey Home" is an imaginative trip worth taking.

> *Jennifer Farley Smith, in* The Christian Science Monitor *(reprinted by permission from* The Christian Science Monitor; *© 1972 The Christian Science Publishing Society; all rights reserved), August 2, 1972, p. 10.*

Long Journey Home: Stories from Black History by Julius Lester ... is in a class by itself. Abandoning familiar biographical territory, Lester seeks out the lives of footnote people, ordinary men and women who might appear only in a Brady Civil War photograph or a neglected manuscript at the Library of Congress. His tales, all drawn from true incidents, are explorations of the human condition in adversity....

In Julius Lester's prose, young people will experience their own kind of poetry: unvarnished truth. With a talent both rare and needed, the author writes from inside his characters, black and white. He is, in fact, bound to connect with readers of all ages.

> *William Loren Katz, in* Book World *(© The Washington Post), September 3, 1972, p. 9.*

[The six stories in *Long Journey Home*] are based on such sources as interviews and footnotes.... Although one monologue, the title story, is slow-moving, the others are dramatic, some poignant and some bitter; the selections are diversified in their settings and alike in their sharply-etched effectiveness.

Zena Sutherland, in Bulletin of the Center for Children's Books *(© 1972 by the University of Chicago; all rights reserved), October, 1972, p. 28.*

The directness and simplicity of [the stories'] flow and the strength of their characterizations derive from a simple but subtle style, which ranges from an elegantly unadorned standard English to a Black English rich in folk awareness. But whether the story is concerned with runaway slaves, or with the problems of post-Emancipation days, or with the reminiscences of Africa, pathos is strengthened by dignity and humor transcended by mordant irony. . . . Above all, the six stories are essentially about the overwhelming desire of a people to be free from the shackles laid upon them by their enslavers—in other words, of their desire to be themselves.

Paul Heins, in The Horn Book Magazine *(copyright © 1973 by The Horn Book, Inc., Boston), April, 1973, p. 146.*

Children's literature of race has so far been, at best, mostly of a rather tentative kind. Even when they have known their minds, writers have hesitated to speak them forcefully. Julius Lester makes up for all that now in a forthright collection of true stories, told with controlled passion. Only in the last story, which tells of a folk-memory of first-generation slave Ibos who salked into the sea and "just walked back to Africa", does bitterness break through. "Ain't nothing here for us black folks but bad luck and trouble".

There is a great deal more to this book than Uncle Tom sufferings. The stories are astonishingly varied. They pick up stages in the history of the American negro from the first slaves to the liberation and its aftermath. . . .

A difficult book this, and a very good one. I hope that conventional parents and teachers will not try to come between it and its potential readers, for it speaks very clearly to a generation which is in [the] process of shedding its own fetters.

The Junior Bookshelf, *December, 1973, p. 409.*

OTHER CITATIONS

Publishers' Weekly, *June 5, 1972, p. 140.*

Brooke Anson, in School Library Journal, *September, 1972, p. 143.*

TO BE A SLAVE (1968)

"To Be a Slave" is made up of the narratives of men, women and children who experienced slavery. These excerpts, many published here for the first time, were selected by Julius Lester, who ties them together in a factual, unemotional manner that throws them into brilliant relief. . . .

Aside from the fact that these are tremendously moving documents in themselves, they help destroy the delusion that black men did not suffer as another man would in similar circumstances, a delusion that lies at the base of much racism today. They help also to explain the depth of the black man's current resentments. Most of them find paral-

lels in their own present life or near past, and realize that the same fundamental myths have kept them enslaved without the actual trappings of slavery.

John Howard Griffin, in The New York Times Book Review *(© 1968 by The New York Times Company; reprinted by permission), November 3, 1968, p. 7.*

Excerpts from original material (usually signed) are arranged chronologically in a moving and explicit documentary record that is given continuity by the author's comments and explanations that link the quoted remarks. . . . From capture to auction, from servitude to freedom, the black man speaks eloquently of his history and his bondage. [*To Be a Slave* is not] better than the [Milton] Meltzer compilations [on American Negro history], but [is] more immediate a picture of slavery. A bibliography is appended.

Zena Sutherland, in Bulletin of the Center for Children's Books *(© 1969 by the University of Chicago; all rights reserved), April, 1969, pp. 129-130.*

[*To Be a Slave* combines] original slave accounts and reports of immediate observers with author's comments (set off in an italic type) that provide continuity and insight in a carefully matched style. In its muted account, the book has the allusiveness of poetry. . . . [It] quietly lays bare the shame of American history while making slavery, suffering, and resistance part of [a] black child's heritage. Its manner of revealing dignity in humiliation, expressing the haunting, ever-present sense of the slave experience in the racial memory, is reminiscent of the Jews' ritual celebration of their history of persecution. (p. 277)

Evelyn Geller, "Julius Lester: Newbery Runner-Up" (originally published in School Library Journal, *May, 1969), in* Authors and Illustrators of Children's Books: Writings on Their Lives and Works, *edited by Miriam Hoffman and Eva Samuels (copyright © 1972 by Xerox Corp.), Bowker, 1972, pp. 275-79.*

The extracts [in *To Be a Slave*] have been carefully chosen and arranged to give an all-round picture of slavery, from the journey in the slave ships till the liberation that made so little difference. A commentary written by Mr. Lester links the extracts, and draws in essential background information.

Nobody could read this book unmoved by pity and indignation. Slavery, like other immense causes of human suffering, can be seen in its true abominable light only when seen and felt in individual terms, and these simple voices, telling with stark directness each his own tale, will surely reach any reader of any age with immense impact. . . . If only Mr. Lester would be content to let us listen; but his commentary is full of misjudgments. In many places useful, it is also aggressive, nagging, insistently underlining morals, attempting to lead and preempt the reaction of the reader.

For example there are the words of Charley Williams, who "wants to see old Master again, anyways", and hear him saying,

Get yourself a little piece of that brown

sugar, but don't let no niggers see you eating it. If you do, I'll whup your black behind!

Mr. Lester breaks in at once, with

> Charley Williams' relationship with his owners was a perverted one, and is an example of the kind of pathetic relationships and people that could exist under slavery.

But surely this conclusion would have more force if Mr. Lester would give his readers breathing space to reach it for themselves.

Or he attaches to a terrible story of the drowning of a number of babies, whose owners "got nary a lick of labor, and nary a red penny for any of them babies", an absurdly bathetic explanatory comment on the level of "Black men, black women and black children were enslaved because it was profitable to other men". Does he perhaps think that children will not understand, or that they need guidance what to think about Charley Williams? Your reviewer believes that children can be trusted more than adults to feel truly, and that they particularly dislike being nannied and preached at.

That said, one must stress that in spite of occasional ineptness in presentation, this book is of inestimable value. One can only hope that it will find its way on to every library shelf, and into the hands of every child, for the understanding that it offers could hasten the day when the sufferings of the Negro are a historical instead of a contemporary outrage.

> The Times Literary Supplement (© *Times Newspapers Ltd., 1970), December 11, 1970, p. 1456.*

To Be A Slave (. . . 1968) provides a much needed balance to the usual glorified biographies of George Washington and Thomas Jefferson. Children reading descriptions of the slave quarters at Mount Vernon and Monticello will find their conceptions of these "perfect" men quite altered.

> *Judith Sloane Hoberman, in* School Library Journal *(reprinted from* School Library Journal, *February, 1975, published by R. R. Bowker Co., a Xerox company; copyright* © *1975 by Xerox Corporation), February, 1975, p. 25.*

OTHER CITATIONS

The Junior Bookshelf, *December, 1970, pp. 386-87.*

Anne Wood, in The Spectator, *October 20, 1973, p. xxi.*

TWO LOVE STORIES (1974)

Two Love Stories by Julius Lester is a schizoid piece of publishing because it attempts to bridge the chasm between those two categories of teenage publishing, the literary and the light romance-cum-adventure type. . . . The gap is unbridgeable in one volume, so the book as a whole will satisfy nobody: the literary reader will admire "The Basketball Game" and reject "Catskill Morning"; the reader of light romance will be carried away on the emotional tide of "Catskill Morning"—a superficial all-White story set in a summer camp—and be impatient with the care, love and

attention to character, detail and symbol which make "The Basketball Game" part of the canon of Black literature. . . .

Julius Lester is passionate about the Black experience and shows himself able to present that experience in fictional form.

> The Times Literary Supplement (© *Times Newspapers Ltd., 1974), September 20, 1974, p. 1003.*

As a study of relationships [*Two Love Stories*] does not entirely convince, but this is probably a reaction of the head rather than the heart, and many readers may well find the emotions depicted are very, very true. They are certainly described with a frankness that was once impossible in such books and I hope this will not result in an obstacle race on its journey to the library shelves.

> *David L. Rees, in* Children's Book Review (© *1975 Five Owls Press Ltd.; all rights reserved), Winter 1974-75, p. 153.*

OTHER CITATIONS

The Junior Bookshelf, *December, 1974, p. 378.*

WHO I AM (1974)

Leafing through [David] Gahr's black-and-white photos— of a naked child running through a meadow (not corny here), of three young toughs posing on a stoop—one might see them as just another collection of attractive shots. But when one takes another look and reads Lester's accompanying poems carefully, the "photopoems" surge with new vitality and the sensitivity of both photographer and poet comes through strongly. One haiku: "on this summer day/ I have no doubt that I will live forever," is in itself not a great poem; neither is the photo of a black girl prancing, full of joy, before a line of clothes drying in the sun. But, taken together and thus enhancing each other, they make a unified, strong statement. Most of the other "photopoems" are at least this effective.

> *Deborah H. Williams, in* Library Journal *(reprinted from* Library Journal, *January 1, 1975, published by R. R. Bowker Co., a Xerox company; copyright* © *1975 by Xerox Corporation), January 1, 1975, p. 54.*

This union [of poems and photographs] conveys beauty, pain, humor, tenderness; every photopoem urges the reader to share in the powerful emotional panorama of life as it is lived by people of different racial backgrounds, ages and sexes. Unfortunately, however, Asians are not represented; the world here is seen as Black, white and brown. . . .

[This] is an engrossing if flawed book. [Mr. Gahr's] photographs reflect the realities suggested by Mr. Lester's language; they are marked by a sharpness and precision that the words lack.

> *Barbara Walker, in* Interracial Books for Children Bulletin *(reprinted by permission of* Interracial Books for Children Bulletin, *1841 Broadway, New York, N.Y. 10023), Vol. 5, Nos. 7 & 8, 1975, p. 18.*

M

McHARGUE, Georgess 1941-

An American author of fiction and nonfiction for children, Georgess McHargue is noted for her writings on folklore and the occult. (See also *Contemporary Authors*, Vols. 25-28, and *Something About the Author*, Vol. 4.)

THE BAKER AND THE BASILISK (1970)

Here condemned for giving birth to the poisonous Basilisk is Master Baker Garbihl's rooster, and between them they make the tale—although the hero is apprentice Hans. . . . [The scenes are hugely] pictured, as is the rooster's day in court. Otherwise [Robert Quackenbush's] illustrations are adequate, but their effect is more decorative than dramatic. All in all, hardly distinctive but pleasantly different: the author of *The Beasts of Never* treats them with the sober respect that makes this all the funnier.

> Kirkus Reviews *(copyright © 1970 The Kirkus Service, Inc.), April 15, 1970, p. 446.*

It may be that the fairy-tale aspects of [this] story—baker's apprentice slays monster to win maiden's hand in marriage—are too commonplace. Or it may be simply that the basilisk itself (part rooster, part reptile) is uninteresting without historical background. We do get a period quality from [Robert Quackenbush's] illustrations. We witness a trial—common in the Dark Ages—in which an unfortunate rooster is convicted of being the basilisk's parent. But on the whole, one feels that the author has tired of her subject and should turn her considerable talents elsewhere.

> *Barbara Wersba, in* The New York Times Book Review *(© 1970 by The New York Times Company; reprinted by permission), May 31, 1970, p. 14.*

OTHER CITATIONS

Neil Millar, in The Christian Science Monitor, *May 7, 1970, p. B3.*

Ruth M. Pegau, in School Library Journal, *September, 1970, p. 151.*

THE BEASTS OF NEVER (1968)

Dragons and unicorns once seemed as real as household pets, and it is the purpose of this fascinating book to find out why. Posing the thesis that mythical beasts were the product of mortal longing—an attempt to explain, or exorcise, natural phenomena—Georgess McHargue has compiled a "history natural and unnatural of monsters mythical and magical" that actually illuminates mankind. . . .

The approach is both scholarly and entertaining: each beast is presented in terms of origin, the superstitions surrounding it, and its eventual demise. And while the author does not look for truths, her discussion of probabilities is brilliant. Drawing from myth, folklore, the Bible, early bestiaries and misguided naturalists, she proves that what does not exist can nevertheless seem real. All children know this, of course, but they will never find it more beautifully stated.

> *Barbara Wersba, in* The New York Times Book Review *(© 1968 by The New York Times Company; reprinted by permission), July 28, 1968, p. 23.*

Engaging, informal accounts of the origin and attributes of dragons, unicorns, basilisks, yales, griffins, sea monsters, and other imaginary "all-animal" beasts are presented in an oversize book embellished with pictures in brown or gray of each creature mentioned in the text. . . . [*The Beasts of Never* covers] fewer creatures in greater detail than Jacobson's *The First Book of Mythical Beasts* . . . and Palmer's *Dragons, Unicorns, and Other Magical Beasts*. . . .

> The Booklist and Subscription Books Bulletin *(reprinted by permission of the American Library Association; copyright 1968 by the American Library Association), October 1, 1968, p. 189.*

OTHER CITATIONS

Kirkus Service, *June 1, 1968, p. 609.*

Clara Hulton, in School Library Journal, *September, 1968, p. 193.*

ELIDOR AND THE GOLDEN BALL (1973)

Georgess McHargue's sure retelling of [this] 12th century Welsh tale avoids both the excessive fragility and the show-offish whimsy that mar most visits to the faery folk (we'll overlook a passage in which "Elidor learned how to catch a falling star and the secrets of the mandrake root . . . where all the lost years are and even who cleft the devil's foot . . .") and [Emanuel] Schongut's fluent pictures—lines, dots and silhouettes that deliberately recall the post-art nouveau conventions of a half century ago—evoke a dreamily remote magical atmosphere.

> Kirkus Reviews *(copyright © 1973 The Kirkus Service, Inc.), September 15, 1973, p. 1036.*

[*Elidor and the Golden Ball* is an] enjoyable Welsh tale about a boy who runs away from a cruel teacher and accidentally witnesses the sacred Faery dance. . . . In a brief epilogue readers are told that Elidor was a real person who grew up to become a priest and scholar; he supposedly told this story to an historian named Gerald of Wales. The retelling here is pleasant and [Emanuel Schongut's] line drawings, though slightly flowery, are decorative and interesting with a graceful flow.

> *Marilyn R. Singer, in* School Library Journal *(reprinted from* School Library Journal, *January, 1974, published by R. R. Bowker Co., a Xerox company; copyright © 1974 by Xerox Corporation), January, 1974, p. 41.*

OTHER CITATIONS

Publishers' Weekly, *September 17, 1973, p. 57.*

The Booklist, *December 1, 1973, p. 388.*

FACTS, FRAUDS, AND PHANTASMS: A SURVEY OF THE SPIRITUALIST MOVEMENT (1972)

Georgess McHargue, who inspired our confidence in the existence of *The Impossible People* and *The Beasts of Never,* here examines the claims of spiritualism in a more critical light and comes up with a carefully hedged maybe. . . . [The] hints of uncanny forces at work are tantalizing, or would be were it not for the prevailing emphasis on frauds, fakes and fools. As it is, it's a well researched and intriguing case study in human gullibility . . . and invaluable background for would-be investigators of occult phenomena.

> Kirkus Reviews *(copyright © 1972 The Kirkus Service, Inc.), May 1, 1972, p. 545.*

A history of spiritualism, [*Facts, Frauds, and Phantasms*] is a genuine rarity—a juvenile title which can stand with adult books as being as nearly a complete popular introduction to a subject as one might wish. The author has treated her subject with thoroughness and a careful consideration of the causes and meanings of this interesting and enduring phenomenon: most satisfying is McHargue's felicitous display of wit and humor. . . .

> *Michael Cart, in* School Library Journal *(reprinted from* School Library Journal, *October, 1972, published by R. R. Bowker Co., a Xerox company; copyright © 1972 by Xerox Corporation), October, 1972, p. 130.*

Spiritualism may or may not be a dead horse itself, but [Georgess McHargue's] treatment of it vibrates with life; filled with intriguing details, the exposition is lively and humorous. Although quick to condemn frauds, the author leaves openings for speculation and occasionally admits that some phenomena—like those performed by Eusapia Palladino—cannot be dismissed as trickery and that they have not yet been explained. Fascinating material treated in a tongue-in-cheek style.

> *Anita Silvey, in* The Horn Book Magazine *(copyright © 1972 by The Horn Book, Inc., Boston), October, 1972, p. 478.*

Comprehensive, well-researched and written with style and wit, this history of spiritualism is one of the best titles dealing with the occult for young people. . . . McHargue's intelligent, carefully detailed study explains it and devotes much-needed attention to contemporary spiritualism. Although intended for a slightly older audience than Daniel Cohen's *In Search of Ghosts* . . . , this book is far superior and should become a standard work on the subject.

> *Michael Cart, in* School Library Journal *(reprinted from* School Library Journal, *November, 1972, published by R. R. Bowker Co., a Xerox company; copyright © 1972 by Xerox Corporation), November, 1972, p. 76.*

OTHER CITATIONS

Zena Sutherland, in Bulletin of the Center for Children's Books, *April, 1973, p. 129.*

FUNNY BANANAS (1975)

"Funny Bananas" strives for originality by setting its story in the American Museum of Natural History. Despite Miss McHargue's extensive descriptions, the natural mysteries and cloistered ambience of that institution fail to come to life, and seem largely irrelevant to Ben Pollock's search for the vandal whose garbage-scattering and wastebasket dumping is disrupting the museum. . . . Ben is bland as breakfast cereal while Carmen, distressingly, is a collection seriatim of female stereotypes ranging from . . . witch to grateful, helpless girlish dependent.

> *Gloria Levitas, in* The New York Times Book Review *(© 1975 by The New York Times Company; reprinted by permission), September 7, 1975, p. 20.*

OTHER CITATIONS

Kirkus Reviews, *April 15, 1975, p. 455.*

Sarah Law Kennerly, in School Library Journal, *May, 1975, p. 70.*

THE IMPOSSIBLE PEOPLE: A HISTORY NATURAL AND UNNATURAL OF BEINGS TERRIBLE AND WONDERFUL (1972)

The "human" counterparts of the *Beasts of Never,* Giants, Faeries and Little People, populate this who's who of mythological beings which weaves together the fragmentary accounts of their existence and nicely differentiates the various subspecies (e.g. Pixie vs. Elf and Brownie vs. Boggart). A purist, McHargue eschews the modern romanticizations of Faery Godmothers and Tinkerbelle, while ranging widely through Celtic and Germanic folklore, Greek mythology, and medieval demonology, and even dipping into African sources for the nine-buttocked Chemosit.... The practical aspects, such as how to identify a werewolf and retrieve infants stolen by faeries, are not neglected, but it's chiefly a carefully guided tour through the esoteric realms of mermaid and manticore. Naturally impossible, but terribly wonderful.

> *Kirkus Reviews (copyright © 1971 The Kirkus Service, Inc.), December 1, 1971, pp. 1262-63.*

Miss McHargue does not merely provide us with the flat surface of history. She also tracks the origins of her impossible people with the determination of a Sherlock Holmes. In a cheery, businesslike way, she guides the reader through a veritable labyrinth of detail—simultaneously explaining that myths, and mythical creatures, are but one of humanity's means of coping with the paradoxes and terrors of existence....

I cannot imagine anyone disliking this book—and will practice witchcraft on them if they do. Like the author's previous work, "The Beasts of Never," the present compendium is a rare blend of scholarship, entertainment, wisdom, gravity and grace.

> *Barbara Wersba, in The New York Times Book Review (© 1972 by The New York Times Company; reprinted by permission), April 2, 1972, p. 8.*

This is a lively-written catalog of those individuals and groups of big and little people, faery folk, good and evil spirits, part animal or sea creatures who live for most of us in the old legends and tales.... Cohen's *Natural History of Unnatural Things* (... 1971) is much more comprehensive and includes some non-legendary creatures popularized by monster movies; on the other hand, McHargue's work includes more varieties of legendary folk and many portions are interesting enough to be read aloud to young audiences.

> *Brooke Anson, in School Library Journal (reprinted from School Library Journal, May, 1972, published by R. R. Bowker Co., a Xerox company; copyright © 1972 by Xerox Corporation), May, 1972, p. 79.*

[Georgess McHargue] provides long-needed definitions for hitherto obscure characters—such as the Transcendent Pig, who "once had the unspeakable audacity to swallow a nephew of the Emperor of Heaven".... Whether discursing on the Blue Men of the Minch, the Brown Man of the Moors, or the shocking misnomer of Gentle Annie, Miss McHargue uses her subject with marvelous humor and an unflagging sense of style. Her imaginative treatment of those who populate our fantasies and folklore is fascinating....

My own reservation is that the author too often seems to "explain away" her creatures by concrete physical manifestations. Tracing the origin of some spirit to early apemen or pre-Christian peoples is ingenious and highly thought-provoking, but it doesn't leave much room for the consideration of Big, Little, and Halfway folk as unsophisticated man's imaginative explanation of the natural forces around him and the psychic mysteries within.

> *Jennifer Farley Smith, in The Christian Science Monitor (reprinted by permission from The Christian Science Monitor; © 1972 The Christian Science Publishing Society; all rights reserved), May 4, 1972, p. B4.*

[Despite] the inherent appeal of the subject matter, [this] book is unlikely to be one that many young readers breeze through at a sitting or two. [Frank] Bozzo's oddly static illustrations, the advanced vocabulary, and the urbane distance the author maintains from her material all conspire to discourage a race to the finish. Its lasting value is as a highly original work of reference.

> *Judith Williams, in Book World (© The Washington Post), May 7, 1972 (Part 2), p. 4.*

[In *The Impossible People*, Georgess McHargue] attempts to determine the origins of the "not-quite-human beings" who populate myth and folklore.... But while all of the material is interesting, most of it is available elsewhere, and the author's chatty style sometimes verges on condescension. In fact, reading the book is like having the history of a brilliant family explained to you by an erudite nanny.

> *Sidney D. Long, in The Horn Book Magazine (copyright © 1972 by The Horn Book, Inc., Boston), August, 1972, p. 380.*

OTHER CITATIONS

The Booklist, *June 1, 1972, p. 862.*

Zena Sutherland, in Bulletin of the Center for Children's Books, *February, 1973, pp. 94-5.*

THE MERMAID AND THE WHALE (1973)

Based on an old Cape Cod sailors' yarn, [*The Mermaid and the Whale*] retains the local color and salty flavor of its Yankee origins. And [Robert Andrew Parker's] shimmering full-color illustrations, executed in ink and acrylic, enhance the mood of enchantment and humor by contrasting a delicate and sensuous mermaid with the phlegmatic Yankee sea captain and the black bulk of the whale. [This book is a] marvelous blend of the storyteller's art with folklore convention.

> *Mary M. Burns, in The Horn Book Magazine (copyright © 1974 by The Horn Book Inc., Boston), February, 1974, pp. 46-7.*

OTHER CITATIONS

Publishers' Weekly, *September 24, 1973, p. 188.*

Kirkus Reviews, *October 15, 1973, pp. 1157-58.*

Ruth M. McConnell, in School Library Journal, *March, 1974, p. 99.*

MUMMIES (1972)

A review of the perversely fascinating subject of mummies

by esoterica collector Georgess McHargue could hardly fail. Yet there are only occasional glimmers of the grotesque here. . . . And contemporary attitudes toward the survival of the body are dealt with only in cursory discussions of the *American Way of Death* and the developing science of cryonics. . . . [Though] the details on preservation techniques are in themselves fascinating, one wishes for more background on the attitudes toward immortality and/or fear of the dead which inspired them in the first place. In all, these Mummies are intriguing, but decidedly lightweight conversation pieces.

> *Kirkus Reviews (copyright © 1972 The Kirkus Service, Inc.), October 1, 1972, p. 1158.*

[In *Mummies*, Georgess McHargue] continues to exploit her flair for combining research with an eminently readable style. Despite a slight accolade to sensationalism—something inherent in the very nature of the subject—she considers mummification in the light of biological, anthropological, and archaeological investigations, and ranges in her pursuit of the subject through many parts of the world. Except for the chapter considering the frozen Siberian mammoths, the book presents the facts and beliefs that prompted man to preserve human bodies after death. . . . The book contains Suggestions for Further Reading and an Index.

> *Paul Heins, in* The Horn Book Magazine *(copyright © 1973 by The Horn Book, Inc., Boston), April, 1973, pp. 152-53.*

[This is a] sufficiently exhaustive account of the phenomenon of mummification, both natural and artificial. . . . The text is interesting, informative, and easy to read, and its impact is effectively augmented by the abundant illustrations which, while gruesome at first sight, invite examination in detail.

> *Sylvia R. Cooper, in* School Library Journal *(reprinted from* School Library Journal, *May, 1973, published by R. R. Bowker Co., a Xerox company; copyright © 1973 by Xerox Corporation), May, 1973, p. 73.*

OTHER CITATIONS

Publishers' Weekly, *December 18, 1972, p. 40.*

STONEFLIGHT (1975)

There is a direct connection between [Janie's] flat, unhappy and oppressively muggy summer in New York and her compensatory fantasy about the stone griffin on her Morningside Heights roof, And McHargue is a bit heavy-handed in emphasizing that [Janie] retreats to the talking Griff whenever the tension and bickering between her parents become too unsettling. At the same time the discrepancy between the flat narration of boring everyday detail and the reported ecstasy [Janie] experiences with Griff make both worlds, at least at first, a bit hollow and unconvincing.

> *Kirkus Review (copyright © 1975 The Kirkus Service, Inc.), March 1, 1975, p. 239.*

McHargue is good at focusing a child's-eye view on Janie's

world and the unstereotyped grown-ups she deals with [in *Stoneflight*]. Just as impressive are the numerous small gems of imagery strewn throughout, combined with a most delicate handling of the fantasy's development; although we never know if the stone creatures live and breathe outside Janie's mind, we are sure that they could.

> *The Booklist (reprinted by permission of the American Library Association; copyright 1975 by the American Library Association), March 15, 1975, p. 762.*

The framework of ["Stoneflight"] has been thoughtfully constructed. Janie's isolation and involvement with art are persuasive. Miss McHargue is most interesting when she is expressing ideas. But the slowness of the pace reduces the drama's momentum. And the language is often labored. Upset with her mother, Janie tries to speak, and "two different answers jam in her mouth fighting to get out like passengers leaving a subway car." (I kept seeing those passengers in her mouth.) Or, "As the weeks went by, things settled into a kind of routine, like plaster of Paris in a mold." Such images don't sharpen action, they trip it up.

In scenes between Janie and her uncle, ideas and feeling blend effectively. More frequently, however, the central characters in "Stoneflight" lack the life to animate the book's promise. "Quickness is a gift" says Griff. In storytelling, too.

> *Karla Kuskin, in* The New York Times Book Review *(© 1975 by The New York Times Company; reprinted by permission), May 25, 1975, p. 10.*

The depiction of an unhappy child whose parents are trying to protect her and only make her feel excluded is candid and perceptive [in *Stoneflight*]; the fantasy is adequately handled, but the two don't mesh, despite the parallel McHargue draws between the real stone creatures and the dangers of becoming petrified into withdrawal.

> *Zena Sutherland, in* Bulletin of the Center for Children's Books *(© 1975 by the University of Chicago; all rights reserved), November, 1975, p. 50.*

OTHER CITATIONS

Susan Davie, *in* School Library Journal, *March, 1975, pp. 98-9.*

Publishers' Weekly, *March 31, 1975, p. 49.*

Virginia Haviland, *in* The Horn Book Magazine, *June, 1975, p. 268.*

*   *   *

MONJO, F(erdinand) N.   1924-

F. N. Monjo, an American editor and author, is known for his easy-to-read books on American historical events.

THE DRINKING GOURD (1970)

Refreshingly, [*The Drinking Gourd* shows] a stopover on the underground railroad without abject blacks or saintly whites. . . . The brave [character], rightfully, is Big Jeff; and slavery is just plain "wicked." In the same upstanding tone, Tommy's father, significantly Deacon Fuller, faces the issue of lawbreaking: the law that says people are property is *wrong*. Rigorous history with a humorous twist, drawn to convey its quiet drama.

> *Kirkus Reviews (copyright © 1970 The Kirkus Service, Inc.), April 15, 1970, p. 450.*

[*The Drinking Gourd* is a] story set in the years just prior to the Civil War, the simplicity of dialogue and exposition, the level of concepts, and the length of the story making it most suitable for the primary grades reader. The illustrations [by Fred Drenner] are deftly representational, the whole a fine addition to the needed body of historical books for the very young.

> *Zena Sutherland, in* Bulletin of the Center for Children's Books *(© 1970 by the University of Chicago; all rights reserved), October, 1970, p. 31.*

In this story, written lucidly and illustrated sympathetically, young Tommy learns the difference between the laws that rule a child's innocent life and those laws that are supposed to govern adult behavior. *The Drinking Gourd* is a straight, unsentimental narrative, with each character clearly established and a climax handled without resort to mawkish language.

The production is excellent. The dialogue is brief and easy to read, linking the narrative without forcing the pace. An intelligent use of grey illustrations [by Fred Brenner] to depict what is taking place in Tommy's imagination contrasts with the muted colour of the pictures showing what is really happening.

> *Margaret Deg, in* Children's Book Review *(© 1971 by Five Owls Press Ltd.; all rights reserved), October, 1971, p. 163.*

OTHER CITATIONS

Lavinia Russ, in The New York Times Book Review, *May 24, 1970 (Part 2), p. 43.*

Virginia Haviland, in The Horn Book Magazine, *August, 1970, p. 382.*

The Booklist, *September 1, 1970, p. 58.*

Trevelyn Jones, in School Library Journal, *December, 1970, p. 71.*

GRAND PAPA AND ELLEN AROON (1974)

Ellen Aroon's plaintive defense of her Presidential Grand Papa recalls, though less painfully, Tad Lincoln's "How could anyone want to hurt my Pa?" In Monjo's *Me and Willie and Pa*. . . . The utter partisan innocence of Thomas Jefferson's favorite granddaughter can in fact become a little wearing, but modern readers will be amused by the workings of a simpler White House. . . . Thomas Jefferson at home can't be expected to inspire the freshness and sparkle of [Monjo's] *Poor Richard in France* . . ., but this genteel and personable sketch has its quieter interest.

> *Kirkus Reviews (copyright © 1975 The Kirkus Service, Inc.), January 1, 1975, p. 23.*

Based on primary sources, including Jefferson's own writings and those of his descendants, [*Grand Papa and Ellen Aroon*] is impeccably authentic and the history, presented from a child's perspective, has an immediacy that will appeal to middle graders. The account is slightly fictionalized to take on the aspect of Ellen's personal narrative but, in all respects, this is vastly superior to Colver's *Thomas Jefferson: Author of Independence* (. . . 1963).

> *Joe Bearden, in* School Library Journal *(reprinted from* School Library Journal, *February, 1975, published by R. R. Bowker Co., a Xerox company; copyright © 1975 by Xerox Corporation), February, 1975, p. 49.*

[Ellen Aroon's] candid remarks about Grand Papa give a great deal of information about [Thomas] Jefferson, but they also have an ingenuous charm of their own, as Ellen prattles on about what Grand Papa is like, and what he thinks of other people, and what other people think of him, and all the things that keep him so busy. Monjo's special ability to invest history with grace and humor adds enjoyment to the usefulness of a book that can give young children accurate information about Jefferson and about the period of his tenure in office.

> *Zena Sutherland, in* Bulletin of the Center for Children's Books *(© 1975 by the University of Chicago; all rights reserved), May, 1975, pp. 151-52.*

OTHER CITATIONS

Publishers' Weekly, *October 21, 1974, p. 51.*

INDIAN SUMMER (1968)

It would be hard to imagine any beginning reader who wouldn't thrill to this story that "really could have happened,". . . . Along with action and suspense, love and loyalty and courage are stressed in an exciting tale and vivid, lifelike pictures. Highly recommended.

> *Polly Goodwin, in* Book World *(© The Washington Post), October 6, 1968, p. 20.*

Indian Summer . . . has excellent pictures by Anita Lobel and more excitement and adventure than most easy readers. On the Kentucky frontier, two boys hear owls hooting in the woods, realize that the owls are really Indians, and warn their family. Unlike too many juvenile book reductions, these Indians do not miraculously become dearest friends of the family, nor have they come on a peaceful mission. The pioneer family (minus father who is off fighting in the Revolution) battle for their lives and cleverly defeat the Indians. Children are fascinated by the Indian wars and this is an exciting story for the very youngest readers.

> *Trevelyn Jones, in* School Library Journal *(reprinted from* School Library Journal, *November, 1968, published by R. R. Bowker Co., a Xerox company; copyright © 1968 by Xerox Corporation), November, 1968, p. 108.*

The setting for [*Indian Summer*] is a log cabin in a Kentucky forest during the time when the American colonies were fighting to gain independence from Britain. While the man of the house is away fighting with the American forces, men of some unidentified tribe skulk around the cabin. The "pioneer" woman outwits them and they retreat hastily into the forest. The author in a fit of incredible cuteness has contrived to work the sound "ugh" into the story.

The message a child gets from this "history" book is that the settlers are good, peaceful people who love their homes and families, and that American Indians are menacing but stupid creatures called "redskins" who can be made fools of by a lone woman. The "pioneer" woman is bravely and courageously defending her home and children. The father is patriotic and dutiful. There is nothing in *Indian Summer* indicating that American Indians are also fathers and mothers with families and homes.

Undoubtedly it is accurate that settlers were threatened by, and afraid of, Indians, but Indians were equally, if not more, threatened by the settlers and they had much more to lose. The history books and story books seldom make it clear that Native Americans in fighting back, were defending their homes and families and were not just being malicious.

> *Mary Gloyne Byler, in her* American Indian Authors for Young Readers: A Selected Bibliography *(copyright © 1973 Association on American Indian Affairs, Inc.), Association on American Indian Affairs, Inc., 1973, p. 8.*

OTHER CITATIONS

Kirkus Service, *August 1, 1968, p. 815.*

The New York Times Book Review, *November 3, 1968, p. 53.*

Zena Sutherland, *in* Bulletin of the Center for Children's Books, *January, 1969, p. 83.*

THE JEZEBEL WOLF (1971)

By singling out a specific episode in [Israel] Putnam's early life—the long chase and final capture of a remarkably intelligent, vengeful she-wolf—[Monjo] has not only presented a nostalgic bit of Americana but also created an engrossing narrative with the structure and cadence of a folk tale. . . . Strong black-and-white illustrations [by John Schoenherr] graphically interpret the short, pungent text which is climaxed by Israel's final confrontation with the desperate wolf. A story with particular appeal for boys.

> *Mary M. Burns, in* The Horn Book Magazine *(copyright © 1971 by The Horn Book, Inc., Boston), October, 1971, p. 477.*

It is a fact that Israel Putnam, General in the Continental Army, told and re-told the story of the wolf hunt; here it is retold as a casual narration by Putnam to his family. The framework . . . adds humor and naturalness to the account, and the story itself is full of action and suspense. The author's appended note includes the information that wolves are not now the menace they were in the days of the Revolutionary War and that every effort should be made to save the species.

> *Zena Sutherland, in* Bulletin of the Center for Children's Books *(© 1972 by the University of Chicago; all rights reserved), April, 1972, p. 127.*

A hunt for a wolf and how that wolf is finally killed hardly seems to be a subject for "an easy to read historical event" or a book suitable to give to a "young history buff". Any young British history buff would be extremely disappointed because there is not much in this book to suggest a sense of history at all. In fact one can imagine much the same chase and kill taking part today, especially if you substitute a fox for the wolf. Israel Putnam may be a name which means something to American youngsters; it is hard to see it meaning anything to British ones. On the other hand it is an interesting tale for those who like animal stories and those who do not mind when the animal comes off worst and is killed in spite of a long and brave fight.

> The Junior Bookshelf, *June, 1974, p. 168.*

OTHER CITATIONS

The Times Literary Supplement, *July 1, 1971, p. 720.*

Kirkus Reviews, *July 15, 1971, p. 740.*

Polly Goodwin, *in* Book World, *November 7, 1971 (Part 2), p. 11.*

The Booklist, *November 15, 1971, p. 293.*

Leone R. Hemenway, *in* School Library Journal, *January, 1972, p. 52.*

Barbara Hardcastle, *in* Children's Book Review, *Summer, 1974, p. 70.*

KING GEORGE'S HEAD WAS MADE OF LEAD (1974)

[King George's] air of piqued pomposity and arsenal of rhetorical flourishes make for a ringing monologue, but the central incident—the melting of New York's lead statue of King George to make Yankee Doodle bullets—is overextended. [Margot] Tomes' tableaux have more action than usual, not to mention ballooned commentary and jokes, and this is an undeniably energetic though somewhat strained performance. Unlike [Monjo's] *Secret of the Sachem's Tree,* this is less a self-sustaining tale than a cleverly got-up history lesson. On that basis, it might work very well for group read-alouds and as an inspiration to have fun on one's own with other unlikely historical perspectives.

> *Kirkus Reviews (copyright © 1974 The Kirkus Service, Inc.), November 1, 1974, p. 1156.*

Like a spoiled child the lead-headed statue of George III impetuously relates events leading to the War for Independence and to his own statuary demise. . . . The condescending rant is a debatable ploy when it strays to pedantry, but the dollops of humor are beguiling, and George's pouty recalcitrance finally buoys this decidedly Yankee, easy-to-read caricature. Although an appended author's note supplies added context to the events, this is more suitable for supplementary, read-aloud dramatics than as a history lesson.

> The Booklist *(reprinted by permission of the*

American Library Association; copyright 1974 by the American Library Association), November 15, 1974, p. 345.

Amply illustrated [by Margot Tomes], this brief history for younger readers offers a clear-cut if lightly expressed view of goings on during Revolutionary War days. . . . A waggish humor emanates from the narrator, who is the head of the statue [of King George]. Set down in verse, the lines occasionally rhyme: "I'm a reasonable man, as I have said/ But my head is, regrettably, made of lead"; "and crowds of my redcoat soldiers have fled,/ all because my royal head/ was—all too disastrously—made of lead."

> *Virginia Haviland, in* The Horn Book Magazine *(copyright © 1975 by the Horn Book, Inc., Boston), April, 1975, p. 158.*

The story of the American revolt against its British rulers is told from a new viewpoint, as the petulant voice of George III gives his account of the unreasonable and disobedient colonists who simply wouldn't cooperate. . . . This is a nice adjunct to the more familiar versions of colonial protest told from the American point of view; there's characterization in the monarch's self-description and the irritable monologue, and there's humor in both the text and the illustrations.

> *Zena Sutherland, in* Bulletin of the Center for Children's Books *(© 1975 by the University of Chicago; all rights reserved), April, 1975, p. 135.*

OTHER CITATIONS

Publishers' Weekly, *November 4, 1974, p. 69.*

Joe Bearden, in School Library Journal, *February, 1975, p. 40.*

LETTERS TO HORSEFACE: BEING THE STORY OF WOLFGANG AMADEUS MOZART'S JOURNEY TO ITALY, 1769-1770, WHEN HE WAS A BOY OF FOURTEEN (1975)

[*Letters to Horseface* is a] skilled divertimento paced by gracefully styled "letters" which Mozart could very well have written at fourteen during his Italian trip with his father from December of 1769 to March, 1771. Monjo has reconstructed with care and spirit the flavor of the cities the Mozarts visited, the frenetic music scene of the times (there's a lively view of an opera audience at their noisy games), the doubtful pleasures attendant on the patronage system, and the peculiarities and problems of opera production. There are insights into the incredible strain placed upon the young musician/composer tirelessly driven to creation and performance by his entrepreneur/violinist father, Leopold. Yet Wolfgang writes "Horseface," his sister, with the buoyancy of a youngster eagerly confronting new sights, places, ideas and dreams. Only occasionally are there poignant Mozartian notes as when he has the pathetically rare joy of friendship with someone his age or as in the response to his father's ". . . your reputation is *made!*": "Poor Papa! Always so hard at work!" Along the way there are cheerful translations of Italian ("servitore umillissimo"), explications of musical terms and hints of opi to come. And throughout there is the boy's seemingly

carefree "Tra-la-la-liera"—both a kind of bravura tune-out on things like overwork on a toothache, and a simple expression of high spirits. The handsome sketches [by Don Bolognese and Elaine Raphael] echo the mood like the most decorative of violin obligatos. With notes and bibliography, for the unhurried and discerning.

> *Kirkus Reviews (copyright © 1975 The Kirkus Service, Inc.), October 15, 1975, p. 1190.*

"Letters to Horseface" carries an initial shock—at least, to a student of Mozart's letters. One rapidly leafs through these pages, not paying much attention. Ah, yes, Mozart's letters to his sister while he was a boy on tour. Then one actually starts reading these letters, and they are not by Mozart at all.

But they very well could be, and it is a tribute to F. N. Monjo's skill and sensitivity that he has carried off the Mozart style so accurately. He has followed the 14-year-old Wolfgang and his father Leopold on their famous trip to Italy during 1769-70 and has written a series of letters purporting to come from the young genius. . . .

Fortunately, Monjo has a good deal of material on which to draw. The primary source materials are, of course, the actual Mozart letters, which have been the scholars' bible ever since they started to be assembled (the three-volume English translation by Emily Anderson came out in 1938), and which tell us more about Mozart than any biography has been able to do.

The young Mozart, as evidenced in his own bubbling, effervescent, sometimes scatological letters, was a bright, observant boy who knew very well how talented he was. He was cocky, full of fun, already absolutely secure and mature in his musical judgments. He was a punster, he loved his big sister Narrerl, and the world was going to be his oyster.

Monjo has caught all of this in these letters to "Horseface," his sister. . . .

What Monjo has done is to reconstruct the trip through young Mozart's mind, and he has done a remarkable job. The letters read as though they actually came from Wolfgang's pen. Young readers will find them easy to take: they go fast, they are light-hearted, and a great deal of information is served up in a painless manner.

In addition, anybody reading this little book will get a good idea of how the mind of a musical genius works. Monjo, like Mozart himself, is not sentimental about the subject. A child like Mozart is born with certain stupendous aptitudes, and he uses them as naturally and unaffectedly as he breathes.

Profuse illustrations by Don Bolognese and Elaine Raphael (husband and wife) are in crayon and ink and are scrupulously accurate in relation to time and place.

> *Harold C. Schonberg, in* The New York Times Book Review *(© 1975 by The New York Times Company; reprinted by permission), November 16, 1975, p. 33.*

OTHER CITATIONS

Publishers' Weekly, *November 17, 1975, p. 97.*

ME AND WILLIE AND PA: THE STORY OF ABRAHAM LINCOLN AND HIS SON TAD (1973)

In the mode of [Monjo's] *Poor Richard in France*, [*Me and Willie and Pa*] is a family portrait of old Abe as he might have been seen by his youngest son Tad. Since Lincoln's informal persona is well known, the view holds fewer surprises here, and many tragedies of his presidency—both on the battlefield and in the White House itself—are less well suited to the colloquial language and limited perspective of a child narrator.... Though Tad's story, which ends with the plaintive cry "How could anyone want to hurt my Pa?" sometimes becomes unbearably painful, it does offer an imaginative, basically honest reworking of familiar Lincoln anecdotes, and [Douglas] Gorsline uses the manner and subject matter of old photographs to achieve an unsettling but highly effective mood.

> Kirkus Reviews *(copyright © 1973 The Kirkus Service, Inc.), November 15, 1973, p. 1269.*

By casting Tad Lincoln as the narrator of [*Me and Willie and Pa,* F. N. Monjo] presents a child's eye view of Lincoln's presidency. Many familiar Lincoln anecdotes are included, yet Tad's innocent observations reveal details about the presidential household normally glossed over.... And Tad's own problems—his speech defect, his failings as a student—are also incorporated into a narrative which is honest and poignant and somewhat more subdued in tone than *The Vicksburg Veteran* or *The One Bad Thing About Father....* [Douglas Gorsline's] illustrations, reminiscent of steel engravings, add an appropriate period flavor. A detailed author's note and a bibliography are appended.

> *Mary M. Burns, in* The Horn Book Magazine *(copyright © 1974 by The Horn Book, Inc., Boston), February, 1974, pp. 42-3.*

[F. N. Monjo's] story of the Lincoln years in the White House is told by a putative Tad Lincoln and illustrated [by Douglas Gorsline] with soft, realistic drawings that capture the serious and formal air of contemporary engravings. Tad's account is ingenuous but not cute, appropriately casual and conversational, and nicely balanced between personal anecdotage and historical coverage.

> *Zena Sutherland, in* Bulletin of the Center for Children's Books *(© 1974 by the University of Chicago; all rights reserved), April, 1974, p. 134.*

OTHER CITATIONS

Publishers' Weekly, *November 12, 1973, p. 37.*

Phyllis Galt, in School Library Journal, *February, 1974, p. 65.*

THE ONE BAD THING ABOUT FATHER (1970)

A child's-eye view of a father is apt to be refreshingly different from the public image of a President of the United States, and this imaginary diary of Quentin Roosevelt portrays Theodore Roosevelt in engaging fashion.... Although the loving and ebullient father almost eclipses the President, the book gives a real sense of both the man and the era. Bully!

> *Zena Sutherland, in* Saturday Review *(copyright © 1970 by Saturday Review, Inc.; reprinted with permission), March 21, 1970, p. 39.*

Quentin Roosevelt never kept a childhood diary, but this invented one will do very nicely: it is consistently childlike, it gives a vivid impression of the vigorous Theodore Roosevelt and some of the flavor of the period, and it is above all a charming picture of family life.... [Monjo's] writing is ingenuous and candid, [Rocco Negri's] illustrations attractive save for some rather blank children's faces.

> *Zena Sutherland, in* Bulletin of the Center for Children's Books *(© 1970 by the University of Chicago; all rights reserved), June, 1970, pp. 163-64.*

OTHER CITATIONS

Kirkus Reviews, *February 1, 1970, p. 103.*

Publishers' Weekly, *February 2, 1970, p. 91.*

Trevelyn Jones, in School Library Journal, *May, 1970, p. 89.*

Lavinia Russ, in The New York Times Book Review, *May 24, 1970 (Part 2), p. 43.*

POOR RICHARD IN FRANCE (1973)

Monjo scores again with this irreverent history told by Franklin's grandson, Benny.... Benny's view of events is based on a skeleton of facts embellished with humorous touches: e.g., he reports that Franklin wouldn't be surprised to see his face painted on chamber pots in a souvenir shop.... On the more serious side, there are excerpts from *Poor Richard's Almanack* and frequent references to Franklin's thoughts on life. The format of chapters coupled with a lively writing style make this a good choice for beginners as well as older, slow readers. Two-color charcoal and pastel illustrations [by Brinton Turkle] on almost every page add greatly to the spirit of the book.

> *Carol Chatfield, in* School Library Journal *(reprinted from* School Library Journal, *December, 1973, published by R. R. Bowker Co., a Xerox company; copyright © 1973 by Xerox Corporation), December, 1973, p. 43.*

[In *Poor Richard in France*, Brinton Turkle's] drawings are authentic in detail and attractive; [Monjo's] text is historically accurate and lively, convincingly told by Benjamin Franklin's small grandson.... Seven-year-old Benny's comments are lively and humorous, and in a perfectly natural way they give a good bit of information about Franklin and about the rebellion against the British.

> *Zena Sutherland, in* Bulletin of the Center for Children's Books *(© 1974 by the University of Chicago; all rights reserved), March, 1974, pp. 115-16.*

OTHER CITATIONS

Publishers' Weekly, *October 8, 1973, p. 97.*

Kirkus Reviews, *October 15, 1973, pp. 1167-68.*

Joyce Alpern, in Book World, *November 11, 1973 (Part 2), p. 5C.*

Ethel L. Heins, in The Horn Book Magazine, *February, 1974, p. 43.*

RUDI AND THE DISTELFINK (1972)

The sense of time and place and the Schimmelpfennig [family] way of life is the whole point [in *Rudi and the Distelfink*], with only a faint thread of a plot . . . to unite the everyday events. . . . The nostalgic parade of incidentals never really takes us back, but it will provide outsiders with an agreeable introduction to the [Pennsylvania Dutch] culture, and of course in the Lancaster area this will be grabbed up like Mutti's snitz pie.

> Kirkus Reviews *(copyright © 1972 The Kirkus Service, Inc.), November 1, 1972, p. 1234.*

Rudi Schimmelpfennig is one of eleven children in a Pennsylvania Dutch family of 1820. His running commentary on family events in each month of the year are accompanied by paintings of the primitive school, appropriate for the simplicity and the bucolic robustness of the text although not outstanding in themselves. Rudi's remarks in the Pennsylvania Dutch dialect are warm and natural, giving a good picture of the family, the farming community, and the customs of the region.

> Zena Sutherland, *in* Bulletin of the Center for Children's Books *(© 1973 by the University of Chicago; all rights reserved), March, 1973, p. 110.*

Monjo captures the Pennsylvania-Dutch life style, but this narrative is not as lively as his *One Bad Thing About Father* (1970) or *The Drinking Gourd* (1969 . . .). While Rowland's *Amish Boy* (. . . 1970) and DeAngeli's *Yonnie Wondernose* (. . . 1944) are more suitable for storytelling, *Rudi and the Distelfink* is enjoyable, and the simple, but colorful, Grandma Moses-style illustrations [by George Kraus] combine with the text to produce a book which actually seems Pennsylvania Dutch in origin.

> Sara Kay Rupnik, *in* School Library Journal *(reprinted from* School Library Journal, *April, 1973, published by R. R. Bowker Co., a Xerox company; copyright © 1973 by Xerox Corporation), April, 1973, pp. 57-8.*

OTHER CITATIONS

Publishers' Weekly, *December 11, 1972, p. 36.*

THE SEA BEGGAR'S SON (1974)

Monjo departs—not entirely successfully—from his usual pattern of humanizing an historical figure in this account of an early Dutch freedom fighter. The situation—Holland's attempts to shake off Spanish oppression in the 16th and 17th Centuries—and the hero—Piet Heyn—are not well known to American children and Monjo complicates the presentation by writing in verse. While the text sticks closely to the facts, too much is contained in too few pages

for easy assimilation. Full-color, detailed illustrations [by C. Walter Hodges] evoke what Holland was like at the time, but the text fails to clearly explain Piet Heyn's role in securing his country's religious freedom or his relationship to William of Orange and King Philip II of Spain.

> Carol Chatfield, *in* School Library Journal *(reprinted from* School Library Journal, *December, 1974, published by R. R. Bowker Co., a Xerox company; copyright © 1974 by Xerox Corporation), December, 1974, p. 42.*

In rolling, resounding verse, Monjo unfurls his patriotic tribute to the Dutch freedom fighters, the Sea Beggars, and to Piet Heyn, son of a herring fisherman from Delft, who chased the Spanish treasure fleet to Havana and captured its gold to finance and reinvigorate the Dutchmen's struggle against King Philip. Neither Hodges' melodramatic crowd scenes nor the ballad rhythms have any particular subtlety (though the rhyme does serve to make the Dutch words pronounceable and fun), but both are zestful and invite children to jump right into relatively unfamiliar historical surroundings.

> Kirkus Reviews *(copyright © 1974 The Kirkus Service, Inc.), December 1, 1974, p. 1257.*

[C. Walter] Hodges' meticulously drawn and historically accurate pictures of the ships and the men of the seventeenth century have drama and vitality; the story of a hero of the Netherlands is told in martial rhythm. . . . [*The Sea Beggar's Son* is an] authentic hero, a stirring tale.

> Zena Sutherland, *in* Bulletin of the Center for Children's Books *(© 1975 by the University of Chicago; all rights reserved), October, 1975, p. 30.*

OTHER CITATIONS

The Junior Bookshelf, *December, 1974, p. 353.*

Anita Silvey, in The Horn Book Magazine, *December, 1974, p. 700.*

Publishers' Weekly, *February 24, 1975, p. 116.*

THE SECRET OF THE SACHEM'S TREE (1972)

Two pages of historical notes follow the text [of *The Secret of the Sachem's Tree*]. Old fashioned names such as Mehitabel will seem strange to modern youngsters, as will the old speech patterns: "'If it had not been for King Philip's head, I were not a widow today!'" It may also come as a surprise to find Father Wadsworth saying "ain't." Nevertheless, Monjo has produced a good narrative that's an interesting piece of history as well.

> Carol Chatfield, *in* School Library Journal *(reprinted from* School Library Journal, *December, 1972, published by R. R. Bowker Co., a Xerox company; copyright © 1972 by Xerox Corporation), December, 1972, p. 73.*

[*The Secret of the Sachem's Tree* is a] Hallowe'en story set in Connecticut in colonial times. . . . The story has historical interest and suspense, it's deftly illustrated [by

Margot Tomes], and it's told in a lively style [by Monjo]; an appended note gives background, and the large clear print adds to the attractiveness and readability of the book.

> *Zena Sutherland, in* Bulletin of the Center for Children's Books (© *1973 by the University of Chicago; all rights reserved), February, 1973, p. 95.*

OTHER CITATIONS

Julia Whedon, in The New York Times Book Review, *November 5, 1972 (Part 2), p. 34.*

Kirkus Reviews, *November 15, 1972, p. 1303.*

Virginia Haviland, in The Horn Book Magazine, *April, 1973, p. 136.*

The Booklist, *May 1, 1973, p. 860.*

SLATER'S MILL (1972)

[Those] few readers who can bear with a plain Quaker background, a 22-year-old hero whose abiding dream is to get rich, and a barely fictionalized plot . . . will find that this recreation of young Mr. Slater's achievement—using the memory of his apprenticeship in England to set up America's first automated spinning mill—is lovingly accurate in the spirit of the Edwin Tunis books, and illustrated [by Laszlo Kubinyi] with the same conscientious regard.

> Kirkus Reviews *(copyright* © *1972 The Kirkus Service, Inc.), February 15, 1972, p. 194.*

The story [of *Slater's Mill*] gives a great deal of information about the technicalities of this landmark in industrial progress, about Quakers (Moses Brown was a Friend) and about the period in which it is set. As a story, however, despite a love interest and some suspense in the perfecting of the machinery, the book moves slowly, its pace slowed by the technical details.

> *Zena Sutherland, in* Bulletin of the Center for Children's Books (© *1972 by the University of Chicago; all rights reserved), October, 1972, p. 30.*

OTHER CITATIONS

Publishers' Weekly, *April 17, 1972, p. 59.*

Elnora M. Portteus, in School Library Journal, *December, 1972, p. 61.*

THE VICKSBURG VETERAN (1971)

Admiration tempered with good-natured raillery all around (not sparing Lincoln's skepticism or Grant's drinking) marks Fred's chronicle of the Vicksburg campaign. . . . Often the grimmer aspects of war, and of this war, impinge: a plantation is sacked to supply the troops, slaves join up, the dead of both sides line the route. To all of this Douglas

Gorsline's battle map and camera-eye drawings add documentary substantiation—but their extent is such that they also interrupt the story. The format being unconventional for an easy reader anyhow, the double-page illustrations (sometimes sans text and with italicized captions) may be handicapping. They can also serve as a valuable (and optional) extension of a flavorful, concretely informative text.

> Kirkus Reviews *(copyright* © *1971 The Kirkus Service, Inc.), February 15, 1971, p. 174.*

Although the story [of "The Vicksburg Veteran"] is true, Fred Grant's diary never existed. The compelling journal is the author's creation done with meticulous research, keen historical insight and a skillful presentation that gives immediacy to the events recounted. Douglas Gorsline provides an added dimension with a map of the campaign and sketches from historical photographs.

> *Irving Werstein, in* The New York Times Book Review (© *1971 by The New York Times Company; reprinted by permission), April 25, 1971, p. 40.*

[Historical] facts become vivid reality in [this] lively, fictional journal, simple enough for younger readers to enjoy and neither condescending in tone nor simplistic in effect. The ingenuous selection of detail . . . artfully suggests the typical impatient adolescent more concerned with recording events than with evaluating issues, although those issues may indeed affect his reactions. [Douglas Gorsline's] handsome illustrations, reminiscent of nineteenth-century steel engravings, visually reinforce the authentic feeling created by the text.

> *Mary M. Burns, in* The Horn Book Magazine *(copyright* © *1971 by The Horn Book, Inc., Boston), August, 1971, p. 378.*

The Vicksburg Campaign of 1863 comes alive in this story, believably written as the diary of General Grant's oldest son. . . . Gorsline's fine pen-and-ink and wash drawings (including views of a slave market, lines inside and outside Vicksburg, a map of the campaign, etc.) add vivid detail to the boy's narrative, which will have definite appeal for slow readers in junior high school as well as for middle graders.

> *Susan L. Pickles, in* School Library Journal *(reprinted from* School Library Journal, *September, 1971, published by R. R. Bowker Co., a Xerox company; copyright* © *1971 by Xerox Corporation), September, 1971, p. 159.*

OTHER CITATIONS

Publishers' Weekly, *February 15, 1971, p. 79.*

Zena Sutherland, in Saturday Review, *April 17, 1971, p. 45.*

Zena Sutherland, in Bulletin of the Center for Children's Books, *June, 1971, p. 160.*

O

O'BRIEN, Robert C. (pseudonym of Robert L. Conly) 1918-1973

An American editor, novelist, and author of children's books, Robert C. O'Brien is best known to children for his *Mrs. Frisby and the Rats of NIMH*, which received the 1972 Newbery Medal and a 1972 Lewis Carroll Shelf Award. (See also *Contemporary Authors*, Vols. 41-44.)

MRS. FRISBY AND THE RATS OF NIMH (1971)

The account of Mrs. Frisby's adventures—a talking-beast tale which blends scientific probability and fantasy—is an unusual addition to the stories of animal communities which have fascinated children for generations.... [This] intriguing adventure [is] made plausible through vivid descriptive prose and meticulous selection of detail. [Zena Bernstein's] fine pen-and-ink drawings are at once interpretive and decorative.

> *Mary M. Burns, in* The Horn Book Magazine *(copyright © 1971 by The Horn Book, Inc., Boston), August, 1971, p. 385.*

Both the story and the tale within it are deftly told [in *Mrs. Frisby and the Rats of NIMH*], fulfilling the first requisite of fantasy by making the impossible believable. The characters are credible, their adventures entertaining, and their conversation natural.

> *Zena Sutherland, in* Bulletin of the Center for Children's Books *(© 1971 by the University of Chicago; all rights reserved), October, 1971, p. 30.*

Robert O'Brien has given us an extraordinary, thought-provoking book, which bears some relationship to Russell Hoban's *The Mouse and his Child*, not merely because of the obvious 'rodent' connections, but because of its ability to comment validly on our times, without once being unfaithful to the rules of the story game.

Recommended for children of eleven up, all adults and literate rats.

> *Margot Petts, in* Children's Book Review *(© 1973 Five Owls Press Ltd.; all rights reserved), December, 1972, p. 185.*

This most unusual story well deserves its Newbery Medal. In the first place, it combines successfully two usually incompatible styles of narration, animals with human names and in human situations, and an accurate study of wild life. Mrs. Frisby is a mouse, and her daily activities—finding meals, nursing a sick child, going to visit a mouse doctor—sound human enough. When Timothy, however, shrivelled with penumonia, looks like a baby again, he appears "scarcely bigger than a marble", and when Mrs. Frisby crosses the farm, by an authentically inconspicuous route, it takes her two hours. Nature and the seasons are vividly described from a mouse's viewpoint. But there is more to the book than a good animal story: there is the clever conception of the rats of NIMH.... The morals are not laboured, but social comment is everywhere, for instance the small group of rats too lazy and comfort-loving to join in the Plan, or the way animals large or small make valuable contributions to the common good. There is no slick ending, but something of a question mark. It is a beautifully written and thought-provoking book.

> The Junior Bookshelf, *February, 1973, p. 49.*

Mrs Frisby, delightful in appeal to middle school readers, could ... lead on to [J.R.R. Tolkien's] *The Hobbit* and Russell Hoban's *The Mouse and His Child*. For like those it examines the place of man (or mouse) in society, is concerned with growth and change, and takes an objective view of the community. Since children today are subject to more pressures and faster changes than ever before in history, they need to be able to cope if they are to survive and this book can help by stimulating ideas and discussion about the world in which we find ourselves.... Readers should enjoy the countryside descriptions and those of the laboratory. Faults there are some—the middle flashback episode is too large and dominating a portion of the book, and as a teacher I deplore the methods used in teaching the rats to read; I'm surprised they ever managed it but then they were super rats.

Finally, I find that far too many children's books are either introspective, retrospective or banal. I found this one broad in outlook, outgoing and original. By the way, it's a jolly good read. I couldn't put it down.

> *Gene Kemp, in* Children's Literature in

Education (© 1973, APS Publications, Inc., New York; reprinted by permission of the publisher), No. 11 (May), 1973, pp. 45-6.

The notion underlying Robert C. O'Brien's *Mrs. Frisby and the Rats of NIMH* . . . is that laboratory rats, raised to a high standard of intelligence and with the ageing process inhibited, might plan to escape and set up an unratlike community of their own. But the story that embodies this notion is told in retrospect by one of the rats involved, in the course of a rather ordinary 'outer' story about Mrs. Frisby the fieldmouse and the rescue of her family from the ploughing-down of their home. The construction is awkward, and there is a lack of memorable characters. One remembers *The Wind in the Willows* for Rat, Mole, Toad and Badger; *Charlotte's Web* for Charlotte and Wilbur; *The Mouse and his Child* for Manny Rat. I do not think any animal in *Mrs Frisby* will be remembered in that way. But there are some nice touches of detail. Look at the farmer's cat Dragon, as seen from a mouse's height:

> He was enormous, with a huge broad head and a large mouth full of curving fangs, needle sharp. He has seven claws on each foot and a thick, furry tail, which lashed angrily from side to side. In colour he was orange and white, with glaring yellow eyes; and when he leaped to kill he gave a high, strangled scream that froze his victims where they stood.

> *John Rowe Townsend, in his* Written for Children: An Outline of English-Language Children's Literature, *(copyright © 1965, 1974 by John Rowe Townsend; reprinted by permission of J. B. Lippincott Company), revised edition, Lippincott, 1974, p. 258.*

Mrs Frisby's home is an underground cavity, not a pretty mock-cottage, yet in her speech, her contacts with other animals, her methodical life, she seems to belong to the same world as Alison Uttley's Grey Rabbit. There is another aspect to this story of the American countryside. The fieldmouse, believable in her mouse-life, also earns by attraction a different kind of reality when she is involved with the science-fiction expertise of the rats. As far as the reader is concerned, Mrs Frisby is definitely in, though not of, the futuristic world of the Rats of NIMH. . . .

The Rats of NIMH are not humanized in the strict sense of the word. They are represented as a super-race, an evolutionary phenomenon resulting from man's interference with nature but capable of using intelligence independently of man. In this sense they belong to science fiction rather than to animal fantasy, to the worlds of Orwell and Andre Norton rather than of Kipling and Kenneth Grahame. Their connection with the human race does not lie in their actions (which are always strictly performed by paws, not hands) but in their philosophy, which in its far-reaching, honest model for a civilization throws, by implication, the searching light of criticism on the human world in general and the rat-race in particular. So, we have here a politico-social allegory, as well as an exciting story in the successful solving of Mrs Frisby's domestic problem. Those rats who are seen as individuals—the dignified Justin; Jenner, the erratic leader of a doomed splinter group; the schoolgirl

Isabella, with her armful of books and her squeaky hero-worship of Justin—are characters as memorable as any in animal fantasy.

> *Margery Fisher, in her* Who's Who in Children's Books: A Treasury of the Familiar Characters of Childhood *(copyright © 1975 by Margery Fisher; reprinted by permission of Holt, Rinehart and Winston), Holt, Rinehart and Winston, 1975, pp. 249, 301.*

OTHER CITATIONS

The Booklist, *July 15, 1971, p. 955.*

Zena Sutherland, in Saturday Review, *September 18, 1971, p. 49.*

Frances Postell, in School Library Journal, *December, 1971, p. 60.*

THE SILVER CROWN (1968)

"Escape literature" is what this blend of high adventure and fantasy would be called if it were aimed at an adult audience. Characters get lost along the way and the ends don't tie up quite as neatly as the reader would like, but like much adult "escape literature," "The Silver Crown" is difficult to put down. . . .

[The] story degenerates into comic book catastrophes and rescues. It is great galloping fun for a while, but the intelligent reader must be prepared to check his brains at the door.

> *Jane Yolen, in* The New York Times Book Review *(© 1968 by The New York Times Company; reprinted by permission), May 5, 1968 (Part 2), p. 36.*

The abruptness of [the opening of *The Silver Crown*] (which is probably less disturbing to children than to protective adults) is masked by the fact that we have not met or learnt anything of [Ellen's] family. More importantly too, Robert O'Brien immediately ensures our interest in Ellen, fifty-five and a half inches tall, just ten and 'knowing all along that she was a queen,' so that the gift of a beautiful, fragile crown comes as no surprise.

From this opening the story moves rapidly and originally, introducing a small but vivid canvas of enemies and friends. . . . There is an intriguing and wholly successful blend of the everyday American scene, with police, telephones and post-offices, and the magical. This includes the powers of the crown itself, its links with ancient cults and the other-worldly wisdom of Otto's 'mother'.

The idea, of a talisman which can be used for good or evil according to the mind of its possessor, is one of the basic themes of story. It is, however, one which Robert O'Brien has handled with deftness and a unique charm which holds the reader. Only the ending which, while appropriate, seems weak and too easily contrived stresses that this book, though published second, was written before *Mrs. Frisby and the Rats of NIMH*. It is a slighter achievement, but nonetheless a stylish, humane, exciting book. . . .

> *Judith Aldridge, in* Children's Book Review *(© 1974 Five Owls Press Ltd.; all rights reserved), Spring, 1974, p. 20.*

OTHER CITATIONS

Jean C. Thomson, in School Library Journal, *April, 1968, p. 133.*

Ruth Hill Viguers, in The Horn Book Magazine, *April, 1968, p. 174.*

The Junior Bookshelf, *February, 1974, pp. 28-9.*

Z FOR ZACHARIAH (1975)

[This] posthumously published story has a familiar plot made fresh. It is set in the U.S. after a nuclear war that has killed everyone else as far as 16-year-old Ann Burden knows.... Ann's resiliency is credibly developed as is the strain of madness in John Loomis in a compelling tale of survival told in the form of Ann's journal.

> The Booklist *(reprinted by permission of the American Library Association; copyright 1975 by the American Library Association), March 1, 1975, p. 687.*

Could you believe such a story [as "Z for Zachariah"]? I can't. Not one bit. Too much reliance on coincidence. Too much like the tired old cliché of the man and woman marooned on a desert isle. And yet—for anyone who loves secret places as much as I do and is willing to accept the situation Robert C. O'Brien has set up without examining it *too* closely—this is a haunting, fascinating book....

Decency, vulnerability and humanity are ... what this whole book is about. Its real triumph is not in the action of the plot, but in the quiet beauties it describes along the way....

With Ann as narrator, this book's style is spare and direct, and yet it sings. Seldom has the word *green*—growing green as opposed to plastic green—taken on such dimension or fresh, minnow-filled water seemed so beguiling. With very few words O'Brien can remind us of the shivery look of a baby crow lost from its nest, of the heady smell of a crab-apple tree in full bloom, of the taste of a newly laid just-cooked egg. Because of this particular talent, "Z for Zachariah" is not just another sci-fi account of the aftermath of nuclear war. It is, instead, a special book to remind us that we tend to rush from day to day without really seeing that what we have around us is fragile, precious and well-worth taking the extra time to appreciate and preserve.

> *Susan Terris, in* The New York Times Book Review *(© 1975 by The New York Times Company; reprinted by permission), March 2, 1975, p. 8.*

It would have been so easy to give a traditional happy ending to this post-atomic-war story of how the last surviving man and girl meet but sixteen-year-old Anne cannot bring herself to accept the responsibility of being a new Eve to the Adam who invades her garden of Eden.

Told in the form of her diary, this story presents with sympathy and sensitivity her reactions to her own solitary existence in a patch of the countryside spared the desolation of the rest of the continent....

This is something of a tour de force in imaginative writing. The reader's attention is held throughout and there are no concessions to sentiment or whimsy.

> The Junior Bookshelf, *June, 1975, pp. 201-02.*

The combination of a survival story and science fiction creates a significant background for a dramatic novel, in which two characters are pitted against one another: Ann with her closeness to earth, her love of nature and of books, her religious feelings; John Loomis with his rational engineering skills and his ruthless will to exploit his surroundings. The title of the book is aptly allusive. Ann tells how she had learned the alphabet in Sunday School "from a picture book called *The Bible Letter Book.* The first page said 'A is for Adam.... The last page of all was 'Z is for Zachariah,' and ... for a long time I assumed that Zachariah must be the last man.''

> *Paul Heins, in* The Horn Book Magazine *(copyright © 1975 by the Horn Book, Inc., Boston), June, 1975, p. 277.*

This is a last-man-on-Earth story for teenagers. Traditionally such stories concentrate on the human relationships which develop. Problems of food-gathering, disposal of dead bodies etc. are secondary to the question: will the new Adam and Eve continue the human race? A is for Adam, the first man, Z for Zachariah, possibly the last, as this story takes a pessimistic turn....

We see that this cold scientific man lacks the qualities needed to make their relationship work. His only interest is self-preservation (he killed a man to get the safe-suit) and satisfaction of his own appetite. The girl would have accepted union if he had been friendly—but now the human race may die out. This book will especially interest those involved in the debate about 'sex-role stereotyping', as it could be said to depict a tragedy caused when a man is poorly educated in the emotions! (and thus an answer to the criticised *Dom and Va* [by John Christopher], which showed the successful union of aggressive male and submissive woman, with love born from hate). Sexual politics apart, this story is well written and exciting. The diary method of narration brings the reader right inside the mind of the naive young country girl. A book which must provoke the question 'what would I do?', it will stimulate young readers and lead on to adult science fiction on the same theme....

> *Jessica Kemball-Cook, in* Children's Book Review *(© 1975 Five Owls Press Ltd.; all rights reserved), Summer, 1975, p. 64.*

[*Z for Zachariah*,] a posthumously published story with a favorite setting of science fiction, a world on which people have survived disaster of their own making, is quite unlike the fanciful and intricate Newbery winner, *Mrs. Frisby and the Rats of NIMH....*

The journal form is used by O'Brien very effectively, with no lack of drama and contrast, and the pace and suspense of the story are adroitly maintained until the dramatic and surprising ending.

> *Zena Sutherland, in* Bulletin of the Center for Children's Books *(© 1975 by the University of Chicago; all rights reserved), November, 1975, p. 52.*

OTHER CITATIONS

Publishers' Weekly, *January 20, 1975, p. 77.*

Pamela D. Pollack, in School Library Journal, *March, 1975, p. 109.*

S

SACHS, Marilyn 1927-

Marilyn Sachs, formerly a children's librarian, is an American author. (See also *Contemporary Authors*, Vols. 19-20, and *Something About the Author*, Vol. 3.)

AMY AND LAURA (1966)

Individual incidents are the happy heart of [*Amy and Laura*]: Amy torn between naming sweet, steadfast Rosa or mercurial, daring Cynthia as her Best Friend; Laura struggling to stay on a bike and her elation when she succeeds. This does not have the structural unity of *Laura's Luck*, but girls who have identified with Amy and Laura in their earlier ups-and-downs will not be disappointed. Amy and Laura remain individuals struggling to reconcile their identity with the inward and outward pressures of growing up. Contemporary, lively, questioning—a superior serial.

> Virginia Kirkus' Service *(copyright © 1966 Virginia Kirkus' Service, Inc.), September 15, 1966, p. 976.*

[This] third book about Amy and Laura Stern develops their sisterhood and their individual personalities. . . . [The] anxieties and joys experienced by Amy and Laura are known to girls everywhere. Natural conversations and a lively pace well within the grasp of average readers assure popular reception of a story that is as realistic as it is readable.

> *Priscilla L. Moulton, in* The Horn Book Magazine *(copyright © 1966, by The Horn Book, Inc., Boston), December, 1966, p. 718.*

The chapters [in *Amy and Laura*] alternately focus on one sister or the other, but the action is not separate; indeed, one of the appeals of the book is that (both in school and at home) there is a continuity of relationship within which there are shifts of motives and moods.

> *Zena Sutherland, in* Bulletin of the Center for Children's Books *(copyright 1967 by the University of Chicago; all rights reserved), January, 1967, p. 79.*

OTHER CITATIONS

Peggy Sullivan, in School Library Journal, *January, 1967, p. 70.*

The Booklist and Subscription Books Bulletin, *January 1, 1967, p. 491.*

Patience M. Daltry, in The Christian Science Monitor, *March 9, 1967, p. 15.*

AMY MOVES IN (1964)

[Marilyn Sachs] follows Amy through her years of trial in a way that shows she's been there. The family scenes have the reality of relatives as they are rather than as the articles on child psychology that Amy's mother reads would have them be. . . . Amy, in her relationship with Laura, who is two years older, is the perfect rendering of the continuously irritated but ineradicable fondness of siblings who must share a bedroom. Amy learns to find her way through the social structure of the 4th grade, which will always be more arbitrary than that of cafe society, and reaches the stage where she can see sticking to her principles as more important than companions to walk home with. This is a very funny book that still offers readers valid insights into people and their behavior. Set near the end of the Depression, it is true to its time and true to the unchanging conditions of childhood.

> Virginia Kirkus' Service, *May 1, 1964, p. 453.*

The way in which Amy solves her problem is described with sympathy and realism; the author's perceptive handling of relationships is, in fact, particularly good. The writing style has vitality, the Stern family is pictured with enough humor to balance the sentiment, and the Bronx neighborhood atmosphere rings true.

> *Zena Sutherland, in* Bulletin of the Center for Children's Books *(copyright 1964 by the University of Chicago; all rights reserved), September, 1964, p. 19.*

THE BEARS' HOUSE (1971)

Though the fantasy [in *The Bears' House*], more the product of desperation than imagination, is fairly thin it helps to cushion Fran Ellen (and the reader) against the inevitable breakup. Despite the desolate environment it's a story of strength, for Fran Ellen's apparently meager resources prove sufficient to her needs and the potential stickiness of neglected waifs fixing their own Kool-Aid lunches is offset by restrained prose and the realistically shabby but affectionate drawings of Louis Glanzman.

> Kirkus Reviews *(copyright © 1971 The Kirkus' Service, Inc.), November 1, 1971, p. 1157.*

This is no ordinary child drifting off into the world of make-believe. Fran Ellen's escape into the bears' house is a journey inward that leaves her sense of real and fantasy worlds precarious. Mama and Papa Bear are the parents she no longer has, the tears she never sheds run down the cheeks of Goldilocks. . . .

What kind of a children's book is this? The best that Marilyn Sachs has written so far, innovative in its use of psychosis. But it is something more—it is a shattering, a tragic book—tragic in the very truth of its picture of the need to love and be loved in return.

Just one more thing—never have I seen what seems so clearly to be an attempt to assassinate a book through illustration. The smug, almost caricatured style of [Louis Glanzman's] drawings serves not only to distort the story. They create an overall appearance that leaves one thinking the book is inane.

> *Ingeborg Boudreau, in* The New York Times Book Review *(© 1971 by The New York Times Company; reprinted by permission), November 7, 1971 (Part 2), pp. 7, 34.*

Although the unrelieved pathos strikes a monotone note, the story [of *The Bears' House*] is touching. The ending seems a bit inconclusive, but there are enough variety and action in the realistic incidents of home and school to give the story substance.

> *Zena Sutherland, in* Bulletin of the Center for Children's Books *(© 1972 by the University of Chicago; all rights reserved), January, 1972, p. 80.*

[*The Bears' House* is a] sober, touching story of a family of city children trying to manage without parents. . . . The grim situation is brightened by sprightly telling, by Fran Ellen's unself-conscious humor, and by the help that eventually comes from her teacher.

> *Beryl Robinson, in* The Horn Book Magazine, *(copyright © 1972 by The Horn Book, Inc., Boston), February, 1972, pp. 52-3.*

OTHER CITATIONS

Publishers' Weekly, *November 1, 1971, p. 55.*

Zena Sutherland, in Saturday Review, *December 11, 1971, p. 46.*

Margaret A. Dorsey, in School Library Journal, *January, 1972, p. 61.*

DORRIE'S BOOK (1975)

For readers . . . Dorrie's trials are amusing rather than upsetting. . . . Presented in the form of a class project written by Dorrie herself, *Dorrie's Book* is a wonderful blend of light-hearted humor and astute perceptions punctuated with perky child-like drawings [by Ann Sachs] that add an authentic touch.

> *Leah Deland Stenson, in* School Library Journal *(reprinted from* School Library Journal, *September, 1975, published by R. R. Bowker Co., a Xerox company; copyright © 1975 by Xerox Corporation), September, 1975, p. 111.*

Stories of single children coming to grips with the arrival of a new brother or sister are not uncommon: Sachs does a comic variation on that theme, carrying it five steps farther. . . . Dorrie's confessional, written as a class assignment, is full of her self-righteous protest at the situation foisted upon her. . . . Sachs' breezy dialog and knack for tuning into the concerns of a spoiled 11-year-old place her as a leading storyteller and interpreter of the middle-class preadolescent experience.

> *Denise M. Wilms, in* The Booklist *(reprinted by permission of the American Library Association; copyright 1975 by the American Library Association), November 1, 1975, pp. 372-73.*

OTHER CITATIONS

Publishers' Weekly, *September 1, 1975, p. 70.*

Kirkus Reviews, *September 15, 1975, pp. 1067-68.*

LAURA'S LUCK (1965)

[Although *Laura's Luck*] is set in a summer camp of the '30's, we'll bet a birdwalk that the discomfort of that milieu are among the eternals and haven't changed a bit. . . . Laura's gradual and real transformation from the odd man out at the first camp fire sing to her last, rather choked up rendition of the camp song, is excellent preparation for how to get along as well as an integral part of a novel typical of the pains and pleasures of growing up. Her story should be in the hands of every girl who is being shipped to summer camp against her better judgement.

> Virginia Kirkus' Service, *August 15, 1965, pp. 820-21.*

[*Laura's Luck* is not] unusual as a camping story, but the good characterizations, the realistic actions and reactions among a group of girls, and the light, humorous style lift the story above the ordinary.

> *Zena Sutherland, in* Bulletin of the Center for Children's Books *(copyright 1965 by the University of Chicago; all rights reserved), November, 1965, p. 49.*

OTHER CITATIONS

Anne Izard, in School Library Journal, *September, 1965, p. 158.*

PETER AND VERONICA (1969)

The further adventures of Veronica Ganz and Peter Wedemeyer are not nearly so engaging as those in *Veronica Ganz* . . . because the focus here is on Peter, who hasn't Veronica's vitality and anti-heroine appeal. . . . There are a few moments of humor, but with Veronica mostly offstage and the spotlight on Peter, the episodic doings of these bland pre-teeners will seem to today's readers as remote as the novel's 1941 setting.

> *Margaret A. Dorsey, in* School Library Journal *(reprinted from* School Library Journal, *April, 1969, published by R. R. Bowker Co., a Xerox company; copyright © 1969 by Xerox Corporation), April, 1969, p. 117.*

Set in the days of frizzy permanents and nickel Cokes, "Peter and Veronica" may seem like historical fiction to most of its audience. Marilyn Sachs wrote it for boys especially, but girls who liked her "Veronica Ganz" . . . will also want to read it. This time Peter Wedemeyer, the smart aleck who used to be tomboy Veronica's inventive enemy, gets top billing as her newfound friend. The story is mostly his; we're not even allowed beyond the front steps of the Bronx apartment where Veronica lives, though we see a lot of Peter's.

Right in current literary fashion, Peter has a Jewish mother, so "prejudiced" she doesn't want Protestant Veronica at her son's bar mitzvah. And that is only part of the episodic plot, peopled by Veronica's holy terror of a little stepbrother and a host of other unsentimentalized children and grownups.

Yet "Peter and Veronica" bears the curse of the sequel. At times it is stilted, and less carefully written than its predecessor, and its characters occasionally turn into cartoons.

> *Nancy Griffin, in* The New York Times Book Review *(© 1969 by The New York Times Company; reprinted by permission), May 25, 1969, p. 32.*

In a vivid sequel to *Veronica Ganz*, Veronica and Peter—now ninth-grade classmates in pre-World War II New York City—have ins and outs over more serious problems, based on religious differences. . . . The author uses an agreeably light touch, creating a precise revelation of the adults, Veronica's tyrannical little brother, and the school crowd in all their spirited responses. The deeper emotions of Veronica's disillusionment and Peter's anger—brewing during a summer of separation—have been handled with a nice perception.

> *Virginia Haviland, in* The Horn Book Magazine *(copyright © 1969 by The Horn Book, Inc., Boston), June, 1969, p. 312.*

[*Peter and Veronica* is not] really, with all its in-jokes and in-thrusts, for the non-Jewish young. But against this must be set the spirited comedy (notably the inventions of a schoolboy chum called Milt), the quick, percipient sketches of fathers and other adults, the real understanding of wounded feelings that can't be set into words—and of the outwardly inexplicable comings and goings of childhood friendships, quite as strange, in their ways, as any of the later moves of love.

> The Times Literary Supplement *(© Times Newspapers Ltd., 1970), October 30, 1970, p. 1267.*

OTHER CITATIONS

Zena Sutherland, in Bulletin of the Center for Children's Books, *April, 1970, p. 133.*

A POCKET FULL OF SEEDS (1973)

With the instinct of an able writer, [Marilyn Sachs] has told [*A Pocket Full of Seeds*] with sensitivity, taste, and even humor—"'People who don't laugh are dead'"—and without a trace of sentimentality.

> *Ethel L. Heins, in* The Horn Book Magazine *(copyright © 1973 by The Horn Book, Inc., Boston), October, 1973, pp. 468-69.*

As I was reading ["A Pocket Full of Seeds"] I felt curiously removed. I finished it and still felt that way. I wondered why, since Marilyn Sachs writes well and cares about the subject. What is missing, I think, is that Mrs. Sachs does not identify deeply enough with Nicole and although the story is written in the "I, Nicole" form, the author never becomes one with her.

> *Johanna Reiss, in* The New York Times Book Review *(© 1973 by The New York Times Company; reprinted by permission), November 4, 1973, p. 48.*

[This is a] touching story, realistic in the way Nicole adjusts to the drastic changes of war and changes from a blithe eight-year-old to a mature adolescent. Style and characterization are deft, and the atmosphere of the place and period are convincingly recreated.

> *Zena Sutherland, in* Bulletin of the Center for Children's Books *(© 1974 by the University of Chicago; all rights reserved), March, 1974, p. 117.*

Mrs. Sach's depiction of life in a small, peaceful French town highlights the tragic intrusion of war; and her characters are sharply and sympathetically drawn.

But a major flaw in this novel is the author's inability to provide some sort of healing resolution in the final pages. The young reader will be left suspended, wondering whether Nicole ever was reunited with her family even though the war ended more than 25 years ago.

> *Jennifer Farley Smith, in* The Christian Science Monitor *(reprinted by permission from* The Christian Science Monitor; *© 1974 The Christian Science Publishing Society; all rights reserved), May 1, 1974, p. F1.*

OTHER CITATIONS

Publishers' Weekly, *July 16, 1973, p. 111.*

Alice Adkins, in School Library Journal, *November, 1973, p. 54.*

Kirkus Reviews, *November 1, 1973, p. 1202.*

THE TRUTH ABOUT MARY ROSE (1973)

Animating Mary Rose's quest are her sharp, amusing observations (many of them gleaned at the keyhole) on both the fun and the frictions of an extended family: her new friendship with cousin Pam, everyone's problems with Pam's mother, and Grandmother's reservations about Father who is Puerto Rican, divorced, and (until now) supported by Mother's dentistry practice (she also pays his alimony). In all, Mary Rose Ramirez is refreshing, perceptive, and a worthy successor to Veronica.

> *Kirkus Reviews (copyright © 1973 The Kirkus Service, Inc.), January 15, 1973, p. 62.*

Marilyn Sachs's thesis that there is no whole truth about any individual, that everyone is a different person to different people, may be valid enough, but as a peg for a story, it presents problems. A reader does, after all, need to discover his own truth about characters in a book—indeed, is that not what a book is about? In this case the reader has already reached conclusions about some of the characters, for Mrs. Sachs has written about them before. . . .

["The Truth about Mary Rose"] might have worked better if, on the one hand, we did not already know that first mean-spirited Mary Rose so well, or if on the other hand we knew more about the second Mary Rose. Why does she need this fantasy? Why is she so upset by the loss of it? Mrs. Sachs in "The Bears' House" has proved her ability to deal sensitively with troubled, fantasy-ridden little girls, but Mary Rose is not troubled; she is simply tiresome. And unfortunately so is her story.

> *Jean Fritz, in* The New York Times Book Review *(© 1973 by The New York Times Company; reprinted by permission), March 11, 1973, p. 8.*

[As] a better-than-average book with a serious subject, *The Truth about Mary Rose* can be recommended. But measured against the standard set by, say, *Charlotte's Web* (a story on a similar subject), Marilyn Sachs's novel is deficient in a sense of felt life. For example, after the episode of the father's artistic success, which is so ineptly done, he fades into the background, to be hauled out again only for some platitudinous advice after Mary Rose's disillusionment. In fact, all the characters are too obviously moved about only by the demands of the plot and theme, and the fine promise gives way, first, to predictability, then to disappointment. And it's a great pity, since the germ of a really superior book is so inescapably *there*; only, it's not enough.

> *Michele Murray, in* Book World *(© The Washington Post), March 11, 1973, p. 13.*

Woven through and around the story of Mary Rose is a rich and perceptive picture of the intricacies of family relationships, a picture peopled with vivid characters. Particularly telling: the obdurately prejudiced grandmother, who repeatedly makes slurring remarks about Mary Rose's father (Puerto Rican) and then asks, "But what did I *say?*" when her daughter remonstrates, who has made a saint of the dead Mary Rose, and who blindly idolizes all her grandchildren.

> *Zena Sutherland, in* Bulletin of the Center for Children's Books *(© 1973 by the University of Chicago; all rights reserved), April, 1973, p. 132.*

Relevancy dominates—and ultimately overshadows—the quasi-sequel to the author's successful, wryly humorous stories of the indestructible, hoydenish heroine, Veronica Ganz. . . . Her daughter Mary Rose, a compulsive eavesdropper, continues the family saga in a first-person narrative overburdened with expository dialogue, stilted conversations, and chic situational clichés. Consequently, Mary Rose emerges as a purveyor of information rather than as a distinct personality. . . . Although her search for mementoes as well as for memories gives continuity to the narrative, Mary Rose's motivation for her obsession with the past is never really explained. . . .

> *Mary M. Burns, in* The Horn Book Magazine *(copyright © 1973 by The Horn Book, Inc., Boston), August, 1973, p. 382.*

Marilyn Sachs's *The Truth about Mary Rose* . . . describes a child's search into the past via grandmother and cluttered attic. Finally, she uncovers a family tragedy that also involves demolishing a myth. Eugene O'Neill for children? Hardly; Marilyn Sachs writes without bitterness, and her characters remain true children even after they discover a painful truth, by a process that has the suspense of a good, if rather sad detective story.

> *Nicholas Tucker, in* New Statesman *(© The Statesman & Nation Publishing Co. Ltd. 1973), November 9, 1973, p. 704.*

OTHER CITATIONS

Margaret A. Dorsey, in School Library Journal, *April, 1973, p. 70.*

The Booklist, *May 1, 1973, p. 860.*

The Junior Bookshelf, *February, 1974, p. 44.*

VERONICA GANZ (1968)

From Peter Wedemeyer's first taunting chant to Veronica Ganz's final (but the first of her life) girl-like giggle, this story of an 11-year-old girl bully has warmth and reality. Several subplots about Veronica's family and divorced parents are skillfully introduced but not resolved. . . . Marilyn Sachs has here fulfilled the promise of her earlier books, but she has erred in pinning this story to the pre-World War II period (by mentioning Woolworth prices, a stepfather's Roosevelt button), because the book might have greater appeal and immediacy for today's readers had it been set in a present-day big city where French lessons in a public elementary school, a curriculum fillip relatively rare in the 1930's, would be not only more credible but more familiar. Adults may quaver at Veronica's bullying but children will recognize and take to their hearts this anti-heroine.

> *Peggy Sullivan, in* School Library Journal *(reprinted from* School Library Journal, *April, 1968, published by R. R. Bowker Co., a Xerox company; copyright © 1968 by Xerox Corporation), April, 1968, p. 131.*

[In *Veronica Ganz*] Mrs. Sachs writes in a light, breezy,

amusing way that makes for easy reading. She is very good at showing family life realistically rather than as people would like it to be. The "everything's going to be all right now" ending, however, may be a bit unrealistic for someone with as much anger inside her as Veronica.

> *Robin Gottlieb, in* Book World (© *The Washington Post), May 5, 1968 (Part 2), p. 18.*

Veronica is growing up around 1940, but except for the prices, and one reference to F. D. R., you would hardly know it. . . . Scarcely conscious of her reputation as the school bully, Veronica has other problems—her fink sister (but did children really call each other finks 30 years ago?), her stuttering little stepbrother, her schoolwork. Angrily she shakes off one teacher's sympathy, plays practical jokes on another, and only fitfully lets us see the good mind and passionate loyalty underneath.

Like so many stories for middle-age girls, the ending of this one is a little too pat. But it has more substance than most.

> *Nancy Griffin, in* The New York Times Book Review (© *1968 by The New York Times Company; reprinted by permission), May 5, 1968 (Part 2), p. 32.*

OTHER CITATIONS

Kirkus Service, *April 1, 1968, p. 395.*

Patience M. Daltry, in The Christian Science Monitor, *May 2, 1968, p. B7.*

Zena Sutherland, in Saturday Review, *May 11, 1968, p. 40.*

Zena Sutherland, in Bulletin of the Center for Children's Books, *June, 1968, pp. 164-65.*

The Booklist and Subscription Books Bulletin, *June 1, 1968, p. 1144.*

                    *   *   *

SERRAILLIER, Ian   1912-

An English poet and author, Ian Serraillier is well known for his retellings of myths and legends. (See also *Contemporary Authors*, Vols. 1-4, rev. ed., and *Something About the Author*, Vol. 1.)

THE BALLAD OF ST. SIMEON (1971)

Ian Serraillier's poem about St. Simeon Stylites comes from his earliest collection—*The Weaver Birds*—and has plenty of the verbal high spirits which were his hallmark from the beginning. Curiously, this most self-contained of poets has always stimulated artists to good creative work. Simon Stern bridges the centuries in his pictures of the primitive saint—who was in a sense the first, and the most consistent of hippies—and surrounds him with all the impedimenta of modern ballyhoo. Simeon's old mother holds a Press conference, and the saint looks down from his pole on to a modern industrial city. The satire is lightly carried and entirely valid. For once, word and picture go hand in hand, each complementing the other.

> The Junior Bookshelf, *February, 1971, pp. 16-17.*

[*The Ballad of St. Simeon*] is told in rollicking verse, both humorous and sophisticated, full of mouth-filling vocabulary (gallimumfery, trumpery, etc.). . . . This will be fun to read aloud if the right audience can be found, but the subject matter limits its appeal.

> *Phyllis Shumberger, in* School Library Journal *(reprinted from* School Library Journal, *September, 1971, published by R. R. Bowker Co., a Xerox company; copyright © 1971 by Xerox Corporation), September, 1971, p. 154.*

[*The Ballad of St. Simeon* is an] oversize book in which the legend of a fourth-century monk is adapted to modern applications, combining the figure of a dragon and people in contemporary costume. The format is that of a picture book, the vocabulary and the length of the story more appropriate for the middle grades reader. . . . The use of modern phraseology is jarring: "See him on his high horse," or, " . . . he can't deny he's scared stiff of the dragon." Yet there is, despite the fact that the common people say, "He ain't no saint," a piquancy in the way Serraillier uses language and a provocation in the theme.

> *Zena Sutherland, in* Bulletin of the Center for Children's Books (© *1971 by the University of Chicago; all rights reserved), September, 1971, p. 15.*

────────────

BEOWULF THE WARRIOR (1961)

To venture on the story of Beowulf in verse, whether for children or adults, is a deed with its own kind of heroism. So many have buckled to, so many have knuckled under. There must be a hundred ways of failing: Mr. Serraillier has hit on one of the ways to succeed. In about 800 lines of well-wrought verse, suitable for reading aloud, and free from the stale smells of lamp and candle, he establishes a manly narrative, with three clean divisions: Grendel, Grendel's Mother, The Fire Dragon. . . . Mr. Serraillier has also preserved the note of royal breeding, of steadfast endeavour and heroic resignation, which is so pronounced in the original poem. He does not attempt translation, save in a phrase here and there, and is at times remote from paraphrase; but as a poem on the Beowulf theme for young readers *Beowulf the Warrior* will take some beating.

> The Times Literary Supplement, *November 19, 1954, p. iii.*

[*Beowulf the Warrior* is a] skillful retelling of the ancient Anglo-Saxon epic about the warrior who thrice crossed the Baltic to the court of Hrothgar, King of the Danes, to rid his land of the monster Grendel, Grendel's mother, and the fire dragon. [Ian Serraillier] . . . deserves full praise here for a condensation which enhances the drama of the original tale by distilling its emotional elements into an heroic, alliterative verse form, supported by [Mark] Severin's stylized drawings.

> *Virginia Haviland, in* The Horn Book Magazine *(copyright, 1962, by The Horn Book, Inc., Boston), February, 1962, p. 61.*

[This is] an impressive retelling of the classic verse

epic.... [Ian Serraillier] has simplified the language yet maintained a style that is powerful and appropriate for the genre; he has preserved the sweep of movement, the flavor of phrasing, the heroic mood. A wonderful book to read aloud.

> *Zena Sutherland, in* Bulletin of the Center for Children's Books *(copyright 1962 by the University of Chicago; all rights reserved), April, 1962, p. 131.*

THE BISHOP AND THE DEVIL (1972)

Narrative verse, which marries so happily with illustration, provides an easy way of introducing poetry to the young. Ian Serraillier's *The Bishop and the Devil* stands constant rereading and would be fun for a seven-year-old who likes mindstretching words. Simon Stern's pictures are just right: good value, this.

> The Times Literary Supplement *(© Times Newspapers Ltd., 1971), October 22, 1971, p. 1328.*

When Ian Serraillier published *The Weaver Birds* in 1944 it was generally acknowledged to be a collection of poems for 'adults', despite the presence of a series of narrative pieces based on nursery and folk tales. Nor would one wish to dispute such an interpretation, since the verse demands of the reader a certain amount of perseverance for the enjoyment of both the technique, with its loose, conversational rhythms, and humour, which is often dependent on a feeling for anachronism.

Converting the narrative poems into picture books is therefore a task which requires clear thinking about the expected readership. No one could pretend that *The Bishop and the Devil,* or its predecessor *The Ballad of St. Simeon,* is likely to have much impact on the conventional picture-book public and Simon Stern's illustrations, which match the casual, but at the same time slightly sophisticated text, reinforce this belief. There has been slight modification to meet the needs of younger readers—three lines which, in the 1944 version, were in French have now been rewritten in English—but explanations about the Swiss legend which is the source of the poem have got no further into the book than its dust-jacket, and even if the verse is read aloud, it can prove demanding on its hearers. One can only assume that the book is designed to stand alongside Helen Oxenbury's *Snark* and Charles Keeping's *Tinker Tailor* as a poetical peppermint for the older child.

> *Brian W. Alderson, in* Children's Book Review *(© 1972 by Five Owls Press Ltd.; all rights reserved), April, 1972, p. 38.*

OTHER CITATIONS

Kirkus Reviews, *October 15, 1971, p. 1118.*

Publishers' Weekly, *November 15, 1971, p. 71.*

The Junior Bookshelf, *December, 1971, p. 367.*

THE CHALLENGE OF THE GREEN KNIGHT (1967)

The lays and romances of the Middle Ages are ideal for the innocent ear, and none more so than *Sir Gawain and the Green Knight.* Its substance is of things half-imagined, half-remembered. Adventure, heroism, love and magic combine in a creation suspended, like dusk, between darkness and light. It is of this world and not of this world; it calls for an unsophisticated response and yet holds secrets.

An attempt, therefore, to open up this poem—just out of reach of those without Middle English—for children excites great expectation. But, alas, it is infernally difficult to translate, and Ian Serraillier has stumbled where others have stumbled before him. His verse translation, concentrated version—call it what you will—has little of the voice of its marvellous original. At best, it sounds like good, updated Chaucer; at worst, it is a hotch-potch of archaism, awkward diction and colloquialism. The illustrations by Victor Ambrus are untrue in spirit and inaccurate in detail.

> The Times Literary Supplement *(© The Times Publishing Company Ltd. 1966), November 24, 1966, p. 1078.*

Of all Ian Serraillier's versions of ancient poems and legends this is the most difficult task. No mediaeval text of the first importance—except perhaps *Piers Plowman*—presents more formidable problems linguistic and aesthetic than *Gawain and the Green Knight.* As usual, and here most wisely, Mr. Serraillier does not attempt a translation or a paraphrase; instead he has written an original poem out of the roots of the remote masterpiece. Instead of the original's subtle elusive alliteration he has used something like blank verse. He keeps something of the mediaeval formality and mannerisms, preserving the grave courtliness in which this startlingly brutal tale is dressed. The result is a slow, powerful, occasionally beautiful poem, the weaknesses of which are built into the theme.

> The Junior Bookshelf, *February, 1967, p. 59.*

This spirited but shortened poetic retelling of the medieval alliterative poem *Sir Gawain and the Green Knight* preserves the subtlety as well as the proportions of the original.... The generally five-stress lines, which frequently rhyme, carry the modern narrative poem vigorously forward through Gawain's searches, adventures, and final reencounter with his challenger. The simple, bright words and sounds, often suggesting Chaucer, re-create the cycle of the seasons, the splendors of medieval castle life, and the hunting of deer, boar, and fox. But beyond fantasy of event and realism of detail, the poem has caught Gawain's sensitive reactions to the testing of his character. Both the richly colored illustrations and the black-and-white drawings [by Victor Ambrus] capture the energy of [Ian Serraillier's] retelling.

> *Paul Heins, in* The Horn Book Magazine *(copyright © 1967, by The Horn Book, Inc., Boston), August, 1967, p. 466.*

Mr. Serraillier has presented [the story of Sir Gawain and the Green Knight] in a loose rhymed form, and employed [an] archaic vocabulary which requires some literary sophistication of the reader. Catalogues of armor and details of hunting are faithfully represented, even though this retelling is less than half as long as the original text. The book is much assisted by [Victor Ambrus'] magnificent illustrations in bright, bold colors.

Walker Gibson, in The New York Times Book Review (© *1967 by The New York Times Company; reprinted by permission), September 10, 1967, p. 38.*

CHAUCER AND HIS WORLD (1968)

[*Chaucer and His World*] combines a capsule biography of Chaucer with a tense graphic description of the age in which he lived. Serraillier relates Chaucer's works to his times touching on both his perceptive portrayal of current modes and customs and his innovations in literary style.... [The] book is of value as background material for Chaucer's writings and as an introduction to more extended biographies such as [Marchette] Chute's *Geoffrey Chaucer of England*....

The Booklist and Subscription Books Bulletin (reprinted by permission of the American Library Association; copyright 1968 by the American Library Association), April 15, 1968, p. 984.

Students beginning to read Chaucer will find the 14th century puzzling country. This orderly account of it will be reassuring both to them and their teachers.... More clearly than ever we see the nine-and-twenty pilgrims and the scenes along the way as they ride toward the shrine of St. Thomas à Becket. Serraillier has chosen material unusual and attractive.... The book will help students to visualize the poems more vividly and to set them within a world over which six centuries have passed.

Edward B. Hungerford, in Book World (© The Washington Post), *May 5, 1968 (Part 2), p. 12.*

In a text much shorter than that of Marchette Chute's *Geoffrey Chaucer of England* ..., [Serraillier] has presented the rich ferment of fourteenth-century England. Using the facts of Chaucer's life as a point of departure, he states briefly, specifically, and clearly the social, historical, and cultural developments of the period. Hints in *The Canterbury Tales* (frequently quoted) are amplified to suggest the importance of such events as the Black Death or the Peasants' Revolt, or to signify the rank or importance of the characters. There is at least one photograph on almost every page: Portraits, manuscripts, architecture, utensils, clothing, weapons illuminate the text and point up the medieval heritage and milieu of the poet.

Paul Heins, in The Horn Book Magazine *(copyright © 1968 by The Horn Book, Inc., Boston), August, 1968, p. 441.*

OTHER CITATIONS

The Junior Bookshelf, *February, 1968, p. 63.*

Zena Sutherland, in Bulletin of the Center for Children's Books, *November, 1969, p. 52.*

THE CLASHING ROCKS: THE STORY OF JASON (1964)

[In *The Clashing Rocks*, Serraillier] gives children a spirited re-telling of the most famous story of all, the adventures of Jason on his quest for the Golden Fleece. The tale is told directly and vigorously in a fine swinging prose, so that the child can follow easily the adventures of the heroes who dared the unknown dangers of land and sea and magic. The ignoble end of Jason is not omitted and adds to the impact of the story.

The Junior Bookshelf, *October, 1963, pp. 205-06.*

The Clashing Rocks by Ian Serraillier fails with the one character of the Witch Princess Medea, because there is no possibility of delving deep enough to succeed with her in any book intended for children. For the rest, this retelling of the story of Jason and the voyage of the Argonauts in quest of the Golden Fleece is told with a magnificent stirring swing to it, a fire, and a poetic simplicity exactly suited to the matter.

The Times Literary Supplement (© *The Times Publishing Company Ltd. 1963), November 28, 1963, p. 981.*

In a simplified style, [*The Clashing Rocks* gives] a fairly extensive version of the voyage of the Argonauts; the details of Jason's life before and after the voyage are given briefly. The writing style is flat, only occasionally having a lyric phrase that gives a sense of legendry.

Zena Sutherland, in Bulletin of the Center for Children's Books *(copyright 1964 by the University of Chicago; all rights reserved), June, 1964, p. 162.*

The flaw in this telling occurs on the very last page. True to the legend [of Jason and the Golden Fleece], Mr. Serraillier has, in the last 25 lines, told of Jason's abandonment of Medea, her murder of Glauke and of her own two children. For one, the details are piled much too quickly, and to see a character, who has been treated as a heroine and a loved one, turn into a monster demands a psychological adjustment not easily forthcoming in the audience the book is aimed at. The ending leaves only an unsettled feeling rather than the roundness and completeness that should be the goal of every well-told tale.

Thomas Lask, in The New York Times Book Review (© *1964 by The New York Times Company; reprinted by permission), September 6, 1964, p. 14.*

THE ENCHANTED ISLAND: STORIES FROM SHAKESPEARE (1964)

The Enchanted Island ... is not a simple book of tales from Shakespeare; nor is it an attempt, such as might be expected from the distinguished author, to convey something of the poetry of the plays. Rather it tries to do a variety of things, to tell a yarn out of *The Shrew*, to look at an episode in history—the Agincourt campaign—from Shakespeare's viewpoint, to follow the sub-plots of *A Midsummer Night's Dream* and *Twelfth Night*, to explore the magic of Prospero's Island. Maybe the author tries too much. This is a book mainly for children who don't know Shakespeare, to be read for its own sake. The child who meets Shakespeare for the first time here will take away an impression of fun, romance, heroism—all conveyed in simple words. Only in the *Tempest* story will he find a touch of mystery and wonder.

If *The Enchanted Island* does not quite succeed, this is because it attempts the impossible. Tales from Shakespeare are a contradiction in terms, for Shakespeare is whole and indivisible. This is nevertheless an interesting and worthwhile failure.

> The Junior Bookshelf, *July, 1964, p. 178.*

[Ian Serraillier] attempts to lure children to enjoy Shakespeare on their own level of understanding. [His] method is to stress the humor, by-pass the romance and simplify the action as much as possible. This is fine for the slapstick in "The Taming of the Shrew" and well enough for giving major roles to Bottom and Falstaff in "A Midsummer Night's Dream" and "Henry IV, Pt. I," but doubtful when the practical joke on Malvolio dominates "Twelfth Night" and the cruelty of Shylock, "The Merchant of Venice." The tragedies of Hamlet, Lear and Macbeth are told straight, history is made fairly clear in "Henry V," as is the moral about high-minded murder in "Julius Caesar." The author certainly succeeds in showing that Shakespeare can be fun, and much more if you care to look for it, but [Peter Farmer's] illustrations are less enticing as the figures are stiff and the color muddy.

> *Aileen Pippett, in* The New York Times Book Review *(© 1964 by The New York Times Company; reprinted by permission), September 20, 1964, p. 26.*

Mr. Serraillier has used material from eleven Shakespeare plays—in some cases retelling the plot, in others, creating a story of some sub-plot. The prose is adequate, but the use of small print and the level of vocabulary difficulty demand readers old enough to enjoy the original version. Even if the young reader does not understand all of the allusive or obsolete language of Shakespeare, he can get as much of the plot from the original as he does here, and can enjoy the power and the poetry of Shakespeare's style.

> *Zena Sutherland, in* Bulletin of the Center for Children's Books *(copyright 1964 by the University of Chicago; all rights reserved), October, 1964, p. 31.*

The uneasiness that adults feel in presenting Shakespeare to children is determined, I believe, by the uneasiness they themselves feel toward him. If their friendship with him is complete, they take the rough with the plain. Shakespeare is intensely subjective; children are subjective. Their ability to accommodate this in the house of their imagination must be accepted prima facie.

This is why I do not like *The Enchanted Island.* . . . Ian Serraillier has put a dozen plays into story-form. They are written without an ear for tone, and goodness knows, Shakespeare's plots without his tonal magic sound like the moanings on a blasted heath. The illustrations, however, by Peter Farmer are strange and beautiful.

> *Henrietta Buckmaster, in* The Christian Science Monitor *(reprinted by permission from* The Christian Science Monitor; *© 1964 The Christian Science Publishing Society; all rights reserved), November 5, 1964, p. 11B.*

OTHER CITATIONS

The Times Literary Supplement, *July 9, 1964, p. 590.*

Margaret Sherwood Libby, in Book Week, *November 1, 1964, p. 14.*

A FALL FROM THE SKY: THE STORY OF DAEDALUS (1966)

Serraillier's clarity [in *A Fall from the Sky*] can be traced to his strict adherence to the storyline and his use of unadorned dialogue. The story of Daedalus, the originator of the practical arts, has never been told more clearly for this age level. By mentioning, without detailing, the part that Pasiphae played in Daedalus' history, the author reclaims the major strengths of the myth—genius turned destructive through jealousy escaping a just death at the even greater sacrifice of his beloved son, Icarus. This reads with a mounting sense of fate, and you can't do better than that in re-telling a myth.

> Virginia Kirkus' Service *(copyright © 1966 Virginia Kirkus' Service, Inc.), February 1, 1966, p. 109.*

OTHER CITATIONS

Roger Jellinek, in The New York Times Book Review, *May 8, 1966 (Part 2), p. 30.*

Della Thomas, in School Library Journal, *September, 1966, p. 253.*

THE GORGON'S HEAD: THE STORY OF PERSEUS (1962)

Ian Serraillier does an excellent job of imitating the strong epic style in re-telling the story of Perseus, "The Gorgon's Head." The book is brief but it has life and motion. William Stobbs's illustrations are forceful and remarkably fine in design, and seem to breathe the same enchanted air as the text.

> *Mary Louise Hector, in* The New York Times Book Review *(© 1963 by The New York Times Company; reprinted by permission), April 28, 1963, p. 38.*

The story of Perseus is told here in thirteen brief episodes, the author having stated in a prefatory note that he had chosen details from varying versions. The illustrations [by William Stobbs] are effective black and white drawings, some of which are beautifully detailed. The retelling is adequate but not impressive, the text preserving the structure and spirit of the genre but having too much simplification and too much dialogue to convey the style of legendry.

> *Zena Sutherland, in* Bulletin of the Center for Children's Books *(copyright 1963 by the University of Chicago; all rights reserved), June, 1963, p. 166.*

OTHER CITATIONS

The Times Literary Supplement, *December 1, 1961, p. x.*

Margaret Sherwood Libby, in New York Herald Tribune Books, *November 11, 1962 (Part 2), p. 5.*

HAVELOK THE DANE (1967)

[In retelling *Havelok the Dane,* Ian Serraillier] labors at an initial disadvantage. Even in medieval times, Havelok, however doughty a hero, was no real competition in song and story for the stalwarts of Arthurian legend. So young readers of today may well find him something less than a man for all story-telling seasons. Still, whatever its ancient faults, there seems staying power in much of this hoary tale. . . . The adapter takes liberties with ye olde rimed version, but with assistance from Elaine Raphael's antiqued illustrations it all goes to prove that there's a lot of life in this old tale.

> *Andrew B. Myers, in* The New York Times Book Review *(© 1967 by The New York Times Company; reprinted by permission), December 10, 1967, p. 38.*

An author who undertakes the re-telling of a legend as old as tenth century should be wary of including windows with glass in them or balconies on crutch houses though there might possibly be isolated instances of such. Apart from such dubious details Mr. Serraillier tells his tale of a hero with a foot on both sides of the North Sea with spirit and pace, albeit the dialogue is occasionally woodenly modern, a cross between the pseudo archaic and the practical. One feels [*Havelok the Dane,* published in Great Britain as *Havelok the Warrior,*] is not this author's happiest work though he has not lost the art of story-telling which his verse epics so incomparably demonstrated.

> The Junior Bookshelf, *December, 1968, p. 385.*

OTHER CITATIONS

The Booklist and Subscription Books Bulletin, *March 15, 1968, p. 870.*

HERACLES THE STRONG (1970)

By integrating Heracles' deeds into an ordered structure—from his strangling of the serpents as an infant, through his years of servitude for the cowardly King Eurystheus, to his final attainment of immortality—[Ian Serraillier] has not only provided . . . comprehensible motivation for the mythological characters but has also given dramatic unity to familiar material. The spirit of the original stories is implicit in spare but vivid prose that has the impact of a visual experience: "Then he hobbled away, snail-slow, weighed down by his years." Strong black-and-white woodcuts [by Rocco Negri] complement the heroic mood of the text.

> *Mary M. Burns, in* The Horn Book Magazine *(copyright © 1971 by The Horn Book, Inc., Boston), February, 1971, p. 49.*

Another retelling of the Heracles legends, this version is not above average and is only slightly more advanced than [Clifton] Fadiman's *The Adventures of Hercules.* . . . The page of acknowledgments appears almost too erudite for the level of readers: Euripides, Robert Graves, Kerenyi and Sophocles; where is Edith Hamilton or Bulfinch? If necessity motivates the consideration of this work, nothing offensive will be found. But do most libraries really need a single volume recounting the labors of Heracles?

> *Sandra Meyer, in* School Library Journal *(reprinted from* School Library Journal, *February, 1971, published by R. R. Bowker Co., a Xerox company; copyright © 1971 by Xerox Corporation), February, 1971, p. 59.*

By telling all the Heracles stories together, from the snakes in the nursery through all the twelve labours to the shirt of Nessus, Ian Serraillier manages to evoke sympathy for his hero. He shows us the sufferings as well as the beefy muscle power of Heracles, hated by the implacable Hera. He finds moments of comedy, as Eurytheus dives into his bronze pot for safety, and moments of tenderness, as when Heracles finds Theseus, his friend, in Hades. A fine and illuminating version.

> The Times Literary Supplement *(© Times Newspapers Ltd., 1971), July 2, 1971, p. 764.*

No one does retellings of ancient tales better than Mr. Serraillier. His versions have a quiet, timeless dignity, and he makes sense of the complicated narrative. Heracles is a particularly difficult subject; there are so many loose ends, and much of the main theme is meaningless without explanation of the hierarchy and the mores of Olympus. Mr. Serraillier keeps it short, avoiding the quagmires of detail, and manages to hold a balance between irony and pathos. It is still a confusing story. Children will be privileged to have so distinguished a guide through the complexities. But is this the best use of Mr. Serraillier's unique talents?

> The Junior Bookshelf, *August, 1971, p. 258.*

The labours of Hercules are so familiar as to be mythological cliché, and so it is exciting to find such an evocatively illustrated and technically sophisticated re-telling as this. Serraillier's Heracles emerges from the clear fast-moving stream of episodes as a man real and sympathetic, not merely strong but ingenious as well. . . . Giving shape to the sequence is Heracles' wish to expiate his guilt for killing wife and sons in a fit of mad rage. In the course of the story he seems preparing for a nobler richness of destiny, and his promise in the Underworld to marry Deianeira heralds the form of this destiny—fatal jealousy, poisoned love-juice, screams of pain on a lonely headland. Here be monsters, but also food for thought. The author's lively re-tellings of the legends of Perseus, Theseus, and Jason have found a worthy shelf-companion.

> *C. S. Hannabuss, in* Children's Book Review *(© 1971 by Five Owls Press Ltd.; all rights reserved), September, 1971, p. 127.*

OTHER CITATIONS

Kirkus Reviews, *November 1, 1970, p. 1199.*

The Booklist, *January 1, 1971, p. 374.*

The Times Literary Supplement, *July 2, 1971, p. 764.*

ROBIN AND HIS MERRY MEN (1970)

Like [Serraillier's] *Robin in the Greenwood* (1968), [*Robin and His Merry Men*] is a dramatic ordering and retelling of traditional ballads. . . . Serraillier's language is both graceful and lively, a tempered combination of the past and the present. None of these songs is in [Anne] Malcolmson's *Song of Robin Hood* but the book's real value is in the stylish presentation of classic adventure crisply and simply told.

> Kirkus Reviews *(copyright © 1970 The Kirkus Service, Inc.), May 15, 1970, p. 557.*

[*Robin and His Merry Men* is a] companion volume to *Robin in the Greenwood*. . . . In the present volume, a retelling of the medieval *Lytell Geste of Robin Hood*—a long extended ballad—[Ian Serraillier] again employs with great skill the ballad stanza and, except for some occasional run-on lines, captures the forthright quality of the original narrative and dialogue. . . . As in the first volume, [Victor Ambrus'] black-and-white and the colored illustrations are vigorous in outline and rich in tonality.

> *Paul Heins, in* The Horn Book Magazine *(copyright © 1970 by The Horn Book, Inc., Boston), August, 1970, pp. 397, 399.*

A medieval ballad, "Lytell Geste of Robin Hood," is the source of this retelling which captures the exciting life of Robin and his famous outlaw band. Serraillier . . . presents four lively tales in easy-to-read verse which retains the style of the ballad. . . . Four full-page color illustrations plus several black-and-white drawings [by Victor Ambrus] effectively echo the mood of these spirited heroic tales, which will be an excellent introduction for students to the ballad form.

> *Nancy Farrar, in* School Library Journal *(reprinted from* School Library Journal, *September, 1970, published by R. R. Bowker Co., a Xerox company; copyright © 1970 by Xerox Corporation), September, 1970, p. 165.*

OTHER CITATIONS

The Booklist, *October 1, 1970, p. 148.*

ROBIN IN THE GREENWOOD: BALLADS OF ROBIN HOOD (1968)

Ian Serraillier's versions of some Robin Hood ballads could only have been made by someone who loves the whole body of early ballad, carol and lay and knows it intimately. One's first reaction is: "He has not rewritten it at all!", so strongly does the enchanted yet rollicking flavour of the greenwood come over. In fact, Mr. Serraillier has very skilfully succeeded in preserving colour, rhythm and phrase while presenting a more immediately comprehensible language. One notices the occasional rearrangement of stanzas into a more logical order, the small omissions, the translation of a medieval phrase into a striking equivalent. . . .

Legend has made Robin Hood into many of the things the English like best, a protester, a sympathizer with the underdog, a sport (his crown is cracked as often as the next man's). Nevertheless, legend could not resist giving him an earl's daughter for mother, who went to the greenwood to bear him. The ballad of Robin's death at the hands of the treacherous prioress, and how he shot his last arrow to show John where he should lie, is splendidly full of foreboding and sorrow and has all the right echoes.

> The Times Literary Supplement *(© Times Newspapers Ltd., 1967), November 30, 1967, p. 1139.*

It takes some research to discover how much of this is Mr. Serraillier and how much the mediaeval balladeer. The modern poet has matched the old anonymous material with extraordinary skill. Here is Robin Hood from tragic birth to lonely death, told in the lilting ballad metre which, let us admit, becomes tedious in time. There is the smell of fresh air and freedom in the verses, and of loyal comradeship, but no mitigation of the brutality which lies at the heart of the old stories.

All this is extremely well done—and so are Victor Ambrus' fine illustrations in line and colour—but readers who know Mr. Serraillier as, now that Eleanor Farjeon has gone, our finest poet writing for the young may feel that this is not the best use of his great talents. He may be, as this book shows, a consummate master of pastiche, but he is so much more.

> The Junior Bookshelf, *December, 1967, p. 382.*

[*Robin in the Greenwood* contains ballads], but without the musical arrangements that accompany the Malcolmson *Song of Robin Hood* (1947) and offering fewer (twelve instead of eighteen) adventures albeit in idioms closer to the original. Serraillier begins with "Among the Lily-Flower," recounting the birth of Robin Hood in the greenwood, and introduces two poems not contained in the Malcolmson collection; the others do appear in the earlier volume, although the two versions usually vary, and Serraillier combines "The Bishop of Hereford" and "The Bishop Who Danced in his Boots" into one ballad. This Robin Hood requires a more sophisticated reader who will find traditional flavor and substance. Ambrus' illustrations add vigor though this hasn't nearly the distinctive appearance of the Malcolmson.

> Kirkus Service *(copyright © 1968 The Kirkus Service, Inc.), April 15, 1968, p. 475.*

[It] is not surprising to find Mr. Ian Serraillier turning to an adaptation of the ballads [about Robin Hood]. . . . It has been a characteristic of Mr. Serraillier's own poetry and of his previous adaptations that the words sound better off the tongue than they look on the page. Both *Beowulf the Warrior* . . . and *The Challenge of the Green Knight* . . . make splendid reading aloud, and the Robin Hood ballads would seem to offer an even richer fund of material, much of it (unlike the earlier books) in need of only the slightest adaptation or "translation."

In making his version Mr. Serraillier has relied heavily upon that marvelous source book of ballad literature, the Child collection; and by a cunning selection of ballads and incidents from ballads he has achieved a reconstruction of the life and adventures of the "popular" Robin Hood, which has a beginning, plenty of middle, and an end. Although he has avoided the narrative complexities of the most famous ballad, the "Lytell Geste," which is long enough to make a book of its own, he has managed to use a number of ballads of like antiquity, where the oral strength is greatest. These are also the tales which seem to give the most natural account of Robin as a character: accepting him seriously and not clogging his story up with the bar-parlor jokes and the Maidmarianry of later versions.

Insofar as the twelve ballads which Mr. Serraillier has chosen are separate episodes, it may be argued that the book does not really hang together as a story; but this is a price which any adapter of the ballads must pay. Much more to the point is the unity of feeling which the author has attempted to give them by sifting them through his own sensibility. In manner of writing, his originals range from fairly easily comprehended, almost doggerel, verse ("Robin Hood and Little John") to the near Middle English of "Robin Hood and the Monk" and the Northern dialect of "Robin Hood and the Beggar," while a number also have verses missing at vital points in their development. Consequently, in comparing these originals with Mr. Serraillier's reconstitutions, we find many verses altered slightly to give a smoother flow to the reading, many more rewritten in a style which is clearly more personal to Mr. Serraillier than to his unknown original author, and a few here and there which he has entirely made up himself. (pp. 283-84)

Some of these changes are felicitous.... On the other hand, some of the ruggedness of the old ballad rhythms has been smoothed out with a consequent loss of the feeling that someone is speaking, and this is not made up for by the inclusion of some very characteristic Serraillier enjambments. These give a most un-balladlike jerkiness in a number of verses:

"You talk like a coward," the stranger said.
"See, like a coward you stand
With your bow and arrow, while I have only
A quarterstaff in my hand."

In places, too, an attempt at the traditional directness of statement has resulted in a triteness which (given the meter) bears a disconcerting resemblance to a Stanley Holloway monologue:

They picked him up, their master dear—
O melancholy task!
What fiendish rogue had laid him low?
There wasn't a soul to ask.

On the whole, however, the evenness of tone with which Mr. Serraillier has recounted the ballads gives the book a unity which would certainly not be present in a literal reproduction of the texts themselves. We are, of course, spared some of the medieval crudities such as the murder of the "litull page" in "Robin Hood and the Monk" and the extra injunction to the monks in "Robin Hood's Golden Prize":

"The second oath that you here must take
All the days of your lives
You never shall tempt maids to sin
Nor lye with other men's wives."

And with these has gone the untranslatable beauty of:

In somer, when the shawes be sheyne,
And leves be large and long,
Hit is full mery in feyre foreste
To here the foulys song:

To see the dere draw to the dale,
And leve the hilles hee,
And shadow hem in the levës green,
Under the grene-wode tre.

While there is much that is enjoyable in Mr. Serraillier's version of these ballads, the question remains as to how far children will find it so. To them the ballad form is likely to appear an unnatural way to treat a theme which has all the components of a picaresque novel. If they have thought about Robin Hood in literary terms at all, it is surely as the hero of stories, not songs. (pp. 285-86)

> *Brian W. Alderson, "Ian Serraillier and the Golden World," in* The Horn Book Magazine *(copyright © 1968 by The Horn Book, Inc., Boston), June, 1968, pp. 281-88.*

OTHER CITATIONS

Martha L. Gardin, in School Library Journal, *September, 1968, p. 195.*

THE SILVER SWORD (1956)

Adventure and peril are Mr. Serraillier's *forte*, yet he writes with restraint [in *The Silver Sword*], and where he can show the best side of a situation, he does. Nobody could take umbrage but a few Storm Troopers. His presentation of Jan, foxlike and sly, loving nothing but animals, yet gradually turning into a human at last, deserves a special credit.

> The Times Literary Supplement, *November 23, 1956, p. iii.*

[*The Silver Sword*] is touched with greatness. It is the story, based on fact, of how four children found their way across Europe from Poland to Switzerland to find their parents after the war. There is nothing idealised about Ruth, Edek, Bronia and Jan. They are real children of the war, living without security or home life, sustained only by hope. They achieve the impossible, and the reader knows that they have the will to do it, that if they "suffer woes which Hope thinks infinite," they will also strive, seek, find and not yield.

This great and inspiring theme is treated with the utmost dignity and unobtrusive eloquence by Mr. Serraillier. Written in a fine, free, colloquial prose with plenty of spirit and even gaiety, it is obviously the work of a poet, who values words and uses them with restraint and economy, who never overplays a scene or overworks an emotion.... It is sometimes said that children should be shielded from the harsh realities of life, that their books, like sundials, should count only with the sunny hours. A book like *The Silver Sword* is sufficient refutation of such a doctrine. It can only enrich and ennoble the reader. "Nothing is here for tears."

> The Junior Bookshelf, *December, 1956, pp. 342-43.*

As a contribution to the understanding of a great international problem, [Margot Benary-Isbert's] *The Ark* is rivalled only by *The Silver Sword* . . ., in which Ian Serraillier brought a poet's sensibility to a true story of a Polish family who, after the war, searched through Europe for their lost parents. The story was written without heroics, but the heroism and endurance of the children shone brightly in Serraillier's unobtrusively lovely prose.

Marcus Crouch, in his Treasure Seekers and Borrowers: Children's Books in Britain 1900-1960 *(© Marcus Crouch, 1962), The Library Association, 1962, p. 126.*

The Silver Sword (1956) belongs to the adventure tradition in that it is essentially a fine narrative; it pushes the bounds of that tradition out as far as they will go. Serraillier had already proved his skill as an inventor of exciting contrived plots. There is no contrivance in *The Silver Sword*. All its episodes belong to the terrible history of Europe in its post-war chaos. The author selected them, matched them with vividly realized characters and clothed them in miraculously simple, dispassionate words. It is a book which one cannot read without profound emotional response and personal involvement, but Serraillier tells the story straight, never overstating the suffering, never adding his personal comment. It is an agonizing story in its very quietness; it is also a story of—in the words of its motto—'abiding hope'. Children's books in the mid-Fifties were still hedged in with taboos; writers were not encouraged to describe the realities of cruelty and pain. *The Silver Sword* deals with these things uncompromisingly. The story is one of tragedy and of heart-stopping tension.

Marcus Crouch, in his The Nesbit Tradition: The Children's Novel in England 1945-1970 *(© Marcus Crouch, 1972), Ernest Benn, 1972, pp. 28-9.*

The one undeniably first-rate war book for children by a British author did not appear until eleven years [after World War II]. This was *The Silver Sword* (1956) in which Ian Serraillier described the trek of three Polish children across Europe in search of their parents, taken away by the Nazis. Though told in a matter-of-fact tone, this impressive story holds enough incident and excitement for half a dozen books; it introduces a succession of people of different nationalities and makes them all interesting; and the children themselves are seen growing up rapidly under the stress of experience.

John Rowe Townsend, in his Written for Children: An Outline of English-Language Children's Literature *(copyright © 1965, 1974 by John Rowe Townsend; reprinted by permission of J. B. Lippincott Company), revised edition, Lippincott, 1974, p. 210.*

In this sincere, humane story, which is founded on fact, the characters of Ruth, responsible and conscientious, of Edek who is dogged by illness and of young, artistic Bronia, stand as representatives of children everywhere whose lives have been disrupted by war. Beside them, Jan stands out as a personality. Skilful pickpocket, ingenious thief, the uncertainty under his jaunty independence is shown by the way he clings to the box of treasures which stands instead of a home; its contents, which include a gold curtain ring, a silver tea-spoon, a feather from the tale of his pet cock (a victim of the war) and three dead fleas caught on a chimpanzee, tell us much about his wayward character. Above all we get to know Jan through the way he changes. For most of the journey he seems exclusively concerned with the fate of the animals he meets and whom he seems mysteriously to understand—from Jimpy his cock to old Jasper, the farmer's dog in East Germany. He seems to be moti-

vated mainly by hatred of the Germans and suspicious of everyone else. But the weeks of travelling with the Balickis teach him that people can be honest and loyal and that there is a meaning in the family pattern.

Margery Fisher, in her Who's Who in Children's Books: A Treasury of the Familiar Characters of Childhood *(copyright © 1975 by Margery Fisher; reprinted by permission of Holt, Rinehart and Winston), Holt, Rinehart and Winston, 1975, p. 150.*

OTHER CITATIONS

Olive Deane Hormel, in The Christian Science Monitor, *May 29, 1957, p. 5.*

Virginia Kirkus' Service, *March 15, 1959, p. 227.*

Zena Sutherland, in Bulletin of the Center for Children's Books, *September, 1959, pp. 20-1.*

SUPPOSE YOU MET A WITCH (1973)

"Suppose You Met a Witch" is based on a Grimm tale but has a language all its own, a lyric, really, which bounces through the story of Roland and Miranda.... It is delightful to read aloud, hard words rolling by so intertwined with easy ones that their meaning is always perfectly accessible. Even if that weren't the case, there is still the happy fact of [Ed] Emberley's remarkable pictures to help things along.

Natalie Babbitt, in The New York Times Book Review *(© 1973 by The New York Times Company; reprinted by permission), December 30, 1973, p. 8.*

Recent years show a timid trend in children's books in which the self-sought horrors of Halloween are gentled with giggling ghosts or wistful witches.... This story-in-verse of what to do when you meet a bona fide witch comes trippingly off the tongue.... [*Suppose You Met a Witch* is] bound to be a new long-term favorite for story tellers at Halloween; however, Emberley's picture spreads are laden with, (and leaden) in a variety of styles from high comic book-styled grotesqueries numblingly over-decorated in full garish color to dramatic silhouettes all too busy to be seen clearly at any distance. The pictorial result traps, makes static, and therefore reduces the chill that a voice can build into [Serraillier's] rhyme.

Lillian N. Gerhardt, in School Library Journal *(reprinted from* School Library Journal, *January, 1974, published by R. R. Bowker Co., a Xerox company; copyright © 1974 by Xerox Corporation), January, 1974, p. 204.*

[Ian Serraillier's] tantalizingly descriptive poetic text [in *Suppose You Met a Witch*] relates the adventures of two resourceful children, Roland and Miranda—from their capture by a witch ("all willow-gnarled and whiskered head to toe") ... through their clever escape, to the eventual fate of the evil witch Grimblegrum. [Ed Emberley's] high-colored illustrations are subtly detailed, leaving many things hidden from view at first glance. While they bear some resemblance to Hansel and Gretel, Roland and Miranda belong to the more adventuresome youth group of today. They are sure to bring pleasure to readers who enjoy getting lost in their own world of fantasy.

> *Barbara Dill, in* Wilson Library Bulletin *(copyright © 1974 by the H. W. Wilson Company), March, 1974, p. 541.*

OTHER CITATIONS

Kirkus Reviews, *October 1, 1973, p. 1093.*

Publishers' Weekly, *October 15, 1973, p. 61.*

Zena Sutherland, in Bulletin of the Center for Children's Books, *February, 1974, p. 101.*

THE TALE OF THREE LANDLUBBERS (1971)

Ian Serraillier writes all too rarely, and has not before provided the text for a picture-book. His three landlubbers, who escape from miseries professional and domestic by going to sea, are promising material and Raymond Briggs gives them accurate and colourful form. But it is all much ado about very little. The landlubbers' argosy is over too soon, and they come back to their old disciplines. Mr. Serraillier's verses are as tough and witty as ever, but they are too few, and the exuberant pictures are out of scale with this thin text. A disappointment after the hopes raised by this distinguished team.

> The Junior Bookshelf, *December, 1970, pp. 347-48.*

In this unsatisfactory variation of "Rub-a-dub dub, three men in a tub," three men set out to sea to escape from their dreary daily lives. . . . The clever, funny paintings are large and colorful in the best Briggs tradition. However, the story is cliché-infested (e.g., the characterization of the butcher's brow-beating wife), the verse is just passable, and the ending is depressing and questionable as it underlines the unattainability of dreams—after only one attempt to realize them. His fans have been led to expect better from Ian Serraillier.

> *Cherie Zarookian, in* School Library Journal *(reprinted from* School Library Journal, *September, 1971, published by R. R. Bowker Co., a Xerox company; copyright © 1971 by Xerox Corporation), September, 1971, p. 154.*

OTHER CITATIONS

The Times Literary Supplement, *October 30, 1970, p. 1261.*

Kirkus Reviews, *February 15, 1971, p. 171.*

THE WAY OF DANGER: THE STORY OF THESEUS (1963)

The story [of Theseus] is full of apparent contradictions, the atmosphere dark with evil. Not in the strictest sense stuff for children; the interpreter needs, like Mary Renault, to have plenty of elbow-room. It is nevertheless in parts a fine story of heroic action and Mr. Serraillier does his most considerable best with it, glossing discreetly over some of the inconsistencies, and bringing out the modern relevance

of parts of it. I admire particularly the way in which he avoids anti-climax in the final chapter. Theseus's ignoble death, murdered by a mean-spirited traitor, is followed by the recovery of his remains after Marathon and their burial in Athens. His shrine becomes a sanctuary for the poor and oppressed "for Theseus had always been their champion."

> The Junior Bookshelf, *October, 1962, p. 204.*

The Way of Danger . . . is the second of a promised series and tells the story of Theseus. Short, divided into short chapters, attractively printed and illustrated, it is altogether well designed to be read by or to children aged between five and seven. The tales of the young giant-and-monster-killer are so good that subsequent anticlimax is hard to avoid, but Mr. Serraillier has made skilful use of the visit to Hades as a counterweight. The moral tone is high. Theseus is brought up to all that is "brave and useful and true": the best possible construction is put upon the desertion of Ariadne: Phaedra does not appear.

> The Times Literary Supplement (© *The Times Publishing Company Ltd., 1962), November 23, 1962, p. 897.*

[This is a] retelling in the modern idiom of the Theseus legend similar in style to Serraillier's verson of "The Gorgon's Head." Details have been expanded, but the story itself has not the grace of style, immediacy of situation, and dimension of character found in [Charles] Kingsley's "The Heroes." Nevertheless, effective black-and-white illustrations [by William Stobbs] and language with a more familiar ring will get a note of response from those for whom the Kingsley title would have little appeal.

> *Marguerite A. Dodson, in* School Library Journal *(reprinted from* School Library Journal, *September, 1963, published by R. R. Bowker Co., a Xerox company; copyright © 1963 by Xerox Corporation), September, 1963, p. 168.*

OTHER CITATIONS

Mary Louise Hector, in The New York Times Book Review, *April 28, 1963, p. 38.*

Margaret Sherwood Libby, in New York Herald Tribune Books, *May 12, 1963 (Sec. 12), p. 19.*

*   *   *

SNEVE, Virginia Driving Hawk   1933-

Virginia Driving Hawk Sneve, an American Indian author, is a member of the Dakota tribe.

BETRAYED (1974)

Sneve's projection of both Indian and white perspectives [in *Betrayed*], while admirable, is studied and sometimes too superficial for the needs of the story. The portrayed dynamics of intertribal politics and religious customs that set up the circumstances leading to the captives' rescue by a related Sioux tribe also seem unconvincing. The author cites the veracity of names and events, but claims credit for character development and situations; and as events progress readers may wish for notes that clearly delineate the boundary between historical fact and fiction. In spite of its flaws, however, this does give dramatic impact to a tragic historical event.

> The Booklist *(reprinted by permission of the American Library Association; copyright 1974 by the American Library Association), November 15, 1974, p. 346.*

Based on a true incident [the 1862 Santee Sioux uprising in western Minnesota], this shows neither side to be all good or all bad; e.g., the Sioux rescuers are mocked for helping white women; some of the captives are treated kindly, some are not; and the betrayal of the title refers to the broken promises of U.S. Indian agents which caused the uprising. As usual, Sneve provides an excellent background to her story which will be a good addition to collections of Indian lore.

> *Roberta Rogow, in* School Library Journal *(reprinted from* School Library Journal, *January, 1975, published by R. R. Bowker Co., a Xerox company; copyright © 1975 by Xerox Corporation), January, 1975, p. 57.*

Except for the old Indian woman Anna (who sounds at times disconcertingly like Bloody Mary in "South Pacific"), the author records Dakota ways and speech in a gravely simple, spring-clear prose of unmistakable authenticity. She tries at all times to deal even-handedly with the fascinating, seemingly irreconcilable motivations of white oppressor-victims, Santee avengers, and part-breed catalyst. The book's flaws are an equivocal (and therefore misleading) title and a less-than-satisfactory ending, which is not so much a resolution as an abrupt dislocation of an otherwise forthright and logical story line.

> *Cathleen Burns Elmer, in* The New York Times Book Review *(© 1975 by The New York Times Company; reprinted by permission), January 19, 1975, p. 8.*

[*Betrayed*] follows a group of white captives taken by the Santee Sioux in the Dakota Uprising of 1862 until they are rescued by a small band of Teton Sioux and clearly shows the provocation (land-grabbing, treachery, broken promises) that drove the Santee to desperation. Characterizations are appealing and the plot holds the interest. However, this reviewer can't help wondering about the motives of the half-white Teton youth Charger, chief rescuer of the captives, who professes indignation at the "cruelty" of the Tetons' brothers, the Santee. This may not be the remarkably white Christian attitude it appears, but I wish Ms. Sneve had explained more of the circumstances in her introduction, as the issue beclouds an otherwise readable book.

> *Georgess McHargue, in* American Libraries *(reprinted by permission of the American Library Association; copyright 1975 by the American Library Association), March, 1975, p. 166.*

OTHER CITATIONS

Zena Sutherland, in Bulletin of the Center for Children's Books, *April, 1975, p. 139.*

THE CHICHI HOOHOO BOGEYMAN (1975)

[*The Chichi Hoohoo Bogeyman* is the] thinnest yet of Sneve's slight tales, with even less of the Indian background that sometimes compensates for her awkward writing and primitive plots.... The car honking is never explained—nor, incidentally, is the family tree which precedes the story but only confuses the relationships by switching two of the three featured daughters.

> Kirkus Reviews *(copyright © 1975 The Kirkus Service, Inc.), August 15, 1975, p. 919.*

[Virginia Driving Hawk] Sneve has again drawn on paranormal events to provide an undercurrent of tension, with better success here than in previous works; but it is her fresh, in-tune portrayal of the girls and their families that makes the slim story line work.

> *Denise M. Wilms, in* The Booklist *(reprinted by permission of the American Library Association; copyright 1975 by the American Library Association), November 15, 1975, p. 458.*

HIGH ELK'S TREASURE (1972)

If young Joe High Elk's loss of the filly in a storm, and the discovery of a horse thief on the nearby wildlife preserve both resolve themselves without much fuss, so does the mystery of High Elk's more valuable hidden treasure—a bundle containing a pictograph record which reveals the identity of the Indian who killed Custer. The High Elks' remarkable heirloom is made more believable than the valuable mink trapped by *Jimmy Yellow Hawk* ..., but none of the family's activities ever amount to anything more than an artificial demonstration of their Sioux Heritage. Best read for the background, if at all.

> Kirkus Reviews *(copyright © 1972 The Kirkus Service, Inc.), September 15, 1972, p. 1100.*

[*High Elk's Treasure*] balances [the] theme of proud heritage with suspense about the old mare that is due to foal, and by an unexpected reunion with a cousin from another branch of the family. There is plenty of action, adequate characterization, a well-developed setting, and good family relationships, but the strength of the book is that it makes clear without a sociological commentary the attitudes of contemporary Indians of different generations, and the solidity of family life that permits this with no generation gap.

> *Zena Sutherland, in* Bulletin of the Center for Children's Books *(© 1973 by the University of Chicago; all rights reserved), February, 1973, pp. 97-8.*

[This] fast-paced, well-constructed story provides an authentic picture of contemporary Indian life. Children looking for another adventure or horse story will enjoy this easy-to-read book and Oren Lyon's sepia pen-and-ink drawings.

> *Mary I. Purucker, in* School Library Journal *(reprinted from* School Library Journal,

March, 1973, published by R. R. Bowker Co., a Xerox company; copyright © 1973 by Xerox Corporation), March, 1973, p. 112.

OTHER CITATIONS

Alan Cheuse, in The New York Times Book Review, *November 5, 1972 (Part 2), p. 14.*

JIMMY YELLOW HAWK (1972)

There's a little information about Reservation life worked [into *Jimmy Yellow Hawk*] through a rodeo and a Pow Wow, and some background about Little Jim and his family is obviously planted in early conversations. In short, this implausibly wish-fulfilling story (how many targets of schoolyard scorn become heroes overnight?) is just a bit of awkwardly fictionalized ethnic instruction, and the portrayal of Little Jim's rancher father—as better off because harder working and more accepting of white ways than the other Indians—won't boost Red power.

> Kirkus Reviews *(copyright © 1972 The Kirkus Service, Inc.), March 15, 1972, pp. 325-26.*

[*Jimmy Yellow Hawk*] is not strong in construction; its strength lies in the picture it gives of a contemporary Indian family that has adjusted to ranch life, and has accepted the benefits of white civilization but given up neither their participation nor their pride in their Indian heritage.

> *Zena Sutherland, in* Bulletin of the Center for Children's Books *(© 1973 by the University of Chicago; all rights reserved), February, 1973, p. 98.*

OTHER CITATIONS

Beryl Robinson, in The Horn Book Magazine, *August, 1972, pp. 383-84.*

WHEN THUNDERS SPOKE (1973)

Sneve's range as a storyteller is limited, and she has used this same theme—the affirmation of Indian identity through the discovery of an old relic—in *High Elk's Treasure*. . . . But there is a serene sincerity about Norman that gives weight to his experience.

> Kirkus Reviews *(copyright © 1974 The Kirkus Service, Inc.), May 1, 1974, p. 481.*

[This is an] engrossing tale about the effects of a relic on a Sioux boy and his family. . . . Norman's decision about what to do with the stick is in keeping with Sioux tradition. The white characters—storekeeper (conniving), tourists (crass and ignorant) and preacher (sanctimonious)—are stereotypes. However, the portraits of Norman's mother, and father, and his grandfather successfully show them caught between two worlds, and the illustrations by Oren Lyons heighten the story's mysterious atmosphere.

> *Roberta Rogow, in* School Library Journal *(reprinted from* School Library Journal, *September, 1974, published by R. R. Bowker Co., a Xerox company; copyright © 1974 by Xerox Corporation), September, 1974, p. 112.*

[The] element of magic [in *When Thunders Spoke*] weakens a story that is otherwise strong in defense of the dignity and validity of the old ways, is candid in depicting the relationship between the Sioux and the white storekeeper with whom they trade, and is rich in cultural detail.

> *Zena Sutherland, in* Bulletin of the Center for Children's Books *(© 1974 by the University of Chicago; all rights reserved), November, 1974, pp. 53-4.*

OTHER CITATIONS

Publishers' Weekly, *May 27, 1974, p. 65.*

* * *

SOUTHALL, Ivan 1921-

An Australian author of articles, short stories, and children's books, Ivan Southall received the Australian Children's Book of the Year Award in 1966 for *Ash Road*, in 1968 for *To the Wild Sky*, and in 1971 for *Bread and Honey*. He has also received the 1969 Australian Picture Book of the Year Award for *Sly Old Wardrobe* and the 1971 Carnegie Medal for *Josh*. (See also *Contemporary Authors*, Vols. 9-12, rev. ed., and *Something About the Author*, Vol. 3.)

GENERAL COMMENTARY

Ivan Southall's novels are very much 'for real'. He offers his readers a criticism of life which is often excruciating (perhaps indulgently so) in its insistence upon the pain, disillusionment and embarrassed failures which are integral to adolescence. He is concerned with deficiency; sometimes in physical and mental terms, for one of his principal characters is spastic and another mongoloid. But he is also relentlessly concerned with deficiency in the larger sense of weakness in personality, of both adults and children. He writes of loss and consequent grief: the loss of parents, the loss of home and even township; the child's own loss of innocence and the painful joy of his self-awareness; and the loss of security experienced by a child as he recognizes the fallibility of his peers and, more devastatingly, of his elders. (p. 49)

However, I would contend that there is [an] area in which Southall's vision is deficient: and indeed that there is a distortion in his criticism of life which seems to me to have been fully rectified only in his most recent books—notably *Chinaman's Reef is Ours*.

For despite my very great admiration of the earlier novels, I have been left with the sense that the writer has offered us a picture which is at once—awkwardly—both optimistic and pessimistic. Optimistic in that he shows us children placed in severely demanding circumstances through which learning, growth and change take place. The children are often profoundly wise; wiser indeed than their parents or teachers. For, pessimistically, the adults of the novels give little evidence of any capacity for growth and change: except for that forced upon them by the example of the children. (pp. 52-3)

[Southall's grown-ups] are, in the main, characterized as being incapable of the exploratory openness which [his] children either have or readily learn. They are mean-spirited, soured by life and lacking vividness. Behind their masks of confidence, they flinch from any challenging experience. Now my objection is not so much that this is how Southall sees adults: rather that he seems to opt for an over-easy nod to his child readers, a knowing, 'Well, kids, that's the way grown-ups are, as you and I know.' It's not so much their masks that I regret, it's the lack of sympathy in showing how experience may have formed the masks. And whilst that is my fundamental complaint, I think I *do* regret that he fails to offer the hope that openness and imagination may be preserved by an adult, so that the consequent possibility of communication between adults and children is there. Where his novels concern children alone, his insight is impressive: but is he not unjust in that he offers only defeated adults and does not explore adults whose variety is as infinite as their children's? . . . Not until *Chinaman's Reef is Ours* does Southall, like one of his characters, open 'a crack in the door of the adult world where lives are a masquerade'. (pp. 54-5)

Ivan Southall's ability is evident not merely in his technique, but also in the directness and sensitivity with which he handles areas children want to read about, and even 'should' read about. [This] ability is clearly enthusiastically recognized by children. If there has been a deficiency in his work in his portrayal of adults, there are signs that he has increasingly resisted the inclination to offer us unsubtle, over-harsh outlines apparently sketched from children's perspectives; and that he has acknowledged that this was to underestimate the sympathy and complexity of understanding of which his child characters, and their identifying readers, are capable. (p. 64)

> *Geoffrey Fox, "Growth and Masquerade: A Theme in the Novels of Ivan Southall," in Children's Literature in Education (© 1971, APS Publications, Inc., New York; reprinted by permission of the publisher), No. 6 (November), 1971, pp. 49-64.*

[Southall's] writing is characteristically masculine, if at times almost femininely sensitive. He is alarmingly intense, having lived each year in the belief that it was nearly his last; and we see in his . . . work the marks of his harrowing, we seem to hear the echoes of old inward battles. . . .

Just how much there is of Southall in his boy characters we cannot be sure, but there seems to be a strong autobiographical element in many of them. And, vividly drawn though they are, I could bear few of them around me for very long. They strike me as humourless, over-earnest and sometimes boring. I feel wary of his creatures, not because Southall himself is a bore—he is anything but that—but partly because he does not seem to laugh readily at himself, and partly because even the resources of his own very full life cannot sustain the range of inner confrontation he has tried to present in his last seven or eight books. We are subjected to emotional nagging. His lads are like feelings rushing in circles looking for the right dimensions to be people in. Southall never reads children's books by other writers—in fact he says he reads hardly anything. Most novelists will admit that they feed on others; the dangers of feeding on oneself are manifest, and I am not the first critic to wonder how much farther Southall can go before he changes direction. It says much for the intensity of his

imagination that he has come so far without running out of energy. . . .

Where he is able to detach himself, as in his treatment of girls, we respond wholeheartedly to the personalities. (p. 184)

If his characters are less attractive than they might have become under a lighter hand, they are in no way shallow. They are drawn with great sympathy and understanding, they fully engage their creator (and—although he may not be at ease in their company—the reader). To Southall they are so real as, once conceived, to lead an independent existence. His stories, he tells us, develop according to their own inner logic—he merely sets up the situation and waits to see what his characters make of it. (*Let the Balloon Go* is an exception—here he knew from the start what would happen, knew what the boy in the tree would make of himself.) They apparently write the book for him; and this leads him into serious difficulties, for there are occasions when we can claim that he does not discharge his responsibilities to his readers—and who are we to blame for that? It takes a lot of courage to begin writing a book without some idea of where it is likely to go—it is rather frightening to be controlled by what you suppose to be your own creation; but what are we to make of the excuse for failure to resolve conflicts, that the action stops where it does simply of its own accord? We are repeatedly faced with crises of leadership for survival which are not fully worked out.

Southall drops us, we do not drop him; for he is a genuine un-put-downable: once a story gets rolling the movement is irresistible. If his situations sometimes seem painfully contrived, we do not make too much of it, for we are so intensely there that we give hardly a thought to the means of arrival—and in any case, some of his situations may be truer to life than we know. (pp. 184-85)

He is magnificent in his handling of tension: the seemingly eternal imminence of the fire; the wracking suspense of the flight in *To the Wild Sky;* and the lower-key dramas of *The Fox Hole* and *Let the Balloon Go*—these rivet the reader, and at the end (the all too often irresolute end) he feels a sudden slackening of the nerves. I cannot agree with those critics who think that Southall overplays the tension; in fact I feel that he can fail to make the most of the possibilities, as in *Hills End,* where he does little more than hint at the impending menace of the sky. (p. 185)

Storms and fires and runaway aircraft do not of themselves create tension; somebody has to be threatened. Where the threat is mortal, gigantic questions are posed, and we desperately need the answers—otherwise we would not be reading the book. We obviously want to examine the nature of the children's response to danger, but unless we are shown the ultimate effect of these responses, what meaning can they have for us? Do the incompetent young inhabitants of Hills End survive the destruction of their township in the wilderness? Southall says he wrote the novel expressly to ask: could they? And he answers the question by bringing adults to the rescue before the kids are really put to the test. We suspect that they, like the plane-wrecked youngsters of *To the Wild Sky,* might not have survived. In neither case are they anywhere near self-sufficient, although in the latter Southall has offered clues to survival—a flight of ducks, hinting at water, and the rediscovery of fire —but they are not convincing in face of the psychological insufficiency of the children. *To the Wild Sky* seems to finish a hundred pages short.

It is difficult to escape the conclusion that he is simply abandoning his characters, or that they are running away from him. These themes of natural catastrophe are as stark as can be: either the children will die, or they will not—there is nothing in between. If the seeds of destruction or survival are not to be found in the makeup of the children themselves—and in these books, despite Southall's skill at developing character, I believe they are not—then it is unfair to ask the reader to decide the outcome. It invariably seems to me that the odds are on death, and that Southall is in some strange way culpable—which is perhaps why he gets the kids off the hook in *Ash Road* and *Hills End,* and turns his back on them in *To the Wild Sky*—confronting us always with the threat of death but never the fact (except when he is anxious to get rid of an inconvenient adult).

Where the open-ended form is wholly legitimate is in the novels of character, where the conflict is between people, as in *Chinaman's Reef;* or within a character, as in *Let the Balloon Go;* or both, as in *Bread and Honey* and *Josh.* These are character-studies of great depth and intensity—necessarily so, for the action takes place in a very short time, mostly in a single day. One can feel that these people are thrust too closely upon the reader, which may account for the fact that we cannot always like them. It may not be their fault, but we expect the decencies to be observed, and we learn to become shy of people who expose their souls on the merest acquaintance. Nevertheless, we try to know them, and, as with the people we live among, we cannot draw firm conclusions. They live on when the day is over, and we close the book wondering how they will get on. These completely human dramas, rather than the more immediately engrossing stories of conflict with elements, are the ones I shall return to with pleasure. (pp. 185-86)

[*Bread and Honey,* 1970, and *Josh,* 1972] are perhaps his most sensitive essays. He seems to me to be at his very best when he is largely occupied with a single character; then we feel the warmth of an unbounded sympathy. (p. 186)

> *Allan Morrison, "Letting the Characters Go: Ivan Southall," in* Children's Book Review *(© 1971 by Five Owls Press Ltd.; all rights reserved), December, 1971, pp. 184-86.*

[Ivan Southall's] four full-length novels for children since *Hills End* have had strong similarities with that book and with each other. *Ash Road* [1966], *To the Wild Sky* (1967), *Finn's Folly* (1969) and *Chinaman's Reef is Ours* (1970) have all been about groups of youngsters faced with disasters which tax their reserves of physical and moral courage to the utmost. A reader acquainted with, say, any two of these five books would have little difficulty in attributing the other three to Southall, even if he had nothing to go on but a plot summary. It is possible to feel that the author has repeated himself, and has sometimes piled on the horror in an effort to combat the law of diminishing returns. A parody of Southall could be written under the title of *Tether's End.* Yet each successive book has explored some new ground, and each has its own interest.

All five novels are cinematic in technique: the point of view roves around, cameralike, from one character or pair of characters to another. It is difficult to use this method effectively when the end-product is to be a book rather than a film, because, for most people, reading is not as compulsive as watching; the attention is jolted when the narrative jumps from one character to another, with the risk of loss of interest. It also requires a more-or-less equal build-up of a number of characters. Southall's ability to manage a large cast, and to make a number of children all interesting and all entirely different, is exceptional. . . . (p. 183)

Ivan Southall is a strong, masculine writer whose style is direct and active, sometimes staccato. His narratives give the impression of moving at high speed under high pressure. At times, as when the fire draws near in *Ash Road* or the boy Gerald takes over from the dead pilot in *To the Wild Sky,* one feels the surge of adrenalin into the bloodstream. His power is extraordinary. Nevertheless I find him difficult to assess and his progress difficult to forecast. Most novelists probably work within quite a narrow range: often narrower than is realized. But Southall's range at present seems *too* narrow. It is hard to see how he can go on facing more and more groups of characters with catastrophe; how he can go on cranking up the same kind of tension. The force and intensity of his imagination have been fully demonstrated; its breadth remains to be proved. Yet clearly he is a gifted and highly intelligent writer. It seems inevitable that before long he will move in a new direction. (p. 189)

> *John Rowe Townsend, "Ivan Southall," in his* A Sense of Story: Essays on Contemporary Writers for Children *(copyright © 1971 by John Rowe Townsend; reprinted by permission of J. B. Lippincott Company), Lippincott, 1971, pp. 182-89.*

ASH ROAD (1966)

You could call this a formula novel because there is a close correlation between all the elements of this story and those of the author's excellent *Hills End.* . . . But it's still a good formula, one which proves out to a sustaining sense of tension and an unusually forceful revelation of personality under stress. The disaster here is a fire which rapidly spread out of control in the windy, hot, long-dry Australian bush area. . . . Particularly well conveyed is the disorganization which affects everyone down the line, and which allowed the damage to be much greater than necessary. But until the end, when a sudden storm puts out the fire just as it reaches the children, the story follows a straight line with a steady accumulation of action.

> Virginia Kirkus' Service *(copyright © 1966 Virginia Kirkus' Service, Inc.), February 15, 1966, pp. 187-88.*

Mr. Southall traces the inexorable spread of the fire [in "Ash Road"] by constantly shifting focus from the older boys who carelessly started it to the children and to the worried adults. The hour-by-hour chronicle of their thoughts and actions as each becomes aware of the peril builds to supreme suspense for the reader. . . .

"Ash Road," rich in homely incidents and personal drama, is a powerful portrayal of youthful courage and resourcefulness. Mr. Southall's description of Australia—the land and the people—has a documentary quality. He has written a memorable, literate story.

> *Margaret F. O'Connell, in* The New York Times Book Review *(© 1966 by The New York Times Company; reprinted by permission), March 6, 1966, p. 34.*

[In *Ash Road*, Mr. Southall] is excellent at preparing the atmosphere for misfortune: and he finds words fit for the fearful natural horrors he has to describe. (The fire sweeps across the land "like a thousand locomotives steaming abreast".) He gives his characters fullness from the beginning, and room to grow. He suggests brilliantly the pure astonishment with which people find themselves involved in danger. But the trouble this time seems to be that he has, before the story is a quarter done, far too many young characters plunged into situations of utter desperation. Among them there is a girl who faces not only the fire but the agony caused by her father's sudden collapse from a stroke; another child lost in the bush; yet another in a state of near-hysterical distress because he was the accidental cause of the fire. Mr. Southall cuts quickly from one to another of these situations—but they are all too awfully the same, in their grim apparent hopelessness: and in the end one simply cannot bear it. A failure, though a most honourable one.

> The Times Literary Supplement *(© The Times Publishing Company Ltd. 1966), May 19, 1966, p. 431.*

OTHER CITATIONS

Allie Beth Martin, in School Library Journal, *April, 1966, p. 108.*

Helen B. Crawshaw, in The Horn Book Magazine, *June, 1966, p. 315.*

Zena Sutherland, in Bulletin of the Center for Children's Books, *June, 1966, p. 170.*

***BENSON BOY* (1973)**

Ivan Southall, so perceptive in exploring areas of fear and insecurity in a boy's mind, goes very close to the bone here, reproducing the thoughts of an eleven-year-old who goes over the top of his known world when his mother begins labour at two in the morning. . . . At every stage, Perry's mind rebels at being pushed into adult situations. He refuses to accept that his mother is unable to make any physical effort to help him, refuses to believe the baby is already present inside her, though he has been carefully prepared previously. Gradually, he grumblingly accepts the inconsistency of the adults he has to deal with and comes to terms with reality, which he finds much better than he thought. We become convinced we are overhearing a real boy, and we can sympathise too with the adults who find him so difficult to convince or move.

> The Junior Bookshelf, *October, 1972, pp. 336-37.*

To make a boy as dim as Perry the hero and sole spokesman [in "Benson Boy"] requires a kind of virtuoso writing [Ivan Southall] has not yet attained. Placing the en-

tire narrative burden on such a protagonist has resulted in a novel as constricted as Perry's own world.

> *Doris Orgel, in* The New York Times Book Review *(© 1973 by The New York Times Company; reprinted by permission), April 29, 1973, p. 10.*

[The] unlikely pile-up of problems [in *Benson Boy*] seems to build naturally out of the situation's urgency and confusion, while even more is happening inside Perry's mind, which is protesting each new disaster and revealing a child's view of children's helplessness and adults' absurdity. Although the mother's patience may strain the reader's, Southall manages to inject humor into the gloomiest moments.

> The Booklist *(reprinted by permission of the American Library Association; copyright 1973 by the American Library Association), July 15, 1973, p. 1074.*

Ivan Southall is at his best in a story like [*Benson Boy*]: a dramatic setting, a tense situation, only a few characters, and a child who calls on unexpected courage and resourcefulness to cope with a problem. . . . The story's span is the one night, but it encompasses problem, conflict, and resolution most deftly constructed and the sometimes-staccato Southall dialogue is just right in the situation. Believable and exciting.

> *Zena Sutherland, in* Bulletin of the Center for Children's Books *(© 1973 by the University of Chicago; all rights reserved), October, 1973, pp. 34-5.*

There is tension at every moment in the story, the resolution of one crisis introducing the boy hero into another critical situation. It is a natural book to read at one sitting and will probably be read by young readers as unexceptionably plausible. If there is anything in the story which may not sit well with young readers, it will probably be the boy's unnecessarily extensive reflections on his own feelings.

The story brings its hero face to face with such human obstacles as the extreme pigheadedness of his father and the feud between his father and a neighbor over political philosophies. These things are on a par with the mother's child-bearing as far as semi-comprehensibility goes. The story is well calculated to bring young readers up to a frontier of unfamiliarity, but in such a way that the discoveries, or not-quite-discoveries, are exciting without being disturbing. The story gains a certain interest from being set in Australia.

> *Tom Heffernan, in* Children's Literature: Annual of The Modern Language Association Seminar on Children's Literature and The Children's Literature Association, *Vol. 4, edited by Francelia Butler (© 1975 by Francelia Butler; all rights reserved), Temple University Press, 1975, p. 204.*

OTHER CITATIONS

Kirkus Reviews, *February 1, 1973, p. 117.*

Publishers' Weekly, *March 5, 1973, p. 82.*

Paul Heins, in The Horn Book Magazine, *June, 1973, p. 273.*

BREAD AND HONEY (1970)

Although we see the action of [*Bread and Honey*] through Michael, his judgment is evidently limited by the awkward shyness for which, in part, his age is responsible; just as John Clement Sumner's picture of other children was limited by his disability [in *Let the Balloon Go*, 1968]. His self-pity depends upon distortion. . . .

The book is chiefly concerned with the emerging relationship between Mick and a girl he meets on the beach; and the crisis the relationship precipitates which the boy must face by asserting his separateness and his strength—in both physical and moral terms—against a bullying trio of boys. The tension between the boy and girl is delicately observed, as is the tension within the boy as he becomes aware of new facets of himself. . . . (p. 61)

But he does not merely break through to the girl and into new areas of himself. For although the adults remain, for the most part, in the background, Mick has attained by the end of the novel a new sympathy with his grandmother in her response to Anzac Day, during which the action takes place. And since we know Mick's judgment to be limited by his awkwardness, we are better able to recognize that not only the grandmother, but also Mick's father and to a lesser extent the father of Mick's neighbour, Ray, have a sensitivity which prompts them to reach out sympathetically to Mick. They are separated from him by experience, but when breakdown in communication occurs it is caused at least as much by Mick's limitations as by theirs. And consequently, when he shares with his grandmother the recognition that Anzac Day is 'a day for forgetting, anyway, same as for remembering' we know that he is coming to terms with growing up himself; that he can acknowledge in a positive way that 'a fellow washed half his life down the sink: every game he ever played, nose-bleeds, hours of sleep, bread and honey, sweat, inky fingers—washed them all down the sink. Swirled them down the plug-hole into the earth and forgot.' (pp. 61-2)

Geoffrey Fox, "Growth and Masquerade: A Theme in the Novels of Ivan Southall," in Children's Literature in Education *(© 1971, APS Publications, Inc., New York; reprinted by permission of the publisher), No. 6 (November), 1971, pp. 49-64.*

Throughout [*Bread and Honey*], [Ivan] Southall suggests that there is a relationship between dying for one's country and the chivalric defense of helpless females, and there certainly is, even though Mick never does come to grips with it, nor does the plot. The parade above the town and the encounter below it remain two separate activities.

The quality of Southall's writing is fine enough to carry even the skeptical reader through the long, feverish episode on the shingle, yet much of Mick's crisis could have been eliminated by a nice change of clothing and a big box of Kleenex.

In sum, the marvel and terror of the bodily changes which take charge of the adolescent, regardless of gender, time, or culture, are circumvented by the story, and the sensitivity of the author lavished instead upon the affirmation of some rather outmoded social precepts. On the other hand, the book would probably be banned in Kentucky.

Feenie Ziner, in Children's Literature: Annual of The Modern Language Association Seminar on Children's Literature and The Children's Literature Association, *Vol. 4, edited by Francelia Butler (© 1975 by Francelia Butler; all rights reserved), Temple University Press, 1975, pp. 195-96.*

CHINAMAN'S REEF IS OURS (1970)

Ivan Southall is one of the more powerful authors writing for young people today; he understands his characters and their problems. They are his creation and it is in this art of creativity that lies his strength. In [*Chinaman's Reef Is Ours*] there is a small scene where one of the characters drops the receiver of a wall telephone and it swings backward and forward uselessly, simply summing up the whole situation. Again as Leah comes out into the sunlight he gives us this marvellous phrase, "her eyes felt bruised by the sunlight". He also uses contrasts to build up atmosphere as when the scene flickers between the children clinging onto a tin roof in the blazing sun and Mr. Gibbs and the boy Peter in the shaded shabby room. All the way through one has this feeling of heat and dust and hopelessness, of small people fighting a big company. . . .

The Junior Bookshelf, *October, 1970, p. 308.*

Anyone who has survived a few rounds with Mr. Southall already should be able to come unscathed through *Chinaman's Reef is Ours,* which is fairly standard Southall and a good deal less gruelling than some of its predecessors. . . .

As often before, Mr. Southall handles a largish cast with great skill and keeps the action going. His writing is terse, masculine, and professional in the extreme. But there is something not quite right about this story. The compression of its events into a single day seems artificial; this is not after all a natural disaster and cannot really share the character of one. The whipping-up of tension appears forced; there is too much running round in circles, too much general stridency. Auntie Sadie, the one strongly-developed character in the opening chapters, plays no effective part in the story.

Yet a human catastrophe has one great advantage over a natural one: it can involve real conflicts, arguable issues, whereas there is no arguing with fire or flood. Does Chinaman's Reef—this "heap of sticks and stones"—deserve to live? Is not life in this neglected, unlovely place a desolating waste of years? What future can it hold for young people? There is plenty here to think about. The sense of a small community is strong, the sense of place still stronger, the sheer Australian-ness strongest of all. The book would be worth reading for that alone.

The Times Literary Supplement *(© Times Newspapers Ltd., 1970), October 30, 1970, p. 1256.*

The emotions and actions of the characters here become so overwrought and convoluted that they detract from the book as a whole.... Factual material is capably enough integrated into the story, but the flaws of characterization and plot make [*Chinaman's Reef Is Ours*] only a fair effort.

> *Susan M. Budd, in* School Library Journal *(reprinted from* School Library Journal, *December, 1970, published by R. R. Bowker Co., a Xerox company; copyright © 1970 by Xerox Corporation), December, 1970, p. 67.*

There is a lack of literal probability in [*Chinaman's Reef Is Ours*]. It is hard to believe that an invading force could or would be sent without warning one Sunday morning to destroy a town and make its people homeless. This seems the kind of conflict to stretch over weeks or months rather than to be fought and finished in a day. The air is one of confusion and over-wroughtness, as if everything had been artificially whipped up into this one brief flurry; as if the author had tried to give human catastrophe the character of a natural catastrophe, which—in peacetime and in what is largely a legal question—it does not possess. (pp. 186-87)

For all its faults, this is a searching novel.... The people are all alive, and, as always, Southall is wonderfully good at showing the individual in action in a social context. But the chessboard technique, in which the pieces are moved forward separately yet all in concert with each other, does not really work here, because there is not a clear enough pattern to the action. (p. 187)

> *John Rowe Townsend, "Ivan Southall," in his* A Sense of Story: Essays on Contemporary Writers for Children *(copyright © 1971 by John Rowe Townsend; reprinted by permission of J. B. Lippincott Company), Lippincott, 1971, pp. 182-89.*

OTHER CITATIONS

Kirkus Reviews, *June 1, 1970, p. 606.*

Publishers' Weekly, *June 1, 1970, p. 67.*

THE CURSE OF CAIN (1968)

[*The Curse of Cain* is a] reverent, exciting retelling of Genesis, embellished by the author's imagination. Strict fundamentalists might be offended by such details as a brown-eyed blond Adam, but young readers will respond enthusiastically to the warmth and human qualities of the biblical figures as presented here.... The period between Abel's murder and the Noah story is telescoped successfully, allowing the flood and its consequences to furnish a dramatic climax for the narrative. The author's cadenced style is a delight to the ear and his final explanatory note expressing his obvious sincerity should soften any dogmatic criticism of this kind of presentation.

> *Mary Ann Wentroth, in* School Library Journal *(reprinted from* School Library Journal, *November, 1968, published by R. R. Bowker Co., a Xerox company; copyright © 1968 by Xerox Corporation), November, 1968, pp. 90-1.*

This most unusual retelling tries to reconcile the various creation stories in the first chapters of *Genesis* with evolu-

tionary theory and archaeological evidence about the birth of mankind. It ingeniously incorporates unresolved facts as being mysterious to the characters themselves. It imagines convincingly what it must have felt like to be Man among animals yet conscious of differing, knowing the dawn of instinct and conscience, inventing words for new experiences, lonely on his own. There is sly humour, such as Adam's difficulties in coping with female logic, and absolute truth to life in his sensations after eating the apple, in Cain's reactions to his father's request that he sacrifices to the God for whom he can find no evidence, and his desolation at the realisation that Abel is dead. Mr. Southall translates these stories into modern terms, in the same way the writers of the mediaeval Miracle Plays interpreted them for their world. Indeed the neighbours' disbelief in Noah reminds one of the vigorous humour of the Noah plays, though the vivid account of the flood is more like a Hieronymus Bosch painting. The book will be best appreciated by those who know *Genesis,* who can appreciate the ingenious interpretation and reconciliation. It will bring a realisation of the universal significance of stories often dismissed as mere fables.

> The Junior Bookshelf, *December, 1968, pp. 385-86.*

Ivan Southall's ... *The Curse of Cain* will help the less imaginative child to find meaningfulness in human things in Adam's loneliness, in Cain's hatred and horror. It will not help him to wrestle with the mysteries of the Fall and the Flood. Here verbiage gets in the way. The myths must speak directly like music, or not at all.

> The Times Literary Supplement *(© Times Newspapers Ltd., 1968), December 5, 1968, p. 1382.*

OTHER CITATIONS

Kirkus Service, *August 15, 1968, p. 901.*

FINN'S FOLLY (1969)

[*Finn's Folly* is the] story of a night of tragedy.... The author uses the technique of construction (short accounts of individual action) that was so successful in *Ash Road* and *Hills End,* here a little less effective, perhaps because of the fact that the dramatic impact is slowed by dialogue that halts rather than helps the action. There is a note of heavy coincidence ... but there is also a strong creation of mood and tension....

> *Zena Sutherland, in* Bulletin of the Center for Children's Books *(© 1970 by the University of Chicago; all rights reserved), January, 1970, p. 88.*

The events [in *Finn's Folly*], objectively considered, are the very stuff of a newspaper account of a roadside accident; but experienced through the senses and the emotions of the adolescent characters, they tingle with immediacy and are gradually unfolded by a series of cumulatively suspenseful episodes. Beyond the slightly melodramatic plot rises the sure characterization of the [children], who not only witness the physical catastrophe of death but realize the momentous changes coming into their lives.... But the starkness of the narrative is overcome by the vividness of the telling, and the world of harsh reality is tempered by human acceptance.

> *Paul Heins, in* The Horn Book Magazine *(copyright © 1970 by The Horn Book, Inc., Boston), February, 1970, pp. 46-7.*

Finn's Folly is to be read for the ambition of its failure. Southall has attempted so much that one supposes an intoxication which allowed one disaster to sweep in upon another until the reader's credibility is snapped. . . . The Fenwicks, the adults whose lives are intertwined with those of the trapped occupants of the truck, face their separate crises; as does Mr. McPhee, the driver. And although so much of the book is uneven, the treatment of the adults here has a greater honesty and certainly a greater optimism than has been evident in the earlier novels. McPhee, Alison's father, is stripped by the accident and deaths he has brought about; the mask which deceives and attracts Alison's schoolgirl friends is torn away. . . . He knows himself to be a failure to his wife, to his daughter: to himself. But for all that, he has been a man who has struggled in his own particular human predicament, and Southall writes of him, exposed, in such a way that we do not despise him for the hypocrisy which has shielded him from his daughter. . . .

The Fenwicks also grow through the situation, although by the time of their intervention the plot has become such a maelstrom of disaster that their personal crises may seem relatively mundane. But at least the Fenwicks are growing and changing through resources in themselves, not simply as pupils of the children. Brittle though his tone is, Fenwick's words to the trapped Alison have an honesty which enables us to believe that adults and children can share their crises. Adults also have imaginations which can respond to experience in terms of changed behaviour. (p. 60)

> *Geoffrey Fox, "Growth and Masquerade: A Theme in the Novels of Ivan Southall," in* Children's Literature in Education *(© 1971, APS Publications, Inc., New York; reprinted by permission of the publisher), No. 6 (November), 1971, pp. 49-64.*

Finn's Folly is a novel I would not read again at any price, precisely because Southall has succeeded so completely in doing what he set out to do, which was to create a nightmare. It is the most powerfully imaginative and penetrating of the 'crisis' stories, and its impact is utterly horrifying. I slept badly after reading it, and I think some readers could be crucified by it—for this is no remote horror, larger than life, but sickeningly real in detail, and all too close to home. As a total situation it is of course unlikely: premonitions of death, the hideous actuality of the parents' deaths; a disintegrating marriage; a retarded child lost in the dark and fog and precipitous country; the monumental selfishness of the adults—all in a single night! If the emotions of the children were not so terribly exposed the thing would be almost laughable. It is, in its perverse way, a great piece of writing, but I cannot see any purpose in it. I certainly did not find it cathartic; but that surely was not the intention, for the child so emotionally constipated as to want such drastic purging is in dire need of professional treatment. Southall himself seems to have benefited from it however, for since the publication of *Finn's Folly* he has eschewed the hor-

rors, and we find ourselves in the homelier company of Josh, and of Michael in *Bread and Honey*, with their boy-sized problems. (p. 186)

> *Allan Morrison, "Letting the Characters Go: Ivan Southall," in* Children's Book Review *(© 1971 by Five Owls Press Ltd.; all rights reserved), December, 1971, pp. 184-86.*

OTHER CITATIONS

Susan M. Budd, in School Library Journal, *September, 1970, p. 177.*

———————

THE FOX HOLE (1967)

Words like "chook" and "beaut" pepper "The Fox Hole," set in what used to be Australia's gold-rush country, and make it sound faintly exotic to American readers. But what they'll remember longest is the terrifying adventure that befalls 10-year-old Ken when he visits his cousins. . . .

[There] are candid yet reassuring glimpses of family friction. Conversation rings true, the writing is unabashedly evocative and adult, characters are as real as your own relations. Ken would call it a beaut book.

> *Nancy Griffin, in* The New York Times Book Review *(© 1967 by The New York Times Company; reprinted by permission), November 19, 1967, p. 60.*

The suspense of the story is breathtakingly maintained, the descriptions, particularly of the boys' camping at night, are brilliant, and the characters, in all their weakness, disturbingly real, but what sort of reading for children, however well done, is this? A boy, always nervous, ends in abject fear for his life, trapped in a horrifying place where murder has been done. From here he has to witness the near breakup of a weak man, first in an emergency and then under the madness of gold, till he is no longer even able to believe in "the goodness of grown-up men". That common humanity, by now seeming almost like heroism, prevails at the very end seems hardly compensation enough.

> *The* Times Literary Supplement *(© Times Newspapers Ltd., 1967), November 30, 1967, p. 1140.*

[*The Fox Hole*] is a very fine book. Though its central character is ten, its truth will be even better appreciated by older readers. The suspense is excellently built-up and held, and the children and adults shown in greater depth than is usual with this type of plot. The fears of a child making his first long journey alone in the Melbourne equivalent of Bank Holiday travel are vividly conveyed, and his realisation of how frightening it is to live with a family he has merely visited for the day, when their standards are so utterly different. . . . The ending is surprising, the naked adult greed and selfishness, overcome just in time by the realisation of more important values. This is altogether a book to stay in the mind.

> *The* Junior Bookshelf, *December, 1967, pp. 402-03.*

The concrete vocabulary appealing to all of the senses, the tenseness of the events, the deft characterization, and the moral crisis that confronts Uncle Bob make [Southall's *The Fox Hole*] a notable addition to fiction from Australia.

> *Paul Heins, in* The Horn Book Magazine *(copyright © 1968 by The Horn Book, Inc., Boston), April, 1968, p. 181.*

The abrupt 'salvation' of Uncle Bob in *The Fox Hole* is all the more unconvincing in contrast to Ken's increasing ability to handle his awkward nervousness. . . . Uncle Bob and Auntie Kath show no sign of the subtle, exploratory relationships which Southall weaves between his children: either with their own children, or with one another. This marriage is typical of those in the novels before *Finn's Folly* [1969]; the assumption seems to be that such long-term relationships cannot sustain—or develop—the vitality of the youthful relationships Southall so precisely explores and celebrates. Adults have closed the doors. The masquerade is played out with anxiety or bitterness, or perhaps an empty sufferance; or, as in this case, with fumbling attempts at communication between the adults. (pp. 56-7)

The final conversion, in which Uncle Bob determines to pretend that the gold is Fool's Gold, recognizing that his wife would 'rather live with an honest battler than a desperate, greedy millionaire' is too neatly and rapidly manipulated; and again, that disturbing sentimentality. . . . His wife is, it could be argued, left to live with a dishonest battler, who is hardly solving a problem by pretending it does not exist. (pp. 57-8)

> *Geoffrey Fox, "Growth and Masquerade: A Theme in the Novels of Ivan Southall," in* Children's Literature in Education *(© 1971, APS Publications, Inc., New York; reprinted by permission of the publisher), No. 6 (November), 1971, pp. 49-64.*

OTHER CITATIONS

Kirkus Service, October 15, 1967, p. 1283.

Zena Sutherland, in Bulletin of the Center for Children's Books, *March, 1968, p. 117.*

HEAD IN THE CLOUDS (1973)

There is a boy at the still centre of an odd, circling book . . ., *Head in the Clouds*. Ray Plumtree is temporarily imprisoned in a wheelchair at home, as the result of a road accident. From his mother's balcony, wistful and angry, he watches his schoolmates stream past, forgetful of him. He studies spells to turn them all into tadpoles—into anything. Then lo and behold! he's turned them all upside down. But his own head feels bursting, and—it's he who's upside down, hanging by one foot from the balcony. He's saved, and the jacket-blurb maintains that this is a "light-hearted story"; but there is something giddy-making about it, in a slow, sick way that some readers may dislike.

> The Times Literary Supplement *(© Times Newspapers Ltd., 1972), December 8, 1972, p. 1490.*

[In *Head in the Clouds*, Southall] uses disjointed sentences

as a film maker uses abruptly-cut film in cinema verité. It is a hard form to follow, and in the case of this book I do not think it is really worth the effort. Certainly the book is much too difficult for the seven-year-old market the publishers suggest.

> The Junior Bookshelf, *February, 1973, p. 30.*

[*Head in the Clouds*] is the plaintive story of nine-year-old Ray Plumtree, member of an accident-prone family, only child, spider caught in his own web. . . . The situation is interesting and the psychology sound, the dialogue is lively —but the book is weakened because so much of it is monologue and because the crucial episode is not quite lucid: is Ray confused by his position to such an extent that he really thinks the world has turned upside down—as he is calling out to warn the assembled children below—or has the story assumed a fantastic turn?

> *Zena Sutherland, in* Bulletin of the Center for Children's Books *(© 1973 by the University of Chicago; all rights reserved), May, 1973, p. 145.*

OTHER CITATIONS

Kirkus Reviews, January 1, 1973, p. 7.

J. Allan Morrison, in Children's Book Review, *April, 1973, p. 43.*

Joseph McLellan, in Book World, *May 13, 1973 (Part 2), p. 7.*

HILLS END (1963)

[*Hills End* is a] good adventure story, set in Australia, about a group of children who share a danger that tests their stamina and their ingenuity. . . . The background and characterization are good; the plot is dramatic and tight-knit; the author uses—most successfully—the technique of moving from one character to another to create suspense.

> *Zena Sutherland, in* Bulletin of the Center for Children's Books *(copyright 1963 by the University of Chicago; all rights reserved), September, 1963, p. 17.*

Unusual peril, fear and uncertainty bring out the children's courage and resourcefulness [in "Hills End"]. The author has the power to get inside his characters, and through them expresses his faith in human nature, in the goodness of man. The book ends, like an echo from the Bible, with a glorification of children as leaders, for they show their parents the way to restore the little town of Hills End.

This is a solid work, strong in action, mood and description. Its message is in direct contrast to that of another, more complex adult novel of isolation—William Golding's "Lord of the Flies"—in which children symbolize the evil in human nature.

> *Robert Hood, in* The New York Times Book Review *(© 1963 by The New York Times Company; reprinted by permission), September 8, 1963, p. 26.*

Hills End is almost a perfect novel of its kind. Although only one adult can be said to play a major role, the feeling of the whole community, adults as well as children, is strong from the start, as indeed it must be in order to give full weight to the blow that falls upon it. The rapid character development and self-discovery of the children under stress are notable. For instance, in a few days and a couple of hundred pages Adrian, the boss's son and 'king of the kids', discovers himself to be a physical coward and moves through deep self-disgust to find himself again as a resourceful organizer; and all this time he remains unmistakably the same boy. (p. 184)

> *John Rowe Townsend, "Ivan Southall," in his* A Sense of Story: Essays on Contemporary Writers for Children *(copyright © 1971 by John Rowe Townsend; reprinted by permission of J. B. Lippincott Company), Lippincott, 1971, pp. 182-89.*

OTHER CITATIONS

Margaret Sherwood Libby, in Book Week, *April 19, 1964, p. 14.*

JOSH (1972)

[The] manner of telling [*Josh*] is original and compelling. The whole story is told in a series of photographic glimpses into the thoughts and emotions that pour through Josh's bewildered brain in the course of five eventful days, and no explanations are given beyond the confused glimpses he himself obtains. This makes the novel something more than an intriguing story—a deeply understanding character study and an analysis of the ingredients commonly present when the generation gap manifests anywhere, and when those of differing backgrounds, ambitions and values meet. Teenagers will find this a stimulating commentary on life, their kind of life, their own problems and confusions, slightly more applicable, of course, to those with an Australian, Canadian or American background, but with wide general appeal. It is the kind of book needed to bridge the current gap between the pure entertainment stories of the young, and general adult reading.

> *Gladys Williams, in* Books and Bookmen *(© copyright Gladys Williams), December, 1971, p. xii.*

Early in the course of [the story], the reader's affection for Josh is solidly established, and a palpable desire for an explanation of the young people's behavior grows. Mr. Southall builds suspense to an almost frustrating level.... But the last page comes with no real denouement at all....

It is as if Mr. Southall were saying it, too: too many loose ends—better to end the book before it is finished than to try to clear things up. It might have worked if he had not created such an intriguing cast of characters and set them in motion in such an aura of inscrutable duplicity. For the plot, whether he intended it, cries for resolutions. Mr. Southall has left the reader hanging after 179 pages of suspense with a murder weapon and a passel of clues but no corpus delicti—and the reaction, on my part, at least, if I may be forgiven an Americanism, was that I'd been had.

> *Natalie Babbitt, in* The New York Times

Book Review (© 1972 by The New York Times Company; reprinted by permission), October 15, 1972, p. 8.

Josh is the story of a fourteen-year-old boy, shy and sensitive, who comes from the city on his first visit to Ryan Creek.... The characters are vividly portrayed, the relationships (whether amicable or inimical) strongly drawn; there is little in the book that indicates the Australian setting save for the dialogue which, almost as much as the exposition, is more heavily staccato and introspective than it is in other Southall books.

> *Zena Sutherland, in* Bulletin of the Center for Children's Books *(© 1972 by the University of Chicago; all rights reserved), November, 1972, pp. 49-50.*

Unfolded in sentences which often substitute present participles for finite verbs, [this] story is essentially an account of Josh's sensations, feelings, and reactions....

Adults, adolescents, and children are presented with such intensity that the paraphernalia and details of everyday life become bigger than life in the consciousness of the oversensitive youth. From Josh's observations and experiences, Aunt Clara and her house full of antique possessions come alive and make of Josh's days at Ryan Creek an agony that somehow or other is turned into a rich comedy.

> *Paul Heins, in* The Horn Book Magazine *(copyright © 1972 by The Horn Book, Inc., Boston), December, 1972, p. 580.*

This noisy, quick-moving, hard-hitting story is written in Ivan Southall's own version of the stream-of-consciousness. The book consists partly of dialogue—pungent, individual and full of overtones—and partly of short sentences, often with present participles as their only verb, which give a startling impression of a boy's thoughts moving along with his actions. The formidable figure of Aunt Clara emerges from a welter of words which suggest, as children's stories rarely do, that any one person's view of another is bound to be partial, imperfect and puzzling.

> *Margery Fisher, in her* Who's Who in Children's Books: A Treasury of the Familiar Characters of Childhood *(copyright © 1975 by Margery Fisher; reprinted by permission of Holt, Rinehart and Winston), Holt, Rinehart and Winston, 1975, p. 164.*

OTHER CITATIONS

Kirkus Reviews, *July 1, 1972, pp. 729-30.*

Publishers' Weekly, *August 14, 1972, p. 46.*

The Booklist, *October 15, 1972, p. 206.*

Michelle Murray, in Book World, *November 5, 1972 (Part 2), p. 8.*

Margaret A. Dorsey, in School Library Journal, *March, 1973, p. 120.*

LET THE BALLOON GO (1968)

As explicit and often crude as this is, it packs a considerable wallop, with implications for the child who isn't crippled, beginning with the right to be wrong. A practical handicap here is the type—so large and dark that you want to hold the book at arm's length; another is the fact that John is twelve: together they may deter the older boy more appropriately skeptical about home sweet home (and the look is dismal enough to deter anyone).

> Kirkus Service *(copyright © 1968 The Kirkus Service, Inc.), November 1, 1968, p. 1227.*

The fierce desire of a handicapped child to try something on his own, unhampered by well-meaning attempts to shield him, is beautifully portrayed here. John's thoughts and fantasies carry the story; his mother is a secondary character, and the neighbors and school friends who watch him fearfully from the ground merely peripheral. Although the book will probably not appeal to the adventure-hungry readers who devour Mr. Southall's other books, handicapped youngsters will certainly derive inspiration from it, and sensitive readers, who do not require run-around action in a story, will empathize deeply with John.

> *Margaret Poarch, in* School Library Journal *(reprinted from* School Library Journal, *March, 1969, published by R. R. Bowker Co., a Xerox company; copyright © 1969 by Xerox Corporation), March, 1969, p. 159.*

Although much of the intensity and suspense of [this] story are because of the fact that it is a spastic child who takes a risk to achieve independence, the importance of the book is in the fact that all young people reaching for maturity want John's chance to say "no" to themselves. The story starts slowly, but builds into a meaningful and dramatic construction, focused on a small, taut area like a pool of light on a dark stage.

> *Zena Sutherland, in* Bulletin of the Center for Children's Books *(© 1969 by the University of Chicago; all rights reserved), September, 1969, p. 18.*

Boys and girls will identify with John's first rebellion against the unfair restrictions placed on his life, and his gallant effort to achieve independence. The fact that this is accomplished in spite of a physical handicap makes the story more appealing. Several attitudes toward physical disabilities are portrayed in the book, as the parents and neighbors show varying amounts of pity, indulgence and embarrassed indifference. Only John's longing to be treated as an ordinary boy illustrates a positive approach. The author also uses symbolism effectively: the balloon and birds represent freedom; the gum tree becomes John's personal Everest, the challenge to prove his worth.

> *John Gillespie and Diana Lembo, in their* Introducing Books: A Guide for the Middle Grades *(copyright © 1970 by Xerox Corp.), Bowker, 1970, p. 101.*

[*Let the Balloon Go*] tells of a sad situation, the central character being spastic, but young people can read the book as a tale of challenge and excitement—because it is that, with a great deal of suspense—and if they get a glimpse at the same time of what it is like to be a spastic, then so

much the better. I know that I felt involved in it to that extent. And no brochure from the March of Dimes campaign, or anything else, has made me feel that the cause is as urgent as I consider it since reading *Let the Balloon Go.*

> *Robert Burch, in* The Horn Book Magazine *(copyright © 1971 by The Horn Book, Inc., Boston), June, 1971, p. 262.*

[*Let the Balloon Go*] is much concerned with perspectives and point of view. Fundamentally, how John sees the world, and how the world sees him. The shifting of viewpoint is the basic device through which the rivetting tension which so engages Southall readers is developed; and through which he explores characters' perceptions of themselves and one another. Here he admits us to the perspective of the spastic boy as he climbs a tree. . . . Southall shows us through the changing mirrors of the book that we all distort; Cecil, whom John thinks is his enemy, actually yearns to be 'his real mate, like soldiers together, like blood brothers'. John certainly gains tremendous insight through his climb and fall. But his mother remains essentially blind; small wonder that John cannot trust her, even at the end. Although in this portrait Southall does allow us to sense the tensions which have eroded the mother's judgment and distorted her love. . . .

Here, although the blindness and the concern for the opinions of others seem to retain the traces of caricature of earlier novels, the writing is free of the staleness which marks [Southall's] treatment of adults. . . . The father too, who is able to learn more than his wife from the incident, is given language which initially still seems to retain a trace of cliche; but somehow that sort of cliche into which we often fall when trying to handle moments of emotion which are almost beyond our capacities. . . . (p. 59)

> *Geoffrey Fox, "Growth and Masquerade: A Theme in the Novels of Ivan Southall," in* Children's Literature in Education *(© 1971, APS Publications, Inc., New York; reprinted by permission of the publisher), No. 6 (November), 1971, pp. 49-64.*

[In *Let the Balloon Go*, John] labours under a gigantic inferiority complex; he lacks assurance and feels no secure tenure of his place in the world, is unable to shake the convict off his back. He is fervour on Anzac Day, a body-worshipper, and a compulsive succeeder. He cannot be Australian enough—if only he knew what being Australian means. And when he is old enough to own a car he will drive it like a maniac. In talking about him Southall speculates on the Australian's attitude to the world: given a population five or six times its present size, he says, Australia would be a great danger to the world. (p. 184)

> *Allan Morrison, "Letting the Characters Go: Ivan Southall," in* Children's Book Review *(© 1971 by Five Owls Press Ltd.; all rights reserved), December, 1971, pp. 184-86.*

[*Let the Balloon Go*] underlines needs, crucial for the handicapped but important to all, for sympathy extending to the whole person, for freedom to make the mistakes from which responsibility may grow, for friendship and for exposure to the testing situations which prompt extraordinary human effort.

The message for parents is clear: to over-protect is to stifle any chance the child has of developing into a responsible, feeling adult. The plea to child readers is to accept handicapped children as people, and to try to get to know them, to understand them, be friends with them.

There is no overt didacticism in the book. The author makes his points largely by taking the reader into John's mind, showing his resentment at being continually watched over by his parents and forbidden to do things, his escaping into fantasy, his wishing to be like other boys, brave, adventurous, a fighter, longing to be accepted, to have real friends, his need of admiration from the opposite sex. Southall posits his thesis unobtrusively but none the less powerfully.

> John Haynes, in Children's Literature in Education (© 1971, APS Publications, Inc., New York; reprinted by permission of the publisher), No. 15, 1974, p. 9.

[In Let the Balloon Go] Ivan Southall uses his particular form of the stream of consciousness, stringing out in a grammatical, continuous and formalized way a mixture of daydreams, imaginary conversations, aggressive posturing, expressions of fear, anger, pique, scorn, shame, coarseness or self-doubt, to give a surprisingly natural impression that we are overhearing what goes on in the boy's mind. The method is perfectly adapted to the study of a boy whose imagination and will are as strong as his body is weak and who proves that he is not 'a peculiar little object . . . who had to be handled carefully like a broken egg' but 'the red-blooded boy who lived inside the one that shook and jerked and smudged his pages.' His brazen shouts—'Ahoy! I'm John Clement Sumner up a tree'—are cries of victory that truly shake the reader.

> Margery Fisher, in her Who's Who in Children's Books: A Treasury of the Familiar Characters of Childhood (copyright © 1975 by Margery Fisher; reprinted by permission of Holt, Rinehart and Winston), Holt, Rinehart and Winston, 1975, p. 159.

MATT AND JO (1973)

Southall takes a breather [in Matt and Jo], playing around with the girl-sick thoughts that preoccupy a fifteen year-old boy on his way to school and the boy-catching ploys and reveries of a girl the same age who has been trying to get his attention since she was ten (or was it two?). . . . Southall observes the boy's ludicrous contortions with amused sympathy and no doubt has the same intentions toward the girl, though at times it seems that if Matt is a comic archetype Jo is more like a shallow stereotype (she reassures herself that "all my bulges are where they ought to be. And not bad either if I do say so" and muses that "Hell hath no fury like a woman scorned. And that's me, brother. You bet!"). Southall makes their first meeting frequently funny but in attempting to make a novel of a pop tune situation he stretches it all exasperatingly thin.

> Kirkus Reviews (copyright © 1973 The Kirkus Service, Inc.), July 1, 1973, p. 692.

For the reviewer of Matt and Jo, the snare lies in being on the same side as the author. Is it really possible to recreate the mental state of first love without seeming, to those for whom it is a present and not a remembered state, to be either nostalgic or patronizing? Patronizing Mr. Southall most certainly is not. As for nostalgia, that may well be in the eye of the beholder. The language seems to me to be of the present and not of twenty years age. This being so Matt and Jo is a shrewd, funny, touching and wholly believable book.

> Ann Carter, in The Times Literary Supplement (© Times Newspapers Ltd., 1974), December 6, 1974, p. 1373.

OTHER CITATIONS

Paul Heins, in The Horn Book Magazine, June, 1974, pp. 288-89.

SEVENTEEN SECONDS (1974)

[These] non-fiction sketches are from the pen of the old rough and tumble Southall, not the reincarnated "quality" writer. . . . The situations are gripping, the pace staccato, the dialogue—"I'll be at the barricade. There's no disgrace; it's not every man's cup of tea . . . Good luck, old boy. . . ."—makes it beastly hard to keep a stiff upper lip. The day when this could be taken straight has passed.

> Kirkus Reviews (copyright © 1974 The Kirkus Service, Inc.), August 1, 1974, p. 814.

In his preface Ivan Southall explains that this is a special edition of Softly Tread the Brave, his treatment of the same subject for adults, and that it is not a gutted version of that book. After the first few pages any such explanation seems unnecessary. This is a tautly-written, highly-exciting and totally absorbing narrative. The seventeen seconds of the title is the length of time that it takes the fuse of a mine to run once it is activated. In that time the mine-disposal expert has to run at least four hundred yards away or die. This is the story of two Australian mine-disposal experts, John Stuart Mould and Hugh Randal Syme. It is founded upon diaries, notes, recorded interviews and official documents. . . . [Southall] calls the book 'a tribute, however inadequate, to the gigantic stature of the human spirit'. It is far from inadequate.

> C. E. J. Smith, in Children's Book Review (© 1974 Five Owls Press Ltd.; all rights reserved), Autumn, 1974, p. 119.

Young readers, for whom the author has prepared this special edition of Softly Tread the Brave, first published in 1960, know Churchill, Hitler, and the Battle of Britain only as history. This taut, suspense-filled narrative, based on diaries, tapes, interviews, and official documents, adds dimension and vitality to that history. . . . Focusing on two men in particular, Hugh Syme and John Mould, the book succeeds in conveying the sense of courage, devotion to duty, and dogged determination which enabled [a small group of Australians] to function day after day under conditions which would have driven lesser men insane. Nor were these men stereotyped danger addicts; they were fully aware that they lived intimately with death. . . . [Seventeen

Seconds is a] gripping documentary, which records not only the observable events but also reflects the *Zeitgeist* of the period—an ineffable blend of stiff-upper-lip humor with genuine patriotism and a special kind of grace under pressure.

> *Mary M. Burns, in* The Horn Book Magazine *(copyright © 1975 by the Horn Book, Inc., Boston), April, 1975, pp. 154-55.*

OTHER CITATIONS

The Junior Bookshelf, *October, 1974, p. 310.*

Margaret A. Dorsey, in School Library Journal, *October, 1974, p. 121.*

THE SWORD OF ESAU (1967)

There are plenty of books of Bible stories retold, but few in which the author makes the story his own without depreciating its value. Ivan Southall's retelling of the stories of Esau, Gideon and Jonah in racy, colloquial language does give one a sense of the perennial quality of the Old Testament which makes its human conflicts as real now as when they were first experienced.

He is most successful with the comic story of Jonah, and the rip-roaring battle tale about Gideon. He tells his stories somewhat garrulously like a Greek, not sparsely and dramatically like a Hebrew. His style lacks the depth and grandeur of myth which belongs to the Hebrew. Perhaps for this reason, the great story of Esau and Jacob seems the least satisfying of the three. However, children who are prepared for leisurely reading will find the whole of *The Sword of Esau* readable.

> The Times Literary Supplement *(© Times Newspapers Ltd., 1968), March 14, 1968, p. 265.*

In easy-flowing, almost racy prose, Ivan Southall retells the stories of Esau and Jacob, Gideon and Jonah. He makes no attempt to alter Biblical traditions; ignoring modern symbolic interpretations of the Jonah story, he has "the mad Hebrew" tossed overboard and swallowed by a "bad-tempered old fish".

Something is inevitably sacrificed by lifting the stories from their context and dressing them in modern language, but as sheer enjoyable yarns for young readers this trio can stand on its own and on its own merit.

> The Junior Bookshelf, *June, 1968, p. 189.*

[Ivan Southall] has retold three famous stories of the Old Testament as mementos of human experience. Deliberately disregarding the severely liturgical quality of the King James Version, he has expanded the narratives by means of a colloquial, conversational style and touches of humor. Never exceeding the Biblical implications regarding the ingenuity of Jacob or Gideon, or the ridiculousness of Jonah, he leads the reader to feel the transformation of each character by the uncanny events in his life—such as Jacob's wrestling with the angel and Jonah's encounter with the whale. And properly enough, and in keeping with the Old Testament spirit, each character's acceptance of the unexpected happenings in his life becomes a revelation of God's purpose.

> *Paul Heins, in* The Horn Book Magazine *(copyright © 1968 by The Horn Book, Inc., Boston), June, 1968, p. 321.*

OTHER CITATIONS

Kirkus Service, *March 1, 1968, p. 267.*

Bernard A. Weisberger, in Book World, *August 4, 1968, p. 13.*

TO THE WILD SKY (1967)

The conclusion [in *To the Wild Sky*]—surprising in a juvenile—is a stand-off: no hope of rescue, a slight hope of survival. Some small silliness—one girl is an eighth aborigine, puts her ear to the ground to hear ancestral murmurings—weakens the story, and the rather adult entanglement of the characters limits its appeal, but their airborne experience is shattering to share.

> Kirkus Service *(copyright © 1967 Virginia Kirkus' Service, Inc.), February 1, 1967, p. 145.*

There is little relaxation of tension [in this book], as personal relationships both at home and within the group are unusually touch-and-go, and everyone's motivation is not only questionable but continually questioned by both the author and the other characters. On the whole, they seem a dud lot, the Robinson Crusoe situation filling them with anything but enterprise and pleasure, but part of the purpose of the book is perhaps the demonstration that something can be broken by sustained stress which is very difficult to rebuild. The staccato sentences and perpetual change of focus present an absorbing picture of this small group of youngsters in their early 'teens, a bit slick at times but compulsive reading. It would be more comforting if they behaved a little better and it does seem Mr. Southall underestimates the resilience and generosity of modern children, but there is no doubt readers of the same age will be somehow sustained to find they are not alone in their fears, envy and distrust of self and others and the discovery that they would very likely behave at least a little better than these Australians might provide some encouragement. There is plenty of food for thought on how human beings act and interact, and how they themselves might react to the events faced by the six very different young people in the book.

> The Junior Bookshelf, *April, 1967, pp. 129-30.*

[*To the Wild Sky*] is disappointing in several ways: it is very slow-moving in the first half, which describes in great detail the difficulties of the flight, and it has an ending that seems awkwardly inconclusive. Although some of the writing is careless (a boy and a girl, twins, are several times referred to as "identical" twins), and much of it seems heavy-handed, there are some incidents that are exciting and some flashes of dialogue or of characterization that seem vivid.

> *Zena Sutherland, in* Bulletin of the Center for Children's Books *(copyright 1967 by the University of Chicago; all rights reserved), May, 1967, p. 147.*

It is not altogether out of place to compare Ivan Southall's Australian novel *To the Wild Sky* with a more optimistic *Lord of the Flies*. It is not, certainly, the same terrible, cosmic parable but in its different way it is pointing to much the same truth about humanity: that we survive not through external circumstances but because of whatever qualities we can dredge out of ourselves. . . .

What makes *To the Wild Sky* such an outstanding book is that never for one moment does Ivan Southall forget that he is dealing with children. It is not the actual physical happenings, brilliant though these are, which give it such conviction, but the mental attitudes. The way even the older ones can seriously spend time and energy on things which, to an adult, would seem inessential, like marking out imaginary rooms of a house on the sand. Such things to them fulfil the same needs as those expressed by the solitary district officer dressing solemnly for dinner in the bush. They have a childish sense of priorities, and yet from one moment to the next each of them can shoot suddenly far ahead into adulthood, and just as quickly back again. This is a book in which children will recognize themselves, but one in which adults may find it disconcerting to recognize their children.

> *The Times Literary Supplement (© Times Newspapers Ltd., 1967), May 25, 1967, p. 455.*

The power of the writing [in *To the Wild Sky*] lies in the author's avoidance of idealization. There is sheer, awful realism without heroics in the account of the flight, given with detail that builds suspense. . . . Although the book lacks the compelling power and breadth of *Hills End* and *Ash Road*, it will hold young readers and allow them to participate again in a legitimately dramatic struggle against supreme odds.

> *Virginia Haviland, in The Horn Book Magazine (copyright © 1967, by The Horn Book, Inc., Boston), August, 1967, p. 476.*

It seems to me that [*To the Wild Sky*] presents the first two acts of a three-act drama. The first act is the flight and the second is the children's stranding and their attempt to sort themselves out. But what of the final act? Is it rescue, or is it—as seen in a premonition by one of the girls—death, slow and dreadful, one at a time? The author has left the last act to be written in the mind of the reader and the few clues he offers are, to my mind, indecisive. But is it legitimate, artistically, to leave the story to be finished by the reader? I do not think it is. To one reader at least it seems that the story is the author's, and that nobody else can say what happens. It is no longer axiomatic that a novel must have a beginning, a middle and an end, but I still believe it is not complete until all that *needs* telling has been told. In this case the significance of the first two acts depends to a large extent on the third. If the children are doomed, they are not the same children as if they survive; the meaning of the story, and of their lives, is different. The ambiguity is too profound to be left unresolved. (pp. 184-85)

> *John Rowe Townsend, "Ivan Southall," in his A Sense of Story: Essays on Contemporary Writers for Children (copyright © 1971 by John Rowe Townsend; reprinted by permission of J. B. Lippincott Company), Lippincott, 1971, pp. 182-89.*

OTHER CITATIONS

Margaret Sherwood Libby, in Book Week, *April 16, 1967, p. 16.*

The Booklist and Subscription Books Bulletin, *June 15, 1967, pp. 1102-03.*

WALK A MILE AND GET NOWHERE (1970)

If readers can get beyond the introspective first chapter, they may be held by the urgency of the author's style, but at best [*Walk a Mile and Get Nowhere*] will have a limited audience. . . . The author displays his usual feeling for drama but in other respects this book is a disappointment. Here inner conflict, instead of natural disaster, is the subject of tension. And instead of Southall's usually neatly constructed, step-by-step plotting, there is just the see-saw pattern of the children's relationship. Many young readers will find this perplexing, exasperating reading.

> *Mary B. Mason, in School Library Journal (reprinted from School Library Journal, January, 1971, published by R. R. Bowker Co., a Xerox company; copyright © 1971 by Xerox Corporation), January, 1971, p. 62.*

In his typically sharp fashion, with telling conversations and detailed scenes, [Ivan Southall] intensifies the picture of Michael's increasing agonies and winds up the novel with finesse. There is much [in *Walk a Mile and Get Nowhere*] to provoke discussion among young readers—questions of stupidities, dishonesties and realities and analogies between personal and national aggressions. Loaded with more seriousness and introversion than the dramas of *Hills End* and *Ash Road*. . . .

> *Virginia Haviland, in The Horn Book Magazine (copyright © 1971 by The Horn Book, Inc., Boston), April, 1971, p. 174.*

The long, detailed scene at the beach slows the book, although it explores with sensitivity the reactions of a thirteen-year-old to boy-girl relations, adult attitudes toward child behavior, and Michael's apprehension about the other boys. Southall never fails to write well, but [*Walk a Mile and Get Nowhere*] lacks the impact of most of his earlier books and it touches too many areas to have cohesion.

> *Zena Sutherland, in Bulletin of the Center for Children's Books (© 1971 by the University of Chicago; all rights reserved), April, 1971, pp. 129-30.*

"Walk a Mile and Get Nowhere" . . . [is] a coming-of-age story that all but collapses under the weight of its emotional baggage. . . . [What] a wailing and throbbing and gasping goes on, more than enough to exhaust our sympathy for poor Michael long before sundown. It's a pity, too, for there are some touching scenes here—Michael's memory of the day his mother died, some of his moments with the fey little girl who gets him mad enough to care for her—but they're pretty well lost in the din.

> *Robert Berkvist, in The New York Times Book Review (© 1971 by The New York Times Company; reprinted by permission), May 2, 1971, (Part 2), p. 14.*

OTHER CITATIONS

Kirkus Reviews, *November 15, 1970, p. 1254.*

Publishers' Weekly, *January 11, 1971, p. 63.*

*   *   *

STEIG, William   1907-

An American artist, cartoonist, and author, William Steig received the 1970 Caldecott Medal for *Sylvester and the Magic Pebble.*

AMOS AND BORIS (1971)

Immediately apparent [in "Amos and Boris"] is this author's progress as a *writer* for children. . . . Before, it was illustrations that offered the primary gratification; now it is description and thoughts expressed that are most noticeable and sustaining. . . .

Steig's illustrations for "Amos and Boris" are deceptive. There's not the posed balladry of "Roland the Minstrel Pig," not the volcanic splash of "The Bad Island" or the colorful romanticism of "Sylvester and the Magic Pebble." . . . Here the palette is muted; a coat of orange paint on the boat, a spot or two for the sun and its reflection on the water. Soft grays, greens and blues predominate for the two friends and the eternal sky and sea.

> *George A. Woods, in* The New York Times Book Review (© *1971 by The New York Times Company; reprinted by permission), October 17, 1971, p. 8.*

Ample pages accommodate wide seascapes and beach scenery, the background for a satisfying story of friendship developed between Boris, a whale, and Amos, a mouse. . . . The words of [William Steig's] text quickly define the occasions of pleasure and trial, while [his] water-color paintings deftly convey changing qualities of light—day and night, sunshine and rain—and a realistic flowing and heaving of seawater. It is a delight to receive from the artist-storyteller another picture book in which a genuine story builds its atmosphere and mood with freshness, compassion, and child interest, and is enhanced by the illustrations.

> *Virginia Haviland, in* The Horn Book Magazine (copyright © *1972 by The Horn Book, Inc., Boston), February, 1972, p. 42.*

[*Amos & Boris* is a] simple, matter-of-fact story. . . . Lovely watercolor pictures and a funny, well-written text which presents its plot coincidences in tongue-in-cheek manner (". . . it just so happened that Boris the whale was flung ashore by a tidal wave and stranded on the very shore where Amos happened to make his home. It also just so happened that when . . . Boris was lying high and dry on the sand . . . Amos came down to the beach . . .") fit together admirably in this faintly Aesopian tale, and children will respond to the true-blue twosome with much pleasure.

> *Ann D. Schweibish, in* School Library Journal (reprinted from School Library Journal, February, 1972, published by R. R. Bowker Co., a Xerox company; copyright © *1972 by Xerox Corporation), February, 1972, p. 61.*

[Amos and Boris'] friendship is based on their respect for each other. Boris admires the "delicacy and quivering daintiness" of Amos; Amos admires the "grandeur, the purpose, the abounding friendliness" of the whale. Circumstances separate them, but by chance Amos is able to rescue his enormous friend and they bid each other a final farewell with tears.

The simple drawings with little detail and the story so rich in vocabulary and word pictures, convey the friendship engagingly. Both friends have the virtues of loyalty and kindness, desirable qualities for children to see expressed pictorially.

[This is a] story which will repay re-reading.

> The Junior Bookshelf, *February, 1973, p. 21.*

OTHER CITATIONS

Publishers' Weekly, *October 4, 1971, p. 59.*

Kirkus Reviews, *October 15, 1971, pp. 1116-17.*

Michael J. Bandler, in Book World, *November 7, 1971 (Part 2), p. 3.*

Jean Stafford, in The New Yorker, *December 4, 1971, pp. 182-83.*

Zena Sutherland, in Bulletin of the Center for Children's Books, *January, 1972, p. 80.*

The Booklist, *January 1, 1972, p. 395.*

THE BAD ISLAND (1969)

On Steig's "rotten, horrible, awful, burning hot, freezing-cold and rocky island," the first flower is as potent as Thurber's last flower. Seeing its quiet beauty, the "monstrous creatures of one crazy kind or another" are irritated and frightened and go berserk, killing instead of clawing at one another, no longer satisfied with mere loathing. Until everyone is dead . . . the rains come . . . flowers blanket the island . . . and the first birds arrive. As a parable this has the flaw of being overdrawn, allowing for no gradation or gradual change—and therefore no redemption; as a story, too, it is relatively static, the first half being a catalog of the evils of the island—a redundancy of grue, at first funny, then repellent, finally tedious. And when the animals freak out, the text takes over, become talky and tendentious and combining current jargon with kiddie talk ("Their whole style of life was threatened and they were all dreadfully nervous, having conniption fits and the worst kind of nightmares"). Actually this is not so much a parable in pictures as a pictured parable, or a labeled, labored lesson.

> Kirkus Reviews (copyright © *1969 The Kirkus Service, Inc.), September 1, 1969, p. 926.*

Man, this is horrorsville. I mean there's no Hilton in this place. Reading William Steig's travelogue description you wouldn't want to visit let alone live here. Not unless you like hot-lava baths, earthquakes, tornadoes, hurricanes, thunder and lightning on the hour—and the ice age at night. The flora and fauna are the worst: the surrounding sea "seething with serpents and sharp-clawed crabs, sting-rays." The things that creep and crawl and galumph over the land are "scaly, thorny, fanged, horned, bug-eyed, barbed, bristling, saw-toothed" and have "scales, or warts or pimples, or tentacles, or talons, or fangs, or extra eyes, arms, legs or tails, or forked tongues." The mosquitoes are pretty bad too. The diet is poison ivy, barbed-wire cactus, each other—with gravel for dessert. Ugliness thrives; pain is prized.

This is a fable, about flower power I suppose because the appearance of a few flowers precipitates an Armageddon with "every rotten one for his own rotten self against every rotten one else." The catalogue of the horrible and hideous runs long, but what saves it are Steig's drawings, lots of them, looking like what you'd see after too many malteds—or something—and in vivid color.

> *George A. Woods, in* The New York Times Book Review *(© 1969 by The New York Times Company; reprinted by permission), October 19, 1969, p. 34.*

THE BAD SPELLER (1970)

[*The Bad Speller* contains a] series of agreeably silly drawings with misspelled captions. Unlike the author-artist's *C D B* . . . this has little ingenuity, depending solely on contrived spelling for its humor. . . . The pitfalls of the English language as-it-is-spelled would be more amusingly demonstrated were there not so many instances of non-phonetic spelling.

> *Zena Sutherland, in* Bulletin of the Center for Children's Books *(© 1970 by the University of Chicago; all rights reserved), November, 1970, p. 49.*

OTHER CITATIONS

Pamela Marsh, in The Christian Science Monitor, *May 7, 1970, p. B1.*

Publishers' Weekly, *May 25, 1970, p. 57.*

C D B! (1968)

Remember "2 Y's U R, 2 Y's U B. . ."? This is more of the same with some harder, and if artist Steig hadn't provided pictorial clues for cryptographer Steig, some of us would still B up N D A-R. Still, fun to D-S-I-4.

> *Kirkus Service (copyright © 1968 The Kirkus Service, Inc.), September 15, 1968, p. 1045.*

The cartoon characters of William Steig . . . here are used in combination with the game of making words out of letter sounds and numbers. Deft and highly entertaining, the book should appeal to those who enjoy word play, have a detective instinct, or simply seek amusement.

> *Zena Sutherland, in* Bulletin of the Center for Children's Books *(copyright 1968 by The University of Chicago; all rights reserved), December, 1968, p. 66.*

OTHER CITATIONS

Zena Sutherland, in Saturday Review, *October 19, 1968, p. 37.*

George A. Woods, in The New York Times Book Review, *November 24, 1968, p. 42.*

DOMINIC (1972)

A throwback to a more leisurely age—say the time that Kenneth Grahame's *Wind in the Willows* was providing Edwardian bedtime reading—*Dominic* is a touchingly innocent work. "Oh Life!" the hero apostrophizes at one juncture, "I am yours. Whatever it is you want of me, I am ready to give." For children of the TV age, whose experiences often consist of the passive absorption of "Life" second-hand, Dominic's headlong philosophy of going out to meet trouble halfway may provide a refreshing new model for action. Whatever happens—bad and good—simply deepens the hound's appreciation of life's beauty and infinite mystery. When his friend Bartholomew Badger, a 100-year-old pig, succumbs to advancing age, Dominic provides the child reader with as understandable a definition of death's poignant finality as he is ever likely to encounter: "His turn was over." For those with turns just beginning, *Dominic* is a loving and lovely primer of life.

> *Selma G. Lanes in* Book World *(© The Washington Post), May 7, 1972 (Part 2), p. 15.*

Having seemingly gone golliwompus, William Stieg has doggedly stuffed into this novel not only too many drawings, some of them fussy, but enough ingredients for a pint-sized "War and Peace." You name it, he's included it. Sermons, fairy tales, the Greek alphabet, romance, *trompe-l'oeil* magic, gourmet menus, news distortion, the peaceable kingdom, Excalibur, ladies' fashion notes from all over, endless catalogues (like this one) and cosmic contemplation. . . .

While portions of the book are crisp and funny or inventive or moving, much of it bogs down in solemn overwriting; and under the upholstery, something goes bump in the night. Dominic makes merry noises, but his restlessness seems finally a little tense, a little forlorn.

> *Nora L. Magid, in* The New York Times Book Review *(© 1972 by The New York Times Company; reprinted by permission), July 9, 1972, p. 8.*

Some of the episodes in this romantic, amusingly illustrated fantasy are indeed humorous; and rakish, self-confident, slightly pompous Dominic is an appealing hero. However, the story is full of often simplistic messages, e.g., money is necessarily a hindrance to free living; etc. The pattern of encounters—triumphant Dominic versus the perennial-loser baddies—becomes tedious, and the animal villains are unfortunately members of those species which already have an undeserved bad reputation among humans: wolves, foxes, stoats, ferrets, weasels.

> *Diane Gersoni Stavn, in* School Library Journal *(reprinted from* School Library Journal, *September, 1972, published by R. R.*

Bowker Co., a Xerox company; copyright ©
1972 by Xerox Corporation), September,
1972, pp. 84-5.

A singular blend of naïveté and sophistication, comic commentary and philosophizing, the narrative [in *Dominic*] handles situational clichés with humor and flair—perhaps because of the author's felicitous turn of phrase, his verbal cartooning, and his integration of text and illustrations. A chivalrous and optimistic tribute to gallantry and romance.

> *Mary M. Burns, in The Horn Book Magazine (copyright © 1972 by The Horn Book, Inc., Boston), October, 1972, p. 470.*

William Steig's "Dominic" . . . is an awfully do-gooding dog, but, leery as I am these days of social messages (for citizens from nine to ninety-nine), I like him very much. . . . Mr. Steig may have intended something portentous here, but I don't think he did, and I really don't care: I am touched when Dominic fondly howls for joy at the sheer beauty of nice smells, and I was very nearly moved to tears when, in a wondrous garden, he comes upon his intended, "in a room where candles flickered and moonlight streamed through stained-glass windows, illuminating a canopied bed where the most beautiful dog he had ever seen lay sleeping. She was black and shimmered in patterns of luminous purple, yellow, green, blue, and carmine from the windows. She looked unreal."

> *Jean Stafford, in The New Yorker (© 1972 by The New Yorker Magazine, Inc.), December 2, 1972, p. 200.*

William Steig offers us a rare feast of delights [in *Dominic*]. Combining a talent for stylish writing with deliciously deadpan drawings, he has produced a story of thievery, skulduggery and virtue triumphant which will enchant many a desperate adult in search of a book with sophistication of thought and language. Yet, at the same time, the story possesses a plot vigorous enough to involve any child of eight or more years. The battles between Dominic, armed only with a lance and as much resourcefulness as a dozen James Bonds, and the magnificently inept Doomsday Gang have much of the panache of [Kenneth] Grahame's siege of Toad Hall [in his *The Wind in the Willows*]. These, and the delightful illogicality of names (a goose called Fox, a pig called Badger and so on) all add up to fun which keeps its originality right to the end.

> *Gabrielle Maunder, in Children's Book Review (© 1973 Five Owls Press Ltd.; all rights reserved), June, 1973, p. 85.*

There is only one note of incongruity in this otherwise perfect delight and that is the lavish honeyed ending which, though in keeping with the pseudo-fairy tale image of the story, is a little too contrived. [Steig] is crisp and witty, his pictures stylish and very much in the spirit of the story. It is a book for fathers to read to the whole family for their mutual delight.

> The Junior Bookshelf, *August, 1973, p. 261.*

OTHER CITATIONS

Kirkus Reviews, *June 15, 1972, p. 674.*

Publishers' Weekly, *August 14, 1972, p. 46.*

Zena Sutherland, in Bulletin of the Center for Children's Books, *October, 1972, pp. 31-2.*

FARMER PALMER'S WAGON RIDE (1974)

There are two wonderful things about Steig. One is the way he draws. The other is that nobody draws like him. The animals [in *Farmer Palmer's Wagon Ride*] are eccentric and endearing. The countryside is Steig country: colorful, spirited, touched by that always individual hand.

> *Eliot Fremont-Smith and Karla Kuskin, in* New York Magazine *(© 1974 by The NYM Corp.; reprinted with the permission of New York Magazine, Eliot Fremont-Smith, and Karla Kuskin), December 16, 1974, p. 108.*

In his offhand, poker-faced manner, Steig narrates the comically hapless journey of porcine Farmer Palmer and his asinine hired hand Ebenezer as they return from town, their wagon loaded with gifts for the Palmer family. . . . The text, longer than that of most picture books, boasts some captivating and original onomatopoeia, lending itself to reading aloud. Full-color illustrations add action, expression, and countryside colors appropriate to the story.

> The Booklist *(reprinted by permission of the American Library Association; copyright 1975 by the American Library Association), January 1, 1975, p. 463.*

[*Farmer Palmer's Wagon Ride* is a] joyous slapstick farce with a breezy text that rushes headlong to the end of the tale and with pictures in which two country bumpkins go from one hilarious misadventure to another—against a background of pastoral beauty.

> *Ethel L. Heins, in The Horn Book Magazine (copyright © 1975 by the Horn Book, Inc., Boston), April, 1975, p. 142.*

While less subtle and more slapstick than Steig's earlier books, this has some of the same quality of nonsensical situation combined with a bland writing style that assumes it is perfectly ordinary to have as a hired hand a talking ass that wears glasses. . . . This hasn't the narrative quality of Steig's stories about Sylvester, Roland, or Amos and Boris, but it's fun, there's wit in the writing, and the illustrations are engaging.

> *Zena Sutherland, in* Bulletin of the Center for Children's Books *(© 1975 by the University of Chicago; all rights reserved), April, 1975, p. 139.*

OTHER CITATIONS

Margaret A. Dorsey, in School Library Journal, *March, 1975, p. 90.*

THE REAL THIEF (1973)

There are lovely phrases in this story. And there are tedious stretches where neither the characters nor the situations come to life sufficiently to keep the reader engrossed. Classically a fable conveys specific truths by using animals that speak or act as human beings. "The Real Thief" touches on many things: the quality and depth of friendship, causes and effects of suffering, the relation of honest intentions to honesty. At one point the author asks "Why did the world go on being so beautiful in spite of the ugliness he [Gawain] had experienced?" Such complex ideas are approached seriously but, perhaps due to their complexity, we are often left mid-thought or with a conclusion that seems clouded.

> *Karla Kuskin, in* The New York Times Book Review *(© 1973 by The New York Times Company; reprinted by permission), September 2, 1973, p. 20.*

For young readers or listeners, [*The Real Thief* is] an involving story with animal characters displaying more real emotions than many supposedly human characters. Steig's gray line-and-wash drawings provide a charming accompaniment to a wholly winning story.

> *Margaret A. Dorsey, in* School Library Journal *(reprinted from* School Library Journal, *November, 1973, published by R. R. Bowker Co., a Xerox company; copyright © 1973 by Xerox Corporation), November, 1973, p. 44.*

[In *The Real Thief* there] is real feeling on the part of all the characters, and the reader's sympathy and understanding are captured from the very beginning. The author invests the theme with an unusual sensitivity, and his style and choice of language are rich and strikingly apt, the whole constituting an inspiring and well integrated composition in every aspect. The black and white drawings are a quiet and unassuming but complementary comment upon the text.

> The Junior Bookshelf, *June, 1975, p. 188.*

OTHER CITATIONS

Kirkus Reviews, *July 15, 1973, p. 756.*

The Booklist, *October 15, 1973, p. 242.*

Sidney D. Long, in The Horn Book Magazine, *December, 1973, pp. 595-96.*

Zena Sutherland, in Bulletin of the Center for Children's Books, *February, 1974, p. 102.*

ROLAND THE MINSTREL PIG (1968)

["Roland the Minstrel Pig"] is somewhat traditional, but Mr. Steig . . . gives it a grand style and infuses it with special graces: the modest accomplishments of Roland's balladry ("I loved her tail, her ears, her snout,/ I loved her form so fair./ She looked at me with glowing eyes;/ I walked as if on air"), moments of peril and poignancy, gentle humor and illustrations that range from the hauntingly lovely to the regally resplendent.

> *George A. Woods, in* The New York Times Book Review *(© 1968 by The New York Times Company; reprinted by permission), April 21, 1968, p. 34.*

[This is an] oversize book with amusing full-color pictures, carefully romanticized; the story is adequately told and—although there are some light touches in the writing—the plot is quite traditional: local pig makes good.

> *Zena Sutherland, in* Bulletin of the Center for Children's Books *(copyright 1968 by The University of Chicago; all rights reserved), July-August, 1968, pp. 181-82.*

The enchanting colors of a perfect midsummer day and the flair and wit of an eighteenth-century fable are combined in a book that is a joy to look at and great fun to read. Roland is a pig *extraordinaire*; a gentle dreamer, he can sing, play the lute, and balance himself on his front legs. . . . Roland's songs, sung at the high points of the story, give the book an extra measure of delight.

> *Sidney D. Long, in* The Horn Book Magazine *(copyright © 1968 by The Horn Book, Inc., Boston), August, 1968, p. 410.*

Although the fox's punishment for following his own nature seems unnecessarily harsh [in *Roland the Minstrel Pig*], all is enjoyably told in the best bedtime manner. Especially satisfying are Mr. Steig's illustrations—each, like his subtle cartoons, worth pondering for cumulative comic effect.

> *Jean C. Thomson, in* School Library Journal *(reprinted from* School Library Journal, *September, 1968, published by R. R. Bowker Co., a Xerox company; copyright © 1968 by Xerox Corporation), September, 1968, p. 126.*

As a creator of picture books William Steig seems to me to be an artist of great talent who has not yet discovered what it is he wants to say. *Sylvester and the Magic Pebble* and *Amos and Boris* had moments of liveliness in the text and consistently enjoyable illustrations, but they were not books one cared to turn to more than a couple of times—and so it is with *Roland*. . . . It is pleasant enough, and Mr. Steig has a distinctive way with words ("'Here, here, what sort of skulduggery is going on in my woods?" roared the King, suddenly confronting Sebastian. "Just a joke, Your Highness," said the fox, "just a joke."'"); the pictures and the page designs are attractive and colourful; but the story has neither enough shape nor enough sense of an ending to make it the truly satisfying picture book that Mr. Steig has it in him to create.

> *Brian W. Alderson, in* Children's Book Review *(© 1975 Five Owls Press Ltd.; all rights reserved), Summer, 1975, p. 56.*

OTHER CITATIONS

Patience M. Daltry, in The Christian Science Monitor, *May 2, 1968, p. B2.*

Polly Goodwin, in Book World, *September 1, 1968, p. 12.*

SYLVESTER AND THE MAGIC PEBBLE (1969)

[If] you're not moved by Sylvester's predicament, by the lion's bewilderment, by moods forlorn and joyous, if you don't take to the logical, easy stance of the animal friends (by chance, I suppose, the blue-coated police are pigs), if you don't appreciate the fair beauty of Steig's landscapes, well, then one will know for sure who's the donkey.

> *George A. Woods, in* The New York Times Book Review *(© 1969 by The New York Times Company; reprinted by permission), February 16, 1969, p. 34.*

Steig's writing style [in *Sylvester and the Magic Pebble*] is crisp and his vividly colored cartoons ably depict seasonal changes, a variety of emotions, and even a bit of contemporary satire—the policemen requested to find Sylvester by his distraught parents are shown as rather blank-looking pigs. It's all in good fun, however, and no rocky moments are likely to result from reading aloud this pleasant story.

> *Pat Byars, in* School Library Journal *(reprinted from* School Library Journal, *May, 1969, published by R. R. Bowker Co., a Xerox company; copyright © 1969 by Xerox Corporation), May, 1969, p. 80.*

What is perhaps ... reassuring for children in *Sylvester* is that his story represents a kind of metaphor for resurrection. Transformed into an unfeeling stone by a bit of misapplied magic, he can neither move nor speak—as dead as any child can imagine being. Yet his parents are miraculously able to restore him. In the literature of childhood, adults and children alike can find temporary refuge from the power of death.

> *Selma G. Lanes, in her* Down the Rabbit Hole: Adventures and Misadventures in the Realm of Children's Literature *(copyright © 1971 by Selma G. Lanes; reprinted by permission of Atheneum Publishers), Atheneum, 1972, p. 208.*

Sylvester is one of those humanised donkeys who wears clothes and lives in a proper house; that is until he finds a magic pebble and is turned into a rock. But all ends happily. The animal characters, the settings, whether of snow scene or domestic interior, are boldly drawn yet full of detail, and, in spite of the sadness that lasts through two-thirds of the pages, the colours are bright and cheerful. Three-year-olds will enjoy shedding tears with the forlorn parents and rejoice with them at the blissful domestic scene on the last page.

> The Junior Bookshelf, *April, 1973, p. 106.*

William Steig ... has a creative gift which makes up for any shortfall in graphic distinction. *Sylvester and the Magic Pebble* (1969) would win no awards if the requirement were a contribution to art history; but this story of the young donkey—really a child—who is turned into a rock and eventually rescued by his parents is appealing, tender, and right on the small child's wavelength.

> *John Rowe Townsend, in his* Written for Children: An Outline of English-Language Children's Literature *(copyright © 1965, 1974 by John Rowe Townsend; reprinted by permission of J. B. Lippincott Company), revised edition, Lippincott, 1974, p. 317.*

The larger animals do not as a rule humanize well in visual terms but William Steig has overcome the inherent difficulties of depicting such an animal managing picnic food or seated in a comfortable house. With the help of suitably devised clothes, spectacles and facial expressions he has turned his donkeys, with kindly satire, into a recognizable suburban family.

> *Margery Fisher, in her* Who's Who in Children's Books: A Treasury of the Familiar Characters of Childhood *(copyright © 1975 by Margery Fisher; reprinted by permission of Holt, Rinehart and Winston), Holt, Rinehart and Winston, 1975, p. 336.*

OTHER CITATIONS

Zena Sutherland, in Bulletin of the Center for Children's Books, *April, 1969, pp. 133-34.*

Ethel L. Heins, in The Horn Book Magazine, *June, 1969, p. 297.*

*   *   *

STEPTOE, John   1950-

John Steptoe is a Black American author and artist.

BIRTHDAY (1972)

If *Uptown* (1970) suffered from an overdose of realism (''I'm gonna grow up to be a junkie, the meanest junkie of them all''), *Birthday* is so awash with idealism that its eight-year-old hero-narrator is hardly more believable than Elsie Dinsmore.... Steptoe's characteristically flat, black-out-lined pictures are interwoven here with decorative African-like motifs and done in darker, chalk-like colors which convey the dignity but not the festivity of the occasion. Of course his powerful style is always impressive and you will want to check out this utopian Yoruba for yourself.

> Kirkus Reviews *(copyright © 1972 The Kirkus Service, Inc.), May 15, 1972, pp. 577-78.*

References to ''the old America'' where people didn't treat Javaka's father like a man '''cause he was Black,'' make [John Steptoe's] feelings about separatism clear. But [his] illustrations, reflecting the richness of the life that Javaka's family and friends have found in their new place, make the point in a much more eloquent way. Full-color spreads have the simplicity of form and intensity of color found in the work of Gauguin; and the artist's use of motifs found in Moorish architecture and design adds a new, dynamic dimension to his style.

> *Sidney D. Long, in* The Horn Book Magazine *(copyright © 1972 by The Horn Book, Inc., Boston), August, 1972, p. 382.*

Javaka's eighth birthday is the occasion for a very special celebration, for he was the first-born in the new town of Yoruba, ''the first child of a whole new thing.'' Yoruba is apparently an imaginary independent black community; however, the black separatist concept is never named nor clearly explained, and most children will not likely understand the situation. The story itself is hollow: there are some general expository remarks about Yoruba, and a bland narration of events on Javaka's birthday. There are no highs or lows and nothing much happens to the characters, externally or internally. The full-color, painterly illustrations, some of which are imaginative and irresistably rich and sensuous, are much more impressive and convincing than the text. But, over-all, this is a sectarian book which strikes no universal chord and fails to transcend party lines and political ideologies.

> *Melinda Schroeder, in* School Library Journal *(reprinted from* School Library Journal, *September, 1972, published by R. R. Bowker Co., a Xerox company; copyright © 1972 by Xerox Corporation), September, 1972, p. 124.*

OTHER CITATIONS

Publishers' Weekly, *October 9, 1972, p. 112.*

Zena Sutherland, in Bulletin of the Center for Children's Books, *January, 1973, p. 82.*

MY SPECIAL BEST WORDS (1974)

The language and activities [in *My Special Best Words*] couldn't be more ordinary, and it's odd perhaps that when the author's stated intent is to convey the naturalness of natural functions he depicts his photo-realistic children with a zappy neon glow (as though seen on a maladjusted color TV) so that even the green "boogas, nasty boogas" running from Javaka's nose are more fluorescent than realistically snotty. Of course Steptoe has always wielded a heavy hand with both his paints and, less impressively but just as boldly, his messages.

> Kirkus Reviews *(copyright © 1974 The Kirkus Service, Inc.), September 1, 1974, p. 941.*

John Steptoe's arresting photo-realism paintings are the highlight of this open and amusing [story]. . . . Best read to an individual child or a small group, this is a beautiful book that has the added plus of showing an affectionate and attentive father who cooks dinner, changes diapers, and does the scolding.

> *Karen Brown, in* School Library Journal *(reprinted from* School Library Journal, *October, 1974, published by R. R. Bowker Co., a Xerox company; copyright © 1974 by Xerox Corporation), October, 1974, p. 108.*

"My Special Best Words" is . . . a delightful book about a girl and a boy, Bweela 3, and Javaka 1, and their father. (There is no explanation as to the whereabouts of the absent mother, an omission which some children may find disturbing.) There is no story line, and one is not needed, for John Steptoe's talent enables us to experience the poetry in the ordinary life of an ordinary home. . . .

[The] entire book is a celebration, from the expressionist colors in Mr. Steptoe's almost photographic illustrations . . . to the matter-of-factness of the language. If one listens to this book with a child's ear, those "objectionable" words will reveal their music too. This book is as exhilarating as an autumn day.

> *Julius Lester, in* The New York Times Book Review *(© 1974 by The New York Times Company; reprinted by permission), November 3, 1974, p. 48.*

The illustrations [in *My Special Best Words*] are so brilliant in use of color, especially in outlining the children's faces, that the captivating Bweela and her brother are almost lost on most pages. While it is refreshing to have the physical functions so important to small children treated honestly, the account of the day (staying with a babysitter, being picked up by Daddy and taken home for baths and dinner) is loosely constructed and has no focus or direction.

> *Zena Sutherland, in* Bulletin of the Center for Children's Books *(© 1975 by the University of Chicago; all rights reserved), May, 1975, pp. 155-56.*

While not a feminist book, the girl is the main character [in *My Special Best Words*] and all children adore having this story read to them because of the real language and the explicitly dealt with subject of toilet training.

> Interracial Books for Children Bulletin *(reprinted by permission of* Interracial Books for Children Bulletin, *1841 Broadway, New York, N.Y. 10023), Vol. 6, Nos. 5 & 6, 1975, p. 11.*

OTHER CITATIONS

Publishers' Weekly, *August 5, 1974, p. 59.*

STEVIE (1969)

"Stevie" . . . offers a subtle paradox. One of the first books set in the ghetto, using black characters, black dialogue and a presumably black life-situation, it certainly stems from black culture. But the simple story the author tells, and pungently illustrates, is of a common experience of young rivalry. Though the author writes and paints out of his own blackness, he pushes black identity beyond the "black is beautiful" stage into a common identity. Which is as it should be. In fact, one might recommend this book for white children.

> *Barbara Novak, in* The New York Times Book Review *(© 1969 by The New York Times Company; reprinted by permission), November 30, 1969, p. 44.*

Here, at last, [is] a recognizable human being drawn from life. Steptoe's *Stevie* was not intended for white children, but the tale it tells—of sibling rivalry and the realization by an older boy that a nuisance of a small brother adds considerable spice to life—has universal appeal. After Stevie leaves, the hero of the tale recalls "the time we played boogie man and we hid under the covers with Daddy's flashlight." And the closing line, "Aw, no! I let my cornflakes get soggy thinkin' about him," brings not black or white but universal laughter. (p. 176)

> *Selma G. Lanes, in her* Down the Rabbit Hole: Adventures and Misadventures in the Realm of Children's Literature *(copyright © 1971 by Selma G. Lanes; reprinted by per-*

mission of Atheneum Publishers), Atheneum, 1972.

John Steptoe, in *Stevie* (. . . 1969), presents a relevant portrayal of the black ethos for the very young. Mild dialect, urban environment, and realistic characterizations emerge to authenticate a black child's experience with a young visitor. While actualizing city life, the universality of Stevie's experience makes this book appealing to all children.

> *Binnie Tate, "In House and Out House: Authenticity and the Black Experience in Children's Books," in* The Black American in Books for Children: Readings in Racism, *edited by Donnarae MacCann and Gloria Woodard (copyright 1972 by Donnarae MacCann and Gloria Woodard), Scarecrow, 1972, p. 45.*

Stevie . . . provides black ghetto children with identification. The writer simply presents a problem familiar to all children—the intrusion of a younger child on a small boy's time, friends, and family and his ambivalent feelings about the situation. To this extent, the book reflects no peculiarly black perspective. Identification for the young black reader rests in the central character's intimate knowledge of the black subculture—his use of informal grammar and idiom, his loosely structured family life, his sophistication and independence in worldly matters, and his brief sketches of the kinds of good times city children make for themselves—from the familiar game of cowboys and Indians to the less usual experience remembered nostalgically by Robert: "And that time we was playin' in the park under the bushes and we found these two dead rats and one was brown and one was black."

The value of such a book is that it assures the ghetto child that he, too, is visible—that he is important enough to be reflected in that literature which has always been made to seem too cultured to admit him.

> *Judith Thompson and Gloria Woodard, "Black Perspective in Books for Children," in* The Black American in Books for Children: Readings in Racism, *edited by Donnarae MacCann and Gloria Woodard (copyright 1972 by Donnarae MacCann and Gloria Woodard), Scarecrow, 1972, p. 23.*

OTHER CITATIONS

Polly Goodwin, in Book World, *February 15, 1970, p. 12.*

TRAIN RIDE (1971)

The illustrations [in *Train Ride*] are stunning, vibrant with color and effective in composition. The story has an all-boy quality: contempt for girls, the relish of a ploy, the fellowship and resourcefulness that emerge particularly when children function as a group. The writing style is adequate, livened only by the cadence of black idiom, a fact that will make the book welcome to some and anathema to others.

> *Zena Sutherland, in* Bulletin of the Center for Children's Books (© 1971 by the University of Chicago; all rights reserved), *October, 1971, p. 34.*

The color paintings [in *Train Ride*] have a dusky, blurry quality which doesn't do justice to either the kids or the city. But Charlie's fast-moving narrative is totally unselfconscious; there are no wasted nor fake words in the teasing/bantering/name-calling dialogue; and New York is described exactly as it would appear to a bunch of impressionable kids whose vitality and energy match the city's own.

> *Diane Gersoni Stavn, in* School Library Journal (reprinted from School Library Journal, *February, 1972, published by R. R. Bowker Co., a Xerox company; copyright © 1972 by Xerox Corporation), February, 1972, p. 73.*

OTHER CITATIONS

Kirkus Reviews, *August 15, 1971, p. 873.*

Publishers' Weekly, *September 27, 1971, p. 67.*

Ethel L. Heins, in The Horn Book Magazine, *October, 1971, p. 477.*

The Booklist, *November 1, 1971, p. 247.*

Polly Goodwin, in Book World, *November 7, 1971 (Part 2), p. 10.*

UPTOWN (1970)

[*Uptown* is an] authentic voice but circumscribed, without extension or illumination for the child. In the vitality, the resilience, the physical beauty—much surpassing *Stevie*—there's an affirmation that is also a denial of shame and ugliness and the book's validation for an adult; it doesn't coalesce (never mind the raw material) for anyone near picture book age and moreover it doesn't express the wanting they put in their poems, the truth they see in their photographs.

> Kirkus Reviews (copyright © 1970 The Kirkus Service, Inc.), *October 1, 1970, pp. 1092-93.*

Steptoe obviously does not intend ["Uptown"] as a cautionary tale for middle-class liberals, but as a mirror in which young blacks might, perhaps for the first time, recognize themselves. This they will surely do—but mirrors, unfortunately, do not transform reality into art. One gathers that Steptoe was honest enough to realize that no conventionally pleasing story could be made from his meager crumbs of spiritual sustenance. Eschewing art, he has rendered instead a sobering picture-book prognosis: ultimately beneficial, but highly painful.

> *Selma G. Lanes, in* The New York Times Book Review (© 1970 by The New York Times Company; reprinted by permission), *November 8, 1970, p. 52.*

Full-color, double-paged paintings [in *Uptown*] are not up to the quality of the author's illustrations in *Stevie* . . ., though they capture successfully the futility implicit in the boys' verbal explorations. The placing of much print on the all-white pages which fall between the pictures detracts also. Most important, however, is the question of the appropriateness of the book's content for children. Children bred in ghettos should have exposure to higher levels of aspiration than those expressed here; those foreign to such situations will neither understand the book's implicit statement nor [empathize] with its protagonists. *Uptown* may be about children but it will find its readers among adults.

> *Barbara S. Miller, in* School Library Journal *(reprinted from* School Library Journal, *December, 1970, published by R. R. Bowker Co., a Xerox company; copyright © 1970 by Xerox Corporation), December, 1970, p. 55.*

Stark and forceful paintings in brilliant colors accompany a story with little line, but with the same strong, assertive mood. It is assertive not because the dialogue between two black boys is positive but because it paints such a harsh, true picture of their position. . . . [*Uptown* tells] no story but [mirrors] the way it is. The format seems juvenile for the concepts and vocabulary level.

> *Zena Sutherland, in* Bulletin of the Center for Children's Books *(© 1971 by the University of Chicago; all rights reserved), March, 1971, p. 115.*

OTHER CITATIONS

Publishers' Weekly, *September 21, 1970, p. 59.*

Florence Heide, in Book World, *November 8, 1970 (Part 2), p. 27.*

Pamela Marsh, in The Christian Science Monitor, *November 12, 1970, p. B1.*

* * *

SUHL, Yuri   1908-

A Polish-born Jewish American historian, Yiddish poet, and English novelist, Yuri Suhl is noted for his writings about the holocaust. He received a 1972 Lewis Carroll Shelf Award for *Simon Boom Gives a Wedding*. (See also *Contemporary Authors*, Vols. 45-48.)

ELOQUENT CRUSADER: ERNESTINE ROSE (1970)

[Ernestine Rose's] wit, like her accent, could be pleasing or cutting, as well-documented quotations attest; her conversations, however, were no doubt less vacuous in actuality than in the reconstructions here. And her early post-Poland years were no doubt more trying than Mr. Suhl's facile passovers would suggest. . . . The omission of unique, individual details relegates this 'biography' to the ranks of sound suffrage literature, at least insofar as its close perspective on the [Women's Liberation] Movement(s) supersedes its personal focus qualitatively and quantitatively.

> *Kirkus Reviews (copyright © 1970 The Kirkus Service, Inc.), March 1, 1970, p. 254.*

Suhl's biography of Ernestine Rose is really the story of early agitation for women's rights. While details of Mrs. Rose's personal life are few, the author gives thorough coverage to the little known but remarkable work of this Polish Jew. . . . Her own words, quoted here from speeches and letters, are the liveliest in a book that should

be of particular interest as historical background for the current Women's Liberation Movement.

> The Booklist *(reprinted by permission of the American Library Association; copyright 1970 by the American Library Association), July 15, 1970, pp. 1409-10.*

The author gets bogged down in some unnecessary detail in the middle [of *Eloquent Crusader*], and there are several instances of less than credible dialogue (Mrs. Rose left no diaries, personal memoirs, or letters). However, in light of the current popularity of the Women's Liberation movement, there will likely be some girls interested in reading about this early crusader for women's rights.

> *Roberta N. Canavan, in* School Library Journal *(reprinted from* School Library Journal, *October, 1970, published by R. R. Bowker Co., a Xerox company; copyright © 1970 by Xerox Corporation), October, 1970, p. 142.*

_____

THE MERRYMAKER (1975)

Simply narrated by the ten-year-old son, this brief yet absorbing tale gives a sensitive picture of Jewish life around the turn of the century, accurately describing the daily experience, the poverty, the small joys. Typical Yiddish humor gives the events a light and joyous touch. Thomas di Grazia's muted, sepia-toned illustrations add dimension to the characters who are portrayed as prototypes of their society.

> *Marilyn Kaye, in* School Library Journal *(reprinted from* School Library Journal, *May, 1975, published by R. R. Bowker Co., a Xerox company; copyright © 1975 by Xerox Corporation), May, 1975, p. 59.*

A warm, thoughtful memory of early twentieth-century Jewish Poland, this will appeal to a special audience that can savor ethnic material and forego action. Di Grazia's expressive brown-and-white illustrations . . . have an appropriately soft-sell effect that emphasizes feelings and people rather than things.

> The Booklist *(reprinted by permission of the American Library Association; copyright 1975 by the American Library Association), May 1, 1975, p. 918.*

OTHER CITATIONS

Publishers' Weekly, *February 3, 1975, p. 75.*

Kirkus Reviews, *April 15, 1975, p. 458.*

_____

ON THE OTHER SIDE OF THE GATE (1975)

[Like] so much of, say, I. B. Singer, [*On the Other Side of the Gate*] is a factually accurate, modern story that reads like a folktale, and that turns the sufferings of Polish Jews under Nazism into a parable of hope and survival. . . . Suhl does include some Poles who are less sympathetic to Jews (to say the least), and he can't be faulted for lack of realism. Within its own limitations, the tale is touching and ultimately inspiring, yet even young readers may find it difficult to reconcile the extreme circumstances with the archetypal impersonality of Hershel and Lena and the consequently restricted emotional range.

> Kirkus Reviews *(copyright © 1975 The Kirkus Service, Inc.), February 1, 1975, p. 128.*

As in *Uncle Misha's Partisans* . . . Suhl describes a kind of tragic triumph in the Jewish resistance during World War II. . . . Strangely impersonal in style and sometimes forced, as in Hershel's exposition on past persecutions, this is still a suspenseful story of physical and emotional survival.

> The Booklist *(reprinted by permission of the American Library Association; copyright 1975 by the American Library Association), April 15, 1975, p. 869.*

Although the first part of the story graphically depicts the brutality of the Nazis and the misery of the Jews, the main thrust of the plot is based on the concept of the natural human will for survival. Both Hershel and Tadeusz were aware of the mixed feelings of the Poles toward the Jews (some were anti-Semitic and others were actuated by Christian compassion), and they had to proceed with unbelievable ingenuity and caution to remove the child from the ghetto. The final paragraph of the story is admirable for its irony and restraint. "Two days later the following item appeared in the *Gazette & Courier* and ran for three days: 'On the morning of May 12, 1942, a male infant was left on the doorstep of Pan and Pani Tadeusz Bielowski, 242 Pienkna Street. The rightful parents are requested to come to the above address to claim their child.'"

> Paul Heins, in The Horn Book Magazine *(copyright © 1975 by the Horn Book, Inc., Boston), June, 1975, pp. 271-72.*

Based on a true episode, this story [of] a young Jewish couple's successful plan to smuggle their infant son out of the Warsaw ghetto is both a tale of danger and courage and a grim picture of the plight of Polish Jews during the German occupation of World War II. . . . [*On the Other Side of the Gate*] shows the range of attitudes among Poles from anti-Semitism to defiant compassion. Suhl creates the atmosphere with caustic conviction and constructs the plot and the characters with solidity.

> Zena Sutherland, in Bulletin of the Center for Children's Books *(© 1975 by the University of Chicago; all rights reserved), September, 1975, p. 20.*

OTHER CITATIONS

Gertrude Serata, in School Library Journal, *March, 1975, p. 110.*

SIMON BOOM GIVES A WEDDING (1972)

[*Simon Boom Gives a Wedding* is a] festive and frothy demonstration of how a compulsion to buy "only the best" can lead to too much of a good thing. In Yuri Suhl's version of the Jewish folk tale Simon Boom goes shopping for his daughter's wedding party and ends up serving some-

thing that is sweeter than sugar, clearer than honey and purer than oil—sweet, clear, pure spring water. . . . [The] Booms' overstuffed homeliness is tempered by Zemach's blushing pinks and soft browns. Refreshing.

> Kirkus Reviews *(copyright © 1972 The Kirkus Service, Inc.), May 15, 1972, p. 578.*

[*Simon Boom Gives a Wedding*, a] noodlehead story illustrated with [Margot Zemach's] humorous and lively pictures, is based on a Jewish folktale. . . . The ending is weak, the story adequately told; its mild humor is helped considerably by the illustrations.

> Zena Sutherland, in Bulletin of the Center for Children's Books *(© 1972 by the University of Chicago; all rights reserved), December, 1972, p. 67.*

OTHER CITATIONS

Publishers' Weekly, May 1, 1972, p. 50.

Rebecca Ricky Friesam, in School Library Journal, *November, 1972, p. 63.*

UNCLE MISHA'S PARTISANS (1973)

The horrors of war never really hit the reader through [this] book's main characters or action; rather the tension of a dangerous adventure pervades, lending a different historical perspective to Second World War Jews as more indomitable than helpless.

> The Booklist *(reprinted by permission of the American Library Association; copyright 1973 by the American Library Association 1973), November 1, 1973, p. 294.*

One of the many recently published, fictionalized reminiscences of World War II, [*Uncle Misha's Partisans*] presents a graphic picture of Jewish partisans in the Ukraine, working to outwit German forces occupying their land. It is full of the heroism and selflessness, the virulent hatred and revenge of wartime. . . . Richly detailed, convincing, and consistently told from a twelve-year-old's point of view, the account has immediacy, poignancy, strong character interest, and suspense.

> Virginia Haviland, in The Horn Book Magazine *(copyright © 1974 by The Horn Book, Inc., Boston), February, 1974, p. 54.*

The Ukraine is the setting for *Uncle Misha's Partisans*, a strongly committed story of World War II told from the point of view of the local people and in particular of the minority population of Jews, whose safety depended on the doubtful goodwill of neighbours. . . . Though the translation reads rather stiffly, the story moves forward at a good pace and the author has done full justice to Motele's feelings, his youthful ardour and expectancies, without holding up the action. It is important to read the story as it is written, as a truly partisan and committed account; the boys and girls in the 'teens who read it are old enough to see differing points of view, and it is a pity that the novels about the war available to them still represent selected points of view.

Margery Fisher, in her Growing Point, *May, 1975, p. 2635.*

There is much in this book which underlines the atrocities suffered by the Jews, and explains their intense hatred of their Nazi oppressors, far more personally than the better-documented horrors of the concentration camps.

Valerie Alderson, in Children's Book Re-

view (© 1975 Five Owls Press Ltd.; all rights reserved), Summer, 1975, p. 77.

OTHER CITATIONS

Kirkus Reviews, *August 15, 1973, p. 888.*

Zena Sutherland, in Bulletin of the Center for Children's Books, *January, 1974, p. 87.*

T

TOWNSEND, John Rowe   1922-

An English journalist, John Rowe Townsend is both a noted author and critic of books for children and young people. (See also *Contemporary Authors*, Vols. 37-40, and *Something About the Author*, Vol. 4.)

GENERAL COMMENTARY

[John Rowe Townsend] has developed over a number of books, until his control over his intentions is assured and sustained. His novels, which are usually about the backgrounds and lives of children from the poorest kind of home, are well written and seemingly based on close observation, and their well-organised plots usually include some theme of interest to those who seek for 'socially conscious' novels for children. But this aspect of them is not overstressed and he is the most successful of the recent 'realistic' writers, because his earlier books can be read at a different level simply as straight and thoroughly exciting adventure stories. Children, therefore, do enjoy them. . . . His earlier books, though their backgrounds were unusual, were not so very different in kind from lesser stories of adventure. Mysterious strangers, misunderstandings, children in conflict with dishonesty, many of the conventional ingredients were used to give interest to his plots though he never allowed them to conflict with the main issues of character that he was really concerned with. But his later work has deepened and strengthened and is noticeably tending towards an older age level.

> *Frank Eyre, in his* British Children's Books in the Twentieth Century *(copyright © 1971 by Frank Eyre), Dutton, 1971, pp. 154-55.*

———————

FOREST OF THE NIGHT (1975)

This is a prose-poem about growing up and all the painful knowledge that has to be learnt. For the adult reader it is beautiful and compulsive reading; but it is an allegory of darkness.

The menace of the tiger, in all its fierce intolerable beauty, is finally faced, and accepted, and the book ends on a note of love and hope. But the horrors encountered on the way will not easily be forgotten.

> *Cecilia Gordon, in* The Times Literary Sup-

plement *(© Times Newspapers Ltd., 1974), December 6, 1974, p. 1374.*

The boy's ordeal [in *Forest of the Night*] has the earmarks, variously, of an initiation ceremony and a mystical experience; he is warned by different anonymous individuals, including a young girl and a fleshly older woman, not to eat or drink for the duration of the night and to find the "right questions" to ask. In the end he obeys an inner command to "go to the buildings" and confronts the beast in the form of a white-haired man in a Blakean dialogue: "'Who came before me?' 'Your father.' 'Who shall come after me?' 'Your son' . . . 'Who made you?' . . . 'He who made the lamb.' . . . 'Did he smile?' 'Yes. He smiled.'" This last exchange is obviously the crux of the matter, and we can't help wondering whether the boy might have done better to stay home and read Blake. Townsend has touched some powerful reference points, but he leaves most of them deliberately vague and his specifics—Blakean symbolism and philosophy—will be unfamiliar to his readers whereas allegory depends on the use of at least some framework recognizable to the intended audience. This is not to say that some young readers won't be attracted to Townsend's prose reverie—where the streetlights are "orange fruits, blur-edged" and the streets themselves "dark twisting forest trails." But they'll be as puzzled as anyone else by the significance of that final dialogue, and the confusion is Townsend's fault, not ours or theirs.

> Kirkus Reviews *(copyright © 1975 The Kirkus Service, Inc.), March 15, 1975, p. 318.*

[*Forest of the Night* is] a strange book, and one that for me hovers on the edge of understanding. I felt that each new paragraph might remove the obscurity, but, like life, it did not follow that the next experience would reveal the pattern behind all previous experience. The book's pattern of search, of hunting and being hunted, of endless corridors, myriad doorways, rooms like Chinese boxes, people at once well-known and unfamiliar, had the elements of nightmare but also the echoes of a hundred legends and myths. In the end, though the outlook was fogged, the map unhelpful, and the destination uncertain, the journey was worthwhile.

> *C.E.J. Smith, in* Children's Book Review

Partly based on William Blake's poem "Tyger," this is a pretentious and dull allegory. . . . Unfortunately, Townsend's message is obscure, though it seems to reflect a Christian acceptance of the human condition and the human community. Worse, the dramatic impact is minimal due to the brevity of the boy's encounters, their similarity, and the lack of detail in characters and events. In short, it has neither the meat nor the meaning of Townsend's well-known and justly acclaimed realistic novels.

> *Margaret A. Dorsey, in* School Library Journal *(reprinted from* School Library Journal, *April, 1975, published by R. R. Bowker Co., a Xerox company; copyright © 1975 by Xerox Corporation), April, 1975, p. 72.*

Forest of the Night is a symbolic narrative of a boy entering manhood, told under the aegis—as it were—of Blake's poem "The Tyger." For not only is the title of the book drawn from the poem, but at various crucial points in the story Blake's phraseology is introduced—with a difference, with a new emphasis. . . .

Whatever Mr. Townsend may have borrowed, he has transmuted. The narrative flows with the intensity of a dream or a nightmare, and the various episodes have moments of transfiguration as well as of terror. Like musical themes, the characters undergo unexpected changes; and at the very hub of the story, as at the hub of the dark city lying under the stars, there lingers another kind of music: "But in this high place silence is not all. Far above the pitch of human ear are sounds, not heard but known of. A planetary music, cold and clear, inaudible but everywhere. A cool and abstract beauty. Opposite to that other beauty hot and fleshed." The author's departure over the perilous seas of fantasy has been made perfect by his safe return home with a story full of power and imagination.

> *Paul Heins, in* The Horn Book Magazine *(copyright © 1975 by The Horn Book, Inc., Boston), April, 1975, p. 133.*

Townsend's prose flows like a dark river in a fantasy of a boy's search—for what? For self-knowledge, for the pain and freedom of maturity, maybe for all these things. There are no names of people or places, just the dark forest in which tigers prowl, and must be conquered. In this allegory based on Blake's poem, the boy must choose to retreat to safety or to go into the ancient and frightening Buildings because it is time, because he is no longer a child. To describe the traps and trials the boy meets, or the strength he shows in being tested would vitiate the impact; [*Forest of the Night*] is not for all readers, but for those who appreciate the nuances of style and symbolism.

> *Zena Sutherland, in* Bulletin of the Center for Children's Books *(© 1975 by the University of Chicago; all rights reserved), July-August, 1975, pp. 186-87.*

OTHER CITATIONS

Publishers' Weekly, *March 31, 1975, p. 49.*

GOOD NIGHT, PROF, DEAR (1971)

Goodnight, Prof, Love [published in America as *Good Night, Prof, Dear*] is [an] absorbing book. The author's involvement in the hero's dilemma, the conflict of daydreams and reality, produces a distinctive novel if not a wholly successful one. . . .

For the telling John Rowe Townsend has chosen, for the most part, a clipped, signalling kind of dialogue to represent the group code of the young, the language of improvised drama. This is less successful than the passages of interior monologue which are very expressive of the boy's feelings, his sexual unease, discontent, longing, his efforts to equate Lynn's robust vitality with idealized womanhood. The parents are too predictably type-cast and sometimes the conflict of values seems over-contrived. Why, for example, must all the café characters be untrustworthy, slightly criminal, insensitive? The book fails to be utterly convincing because the author has one eye on the needs of his readers and has let the awareness of these come between him and the full realization of his theme.

> The Times Literary Supplement *(© Times Newspapers Ltd., 1970), October 30, 1970, p. 1258.*

Mr Townsend has devised a love story as haunting and aching as any I have read in ages. Told almost entirely in dialogue, with but the barest touches of description, it achieves an extraordinary poetry that really does recapture the passionate bewilderment of adolescent love. Though not so broad in its scope as Mr Townsend's *The Intruder*, it succeeds, I think, in cutting even deeper.

> *Leon Garfield, in* New Statesman *(© The Statesman & Nation Publishing Co. Ltd. 1970), November 6, 1970, p. 608.*

The plot [of *Good Night, Prof, Dear*] is well developed—it begins slowly and builds to a high-pitched climax. And all the characters are extremely credible, from the sensitive, daydreaming boy to his hysterical mother and well-meaning but ineffective father. The style is interesting, with convincing dialogue and good description. And the author's use of stream of consciousness to show Graham's fantasies and incessant bouts of conscience is generally effective, though it probably would be confusing for slow readers.

> *Charlotte C. Levy, in* School Library Journal *(reprinted from* School Library Journal, *April, 1971, published by R. R. Bowker Co., a Xerox company; copyright © 1971 by Xerox Corporation), April, 1971, p. 122.*

Mr. Townsend must . . . be congratulated for attempting so tricky a theme [in *Good Night, Prof, Dear*]. The contrast between Graham, fumbling in the fog of adolescent emotions, and Lynn, brash as a Blackpool trinket stall, is sustained, convincing and, at times, pathetic. The staccato prose style and the preponderance of dialogue will no doubt catch the attention of older teenage readers; adults may find them slightly irritating—but this is a book (and a sensitively conceived book) for the under-eighteens: it explores one corner of the teenage jungle of doubt and despair intelligently and compassionately.

> The Junior Bookshelf, *June, 1971, p. 122.*

In a narrative essentially keyed to high-school readers, [John Rowe Townsend] has told a story in which the commonplaces of a surface realism are skillfully arranged to denote the emotional experiences and psychological crisis in the life of a boy "not quite seventeen." . . . Frankly acknowledging the sexual and social facts of life, restrained in treatment, emotionally honest, the narrative [in *Good Night, Prof, Dear*] permits the ironies of the situation to speak for themselves.

> *Paul Heins, in* The Horn Book Magazine *(copyright © 1971 by The Horn Book, Inc., Boston), June, 1971, pp. 294-95.*

OTHER CITATIONS

Kirkus Reviews, *January 15, 1971, pp. 57-8.*

Publishers' Weekly, *March 22, 1971, p. 53.*

Sidney Offit, in Book World, *May 9, 1971 (Part 2), p. 18.*

Zena Sutherland, in Bulletin of the Center for Children's Books, *July-August, 1971, p. 179.*

GOOD-BYE TO THE JUNGLE (1967)

[Mr. Townsend] understands these young teenagers [in *Good-bye to the Jungle*, published in Great Britain as *Widdershins Crescent*], their problems and their background. He writes sympathetically yet never condescendingly. Sandra, the girl, who is ashamed of her home and the way they live, and who tries desperately to hold the family together and give the younger ones a higher standard both mentally and morally, is a character many teachers must have met and admired. Teenagers, too, will feel a greater affinity with this family than with those dreadful "horsey" families so popular with authors and publishers. These are real people in a real situation, uprooted from their familiar settings and moved to a brand new environment. This is happening all over Britain and one must be grateful to the author for tackling this problem and treating it so unsentimentally and yet with such deep understanding, almost tenderness. Some of the adult characters are rather over-drawn.

> The Junior Bookshelf, *December, 1965, p. 376.*

No one could accuse John Rowe Townsend of presenting a prettied up view of life for the children of and for whom he writes. The family of four who appeared first in Mr. Townsend's excellent first children's book, *Gumble's Yard* [published in America as *Trouble in the Jungle*], appear again in *Widdershins Crescent* [published in America as *Good-bye to the Jungle*]. They have been moved from their old, tumbledown home to a new housing estate, an opening which for many authors would have been the triumphant end of another story. Mr. Townsend knows, and says, that a change of place does not necessarily mean a change of heart. . . . This is a story of the sort of thing that really happens; both the characters and the events are presented as mixtures, hateful and sympathetic, sad and funny, potentially both evil and good. There is injustice, Mr. Townsend says to his readers; the innocent suffer with the guilty, there is squalor and poverty and misery. But, he says, there is hope, there is courage and there is love. Besides making

these unusual statements Mr. Townsend has written an excellent story with lively and credible characters; he has a beautiful sense of timing, and he writes in a style which is always a pleasure to read.

> The Times Literary Supplement *(© The Times Publishing Company Ltd. 1965), December 9, 1965, p. 1142.*

Walter and Doris bicker continually [in *Good-Bye to the Jungle*], but they are somehow likable in spite of their slipshod ways and are very well portrayed. Kevin, the narrator, observes his milieu meticulously and points up some of the truths about the poor that are overlooked by pat formulas. Poverty is handled realistically and with dignity and so are the strains involved in casting off its stigma.

> *Elinor Cullen, in* School Library Journal *(reprinted from* School Library Journal, *May, 1967, published by R. R. Bowker Co., a Xerox company; copyright © 1967 by Xerox Corporation), May, 1967, pp. 68-9.*

["Good-bye to the Jungle"] is a rare and startling book. It shows how dreams are not smashed but just crumple; how people do not change radically, but just in little ways; how goodness and badness intermingle in each human being. For its intimate glimpse of the harangues, tears and small joys of slum people, for its view of the unquenchable hope which drives human beings toward tomorrow, for its genuine dialogue and total honesty, this book deserves extra praise.

> *Jane Manthorne, in* The New York Times Book Review *(© 1967 by The New York Times Company; reprinted by permission), May 7, 1967, p. 14.*

The characterizations [in *Good-bye to the Jungle*] are excellent. Walter and Doris, among the most degraded "parents" to be found in juvenile fiction, are entirely believable. The children are as different from each other as children inevitably are, and their loyalty to each other gives them the strength to present a united front to a world that has often been unkind. There is not a trace of false sentiment, nor yet is the story overly grim. It is often exciting, sometimes funny, and always absorbing. Kevin and Sandra with their pride and pluck and dogged resolution are real and memorable.

> *Ruth Hill Viguers, in* The Horn Book Magazine *(copyright © 1967, by The Horn Book, Inc., Boston), June, 1967, p. 356.*

["Good-bye to the Jungle" develops] into a mystery that is never solved. Children may be disappointed in the ambiguous, though fitting, ending, but then again they may not. One should not underestimate children any more than one should underestimate writers of children's books. "Good-bye to the Jungle" should dispel the notion that people who write for children are necessarily less writers than the people who write for adults.

> *Janet Malcolm, in* The New Yorker *(© 1967 by The New Yorker Magazine, Inc.), December 16, 1967, p. 164.*

OTHER CITATIONS

Kirkus Service, *February 15, 1967, p. 212.*

The Booklist and Subscription Books Bulletin, *September 1, 1967, p. 67.*

HELL'S EDGE (1969)

One could commend Mr. Townsend's novel of life in a West Riding Township with more conviction were it not for a kind of faintly sickening predictability in the sequence of events portrayed. It is just that little bit too romantic in construction to be outstanding among present day books in the teen-age range. His young people, Amaryllis and Norman, are sympathetically drawn if not particularly complete characters. They would have been the better, too, for a little more inbred respect for the law; swimming in private waters is one thing, but breaking and entering is quite another, however noble the motive. The motive, indeed, is also in the romantic vein: the effort to secure a document which will prove that an ancestor of the haughty and neurotic young man of the big house really did will part of his coveted parkland to the town. Hallersedge (Hell's Edge) is well drawn as a town and the northern flavour of the setting is conveyed without the too obvious use of dialect or catchwords, though its adult members creak a little at times. Such comments as these probably make the book sound rather less of an achievement than it truly is. It has pace and colour and [a] high degree of readability.

> The Junior Bookshelf, *November, 1963, p. 296.*

To a thoroughly rousing adventure story, replete with pursuits by foot and car, John Rowe Townsend adds a memorable community of people—rugged, forthright Yorkshire folk, who for generations traded legends and gossip, took their pint at the Feathers, called each other "love" and resisted new ideas. Into their snug world Townsend injects the audacity of youth and the gentle winds of change. And the concluding reverie of his heroine points to the value of diversity: "It didn't just take North and South to make a world. It took all that they symbolized. It took both tough and tender, both practical and romantic."

> Jane Manthorne, in The New York Times Book Review (© *1969 by The New York Times Company; reprinted by permission), August 31, 1969, p. 16.*

[*Hell's Edge*] has a smooth blending of diverse elements. . . . There is pace and momentum in the plot, a setting that is realistic and contemporary, and a wonderful array of characters, their speech just enough tinged with local idiom to be flavorsome rather than quaint.

> Zena Sutherland, in Bulletin of the Center for Children's Books (© *1969 by the University of Chicago; all rights reserved), September, 1969, p. 19.*

THE INTRUDER (1970)

As plots go, this one might have served Mr. Townsend well enough. Arnold's adolescent naiveté and mounting frustra-

tion as he attempts to deal with a cynical and physically powerful adult are well presented—but the author seldom gets beneath the facades of his principals. Nor will the reader really understand why the title character (who, it turns out, has the evidence of his true identity in his wallet) has risked everything in his attempt to kill both Arnold and Mr. Haithwaite, in order to take over the old man's affairs and profit by them.

Once this dark purpose is revealed, the well-worn story-line seems little more than synthetic drama devised for its own sake. This reader expected a good deal more from Mr. Townsend, who gave us such an unusual version of a treasure hunt in "Pirate's Island."

> Eleanor Cameron, in The New York Times Book Review (© *1970 by The New York Times Company; reprinted by permission), April 26, 1970, p. 30.*

The Intruder . . . is a fairly complex story which does not preach. Yet most of its people are so clearly drawn in the round, from life, that their actions and reactions inevitably teach lessons about living.

Mr. Townsend has given us a solid young fisherman hero and a splendid working class villain, sinister, menacing, yet also faintly pathetic. The plot moves; tension rises and is held taut; a couple of exquisite red herrings are insinuated across the trail. The outcome surprises us. It also satisfies, though a little bleakly. The climax, swift and dramatic, drowses into the slow turning of generations.

Unsentimental, unsweetened, uncompromisingly honest, *The Intruder* . . . is a work of quality.

> Neil Millar, in The Christian Science Monitor (*reprinted by permission from* The Christian Science Monitor; © *1970 The Christian Science Publishing Society; all rights reserved), May 7, 1970, p. B6.*

"Sea, sand, stone, slate, sky" are the first and last words of [this] fine book, and describe its flavor well. . . .

John Rowe Townsend shares with a handful of other writers for children a gift for creating people, not characters. But few share with him his knack of making background into foreground. The book's people are fully credible. But its most durable elements are sea and sand, stone and slate and sky.

> Digby B. Whitman, in Book World (© The Washington Post), *May 17, 1970 (Part 2), p. 20.*

Set in a village in England, on the coast of the Irish Sea, [*The Intruder* is] a dramatic and compelling story with fine characterization, an imaginative plot, and a remarkable evocation of atmosphere and mood. . . . The intruder is so plausible that none of the adults to whom Arnold turns for help take him seriously, although it is clear to the reader that the man is not only evil but criminal. The solution is unexpected but plausible, the exciting ending a fitting one to a tale pregnant with suspense.

> Zena Sutherland, in Bulletin of the Center for Children's Books (© *1970 by the University of Chicago; all rights reserved), July-August, 1970, p. 186.*

[*The Intruder*] deals with a boy who is an isolated individual, living close to a terrain and sharing its life. . . . [It is a] novel, realistic and laconic in manner, [which explores] the hesitancies of youth and [acknowledges]—in the manner of Thomas Hardy—the power of nature and of fate.

> *Paul Heins, in* The Horn Book Magazine *(copyright © 1970 by The Horn Book, Inc., Boston), August, 1970, p. 396.*

In *The Intruder,* Townsend begins with "Sea, sand, stone, slate, sky." Both the staccato introduction and the paragraphs that follow, giving geographical details and historical background, lend emphasis to the importance of the place. The two-page chapter ends, "Sea, sand, stone, slate, sky. That is the landscape," a further emphasis by setting the description apart. Facing the opening lines is a map, another clue to the fact that the setting is important. Townsend assumes that his reading audience will appreciate this, and he creates, in the two pages, an atmosphere that invites an expectation of suspense that depends on the kind of reading experiences older children have had.

> *May Hill Arbuthnot and Zena Sutherland, in their* Children and Books *(copyright © 1947, 1957, 1964, 1972 by Scott, Foresman and Co.), 4th edition, Scott, Foresman, 1972, p. 24.*

In setting, characterization and narrative power *The Intruder* is one of the outstanding books of its decade. It commands admiration but not, for me, affection. There is a coldness in it which is repellant. A convincing case-history, it lacks the quality of involvement. One does not identify with Arnold, still less with Sonny. . . . *The Intruder* is a masterly novel, but its message is arid. Arnold gets a chilly satisfaction from his job, which 'will live as long as he does, and that is enough'. It is not, one hopes, enough to satisfy the young reader.

> *Marcus Crouch, in his* The Nesbit Tradition: The Children's Novel in England 1945-1970 *(© Marcus Crouch 1972), Ernest Benn, 1972, p. 208.*

This magnificent story is narrated through Arnold's thoughts, through the comments of other people and in the increasingly terse, manic sentences which are as ugly as Sonny's fixed artificial eye and his harsh voice. The book has an intensely visual quality. There is little direct description but the words chosen to build a picture of the sands and the shabby village, of the people whose lethargic attitude to life makes them so vulnerable to the unruly actions of a psychopath, are placed unerringly so as to stir the imagination. This is a macabre contest between a lad who accepts his ambiguous background and a man who needs to steal his name to support a monstrous self-will and an equally monstrous inadequacy as a human being. Sonny comes as near to pure evil as any of the characters in children's fiction who have been drawn plainly and directly without the overtones of fantasy.

> *Margery Fisher, in her* Who's Who in Children's Books *(copyright © 1975 by Margery Fisher; reprinted by permission of Holt, Rinehart and Winston), Holt, Rinehart and Winston, 1975, p. 29.*

OTHER CITATIONS

Kirkus Reviews, *February 1, 1970, p. 112.*

Arlene Ruthenberg, in School Library Journal, *April, 1970, p. 125.*

Publishers' Weekly, *April 27, 1970, p. 79.*

Zena Sutherland, in Saturday Review, *May 9, 1970, p. 69.*

The Booklist, *June 1, 1970, pp. 1217-18.*

PIRATE'S ISLAND **(1968)**

The story [*Pirate's Island*] is exciting, well-articulated, well-documented: this is a North Country town all right. But beneath quick talk, quick event, lies a sturdy belief in the eternal variety of human nature.

> *Margery Fisher, in* The Christian Science Monitor *(reprinted by permission from* The Christian Science Monitor; *© 1968 The Christian Science Publishing Society; all rights reserved), May 2, 1968, p. B10.*

In his special sphere of juvenile literature, Townsend is without peer and indeed almost without company. His adventure stories are magnificently credible, because his adventurers are the children all around us. Fat boys suffer as much from unimaginative writers as they do from their schoolmates, but [in *Pirate's Island*] Gordon is presented neither comically nor tragically; only matter-of-factly as an unhappy child needing understanding and help. The indomitable Sheila, too, escapes the Orphan Annie stereotype; in her own way she is as wonderful as Mrs. Konigsburg's unforgettable Jennifer (in *Jennifer, Hecate, Macbeth, William McKinley, and Me, Elizabeth*). Best of all, both children are alive in the literal sense that, like all living things, they grow and change as the story advances. A strongly satisfying little book.

> *Digby B. Whitman, in* Book World *(© The Washington Post), May 5, 1968, p. 24.*

A pampered pork-butcher's son and a fey little girl whose only escape from her shabby existence is "Treasure Island" come together in this return to the Jungle, that "citadel of slumdom" in a tough city of northern England first introduced to older readers in "Good-bye to the Jungle." This serio-comic adventure stars plump Gordon, who rises above his complacent life of comics and sweets, and Sheila, who surmounts her barren, tormented existence to build a raft and float forth on a treasure hunt. They also outwit and outrun local no-goods to retrieve an old man's life savings. In the author's setting of rat-ravaged alleys, where policemen and rent collectors travel in pairs for safety; in his characters, who can curse and brawl and beat children; in his picture of poverty, which creates numb, blank-eyed mothers and sickly little ones, Townsend brings the dimensions of reality to children's books.

> *Jane Manthorne, in* The New York Times Book Review *(© 1968 by The New York Times Company; reprinted by permission), May 12, 1968, p. 30.*

[John Rowe Townsend's] work is always of a high standard

... but I find its pulse intermittent: narrative isn't one of his strong points; he's happiest with character and mood and the way children talk to one another. But in *Pirate's Island* ... the beat is loud and strong, and the story line—about the fat and derided son of the local sausage-maker—fairly pumps up the blood-pressure. There's some well-observed junior tribal behaviour, and a quick concession to puberty in the idea that girls can be both civilising and exciting. The end is very deft, though I resent its implication that the way to manhood is to be a boys' boy rather than a girls' boy.

> *Michael Baldwin, in* New Statesman (© *The Statesman & Nation Publishing Co. Ltd. 1968), May 24, 1968, p. 695.*

Mr. Townsend has come to be regarded as one of England's finest contemporary writers of and about books for children. ... He has acute perception of the way children behave and control their lives in the midst of adversity. In addition, his plots, characterization, and writing skill are excellent. ...

Two themes are developed [in *Pirate's Island*]. The first, eloquently detailed, states that intelligent compassion, rather than blind sentimentality, should be extended to those living in poverty of body and spirit. The second theme, also well-developed, deals with the realization that incarceration in a penal institution ... may not always be a wise solution. The natural resiliance of children when the proper kind of loving care is available is stressed.

> *John Gillespie and Diana Lembo, in their* Introducing Books: A Guide for the Middle Grades *(copyright © 1970 by Xerox Corp.), Bowker, 1970, pp. 179, 182.*

OTHER CITATIONS

Kirkus Service, *March 1, 1968, p. 263.*

Gertrude B. Herman, in School Library Journal, *April, 1968, p. 133.*

The Booklist and Subscription Books Bulletin, *April 15, 1968, pp. 999-1000.*

Zena Sutherland, in Saturday Review, *May 11, 1968, pp. 40-1.*

The Junior Bookshelf, *June, 1968, pp. 190-91.*

Zena Sutherland, in Bulletin of the Center for Children's Books, *July-August, 1968, p. 182.*

Virginia Haviland, in The Horn Book Magazine, *August, 1968, p. 423.*

THE SUMMER PEOPLE (1972)

The games [Philip and Ann] play, and the contrast of these games to the reality of their world (headlines about the coming Hitler war play counterpoint to the entire novel), give their story perspective and dimension.

"The Summer People" is clear, honest and delicate. Philip Martin is a three-dimensional protagonist who knows how to do justice to those he loves.

> *Bruce Clements, in* The New York Times

Book Review (© *1972 by The New York Times Company; reprinted by permission), November 19, 1972, p. 10.*

Realistically, the closing letter from Philip to his son [in *The Summer People*] divulges the fact that Sylvia and Philip did marry, but that the son married Ann's daughter seems contrived and coincidental and the epistolary framework weakens the story. The setting and the characters are well drawn, although Ann is a weak character and her relationship with Philip rather ponderously developed. The family scenes are very good indeed, and the writing is polished yet deceptively casual.

> *Zena Sutherland, in* Bulletin of the Center for Children's Books (© *1972 by the University of Chicago; all rights reserved), December, 1972, p. 67.*

Neatly presented as an adult's confession of what happened at a quiet seaside village in August, 1939, this jigsaw of emotional tangles is basically a double romance with Philip Martin, rising seventeen, at its heart. ...

Mr. Townsend handles a tricky theme with disciplined insight; he contrasts his adolescents effectively and refrains from turning any of them into cardboard caricatures, though he comes very near to doing this with the adult Mr. Fox; he explores the flirtation of the hearty Sylvia and the somewhat bewildered Harold to just the right depth, leaving his more serious analysis for the sincere love of Philip and Ann.

> The Junior Bookshelf, *February, 1973, p. 56.*

There's a fine sense of place here, the hero is refreshingly unremarkable, and the well-written story shows that the duration of a relationship has nothing to do with its intensity or impact on one's life. However, some readers may be impatient with the lack of action, the dated social mores, and Phil's propensity to feel guilty without reason.

> *Diane Gersoni Stavn, in* School Library Journal *(reprinted from* School Library Journal, *March, 1973, published by R. R. Bowker Co., a Xerox company; copyright © 1973 by Xerox Corporation), March, 1973, p. 121.*

In a tone reminiscent of Elizabeth Bowen's *The Death of the Heart*, [John Rowe Townsend] describes characters tensed between innocence and knowledge, adolescence and maturity, stability and destruction. Throughout, a feeling of sadness and acceptance shadows [*The Summer People*]; a feeling that is only partially blunted by the rather contrived ending. ... But, perhaps in the long run, the tidiness of the ending becomes part and parcel of Philip's observation that in spite of tragedy, love, or human frailty, in the England he recognizes, "Cricket goes on forever." Exceptionally well-written—a powerful and disciplined approach to the business of the novel.

> *Sheryl Andrews, in* The Horn Book Magazine *(copyright © 1973 by The Horn Book, Inc., Boston), April, 1973, p. 129.*

OTHER CITATIONS

Kirkus Reviews, *September 15, 1972, p. 1107.*

Publishers' Weekly, *October 16, 1972, p. 49.*

M. H. Miller, in Children's Book Review, *April, 1973, p. 48.*

TROUBLE IN THE JUNGLE (1969)

[*Gumble's Yard,* published in America as *Trouble in the Jungle,* presents] a real situation which has faced hundreds of children, but has it ever before been presented for other children to read? There is a subsidiary plot of smugglers, crooks with flick knives and stolen diamonds which one could have done without, but which is less out of place in this setting than in the usual middle-class, country-holiday-with-ponies background. The end of the book is perfect: undramatic, perhaps saddening, but perfect and poetically right. Perceptive children will feel that this is what life is really like.

> The Times Literary Supplement (© *The Times Publishing Company Ltd. 1961), December 1, 1961, p. xx.*

Realistically, there is no pat ending [to *Trouble in the Jungle*]; the delinquent, shiftless father and his mistress come back and a young curate advises Kevin to return to the fold: it may be the Jungle (the slum neighborhood) but at least it is a home where the family can stay together, and there may be slovenliness and neglect, but there is no cruelty. The milieu is deftly established, the characterization and dialogue are good, and the plot has pace and suspense.

> *Zena Sutherland, in* Bulletin of the Center for Children's Books (© *1970 by the University of Chicago; all rights reserved), February, 1970, p. 106.*

A precarious life and an early acquaintance with the contrivances of poverty have not warped any of the children, nor are the two stories about them [*Trouble in the Jungle* and *Good-bye to the Jungle*] drab or morbid; the narrative is far too lively, the characters too full of life and bounce for that. Kevin and Sandra may be old for their age but they still respond in a natural, excited way to the surprises of Gumble's Yard and the curious behaviour of Alderman Widdowson. As for the younger cousins, Harold is totally believable, a child with an exceptional brain who never doubts that everyone will put their minds to finding the means for him to take the offered place at the Grammar School, a child whose dreams of being the great inventor Sir Harold Thompson are merged with a more normal addiction to space-ship noises, while his sister, obstinate little Jean, lavishing her affection on a battered alley-cat, has her own way of compensating for a life of uncertainty. There is no attempt to conceal the lack of support and affection which the children suffer but they learn to depend on the affection they have for each other. In a story as alive and vivid as this, this is no abstract conclusion.

> *Margery Fisher, in her* Who's Who in Children's Books *(copyright © 1975 by Margery Fisher; reprinted by permission of Holt, Rinehart and Winston), Holt, Rinehart and Winston, 1975, p. 167.*

TRAVERS, P(amela) L(yndon) 1906-

P. L. Travers, an Australian-born Englishwoman, is a writer, journalist, critic, and poet best known for her books about Mary Poppins. (See also *Contemporary Authors*, Vols. 33-36, and *Something About the Author*, Vol. 4.)

GENERAL COMMENTARY

Mary Poppins is . . . the embodiment of authority, protection, and cynical common sense; her powers are magical. Basically, she is the Good Fairy, whom we are all seeking, but in priggish human guise. Practical, neat and brisk, sure and independent, omniscient, haughty and vain . . ., she is the queller of her charges' vanities, the minister of punishment and reward, the rescuer from peril, the deflater of whimsy, dreaming and nonsense—and the purveyor of something akin but vastly superior to all of these when occasion warrants. . . .

A few episodes [in the books about Mary Poppins] are weakened by what Mary Poppins herself would not have allowed—the sentimental fallacy; but on the whole this is brilliantly resisted. Actually, the poetry of the author's imagination comes out, not always where poetry is intended, but in the range of idea, and in the marriage of idea and dialogue. . . .

But, poetry apart, the author has set foot in several important fields, involving parent, child, and servant. The relation of servant and child can be, indeed, both intimate and profound—a closer one than all other early ties. The mother in these books makes a poor showing compared with the nursemaid who lives with the children; she has little authority; she does not even understand the infant's language. . . . The other notable feature in the Mary Poppins saga is the position of the child itself. Here, the author writes with immense understanding but without false sentiment. The child has its place, but not—unusually for to-day—the dominating one. These pleasant boys and girls who are her charges get no favours from the supernatural world simply by virtue of their youth and charm, but by being Mary Poppins's friends.

> The Times Literary Supplement, *November 28, 1952, p. iii.*

[A] sturdy realism anchors to the earth the tugging, sky-bound stories about Mary Poppins by P. L. Travers. Mary Poppins occupies in the Banks family the place filled in [E.] Nesbit's books by the Mouldiwarp, the Psammead and the Phoenix. Like them, she is crusty, unpredictable and fond of speaking her mind. Magic is something she is obliged to perform and which she feels will do her charges no good. But she cannot help being magic, for she is an elemental. Sun and stars defer to her at a sky-fête; she is an old friend of the Greek gods; she appears out of the sky on a kite-string; she orders the elements and promotes the unlikely everywhere. That is one side of her. The other side is the Nannie, with her expressive sniff, her despotic commands, her love of the last word. . . .

These lively stories take you into a madder, more completely fantastic world than the world of E. Nesbit, though with the same homely domestic foundation. There is *Bad Wednesday,* a terrifying piece, when Jane is whisked into the world of a Royal Doulton bowl; there is *Mrs Lark's Andrew,* a splended piece of nonsense about a respectable dog and a mongrel; there is *The Marble Boy,* an incident in the park which combines sharp social comedy with a deep apprehension of the antique; there is the vivid *Hallowe'en,* where comic characters and natural objects all obey Mary Poppins as, with her Dutch doll hair and her immovable, bourgeois hat, she foots it through the night. She is always respectable. When, in *Peppermint Horses,* she whirls the children up into the sky, she is still very much the Nannie. . . .

These stories depend mainly on the character of this strange personage, and because her character is so important, Mary Shepard's illustrations are of the first importance too, for they present Mary Poppins to us visually in a way that establishes her for ever. It is because of Mary Poppins, because she is as she is, that these books are at once gay and serious, superbly entertaining, but always probing into depths of mystery and poetry.

> *Margery Fisher, in her* Intent Upon Reading: A Critical Appraisal of Modern Fiction for Children *(copyright © 1961 by Margery Fisher), Hodder & Stoughton Children's Books (formerly Brockhampton Press), 1961, pp. 148-49 (published in America by Franklin Watts, 1962).*

In four exquisite books . . . P. L. Travers developed a most original and consistent heroine. Mary Poppins is . . . terribly convincing in her severity and high standards, putting down her wards with ruthless efficiency, perfect but for her yard-wide vein of conceit; she is also, and this is one of the most delicious surprises in children's literature, magical.

> *Marcus Crouch, in his* Treasure Seekers and Borrowers: Children's Books in Britain 1900-1960 *(© Marcus Crouch, 1962), The Library Association, 1962, p. 62.*

As in [John] Masefield's books [*The Midnight Folk* (1927) and *The Box of Delights* (1935)], magic and fantasy mingle with everyday life [in P. L. Travers' books]. But in *Mary Poppins* and its four sequels not only is it the magic of happy fantasy, but it is apt to make itself apparent—with perfect propriety, and absolute conviction—at any moment and as a part of the normal, everyday doings of the Banks family who are under the charge of this truly remarkable Nannie. The amazing achievement of the series is the way in which it captures with such simplicity and conviction the younger child's world of fantasy in which nothing *is* impossible, and the magic which happens in the imagination and is always about to happen in the actual world. The genius and inspiration of P. L. Travers lies in having captured this borderland of fancy with absolute verisimilitude and with never a suggestion of adult invention or condescension.

> *Roger Lancelyn Green, in his* Tellers of Tales: British Authors of Children's Books from 1800 to 1964 *(copyright 1946, © 1965 by Edmund Ward, Publishers, Ltd.; reprinted courtesy of Kaye & Ward Ltd.) revised edition, Kaye & Ward Ltd., 1965, p. 273.*

Mary Poppins appears to have a good deal of acid in her nature until you know her well, as children do—brusquely spoken, unreasonably vain, putting up with no nonsense, but past mistress of such magnificent and sometimes beautiful nonsense as never was.

> *Annis Duff, in her* Longer Flight: A Family Grows Up With Books *(copyright 1955 by Annis Duff; reprinted by permission of The Viking Press, Inc.), Viking, 1966, p. 237.*

Mary Poppins is one of the oddest figures in the whole of children's literature and quite an antiquated one to find in the age of modern technology. One is tempted to ask if, in her combined capacities as magician and strict children's nurse, she is a latter-day descendant of those curious characters in *Alice in Wonderland,* or if she symbolizes the natural relapse of modern man into a world of fantasy. Since the creator of the books is a woman with both her feet firmly in our own age it may well be surmised that a close familiarity with the English tradition is sending her in search of the modern equivalent for the fairy tale. . . .

P. L. Travers is convinced that conscious recollection of the world of dreams and fairy tales and of those things which we see with our inward eye can do nothing but good. She is as convinced as the French Père Castor that an understanding of nature will do much to soothe the restless spirit of the modern child. In her work we find the two concepts united in poetic garb. When she describes the morning mist in the park or the East or the West winds, then these are masterpieces of natural description for adult readers as well as children, so that her books may be placed in that rare category which used at one time to be labelled: 'For children from 7 to 70.' . . .

> *Bettina Hürlimann, in her* Three Centuries of Children's Books in Europe, *translated and edited by Brian W. Alderson (English translation © Oxford University Press 1967), Oxford University Press, 1967, pp. 79-80.*

Mary Poppins, a nursemaid with magical powers of an unexpected kind, is a most endearing character, and Pamela Travers was extremely lucky in her illustrator, Mary Shepard, who caught to perfection the turned-up nose and consequential air that distinguish Mary Poppins from most other magical personalities. For she is inordinately vain, anything but good-tempered, and the justice she administers is of an incalculable kind, doled out by fits and starts in just such a way as no doubt the Olympian authority of more prosaic nannies must appear to children. She is an inspired conception, and the books in which she appears have a deserved place in the hearts of present-day children.

> *Frank Eyre, in his* British Children's Books in the Twentieth Century *(copyright © 1971 by Frank Eyre), Dutton, 1971, p. 70.*

ABOUT THE SLEEPING BEAUTY (1975)

Although blessed with the fascinating idea of including five other versions of the Sleeping Beauty story in translation . . ., P. L. Travers must have forgotten to invite a fairy godmother to the christening of her own new version. . . .

[Instead] of creating a fresh and vibrant "sub-created world"—without which, Tolkien believed, nothing either meaningful or magical could ever be communicated—P. L.

Travers furnishes us with a gimcrack silk and damask Arabian court setting, inhabited by bright-liveried servants, salaaming Viziers, guests "proffering" gifts, and a "dark slave" named Bouraba who is clumsily forced to act the role of a kind of Jungian shadow or animus figure to the heroine. . . .

But if she has substituted flummery for "attic clutter," and if her depiction of Sleeping Beauty and the Wise Woman in the tower attic is light years away in radiance and intensity from a similar scene in the Victorian visionary George MacDonald's astonishing "The Princess and Curdie," still P. L. Travers is capable of many breathtaking moments. . . .

P. L. Travers's profoundly Sufic and Gurdhieffian interpretation of the tale is fascinating . . ., an interpretation which the author amplifies in her "Afterword". . . .

If this "Afterword" is not quite up to the level of the great essays on fairy tales by Tolkien and C. S. Lewis (or even of the author's own reprinted lecture, "Only Connect"), it is nevertheless filled with extraordinary insights into the nature of the Wise Woman (or Fairy Godmother), the "necessary antagonist" seen as an aspect of the Hindu goddess, Kali, and into the notion of how acts in time can, with the gift of grace, conform to eternal meaning (a notion, although Travers doesn't mention it, that is at the heart of Shakespeare and Milton).

We must be grateful that P. L. Travers has not forgotten that the fairy tale is the primer of the picture-language of the soul in the words of Joseph Campbell. And following her lead we may well see in the character of the princess (called Rose by both Travers and the Grimms)—who sleeps in trance surrounded by briars and hedges—the hermetic rose cross itself, an emblem of the soul, whose nature is revealed in the beautiful and ancient esoteric text that reads "Suffering is the golden cross upon which the rose of the Soul unfolds."

> *Jonathan Cott, in* The New York Times Book Review *(© 1975 by The New York Times Company; reprinted by permission), September 28, 1975, pp. 27-8.*

Well written and thoughtfully analyzed, [*About the Sleeping Beauty*] belongs in libraries which collect folk literature for specialists. It is not, however, a book which will appeal to children, who may find the cannibalism and the sexual overtones of the less familiar variants disturbing.

> *Margaret Maxwell, in* School Library Journal *(reprinted from* School Library Journal, *October, 1975, published by R. R. Bowker Co., a Xerox company; copyright © 1975 by Xerox Corporation), October, 1975, p. 109.*

Instead of bringing out the old tale's patina Travers merely covers it over with redundant words ("the frog unceremoniously . . . turned his back") and interpretations ("in him, all men stood gazing at their hearts' desire—or perhaps their inmost selves"), fine sounding pseudo-archaicisms ("and at length the time of maidens was upon her"), cliches ("she trembled—was it fear or joy?"), coy allusions ("kind hearts are all very fine. But who will give her a coronet?"), tendentious and questionable pronouncements ("Since a

man cannot grieve continually—though the same thing is not true of women" . . . "no baby can resist flattery" . . . "There is no good love without good luck"), analytical clutter ("Light is light because of the dark" . . . "Violet is as necessary to the rainbow as any of the other colours. It is either the beginning or the end, depending how you look at it"), and long, empty discourse on the Wise Women's role in life or the meaning of time. Even her appended essay is repetitive and windy, the few small insights it does purvey buried in self-infatuated blah. As regards style and structure Lillian Smith in *The Unreluctant Years* has written far more tellingly about "The Sleeping Beauty" and as for those "hidden meanings" Travers never approaches the promised "crux"—or confronts the function of the prince, here simply a "mysterious figure" who has no hero's task to perform: "All he has to do is come at the right time." That's all?

> *Kirkus Reviews (copyright © 1975 The Kirkus Service, Inc.), October 15, 1975, p. 1202.*

FRIEND MONKEY (1971)

["Friend Monkey"] has its share of failings. Most of the characters are assigned only one distinguishing trait . . . and soon get tiresome; when Mrs. Linnet complained of overwork with the stock phrase "I have only one pair of hands" for the fourth or fifth time, I had enough of her and her two hands, as I soon had enough of the misfortune-bearing Monkey.

The book's most serious flaw is the writing. Miss Travers is an excellent story teller, and there are pleasant touches of fantasy and whimsy, but her adjectives run to the would-be poetic: some monkeys have "sodden shoulders" and a bird does a "skiey dance." Her metaphors seem strained—"Motionless as a model ship inside a whiskey bottle" occurs on one page; "as motionless as a painted child beside a painted monkey," on another . . . Both, of course, are echoes of Coleridge's as idle as a painted ship upon a painted you-know-what.

> *Susan Sheehan, in* The New York Times Book Review *(© 1971 by The New York Times Company; reprinted by permission), November 7, 1971 (Part 2), pp. 6, 26.*

Despite the activity of the plot (nothing is ever allowed to simmer; something is always boiling over) the incidents [in *Friend Monkey*] are ludicrous without being funny. The borrowings, obviously from Dickens and Hugh Lofting, live uncomfortably with the mystical suggestion that Friend Monkey, who fails to attain the simian grandeur of the gorilla in [L. M. Boston's] *A Stranger at Green Knowe*, is a reincarnation of the helpful monkey lord in the Indian epic *The Ramayana*. The story proffers superficial narrative pleasure for an uncritical reader. What is lacking—of course—is the wonderful deadpan magic of Mary Poppins.

> *Paul Heins, in* The Horn Book Magazine *(copyright © 1972 by The Horn Book, Inc., Boston), February, 1972, pp. 53-4.*

It is disappointing that, though parts of [*Friend Monkey*] are as good as anything [Mrs. Travers] has written, it just does not succeed as a whole. She tries to combine two distinct conceptions of Friend Monkey. He is a Mowgli-like waif abandoned by his tribe in a tropical storm, with the realistic reactions to other animals and to humans one would expect from him as an animal (there is more than a trace of sentimentality here). And he is a mysterious embodiment of a Hindu Lord of the Monkeys with a well-developed racial memory. He has also a third character, linked with the last by the concept of ''abundance'', his well-meaning and invariably excessive or misplaced desire to help. These different attributes never seem to fuse, but disturb the unity of the story.

> The Junior Bookshelf, *October, 1972, p. 338.*

OTHER CITATIONS

Timothy Foote, in Time, *December 27, 1971, p. 61.*

Zena Sutherland, in Bulletin of the Center for Children's Books, *January, 1972, p. 81.*

Gladys Williams, in Books and Bookmen, *May, 1972, p. xii.*

John Fuller, in The Listener, *November 9, 1972, p. 644.*

I GO BY SEA, I GO BY LAND (1964)

[This] book's quality lies in the delicate way Miss Travers has captured the particular outlook of English children seeing America through English eyes; yet all emerges as the universal experiences of any children displaced from any country.

> *Shulamith Oppenheim, in* The New York Times Book Review *(© 1965 by The New York Times Company; reprinted by permission), March 21, 1965, p. 26.*

The style [in *I Go by Sea, I Go by Land*] is gravely quaint, maintained with a high degree of consistency as the narrative of a girl of eleven—the consistency aided by misspellings used with restraint. The story has some humor, some sentiment, and an impartial loyalty to both countries. Much of the book will evoke poignant memories for an adult; much of this the child reader will miss, but as a record of wartime impressions or as a good story the book stands, memories or no.

> *Zena Sutherland, in* Bulletin of the Center for Children's Books *(copyright 1965 by the University of Chicago; all rights reserved), May, 1965, p. 137.*

OTHER CITATIONS

Margaret Sherwood Libby, in Book Week, *April 4, 1965, p. 19.*

MARY POPPINS (1934)

[P. L. Travers] is able to take commonplace events, such as birthday parties and shopping trips and, with a twist of imagination, move each into the world of fantasy. Youngsters enjoy Mary's no-nonsense attitude toward life, and they also identify with Jane and Michael, who occasionally

succumb to bouts of bad temper and disobedience. The zoo incident contains some wise words about man's relations with other animals.

> *John Gillespie and Diana Lembo, in their* Introducing Books: A Guide for the Middle Grades *(copyright © 1970 by Xerox Corp.), Bowker, 1970, p. 258.*

[A] racist nightmare in which Third World people turn—without the slightest provocation—into monsters to punish a white child remains unaltered in the new [1972 paperback] version of *Mary Poppins*. Viewed as the product of a cultural fantasy, as an expression of racist fears of retribution, this scene may make perfect sense; but if this view is accepted or not, it is clearly irresponsible to teach children to identify their fears of punishment with Third World people.

> *Albert V. Schwartz, in* Interracial Books for Children Bulletin *(reprinted by permission of* Interracial Books for Children Bulletin, *1841 Broadway, New York, N.Y. 10023), Vol. 5, No. 3, 1974, p. 5.*

The humour [in *Mary Poppins*] is partly that of paradox—that a mere nursemaid should be so godlike in her powers and attitudes—but mostly comes from a comic and inventive use of magic. Mary Poppins is clearly not a contemporary figure, and her setting—supposedly a hard-up suburban household which nevertheless manages to employ cook, housemaid and gardener as well as Mary Poppins herself—now seems as remote as Samarkand. The American popularity of [this book] may owe something to, and may even propagate, illusions about English domestic life.

> *John Rowe Townsend, in his* Written for Children: An Outline of English-Language Children's Literature *(copyright © 1965, 1974 by John Rowe Townsend; reprinted by permission of J. B. Lippincott Company), revised edition, Lippincott, 1974, pp. 175-76.*

Among the many positive statements with which Mary Poppins educates her charges is 'everybody's got a Fairyland of their own', but hers is exceptional, for it is, simply, the real world turned upside-down, irradiated, enlivened and revolutionized. In spite of her chronic sniff of disapproval, she has a carefully hidden sense of fun, and a sense of justice. She dispenses rewards for virtue as readily as punishments, and in both cases they are unusual and unexpected. . . . She is no vulgar waver of magic wands, even if her parrot-head umbrella seems to have unusual properties. Her inscrutable, conceited face keeps its secrets, though it does break into an occasional smile of pleasure and relax into something like affection when her charges show their need of her. . . .

'Supposing you weren't Mary Poppins, who would you choose to be?' one of the children asks her; 'Mary Poppins' is the instant reply. It is unfortunate that film makers have decided that she should become somebody else—a conventionally pretty, whimsical young woman instead of an ageless personality looking like a Dutch doll, a stereotyped heroine as full of songs and synthetic charm as Mary Poppins is stiff and uncompromising.

Perhaps it is even out of place to suggest that Mary Poppins is an ironical composite of all the most characteristic attributes of that lost species, the old-fashioned Nannie. At least it would be true to say that she shares with the ideal Nannie the capacity for being always right, always having the last word and being, seemingly, immortal.

> *Margery Fisher, in her* Who's Who in Children's Books *(copyright © 1975 by Margery Fisher; reprinted by permission of Holt, Rinehart and Winston), Holt, Rinehart and Winston, 1975, pp. 217-18.*

MARY POPPINS FROM A TO Z (1962)

[This is] a unique series of one-page alphabetical skits. . . . Mary Poppins herself is as unpredictable, dictatorial, puzzling and fascinating as ever—she even delights the children with a Topsy-Turvy Tuesday. These alliterative antics (the form is catching) are funny, imaginative, occasionally poetic, tickling the ear even as they twist the tongue. Although quite young children love such exercises, it would be best to save these until they know the stories to get the full flavor. Mary Shepard's illustrations, while too busy in design to be entirely satisfying, evoke very fond recollections.

> *Ellen Lewis Buell, in* The New York Times Book Review *(© 1962 by The New York Times Company; reprinted by permission), September 30, 1962, p. 28.*

That magical nurse, counselor, and friend of children everywhere, heroine of three other books, is with us once more. This witty alphabet book in twenty-six short episodes uses several words for each letter, and most words are characters from the earlier books. Marvelous nonsense that is great fun.

> *Charlotte Jackson, in* The Atlantic Monthly *(copyright © 1962, by The Atlantic Monthly Company, Boston, Mass.; reprinted with permission), December, 1962, p. 176.*

[This is an] alphabet book in which a page of delightful illustration [by Mary Shepard] is faced by a page of text; each of the latter employs many examples of a letter of the alphabet, capitalizing that letter. For example, "P is for Park. Along the Path the Policeman Paces, a Pillar of the Lar . . . " etc. There is the usual charm of the indomitable Mary Poppins, but the book seems not exactly suited to the usual Travers audience who can read independently, since they may feel themselves above an alphabet book. For the children to whom the book is read aloud, the writing is a bit sophisticated: "If East Winds and Elderly Professors wish to Express Enthusiasm, they are Entitled to do so."

> *Zena Sutherland, in* Bulletin of the Center for Children's Books *(copyright 1962 by the University of Chicago; all rights reserved), December, 1962, p. 66.*

OTHER CITATIONS

Alice Dalgliesh, in Saturday Review, *November 10, 1962, p. 37.*

Margaret Sherwood Libby, in New York Herald Tribune Books, *November 11, 1962 (Part 2), p. 31.*

MARY POPPINS IN THE PARK (1952)

[*Mary Poppins in the Park* contains six] delicious stories about the fabulous Mary Poppins and the Banks family that should make her many young fans rejoice. [It has] all the bounce, verve, and delightful madness of her first two volumes with a new note of tender association in her relationship to the Banks children. . . . Wonderful for reading aloud.

> Virginia Kirkus' Bookshop Service, *October 15, 1952, p. 681.*

If sometimes in these six new stories [Mary Poppins'] unpredictable moods seem a little too predictable, she still has the power to transform the ordinary into something rich and strange.

No one then will be in the least surprised at the extraordinary happenings in a commonplace London park. Some of the devices may be a trifle worn, as when a pair of china figurines come to life, but you can generally trust Mary Poppins to give them a new twist. Traditional fairy tale characters—the prince disguised as a swineherd, the discontented geese—are gently satirized under her sharp inspection; shadows become the real substance of Hallowe'en. When Mary Poppins is about her young charges can never tell where the real world merges into make-believe. Neither can the reader, and that is one of the hallmarks of good fantasy.

> *Ellen Lewis Buell, in* The New York Times Book Review *(© 1952 by The New York Times Company; reprinted by permission), November 16, 1952 (Part 2), p. 36.*

The rejoicing with which children will greet the appearance of this fourth *Mary Poppins* will be followed by their pure satisfaction and refreshed sense of wonder as they reenter her special realms of magic. She is the same efficient nursemaid, respectable, neat and as satisfied as ever—in a new tulip-trimmed hat. And the five Banks children are at the very ages at which they were left in the last volume. Again Mary Poppins looks reasonably on unique fantasies built of dreams and wishes, imaginings and storybook people come to life. . . . [Mary Shepard's] drawings, with their happily careful details, further the book's inimitable spell.

> *Virginia Haviland, in* The Horn Book Magazine *(copyright, 1952, by The Horn Book, Inc., Boston), December, 1952, pp. 406-07.*

OTHER CITATIONS

Anne Carroll Moore, in The Horn Book Magazine, *December, 1952, p. 395.*

*   *   *

TREECE, Henry   1911-1966

An English schoolmaster, poet, critic, editor, and author of historical novels for both adults and children as well as historical nonfiction, short stories, and plays, Henry Treece was noted for his close studies of the Viking and Roman periods in history. (See also *Contemporary Authors*, Vols. 1-4, rev. ed., and *Something About the Author*, Vol. 2.)

GENERAL COMMENTARY

[Henry Treece] can be compared to a writer slightly older

than himself, Alfred Duggan, who, also beginning late, wrote a shelfful of outstanding historical novels which showed rare sympathy with the early centuries of our civilization. Looking to the Norse sagas, to the chronicles which record the asperities of life down to the 11th century, Treece did for children what Duggan had done for adults: he brought his lively imagination to bear on peoples and periods which for most of his readers must have seemed cold and dry; he clothed them in a glowing reality.

Probably he wrote too much. A certain recurrent pattern can be discerned in [his books]. . . . There may well be a boy, or a very young man, much put upon by his elders; there will be beatings and insults, rocky coasts and high seas, the vindication of heroism during long voyages over land and water. The style, too, sometimes becomes turgid, when Treece stays too close to the Viking manner of narration. He greatly admired what he calls the "craft and gusto" of the *Skald*; he responded to the grim humor of these ancient northerners. At his best, he matches these virtues with aplomb, and in his trilogy dealing with Harald Sigurdson—*Viking's Dawn* . . . , *The Road to Miklagard* . . . , and *Viking's Sunset* . . .—he has sustained an unflagging narrative with ease. In the light of such successes he will be forgiven an occasional lapse into Old World jargon. . . .

His years as a schoolmaster left their mark on Treece: he valued accuracy, and he was not above pointing a moral. But, above all, he was a gifted writer, with keen insight into the kind of writing which holds a child's attention. His long line of books for the young are as good as any written in his time, and better than most.

Allan Pryce-Jones, in Book Week *(© The Washington Post), October 30, 1966 (Part 2), pp. 6, 8.*

In one field in particular [Henry Treece] was making himself a master, in his Viking stories. Perhaps his ability to get inside the Viking skin, to produce an utterly convincing extension of the saga tone of voice, is due to his own evident delight in fast, suspenseful, surprising action: and also, surely, to an imaginative sympathy with their way of meeting life.

The picaresque, take-what-comes kind of action arising from the Northmen's voyages of discovery, plunder, or revenge, is almost bound to make a rapid episodic story, and suited Treece. He first uses the voyaging pattern in *Viking's Dawn*. . . . The modern writer for the young is hard put to it to make plunder and treachery part of his story without seeming to extol them. Treece manages this problem well. . . . The [shipwreck] incident is told with the starkness of a ballad and shows how Treece's often overcolourful writing gains in pungency and strength when he willingly submits to the saga style—an objective, allusive economy. (pp. 256-57)

The last tale of Harald, [*Viking's Dawn* and *The Road to Miklagard* were the first two], *Viking's Sunset*, is splendid. . . . Henry Treece has forged and used a pointed weapon of conversation between his Northmen which has a flash and twist and bite peculiar to itself. Inspired by the old sagas, yet individual and more expansive, the flavour of this talk is as recognizable as a favourite wine. Maturing with time, it has perhaps reached perfection in *Swords from*

the North. Irony is its basic ingredient: 'the men of the North were not given to self-pity', as Treece remarks, and the ironical, stoical attitude is part of their very nature. But its shifts and variations are like the glitter of sword-play. It ranges from plain irony—'A man would not know unless he was told . . . ' replies Summerbird of Harald Hardrada's protest that he is a Christian—to the euphemism that brings a shiver: 'And I speak for my brothers, who do not wish to talk . . . ' says a warrior in his death-verse, his brothers being dead. It includes a constant grim or comic use of understatement . . . and a balancing use of gloriously exaggerated bombast. (pp. 259-60)

Treece's great achievement in individual characterization in these tales is [his] re-creation of the Norway giant King Harald Hardrada into so awesome yet lovable a figure: audacious, joyous, poetical, warm-hearted, immensely brave, yet also hard, calculating, savage, and proud. In *The Last of the Vikings,* a haunting and shapely book (perhaps artistically the best of these), the author draws all Harald's young life into the compass of his thoughts on the battlefield of Stamford Bridge, where he is to die. *Swords from the North* tells of Harald as head of the Varangian guard in Byzantium and remains episodic—but what episodes and changes of mood! Scenes of violence, mystery, stark drama, controlled pathos, and wild comedy follow one another with unflagging gusto, related with crisp, ironic invention. (p. 260)

In what appears to be his last story of all, *The Dream-time,* Treece, touchingly enough, has written a lucid poetical fable, set back in the dawn of time, about a 'maker' among warriors. In it there are some statements of simple profundity about the artist among ordinary men. . . .

Treece's other earlier historical stories are ambitious in theme, sometimes uncritically bold in scope, giving an impression of impatience to reach the end. This may be because they have a recurring tendency to compress too much material into too short a book, with a consequent sacrifice of depth to breadth, both in plot and characterization. This is in turn partly due to his fascination with themes from cross-roads in history and the desire to hitch his young heroes on to those historical characters of huge stature who are so often centred there. (p. 262)

"Henry Treece: Lament for a Maker," in T. L. S. 5, Essays and Reviews from The Times Literary Supplement 1966 *(© The Times Publishing Company Ltd. 1966), pp. 128-35 (and reprinted in* Only Connect: Readings on Children's Literature, *edited by Sheila Egoff, G. T. Stubbs, and L. F. Ashley, Oxford University Press, 1969, pp. 256-64).*

Treece's books for children often have an adult counterpart with a fuller emotional treatment of his theme. His work groups itself naturally according to the periods which most strongly roused his imagination—Ancient Greece, Bronze Age and Roman Britain, the centuries of Viking activity. . . . It was not through paucity of material that he chose to use the same subject several times, though a researcher can hardly be blamed if he plays the thrifty housewife with his unused notes. Each time Treece wrote of ancient man, to take one example, he was experimenting with ways of relating the cycle of the seasons to man's birth and his passage towards death. (p. 20)

During the twelve years when Treece was writing for the young he grew gradually bolder and easier in his choice of material for them but he always considered their tastes, capacities and interests. As a teacher he knew how to bring the past to life *actively,* in scenes where period details would seem most natural. The accepted formula of the 1950s by which historical events were arranged round a young hero must have seemed to him congenial and convenient. For his first story [*Legions of the Eagle*], then, he created his typical Belgic boy, Gwydion, and gave him two comrades—a slave and friend Math the Silurian, an enemy turned friend, Gaius, son of a Roman centurion on active service in Britian. This particular grouping of characters allowed the teacher in Treece to range over a wild field of detail—domestic, historical, behavioural. It allowed the story-teller that geographical sweep which is one of the most recognisable points of any Treece novel. . . . It allowed the historical philosopher to develop his thesis about the uselessness of war. . . . Finally, it allowed Treece as a children's writer to enlarge the emotional understanding of his readers in a way that would not puzzle nor upset them; the boys in the story face danger and loss and forge their friendship in a way that belongs to boyhood as much as to history. (pp. 22-3)

Treece's journeys into the past took him most often to what he called the 'crossroads of history', the significant moments when cultures and races met. He was not so naïve, of course, as to think of historical change literally in terms of 'moments', but as a novelist he was prepared to imagine points in time when, as he put it, 'within the great exterior Movements of history, individuals of opposing sides meet and learn from one another, merge and comes to terms'. This broad view of the past corresponded with his apprehension of the basic cycles of nature and man—spring and winter, growth and decay, birth and death. He saw the past in terms of human beings and chose representative men and women who would stand at one of the 'crossroads'. . . . (p. 33)

His historical novels can be defined in two words—journeys and confrontations. The pattern is particularly clear in an early trilogy—*Viking's Dawn* (1955), *The Road to Miklagard* (1957) and *Viking's Sunset* (1960). In these books historical fact, in outline and in detail, supports the fictitious adventures of Harald Sigurdson, a boy of fifteen when he first boards a longship, a warrior of about forty when he dies far from his homeland. (p. 34)

If Treece compels our belief in these three Viking voyages, it is not because of their hero. The three stages of Harald's life are knit together in date but each book seems to be about a different person. There are none of the perceptible changes which would be expected if this were a trilogy depending on character. Harald is a useful link between stories which are, really, about Vikings in their ships. It is the voyaging that matters, whether its motive is a quest for living space, herring shoals, revenge or gold. (p. 35)

The simple code of loyalty demonstrated in Treece's stories is not unlike the equally simple code binding the cowboy of the traditional Western film—a genre which Treece delighted in and hoped one day to try. Robbers, marauders, invaders the Vikings were and Treece does not try to hide this; but he sees also their courage and their group-loyalty and that impulse to explore the unknown which drove them as much as the desire for gain. (pp. 35-6)

Human behaviour in a historical context—this is the way Treece approaches the past. He is at his most confident when he can go off at a tangent from textbook history—as he does in *Hounds of the King* (1955) or *Man with a Sword* (1962). (p. 41)

He had always been fascinated by men who, as it were, demonstrated death through performance—matadors, for instance, or professional boxers—and the Viking with his verbal challenges and his uncontrollable rages was another human animal whose aggressive display might either avert or accelerate conflict. Well aware of the peaceful and constructive aspects of the Norseman's life, Treece was inspired to describe him, rather, as a fighting man, neither glorifying war nor ignoring the virtues it could reveal. It was his purpose to describe the disease, not to offer a remedy for it. . . . There seems to have been a real compulsion in Treece to face both his interest in the mood and technique of war and his hope for peace in the ambiguity of the berserk nature. (p. 47)

After he turned from poetry to prose Treece wrote adult and junior stories concurrently with equal method and drive. His versatility never led him to relax his high standard of writing. He brought the same care to a short story for a seven-year-old as he did to a long mature novel; his search for the best possible style and form was equally determined. His early fiction, for whatever readership, showed the fault of superfluity. He had to learn to discipline his delight in a pictorial past, to select from an overplus of material, to let action speak for itself instead of loading it with explanation. He had always tried to avoid a latinate, polysyllabic style but even so his early books show the indulgence of a man in love with words. (p. 70)

The Golden One and *Man with a Sword* show at its best Treece's more extended, decorated, narrative style. Under the influence of the sagas he came more and more to believe that action should be the basis of his story and he worked to achieve a concise prose (foreshadowed in *Viking's Sunset*) in which every descriptive word, every spoken word should count. When he returned to the fuller type of narrative, as he did in *Swords from the North,* he kept a tight rein on background detail and, above all, on his characters.

It would not be true to call Treece's characters 'types'—in any case the word as we tend to use it now has a derogatory sound; but they are not deeply analysed as individuals. Often they *represent* a stage in the development of a tribal or a movement. So tight is the bond between action and character in Treece's stories that we often have the illusion that people are developing radically when in fact it is their circumstances which are changing. Events drive Hereward towards old age: at the end he is still the same 'man with a sword'. We overhear the thoughts of Runolf, of Hardrada, of Theodora, but as they think aloud they are seen either in motion or in a state of arrested animation. We recognise them by their actions, often by their facial expressions, more often still by their speech.

This speech, however, is not idiosyncratic; it is essentially group-speech. Hero and villain, friend and enemy will use the typical Viking irony and understatement. They will use the colloquialisms, many of them dialectal, with which Treece often indicated the mood of an episode. In seeking words to put into the mouths of Roman centurion, Viking marauder, Norman soldier, which would not destroy the illusion of their existence, Treece ranged from the extremes of ceremonial address to the extremes of brutish utterance. In his first book for the young, Belgic boy and Roman lad talk as if they were extemporising in a History lesson: trial and error brought him to the purposive, racy talk in *Man with a Sword* and the savage shocks and vagaries of the language of communication in his adult novel, *The Green Man*. He struck with confidence the note of unreason, suggesting feigned lunacy in Amleth and emphasising the temporary madness of Hereward by a careful breaking up of syntax and a conscious waywardness of diction. As his characters speak we hear, sometimes, the thoughts they would not, or cannot, express. (pp. 71-3)

Treece wrote about man the aggressor. In his interpretation of the past—the serious interpretation of a good amateur historian—the Romans fought for law and order in a spirit not notably humane; the Vikings fought, often, for the sheer love of fighting. Behind objections to scenes in his stories which he regarded as 'honest blood-letting' lies the more far-reaching criticism that he has no 'message' for children; as one critic commented in regard to his Hereward, 'for young readers a hero must be someone to admire and imitate'. Treece's uncompromising view of the past did not suit, and no doubt never will suit, the view that children's stories must be not only harmless but also actively moral. Moreover, present-day liberal attitudes and concepts of international affairs necessarily raise problems for the historical novelist. . . . Treece . . . wrote in the belief that children were capable of making a sane and intelligent appraisal of scenes of conflict without direct guidance. (p. 79)

If Treece did not insert a 'message' for the young in his stories, he had something to say to them none the less. He knew they could enjoy stories in many ways and on many levels. He chose to *suggest* ideas to them in the emotional content and texture of his books. (p. 81)

In the children's world Henry Treece will live on as a story-teller. The story-teller establishes an identity with his subject and with his audience. Treece wrote (of one of his adult books) that Jason was 'more actual to me than Queen Anne', and again 'I *know* about Jason—in the way that a poet knows about things, because he is part of them.' Children of many ages and abilities enjoy his books because he knew children as well as he knew the people of the past. (p. 84)

> *Margery Fisher, "Henry Treece" (© Margery Fisher 1969), in* Henry Treece, C. S. Lewis and Beatrix Potter, *by Margery Fisher, Roger Lancelyn Green and Marcus Crouch, Bodley Head, 1969, pp. 7-84.*

[Henry Treece] wrote many books but only the best of them achieve any real stature. Too many of them have the air of a professional exercise, and his plots lack subtlety and skill, being, for all their basis on genuine research and true historical understanding, much nearer in their treatment of character and dialogue to the older tradition of historical novel.

> *Frank Eyre, in his* British Children's Books in the Twentieth Century *(copyright © 1971 by Frank Eyre), Dutton, 1971, p. 109.*

Henry Treece is distinguished both for the sonorous quality of his prose and for his ability to create convincingly the mood and language of the distant past. . . .

Like Rosemary Sutcliff, he is so steeped in history that his stories have a remarkable unity: details of dress and architecture, language, and references to other events have a consistency that makes his books convincing and alive.

> *May Hill Arbuthnot and Zena Sutherland, in their* Children and Books *(copyright © 1947, 1957, 1964, 1972 by Scott, Foresman and Co.), 4th edition, Scott, Foresman, 1972, p. 507.*

There seemed always a sense of inadequacy, or at least of holding too much in reserve [in Treece's books]. Perhaps Treece, like other authors who work in the field of adult books, was inhibited by a vision of his young readers and tried, as the finest writers for children do not, to write for them rather than for himself. Certainly the adult novels he was writing at the same time, in which he retold the stories of the Golden Fleece, Electra and Hamlet, are brilliantly successful in just the way that the children's stories are not, in that they show an author clearly in control of his material and giving it the full force of his imagination, intellect and technique. Treece had started his literary career as a poet; in *The Green Man* the reader is aware of this, but *The Last of the Vikings* (1964), which has a subject almost as fundamental, remains obstinately earth-bound.

> *Marcus Crouch, in his* The Nesbit Tradition: The Children's Novel in England 1945-1970 *(© Marcus Crouch, 1972), Ernest Benn, 1972, p. 67.*

THE BURNING OF NJAL (1964)

The events in which Njal and his family were involved cover a period from 930 to 1017, a good span of lives and incidents, and it hardly needs the workmanlike introduction to assist the picture of Icelandic society, customs and laws which the re-telling of Njal's story contains within itself. Of incident there is plenty, but the line of narrative remains clear and clean throughout. Blood and bravery, underlined by savagery mixed with a rigid code of honour, give the reader not only a comprehensive view of the period but provide a good yarn as well.

> The Junior Bookshelf, *July, 1964, p. 181.*

Henry Treece has rendered the story of Burnt Njal with a fidelity to the original which does nothing to spare the reader. Here is a curious situation, of a country in which the most ruthless blood-feuds are pursued within rigid conventions enforces as law. The ultimate absurdity is reached when the murderers of Njal and his family, a particularly brutal gang even by the standards of their day, win the case against the avengers on a technicality. No wonder the hearing broke up in bloody confusion! All this would be intolerable to a modern reader, of any age, were it not for the grim humour and the harsh eloquence which Mr. Treece has echoed so well.

> The Times Literary Supplement *(© The Times Publishing Company Ltd. 1964), July 9, 1964, p. 595.*

This is a retelling of *Njal's Saga,* considered by many to be the finest of the medieval Icelandic sagas.... In spite of the author's acknowledged skill, the book is so filled with repetitious incidents, convoluted plots, and a confusing host of characters that its appeal to younger readers will be limited.

> *John T. Gillespie, in* School Library Journal *(reprinted from* School Library Journal, *January, 1965, published by R. R. Bowker Co., a Xerox company; copyright © 1965 by Xerox Corporation), January, 1965, p. 116.*

OTHER CITATIONS

Zena Sutherland, in Bulletin of the Center for Children's Books, *February, 1965, p. 93.*

The Booklist and Subscription Books Bulletin, *July 1, 1965, p. 1030.*

THE CENTURION (1967)

[Drucus Pollio's] mature reflections and regrets—that he never had a family, that the lion-haired Briton should die—will be a revelation to the child unused to looking into the mind of a middle-aged man. Despite a trite ending in which Drucus Pollio saves the life of the lion-haired youth's brother and takes him as a son, the portrait of a courageous, great-hearted, weary man is affecting, his experiences as a non-combatant often exciting, the backdrop and set authentic. The absence of young characters has a double-edged effect: no one to empathize with, someone to extend sympathy to. This might be the first Treece for the right younger boy.

> *Kirkus Service (copyright © 1967 Virginia Kirkus' Service, Inc.), May 1, 1967, p. 567.*

The plot [of *The Centurion*] is shorter and less complicated than that of other stories by the author, and perhaps therefore the story would appeal to those not yet introduced to his books. This one, however, matches others by Treece in giving a complete feeling for the time and place.

> *Helen B. Crawshaw, in* The Horn Book Magazine *(copyright © 1967, by The Horn Book, Inc., Boston), August, 1967, p. 472.*

OTHER CITATIONS

Zena Sutherland, in Bulletin of the Center for Children's Books, *October, 1967, p. 34.*

Robert Berkvist, in The New York Times Book Review, *October 8, 1967, p. 40.*

The Booklist and Subscription Books Bulletin, *January 15, 1968, p. 596.*

THE DREAM-TIME (1968)

Henry Treece's last story, a strangely haunting fable of early men called *The Dream-Time* ..., is now issued with suitably archetypal, and often very beautiful, drawings by Charles Keeping, together with some evocative symbols drawn by Treece himself, and with an illuminating postscript by Rosemary Sutcliff. This story of a boy who would

rather create than fight, a maker not a breaker, is the kind of dream one would expect from a poet, a lover of history and a lover of man. It is simple in language and thought, and its simplicity seems to reflect that uncomplicated wisdom we sometimes attain between sleep and waking.

> The Times Literary Supplement *(© Times Newspapers Ltd., 1967), November 30, 1967, p. 1139.*

[*The Dream-Time*] is not a straightforward story set in a specific period, but a kind of allegory, in which the hero seems to live through several ages, even changing his name, in the course of his adventures, until, like Pilgrim, he arrives at what appears to be some kind of celestial city. He has a breadth of mind far in advance of the circumscribed language in which he has to express his ideas. Not very subtly he represents a plea for a greater understanding and brotherhood between men, and is more a point-of-view personified than a flesh and blood creature. The author seems to have been moving away from the straight historical novel towards history used merely as a basis for works of greater significance, and it may be conjectured that he would have developed a power and vigour in this field as great as or greater than he had already shown in the other. *The Dream-Time* is interesting as a first essay in this direction, and is well worth-reading, not only by children, who will enjoy it for itself, but by grown-ups, who will see in it a promise that it is sad to know will now never be fulfilled.

> The Junior Bookshelf, *April, 1968, p. 123.*

[The] distinction between savage belligerence and almost dreamy-eyed peaceful strivings is quite clearly drawn [in *The Dream-Time*]. Much will be too contrived for some tastes: e.g. Crookleg, who almost loses a finger as punishment for his drawings, meets up Blackbird who has lost a toe as punishment for her dancing. As interpolation of historical thought, however, it has presence.

> *Kirkus Service (copyright © 1968 The Kirkus Service, Inc.), August 15, 1968, p. 902.*

Without any regard to historical sequence but based on current knowledge of prehistoric cultures, [*The Dream-Time*] story tells of the experiences of Crookleg, later called Twilight.... The simplicity, concreteness, and directness of the storytelling style is excellent; yet, there is an implicit allegorical meaning behind the dreams and intuitions of Twilight: "Spearsticks will save no man. But his dream will if he can only find the courage to hold it when the wolves glare into his eyes."

> *Paul Heins, in* The Horn Book Magazine *(copyright © 1968 by The Horn Book, Inc., Boston), October, 1968, p. 561.*

The Dream-Time (1967) was [Treece's] last book. It was possibly not quite finished, for there are small hints in it of uncompleted revision. It is not entirely successful. It certainly opens a door through which we glimpse a different kind of Treece story, and one infinitely richer, wiser, more fundamentally poetic in concept, than anything which had gone before....

In *The Dream-Time* Treece was extraordinarily successful

in purging his words of modern concepts and colouring. Accepting that his hero, Twilight, has the vision of a genius, he allows no ideas or images of the modern world to creep in. The thoughts of these people are deep and complex, arising from their concern with basic necessities like God and survival and fear, yet the whole story is told with the utmost simplicity, almost entirely in monosyllabic words; this is no artificial literary device but an inevitable response to the demands of the theme.

> *Marcus Crouch, in his* The Nesbit Tradition: The Children's Novel in England 1945-1970 (© *Marcus Crouch 1972), Ernest Benn, 1972, pp. 67, 69.*

Henry Treece's last book, *The Dream-time,* published posthumously in 1967, was praised highly; too highly. It is the story of a Stone Age boy who does not wish to be a warrior; and if one sets it beside a book by a person steeped in knowledge of a primitive community, such as Donald Stuart's *Ilbarana: an Aborigine's Story* (1972), one sees that it does not represent modes of thought and feeling which are possible against such a background. The central character of *The Dream-time* is a man of peace, an artist-for-art's-sake, who wishes that men and women could be equals and speak the same language; and this requires emotional and psychological anachronism. The hero is a representative of modern attitudes planted in a primitive community. Possibly the story should be seen as an extended fable; even so, it does not quite ring true.

> *John Rowe Townsend, in his* Written for Children: An Outline of English-Language Children's Literature *(copyright © 1965, 1974 by John Rowe Townsend; reprinted by permission of J. B. Lippincott Company), revised edition, Lippincott, 1974, p. 222.*

In this spare, concentrated, poetically conceived story, the tribes which Crookleg encounters belong in a wide spread of time, from the late Stone Age to something resembling the Bronze Age. Their diversity emphasizes one of the principles which Crookleg works out for himself; he wishes 'that all people, the men and women and hares and owls and dogs, could agree to speak the same words. . . . Perhaps no one would fight then.' In his journey he discovers his own family pattern, which is not one of custom and blood-relationship but one of love and responsibility, and he finds justification for his compelling creative instinct. Within a magnificently taut, pictorial evocation of ancient worlds Crookleg takes his place as the seeker, who pushes ahead of his fellow men on the evolutionary journey—a journey not only towards better command of human relations and communication but also towards the difficult harnessing of reason and thought. Crookleg is learning to recognize his own personality, his own ideas, and to translate them into the words available to man at the beginning of time.

> *Margery Fisher, in her* Who's Who in Children's Books: A Treasury of the Familiar Characters of Childhood *(copyright © 1975 by Margery Fisher; reprinted by permission of Holt, Rinehart and Winston), Holt, Rinehart and Winston, 1975, p. 75.*

OTHER CITATIONS

Zena Sutherland, in Bulletin of the Center for Children's Books, *October, 1969, p. 53.*

FIGHTING MEN: HOW MEN HAVE FOUGHT THROUGH THE AGES (with Ewart Oakeshott, 1965)

As the authors point out, no matter how great the desire for peace in any age, the arts of war exert a fatal fascination, especially on the male imagination. The seven types of fighting men described here are lost to modern warfare, their functions difficult to imagine. Mr. Treece and Mr. Oakeshott have combined forces to track down and delineate everything that is known about: charioteers, Roman soldiers, Vikings, cavalry, bowmen, pikemen, and musketeers. The book is especially good in describing the fighting skills required by the special weaponry of each major group or period—what it *felt* like to be one of these warriors. Excellent.

> Virginia Kirkus' Service, *August 15, 1965, p. 832.*

[This] book does not describe exactly how troops were employed or [specifically] how they fought . . .; it gives, rather, a general description of important battles and events. The emphasis is on English history. Techniques of warfare through the medieval period in Europe are described, with brief mention of weapons of later periods.

> *Charlotte A. Gallant, in* School Library Journal *(reprinted from* School Library Journal, *February, 1966, published by R. R. Bowker Co., a Xerox company; copyright © 1966 by Xerox Corporation), February, 1966, pp. 87-8.*

THE FURTHER ADVENTURES OF ROBINSON CRUSOE (1958)

As a sequel to [the Defoe work, *The Further Adventures of Robinson Crusoe*] is rather successful: the flavor of the original appears throughout, although the technique is a bit labored. . . . [This is a] good adventure story for those who like action on every page and are able to accept the idea of Crusoe rampant again.

> *Zena Sutherland, in* Bulletin of the Center for Children's Books *(published by the University of Chicago), October, 1958, pp. 38-9.*

[*The Further Adventures of Robinson Crusoe*] is an excursion into outright romance, taking Robinson Crusoe and Friday from a snug Yorkshire estate back to the islands of the New World on a search for pirate gold. Unfortunately, the story is of dubious value, compared to its classic predecessor, for it lacks the imagination and scope of the original, and there is an excessive display of violence. Boys may want to read this sequel for its own sake, simply as a spine-tingling tale replete with treasure-hunting, mutiny, and hairbreadth escapes. Mr. Treece is undeniably an accomplished storyteller, and his prose is as colorful as ever, but this time, with the historical element lacking, his work seems to lack the stature that marks the difference between desirable literature and mere escape fiction.

Marion West Stoer, in The Christian Science Monitor *(reprinted by permission from* The Christian Science Monitor; © *1958 The Christian Science Publishing Society; all rights reserved), November 6, 1958, p. 18P.*

Extreme credibility is the essence of "unabashed Defoe's" masterpiece. We read and re-read it for its truth to human nature, for the circumstantial detail that makes it more real than reality. These considerations did not, however, trouble Henry Treece when he contrived his sequel to *Robinson Crusoe* [published in Great Britain as *The Return of Robinson Crusoe*]. He bestows on Crusoe a long-lost brother, and on Friday a long-lost island kingdom containing buried treasure carelessly left behind by Henry Morgan. It is difficult to see why Mr. Treece did not give this odd *mélange* an independent existence, instead of claiming for it a pedigree which very few tales could live up to. The story is readable enough on its own merits, but cannot withstand the inevitable comparison.

The Times Literary Supplement, *November 21, 1958, p. xix.*

THE GOLDEN ONE (1962)

We all respond with unusual delight to the kind of books we would have loved as children. ["The Golden One"] is such a one for me. The exhilarating sense of partaking in historic events, the exotic setting, the violence and the tenseness of the drama were what I longed for at the age of [twelve], and a little older. Perhaps some young readers of today have similar tastes. Many of them are ardent fans of Mr. Treece, we know, and this is the most convincing and exciting of his tales.

Margaret Sherwood Libby, in New York Herald Tribune Books *(© 1962, New York Herald Tribune, Inc.), May 13, 1962 (Sec. 12), p. 25.*

The complexity of the political situation and the rapid pace of incident upon violent incident are a bit over-powering [in *The Golden One*]. Colorful and dramatic as the story is, it lacks the strength and unity that made the Viking cycle (*Viking's Dawn, The Road to Miklagard,* and *Viking's Sunset*) so impressive.

Zena Sutherland, in Bulletin of the Center for Children's Books *(copyright 1962 by the University of Chicago; all rights reserved), June, 1962, p. 167.*

OTHER CITATIONS

The Times Literary Supplement, *December 1, 1961, p. viii.*

Virginia Kirkus' Service, *April 15, 1962, p. 389.*

HORNED HELMET (1963)

In form and selection of detail [*Horned Helmet*] is no mean achievement, tracing the fortunes of a boy of the north, adopted by a band of roving Vikings, with a rare unity and dramatic sense. Economy of incident and description have for once hardly detracted from the completeness of the sto-ry's general atmosphere and one feels that here is a story conceived as a whole and written out as a fluid narrative into which a reader can interpolate his own ideas of what might be omitted without feeling the author has let him down. Mr. Treece claims to have written the story as far as possible in the style of the ancient sagas from which the background of his own tale is drawn. He has retained the sense of wandering and of men at the mercy of events while trimming off the repetition and digression from which the sagas seem to suffer to the modern mind. Though his tale is of a boy he does not shirk the reality of incidents which were in truth bloodthirsty and ruthless in impact as part and parcel of those times. Consequently the sense of history is as strong as the sense of romance, producing something which is as much an entertainment as a source of information.

The Junior Bookshelf, *October, 1963, pp. 218-19.*

Set at the beginning of the eleventh century, [*Horned Helmet* is] a fast-paced story of an orphaned Icelandic boy who ships with a Viking crew.... The writing style has a virility and a simplicity that are eminently suitable for the historical period and the Viking theme; the story is unusually tight-knit and is completely convincing.

Zena Sutherland, in Bulletin of the Center for Children's Books *(copyright 1964 by the University of Chicago; all rights reserved), January, 1964, p. 86.*

This story is for the reader who is not literate enough or has not the patience to read a detailed story like Treece's fine "The Road to Miklagard" but it is both more exciting and stronger in character and setting. Few young readers will be able to put it down if they read the first few pages where young Beorn, fleeing for his life, finds himself kidnaped or rescued (it is hard to tell which it is at first) by raiding Vikings. His adventures with the marauders include his strange relationship with Stared, a baresark, one of those semi-madmen feared and respected by the other warriors. Over-brutal for some tastes, but convincing.

Margaret Sherwood Libby, in Book Week *(© The Washington Post), February 23, 1964, p. 18.*

OTHER CITATIONS

The Times Literary Supplement, *November 28, 1963, p. 971.*

Elizabeth Hodges, in The New York Times Book Review, *January 19, 1964, p. 20.*

Ethel L. Heins, in The Horn Book Magazine, *April, 1964, p. 185.*

THE INVADERS: THREE STORIES (1972)

This somewhat over-edited book contains three short stories by Henry Treece, one of which has not previously been published. Accompanying them is an illuminating and sympathetic essay by Margery Fisher, outlining Henry Treece's life and work, and placing the stories in the context of his career. Each story is also supplied with an independent introduction, bearing neither Margery Fisher's name, nor anyone else's, the purpose of which is unclear, since it is hardly credible that any reader needs to be told: 'The scene is set near the Welsh border and the town of Vricon (Wroxeter) in Shropshire. The story is told from the Roman point of view' or 'The action of 'The Black Longship' takes place off the coast of Northumberland late in the year', when they have only to turn the page to find the story itself, which sets its scene, and establishes its viewpoint very adequately on its own. Of the three stories two are very good, and one—'The Black Longship'—is magnificent, a small masterpiece, showing Treece's mature powers at their best. Charles Keeping has contributed illustrations which particularly harmonise with Treece's work. Both artists deploy great technical fluency with a burning inner ferocity. 'The Black Longship' was probably Treece's last completed piece of work, and it deserves wider publication than it has so far received.

> *Jill Paton Walsh, in* Children's Book Review *(© 1972 by Five Owls Press Ltd.; all rights reserved), October, 1972, p. 157.*

Dealing with Treece's familiar historical themes of conquerors and conquered, the former never really winning psychological victories over the latter, these three stories are set respectively during the eras of Roman domination over the Celts, Viking raids, and Norman conquest. . . . The last story is the most forceful, but they're all low-key compared with Mr. Treece's full-length books. . . . Margery Fisher's introductions—to the book and to each story —serve to make this almost as much a critique of Treece's work as a collection of his stories. Otherwise it's a thematic rerun.

> Kirkus Reviews *(copyright © 1972 The Kirkus Service, Inc.), November 15, 1972, pp. 1313-14.*

The three stories [in *The Invaders*] belong to different periods of [Henry Treece's] stylistic development, as is explained in Margery Fisher's judicious Introduction. But all of them . . . are representative of the conflicts and accommodations among various peoples in early British history. . . . The stories are no mere period pieces, but realistic narratives of strong men and women aware of being caught in the web of history. . . . The only flaw in the arrangement of the book is the interpolation of introductory material before each story; after an excellent general introduction, the stories should have been allowed to speak for themselves.

> *Paul Heins, in* The Horn Book Magazine *(copyright © 1973 by The Horn Book, Inc., Boston), April, 1973, pp. 143-44.*

THE LAST VIKING (1966)

In *The Last of the Vikings* [published in America as *The Last Viking*] Mr. Henry Treece has chosen his material with brilliance and has used it with great artistry and imaginative freedom. . . .

Mr. Treece achieves the perspective of the saga writers— their scope and fling—in a manageable space, by this presentation. What is more important, he catches their spir-

it. . . . Violent actions smash down almost nonchalantly like following waves, and the pattern in the whole is most subtly and believably underlined with omen and dream and supernatural event. He catches too the objective irony of their tone, their wise hardness about life. . . .

Mr. Treece matches epic deeds with epic language, and has an unfailing ear for convincing dialogue, never too modern, never falsely archaic.

> The Times Literary Supplement *(© The Times Publishing Company Ltd., 1964), November 26, 1964, p. 1073.*

[In "The Last Viking," Harald Hardrada's] adventures are described in all their rude and bloody violence, relieved occasionally by rowdy humor, as in the account of Yuletide feasting at the court of King Jaroslav. . . .

Historically accurate and crowded with bold exploits and rugged characters, this is heady fare for adventure-hungry older boys. Charles Keeping's fierce and shaggy Vikings share honors with the author's turbulent story.

> *Elizabeth Hodges, in* The New York Times Book Review *(© 1966 by The New York Times Company; reprinted by permission), May 8, 1966 (Part 2), p. 14.*

OTHER CITATIONS

The Junior Bookshelf, *October, 1964, p. 238.*

Helen B. Crawshaw, in The Horn Book Magazine, *August, 1966, p. 441.*

Zena Sutherland, in Bulletin of the Center for Children's Books, *September, 1966, p. 20.*

MAN WITH A SWORD (1964)

You need an open mind to enjoy this book, because Mr. Treece's Hereward, although arguably authentic, is far from the romantic and patriotic hero of more conventional interpretations. He is, in fact, like so many of Mr. Treece's heroes, a remarkably unlikable character, and for young readers a hero must be someone to admire and imitate. The defence of the Fens is only one episode in this complicated story which conveys the brutality and anarchy which were brought temporarily to an end by the Conqueror.

Sincerely written, this book seems to be yet another of Mr. Treece's near misses. Although he has the equipment of the scholar and the poet he lacks one vital quality in a writer, the power to evoke sympathy.

> The Junior Bookshelf, *November, 1962, p. 270.*

Hereward, as an embittered old man, is an unlikely hero for young readers; rather, William [the Conqueror] stands as the noble character. Although the plot is complex, the characters are many, and the purpose is vague, Hereward's adventures provide first-rate entertainment. A masculine, robust telling is accentuated with dry, understated humor; constantly changing scenes permit glimpses into several warring kingdoms and give an over-all view of the times. For perceptive readers, there are acute observations on the ways and weaknesses of men and a poetic prose that rings with the haunting voices of a troubled past.

Priscilla L. Moulton, in The Horn Book Magazine *(copyright © 1964, by The Horn Book, Inc., Boston), October, 1964, p. 511.*

The historical details [in *Man with a Sword*] are superbly minute and authoritative, the characters and dialogue are good, and occasional descriptive passages have a fine sweeping grandeur. The weakness of the book is in the plethora of incidents: the intrigues, the battles, the feuds, the dates, the places, and of the many characters.

Zena Sutherland, in Bulletin of the Center for Children's Books *(copyright 1965 by the University of Chicago; all rights reserved), January, 1965, p. 80.*

Henry Treece's picture of Hereward in *Man with a Sword* belongs as obviously to our own time, drawing on new interpretations of the sagas as well as on modern ideas of mental alienation. It is, nonetheless, a splendidly co-ordinated, skilfully constructed study in character, based on the established fact that Hereward was a warrior. Henry Treece sees him not romantically but with historical understanding. Adding to the few available facts a measure of novelist's intuition, he draws the picture of a man of cool courage and sudden furies (the berserk temperament which he depicts so often in his novels) who hired himself out as a swordsman and whose manic state was intensified after he was severely wounded by the Godwins. . . . In the last years of his life, when as a solitary, beleaguered figure in the Ely marshes he seeks William to make terms for his starving men, he seems a far more complex and dignified figure than Kingsley's pathetic automaton [in *Hereward the Wake*], and the description of the 'two old fighting-men', William and Hereward, wearied by the past, 'beating time with their wine-horns and carolling away at a ditty that the rest of the world had forgotten', shows more imagination than Kingsley's stiff, patriotic portrait does. Treece saw Hereward as a man always ready to assert his Englishness against the Normans but as an individual first and foremost, dominated by the ebb and flow of his berserk temperament. Edgar Atheling's words when Hereward finally relinquished his fierce hold on life—'Hereward is the stuff of which the Gods make Kings, when it pleases them'—confirms him in history: Treece's magnificent novel also confirms him as a man.

Margery Fisher, in her Who's Who in Children's Books: A Treasury of the Familiar Characters of Childhood *(copyright © 1975 by Margery Fisher; reprinted by permission of Holt, Rinehart and Winston), Holt, Rinehart and Winston, 1975, pp. 139-40.*

OTHER CITATIONS

The Times Literary Supplement, *November 23, 1962, p. 898.*

The Booklist and Subscription Books Bulletin, *February 1, 1965, p. 530.*

MEN OF THE HILLS (1958)

One of the difficulties facing the historical novelist who attempts to interpret the remote past is that of making accept-

able or even intelligible a society so different from the present. And so often he errs in making the past too familiar. Mr. Henry Treece, in *Men of the Hills*, is not tempted into such error, and he describes his Hunter Folk and Cattle Folk objectively, neither excusing nor concealing the savage strangeness of their behaviour and their codes. . . . It is a brutal story, in which only the hopeful conclusion seems contrived. Its weakness is that none of the characters claims the reader's sympathies, its strength that one reads with interest about people so completely lacking in charm.

The Times Literary Supplement, *May 31, 1957, p. vi.*

The boys' courage and friendship brighten what could have been a bleak and brutal novel. But [Henry Treece] knows how to control a story; he weaves careful research with excitement into his powerful saga. He shows the daily lives of prehistoric people and the clash of cultures, although he may have oversimplified the overlapping of the New Stone and early Bronze Ages. Reconstructing unrecorded times is risky, but Mr. Treece is bold enough to gamble—and both he and the reader win. This is imaginative, well-handled, challenging stuff.

Eric Hood, in The New York Times Book Review *(© 1958 by The New York Times Company; reprinted by permission), March 9, 1958, p. 34.*

The author has created a vividly realistic picture of a prehistoric time [in *Men of the Hills*] and Lalo and Cradoc are well-drawn characters. The book is something more than an exciting adventure story, however, since Lalo and Cradoc are used to indicate the germination of certain views of religion, personal relationships and technological progress which have evolved with the growth of civilization.

Zena Sutherland, in Bulletin of the Center for Children's Books *(published by the University of Chicago), June, 1958, p. 115.*

OTHER CITATIONS

Virginia Kirkus' Service, *January 15, 1958, p. 37.*

PERILOUS PILGRIMAGE (1959)

Henry Treece . . . lends a superbly confident sense of time and events to this poignant portrayal of the Children's Crusade. . . . The betrayal of the children, their imprisonment by the Moslems, the failure of the decisive miracles to occur are told here in a richly emphatic prose, which, despite the author's thesis that this daring undertaking was a misguided failure, sustains a feeling of unique spirituality and grandeur. A fortunate union of poetry, prose and history.

Virginia Kirkus' Service, *March 1, 1959, p. 178.*

[*Perilous Pilgrimage* is the] story of a brother and sister who joined the Children's Crusade led by Stephen of Cloyes. . . . The plot is rather lurid and overdrawn, although the style of writing is good enough to hold the reader's attention. The first part of the book is the more interesting, since it makes the atmosphere of the march of the crusading children truly vivid. Characterization is exaggerated. Not quite as good as the author's usual excellent storytelling and writing style, but a good adventure story.

> *Zena Sutherland, in* Bulletin of the Center for Children's Books *(published by the University of Chicago), April, 1959, pp. 142-43.*

There are many exciting incidents in ["Perilous Pilgrimage"] and the backgrounds, especially that of the Near East, are interesting and unusual. Even so, possibly because the ending is contrived and because Stephen and the piper remain shadowy the book as a whole is episodic and, despite its basis in fact, unconvincing.

> *Lavinia Davis, in* The New York Times Book Review *(© 1959 by The New York Times Company; reprinted by permission), May 3, 1959, p. 32.*

RIDE INTO DANGER (1959)

[This] story of medieval England, straining toward unity, yet alive with diverse factions, maintains the high quality of the [author's] two former books [for young people]. From Henry Treece's portrayal of Edward III's England, a vivid tapestry of chivalric tradition unfolds, made articulate and immediate by his vivid depiction of character, his dramatic handling of plot, and his deft interweaving of fiction with history.

> Virginia Kirkus' Service, *September 15, 1959, p. 703.*

OTHER CITATIONS

Zena Sutherland, in Bulletin of the Center for Children's Books, *December, 1959, p. 69.*

THE ROAD TO MIKLAGARD (1957)

From the first paragraph [of *The Road to Miklagard*] it is evident that the Viking hero will voyage oversea by Ireland and Moorish Spain to Constantinople, and return by way of the Russian rivers. It is a pity that Mr. Treece seems to see nothing wrong in raiding as a way of life, and implicitly advises his readers to go and do likewise. Perhaps he does not realize the labour and hardship inseparable from the Viking cruise, for he brings his longship from Norway to Ireland in five days, and the crew are not conscious of having broken a record.

> The Times Literary Supplement, *November 15, 1957, p. xiv.*

For sheer, exuberant action and narrative pace, this saga-like tale can hardly be topped. The qualities that made up the viking spirit—wanderlust, fatalism, naïveté, and a bent for looting and violence—are superbly conveyed. With its helpful map and evocative drawings, Mr. Treece's story is guaranteed to open new horizons.

> *Howard Boston, in* The New York Times Book Review *(© 1958 by The New York Times Company; reprinted by permission), January 19, 1958, p. 24.*

OTHER CITATIONS

Virginia Kirkus' Service, *September 1, 1957, p. 642.*

Zena Sutherland, in Bulletin of the Center for Children's Books, *April, 1958, p. 87.*

SPLINTERED SWORD (1967)

There is a complete lack of realism about the adventures of Runolf, the Orkney boy who runs away from home to become a Viking in the closing years of the eleventh century; a lack of realism too in the whole swashbuckling rabble with which he is caught up. . . . The characters of Runolf, Nial and Thiolve are well drawn, others less clearly defined. Though the story has pace and action it lacks shape. It tends to be the story of Runolf rather than of the sword, and as such there seems no good reason why it should end where it does; it is only on second thoughts that the reader realizes it is because the sword has been destroyed.

> The Junior Bookshelf, *August, 1965, pp. 225-26.*

[*Splintered Sword*] is set around Scotland and the Hebrides at the time of the Scandinavian invasions during the late Middle Ages. It is not quite satirical in tone, but offers a strong sense of realism about a period often beclouded by legend, and will probably be particularly enjoyed by those who have some familiarity with the historical background.

> Virginia Kirkus' Service *(copyright © 1965 Virginia Kirkus' Service, Inc.), December 1, 1965, p. 1190.*

In *Splintered Sword* [Treece] shifts his gaze from the last of the famous Vikings and directs our eyes through a tattered peephole to the bitter dregs of the Viking way of life, a dream still harrying some men long after it is over. The story of Runolf, an Orkney shepherd, unloved foster-son, murderer and outlaw, is a clear-sighted piece of historical and psychological truth, to set beside the stories of earlier Viking success.

> The Times Literary Supplement *(© The Times Publishing Company Ltd. 1965), December 9, 1965, p. 1146.*

To Treece's credit, things [in "Splintered Sword"] are called by their authentic, curious names (curraghs, shield-bosses, bladder-wrack), which brightly stud a genuinely literary style. To his greater credit, the authentic brutality of the age is not scanted. Indeed, only the pain and danger are impressive, and when this runs thin, the characterizations run thinner. Boys will long for the next bloodletting as ardently as the author advances the dawn of a new civilization. Charles Keeping's illustrations are exuberantly violent, if sometimes irrelevant to the story.

> *Erik Andersenn, in* The New York Times Book Review *(© 1966 by The New York Times Company; reprinted by permission), March 20, 1966, p. 26.*

[*Splintered Sword* is a] well-written tale of the Viking period. . . . In a realistic ending Runolf accepts the fact that the old days of fire and pillage are over and that a warrior must also learn skills and responsibilities. This book follows the fine tradition of the other Treece Viking tales. The narrative has a poetic quality; the nature imagery is especially beautiful. The situations and characters present a fascinating picture of this period of history.

> *Elizabeth M. Guiney, in* School Library Journal *(reprinted from* School Library Journal, *April, 1966, published by R. R. Bowker Co., a Xerox company; copyright © 1966 by Xerox Corporation), April, 1966, pp. 109-10.*

OTHER CITATIONS

Helen B. Crawshaw, in The Horn Book Magazine, *August, 1966, p. 441.*

Zena Sutherland, in Bulletin of the Center for Children's Books, *November, 1966, p. 50.*

SWORDS FROM THE NORTH (1967)

This tale, based on the Heimskringla—misspelled in the introduction—is a wonderful evocation of period, place and people, and covers a surprising variety of episodes without slackening for a moment. The madness of Harald is made acceptable—evidently the "old saga-men" knew how to take this sort of thing in their stride—and the complexity of the Byzantine manoeuvres is made clear. There is continual pleasure in the Scandinavian back-chat of his supporters, and real emotion when his major comrades fall. After reading of Harald's own fall in *Last of the Vikings* it is invigorating to discover him again here, so very much alive, and his whole era brought to life around him, not only Byzantium, Harald's Miklagard, to whom he brings his men as members of the Varangian Guard, but Cyprus, Sicily and Jerusalem—how these Vikings got around, and considering how involved and corrupt the more civilised countries were in their day, how well their stark philosophy served them, and how well Mr. Treece served it *and* them.

> The Junior Bookshelf, *April, 1967, pp. 130-31.*

The final book in the Hardrada Trilogy (*Man With a Sword*, 1964, and *The Last Viking*, 1966), this epic story [retains] the historic realism of the earlier books.... Though parts of the story are brutal and stark, the author has created a superior historical novel for superior readers. The dark drawings by [Charles] Keeping continue with the visual force of his illustrations for the previous books in the trilogy.

> *Patricia Dahl, in* School Library Journal *(reprinted from* School Library Journal, *May, 1967, published by R. R. Bowker Co., a Xerox company; copyright © 1967 by Xerox Corporation), May, 1967, p. 71.*

[In *Swords from the North,* the] suspense is high and the exotic panorama colorful to the point of being gaudy. [Treece] is at his best in portraying the dauntless spirit of the Vikings, their ironical sense of humor and fierce loyalty. Despite occasional lapses when they are made to appear unnecessarily endearing, the proper sense of doom-laden fortitude clings to them.

When we are disappointed it is perhaps because Mr. Treece's approach is too intimate. Heroic and semilegendary characters should be viewed from a slight distance, dispassionately, if we are to be convinced of their grandeur and impressed by the sweep of their actions. Here, the splendid austerity of the saga becomes tainted with the exoticism of romance and the close view reveals details that sometimes seem uncomfortably fabricated. There are a number of impressive scenes and the story deserves top marks for entertainment, but in the end one has the suspicion that this Byzantium is geographically a bit too close to Hollywood.

> *Houston L. Maples, in* Book Week *(© The Washington Post), July 16, 1967, p. 14.*

OTHER CITATIONS

Kirkus Service, *February 15, 1967, p. 213.*

Robert Berkvist, in The New York Times Book Review, *May 21, 1967, p. 30.*

Jane Manthorne, in The Horn Book Magazine, *August, 1967, p. 477.*

Zena Sutherland, in Bulletin of the Center for Children's Books, *January, 1968, p. 86.*

VIKING'S DAWN (1956)

The book's plot is slight, and what there is follows the loose picaresque pattern. The characterizations also are sketchily developed. Yet "Viking's Dawn" has a power and echoing quality which puts it far ahead of most juveniles.... Man's strangely noble restlessness—noble in spite of the greed that is often his most obvious motive—is evoked against a dim and swirling background of stormy seas and primitive Scottish communities.

Norseman, Lapp, and Celt all intermingle in this story of a vanished age, and the reader senses what it was like to live in a world where the strong sword arm was the only form of social security—and the sword arm often was not enough.

> *Chad Walsh, in* The New York Times Book Review *(© 1956 by The New York Times Company; reprinted by permission), November 18, 1956 (Part 2), p. 34.*

OTHER CITATIONS

The Times Literary Supplement, *November 4, 1955, p. iv.*

Virginia Kirkus' Service, *July 15, 1956, p. 480.*

Bulletin of the Center for Children's Books, *December, 1956, pp. 57-8.*

VIKING'S SUNSET (1961)

In *Viking's Sunset* Henry Treece tells a thrilling tale.... But it is very naughty indeed to use the faked Minnesota rune-stone as evidence of Viking penetration into America; that kind of misinformation may lodge for ever in a young mind. In other respects Mr. Treece misinterprets history merely to get his story moving. It is pardonable to antedate the discovery of Iceland, especially after he has called attention to the liberty in his introduction. But he implies that

Eskimoes and Red Indians spoke much the same language, merely because it would hold up his plot if the voyagers had to sit down for the winter to learn another tongue; and his Eskimoes are much too civilized, waging war and brewing an intoxicating drink. But the Vikings are lively enough, especially in conversation. Adventurous boys will enjoy this book, but they must be reminded again and again that the background is false to history.

> The Times Literary Supplement (© *The Times Publishing Company Ltd. 1960), May 20, 1960, p. ix.*

There are here excitement in abundance, a sense of almost constant danger, bits of humor. Most of all there is a brooding sense of doom and the reader senses that however valiantly the warrior may fight, death stalks at his elbow and there will be no return to Norway. . . . The book is stark, in line with nature's pitilessness. The style heightens the mood; it may seem stilted to some young people but in its poetic quality it is reminiscent of the old epics and sagas and it delivers the story with uncommon impact.

> *Chad Walsh, in* The New York Times Book Review *(© 1961 by The New York Times Company; reprinted by permission), May 7, 1961, p. 26.*

OTHER CITATIONS

Virginia Kirkus' Service, *March 15, 1961, p. 265.*

Zena Sutherland, in Bulletin of the Center for Children's Books, *April, 1961, p. 150.*

The Booklist and Subscription Books Bulletin, *June 15, 1961, p. 644.*

Charles R. Dietz, in School Library Journal, *September, 1961, p. 139.*

WAR DOG (1963)

As a story of Bran, the war-dog of the Catuvellauni, [this] book is a pleasant if rather simple story. As an historical novel for children it is as thin as an ice-cream wafer and about as sustaining. Set around and between such events as the defeat of Caratacus at Camulodonum and Vespasian's victory over Mai Dun, one would expect from it a full background of savagery and civilisation in conflict. The upshot is a tame rendering of the battles and a good deal of apparently irrelevant trivia introduced more for novelty than for truth. The action proceeds rather like that of a one-act play whose author is consciously adding one slight twist after another to spin out the suspense. There is something vaguely familiar about it all. Mr. Treece writes well, as always, but it is difficult to feel convinced that the full sympathy of a young reader will be engaged either by the dog or by the Tribune, Marcus Titus, whose allegedly desperate mission behind the British lines fizzles out so soon. Some writers can make the reader feel they live the lives of the animals they picture; Mr. Treece does not, and it is a great pity he has made Bran rather than Marcus, even, the focus [of] his writing on this occasion.

> The Junior Bookshelf, *July, 1962, p. 147.*

Anyone opening a book by Henry Treece is sure of a good

story superbly evoking the past, and generally, though not always, that it will be beautifully written—the adverb is used not loosely but with Mr. Treece's own care for the exact choice of words: he uses style as a precision instrument, and his English is always a pleasure to read. . . .*War Dog* is mercifully without its occasional tendency to dwell on brutality like a dog rolling in nastiness. Battle, grief, wounds and sudden death are all there, but they are treated clearly and quickly and allowed to pass. The plight of the hound, Bran, after the death of his British master is at times almost painfully moving, and from the first he emerges as a character in his own right, without ever being put to the indignity of being made to think or feel as a human. But alas! Nobody else quite succeeds in stepping clear of the printed page. Marcus Titus, the young Roman tribune who becomes Bran's second master, comes nearest to it, but his first master, Gwyn the Golden, scarcely emerges at all, and the other characters form a background of powerful but unfinished sketches. This, perhaps, is because the book is too short. There is no time to develop the characters or get to know them, nor even to introduce somewhere in the early part of the story the sister of Gwyn, who is to step unannounced out of nowhere, only four chapters from the end, to marry the wounded tribune. It is too short also for the very simple reason that one enjoys it and would like more.

> The Times Literary Supplement (© *The Times Publishing Company Ltd. 1962), November 23, 1962, p. 899.*

The historical background [in *War Dog*] is fascinating, the period details are of interest, and the plot is restrained. The book is weakened by the rather sentimental and florid writing, especially in the ascription of human, or near-human thought processes to [the dog] Bran. "In the dog's heart there was a glow of pleasure that he and Bel should be with Gwyn, and the King at this time."

> *Zena Sutherland, in* Bulletin of the Center for Children's Books *(copyright 1963 by the University of Chicago; all rights reserved), September, 1963, pp. 19-20.*

WESTWARD TO VINLAND (1967)

The supernatural (prophecies, destiny, Christian and Pagan gods) shares responsibility for history with men's actions in this fictionalized account of Iceland's founder—Eirik the Red—and his explorer sons, who sail west to Vinland three times. The telling has a legendary quality reminiscent of a famous Greek voyage, and the characterization is appropriately frieze-like. Sometimes it oversteps credibility (a son *literally* dreamed up); generally it's too slow moving, fraught with forewarning and filled with death, for wide enthusiasm.

> Kirkus Service (*copyright © 1967 Virginia Kirkus Service, Inc.), July 1, 1967, p. 748.*

Based on the Icelandic narratives *Eirik's Saga* and *The Greenland Saga* the chronicle of the Viking migration westward to Greenland and the southern coast of New England is the story of a people living in a state of turmoil and transition. . . . Their tragic struggle is embodied in the strongly depicted characters of Eirik, who has killed more than one man; his son Leif the Lucky, a seafaring adventurer and king of his people; and Eirik's daughter Freydis, a fierce barbarous woman, who in her courage and fury suggests Lady Macbeth. The three parts of the story—the settling of Greenland, the discovery of Vinland, and the unsuccessful attempt by Karlsefni to colonize the new land—have been recently retold, but the intermingling of strong individual characterization with Viking customs and beliefs, along with a grim humor, gives this retelling the austere intricacy and richness of ancient Scandinavian jewelry.

> *Paul Heins, in* The Horn Book Magazine *(copyright © 1967, by The Horn Book, Inc., Boston), October, 1967, p. 603.*

OTHER CITATIONS

James Playsted Wood, in Book World, *November 5, 1967 (Part 2), p. 44.*

THE WINDSWEPT CITY: A NOVEL OF THE TROJAN WAR (1968)

Taking a stance between Homer and present-day historians, Mr. Treece posits a Trojan War sparked both by Helen's abduction *and* by trade rivalry, a wooden horse that was a scaling tower surmounted by a horse's head (in mockery of Hector the Horse Tamer).... It's less effective as fiction than as an anti-heroic polemic, only effective for youngsters who know their Homer and can appreciate the transformation.

> Kirkus Service *(copyright © 1967 Virginia Kirkus' Service, Inc.), December 1, 1967, p. 1426.*

Told from the point of view of a Thracian slave boy, the property of Helen, the story of the fall of Troy retains its original power.... In [*The Windswept City*], Cassandra, Priam, Aeneas, and the other characters familiar from the *Iliad* relive their tragic destiny in the immediacy of the slave boy's experiences; the strategem of the wooden horse is given a new, plausible explanation; and the Greeks are seen as commercial rivals of the Trojans as well as seekers of vengeance for Helen.

> *Paul Heins, in* The Horn Book Magazine *(copyright © 1968 by The Horn Book, Inc., Boston), April, 1968, p. 181.*

The minimal value of [*The Windswept City*] is in the main (and most familiar) events of the struggle and the victory of the Greeks. The story is dramatic, the style of writing egregiously contrived. "Then Helen got up and paced around the room awhile, swishing her skirts and frowning." Also, dialogue is often used to give information in a quite artificial fashion: "... if you are so certain that Troy is doomed, why do you not tell your father, King Priam? Why do you not tell your mother, Queen Hecabe, or your great warrior brothers, Hector ..." etc.

> *Zena Sutherland, in* Bulletin of the Center for Children's Books *(copyright 1968 by the University of Chicago; all rights reserved), May, 1968, p. 150.*

*　　*　　*

TUNIS, Edwin   1897-1973

Edwin Tunis, an American author and illustrator, was well

known as a social historian, chiefly for children. (See also *Contemporary Authors*, **Vols. 5-8, rev. ed., and** *Something About the Author*, **Vol. 1.**)

CHIPMUNKS ON THE DOORSTEP (1971)

Though [Tunis'] observations are supported by purposive reading and concur with modern ethology, [his] approach is that of an old-fashioned naturalist: "Obviously, Chippy is a born digger and loves his work," we are told at one point, and at another that "any problem not included in the chipmunk's book of instructions seems to baffle him." Frequent headings such as "teeth," "brains," "swimming," and "drinking" make the book easy to scan, but its tone [invites] more leisurely perusal.

> Kirkus Reviews *(copyright © 1971 The Kirkus Service, Inc.), April 15, 1971, p. 441.*

Writing from day-to-day observation and from careful research Tunis describes the physical characteristics and the habits and behavior of chipmunks, covering every aspect of their lives. The affectionate, informal close-up, illustrated with charming colored drawings throughout, gives evidence of the pleasures and rewards of firsthand nature observation and offers reading enjoyment to anyone, young or old, interested in chipmunks.

> The Booklist *(reprinted by permission of the American Library Association; copyright 1971 by the American Library Association), July 15, 1971, p. 956.*

[*Chipmunks on the Doorstep* is a] book of special distinction in itself as well as for the nature-lover. No casual study of an animal species, it is the result of intensely devoted observation and research.... The profusion of [Edwin Tunis'] small full-color drawings, supporting [his] statement that it is the chipmunk's personality that recommends him, provide clear biological information about Chippy's gaits, tracks, cheek pouches, and eating, drinking, and mating habits. No detail has seemed too small or unimportant.

> *Virginia Haviland, in* The Horn Book Magazine *(copyright © 1971 by The Horn Book, Inc., Boston), August, 1971, p. 398.*

[*Chipmunks on the Doorstep* is a] delightful, complete portrait of one of nature's most endearing creatures. The author's direct observations, backed by his research, are the basis for this study of the *modus operandi* of the eastern chipmunk. His personal, journal-like treatment of the subject is slightly reminiscent of Glen Rounds's *Beaver Business*.... The information is presented in many short chapters, each about one specific aspect [of chipmunks] ("Grooming," "Attitudes," "Vocalizing," "Life Span and Death," etc.) and each accompanied by several captivating though precise spot drawings in browns and greens.

> *Ann D. Schweibish, in* School Library Journal *(reprinted from* School Library Journal, *September, 1971, published by R. R. Bowker Co., a Xerox company; copyright © 1971 by Xerox Corporation), September, 1971, p. 168.*

Tunis has made his chipmunks homey. We see them as he sees them: in the yard, responsive to his motions, individual, each with a pet name. He helps us to see as well as he does, deeply and carefully. The chipmunks are sunnily drawn from life in all kinds of action and in subtle and convincing color: among rocks and acorns, in battle with chipmunk neighbors, rushing a robin. A few pages on how to tame a chipmunk are entertaining and plausible; they stand as a sign of the rapport the author has achieved.

> *Philip and Phylis Morrison, in* Scientific American *(copyright © 1971 by Scientific American, Inc.; all rights reserved), December, 1971, p. 108.*

OTHER CITATIONS

Paul Showers, in The New York Times Book Review, *May 16, 1971, p. 8.*

Publishers' Weekly, *June 21, 1971, p. 71.*

COLONIAL CRAFTSMEN AND THE BEGINNINGS OF AMERICAN INDUSTRY (1965)

[This is an] oversize book that is impressively handsome and that should be tremendously useful; well-organized and superbly illustrated, the text is comprehensive, lucid, and detailed. The book is divided into six sections: a general appraisal of crafts and industries in the New World, country work, town shops, bespoke work (specially ordered), group work, and manufactories. An extensive index is appended.

> *Zena Sutherland, in* Bulletin of the Center for Children's Books *(copyright 1965 by the University of Chicago; all rights reserved), May, 1965, p. 138.*

High-schoolers will have trouble getting this book away from their parents. . . . Drawings and text are exceptionally good and constant conversation pieces. The patience, ingenuity, and pride that went into early American tools and products are matched only by Edwin Tunis's research and accurate descriptions.

> The Christian Science Monitor *(reprinted by permission from* The Christian Science Monitor; *© 1965 The Christian Science Publishing Society; all rights reserved), September 16, 1965, p. 7.*

OTHER CITATIONS

Alice Dalgliesh, in Saturday Review, *April 24, 1965, p. 45.*

Margaret Sherwood Libby, in Book Week, *May 9, 1965 (Part 2), p. 6.*

The Booklist and Subscription Books Bulletin, *May 15, 1965, p. 916.*

Elnora M. Portteus, in School Library Journal, *May, 1966, p. 120.*

COLONIAL LIVING (1957)

In [a] lively text complemented with over 230 clearly detailed pen drawings, [Edwin Tunis] depicts everyday life in seventeenth- and eighteenth-century America. Organizing a

wealth of material geographically as well as chronologically, he describes the people who settled the 13 colonies—their houses and furniture, occupations, crafts, tools, food, clothing, and social customs. [This is a] simple but informative and enjoyable book for browsing and an authentic reference source.

> The Booklist and Subscription Books Bulletin *(reprinted by permission of the American Library Association; copyright 1957 by the American Library Association), October 15, 1957, p. 104.*

[*Colonial Living* is immediately] absorbing and perhaps the most widely useful of this author-artist's four excellent illustrated histories. Over 200 pen drawings, well set on large double-column pages, catch the eye with their liveliness and meticulous detail. With their precise captions they add a vast amount of information to that in the text—about house construction, food preparation, clothing, lighting devices, spinning, weaving, etc.—for New England, New Netherland, and the Southern Colonies during the seventeenth century, and Pennsylvania and the Coastal Colonies in the eighteenth. The mechanical gadgets and craft processes will intrigue many; costume names and details, information about churches, schools, and "diversions" will answer frequent questions.

> *Virginia Haviland, in* The Horn Book Magazine *(copyright, 1957, by the Horn Book, Inc., Boston), December, 1957, p. 497.*

Mr. Tunis delights the curious-minded in his "Colonial Living." In this big, generously illustrated volume, . . . he tells us how the American colonists lived: of the furniture they used, the houses they built, the clothes they wore, the crops they planted—and also why. Not every one will want to know exactly how wool was turned into clothing—Mr. Tunis is very thorough here—but it does make a woolen cape seem like a real achievement.

Here is recreated the pattern of everyday living so that we come to a closer understanding of these doughty people, the tasks they performed and their pleasures, too.

> *Ellen Lewis Buell, in* The New York Times Book Review *(© 1958 by The New York Times Company; reprinted by permission), January 19, 1958, p. 24.*

OTHER CITATIONS

Learned T. Bulman, in School Library Journal, *October, 1957, p. 151.*

Zena Sutherland, in Bulletin of the Center for Children's Books, *May, 1958, p. 103.*

FRONTIER LIVING (1961)

The careful research and comprehensive treatment of the subject, the handsome illustrations and maps, and the extensive index that notes page numbers of the illustrations indicate that [*Frontier Living*] can be used as reference material. It is well-organized, and the combination of romantic historical material and straightforward style is judicious. While the vocabulary will be beyond some fifth grade readers, the subject interest and organization of material makes the book useful at that level for ready reference.

> *Zena Sutherland, in* Bulletin of the Center for Children's Books *(copyright 1961 by the University of Chicago; all rights reserved), December, 1961, p. 67.*

[*Frontier Living* is another] brilliant achievement, a companion to *Colonial Living*, in bringing history to life through lively commentary and abundant meticulous illustration of daily work, amusement, religion, and government. For the long line of frontiers stretching away from the seacoast—from the Piedmont, over the Appalachians, to the Mississippi and the prairies, and on to the Far West—Mr. Tunis conveys the spirit as well as the physical details of living in untamed areas, the ingenuity, hard work, and courage of those who built there.

> *Virginia Haviland, in* The Horn Book Magazine *(copyright, 1962, by The Horn Book, Inc., Boston), February, 1962, p. 63.*

Frontier Living . . . is a valuable and substantial account of daily life on the edge of the American wilderness as it gradually receded toward California. This book is not only full of uncommon information; it is surprisingly candid. Unlike most books in its category, it neither patronizes nor sentimentalizes the Indians, whose side it takes against the whites where it is necessary to do so. The Kentucky settlers are described as drunken and brutal, while it is revealed that the towns farther west were often bothered by gamblers and prostitutes. The directors of the Union Pacific and Central Pacific are described as thieves and exploiters who co-operated with the California legislature to rob the public, while the United States senate is shown to have been frequently faithless in its treaties with the Indians. In its attention to detail and the cleanliness of its style, *Frontier Living* is a considerable achievement—one of those books that are likely to inspire strong feelings of social justice and patriotism in certain young readers by providing them not only with a sense of their uniqueness but with a link to the common welfare.

> *Jason Epstein, in* Commentary *(reprinted by permission; copyright © 1963 by the American Jewish Committee), February, 1963, pp. 120-21.*

The immense amount of detail produced in *Frontier Living* (1961) reflects painstaking research; the text contains little conjecture, but only fact upon fact about all aspects of frontier living. . . .

The black and white line drawings are of uniform excellence and accuracy, whether of a panoramic view of moving half of a canal boat over a mountain, or detailing the intricate works of a small arsenal of early western arms. The author's captions are revealing, too, and often humorous. Of the illustrations of the Bowie Knife, he wrote: "The mild and quiet Colonel Bowie didn't design this toadsticker; he gave it his name by way of the mayhem he did with it."

> *May Hill Arbuthnot and Zena Sutherland, in their* Children and Books *(copyright © 1947, 1957, 1964, 1972 by Scott, Foresman*

and Co.), 4th edition, Scott, Foresman, 1972, p. 611.

OTHER CITATIONS

Margaret Sherwood Libby, in New York Herald Tribune Books, *November 12, 1961 (Sec. 12), p. 24.*

Laura E. Cathon, in School Library Journal, *December, 1961, p. 46.*

The Booklist and Subscription Books Bulletin, *December 15, 1961, p. 260.*

INDIANS (1959)

A highly attractive and comprehensive study of American Indian life in the period pre-dating the arrival of the European settlers, this book is liberally illustrated in black and white by the author. The various tribes of Indians are indicated, their economic and athletic activities described, and generous examples of their crafts are analyzed. Edwin Tunis writes knowingly both of the material and cultural aspects of American Indian life in this informative and respectful book.

> Virginia Kirkus' Service, *March 15, 1959, p. 355.*

[In *Indians*] Mr. Tunis gives a detailed, careful treatment of material culture; when he leaves that for non-material matters, he runs into trouble. His opening section on religion, for instance, is bad; he writes as if there were a single "Indian religion," and that religion, as he describes it, is in fact non-existent.

In treating so great a subject in so short a space, one is forced into dangerous generalizations. On the whole, the author has handled them well, but some go pretty far astray. Taking one tribe as the type for a whole area leads to some misrepresentations. For instance, the Hopis, here used to typify the Southwest, differ greatly from the Eastern Pueblos and the Pueblos as a whole are quite unlike the Navahos, Apaches, Pimans and Yumans of the area. Some slight references to these differences should have been included.

The book is jam-packed with factual information (which may be why the writing seems pedestrian) and the explanations are always clear. . . . I can imagine curious-minded youngsters poring over this book with pleasure. The text is well supported by the author's numerous, clear, detailed illustrations.

> *Oliver La Farge, in* The New York Times Book Review *(© 1959 by The New York Times Company; reprinted by permission), July 12, 1959, p. 20.*

[This is a] beautiful and useful book. Comprehensive recording, lively writing style and profuse, accurate illustrations combine to serve as a reference source as well as an immensely readable history of the Indian groups of the United States. . . . Individual tribes are referred to when there is special reason, and information about them is available through the extensive index. Illustrations are listed in full, and all of the listed illustrations are informatively captioned. The handsome format is an additional attraction.

Zena Sutherland, in Bulletin of the Center for Children's Books *(published by the University of Chicago), September, 1959, pp. 22-3.*

SHAW'S FORTUNE: THE PICTURE STORY OF A COLONIAL PLANTATION (1966)

With his usual eye for interesting detail, Edwin Tunis has created a vivid panorama of life on a particular Virginia plantation in 1620, 1650 and 1752. In a small scope he answers multitudinous questions of what—tools, furnishings, dress; of how—planting, weaving, learning; and of why—economic and social background. Regarding the latter, he is careful to point out that the slaves were not content with their status. All librarians will want to take their children on this leisurely, lucid guided tour.

> Virginia Kirkus' Service *(copyright © 1966 Virginia Kirkus' Service, Inc.), September 1, 1966, p. 905.*

In his account of the Shaw family and their world Tunis uses the present tense and occasional dialog to give the effect of a narrative to the essentially factual, short-sentence text. As in his excellent pictorial histories for older readers the many handsome drawings, shown to advantage in the wide picture-book format, are meticulously researched and finely detailed.

> The Booklist and Subscription Books Bulletin *(reprinted by permission of the American Library Association; copyright 1966 by the American Library Association), December 15, 1966, p. 454.*

OTHER CITATIONS

George F. Scheer, in The New York Times Book Review, *November 20, 1966, p. 55.*

Virginia Haviland, in The Horn Book Magazine, *December, 1966, p. 718.*

The Best in Children's Books: The University of Chicago Guide to Children's Literature 1966-1972, *edited by Zena Sutherland, University of Chicago Press, 1973, p. 406.*

THE TAVERN AT THE FERRY (1973)

In [*The Tavern at the Ferry*] Tunis handles the site of Washington's crossing with the same loving precision and inspired authority that distinguished his previous beautifully produced and illustrated recreations of early American life. . . . Tunis recalls the textures of domestic and public life in fascinating detail . . .; in his background digressions (the course of the Revolutionary War up to the crossing is summarized at some length) historical byways are explored in the same spirit. . . . Tunis' pencil and wash drawings are handsome and meticulously faithful as always, and his chapter-heading tavern signs (the names all authentic, the symbols original) are a typically felicitous extra.

> Kirkus Reviews *(copyright © 1973 The Kirkus Service, Inc.), September 1, 1973, p. 978.*

Painstaking research into [the tavern's] origins and development yield a socio-historical account that first introduces the Bakers and then expands in time and scope to include their descendents, neighboring enterprises, and finally the intrigue surrounding Washington's Revolutionary War attack on nearby Trenton. Meticulous pen-and-wash drawings and occasional inserts of frontier dialect somewhat relieve the plethora of detail describing daily life and major events over those years. [*The Tavern at the Ferry* is a] precise reconstruction of frontier and Colonial history for the dedicated juvenile historian.

> The Booklist *(reprinted by permission of the American Library Association; copyright 1973 by the American Library Association), November 15, 1973, p. 343.*

Tracing the development of the taverns and ferry-crossings along the Pennsylvania and New Jersey sides of the Delaware River, [Edwin Tunis] perforce traces the growth of transportation, of commerce, and—finally—of rebellion in the colonies. By focusing on a few families in one particular part of the country, he gives the reader a sense of a much larger drama: the evolution of the early settlers of this country into Americans. . . . [*The Tavern at the Ferry*] is handsome, a companion volume in format to *The Young United States;* and, as in all Tunis' books, the text is copiously illustrated with softly shaped pencil drawings.

> *Sidney D. Long, in* The Horn Book Magazine *(copyright © 1973 by The Horn Book, Inc., Boston), December, 1973, pp. 601-02.*

As all Tunis books are, [*The Tavern at the Ferry*] is profusely illustrated with pictures that give, in their meticulous detail, authoritative information about clothing, buildings, weapons, vehicles, and other artifacts of the period. And they are handsome. . . . The pace is stately through most of the book, but excitement is added in the final pages, in which the events preceding the Battle of Trenton, and the battle itself are described. Useful for social studies, fascinating for the history buff or the reader interested in Americana, well organized and written, this is a handsome book with minor reference use.

> *Zena Sutherland, in* Bulletin of the Center for Children's Books *(© 1973 by the University of Chicago; all rights reserved), October, 1973, p. 35.*

OTHER CITATIONS

Publishers' Weekly, *October 8, 1973, p. 96.*

George Gleason, in School Library Journal, *December, 1973, p. 57.*

Scott O'Dell, in The New York Times Book Review, *February 17, 1974, p. 10.*

WHEELS: A PICTORIAL HISTORY (1955)

[This] pictured history of wheels takes its place at the top of the list that youngsters call "browsing books." It is not to be read straight through at one time or even at several sittings. Rather it is a book to dip into, to go back to again and again. . . .

Although the text is for the teen-aged and older readers, the book appeals to any age, for as one young man of 6 said of the drawings, ''They are little stories themselves.'' A diverting and dramatic presentation of a complex subject.

> *Iris Vinton, in* The New York Times Book Review (© *1955 by The New York Times Company; reprinted by permission), August 21, 1955, p. 24.*

[This is a] readable, beautifully illustrated history of the use of wheels in transportation. The book is more a history of transportation than a history of wheels, since no mention is made of the use of wheels in industry. There is an emphasis throughout on private vehicles, with infrequent references to public conveyances of earlier days, and nothing about trains and airplanes of modern time. As a history of the development of carriages, wagons, and automobiles, the text is satisfactory, and the excellent pictures would give the book value even without the text.

> Bulletin of the Center for Children's Books *(published by the University of Chicago), April, 1956, p. 88.*

OTHER CITATIONS

Virginia Kirkus' Service, *May 15, 1955, p. 330.*

Jennie D. Lindquist, in The Horn Book Magazine, *August, 1955, p. 274.*

THE YOUNG UNITED STATES: 1783 TO 1830 (1969)

No one is better at portraying the daily life and artifacts of our 18th-century and 19th-century forebears than Mr. Tunis. . . . The tools, homes, household articles and clothing of early settlers, frontiersmen, villagers and town dwellers are knowledgeably and clearly shown. The author gives almost encyclopedic coverage of broad areas of history and culture; indeed he includes so much that some oversimplification inevitably results. And although he is obviously enamoured of the achievements and virtues of our ancestors, he does not always avoid 20th-century assumptions and predilections. Yet, over-all, here is a readable, useful—and very handsome—account of our nation's early years.

> *Nash K. Burger, in* The New York Times Book Review (© *1969 by The New York Times Company; reprinted by permission), November 30, 1969, p. 42.*

The success of the text [of *The Young United States, 1783 to 1830*] lies in [Edwin Tunis'] ability to share his knowledge with the reader through prose that is never pedantic, but marked by dry wit and a gift for characterization. . . . Naturally, whenever the author-artist wants to illustrate a point—he does. And the illustrations reflect the exuberance and energy of the time as well as the attention to detail which distinguished *Shaw's Fortune* and *Frontier Living.* The book is a unique example of nonfiction that is, at the same time, an imaginative and intensely personal artistic creation.

> *Sidney D. Long, in* The Horn Book Magazine *(copyright © 1970 by The Horn Book, Inc., Boston), April, 1970, p. 151.*

OTHER CITATIONS

Zena Sutherland, in Bulletin of the Center for Children's Books, *December, 1969, p. 68.*

The Booklist, *February 1, 1970, p. 667.*

W

WALSH, Jill Paton   1939-

Formerly a teacher, Jill Paton Walsh is an English author. (See also *Contemporary Authors*, Vols. 37-40, and *Something About the Author*, Vol. 4.)

THE DOLPHIN CROSSING (1967)

[*The Dolphin Crossing* is a] story set in England in 1940, in which two adolescent boys participate in the evacuation from the beaches of Dunkirk. . . . The contrast between these boys of such different backgrounds is sharply drawn, and the characterization and dialogue are good; the picture of wartime Britain is vivid. There is a slow building toward the drama of Dunkirk that makes the contribution of such boys believable, since it makes clear the quiet courage of British citizens.

> *Zena Sutherland, in* Bulletin of the Center for Children's Books *(copyright 1968 by The University of Chicago; all rights reserved), January, 1968, p. 87.*

In a well-told story that opens in an English coastal town during [the] fateful spring [of 1940], two boys from incongruously different backgrounds are brought together by the circumstances of war. . . . [More] than anything else, the story emphasizes, as any good war story must, that transcending patriotism, courage, and idealism, is the realization of the uselessness and the ultimate waste of war. Separated in both time *and* space from this historic episode, young American readers might well be even more interested in the book than their British contemporaries.

> *Ethel L. Heins, in* The Horn Book Magazine *(copyright © 1968 by The Horn Book, Inc., Boston), February, 1968, p. 72.*

The unwavering heroism of British civilians during "their finest hour" is sensitively portrayed [in *The Dolphin Crossing*] as are the personal relationships of the main characters, and the suspense and danger of the Channel crossing and rescue operation are vividly conveyed.

> The Booklist and Subscription Books Bulletin *(reprinted by permission of the American Library Association; copyright 1968 by the American Library Association), March 15, 1968, p. 872.*

OTHER CITATIONS

Marian Herr Scott, in School Library Journal, *December, 1967, p. 87.*

THE EMPEROR'S WINDING SHEET (1974)

Ms. Walsh brilliantly projects the dying splendor of Constantinople and the agony of its fall [in *The Emperor's Winding Sheet*]. . . . Walsh's ability to make the inevitable so exciting and the remote so vivid is impressive, and her prose becomes her subject like a technicolor film so consistently sumptuous that almost any moment might be selected as a still to represent the whole.

> Kirkus Reviews *(copyright © 1974 The Kirkus Service, Inc.), May 1, 1974, pp. 490-91.*

In 1453 Byzantium fell finally to the Turks, and a pair of purple shoes alone distinguished the Emperor Constantine's corpse amongst the pile of dead beneath the broken walls of the city. By a slim device of dropping an English boy at the foot of the Emperor, Mrs. Walsh sets out to share with a youthful reader her own fascination with the death throes of the Roman Empire in the East. Even if Piers Barber, a lad from Bristol, is adopted as the Emperor's stoicheon, the talisman whose continued presence by the side of his master ensures his safety and that of the city, the real hero, as it was for Yeats, is the city itself and its magical king with whom its very existence is identified.

In a sense this is almost too good a book for children. Both theme and presentation will yield to adult sensitivity. It is all so long ago and the framework of values with its eunuchs and theological disputes makes it a difficult world for a television-conditioned child to enter with any sort of understanding. The style is scholarly but direct and dramatically visual.

> The Junior Bookshelf, *June, 1974, p. 173.*

Entwining the fate of the Eastern Roman Empire with the personal adventures of an English boy who had sailed away from far-off Bristol, [Jill Paton Walsh] conveys a powerful sense of the possible interplay between tragic history and private experience. . . . The richly detailed narrative captures the physical as well as the cultural ambience of [Constantinople]. . . . A wide historical canvas accommodates both ceremonial and military scenes that are panoramic and powerfully moving at the same time. . . . [This is for] the unusual reader who is a lover of history.

> *Paul Heins, in* The Horn Book Magazine *(copyright © 1974 by The Horn Book, Inc., Boston), June, 1974, p. 289.*

With the sprawling richness of Herodotus yet styled with the discipline of the *Annals* of Tacitus comes *The Emperor's Winding Sheet*, a tale of the death of a city. . . . As with *The Dolphin Crossing*, war is used dramatically; it is a place full of real terrors, and not tied down with wishy-washy abstractions about courage and endurance. It is also something which is not allowed to constrict the hero into a convenient lens. . . . A period has been brought to life in this book, and yet by paradox, like Gustave Flaubert's *Hérodias* with its continuous use of *mot juste* which only succeeds to emphasise the otherness of that far-distant time of Herod Antipas. *The Emperor's Winding Sheet* is too richly-textured to be a story. It is a series of annals with a research interest that will conduct an interested young reader through facts—and more than a few demanding emotions.

> *C. S. Hannabuss, in* Children's Book Review *(© 1974 Five Owls Press Ltd.; all rights reserved), Summer, 1974, p. 71.*

[*The Emperor's Winding Sheet*] gives a detailed account of the religious and political complications that faced Constantine and a vivid picture of the inexorable progress of Turkish conquest, but it is weakened by the use of conversation to give background information, and—to a lesser extent—by an occasional use of a word that seems obtrusively anachronistic.

> *Zena Sutherland, in* Bulletin of the Center for Children's Books *(© 1974 by the University of Chicago; all rights reserved), September, 1974, p. 19.*

OTHER CITATIONS

Diane I. Weber, in School Library Journal, *April, 1974, p. 72.*

Publishers' Weekly, *May 6, 1974, p. 68.*

Elizabeth Hall, in Psychology Today, *October, 1974, p. 144.*

FIREWEED (1970)

[*Fireweed*] is moving and sensitive in its foreground relationship, a 'brief encounter' friendship between two adolescents during the London blitz, and vivid in background detail. It also suggests a valid connection between them through the fireweed of the title, a plant growing only out of the scars of ruin and pain, whether caused by bombs or people. Yet there is some cheating, also, for the opting-out situation which brings and holds the boy and girl together, alone against hostile authority, is essentially expressive of modern, not wartime attitudes. This makes for strong emotional validity for young readers, which is important, but at

a cost. For the emotional truth is isolated from the outside world, there is much skating over of class divisions, in the author's mind, as much as in the details of the story, which amounts to a kind of pretence. So although one has a rare sense of the boy's fluctuation and growing complexity of feeling, he seems strangly unrooted, to me, in the London he is supposed to have lived in always.

> *Marie Peel, in* Books and Bookmen *(© copyright Marie Peel), February, 1970, p. 36.*

The call to class [in *Fireweed*] is un-American but not untranslatable (into more subtle cultural pressures), and the bond between Bill and Julie, *their* finest hour, irradiates the scene: "The oddest thing was that the leaves turned gold and fell off while Hitler's bombers filled the sky." He is fifteen, she is somewhat younger, and theirs is a romance their counterparts can credit.

> *Kirkus Reviews (copyright © 1970 The Kirkus Service, Inc.), March 15, 1970, p. 331.*

[*Fireweed*] is tender, moving, painfully real. The values presented arise from the boy's and girl's sacrifices for each other and from the warmth and kindliness of the adults who befriend them; superbly captured are the familiar or humorous little things that endure even in the midst of horror. Young people always revel in stories of self-preservation by their contemporaries, and they will thoroughly enjoy this superior work.

> *Loretta B. Jones, in* School Library Journal *(reprinted from* School Library Journal, *May, 1970, published by R. R. Bowker Co., a Xerox company; copyright © 1970 by Xerox Corporation), May, 1970, p. 87.*

Jill Paton Walsh has a talent for buttonholing which the ancient mariner would have envied, and her book *Fireweed* . . . justifies, at least for once, all those adult readers who turn for their reading to the children's shelf and insist that they find good well-plotted novels there.

In one sense it is the old desert island story Mrs. Paton Walsh is telling. Her two young teen-agers are struggling to survive in wartime London. Both have "escaped" evacuation, and live an existence threatened by the blitz and by "interfering adults." . . .

And all the time she is keeping the story going, Mrs. Paton Walsh is using her remarkable facility with minor characters and small significant events to sweep us up into the London of the 1940's. But, though she does not glamorize war, she does not rub our noses in its horror either.

In a sense this is almost a love story—but not quite. Her Bill and Julie are too unselfconscious to be really in love until the very end of the story. And when the realization comes it is too late, for the book closes on a note of sadness —tragic sadness, not depressing sadness.

> *Pamela Marsh, in* The Christian Science Monitor *(reprinted by permission from* The Christian Science Monitor; *© 1970 The Christian Science Publishing Society; all rights reserved), May 7, 1970, p. B6.*

[The] ending [of *Fireweed*] is as poignant, as bitter, and as inevitable as a classic tragedy. The setting is at once theatrical and realistic, the theme touching, the plot simple and effective. Moreover, the writing has an effortless, colloquial flow.

> *Zena Sutherland, in* Saturday Review *(copyright © 1970 by Saturday Review, Inc.; reprinted with permission), May 9, 1970, p. 69.*

Some of the adult characterizations [in *Fireweed*], especially Julie's mother, are never satisfactorily realized or explained. But more important is the fact that the war, no mere background, is part and parcel of the story; and [Jill Paton Walsh] uses historical detail selectively and imaginatively. Throughout most of the book she lets her narrator describe with almost casual restraint the siege of [London during World War II] and the patience, humor, exhaustion, silent suffering, and bravery of its people.

> *Ethel L. Heins, in* The Horn Book Magazine *(copyright © 1970 by The Horn Book, Inc., Boston), June, 1970, p. 284.*

Anyone can write about adolescent sexuality. Love is a rarer and harder subject—and what develops between Bill and Julie, half understood, is a true form of love. . . .

There are improbabilities here—and there are times when the background descriptions have an air of old newsreels and the first-person narration slips out of focus. Yet "Fireweed" is an outstanding novel for young people: original, haunting, poetic.

> *John Rowe Townsend, in* The New York Times Book Review *(© 1970 by The New York Times Company; reprinted by permission), July 5, 1970, p. 14.*

[In *Fireweed*] Bill realizes that he will not be accepted [by Julie's family], and is smitten with dismay when Julie seems to be rejecting him also—a sad, believable, and sharply etched ending to a convincing and dramatic story, beautifully constructed and conceived.

> *Zena Sutherland, in* Bulletin of the Center for Children's Books *(© 1970 by the University of Chicago; all rights reserved), November, 1970, p. 51.*

The London blitz of 1940 provides a disorderly background for this tremulous love story of two homeless, middle adolescents who seek survival by combining forces. . . . *Fireweed* is chastely simple. The author involves a reader in the contest for survival faced by her two major characters without using four-letter words or suggesting incidents of premarital sexual activity. *Fireweed* is a good book about adolescents involved in a major world crisis. These kids are too busy staying alive to revel in sensuality.

> *John W. Conner, in* English Journal *(copyright © 1973 by The National Council of Teachers of English), February, 1973, p. 309.*

OTHER CITATIONS

Ellen Lewis Buell, in Book World, *May 17, 1970 (Part 2), p. 3.*

Publishers' Weekly, May 18, 1970, p. 38.

The Junior Bookshelf, June, 1970, p. 109.

The Booklist, June 1, 1970, p. 1218.

GOLDENGROVE (1972)

Jill Paton Walsh's *Goldengrove* . . ., with its echoes of Gerard Manley Hopkins' poem of lament and rejoicing, is a nice English story full of description of the Cornwall cliffs, a girl's first crush, and a family secret, rather in the style of Ruth M. Arthur's popular girls' books, but it lacks the imaginative sweep of the best books about boys.

> *Michelle Murray, in* Book World *(© The Washington Post), November 5, 1972 (Part 2), p. 8.*

Jill Paton Walsh . . . has not forgotten [childhood]—and I am rather in awe of her. She writes as though she were still 12 years old, choking back angry tears and incapable of dissembling. . . . [Her] knowledge of the young floods ["Goldengrove"] with absolute truth. . . .

[It] is neither plot nor character that makes "Goldengrove" such a brilliant novel. Mrs. Walsh has chosen a technique whereby her material is presented on several levels, and not only is this ingenious, but it serves her talents to perfection. Set in the present tense, the story weaves in and out of the thoughts of its characters, all the while holding a steady narrative line and creating vivid atmosphere.

> *Barbara Wersba, in* The New York Times Book Review *(© 1972 by The New York Times Company; reprinted by permission), November 5, 1972 (Part 2), p. 6.*

The personalities of all the characters [in *Goldengrove*] are deftly developed through dialogue and their actions. However, the author's use of stream of consciousness presents difficulties for young readers, as do the many descriptions which slow the action. Nevertheless, mature older teens who can appreciate the style will find the story rewarding.

> *Sister Avila, in* School Library Journal *(reprinted from* School Library Journal, *December, 1972, published by R. R. Bowker Co., a Xerox company; copyright © 1972 by Xerox Corporation), December, 1972, p. 69.*

The author's own vivid recollection of a place in Cornwall creates a background of sea and harbor that is inseparable from her story [*Goldengrove*]. . . . Taking part of her theme (and even the name of the house and the heroine) from Gerard Manley Hopkins' brief poem, "Spring and Fall: to a young child," the author evokes a mood of autumnal melancholy mixed with the first painful awareness of growing up. Throughout the story, the present tense and fusion of the characters' thoughts—spoken and unspoken—into single, often breathless, sentences lend immediacy and great emotional intensity.

> *Ethel L. Heins, in* The Horn Book Magazine *(copyright © 1972 by The Horn Book, Inc., Boston), December, 1972, pp. 601-02.*

This book gave me little pleasure and no satisfaction, but it is unusual, and others may find it very rewarding, especially devotees of Virginia Woolf. It is about Madge, aged sixteen, and Paul, a little younger, who are brother and sister, but think they are cousins, having been deceived by their divorced parents.

The story is written in the present tense throughout, and the impression it leaves is of a negative and essentially artificial tale of deceived young people and blind older people. The climactic message, "The best of us cannot be trusted with another's happiness," would be more acceptable if we had been shown "the best of us" trying to be trustworthy. The book is full of symbols, which never seem strong enough to bear their significance, including, believe it or not, a lighthouse. I suspect this is a novel for adults which could be read by girls of about sixteen.

> *The Junior Bookshelf, February, 1973, p. 58.*

Strangely enough, most of the books describing how children become adolescents are intended for adults; the elusive psychology of the transition combines with the motive of nostalgia to ensure that this is often so. *Goldengrove* is one of the few books to take this subject and at the same time remain a children's book. But only just. . . .

Literary, with Virginia Woolf's lighthouse and with her style that yet so delicately reflects Madge's gradual perception of the subjective realities of adulthood, ambitious and elusive, *Goldengrove* is a testing story for a sensitive teenager like Madge and fine proof of the author's developing talent.

> *C. S. Hannabuss, in* Children's Book Review *(© 1973 Five Owls Press Ltd.; all rights reserved), February, 1973, p. 15.*

The impression I have is that the book's sadness is over the lapse of time, the loss of childhood, the burden of knowing about grief: the *cost* of growing up. It is impossible for an adult to read *Goldengrove* without thinking of Virginia Woolf; the style, the feeling, even the setting weave themselves into a fine mesh of correspondences; but Jill Paton Walsh remains her own woman, the book is hers alone.

> *John Rowe Townsend, in his* Written for Children: An Outline of English-Language Children's Literature *(copyright © 1965, 1974 by John Rowe Townsend; reprinted by permission of J. B. Lippincott Company), revised edition, Lippincott, 1974, p. 298.*

OTHER CITATIONS

Kirkus Reviews, *November 1, 1972, p. 1246.*

Jean Stafford, in The New Yorker, *December 2, 1972, p. 208.*

Publishers' Weekly, *December 4, 1972, p. 61.*

Alison Lurie, in The New York Review of Books, *December 14, 1972, p. 41.*

The Booklist, *January 15, 1973, p. 495.*

Zena Sutherland, in Bulletin of the Center for Children's Books, *February, 1973, p. 98.*

HENGEST'S TALE (1967)

The author of *Hengest's Tale,* assuming that the Hengest who came to Britain is the same as he who appears in an episode in *Beowulf* and the fragment called *The Fight at Finnsburg,* has pieced these together in a richly imagined setting, to make this ancient tale of treachery and vengeance live again. Moreover, Hengest tells his own story, as he lies dying in Britain: and the immediacy of this first person narrative shows us a real Hengest, cruelly caught between his duty to avenge the death of his lord, Hnaef, and his love for his boyhood friend Finn. . . .

Life at the Jutish Court and on the Baltic coast of Frisia, at this time when the Romans had retreated, is evoked with fascinating detail. In a setting concretely everyday, yet pierced with foreboding, the author expands the stark words of the Saxon poems into scenes of immense drama. Other imagined episodes of strangeness and beauty ring in the mind: the berserk Danes smashing up weapons in the mountains: the wanderer Gefwulf's return in his ghostly ship: the sea freezing round Finnsburg. The greatest triumph in so remote and fate-haunted a tale is that the characters all live: Finn, noble and generous in a Roman tradition; Hildeburgh his wife, like him; Hnaef, blindly storing up trouble for himself; Hengest, changing from eager life-love to bitter despair.

The author has shown these men's own failings as the causes of their doom. Hengest knows himself rightly cursed when Finn's father wishes that his two-faced heart shall never again find wholeness and peace; for he has seen his heart's guidance, and not followed it.

> *The Times Literary Supplement (© The Times Publishing Company Ltd. 1966), November 24, 1966, p. 1079.*

With the savage thrust of a [Henry] Treece, [Jill Paton Walsh] spills forth a tale of loyalty and deceit, of graciousness and cruelty, of a new civilization nascent. Seldom has the gloom and fear of the Dark Ages been induced with such immediacy, nor the shifting demands of primitive loyalty and honor been so effectively juxtaposed; and seldom, indeed, does historical fiction sustain such knife-edge suspense throughout.

> *Kirkus Service (copyright © 1967 Virginia Kirkus' Service, Inc.), January 15, 1967, p. 68.*

Blood, blades and betrayals are the hallmarks of this story of Hengest the Jute, invader and settler of fifth century Kent. In this tale, drawn from the mists of English myth and legendary history, Hengest emerges as no simple hero of old, but a complex man capable at once of deep loyalty and broken oaths, of bloody outrages and bitter remorse. . . . [This is] a highly serviceable tale, spare and direct in the telling, with touches of Old English language ("hall Gold-gleamer," "word-hoard") that lend a ring of authenticity. The descriptions of cut throats, hangings and split skulls are hardly for the weak-stomached, but here for a boy's reading is brief, if gory, adventure.

> *Arthur T. Leone, in* The New York Times Book Review *(© 1967 by The New York Times Company; reprinted by permission), April 9, 1967, p. 26.*

From a story found in the oldest English poetry, the author weaves an adventure tale of fifth-century warriors. It is a story of bloodshed, revenge, and death, told by Hengest—ruler of Kent and one of the earliest Saxon invaders of Britain—as he looks back over his life with its battles, the breaking of the truce, and his own murder of his best friend. The language is somewhat stilted, to convey the style of an old epic, but it's an exciting, often spine-tingling, adventure.

> *Nan Sturdivant, in* School Library Journal *(reprinted from* School Library Journal, *October, 1967, published by R. R. Bowker Co., a Xerox company; copyright © 1967 by Xerox Corporation), October, 1967, pp. 192-93.*

OTHER CITATIONS

Paul Heins, in The Horn Book Magazine, *August, 1967, p. 478.*

Zena Sutherland, in Bulletin of the Center for Children's Books, *November, 1967, pp. 50-1.*

TOOLMAKER (1974)

There are great difficulties involved in writing about the earliest human beings. What names shall we give them? How can we make them speak realistically? Jill Paton Walsh has solved both these problems through simplicity. Her characters have short, one syllable names, and speak in brief, simple sentences. This necessary austerity is balanced by the depth she gives to their personalities. . . .

[*Toolmaker*] is a pleasant story and as realistic a re-creation of the Early Stone Age as anyone accustomed to our sophisticated society is likely to achieve.

> The Junior Bookshelf, *April, 1974, p. 101.*

The recounting of events leading to [the survival of an abandoned member of a stone-age tribe] is, despite its understated and deceptively simple format, structured around a fairly complex theme—more appropriate for fifth and sixth graders than first impressions might suggest. For this age group, [*Toolmaker*] is an effective exploration of man's earliest attempts to change through challenge. [Jeroo Roy's] paper-cut illustrations, four of which are in full color, underscore the somber dignity of the text.

> *Mary M. Burns, in* The Horn Book Magazine *(copyright © 1974 by The Horn Book, Inc., Boston), June, 1974, pp. 284-85.*

[*Toolmaker*] has an adequate plot, the writing style is competent although this hasn't the impact of Walsh's contemporary stories for older readers, and the principles of division of labor and cultural diffusion are smoothly introduced.

> *Zena Sutherland, in* Bulletin of the Center for Children's Books *(© 1974 by the University of Chicago; all rights reserved), September, 1974, p. 19.*

[*Toolmaker* is a] slight, but satisfying story set in prehistoric times which centers on how specialization of tasks

might have begun. . . . [Jeroo Roy's] cut-paper illustrations, some in color, are good in design, and the well-constructed story offers an absorbing glimpse of the Stone Age.

> *Shirley M. Wilton, in* School Library Journal *(reprinted from* School Library Journal, *September, 1974, published by R. R. Bowker Co., a Xerox company; copyright © 1974 by Xerox Corporation), September, 1974, p. 94.*

OTHER CITATIONS

Publishers' Weekly, *March 4, 1974, p. 75.*

Kirkus Reviews, *April 15, 1974, p. 427.*

WORDHOARD: ANGLO-SAXON STORIES (with Kevin Crossley-Holland, 1969)

Wordhoard . . . is a collection of Anglo-Saxon stories, based mainly on true events, and showing a loving absorption by both authors of the historical texts. They claim to be in chronological order, but surely "Leof's Leavetaking" (the kernel of whose idea is presumably the Anglo-Saxon poem "Deor" and whose setting, in view of the reference to the Wuffing kings, is perhaps the late seventh century) should come before "Asser's Book", which is related by King Alfred just after the Welsh monk arrives at his court—the late ninth century. Likewise, Aelfric, who figures in "The Childmaster", was teaching at Winchester before the battle of Maldon, the period of "The Horseman." This confusion might matter to young history enthusiasts, trying to piece together the long period from about 520 to 1066. The stories are varied in mood and technique. Mrs. Paton Walsh tells a direct and pathetic tale of a defeated British war leader who comes back to a Saxon settlement to discover what has become of his descendants. "The Woodwose" (has this good name an Anglo-Saxon source?) seems to be the only story without a specific text behind it. Her story "The Childmaster," of an unwilling boy-monk at Winchester won over to his new life by the patient kindness of the inspired teacher Aelfric, is a quieter story, with great atmosphere, and shows Aelfric's Colloquy in actual use.

"Thurkell the Tall", the tale of the murder of Aelfheah, archbishop of Canterbury, is the darkest drama she attempts and is excellently done. Her stories have the pathos and drama, and the elegiac sense of doom, which was apparent in her fine book *Hengest's Tale*.

> The Times Literary Supplement *(© Times Newspapers Ltd., 1969), October 16, 1969, p. 1195.*

Deeply absorbed in Anglo-Saxon history and literature, [Jill Paton Walsh and Kevin Crossley-Holland] have each written four stories. Some are focused on actual people—Bede and Caedmon, Alfred and Asser, Harold and William the Conqueror. Others are suggested by the poetry and prose of the era. Each one deals with a typical but crucial situation. . . . The stories, skillfully told and subtle in construction, form a unified historical sequence, and bring to life the rigorous splendors of the Old English period. The occasional Anglo-Saxon expressions add zest to, rather than impede, the flow of the prose.

> *Paul Heins, in* The Horn Book Magazine

[*Wordhoard* is the] first successful attempt to present a sensitive vision of Anglo-Saxon life to teens. Each of the eight stories (four by Walsh, four by Crossley-Holland) is poignant, and has a literary value not dependent on its genre: for that reason, the stories present an effective picture of "the way it was" in England a thousand years ago.... Teachers and librarians now have the means to bring the Anglo-Saxon experience alive for today's youth through stories worth having simply for themselves.

Bruce L. MacDuffie, in School Library Journal (reprinted from School Library Journal, February, 1970, published by R. R. Bowker Co., a Xerox company; copyright © 1970 by Xerox Corporation), February, 1970, pp. 91-2.

*   *   *

WILDER, Laura Ingalls   1867-1957

An American author, Laura Ingalls Wilder is known and loved for her "Little House" books. In 1954 she received the first Laura Ingalls Wilder Award, created in her honor. Mrs. Wilder's *Little House on the Prairie* was adapted for television in 1975.

GENERAL COMMENTARY

In her five volumes for children ..., *The Little House in the Big Woods, The Little House on the Prairie, Farmer Boy, On the Banks of Plum Creek,* and *By the Shores of Silver Lake,* Laura Ingalls Wilder ... has caught the very essence of pioneer life; the feeling of satisfaction brought by hard work, the thrill of accomplishment, and of safety and comfort made possible by resourcefulness and exertion.

Anne Thaxter Eaton, in her Reading With Children (copyright 1940 by Anne Thaxter Eaton; reprinted by permission of The Viking Press, Inc.), Viking, 1940, p. 176.

In realistic fiction, some aspect of life should be presented wholly and honestly, with convincing sincerity, with authentic, inescapable realism. This accomplishment is the real reason for the wide appeal of Laura Ingalls Wilder's books.

Elizabeth Nesbitt, in The Contents of the Basket: And Other Papers on Children's Books and Reading, edited by Frances Lander Spain, The New York Public Library, 1960, p. 79.

Memory is capricious. Often, in older people, the brilliance of detail about one's earliest years is one of the strangest tricks that it plays. This living remembered detail about things done, things made, things seen—the trick is never pointlessly used—is one of the most compulsive features of Mrs. Wilder's style. It suggests, perhaps, why—though our own time is rich in autobiographical records of early days—not so many of them can, like Mrs. Wilder's, be read at two very different levels.

Unlike most books about childhood, hers are genuinely books for the young; the troubles and joys of Laura's daily life are of a kind and on a scale that any child can appreciate. And yet, although the author never diverges from the single view, never records any adult conversation or thought that she would not have heard or known, an adult will all the time be aware of the parents' tensions too.

The Times Literary Supplement (© The Times Publishing Company Ltd. 1962), June 1, 1962, p. 412.

Mary, Carrie and Grace are individuals, but it is Laura who brings the ["Little House"] stories to life and with whom most children will identify themselves. She has something of the vitality, honesty and independence of Jo in *Little Women*, and she is brave and quick-witted. The more gentle of household tasks are a trial to her, sewing makes her feel like "flying to pieces" and sometimes "wickedness boils up in her," a trait which will please any normal child. (p. 238)

[The] story that runs through the eight books ... is an absorbing one, full of humour, drama and warmth, and set against a constantly changing background. The end of each book holds the promise of new adventures in the next. There is an immediacy, a directness about the way in which the story is told that makes the reader feel that he is *listening* to a storyteller. (p. 242)

There is no lack of adventure in these books, for it rises naturally from the environment and is never exaggerated for effect. Life has a "Crusoe" element, for nearly everything must be made and Pa and Ma have a genius for improvisation.... Physical conditions—intense cold, suffocating heat, hunger and well-being—are conveyed so vividly that we find ourselves experiencing the same sensations in sympathy. All the seasons are here in their cruelty and their beauty, for Laura has the seeing eye of the poet. Again and again the story is illumined by some moment of joy, a vivid experience of childhood, not merely remembered nostalgically but re-created from the heart by the writer who was once Laura the child.

Surely the charm of these books lies in their warm humanity and faithfulness to life. Here are real people sharing joys and sorrows within an atmosphere of emotional security. One of the greatest merits of the stories is the way in which the characters mature as the narrative goes on, a characteristic rare in modern children's books. To read Laura Ingalls Wilder's books, with their tenderness and humour and their moving pictures of a girl growing up, is a satisfying and delightful experience. (pp. 242-43)

Eileen H. Colwell, "Laura Ingalls Wilder," in The Junior Bookshelf, November, 1962, pp. 237-43.

Few books have provided more sheer excitement ... than Laura Ingalls Wilder's stories of homesteading, first in Wisconsin, then in Indian territory, then still farther west, in Dakota. Here, indeed, are "books that shall be classic for the young." Courage, humor, resourcefulness and an unbreakable endurance flow in a strong undercurrent through all these accounts of adjustment to a series of new and difficult circumstances, and food is here ... the index to the ups and downs of prosperity. It is no longer just an element of pleasure and gracious occasions; it is a constant, fundamental need. When food is scarce, you share anxiety and suffering with the gallant family, and when it is plentiful their deep thankfulness somehow becomes your own. What they had to eat, and the circumstances in which they ate it, are described in faithful detail, and they are important and revealing to the reader because meals eaten seventy years ago are still, to the writer, a matter of vital consequence. . . .

What a shining tradition we inherit from the pioneers, who flavored their lean meals with fortitude and imagination, and their fat meals with thankfulness and enjoyment! Today's children find their pride in it through books like Laura Ingalls Wilder's, written with zest and affection and a true sense of proportion.

> *Annis Duff, in her* Bequest of Wings: A Family's Pleasures with Books *(copyright 1944 by Annis Duff; reprinted by permission of The Viking Press, Inc.), Viking, 1966, pp. 126-27, 129.*

No child in the United States should miss the Wilder *Little House* series, splendidly and authentically illustrated by Garth Williams. The eight books carry the Ingalls family from Wisconsin westward into Indian country and beyond. . . . This pioneer saga is filled with blizzards, drouths, crop failures, Indian perils, and all the other vicissitudes of frontier life, but family courage never fails. Ma's gift for homemaking, Pa's wonderful fiddle music and singing, and warm, cheerful affection and trust keep the Ingalls family hopeful and determined, come what will. Here in these books, children will find security of the heart and of the emotions, the kind of security that weathers every storm. If only one book in the series is read, don't let a child miss *The Long Winter*. It is the summation of the quiet, unsung heroism of thousands of nameless people who ventured into the wilderness and took and held the land.

> *May Hill Arbuthnot, in her* Children's Reading in the Home *(copyright © 1969 by Scott, Foresman and Co.), Scott, Foresman, 1969, pp. 132-33.*

To me, the compelling power of place, of the particular place Laura Ingalls Wilder wrote of in each of her books in the *Little House* series, is absolutely astonishing, especially when, as in the earlier books, she was evoking it for quite young readers. But the youth of her audience could make no difference to Mrs. Wilder, so possessed was she by the living surround of these remembered places. . . .

[What] Laura Ingalls Wilder had to say about the places of her childhood in each of her books was a profound part of herself and therefore a part of her story. Place moves and breathes within the story; it is not simply background, not a backdrop, never static.

> *Eleanor Cameron, in her* The Green and Burning Tree: On the Writing and Enjoyment of Children's Books *(copyright © 1962, 1964, 1966, 1969 by Eleanor Cameron; reprinted by permission of Little, Brown and Co. in association with The Atlantic Monthly Press), Little, Brown, 1969, p. 171.*

Among the historical stories affording a genuine portrait of American pioneer life is the series of books by Laura Ingalls Wilder. Frequently known as the "Little House Books," the series is unexcelled in the use it makes of authentic background details, lifelike characterization, and themes appropriate to the sturdy pioneers. . . .

In the "Little House Books" family life is honored and the emphasis is on family unity and joint human efforts in keeping soul and body together. And through it all, a warm sense of comfort and security is projected as young readers are touched by the integrity and the sincerity expressed in these stories.

> *Constantine Georgiou, in his* Children and Their Literature *(© 1969; reprinted by permission of Prentice-Hall, Inc., Englewood Cliffs, New Jersey), Prentice-Hall, 1969, pp. 312-13.*

A child's everyday home life plays so essential a part in his psychological balance and emotional security that for him the simple fact of naming familiar objects is a satisfaction—hence his tendency to count, collect and list. In this respect the masterpiece of realistic literature for children is assuredly the *Little House* series by Laura Ingalls Wilder, an untutored writer who might be seen as the Grandma Moses of fiction. The daughter of settlers turned farmers, she drew upon her store of childhood memories to write unsophisticated yet subtle books which are stories about things: Laura, her parents and her little sisters re-invent reality while accomplishing their daily tasks inside their diminutive home, stranded in the middle of the great Wisconsin forest, like an island in the ocean. Literary reminiscences play no part in her natural ability to observe each gesture with a little girl's inquisitive eyes, and when she offers her simple descriptions of hunting, preserving meat for the winter, bartering butter and weaving straw hats for protection against the sun, it is not in imitation of *Robinson Crusoe* but is an unconscious echo of the survival theme that was the subject of one of the greatest books of all time.

> *Isabelle Jan, in her* On Children's Literature, *edited by Catherine Storr (originally published in French by Les Editions ouvieres; copyright © 1969; translation copyright © Allen Lane, 1973), Schocken, 1974, p. 119.*

To the great collection of books based on memories and family records, Laura Ingalls Wilder . . . made the most unusual contribution. . . .

No other writer for children has given such a complete picture of a period in America's past, of a time when the individual drew his security from the strength of his closely knit family life, when outside influences emphasized family unity instead of destroying it. At the same time Mrs. Wilder told stories that children enjoy; her realism is charged with tenderness and humor.

> *Ruth Hill Viguers, in* A Critical History of Children's Literature, *by Cornelia Meigs, Anne Thaxter Eaton, Elizabeth Nesbitt, and Ruth Hill Viguers, edited by Cornelia Meigs (copyright © 1953, 1969 by Macmillan Publishing Co., Inc.), revised edition, Macmillan, 1969, pp. 526-28.*

[Laura Ingalls Wilder's] prose has a natural simplicity and goodness that [sets] it apart from the studied simplicity that often infects writing for children. In her books there are no traces of condescension—no patronage, no guile, and no cuteness. She speaks to us directly and brings her affectionate memories alive by the power of overwhelming detail and with a dramatic force that derives from honesty and accuracy. . . . The Wilder books, with their unaffected charm and their recapturing of a time long gone, will always stand as an inspiration and a guide to the rest of us.

> *E. B. White, in* The Horn Book Magazine, *(copyright © 1970 by The Horn Book, Inc., Boston), August, 1970, pp. 349-50.*

The ["Little House"] . . . are something more than warmhearted. At the most immediate level, they are entrancing tales of a vanished way of life. You learn how to slaughter a pig (and to play ball with a pork bladder), how to train oxen, milk-feed a pumpkin, build a door with a latchkey, dig a well. You meet bears, Indians, wolves, locusts. There are blizzards in which you can't see your hand in front of your face, hailstones that knock a man out, tornadoes that strip off a boy's clothes. You know what it's like to sleep on the floor of the prairie, to learn in a one-room schoolhouse, to treasure glass windows, to go hungry. . . .

Quiet adherence to the routines of daily life abuts adventure and hardship. The adventures are sensational, yet they are told without flourish. They are tucked into their place, not altering the discipline and merriment of the family. Their private values remain untouched by whatever outside forces appear. There must have been doubts over the treacherous life through which Pa led his family. But Laura celebrates the twinkle in her father's eye and the rare independence of his spirit. . . .

[The] faithfulness of these books to young Laura's sensibility is a large part of their charm. For the story is told through the eyes of Laura; each book seems to duplicate in tone the age Laura was at the time the story takes place. Book by book, the narrative grows gradually in difficulty. . . .

Mrs. Wilder's carefully controlled relinquishment of her adult sensibility makes the life she once led available to every child. And yet the adult voice behind the child's never condescends; she simplifies, omits what may be too difficult for a young listener to understand, but never shirks an experience. The result is a prose that is always dignified and restrained, often eloquent, a rarity in children's literature. Gradually you understand your pleasure: you are reading something that promised to be entertainment and that turns out to be art.

> *Susan Bagg, in* The Atlantic Monthly *(copyright © 1975, by The Atlantic Monthly Company, Boston, Mass.; reprinted with permission), February, 1975, pp. 117-18.*

The easy flow of her language and the enormous recall of details of her life deceive the reader into imagining that Laura Ingalls Wilder must have found writing her autobiographical novels for children a matter of no more than sitting down to record exactly what she meant, in order from the earliest memories until her marriage. (p. 105)

Any child notices the difference [in *The First Four Years*],

and may accept it, through his great faith in Mrs. Wilder. But the adult is struck by its relative flatness, the lacklustre quality of its language, the very different character of Laura from the one he has learned to know and love, the disheartening series of misfortunes. One is also struck by many episodes' being told again, less well it seems than the first time. The impulse to discover the character of the dissimilarities leads one to compare familiar portions of *The First Four Years* with the same events as they are related in *These Happy Golden Years*, published during her lifetime. The latter novel is drawn in part from events also related in *The First Four Years,* and revised by Mrs. Wilder in a manner that presumably satisfied her exacting standards of language, form, and mood. (pp. 105-06)

The reader of *The First Four Years* knows that Chapter One, "The First Year," gives an account of another event he has read of before—the preparation for the wedding in Chapter 31 of *These Happy Golden Years*. But the major surprise is in characterization, especially that of Laura. (p. 106)

This Laura, practical, cautious, doubtful almost to the point of appearing ready to decide not to marry at all—one might say "modern"—is not the Laura of Chapter 31 in *These Happy Golden Years,* which covers the same ground. . . . The revised Laura still is strong and independent but not penurious, and her love bears the marks of courage, optimism, and endurance, as well as genuine devotion. (p. 108)

Collation of passages describing events common to both *The First Four Years* and *These Happy Golden Years* reveals at least five distinctions between them. Most prominent is the poetic and philosophic dimension which characterizes the latter. Regularly, those portions which we have examined are specified in *Golden Years* with considerable detail, named characters, conversation. In short, they are dramatized. In that book, too, information which may have been judged to be unpleasant, inappropriate, or lacking in appeal to children is omitted. Portrayal of character is altered in the interest of consistency or vividness, except in cases where omission because of unpleasantness, inappropriateness, or lack of appeal takes precedence. Finally, the sense of form controls . . . firmly . . . the relation of parts to each other and to the whole—whole book, whole series— with consequences for point of view as well. (pp. 109-10)

[Laura Ingalls Wilder's] control is natural and so instinctively right that negative criticisms, such as may be made about the characterization of Ma, are absorbed and balanced out in the portrayal of a hardy and loving family that did more than survive: they carried a cultural tradition into a new world of experience, where it gave them strength to endure and create. They became a touchstone both of literature and of life for American children. (p. 118)

> *Rosa Ann Moore, "Laura Ingalls Wilder's Orange Notebooks and the Art of the Little House Books," in* Children's Literature: Annual of the Modern Language Association Seminar on Children's Literature and The Children's Literature Association, *Vol. 4, edited by Francelia Butler (© 1975 by Francelia Butler; all rights reserved), Temple University Press, 1975, pp. 105-19.*

Few stories taken from real life are as honest as the stories of the Ingalls family, which were written down by the author in her late middle age. The continuity of the books and their unity of feeling are not due to memory alone, nor are they simple catalogues of events. They are essentially a record of *family* life in which Laura's lively personality is defined in the way she reacts to the many homes she knows, the way she trusts and relies on her parents to make a true home wherever they go. The concrete details of life in the woods, by the river, on the prairie, hold an endless attraction for children because of their intriguing difference from the world of today, but just as important is the feeling of love and security that runs through the books.

> *Margery Fisher, in* Who's Who in Children's Books: A Treasury of the Familiar Characters of Childhood *(copyright © 1975 by Margery Fisher; reprinted by permission of Holt, Rinehart and Winston), Holt, Rinehart and Winston, 1975, pp. 170-72.*

BY THE SHORES OF SILVER LAKE (1939)

[*By the Shores of Silver Lake*] is full of small homely domestic incidents and the author arouses an appreciation of simple things and a thankfulness for the good. The story is spoilt by a tendency to the sentimental and perhaps because of this never makes absolute contact with the reader, in spite of the fact that it is true to life. It remains a period piece that has severed its connection with the present day. Yet historically the story throws detailed light on a scene of those times and without the sentimentality would have made a bolder bid for appreciative recognition and wider acceptance. The illustrations by Garth Williams are in keeping with the text, caught and held by the atmosphere of the author's world.

> The Junior Bookshelf, *June, 1961, p. 158.*

THE FIRST FOUR YEARS (1971)

"The First Four Years" . . . is but the framework of a novel compared to the classic story of [Mrs. Wilder's] childhood. Laura's strength was always her ability to see with the eye of wonder and to memorably communicate what she saw. With her poetic seeing gone, we have nothing left but a flatly told procession of disasters, most of which we have experienced with her in one form or another in previous books. . . .

The book satisfies simple curiosity, but adds neither depth of vision nor understanding of a relationship. As for Laura, we already understand her as deeply as we ever will.

> *Eleanor Cameron, in* The New York Times Book Review *(© 1971 by The New York Times Company; reprinted by permission), March 28, 1971, p. 28.*

Although this hasn't the lively antics of little girls to give it quite the same appeal as the Little House books, it has the same direct, ingenuous quality, the same satisfying observance of detail, and the same family-centered warmth.

> *Zena Sutherland, in* Bulletin of the Center for Children's Books *(© 1971 by the University of Chicago; all rights reserved), May, 1971, p. 147.*

In this episodic, journal-like account of her first years of marriage . . . [Laura Ingalls Wilder] describes the pleasures, problems, and sadnesses shared with her Almanzo ("Manly") during the period they were trying to develop their land claim. . . . The vast number of devotees of the earlier books will rejoice in the important autobiographical sequel to *These Happy Golden Years*. One must acknowledge, too, the very real documentary value of the precisely presented details of the economics and philosophy of farm life. . . . [It] is appropriate to have Garth Williams' illustrations tying this book with the others, although they fall far short of his preceding work.

> *Virginia Haviland, in* The Horn Book Magazine *(copyright © 1971 by The Horn Book, Inc., Boston), June, 1971, pp. 289-90.*

[*The First Four Years*] possesses those same characteristics of sincerity and simplicity, that same grasp of detail and ability to vivify, that informs the previous books. . . . Mrs. Wilder died before this account of her marriage could be revised so it is presented in its original draft. Even so it is a worthy addition to the series and makes one wish there could be more.

> *C.E.J. Smith, in* Children's Book Review *(© 1973 Five Owls Press Ltd.; all rights reserved), September, 1973, pp. 121-22.*

[*The First Four Years* is a] sequel to the eight books about Laura Ingalls Wilder's pioneer childhood and youth which ended with the marriage of Laura and Almanzo. . . .

The final book is only the first draft, discovered after the author's death. It lacks something of the charm and personality of the previous books, perhaps because Laura Ingalls Wilder never revised and rewrote it as she did the others. . . . Does the child reader want to know "what happened next"? Is not the ending of *These Happy Golden Years*, in which two young people face a life together in which the next stage is left to the child's imagination, the right one?

> The Junior Bookshelf, *October, 1973, pp. 341-42.*

OTHER CITATIONS

Kirkus Reviews, *January 15, 1971, p. 58.*

Zena Sutherland, in Saturday Review, *March 20, 1971, p. 31.*

Publishers' Weekly, *March 22, 1971, p. 53.*

The Booklist, *April 15, 1971, p. 705.*

LITTLE HOUSE IN THE BIG WOODS (1932)

[*Little House in the Big Woods*] is an extremely good book, with an excellence which is so unobtrusive that it may well go unnoticed. There is plenty of excitement, but no spurious thrills, and encounters with bears and other perils are not more important than the business of harvesting maple sugar or the thrills of a square-dance. Mrs. Wilder's observation is precise and true, her human values are sound. She paints an entirely satisfying picture of family life, life which is lived with little more than the barest necessities, but which is seen to be full of the finest riches.

The Junior Bookshelf, *October, 1956, p. 221.*

OTHER CITATIONS

The Times Literary Supplement, *May 11, 1956, p. x.*

LITTLE HOUSE ON THE PRAIRIE (1935)

Little House on the Prairie is more informative and less of a story [than *Little House in the Big Woods*], but none the worse for it. It is a clever reconstruction, charmingly illustrated [by Garth Williams], of what it was like to trek West from Wisconsin in a covered wagon, across the Mississippi to the grass lands of Kansas. . . . Prairie wild life is vividly described; the gophers, the hawks, the panthers and the wolves; so too is the quiet everyday life of the pioneer and his family.

The Times Literary Supplement, *November 15, 1957, p. xvi.*

LITTLE TOWN ON THE PRAIRIE (1941)

Laura in adolescence is as delightful and human as ever, one of the outstandingly complete portraits in children's literature, and the community in which she lives is realised in minute detail. Plenty of stories, like this, are based on fact, but Mrs. Wilder's books have an artistic truth as well.

The Junior Bookshelf, *July, 1963, p. 163.*

THE LONG WINTER (1940)

Laura Ingalls Wilder has written a wonderful series of stories based on her own childhood, beginning with *Little House in the Big Woods,* and continuing in this, the fifth book, describing a terrible season of blizzards in Dakota. Every detail shines clearly, so that the pages almost crackle with frost as one reads; and how dreary the confinement to the cabin and the dullness of a poor diet must have been to the families in that part of the world. . . . These books are well worth reading, for boys and girls of ten or so, both for their content and style. They may well prove some of the best books describing real life on the prairies that have been written for this generation.

The Junior Bookshelf, *October, 1962, pp. 207-08.*

The Long Winter [is] perhaps, through its concentrated theme, the most impressive of [Wilder's] vivid and memorable narratives. . . .

The intensity of a drama need not depend on its scale. In a story like this, every meal, every gift devised for occasions, each substitute for heating or light, has a quality of adventurous surprise. When the melting spring wind comes the reader may be as dazzled by the outside world's reappearance as if this classic sojourn of Laura's family had been his own.

The Times Literary Supplement (© *The Times Publishing Company Ltd. 1962), November 23, 1962, p. 901.*

The best of all the [Little House] books is *The Long Winter* (1940), which tells how the Ingalls family survive through month after month, blizzard after blizzard, on open prairie with no trains getting through and no supplies. . . .

Like the other books, but more deeply and impressively, *The Long Winter* is about family solidarity, the warmth of love opposed to the hostile elements. The story intensifies until at last there is the one enemy, winter; the one issue, survival. The writing is clear, plain, and as good as bread.

> *John Rowe Townsend, in his* Written for Children: An Outline of English-Language Children's Literature *(copyright © 1965, 1974 by John Rowe Townsend; reprinted by permission of J. B. Lippincott Company), revised edition, Lippincott, 1974, pp. 180-81.*

ON THE WAY HOME (1962)

Here is Laura's journal begun July 17, 1894, in a little five-cent memorandum book, when with her husband and daughter Rose she made the trip by covered wagon from the drought-stricken Dakota territory to Mansfield, Missouri, where she would write those classic pioneer stories and live out her long life. The journal entries are filled with homely details of weather, crops, foods, and people met—all vivid and meaningful and related in spirit to her later writing. Rose Wilder Lane's introduction explains the move to the Ozarks, and her lengthy concluding portion of her own memories carries on where her mother's record ends to describe the purchase of land and the first months of work, thus rounding out the account. A most unusual bit of Americana, from a beloved author.

> *Virginia Haviland, in* The Horn Book Magazine *(copyright © 1962, by The Horn Book, Inc., Boston), December, 1962, p. 614.*

A narrative of Rose Wilder Lane's childhood memories, preceding and following [Mrs. Wilder's] diary, adds meaning to the times, places, and events surrounding the family journey and its written record. The diary will have more appeal for older readers of "These Happy Golden Years" and [Mrs. Lane's] "Let the Hurricane Roar" than to youngsters who are still enjoying the earlier "Little House" books, for the journal is understandably rather mature in fact and observation. The narrative of Rose Wilder Lane, which really summarizes the experience chronicled in her mother's diary, will be of interest to younger readers as well as to older girls reading romantic frontier stories.

> School Library Journal *(reprinted from* School Library Journal, *March, 1963, published by R. R. Bowker Co., a Xerox company; copyright © 1963 by Xerox Corporation), March, 1963, p. 189.*

["On the Way Home"] is a recently-discovered diary kept by Laura Ingalls Wilder. . . . Her daughter, Rose Wilder Lane, has provided her own memoir or a "setting," and actually this is the most interesting part of the book. Mrs. Wilder's diary, while revealing an eye for detail and a feeling for the land, is more meaningful for adults. Mrs. Lane's own narrative gives us the muted drama of the times and the country, a sense of adventure, of comradeship and of courage.

> Ellen Lewis Buell, in The New York Times Book Review (© 1963 by The New York Times Company; reprinted by permission), April 14, 1963, p. 56.

THESE HAPPY GOLDEN YEARS (1943)

It is a delight to have the final volume of the *Little House* series and so meet once more the lovable and courageous person who wrote her own story in them so unforgettably. . . .

Behind this book, as in all the others, is the warmth and love and appreciation of beauty which makes each story an experience for the reader. In spite of the author's long experience of hardship and heartache, she can still say at the end of this book, "It is a beautiful world." The values and truths implicit in these books cannot but be helpful to the children who read them.

> The Junior Bookshelf, *July, 1964, p. 183.*

[*These Happy Golden Years* is] written with sensitivity and affection. . . . Although the book ends with Laura reaching the mature age of eighteen, and marrying her faithful Almanzo, the very simple style in which it is written and the loving attention to minute detail in the descriptions of everyday life seem to refer this new instalment about Laura to readers considerably younger than the heroine herself.

> The Times Literary Supplement (© The Times Publishing Company Ltd. 1964), July 9, 1964, p. 602.

Mrs. Wilder's autobiographical story of courtship in the late 1800's creates a sentimental portrait of a loving family in the tradition of *Little Women*. Although the characters, Laura Ingalls and Almanzo Wilder, belong to a bygone era, they personify the many conflicts that all young people face when they approach adulthood. . . .

In addition to the romantic theme, the author's emphasis on a warm-hearted family relationship makes this book an excellent choice for young readers. The personal fortitude and courage required of pioneers is also well depicted.

> John Gillespie and Diana Lembo, in their Juniorplots: A Book Talk Manual for Teachers and Librarians (© 1967 by the R. R. Bowker Co.), Bowker, 1967, pp. 123-24.

*   *   *

WILDSMITH, Brian   1930-

An English painter, author, and illustrator, Wildsmith is noted for his exuberant color pictures. He received the 1962 Kate Greenaway Medal for *Brian Wildsmith's ABC*.

GENERAL COMMENTARY

Although Brian Wildsmith is not the first or last to be fascinated by the words that signify groupings of creatures, he is one of the most articulating of artists. His "Birds," which ranges from a wedge of swans to a company of parrots, was included in The New York Times list of Best Illustrated Children's Books for 1967. A short time later came "Wild Animals," with such provocative collectives as a nursery of raccoons, an ambush of tigers, a troop of kangaroos, a corps of giraffes. The urge to cite more of these poetic pluralities is almost irresistible; parlor games have been based successfully on far less incentive.

Now a third Wildsmith variation on the theme with "Fishes," which includes a school of butterfly fish, a glide of flying fish, a hover of trout, a herd of sea horses, and odder and odder assemblies. The format is identical with that of the earlier two books, including a conversational and informative foreword to the reader explaining—or speculating—on how these group names came into being. These introductions are useful, and word addicts of all ages will be pleased to read and reread them.

But, and here is the nub, these are picture books, and from the format it would seem that they are directed to nursery and kindergarten level. The illustrations for all three books are very much of a piece: bright and sprightly, leaning a bit to the caricatured side. For my own taste, I would prefer them more anatomically defined; more naturally correct; more scientific, that is to say more beautiful. I wonder, did Mr. Wildsmith feel that he had to "draw down" to the Saturday morning TV watchers association of classic cookie munchers and chocolate-milk swiggers? . . .

Finally, the titles for this triplicate offering: "Brian Wildsmith's Birds," "Brian Wildsmith's Wild Animals," "B. W.'s Fishes." A touch overly proprietary, no? I had thought we were all creatures of some slightly higher force.

> Eve Merriam, in The New York Times Book Review (© 1968 by The New York Times Company; reprinted by permission), August 18, 1968, p. 34.

Although he says he has "abstract tendencies," Brian Wildsmith's illustrations are strongly brilliant and representational. He sees the pictorial form as being at one with the text, yet each a thing unto itself—complementary—and each able to exist without the other. All of his work is in full color; a Wildsmith trademark is the use of bright contrasting colors in a harlequin pattern. In his technique, gouache is used, moving from impasto down to almost translucent watercolor effects. The subjects he treats lend themselves to strong impact. . . .

> May Hill Arbuthnot and Zena Sutherland, in their Children and Books (copyright © 1947, 1957, 1964, 1972 by Scott, Foresman and Co.), 4th edition, Scott, Foresman, 1972, p. 74.

Brian Wildsmith is more painter than draughtsman, and much more painter than storyteller. The richness of his *A.B.C.* was astonishing when it first appeared in 1962; there was nothing else quite like his kettle aglow with heat or his lion on the next page aglow with sun. Since then Wildsmith has produced a *1 2 3* (1965) and books of *Birds* and *Wild Animals* (1967), *Fishes* (1968) and *Puzzles* (1970), all lovely books in themselves but not showing any spectacular advance. *The Circus* (1970) was especially successful; the vividness, vigour and larger-than-lifeness of the circus as a subject were ideally suited to Wildsmith's talent for producing brilliant set-pieces unimpeded by story.

Wildsmith has illustrated several folktales, but gives the impression of turning constantly aside to pick flowers. This happens almost literally in *The Miller, the Boy and the Donkey* (1969), which at one point shows man and boy riding across a rich deep flowerscape that is irrelevant to the story but is the principal interest of the double-page spread on which it appears. In *The Hare and the Tortoise* (1969), when the hare stops to eat carrots, we see a cross-section of growing, glowing carrots in the juicy black jewelled earth. Nothing could be farther from the idea of a race, and we may well wonder whether (endearingly) the artist shares the hare's tendency to be sidetracked. Wildsmith's own story in *The Little Wood Duck* (1972)—about the duckling that can only swim in circles but thereby makes the bad old fox dizzy—really will not do at all as a story. Yet the face of the dizzy fox is marvellous; almost enough to make the book go round and round in the reader's hands.

> *John Rowe Townsend, in his* Written for Children: An Outline of English-Language Children's Literature *(copyright © 1965, 1974 by John Rowe Townsend; reprinted by permission of J. B. Lippincott Company), revised edition, Lippincott, 1974, pp. 323-24.*

No longer do I open a picture book by Brian Wildsmith with the pleasurable thrill of anticipation which greeted *The Lion and the Rat* or *The North Wind and the Sun*. The brilliant blending of colour is still there, with all the artistic skill, but somehow there is a sameness which turns expectation sour. If one had never seen a Wildsmith picture book before, either of these new offerings [*Squirrels* and *Python's Party*] would seem outstanding, and yet, because one feels that there has been no progression in style, one is continually frustrated, almost cheated. They are like a beautiful, but un-lived-in house.

> *Valerie Alderson, in* Children's Book Review *(© 1975 Five Owls Press Ltd.; all rights reserved), Spring, 1975, p. 37.*

BRIAN WILDSMITH'S ABC (1963)

[This is an] alphabet book with jewel-like pictures on brightly colored pages of different hues. Skillful librarians will use this in story hours to develop imagination (e.g. the unicorn) and appreciation of color (e.g. the picture of the turtle or the snail). A simple and beautiful book that children will enjoy looking at again and again.

> School Library Journal *(reprinted from* School Library Journal, *March, 1963, published by R. R. Bowker Co., a Xerox company; copyright © 1963 by Xerox Corporation), March, 1963, p. 166.*

Mr. Wildsmith makes a bold and effective use of both form and color [in *A.B.C.*]. The book is conceived as a whole, brilliantly colored paper and type being used to complement the pictures themselves. The effect is highly individual, and the book should prove a joy to young children and also to many of their elders.

> *Sheila M. Rawson, in* The Christian Science Monitor *(reprinted by permission from The*

Christian Science Monitor; *© 1963 The Christian Science Publishing Society; all rights reserved), October 12, 1963, p. 9.*

Brian Wildsmith's ABC is exotic in conception and striking in its visual impact. Bold, recognizable pictures of many familiar animals and things, drawn in Wildsmith's vibrant style, provide an excellent beginning for a modern child's first encounter with the alphabet.

Wildsmith reaches children struck by the staccato designs in their neon-lit environment where bold, vivid forms vie for attention. And to focus young eyes on the alphabet, this book offers full, double-page spreads for upper and lower case letters, each beginning the name of an imaginatively drawn object or living thing and set against a backdrop of luminous color.

> *Constantine Georgiou, in his* Children and Their Literature *(© 1969; reprinted by permission of Prentice-Hall, Inc., Englewood Cliffs, New Jersey), Prentice-Hall, 1969, pp. 72-3.*

This is the ABC that is perhaps the most widely known, and [a] main introduction to Wildsmith's style of hitting the reader with intoxicating colour. Here he contrasts boldly the opposite colours of midnight blue and gold, fuschia and blue, jade and purple, setting the pace for other illustrators to follow. The objects portrayed have characters of their own, the cat glares out from the page, the dog is baleful and sad, the owl rather smug.

> *Pat Garrett, in* Children's Book Review *(© 1971 by Five Owls Press Ltd.; all rights reserved), April, 1971, p. v.*

Brian Wildsmith's ABC is a heady experience with color, an ABC book with the simplest of texts and the most glorious rainbow of subtle tints and hues. . . . One of the great pleasures of this book is to flip the pages slowly and enjoy the changing colors.

> *May Hill Arbuthnot and Zena Sutherland, in their* Children and Books *(copyright © 1947, 1957, 1964, 1972 by Scott, Foresman and Co.), 4th edition, Scott, Foresman, 1972, p. 48.*

OTHER CITATIONS

The Junior Bookshelf, *December, 1962, p. 309.*

Margaret Sherwood Libby, in New York Herald Tribune Books, *May 12, 1963 (Sec. 12), p. 6.*

Alice Dalgliesh, in Saturday Review, *June 22, 1963, p. 46.*

BRIAN WILDSMITH'S BIRDS (1967)

Wildsmith's *Birds* are of great beauty, and subtly show how different species came by their group names (a wedge of swans, a walk of snipe, a watch of nightingales); beautiful pictures to hang on the wall, but not a book. And most particularly not a child's book; to appreciate these paintings one needs to know the birds already, and at least something about their habits. But they are lovely pictures.

The Times Literary Supplement (© *Times Newspapers Ltd., 1967*), *May 25, 1967, p. 452.*

[If] this does not advance the picture-book as an art form, it represents the highest reach to date of this generation's most remarkable book-artist. Wildsmith has never drawn with greater assurance and with better control of his characteristic mannerisms. His birds are accurate, amusing, beautiful, and they are given settings which are at once fitting and exquisite. The design of each page—or rather pair of pages—is a lesson in composition equally persuasive and delightful. With what mastery Wildsmith uses natural forms as the material for highly artful designs. And what fun it all is. Lucky children to be born into a world which has birds and Brian Wildsmith in it.

The Junior Bookshelf, *August, 1967, p. 239.*

Brian Wildsmith's picture-books are among the brightest happenings in children's illustrating in recent years. His latest outpouring, called simply *Birds* . . . is a book likely to become a family affair. Mr. Wildsmith is fascinated by the terms used to describe various collections of birds—a stare of owls, a party of jays, a walk of snipe, a wedge of swans etc. His pictures illustrate both birds and terms. The owls stare, jays are obviously having a party, snipe walk their long-legged way across the page, and a wedge-shaped flotilla of swans floats on a blue pond. Children will need some adult help to get the point of a sedge of herons, but an unkindness of ravens is quite straight-going. Mr. Wildsmith doesn't offer easy entertainment but glorious eyefuls of color and pattern. This is a book that young children can look at and talk about with their parents. It is also a book that they can come back to on their own as they grow older.

Patience M. Daltry, in The Christian Science Monitor (*reprinted by permission from* The Christian Science Monitor; © *1967 The Christian Science Publishing Society; all rights reserved*), *August 31, 1967, p. 5.*

One picture is worth a thousand words and though only one line of text appears on each double-page spread of this book, Wildsmith's delightful illustrations are worth at least that thousand. After an introduction noting their possible origin, ancient expressions such as "a nye of pheasants" or "a fall of woodcock" are brilliantly illustrated with such colorful and humorous paintings that one wishes the book had been enlarged to include more than the 12 selections given here.

Ann D. Schweibish, in School Library Journal (*reprinted from* School Library Journal, *September, 1967, published by R. R. Bowker Co., a Xerox company; copyright © 1967 by Xerox Corporation*), *September, 1967, p. 114.*

Beautiful, beautiful. Brian Wildsmith has painted a series of pictures of birds—not single birds, but groups of birds. A wedge of swans, a siege of bitterns, a walk of snipe. The pages are sometimes crammed with jewel-tone colors, but some are even more effective in showing the birds as a frieze against an almost-monotone background. The humor

will appeal to those readers who enjoyed [Eve] Merriam's *A Gaggle of Geese* (. . . 1960) in which there are many more terms.

Zena Sutherland, in Bulletin of the Center for Children's Books (*copyright 1967 by the University of Chicago; all rights reserved*), *October, 1967, p. 35.*

OTHER CITATIONS

Kirkus Service, *July 1, 1967, p. 737.*

Polly Goodwin, in Book World, *September 10, 1967 (Part 2), p. 36.*

The Booklist and Subscription Books Bulletin, *September 15, 1967, p. 132.*

Marion Marx, in The Horn Book Magazine, *October, 1967, p. 585.*

BRIAN WILDSMITH'S CIRCUS (1970)

At his best Brian Wildsmith is the master of them all, but one has the feeling that his art has taken a wrong turning. There are some brilliant pictures in *The Circus* yet, but for the possession of covers, it is hardly a book at all. The patterns are lovely and exciting; they lack the inner discipline which marks the work of the great picture-book maker. This very fine and intelligent artist needs a pause for self-appraisal and a conscious effort to back out of the "No Through Road" into which he has wandered.

The Junior Bookshelf, *October, 1970, p. 278.*

Brian Wildsmith is a disciple of the sun; his pictures, in *The Circus*, give a brilliant impression of the glamour and excitement of the sawdust ring. "But there's no story"; no, but if you study the pictures carefully you can imagine yourself at a real, live performance, so skilfully does the artist translate the performers' feats of balance and control to the page.

The Times Literary Supplement (© *Times Newspapers Ltd., 1970*), *October 30, 1970, p. 1260.*

All the superlatives have already been employed about Brian Wildsmith's pictures, but this is a breathtaking book, amusing and full of vigour. The circus wends its way between two brief lines of text—'The circus comes to town' and then, after it has receded into almost filmic distance. 'The circus goes away'. Act follows act as the pages are turned, bringing alive the true spirit of circus which is a much more vital and glorious essence than the disappointing reality often proves to be. Against the brilliance of such illustration, text would have been absolutely superfluous: the very colours seem to conjure sound.

Anne Wood, in Books and Bookmen (© *Anne Wood*), *November, 1970, p. 56.*

Brian Wildsmith . . . has produced a pretty set of coloured plates in *The Circus* . . ., with nine words of text. [The publisher's blurb says that this book] '. . . reveals his genius for arousing the interest and enlarging the vision of young children'—I'm sorry, but how? Because he paints better than they do? The middle-class children who get a book like this as a present will probably have seen a circus in real life and drawn their own conclusions—with felt pens.

> *John Coleman, in* New Statesman (© *The Statesman & Nation Publishing Co. Ltd. 1970), November 6, 1970, p. 612.*

Since the entire text of Brian Wildsmith's latest book consists of nine words, it is a picture book in the strictest sense. Not for those children who like to be able to find some thread of plot, even the slightest, to connect the illustrations—but for those happy to feast the eye on this parade of circus performers, the artist's style is as richly colourful as ever, with the animals and artistes all wearing the same engagingly wistful expression.

> *Anthea Bell, in* The School Librarian, *December, 1970, p. 502.*

Who needs words? The brilliant water color pictures [in *Brian Wildsmith's Circus*] leap from the page, the costumes glowing with color, the jugglers and acrobats tense with action, the big cats vibrant and snarling, the clowns and bareback riders splendidly poised.

> *Zena Sutherland, in* Bulletin of the Center for Children's Books (© *1971 by the University of Chicago; all rights reserved), June, 1971, p. 164.*

OTHER CITATIONS

Publishers' Weekly, *September 21, 1970.*

The Booklist, *January 1, 1971, p. 375.*

Virginia Haviland, in The Horn Book Magazine, *February, 1971, p. 46.*

Barbara Gibson, in School Library Journal, *April, 1971, p. 101.*

Zena Sutherland, in Saturday Review, *May 15, 1971, p. 46.*

BRIAN WILDSMITH'S FISHES (1968)

Brilliant color and the rich quality of dramatic painting make a perfect presentation of the varied patterns and movements of 14 kinds of fish in *Brian Wildsmith's Fishes*.... An intriguing two-page foreword explains with a light touch the origin of the various names that sportsmen, zoologists and and poets have given groups of fishes, so no further text is necessary except the collective noun unsed with each appropriate breed. The double spreads show both the color and variety of fish and the infinite variety in the water itself. Here is an artist enamored with beauty and so gifted he can share his vision of it.

> *Anne Izard, in* Book World (© *The Washington Post), November 3, 1968 (Part 2), p. 4.*

Like several previous books by Wildsmith, this offers group names (a spread of sticklebacks, a battery of barracuda, or a hover of trout) and a series of stunning double-page spread illustrations. Despite the preface, which gives addi-

tional terms, the value of the book depends less on the small amount of information it gives than it does on the paintings. Well worth inclusion in a collection of art books, the pictures are a triumph of imaginative embroidery on natural beauty.

> *Zena Sutherland, in* Bulletin of the Center for Children's Books (© *1969 by the University of Chicago; all rights reserved), April, 1969, p. 135.*

OTHER CITATIONS

Kirkus Service, *August 15, 1968, p. 894.*

BRIAN WILDSMITH'S MOTHER GOOSE: A COLLECTION OF NURSERY RHYMES (1965)

[Children] ought to revel in Mr. Wildsmith's magnificent blurs of colour and his humorous detail [in *Mother Goose*]. If there be some awkward child who refuses this book, his elders will have more time to enjoy it. Of course there are nursery rhymes as well, some not so well known, but the pictures are the *raison d'être* of this publication. And a very good reason, too.

> The Junior Bookshelf, *December, 1964, p. 366.*

This is a newly illustrated edition of an old favorite, sure to please both children and adults. Some highly original artistic conceptions of the old rhymes, the wonderful action in animal and human figures, and Mr. Wildsmith's usual harmony of color place this among the most beautiful Mother Goose picture books.

> *Elsie T. Dobbins, in* School Library Journal *(reprinted from* School Library Journal, *March, 1965, published by R. R. Bowker Co., a Xerox company; copyright © 1965 by Xerox Corporation), March, 1965, p. 180.*

Highly individual in its harlequin patterns, this is a most pleasing *Mother Goose*, with (in general) one rhyme to a page and each page in color. Children will like the play of expression also: Jack Horner's delight in his plum. Even the back views of characters are expressive.

> *Alice Dalgleish, in* Saturday Review *(copyright © 1965 by Saturday Review, Inc.; reprinted with permission), April 24, 1965, p. 44.*

[Wildsmith's] full-blown, decorator-color images [for *Mother Goose*] grossly underestimate the poetry by grossly overshooting the mark; such irreverent treatment of Mother Goose as a mere excuse for noisy posturing is irritating. On most pages the verses are scrunched down at the bottom, denoting only too clearly their unimportance in relation to the pictures.... This pretentious book is Cinemascope Mother Goose, Mother Goose gone Wildsmith, and she has lost her identity in the process.

> *Maurice Sendak, in* Book Week (© *The Washington Post), October 31, 1965 (Part 2), p. 40.*

OTHER CITATIONS

The Booklist and Subscription Books Bulletin, *March 1, 1965, p. 664.*

Patience M. Daltry, in The Christian Science Monitor, *March 25, 1965, p. 7.*

May Hill Arbuthnot and Zena Sutherland, in their Children and Books, *4th edition, Scott, Foresman, 1972, p. 119.*

BRIAN WILDSMITH'S 1, 2, 3'S (1965)

At first sight you might think that *1 2 3* is a picture book which just used the counting idea as an excuse for lovely patterns. A closer look reveals that this is both a book of exquisite visual delights and an educational stimulant. The brilliantly coloured shapes, with their dazzling harlequin patchworks, are most lovely in themselves. They will shock the young child into an awareness of the beauties of form and tone, and will set him out on voyages of mathematical discovery—simple enough voyages, it is true, but excitingly purposeful.

> The Junior Bookshelf, *June, 1965, pp. 144-45.*

[*1 2 3* is] another triumph for an exceptional talent. Number as colour is now the secret language of children which mystifies prosaic adults. The artist is in the know. This group of abstract paintings, with the basic shapes in brilliant *Gestalten* make one want to learn to count all over again. There should be extra copies in classes where there are children with reading difficulties.

> *Margaret Meek, in* The School Librarian and School Library Review, *July, 1965, p. 251.*

The numbers one to ten are illustrated [in *Brian Wildsmith's 1, 2, 3's*] with simple basic forms and brilliant color in a kaleidoscopic presentation of counting for the beginner.... Although it may not be possible to predict the importance of the book as an introduction to mathematics, it can stand alone as an introduction to form and color.

> *Helen B. Crawshaw, in* The Horn Book Magazine *(copyright © 1966, by The Horn Book, Inc., Boston), April, 1966, pp. 190-91.*

It is almost as though Brian Wildsmith has set himself a puzzle, to produce a counting book by restricting himself to just three basic shapes, the triangle, rectangle and circle. The result, however, is quite intoxicating and is amongst his very best work. These basic shapes form the objects which in turn are themselves made up of a mosaic of brilliantly coloured shapes, the bolder colours forming superimposed patterns of their own, and the effect is quite beautiful, a kaleidoscope of colour set against strongly contrasting backgrounds. Wildsmith has a sure, instinctive gift for colour, and the objects have form and give an indication to children of what can be achieved with shapes, area and perspective.

> *Pat Garrett, in* Children's Book Review *(© 1971 by Five Owls Press Ltd.; all rights reserved), October, 1971, p. vi.*

OTHER CITATIONS

School Library Journal, *September, 1965, p. 146.*

Charlotte Jackson, in The Atlantic Monthly, *December, 1965, p. 153.*

Zena Sutherland, in Bulletin of the Center for Children's Books, *April, 1966, pp. 139-40.*

Della Thomas, in School Library Journal, *March, 1971, p. 96.*

BRIAN WILDSMITH'S PUZZLES (1971)

Brian Wildsmith . . . returns to his best form in *Puzzles*. He is still making a set of pictures rather than a book, but what pictures! The slender link between them is that each contains the answer to a question, but neither question nor answer is of great importance. What matters is that in these pages children will be subjected to the impact of a great artist's passion for colour and form, and those who have eyes to see will not remain unmoved by the experience.

> The Junior Bookshelf, *February, 1971, p. 25.*

With *Puzzles*, Brian Wildsmith has at last cast off the pale shadows with which he seemed to be shrouding himself and burst forth in all the glorious rich colours with which he was originally associated. Looking at these vivid spreads it is easy to understand the children who are reputed to lick the pages of some picture books in an ecstacy of enthusiasm.... [*Puzzles* is a] brilliantly attractive book which can provide glowing colourful experience for any child from two upwards.

> *Valerie Alderson, in* Children's Book Review *(© 1971 by Five Owls Press Ltd.; all rights reserved), February, 1971, p. 16.*

Children will be utterly enchanted by the lavish drawings in *Brian Wildsmith's Puzzles* . . ., a bright collection of sight gags and tricks that should keep the young reader nicely occupied. Parents, however, may have to explain the answers the first time to pre-schoolers.

> *Michael J. Bandler, in* Book World *(© The Washington Post), November 7, 1971 (Part 2), p. 2.*

In kaleidoscopic color Wildsmith sets forth a sundry of things to look at and for: things to count, choices to make, footsteps to follow. [The book will be good] for a day in bed or for the child who is wild about workbooks. The language of comments and questions is so banal that the book is better off without text. Just looking, thanks!

> *Joan Bodger Mercer, in* The New York Times Book Review *(© 1971 by The New York Times Company; reprinted by permission), November 7, 1971 (Part 2), p. 46.*

OTHER CITATIONS

Publishers' Weekly, *August 30, 1971, p. 274.*

Marjorie Lewis, in School Library Journal, *October, 1971, p. 107.*

The Booklist, *October 15, 1971, p. 207.*

Zena Sutherland, in Saturday Review, *October 16, 1971, p. 56.*

Jean Stafford, in The New Yorker, *December 4, 1971, p. 188.*

Virginia Haviland, in The Horn Book Magazine, *February, 1972, p. 43.*

BRIAN WILDSMITH'S THE TWELVE DAYS OF CHRISTMAS (1972)

Ultimately, what every reader, whatever his taste in stories, demands of a picture book is that it should be good to look at. Brian Wildsmith's *The Twelve Days of Christmas* . . . fulfils brilliantly this basic requirement. Mr. Wildsmith is one of those rare artists who appreciate the value of uncluttered expanses of page, and here brightly jewelled patches of colour contrast with satisfying, untouched matt surfaces to give a glowing reminder of the magic of Christmas.

> The Times Literary Supplement (© *Times Newspapers Ltd., 1972), July 14, 1972, p. 808.*

The pictures [in *The Twelve Days of Christmas*] are rather less formal than [Wildsmith's] most recent work and the mannerisms are mostly under control. The colour is as gorgeous as his best. Surprisingly he returns briefly to line. On each reverse page he sketches the accumulated gifts in the margins of the verses. It is all gay, relaxed and, perhaps, much ado. As so often with this infinitely gifted artist, one feels that huge forces are being held in reserve.

> The Junior Bookshelf, *October, 1972, p. 300.*

"The Twelve Days of Christmas" . . . is the Beautiful Christmas Book for this season. In spite of the fact that his style is so familiar (has, in fact, spawned a whole school of illustration), Wildsmith's paintings with their geometric designs and brilliant patchworked colors remain unique; his treatment of his subject is continually surprising and original. . . . As the days and presents and verses pile up, the momentum of the paintings increases until the 12 lords a-leaping seem to have enough energy to remain suspended indefinitely. The text is wrapped between eight pages of giant-sized Christmas tree ornaments; and the impression overall is of having been invited to a gallery for a special Christmas exhibition.

> *Sidney Long, in* The New York Times Book Review (© *1972 by The New York Times Company; reprinted by permission), December 3, 1972, p. 8.*

OTHER CITATIONS

Alice Miller Bregman, in School Library Journal, *October, 1972, p. 126.*

Zena Sutherland, in Bulletin of the Center for Children's Books, *November, 1972, p. 51.*

Virginia Haviland, in The Horn Book Magazine, *December, 1972, p. 582.*

BRIAN WILDSMITH'S WILD ANIMALS (1967)

A companion to the book on birds, this one gives the collective term for sixteen animals and fourteen vivid double-page spreads conjuring up the animals themselves. The terms happen to be less exotic on the whole, though some are very apt: a sloth of bears, an ambush of tigers, shrewdness of apes and skulk of foxes, etc. but of course the pictures are the main reason for purchase and justify it fully. Mr. Wildsmith is best with non-humans and an oblong format seems to stimulate him; the subjects' disposition of the page, the use of pattern, texture and colour and the feeling of movement are all most effective here. The pictures would look well enough on a wall but seem essentially designed for the pages of a book, and this particular book at that. . . . These books are real eye-openers and should make many children more aware of colour, design and movement both in and out of books.

> The Junior Bookshelf, *February, 1968, p. 34.*

Mr. Wildsmith is not the first artist to be intrigued by the "terms of assembly" of the animal world; but no other artist has so magnificently expressed this fascination. The words—some archaic and long forgotten—referring to a group of creatures often stress the peculiar quality of the animal itself. A brilliant and thoughtful imagination has created—beyond mere representation—a collection of visual characterizations such as "a sloth of bears," "a nursery of racoons," "an ambush of tigers," . . . and "a skulk of foxes." The artist has added subtlety to the splendor of his colors; and he has continued his new enthusiasm for composition and page design, first apparent in the recent *Brian Wildsmith's Birds*.

> *Ethel L. Heins, in* The Horn Book Magazine (copyright © *1968 by The Horn Book, Inc., Boston), April, 1968, p. 171.*

OTHER CITATIONS

The Times Literary Supplement, *November 30, 1967, p. 1152.*

The Booklist and Subscription Books Bulletin, *January 15, 1968, p. 596.*

Polly Goodwin, in Book World, *February 25, 1968, p. 16.*

Zena Sutherland, in Bulletin of the Center for Children's Books, *April, 1968, p. 136.*

THE HARE AND THE TORTOISE (1966)

The Hare and the Tortoise is the latest of Wildsmith's fables and the best. He is now out of his "Harlequin" period, many of his admirers will be delighted to learn. His style is freer of mannerisms. Instead of geometrical shapes he builds up his backgrounds now out of natural forms, stylised flowers and grasses which give each picture an extraordinary richness and depth. This book is great fun, too. The artist has not only found most satisfactory forms for his principals—including a tortoise displaying massive reliability in every inch—but surrounded them with a most delectable collection of farmyard and wild creatures. As usual the pages are a riot of gorgeous colour. This is not mindless prodigality, however; each opening, and the progression from page to page, are the result of careful thought and fine taste. Children will love the gaiety and the richness of this lovely book, and from it will gain a sharper awareness of the beauties of form and colour.

> *The Junior Bookshelf, February, 1967, pp. 28-9.*

The extraordinary subtlety and variety of tone, colour and texture, the imaginative light that plays over Brian Wildsmith's work have here [in *The Hare and the Tortoise*] full range and scope. Look at the plodding tortoise and the sleeping hare to see why this old tale has a new appeal. Most other picture books have a medieval aspect by comparison.

> *Margaret Meek, in The School Librarian and School Library Review, March, 1967, p. 125.*

OTHER CITATIONS

The Times Literary Supplement, *November 24, 1966, p. 1082.*

The Booklist and Subscription Books Bulletin, *June 1, 1967, p. 1054.*

THE LAZY BEAR (1974)

For once [Wildsmith] has quite a good story [in *The Lazy Bear*], but the book is really an excuse for some masterly animal portraits in a rich and stylised forest. Marvellous—but is Mr. Wildsmith in danger of losing a little of his fine sensitivity towards colour? In a lesser artist the effect might almost seem garish.

> *The Junior Bookshelf, February, 1974, p. 10.*

Wildsmith's fable about a bear who finds a wagon and invites his friends the raccoon, the deer and the goat to share his rides, but exploits them by making them push him uphill, might carry more weight if the author/illustrator showed more interest in his characters' thoughts and behavior. As it is, not only the animals' expressions but even their standardized figures have to take a back seat to his showy artificial landscapes, which look more like the wild dream of an extraterrestrial color freak than the setting for an essentially conventional lesson in sharing.

> *Kirkus Reviews (copyright © 1974 The Kirkus Service, Inc.), September 1, 1974, p. 942.*

The over-obvious intent [in *The Lazy Bear*] is to socialize, but Wildsmith's stylized double-page spreads in glowing color help take the curse off this lesson on selfishness and bullying. . . . The effect on youngest listeners is unlikely to be an instant commitment to sharing, but, as usual, Wildsmith's pictures show and share well for group use.

> *Lillian N. Gerhardt, in School Library Journal (reprinted from School Library Journal, November, 1974, published by R. R. Bowker Co., a Xerox company; copyright © 1974 by Xerox Corporation), November, 1974, p. 52.*

OTHER CITATIONS

Publishers' Weekly, *September 9, 1974, p. 67.*

Karla Kuskin, in The New York Times Book Review, *November 3, 1974, p. 57.*

Beryl Robinson, in The Horn Book Magazine, *December, 1974, p. 687.*

Zena Sutherland, in Bulletin of the Center for Children's Books, *April, 1975, p. 140.*

THE LITTLE WOOD DUCK (1973)

As an example of the handicapped hero genre [*The Little Wood Duck*] cannot be rated very high for creative imagination but the development of the story is sufficiently well controlled to sustain the child's interest and the text reads aloud quite well, although it lacks any distinctive tone of voice.

If the book were not illustrated by Brian Wildsmith that would be that—but even at less than his best Mr. Wildsmith creates some very lovely effects. In particular, his treatment of the mother duck has led to some warm and satisfying compositions in the earlier part of the book and the three double-page spreads of the fox also suggest a serious involvement of the artist with his subject. However, the introduction of a miscellaneous menagerie in the middle of the story starts to look like a rather perfunctory cliché—effective enough when an essential feature of the narrative, as in *The Lion and the Rat*, but perhaps suggesting a lack of freshness and invention when it is reworked in a somewhat mechanical manner—as here or in *The Owl and the Woodpecker*.

> *Eleanor von Schweinitz, in Children's Book Review (© 1973 Five Owls Press Ltd.; all rights reserved), December, 1972, p. 181.*

Like other Wildsmith books, [*The Little Wood Duck*] is distinguished for brilliant use of color and the combination of abstract and representational details. The story is a variant on a familiar theme: a young animal has a nonconforming behavior trait that is disapproved, but later he wins approbation because the despised trait proves to be useful. . . . A story like this isn't to be taken too seriously, of course, yet the pattern has its hazards: should the "different" duck—or child—be accepted only when his difference has utility?

> *Zena Sutherland, in Bulletin of the Center for Children's Books (© 1973 by the University of Chicago; all rights reserved), October, 1973, p. 36.*

OTHER CITATIONS

Gabrielle Maunder, in The School Librarian, *March, 1973, p. 93.*

Publishers' Weekly, *June 11, 1973, p. 153.*

Eleanor Glaser, in School Library Journal, *September, 1973, p. 119.*

The Booklist, *October 1, 1973, p. 176.*

THE OWL AND THE WOODPECKER (1972)

Brian Wildsmith . . . has found a theme which suits him

well [in *The Owl and the Woodpecker*]. It is a pity that he lacks . . . felicity with words. His text is flat in the extreme, but his pictures are in his finest manner. . . . Wildsmith's designs for the forest and its denizens are as good as he has done. They have great strength and depth, and his mannerisms are firmly under control. No one today conveys more convincingly the texture of living things, owls and badgers and leaves and tree-trunks.

> The Junior Bookshelf, *February, 1972, pp. 20-1.*

The Owl and the Woodpecker [is] a simple, unambitious little tale of birds who quarrel but learn in the end to be friends, but to his story Wildsmith adds brilliant, glowing, mysterious yet happy pictures that lure a child on to explore them as surely as, in reality, a forest might do. And, just as he won't on one visit discover anything like all the forest's treasures, here are pictures to which he will come back again and again. I think, however, that this is a book I'd select primarily for a visual child. Those less keen of eye, less imaginative, might find it rather beyond them.

> *Gladys Williams, in* Books and Bookmen *(© copyright Gladys Williams), February, 1972, p. 96.*

Brian Wildsmith's pictures are always a joy to look at, vibrant with lavish color in strong tones. The story they illustrate [in *The Owl and the Woodpecker*] is less strong. . . . The slight plot moves contrivedly, although it is adequately written, the ending [is] a bit pedantic.

> *Zena Sutherland, in* Bulletin of the Center for Children's Books *(© 1972 by the University of Chicago; all rights reserved), December, 1972, p. 68.*

OTHER CITATIONS

The Times Literary Supplement, *December 3, 1971, pp. 1514-15.*

Publishers' Weekly, *January 31, 1972, p. 247.*

PYTHON'S PARTY (1975)

Even though Wildsmith's showy watercolors have begun to suffer from overexposure, the tricks he puts his jungle animals through as they perform at Python's party afford a splendid chance for dashing double-page displays. . . . Elephant's arrival after the consequently overstuffed Python has gone to sleep helps the animals escape without any uncharacteristic repentance on the reptile's part, and the tricks that Wildsmith plays with Python's form and patterns are just what's required to make him stand out from the splashy crowd.

> Kirkus Reviews *(copyright 1975 The Kirkus Service, Inc.), October 1, 1975, pp. 1125-26.*

OTHER CITATIONS

Publishers' Weekly, *October 27, 1975, p. 53.*

SQUIRRELS (1975)

Arresting close-ups of furry orange squirrels are the forte of Wildsmith's latest graphic display. Distance scenes of the creatures going about their business seem to lose drama along with clarity when neon-colored washes form branches or trunks—though in some of the treescapes, where a blur is the backdrop for concrete detail, the sharpness remains. While the minimal text is secondary to the color spreads, it imparts enough factual material to constitute a suitable introduction for young listeners.

> The Booklist *(reprinted by permission of the American Library Association; copyright 1975 by the American Library Association), June 15, 1975, p. 1078.*

[In *Squirrels*,] Wildsmith paintings—exquisite as always—depict squirrels in their seasonal habitats. Beautiful squirrels they are, too, particularly the young ones, scampering in their red-gold fur, busy with their squirrely duties—poking, collecting, swimming with their tails held high amid impressionistic reeds and rushes. Unfortunately, the treatment, supposedly factual, is careless, e.g., American red squirrels have side stripes which Wildsmith's do not and a squirrel's nest is called a "drey" which is an alternative spelling for "dree," an archaic term not in common parlance. [*Squirrels* is] strictly for browsers.

> *Marjorie Lewis, in* School Library Journal *(reprinted from* School Library Journal, *September, 1975, published by R. R. Bowker Co., a Xerox company; copyright © 1975 by Xerox Corporation), September, 1975, p. 93.*

The many uses of a squirrel's tail—as a parachute, a sail, or a blanket—are some of the facts about the buck-toothed creature revealed in the text. The artist clearly envisions squirrels as brightly-colored, fluffy, often fat lumps of fur. In his characteristic style, he has depicted another member of the animal kingdom in drawings of great beauty, but he has ignored the true nature of the animal observed.

> *Anita Silvey, in* The Horn Book Magazine *(copyright © 1975 by the Horn Book, Inc., Boston), October, 1975, pp. 482-83.*

OTHER CITATIONS

Kirkus Reviews, *April 1, 1975, p. 370.*

Publishers' Weekly, *April 14, 1975, p. 54.*

Zena Sutherland, *in* Bulletin of the Center for Children's Books, *November, 1975, p. 56.*

*   *   *

WILLARD, Barbara

Barbara Willard is an English author who writes for both adults and children. She is also an actress, and has written and produced amateur plays.

GENERAL COMMENTARY

If I call Barbara Willard the Louisa Alcott of our time it is not only because her Tower family so strongly recalls *Eight Cousins* and one of its most engaging members is called Jo. Primarily it is because she is in the truest sense a writer of family stories, demonstrating the diversity that exists within resemblances, illustrating the conflict of temperaments within the protective family circle. Barbara Willard is a virtuoso when it comes to family relationships. Indeed, I suspect she sometimes sets herself problems for the fun of it. . . . In any cross-section of a family she is mindful of the traits and talents which account for individual status and for those constantly shifting alignments that keep a household from stagnation. . . .

Though the ties of family are always recognizable as such, Barbara Willard never makes her boys and girls typical. Theirs are the hostilities and alliances of individuals, properly motivated. (p. 343)

Barbara Willard's books should be defined as family novels rather than family chronicles. Louisa Alcott was first and foremost a chronicler and her best known books, *Little Women* and its sequels, depend on time-sequence rather than on a tighter type of plot, but Barbara Willard prefers to work towards a single climax to which situations and clashes of character all contribute. Even the three early post-Ransome holiday adventures about Snail and the Pennithornes [*Snail and the Pennithornes, Snail and the Pennithornes Next Time, Snail and the Pennithornes and the Princess*] have a developing plot behind a peripatetic pattern—a literary deadline in the first, a soft fruit crop endangered by a strike in the second, a summer pageant in the third. Sometimes the whole plan of a story will be indicated in the first few pages. (pp. 343-44)

Tensions in a family are more dramatic if that family is seen as a community at a moment of crisis. With Barbara Willard that crisis is very often the arrival of an outsider, the device being used lightly or gravely according to the dimensions of each book. . . . There is plenty of material in [the] novels [*The Pet Club, The Family Tower, The Toppling Towers*], in which the author has faced the issues of today (strikes, takeover bids, the colour problem) strictly as they arise from the alignment of her characters. It is because the characters come first that the books have so much vitality and such truth of emotion. (p. 344)

Barbara Willard's lifelong love of Sussex provides her with a setting not superimposed but integral to the majority of her stories. Market town, village, hamlet and seaside resort, the county is vividly realized, sometimes in dialect, often through local occupations (charcoal-burning, iron-founding, fruit-picking), always with bird sound, flowers, roads and weather. The holiday adventures in *The Summer with Spike* or *Surprise Island* or *A Dog and a Half* are hardly original; boating enterprises, village fêtes, domestic pets—we have met these before. But the stories have an authentic ring because they take place in a setting we can really believe in. Barbara Willard knows how a village works; how interests merge, how feuds arise and fade away, how children lead their secret existence in a familiar world. (p. 345)

None of the rich layers of detail in her stories has got there by accident. She is a good story-teller and a fine technician, well aware that each book must have its own shape and style. In *Charity at Home* we can see a skilled novelist using the devices of dramatic irony, timing, personal idiom, documentation to transcend the restrictions of the junior novel. At the opposite end of the scale, her expert planning can be seen in two of her shortest and simplest tales. *The Penny Pony* is a little gem. The opening, with two children gazing longingly at a battered pony-pram in a junk shop,

coils neatly round to the end, where Cathy and Roger, with a real pony at their disposal, affectionately remember the tin one which their imagination brought to life. The transition from toy to live horse is natural and depends as much on the character of boy and girl as it does on external agencies. How well this author understands the way small children think and feel. And how well she caters for those other small children who will read the book—the children of seven or eight who take so much of their vocabulary and their sense of style from the books they read. Barbara Willard is as scrupulous with her words and sentences in a book as brief as this as she is in her full-scale novels for the 'teens. Her unobtrusive style, if it is considered carefully, gives up treasures of expression, endless subtleties of dialogue, within an essential simplicity. (pp. 345-46)

Barbara Willard moved into the sphere of children's books . . . when she was already an experienced and versatile novelist. [She] has adapted her technique to suit a reading range from five to fifteen without losing any of her shrewdness or her humour. She has faced the challenge of restricted length and vocabulary with notable success. Her work with the stage has been a particular advantage to her in her books for the young. How often one feels that she sees her characters dramatically—in the Tower tales, for instance, when the cousins are collected in the garage, on a picnic, at a car rally, we are aware of their movements, gestures, expressions, tones of voice, all the time. (p. 346)

Barbara Willard is no revolutionary in the field of writing for children. She has always worked within orthodox categories and kinds and has always added to them her special pointed style, her shrewd observation of human behaviour and an affection for people which is quite without sentiment and is touched with a pleasantly wry humour which should suit the present-day reader very well. As a novelist for the young she has made a special place for herself as a reliable craftsman and a sound judge of human affairs. (p. 347)

> *Margery Fisher, "Barbara Willard," in* The School Librarian, *December, 1969, pp. 343-48.*

It was Rumer Godden who advised those who read and review children's books to treat them like Persian carpets: design, she said, and colour are important—but what really counts is the perfection of the stitching, for if the stitching is less than perfect the carpet will soon disintegrate. Barbara Willard is one of the few craftsmen writing for young people today whose stitching can be examined under a magnifying glass and found flawless.

> The Times Literary Supplement (© *Times Newspapers Ltd., 1972), December 8, 1972, p. 1489.*

Some writers have a talent for place, some for period. Barbara Willard has both. Her sense of place is so strong she doesn't have to describe things much, they are simply part of the action and atmosphere; and her knowledge of the past can be lightly worn because it too is part of the atmosphere.

> *Isabel Quigly, in* The Spectator (© *The Spectator), December 22, 1973, p. 822.*

CHARITY AT HOME (1966)

[The] people [in *Charity at Home*] are sufficiently nice to be likable, not so perfect as to be unbelievable. Charity finds that she has artistic ability. She is, she decides, different from the rest of the family. Her explanation of this phenomenon is comical, in a touching way. The plot is thickened, a trifle artificially, and there is a dramatic climax. What one remembers in retrospect, however, is not the mystery but the study of a young girl growing to maturity in a quiet, happy home.

> The Times Literary Supplement (© *The Times Publishing Company Ltd. 1965*), *December 9, 1965, p. 1135.*

[Barbara Willard] is very much in sympathy with the anxieties and problems of this 15-year-old girl, and teenage readers will see in Charity some of their own moods and struggles. All the members of the family are well characterised and even when involved in a plot to rob their kind neighbour, Mr. Tressider, the story never becomes stilted or unrealistic.

I found the adult characters particularly attractive and unusually well developed for a children's book. They were a necessary part of the story, and not just a troublesome addendum as they so often appear.

> The Junior Bookshelf, *February, 1966, p. 62.*

In a thoroughly satisfying denouement, which brings unexpected heroes to the fore, Charity willingly accepts reality. Suspense and humor, fast-moving plot, well-delineated characters, taut emotions—all help to make a totally absorbing tale about a modern Cinderella.

> Priscilla L. Moulton, *in* The Horn Book Magazine (*copyright © 1966, by The Horn Book, Inc., Boston*), *December, 1966, p. 722.*

Perhaps the most subtle of Barbara Willard's longer books so far is *Charity at Home*. Here is the theme of the outsider again, but seen from the inside, through Charity's eyes; emotionally, though not actually, this is a first person narrative. The Hollidays in their Sussex village setting are finely realized—the thoughtful policeman father, his son Keith now imitating, now resenting him, the quiet, sensitive mother, the little sister, spoiled, whiney, more than a little lonely. In this group Charity is the outsider—but only to herself. Auntie Joyce, her dead mother's sister, treats her as a daughter; but Charity, discovering in herself a talent for sculpture and at an uneasy stage in her emotional development, cannot laugh herself out of the fancy that she is really the daughter of Mr. Tressider of the Big House, who has always been especially kind to her. Skilfully the author shows how the seed of the idea is sown in Charity's rather confused mind by the lad Derek, just out of approved school and picking up the threads of an old friendship. Tensions within the family and outside it arise from the characters and promote action, making this an unusually mature and satisfying junior novel, planned with technical brilliance. (p. 345)

> Margery Fisher, "Barbara Willard," *in* The School Librarian, *December, 1969, pp. 343-48.*

OTHER CITATIONS

Virginia Kirkus' Service, *August 15, 1966, p. 835.*

Marilyn Gardner, *in* The Christian Science Monitor, *November 3, 1966, p. B 12.*

The Booklist and Subscription Books Bulletin, *February 1, 1967, pp. 585-86.*

Zena Sutherland, *in* Bulletin of the Center for Children's Books, *April, 1967, p. 131.*

A COLD WIND BLOWING (1973)

[*A Cold Wind Blowing*] shows poignantly how the lives of ordinary people are deeply, even tragically, affected by . . . great events. The displaced monks and nuns, hunted and fearful, the King's agents grown fat and self-righteous in their business are credible within the historical framework yet representative of those caught up in a major upheaval in any period or country. . . . Despite the periods of happiness and success, the creation of a warm family atmosphere, the loving accounts of the countryside and harvest, there is indeed a cold wind blowing through the story as the relationship in which Piers is involved moves to a grimly inevitable conclusion.

As a historical novel which depicts the social rather than the political implications of Henry VIII's actions, the book is absorbing. It is equally successful in exploring timeless human relationships, the distortion of emotions by causes or misapplied principles, the futile ease with which lives can be lost.

> Judith Aldridge, *in* Children's Book Review (© *1973 Five Owls Ltd.; all rights reserved*), *February, 1973, pp. 16-17.*

The effects of national events—the persecution of the clergy—on the lives of ordinary people are realistically shown [in *A Cold Wind Blowing*]. Family relationships are particularly well drawn, and the unhappy romance of Piers and Isabella is moving without being maudlin.

> Nancy Berkowitz, *in* School Library Journal (*reprinted from* School Library Journal, *January, 1974, published by R. R. Bowker Co., a Xerox company; copyright © 1974 by Xerox Corporation*), *January, 1974, p. 61.*

Although the period details are strongly depicted and the dialogue richly appropriate, the historical aspect of the writing does not outweigh the narrative [in *A Cold Wind Blowing*]; the book hasn't the starkness or grandeur of Greek tragedy, but it has the same inevitability.

> Zena Sutherland, *in* Bulletin of the Center for Children's Books (© *1974 by the University of Chicago; all rights reserved*), *March, 1974, p. 120.*

OTHER CITATIONS

The Junior Bookshelf, *February, 1973, p. 61.*

Kirkus Reviews, *September 1, 1973, p. 974.*

Beryl Robinson, *in* The Horn Book Magazine, *December, 1973, p. 598.*

A DOG AND A HALF (1971)

[*A Dog and a Half*] is a well told simple story with a good measure of excitement when Brandy outwits a thief. The adults play a large part in the plot and are always very believable and comfortable characters.

> The Junior Bookshelf, *March, 1964, p. 89.*

The naturally appealing elements of the pet story combined with the children's worries about their continued ownership of Brandy are capped by quickened tension over the theft of valuable experimental seedlings from the nursery and by Brandy's subsequent heroism. The brisk tempo of the storytelling, the very real children, the dog for whom the author must have had a model, and the wholly credible situations make for a popular type of story for a wide range of young readers.

> *Virginia Haviland, in* The Horn Book Magazine *(copyright © 1971 by The Horn Book, Inc., Boston), August, 1971, pp. 386-87.*

The story [of *A Dog and a Half*] has pace, suspense, and child-plus-dog appeal, but the plot is contrived: Brandy's owner, who has had to give him away to the children, is a sweet old widow whose husband had also been a nurseryman, and she is invited to live in a trailer on the family property and help in the [family greenhouse] business.

> *Zena Sutherland, in* Bulletin of the Center for Children's Books *(© 1971 by the University of Chicago; all rights reserved), September, 1971, p. 19.*

OTHER CITATIONS

The Times Literary Supplement, *July 9, 1964, p. 604.*

Kirkus Reviews, *February 1, 1971, p. 107.*

Cherie Zarookian, in School Library Journal, *September, 1971, p. 168.*

DUCK ON A POND (1962)

Barbara Willard hovers on the brink of excellence. She has intelligence, social conscience, understanding of children. What she lacks is literary invention; her stories never get that inner glow which distinguishes the really good book.

Duck on a Pond is an average sample of her work. The scene is suburbia, unromantic acres of brick enlivened only by the common with its pond. Tim is an odd-boy-out, with his passion for wild birds and his liking for his own company. Janie, next door, makes an excellent foil; it is one of the charms of the book that the friendship of a boy and a girl should be shown as so charming and natural a thing. The story, about a goldeneye duck which Tim finds and adopts, and the journey to the Severn Wildfowl Trust, is thin, not too well-developed, and too much dependent on coincidence.

> The Junior Bookshelf, *July, 1962, pp. 147-48.*

The story line is firm, the nature study fascinating [in *Duck on a Pond*]; in addition, the characterization in the book is sharply perceptive and the relationships between the children and between children and adults is realistic and perspicacious.

> *Zena Sutherland, in* Bulletin of the Center for Children's Books *(copyright 1962 by the University of Chicago; all rights reserved), October, 1962, p. 36.*

OTHER CITATIONS

The Times Literary Supplement, *June 1, 1962, p. 397.*

Elizabeth F. Grave, in School Library Journal, *October, 1962, p. 192.*

EIGHT FOR A SECRET (1961)

[*Eight for a Secret* is a] most entertaining story about a group of English children, all very different, all vividly real. . . . The author has a real flair for writing realistic conversation that conveys the personality of her characters. An unusual element in the book is the casual and happy relationship of Eillie to the brother and sister-in-law with whom she lives, and even more to her love for their baby. The affection—and the baby—are treated with light and irreverent humor.

> *Zena Sutherland, in* Bulletin of the Center for Children's Books *(copyright 1961 by the University of Chicago; all rights reserved), October, 1961, p. 35.*

Characters must be developed economically in children's stories; there is room to draw only one or two in depth each time. We accept readily the definition of personality by sharp salient points, when this is done well. Using this method, in *Eight for a Secret* Barbara Willard introduces children ranging from the Vicarage twins of fifteen to pram-bound Pam from the housing estate, and shows how they find common ground in spite of differing backgrounds. This kind of shorthand animates her briefest junior tale. (p. 343)

> *Margery Fisher, "Barbara Willard," in* The School Librarian, *December, 1969, pp. 343-48.*

OTHER CITATIONS

The Times Literary Supplement, *November 25, 1960, p. xii.*

Pamela Marsh, in The Christian Science Monitor, *May 11, 1961, p. 7B.*

Margaret Warren Brown, in The Horn Book Magazine, *August, 1961, p. 345.*

The Booklist and Subscription Books Bulletin, *September 15, 1961, p. 74.*

THE FAMILY TOWER (1968)

Barbara Willard is a past master of the family story, and one or two of the characters [in *The Family Tower*] are as well drawn as ever, but this family has so many members that to meet them all in the space of 140 pages is confusing, and the family tree on the end-papers does not really help to clarify matters.

> The Junior Bookshelf, *June, 1968, p. 193.*

The Tower cousins are a pretty extrovert lot. They are almost all ambitious to follow on in the family motor firm and their hierarchy has been determined over many years. By contrast, Emily, as only child, has been brought up in Ghana and at ten is far more mature than the attractive but domineering fourteen-year-old Jo, who hopes to become the new leader of the cousins now that Camilla is married. Emily's reserve, her alarming gift of second sight, make her doubly alien. Inevitably the two girls have to work out a relationship, their rivalry all the stronger for being unexpressed and unacknowledged. Here is the theme of *The Family Tower*. (p. 344)

> Margery Fisher, "Barbara Willard," *in* The School Librarian, *December, 1969, pp. 343-48.*

OTHER CITATIONS

Kirkus Service, *April 1, 1968, p. 405.*

The Times Literary Supplement, *June 6, 1968, p. 579.*

FLIGHT TO THE FOREST (1967)

Vividly re-creating the atmosphere of fear and suspicion between Royalist and Puritan in Cromwell's England, Miss Willard has also shaped interesting characters with believable problems. The reader should not be discouraged by the first few bursts of period dialect—fortunately, they don't last, and the story is a good one.

> Margaret Berkvist, *in* The New York Times Book Review (© *1967 by The New York Times Company; reprinted by permission), September 24, 1967, p. 34.*

The characters [in *Flight to the Forest*] are well drawn; what happens to Rafe's sister and mother is important to the reader, but most deeply felt is the personality of old Gregory Trundle. Many books have been set in Cromwell's time; but in singling out a group of people whose careers were destroyed and lives endangered by the regime, the author has told an unfamiliar and exciting story.

> Ruth Hill Viguers, *in* The Horn Book Magazine (copyright © *1967, by The Horn Book, Inc., Boston), October, 1967, p. 599.*

Set in Cromwell's Commonwealth England, this is [Barbara Willard's] first historical novel. While it is in many ways her weakest book, it does offer some fascinating characters and some unusual insight into the period. . . . Gregory is by far the most interesting personality, an aging, second-rate, yet totally dedicated actor. Rafe's personal conflict over whether to join his grandfather's clandestine profession is also handled well. Despite plot contrivances the book succeeds very well in conveying the spread of popular extremist feeling during that period.

> Elinor Cullen, *in* School Library Journal (*reprinted from* School Library Journal, *February, 1968, published by R. R. Bowker Co., a Xerox company; copyright © 1968 by Xerox Corporation), February, 1968, p. 101.*

OTHER CITATIONS

Kirkus Service, *May 15, 1967, p. 610.*

THE GROVE OF GREEN HOLLY (1967)

Gregory is a big character, perhaps rather too big to live comfortably within the confines of a children's novel. He needs space in which to spread himself, and he deserves closer analysis than would be appropriate in this context. It is, however, wiser to accept the riches offered than to crave those withheld, and *The Grove of Green Holly* is in its own right a remarkably good book. . . .

[The] conflict [between Gregory and Rabe] is worked out in the terms of an absorbing and often exciting adventure story. Miss Willard knows her Sussex and her period equally well, and shares with the reader her intense feeling for the strange forest country in the throes of an industrial revolution. Authentic as history, this is still more a convincing study of people and an investigation of motives.

> The Times Literary Supplement (© *Times Newspapers Ltd., 1967), May 25, 1967, p. 447.*

The Grove of Green Holly stands out among Barbara Willard's few historical novels for the young and this exceptionally fine tale can surely not be her last in this genre. In this tale of the Civil War, drama is technically and emotionally supreme. . . . With the stage as an utterly convincing historical background, the book is divided into crucial scenes—the meeting with Charles II, the rehearsal for *Lear* untimely stopped, Gregory's last moment of tragedy and triumph in the holly grove. Barbara Willard uses visual detail dramatically to carry her story, to promote feeling from it and to set the historical scene. This she does magnificently. Her book may well be the exception that proves the rule that it is unwise to mix historical and fictional characters. The scene at Shoreham, where Gregory brings his skill in make-up to the service of the King, is brilliant in its pictorial force. Through the eyes of young Ralph we see the towering, swarthy fugitive and the old actor face to face, spotlighted in the darkness of the inn chamber where anxious faces advance and recede and voices echo. Words which subtly suggest the seventeenth century without imposing any strain on the reader's belief give a final touch of truth to this imagining of the past. (p. 345)

> Margery Fisher, "Barbara Willard," *in* The School Librarian, *December, 1969, pp. 343-48.*

HETTY (1963)

A large Victorian household in an English seacoast town provides a richly detailed setting for Barbara Willard's *Hetty*. . . . There are appropriate touches of gaslight melodrama when a ne'er-do-well's embezzlements crumble the family fortunes and a long-lost uncle returns to set everything right. Very much of the period is the concern for family reputation and the thorny social distinctions between wealthy families and those "in trade," as incorrigible Hetty, the young heroine, learns to her sorrow.

> Houston L. Maples, *in* Book Week (© *The Washington Post), November 10, 1963 (Part 2), p. 26.*

[*Hetty* is a] smoothly written story of family life in Victorian England. . . . The style, the characterization, and the period details are of more interest than the plot, which is episodic but is tied together rather slightly by the fall and rise of the Jebb [family] finances. Indeed, the only weakness of the book is in the pat appearance—just as Mr. Jebb has decided he must sell the store—of Mrs. Jebb's long-lost brother, who returns a rich man, retrieves the family fortunes, and marries his old love, Cousin Laura.

> Zena Sutherland, in Bulletin of the Center for Children's Books (copyright 1963 by the University of Chicago; all rights reserved), December, 1963, p. 68.

Everything about this story is alive and real: the re-creation of the period and place; the varied, interesting characters (the grandparents are especially delightful); and Hetty's painful growing out of her hoydenish ways. A most satisfying story for girls between ten and twelve.

> Ruth Hill Viguers, in The Horn Book Magazine (copyright © 1963, by The Horn Book, Inc., Boston), December, 1963, p. 601.

OTHER CITATIONS

The Junior Bookshelf, November, 1962, pp. 271-72.

The Times Literary Supplement, November 23, 1962, p. 903.

THE HOUSE WITH ROOTS (1959)

The same happy, well-knit family seems to crop up constantly in children's books under different names. There is the Funny Child, the Practical Child, the Sensible and the Sensitive one. But the children in "The House With Roots" are entertaining enough to be more than caricatures, their bright ideas and the results of their bright ideas surprising enough to keep the plot moving. And since Barbara Willard is English, writing about England, the background has a genuinely different feel for 8-12-year-old Americans.

> Pamela Marsh, in The Christian Science Monitor (reprinted by permission from The Christian Science Monitor; © 1960 The Christian Science Publishing Society; all rights reserved), February 4, 1960, p. 11.

[The House with Roots is an] entertaining story of an English family with four children. . . . The children are remarkably vivid and individual, and the writing style is lively, the one weakness of the book being that the characters are obtrusively British in their conversation, often precocious and occasionally both.

> Zena Sutherland, in Bulletin of the Center for Children's Books (published by the University of Chicago), March, 1960, p. 123.

This is one of the most engaging family stories I have read in a long time. Events are neither very unusual nor exciting, but just getting acquainted with each of the four Pryde children and their parents, in their ancient and fascinating house, makes very good reading. The godparents, too, are interesting and play rather special roles in the fortunes of the family. . . . Each member of the family emerges as a

distinct personality, the relationship between adults and children is exceptionally good, and the setting of modern English life against an old Sussex town very interesting.

> Ruth Hill Viguers, in The Horn Book Magazine (copyright, 1960, by the Horn Book, Inc., Boston), June, 1960, p. 219.

In this breezy tale of an English family pulling together in adversity, the adventures are believable, the hobbies universally interesting and the old house a genuine character, beautifully described. The only trouble is with the humans who seem just a bit priggish. Readers in the middle years bracket will take in stride the unfamiliar slang of the young Prydes and the English equivalents of "filling station," "baby buggy," "garbage collector," "eraser," etc., but they may be surprised at the inordinate time out for tea-making.

> Mary Welsh, in The New York Times Book Review (© 1960 by The New York Times Company; reprinted by permission), June 5, 1960, p. 32.

The book which [Barbara Willard] herself likes to think of as her first—the first, that is, which presented a live and contemporary world to the young—owes very much to its small town atmosphere. The House with Roots reflects the perennial war between progress and history in the familiar plot of an old house threatened by a new ring road. The balance tilts in favour of the old, but only when the house is found to rest on unspoilt monastic foundations. This is a romantic story but not an unreal one, for children and adults belong to Wellowford and their place in the community is made clear from the start. (p. 345)

> Margery Fisher, "Barbara Willard," in The School Librarian, December, 1969, pp. 343-48.

IF ALL THE SWORDS IN ENGLAND (1962)

[This] is a passably good historical novel about the struggle between England's Henry II and Thomas Becket, the Archbishop of Canterbury. While the angle of vision is that of Roman Catholicism, the book is an eminently fair account of the events. The roles of villain and hero have to be assigned in accordance with whether one prefers dominance by the Church or the State. . . .

The book suffers from the fact that the real drama of the quarrel between the two is merely stated. The story should, perhaps, have begun earlier and pictured the stuff of their enmity. Though, from the author's viewpoint, the Archbishop is the hero, he appears austere, remote—even arrogant; there must have been a more warmly human side that could also have been presented. As it is, the reader is likely to conclude—rightly or wrongly—that the saint was consciously or unconsciously trying to provoke his own martyrdom.

> Chad Walsh, in The New York Times Book Review (© 1961 by The New York Times Company; reprinted by permission), April 16, 1961, p. 30.

This is good storytelling, dealing with the conflict between loyalty to Church and allegiance to King arising from the *Constitutions of Clarendon.* Interest lies also in the deep attachment between Simon and his twin who had been taken into Henry II's court.

> The Horn Book Magazine *(copyright, 1961, by the Horn Book, Inc., Boston), June, 1961, p. 267.*

OTHER CITATIONS

Virginia Kirkus' Service, *January 15, 1961, p. 61.*

Zena Sutherland, in Bulletin of the Center for Children's Books, *March, 1962, p. 119.*

THE IRON LILY (1974)

The Iron Lily . . . demands a readership sufficiently mature to appreciate the involved inheritances and family relationships, legitimate and illegitimate, of Barbara Willard's wealden forest iron workers. This is the fourth of her 'Forest' novels and combines strong delineation of character with vivid description of 16th-century rural England. The dialogue, with its rustic directness, is particularly skilful, steering a sure course between the rival dangers of overornate archaism (sometimes called the twere and werty) and jarring contemporary idioms.

> *George van Schaick, in* New Statesman (© *The Statesman & Nation Publishing Co. Ltd. 1973), November 9, 1973, p. 702.*

[*The Iron Lily*], the fourth [book] dealing with the people of [Mantlemass], has all the strength and richness of its predecessor, *A Cold Wind Blowing.* . . .

The story is splendidly constructed, every detail of Lilias's early character and experience being used to justify or prepare for later events. The setting too is superbly presented. South-eastern England, now ruled by Elizabeth, is scarred by iron-workings, and their grimness, smoke and noise are vivid contrasts with the tranquil landscapes around. It is as master of an iron-foundry that Lilias becomes wealthy, but her nickname, the Iron Lily, reflects her character as well as her position.

Lively though all the characterisation is and vigorously presented though all relationships are, it is Lilias with her crooked shoulder and uncompromising outlook who dominates the book. Barbara Willard conveys the nature of despair and resolution to succeed with total success. She ensures that we share Lilias's emotions, yet also those of Ursula when, with shocking suddenness, she is left as a servant at Penshurst (where Lilias had worked) in order to cure her of love for the wrong man.

In all, this is an absorbing and exciting book, not easily put down, and it concludes on a warm note which compensates for the bleakness at the end of *A Cold Wind Blowing.*

> *Judith Aldridge, in* Children's Book Review (© *1973 Five Owls Press Ltd.; all rights reserved), December, 1973, p. 182.*

Lilias is a strong hard character whom we only get to know slowly as the book unfolds. Her daughter, Piers and Richard Medley and all the family from Mantlemass are

much warmer people, but it is "the Iron Lily" who dominates them all. . . . [This is a] fascinating book, completely steeped in the period, [and] the author uses the dialect quite naturally both in speech and descriptive passages. Girls of twelve and over, especially the more thoughtful, will enjoy it, although one reader said if she had not read the earlier novels she would have found it difficult to follow. However it is good to have writing of such high quality for this age group. Miss Willard has a very deep feeling for both her characters and their relationship to each other and to their setting.

> The Junior Bookshelf, *April, 1974, p. 123.*

The writing style [in *The Iron Lily*] is sometimes too consciously historical, especially in the use of archaic words and expressions; also, the political, military, and religious matters of the day are treated as inconsequential but obligatory additions to the story. Still, characterization—especially that of Lilias—is good, the period well drawn, and the mystery of Lilias' origins a suspenseful theme.

> The Booklist *(reprinted by permission of the American Library Association; copyright 1974 by the American Library Association), December 15, 1974, p. 427.*

Lilias's character, suggested by the title *The Iron Lily,* is shown in her behaviour, her manner of speech and her appearance. She outfaces the protests of her work-people in the forest when she decides to hire foreign labour; from loyalty and good business sense, she uses as a symbol and trademark the delicate iron lily which her husband fashioned; she tries to rule the future of her headstrong daughter Ursula as she rules her life and her longings. In this notable portrait of a woman working for her living through the reigns of Mary and Elizabeth Tudor certain traits inherited both from her mother and from her true father, Piers Medley, are carefully and convincingly blended.

> *Margery Fisher, in her* Who's Who in Children's Books: A Treasury of the Familiar Characters of Childhood *(copyright © 1975 by Margery Fisher; reprinted by permission of Holt, Rinehart and Winston), Holt, Rinehart and Winston, 1975, p. 173.*

OTHER CITATIONS

Kirkus Reviews, *November 1, 1974, p. 1162.*

Beryl Robinson, in The Horn Book Magazine, *February, 1975, p. 57.*

Zena Sutherland, in Bulletin of the Center for Children's Books, *February, 1975, p. 101.*

THE LARK AND THE LAUREL (1970)

Tender, solemn romance and well-sustained mystery add spice to this good historical novel. . . . The author's description of the domestic details of one facet of English country life at the beginning of the Tudor era is particularly interesting, and in Dame Elizabeth, she has given readers a solid portrait of the Renaissance woman, a vital force in Europe for well over 100 years.

Nancy Berkowitz, in School Library Journal *(reprinted from* School Library Journal, *May, 1970, published by R. R. Bowker Co., a Xerox company; copyright © 1970 by Xerox Corporation), May, 1970, p. 88.*

From the very first sentence of *The Lark and the Laurel* . . . it is obvious just how practiced a storyteller Miss Willard is. "Cecily had been brought to Mantlemass at dusk." "Brought to Mantlemass"—at once we feel Cecily's helplessness. Mantlemass has a properly medieval taste, and dusk is the right time for shady goings-on. And never does Miss Willard fall below the standard of the opening as she unravels an entrancing tale. . . .

Pamela Marsh, in The Christian Science Monitor *(reprinted by permission from* The Christian Science Monitor; © 1970 The Christian Science Publishing Society; all rights reserved), May 7, 1970, p. B6.*

There are few writers better than Miss Willard in the field of the novel for the twelve to fifteen year old of average or slightly below average ability. She always creates living characters in stimulating and unusual situations. . . .

The main theme [of *The Lark and the Laurel*] is the development of the girl's character, it is truly like the setting free of a caged bird, against the backcloth of everyday life in a remote part of fifteenth-century England. The vivid portrayal of life will fascinate most readers. The author imparts a vast quantity of information with her narrative, and this is one book one would strongly recommend to students engaged in a project on this period.

The Junior Bookshelf, *August, 1970, pp. 234-35.*

With her practical, home-spun skirts above her ankles and her natural air of authority, Dame FitzEdmund, a woman earning her living in a man's world, is a particularly interesting character in the late fifteenth century. She can be matched by other characters later in the sequence of Mantlemass stories—for example, Lilias Rodman . . . —and Barbara Willard has used them to illustrate certain economic and social truths as well as developing their several personalities. Dame Elizabeth remains important above all as the founder of the Mantlemass dynasty, which the author has followed to the middle of the seventeenth century. As the chronicle of a family it shows brilliantly the intricacies of marital lines and the continuance of certain inherited characteristics, both physical and psychological.

Margery Fisher, in her Who's Who in Children's Books: A Treasury of the Familiar Characters of Childhood *(copyright © 1975 by Margery Fisher; reprinted by permission of Holt, Rinehart and Winston), Holt, Rinehart and Winston, 1975, p. 102.*

OTHER CITATIONS

Kirkus Reviews, *April 15, 1970, p. 466.*

The Booklist, *June 15, 1970, p. 1282.*

THE POCKET MOUSE (1969)

[Barbara Willard's] *The Pocket Mouse,* is shaped round three objects—a toy mouse made of coloured felt, a harvest mouse, a joke mouse made of string; each satisfies Colin in a different way for differing reasons and the episodes are arranged skilfully to lead properly one from another. The text is simple and economical but the value of a graceful, accomplished prose is felt in every sentence. . . . (p. 346)

Margery Fisher, "Barbara Willard," in The School Librarian, *December, 1969, pp. 343-48.*

[*The Pocket Mouse* is] the story of a small boy who goes to visit his grandfather and finds the housekeeper forbidding. . . . The pace is sedate, [Willard's] writing competent, [Mary Russon's] illustrations attractive; the story is ostensibly about Colin and his desire for a pet, but it shifts its emphasis to the relationship between adult and child.

Zena Sutherland, in Bulletin of the Center for Children's Books *(© 1970 by the University of Chicago; all rights reserved), June, 1970, p. 169.*

THE RICHLEIGHS OF TANTAMOUNT (1967)

[There] is a crispness about this well-to-do household, an uncomfortable reality, even while they are cocooned by rank and hosts of servants. The first paragraphs neatly outline not only the four Richleighs but the mid-nineteenth century standards of landed gentry. . . . Their Swiss-Family-Robinson existence with the aid of Nancy and Dick, motherless children of a distant sailor, should . . . be improbable, but the pair's pride and the Richleighs' unwitting arrogance, and the sad little story of Edwin's first love, constantly remind us of reality. The rich scenes of Tantamount's internal decay, the gradual discovery of its terrible secret and the real danger at the end make a lurid plot. The cosseted children grow up convincingly when forced into independence, and learn that wealth does not mean they can possess people as well as things. The rigidity of their upbringing is as stern as Nancy and Dick's poverty: eight year-old Maud's being forced to give her dearest toy to a poor child is a harrowing scene.

The Junior Bookshelf, *February, 1967, pp. 63-4.*

This is a departure and an expansion for Barbara Willard: her previously displayed gift for psychologically perceived domesticity gives substance to situations ranging from farce to melodrama in the earlier episodes, deepens to tenderness and compassion before the close. It's her strongest book since *Storm from the West.*

Kirkus Service *(copyright © 1967 Virginia Kirkus' Service, Inc.), March 15, 1967, p. 351.*

Set in a gloomy, isolated castle in the late nineteenth century, [*The Richleighs of Tantamount* is] a rather long-winded tale of the Gothic variety. . . . The fustian and artificial plot cannot quite be overcome by the author's ability to write, frequently, an illuminating descriptive passage.

Zena Sutherland, in Bulletin of the Center for Children's Books *(copyright 1968 by The University of Chicago; all rights reserved), April, 1968, p. 136.*

The Richleighs of Tantamount, a book with a very strong visual quality, is dominated by a Gothicized castle in North Cornwall and the stretch of sand beneath its cliffs; in this vivid setting the four aristocratic children explore the background and outlook of Dick and Nancy Treloar, whose father is a sailor, with as much apprehension and excitement as they explore for the first time the delights of dirt and untidiness and childhood freedom. (pp. 346-47)

> *Margery Fisher, "Barbara Willard," in* The School Librarian, *December, 1969, pp. 343-48.*

OTHER CITATIONS

The Times Literary Supplement, *November 24, 1966, p. 1070.*

Mary S. Cosgrave, in The Horn Book Magazine, *June, 1967, p. 356.*

THE SPRIG OF BROOM (1972)

This original "mystery story" set in the early Tudor period was inspired by the finding of an ancient grave in a village churchyard in Kent which bore the name of Richard Plantagenet, a king of England. . . .

While the story is the main interest as in all Barbara Willard's books, the historical setting is convincing and vivid. The characters are people of their time, not figures transplanted from the twentieth century to another period. The whole story is an original and credible re-creation of what *might* have happened in this byway of history.

> The Junior Bookshelf, *December, 1971, p. 407.*

[*The Sprig of Broom*] by Barbara Willard is of mixed quality. The main characters, Medley Plashet and his companions, are well-drawn; their talk is vigorous and natural; they mature convincingly with events; and their emotions are warmly portrayed. The setting, a country community in Tudor times, comes to life also.

The plot, however, lacks tension and fails to blend the story of Medley with the political intrigues which affect the life of his father. The opening indicates that his father is an illegitimate son of Richard III. The story then jumps twenty-one years to Medley's boyhood, showing his attempts to unravel the mystery of his father's behaviour and his true name. Since the reader already knows this, and since Medley's search does not gather momentum until the final third of the book, suspense is lost, though mystification is provided by unexplained visitors and obscure statements by the boy's father.

> *Judith Aldridge, in* Children's Book Review *(© 1971 by Five Owls Press Ltd.; all rights reserved), December, 1971, p. 196.*

In *The Sprig of Broom* . . . Barbara Willard builds an unusual mystery story on an intriguing entry in the Eastwell Parish Register of 1550 which suggests that Richard III may have had an unacknowledged morganatic heir. . . .

The charm and chief merit of the story lies in the author's vivid picture of country life in Tudor England and in her

ability to project the fears, understand the dangers and temptations of any man in those days who might have been regarded as having any possible claim to the long disputed throne.

> *Gladys Williams, in* Books and Bookmen *(© copyright Gladys Williams), December, 1971, p. xii.*

Friends of Richard III, followers of the Mallory family fortunes and fans of a well turned bend sinister and royal will be pleased to see the younger generation so neatly and favorably disposed of [in *The Sprig of Broom*], but Medley himself is neither remarkable nor particularly plausible. He draws his strength from the sturdy scenery of the English countryside and the controversial aura of his illustrious ancestor.

> Kirkus Reviews *(copyright © 1972 The Kirkus Service, Inc.), October 1, 1972, p. 1155.*

In addition to the tantalizing mystery, [*The Sprig of Broom*] presents history, romance, and a masterful re-creation of life lived long ago. The characters are real and solid, and the story can be read for the engrossing plot and rich background. [Barbara Willard] has shown great skill in revealing gradually the information that leads to the solution of the mystery.

> *Beryl Robinson, in* The Horn Book Magazine *(copyright © 1973 by The Horn Book, Inc., Boston), February, 1973, p. 60.*

This quiet, dignified, mysterious character [Dick Plashet] derives from a tradition that a son of Richard III did work in Sussex at the mason's trade, being buried at Eastwell in Kent in 1550 under the name of Richard Plantagenet. It is a remarkable feat of imagination and historical intuition that has presented a character so diverse. Dick Plashet is linked with those unhappy pretenders of the late fifteenth century and gains credibility by association with them; but where historians can only guess at the motives of Perkin Warbeck and Lambert Simnel, Barbara Willard has drawn her fictional character in depth, giving us clues from the beginning of his strange story to the man's strength and his weakness, his courage in protecting his family and his knowledge that he could be tempted by the promise of rank and fortune.

> *Margery Fisher, in her* Who's Who in Children's Books: A Treasury of the Familiar Characters of Childhood *(copyright © 1975 by Margery Fisher; reprinted by permission of Holt, Rinehart and Winston), Holt, Rinehart and Winston, 1975, pp. 83-4.*

OTHER CITATIONS

Patience M. Canham, in The Christian Science Monitor, *November 8, 1972, p. B6.*

Publishers' Weekly, *January 1, 1973, p. 57.*

The Booklist, *January 15, 1973, p. 495.*

STORM FROM THE WEST (1964)

The theme of *The Battle of Wednesday Week* [published in

America as *Storm from the West*] has possibilities. Three (English) children of a widowed mother and four (American) of a widower father find themselves members of one family through the marriage of these parents. The seven young people are prudently left for the summer in a cottage on the wild west coast of Scotland to resolve their relationship. Which they do. But the restrictions of time—the choice of the holiday adventure form—the necessity for a quick and happy solution—all these keep the book to a merely efficient level, lively, not memorable.

> The Times Literary Supplement (© *The Times Publishing Company Ltd. 1963*), *November 28, 1963, p. 978.*

Miss Willard opens [*Storm from the West*] with a situation fraught with difficulties: the marriage of a widow with two children to a widower (American) with four; and a locale (Scotland) which gives all parties full scope for the trial and error of matching up. The author brings both adults and children into fierce conflict before enabling them to find ways and means of accepting one another and the situation in which they find themselves. The reader can thus enjoy a full-blooded contest of wills and personalities complicated by natural and local hazards, as well as the lavish pleasure of a wild and picturesque setting. A well-planned and well-written book; the author knows children.

> The Junior Bookshelf, *December, 1963, p. 354.*

OTHER CITATIONS

The Booklist and Subscription Books Bulletin, *November 15, 1964, p. 316.*

Zena Sutherland, in Bulletin of the Center for Children's Books, *September, 1965, p. 24.*

THE SUMMER WITH SPIKE (1962)

At first glance this looks like an ideal story for 10-12-year-old boys. The friendship of Perry and Spike starting with a rough and tumble fist fight grows into a companionable and memorable summer for two rather lonely boys. But somehow too many quaint characters crowd into the story. Perry's witty older brother talks too much. The problems of a 17-year-old sister require more attention than a young reader might think they merit. Even the promise of a final exciting clash between a town parade and evacuating trailer camp families fizzles out in the rain. While there is charm in this story of life in an English village, and whimsical humor in the slow-paced unraveling of a mystery that isn't really very mysterious, the average boy will probably find it too descriptive and too long. Girls might like it better.

> Morley John, in The Christian Science Monitor (*reprinted by permission from* The Christian Science Monitor; © *1962 The Christian Science Publishing Society; all rights reserved*), *May 10, 1962, p. 4B.*

In this well-knit, slightly English-villagey story, two boys have a happier than expected summer and, as new friends, become "blood brothers" in spite of entirely different backgrounds.... They are well-drawn individuals, strong in their energies and imagination, Spike having a delightful interest in nature.

> Virginia Haviland, in The Horn Book Magazine (*copyright © 1962, by The Horn Book, Inc., Boston*), *August, 1962, p. 376.*

OTHER CITATIONS

The Times Literary Supplement, *December 1, 1961, p. xx.*

Virginia Kirkus' Service, *March 15, 1962, p. 282.*

Zena Sutherland, in Bulletin of the Center for Children's Books, *November, 1962, p. 51.*

THREE AND ONE TO CARRY (1965)

[*Three and One to Carry* is a] family story set in the south of England; written in a lively style, the book has characterization that is perceptive, relationships that are warm and realistic, and a plot that is modestly dramatic.... Woven neatly into the story are a slight mystery and a modicum of love interest, both concluded believably but with a fillip.

> Zena Sutherland, in Bulletin of the Center for Children's Books (*copyright 1966 by the University of Chicago; all rights reserved*), *February, 1966, p. 108.*

The theme of *Three and One to Carry* is introduced literally with a bang. Arthur falls off a ladder in the barn at Winterpicks and breaks his thigh. This means, as Simon and Prue at once realize, that they must not only look after this unlikeable protégé of their sister's but must also try to like him. The miserable Arthur is a misfit, vastly different from the Lodges in background, education and temperament, and the way he is influenced by and influences them provides a psychological pattern to match the pattern of events in the book. (p. 344)

> Margery Fisher, "Barbara Willard," in The School Librarian, *December, 1969, pp. 343-48.*

OTHER CITATIONS

Virginia Kirkus' Service, *July 1, 1965, p. 629.*

The Booklist and Subscription Books Bulletin, *November 15, 1965, p. 334.*

Kathleen Urban, in English Journal, *January, 1966, p. 111.*

THE TOPPLING TOWERS (1969)

[This is an] uneven novel of a close-knit family of cousins living in a present-day small town in England.... At its worst, this story is pure soap opera (for example, the return of widowed cousin Anthea from America, mink-clad and pregnant); at its best, it offers a perceptive look at pride, simultaneously morale-building and snobbish. There are some authentic glimpses of maturing young people and the dialogue is good, but the author has attempted too much, and *The Toppling Towers* thematically collapses.

> Sarita M. Worthing, in School Library Journal (*reprinted from* School Library Journal, *May, 1969, published by R. R. Bowker Co., a Xerox company; copyright © 1969 by Xerox Corporation*), *May, 1969, p. 107.*

The writing style and the characters [in *The Toppling Towers*] are delightful, but the book is so heavily laden with sub-plots (a cousin from the United States whose husband, thought killed, turns up; an African friend who cannot adjust to life in England; the death of one of the cousins; a love interest) that the story is overburdened.

Zena Sutherland, in Bulletin of the Center for Children's Books *(© 1969 by the University of Chicago; all rights reserved), October, 1969, p. 34.*

Z

ZIM, Herbert S(pencer)   1909-

An American science instructor, editor, and author of articles and reviews, Herbert Zim is noted for his books on science and natural history. (See also *Contemporary Authors,* **Vols. 15-16, and** *Something About the Author,* **Vol. 1.)**

ALLIGATORS AND CROCODILES (1952)

The interesting subject and easy style [in *Alligators and Crocodiles*] will appeal to most third grade readers. The book's value as remedial reading is greatly reduced by the primer size type which older readers will label as babyish. Excellent illustrations [by James Gordon Irving].

> Bulletin of the Center for Children's Books *(published by the University of Chicago), September, 1952, p. 11.*

Alligators and crocodiles are fully described here in large type and numerous pictures. The author, as usual, makes his information both enlightening and easy to understand, while the artist [James Gordon Irving] provides scientific diagrams and habitat drawings to give lifelike impressions of these creatures, so interesting to children.

> *Virginia Haviland, in* The Horn Book Magazine *(copyright, 1952, by The Horn Book, Inc., Boston), December, 1952, pp. 417-18.*

OTHER CITATIONS

Virginia Kirkus' Bookshop Service, *August 1, 1952, p. 453.*

ARMORED ANIMALS (1971)

This typical show-and-tell book differs little in style and makeup from those of the genre published 20 years ago. The title is more restrictive than the text for in the first 15 pages it provides a cursory survey of animal integuments from unicellular invertebrates to elephants, and also digresses into the topics of protective coloration, mimicry, chemical protection, and warning behavior. The remaining three-fourths of the text is descriptive of the real "armored" species such as mollusks, coelenterates, crustaceans, some insects, fishes, reptiles, and a variety of mammals. The text is accurate and informative, but since there are so many attractive books illustrated in color, a young-

ster is not likely to select this dull number for recreational reading. It's pretty superficial too.

> Science Books *(copyright 1971 by the American Association for the Advancement of Science), Vol. VII, No. 1 (May, 1971), pp. 57-8.*

[This is a] fine consideration of all types of animals protected by some sort of armor, from the simplest one-celled, armored invertebrates to complex vertebrates. The simple, well-written text briefly alludes to other protective mechanisms (camouflage, speed, mimicry, chemical means, etc.), and to the general classification of animals into vertebrates and invertebrates. . . . The question is raised as to whether armor is a help or hindrance as far as evolutionary survival and progress are concerned, but readers are left to formulate their own conclusions based on the evidence presented.

> *Lea R. Pastorella, in* School Library Journal *(reprinted from* School Library Journal, *September, 1971, published by R. R. Bowker Co., a Xerox company; copyright © 1971 by Xerox Corporation), September, 1971, p. 169.*

OTHER CITATIONS

Kirkus Reviews, *April 1, 1971, p. 378.*

The Booklist, *June 15, 1971, p. 873.*

BLOOD (1968)

Typically, Mr. Zim here presents a steady stream of facts and ideas about blood. [René Martin's] illustrations are quite informative and suffer only from their black and white drabness. As is often the case with such short, full presentations, it makes very dry reading, which is true even though the author diverges from the narrow physiological attributes of the life fluid to include cultural notes (Asian nuptial blood ceremonies) and even fantasies (the vampire bat fiction). Useful if not pulsating.

> Kirkus Service *(copyright © 1968 Virginia Kirkus' Service, Inc.), March 15, 1968, p. 341.*

OTHER CITATIONS

Science Books, *Vol. 4, No. 1 (May, 1968), p. 55.*

The Booklist and Subscription Books Bulletin, *July 15, 1968, p. 1289.*

Zena Sutherland, in Bulletin of the Center for Children's Books, *December, 1969, p. 70.*

BONES (1969)

A useful supplemental text for elementary science units, this is also an alluring presentation of a topic that may have little initial appeal to readers. In a very brief space, however, a wide variety of information about bones is introduced that will interest readers and give them a feeling for the living aspects of bones; children might be inspired to do further reading about fossils or animal anatomy and physiology.

> *Daryl D. Smith, in* School Library Journal *(reprinted from* School Library Journal, *May, 1970, published by R. R. Bowker Co., a Xerox company; copyright © 1970 by Xerox Corporation), May, 1970, p. 98.*

It is possible to take a chicken bone, put it into weak acid for a week and then remove the bone, curve it like a piece of rubber, or tie it into a knot. This is due to the fact that the acid will have dissolved most of the mineral in the bone. This is just one of the fascinating facts with which Dr. H. Zim arouses an interest in bones and their purpose in the body. . . . Here is a book of interest to everyone, children and adults, but written in such a clear, simple, intriguing way, with delightful illustrations [by R. Martin], that the youngest child, upwards, will be absorbed by it.

> The Junior Bookshelf, *June, 1970, p. 157.*

[Herbert Zim] gives his subject very full, perhaps over-full, treatment, dealing with the skeleton, bone structure, movement and growth, and extending to the use of bones as ornaments and musical instruments. The facts are here right enough [and the book includes] an index for easy reference but as a straight read through *Bones* is a bit daunting.

> The Times Literary Supplement *(© Times Newspapers Ltd., 1970), July 2, 1970, p. 722.*

OTHER CITATIONS

Harry C. Stubbs, in The Horn Book Magazine, *April, 1970, p. 184.*

CARGO SHIPS (with James R. Skelly, 1970)

[*Cargo Ships* explains what] every landlubber needs to know—from why a steel ship doesn't sink to how to get a captain's stripes—conveyed in masterful diagrammatic drawings [by Richard Cuffari] and businesslike explanations. Assuming no prior knowledge on the part of the reader, specifics are provided on parts of the ship, markings (load lines and draft marks) and what they signify, equipment and how it operates, engines from the pioneer reciprocating steam installations to diesels and those powered by electric drive.

> Kirkus Reviews *(copyright © 1970 The Kirkus Service, Inc.), April 1, 1970, p. 388.*

There are many popular picture books about ships and shipbuilding for children, but this one is different. It has good solid factual information in adequate detail. The various types of ships are described. Comparisons are made of the cargo capacity of airplanes and ships, and there is an explanation of buoyancy as it relates to shipbuilding and cargo capacities. Details of the different types of hulls, bows and sterns, and the reasons for those differences or variations are another worthwhile feature. The various types of cargo ships and their adaptation to handling different cargoes, cargo handling equipment, and other related details are thoroughly explained, and adequately labelled line drawings facilitate the explanations. . . . Information on careers in the merchant marine and how one qualifies for work at sea is there, too. The book is therefore good for elementary information on [the] great variety of cargo ships currently in use, as well as a first look for many boys at what is involved in a career at sea, which is attractive to many boys and men. It is printed in large type for easy reading and because of its subject matter should be useful for teaching reluctant readers because it may contain something many of them would "like to know."

> Science Books *(copyright 1970 by the American Association for the Advancement of Science), Vol. 6, No. 1 (May, 1970), p. 60.*

OTHER CITATIONS

The Booklist, *June 15, 1970, p. 1282.*

The Junior Bookshelf, *December, 1972, p. 392.*

COMMERCIAL FISHING (with Lucretia Krantz, 1973)

The imprecise opening definition—"fishing for food and other industrial purposes is called commercial fishing"—can be taken as fair warning of the authors' slack, unincisive treatment. Otherwise this latest of Zim's countless juvenile surveys has the nice easy look of his *How Things Work* series but no new perspective to give it an edge over existing titles. The authors make only passing mention of the problems of pollution and overfishing . . . , nor is there any reference to boundary disputes, the economics of the industry, or even how fish are marketed. Instead, . . . the authors offer a mechanical (in both style and focus) review of new ways of finding fish (radio, sonar, chopper spotting), improvements on the old ways of catching them (here a rundown on different hooks and nets), and a quick skim over varieties of fish in the catch, non-food uses, oyster farming, and (unhelpfully—"Fishing is work for men who like the sea, the wind, and waves") fishing as a career.

> Kirkus Reviews *(copyright © 1973 The Kirkus Service, Inc.), October 1, 1973, p. 1104.*

OTHER CITATIONS

Darwin Jones, in School Library Journal, *January, 1974, p. 55.*

CORALS (1966)

Corals is a traditional children's book that superficially describes these interesting animals, their habitat, representative living and fossil specimens, the location of major coral islands and reefs, and some of the other invertebrates and fishes that live in association with the corals, and the formation of coral reefs and atolls. Incidental reference is made to the voyage of the *Beagle*, and the book terminates with mention of lighthouses and buoys that mark the locations of coral reefs, and the statement that "each year more and more visitors come to coral reefs from Florida to Australia." This is too much material for a 63-page book especially since about half of the space is devoted to rather amateurish black-and-white illustrations [by René Martin]. The book has no logical or sequential organization. Apparently Dr. Zim tried to compromise exactness in order to make the book palatable to younger students. It lacks lucidity—he has made it too dull and confusing for younger readers, and too superficial for students in upper elementary grades. There is no bibliography, but there is an index.

> Science Books *(copyright 1966 by the American Association for the Advancement of Science), Vol. 2, No. 3 (December, 1966), pp. 195-96.*

OTHER CITATIONS

Gladys Conklin, in School Library Journal, *October, 1966, p. 242.*

The Booklist and Subscription Books Bulletin, *December 15, 1966, p. 454.*

CRABS (with Lucretia Krantz, 1974)

This well-integrated mix of concrete language and clear, relevant drawings could serve as a model for elementary science writers. Zim and Krantz introduce an impressive variety of topics . . . and they manage to combine clear, fascinating explanations of mechanical processes (such as the ghost crab's acrobatic walk) with discussions of more complex topics that can be adequately understood on a simple level yet stimulate one's curiosity to know more. Extra material on crab species and evolutionary ancestors is included in a small print supplementary chapter, all measurements are expressed in metric units—an innovation which should help youngsters become familiar with the system, and unlike so many non-fiction illustrations, [René] Martin's drawings really relate to and extend page-by-page the message of the text.

> Kirkus Reviews *(copyright © 1974 The Kirkus Service, Inc.), April 1, 1974, p. 367.*

This is a curious little book. The large font and simple, crisp illustrations [by René Martin] suggest to the casual examiner that *Crabs* is a superficial story written for pre-school children. Actually the information content is quite advanced. The crabs' relatives, structure and many aspects of their biology are discussed in a remarkably informative fashion. The discussions answer a variety of questions, telling how crabs vary, what they feed on, how they move, how they breathe, what senses they use, how many kinds there are and what are their principle enemies. A short section even covers a classification describing the major groups in a simple, easily remembered format. Thus, while the book could be read by an elementary school student,

the student's capacity to remember the material might limit its utility. If only half the knowledge gleaned is remembered, the reader will know as much or more about crabs as does the average college student taking an introductory course in zoology.

> Science Books *(copyright 1974 by the American Association for the Advancement of Science), Vol. X, No. 3 (December, 1974), p. 257.*

OTHER CITATIONS

Juliet Kellogg Markowsky, in School Library Journal, *September, 1974, p. 96.*

Harry C. Stubbs, in The Horn Book Magazine, *April, 1975, pp. 169-70.*

DINOSAURS (1954)

[This] authoritative once-over on the age of giant reptiles is very informatively illustrated with James Gordon Irving's pencil drawings and undaunted when it comes to explanations of more obscure evolutionary processes. From fossil finding on through to the influence of cerebral development on survival, both Zim and Irving are quite explicit—and anyone going with them will emerge knowing more about this particular 100 million years in the world's history than he did before.

> Virginia Kirkus' Bookshop Service, *February 1, 1954, p. 64.*

Among the many books that Herbert Zim has written in various scientific fields, *Dinosaurs* (1954) is a good example of the logical organization, simple and succinct writing, and provision of background information that make his approach admirably suitable for presenting complex information to a reader unfamiliar with the subject.

> *May Hill Arbuthnot and Zena Sutherland, in their* Children and Books *(copyright © 1947, 1957, 1964, 1972 by Scott, Foresman and Co.), 4th edition, Scott, Foresman, 1972, p. 613.*

OTHER CITATIONS

Virginia Haviland, in The Horn Book Magazine, *April, 1954, pp. 100-01.*

Bulletin of the Center for Children's Books, *July, 1954, p. 97.*

HOISTS, CRANES AND DERRICKS (with James R. Skelly, 1969)

In spite of the large print and simple sentence construction, this is not a book for young children, but requires considerable mental effort on the part of the reader. . . . One wonders what readership is imagined for sentences such as "Mechanical advantage is the relation of the pull or effort to the load", or what's going to happen for a child once he's learnt that 100ft of polyester rope weighs 31lb. against dacron rope's 30. [Gary Ruse's] diagrams are particularly helpful, but the book must be counted as one of the less successful of Zim's efforts.

The Times Literary Supplement (© *Times Newspapers Ltd., 1971), July 2, 1971, p. 778.*

[Zim and Skelly] have made a clear and workmanlike job of this outline of various types of hoist, crane and derrick. Their construction, uses and capacities are described, and the text is most effectively assisted by the very clear line drawings by Gary Ruse. While the book will be a fascination for the more technically-minded young, it will be equally good for instructing the others in the way these equipments are used, and the principles on which they are made.

The Junior Bookshelf, *August, 1971, p. 260.*

OTHER CITATIONS

Paul Showers, in The New York Times Book Review, *November 9, 1969, p. 52.*

Science Books, *Vol. 6, No. 4 (March, 1970), p. 341.*

LIFE AND DEATH (with Sonia Bleeker, 1970)

Drs. Zim and Bleeker [Dr. Sonia Bleeker is also Mrs. Herbert S. Zim], as biologist and anthropologist, have pooled their understanding of life processes and death practices in a synthesis so forthright it allays fears, so tactful it strengthens respect, so thorough it spares the parent from explaining what he may be unwilling or unequipped to discuss. The facts of life—as against non-life—lead to the data of death: comparative lifespans among animals, rates of life expectancy time-wise and place-wise. . . . [*Life and Death* is invaluable] preparation for a death in the family and for that ultimate demise, one's own.

Kirkus Reviews *(copyright © 1970 The Kirkus Service, Inc.), April 1, 1970, p. 388.*

''Life and Death'' does a good job of avoiding the clichés of false sentiment and concentrating on the many observable facts about dying and death which may so easily trouble children confronted with them for the first time. . . .

About a quarter of the book is devoted to our costly and elaborate ceremonies for disposing of corpses. . . . This is put in fascinating perspective by a succeeding section which describes not only the burial rituals of the ancient Egyptians and Iroquois, the Maoris, Hindus, Pygmies, Navajos and Chukchees, but the various beliefs regarding the spirits that are thought to survive the body. It all adds up to a thorough and candid presentation, as reassuring as it is unemotional.

Paul Showers, in The New York Times Book Review (© *1970 by The New York Times Company; reprinted by permission), April 26, 1970, p. 30.*

This is a long-needed book dealing matter-of-factly with a subject usually treated, in books for the young, with careful circumlocution or saccharine tenderness. Mr. and Mrs. Zim are crisp and clear in their discussions of life-spans, the aging process, the end of life-functions, and the roles of doctors, ministers, and morticians. . . . The illustrations [by René Martin] are static, the diagrams useful. A serious flaw

in an otherwise excellent book is its failure to point out that it is not necessary to employ an undertaker, and that one can bequeath one's body for use in medical research.

Zena Sutherland, in Saturday Review *(copyright © 1970 by Saturday Review, Inc.; reprinted with permission), June 27, 1970, p. 39.*

[This] is a unique, partially successful discussion of life but mostly death, including physical and cultural aspects of the latter. Some of the chemical information about life in the text or in charts is too technical to leave unexplained: e.g., the mention of DNA and RNA with too little amplification. The discussion of aging is not really comprehensible because of the lack of information on the function of cells in life. No real explanations are given of how hair turns grey or white, why skin wrinkles, what happens when old people shrink in height; there is just the statement that cells and organs function less well as one ages. In general, the frame of reference is death from old age. Considerable space is devoted to the function of a funeral home (including the training of its director) and cematary burials, which seems disproportionate in view of the need for more detailed explanation of various terms and concepts used throughout the book. The last section on belief in spirits and soul is very well done. Many charts and adequate drawings [by René Martin] illustrate the text which, all in all, will be useful as an introductory treatment of a subject that excites juvenile curiosity.

Isadora Kunitz, in School Library Journal *(reprinted from* School Library Journal, *September, 1970, published by R. R. Bowker Co., a Xerox company; copyright © 1970 by Xerox Corporation), September, 1970, p. 110.*

OTHER CITATIONS

The Booklist, *July 1, 1970, p. 1343.*

Zena Sutherland, in Bulletin of the Center for Children's Books, *October, 1970, p. 36.*

Harry C. Stubbs, in The Horn Book Magazine, *February, 1971, p. 70.*

LIGHTNING AND THUNDER (1952)

This is an intriguing book in its dramatic and beautiful pictures by James Gordon Irving, which by its very appearance will lure the inquiring youngster through a text that is quite a reach for third and fourth graders (and in format that is the age level at which the book seems to aim). Zim has the ability, however, to present scientific facts in an appealing package, and much of the data on causes and effects, on what happens and how, will be understood, and make the terrifying beauty of thunder storms a force to respect and admire.

Virginia Kirkus' Bookshop Service, *January 1, 1952, p. 2.*

[*Lightning and Thunder*] combines an easy style with an interesting subject to make a book that will be read from the elementary grades through high school. Graphic illustrations [by James Gordon Irving] and clear text explain the causes and effect of thunder and lightning. Unfortunately some of the most important illustrations—the do's and don'ts to be followed during a lightning storm—are on the end papers only.

> Bulletin of the Center for Children's Books *(published by the University of Chicago), February, 1952, p. 48.*

MACHINE TOOLS (with James R. Skelly, 1969)

The book's format (with the large, open type), simple illustrations that show young people, and easy writing style make this suitable for the intended readers who will also relate to examples given of the products of machine tools: bicycles, notebook binders. However, the vocabulary becomes complex and undefined terminology used excessively: "The machinist carefully positions a die on the bolster, and then fastens the punch on the bottom of the ram." Fortunately, [Gary Ruse's] illustrations provide a visual reference that helps to explain the text, but average upper elementary students still won't understand the workings of some of the machines.

> *Donald J. Schmidt, in* School Library Journal *(reprinted from* School Library Journal, *December, 1969, published by R. R. Bowker Co., a Xerox company; copyright © 1969 by Xerox Corporation), December, 1969, p. 61.*

OTHER CITATIONS

Science Books, *Vol. 5, No. 1 (May, 1969), p. 69.*

MEDICINE (1974)

Not medical practice but medication ("drugs" or "remedies") is Zim's subject here. . . . Though avoiding the issue of drug companies' general irresponsibility, Zim does point out the possibility of undesirable side effects, the uselessness of many over-the-counter drugs, and the dangers of abuse or overreliance on medicines. It's all done with a welcome absence of awe for "good" drugs, hysteria over "bad" drugs, or any kind of preaching.

> Kirkus Review *(copyright © 1974 The Kirkus Service, Inc.), December 1, 1974, p. 1258.*

Not a survey of the field of medicine but of medicinal products, this discusses the various ways in which medicines are used (taken by mouth, injected by a hypodermic syringe, etc.) and the care with which dosage is decided. . . . The book contains much sensible advice, and the material is authoritative and well organized; the writing style is not difficult to read because of complexity, but it is sedate and the pages quite solid with close although large print. A single-page index is appended.

> *Zena Sutherland, in* Bulletin of the Center for Children's Books *(© 1975 by the University of Chicago; all rights reserved), February, 1975, p. 103.*

[In *Medicine*] Zim wisely emphasizes that many people take medicines they don't really need and mentions that even vitamins can be poisonous in excessive amounts. In discussing the potential dangers of medicines, the text remains calm and objective and does not turn into the usual propaganda piece against drug abuse.

> *Isadora Kunitz, in* School Library Journal *(reprinted from* School Library Journal, *March, 1975, published by R. R. Bowker Co., a Xerox company; copyright © 1975 by Xerox Corporation), March, 1975, p. 103.*

For all students . . . Zim's excellent book clearly and accurately tells a great deal about the scope and use of medicines in medical practice. He discusses patent medicines, antibiotics, biological preparations—vaccines—and many other therapeutic and nontherapeutic agents taken by Americans and prescribed by physicians. The physiology of the human body is explained simply, as it is relevant to the drug being described. This is not a book about medicine as a profession, but the author does describe some of the ways in which physicians can treat their patients. He also discusses the interesting and important matter of self-medication by patients who unthinkingly seek an elixir which will solve their problems or make their lives more tolerable.

> *William Fleeson, in* Science Books & Films *(copyright 1975 by the American Association for the Advancement of Science), Vol. XI, No. 1 (May, 1975), p. 39.*

MONKEYS (1955)

[This book] covers the subject of monkeys in the adequate and quietly humorous way we expect from the author. Monkeys as primates are discussed first and their special characteristics are brought out. Then special types of Old World and New World monkeys gives a sampling of the many extant varieties, and final passages on their use in scientific experiments and as pets relates them more closely to human experience. Drawings by Gardell D. Christensen are very much alive.

> Virginia Kirkus' Service, *May 1, 1955, p. 305.*

OTHER CITATIONS

Jennie D. Lindquist, in The Horn Book Magazine, *August, 1955, p. 274.*

Bulletin of the Center for Children's Books, *September, 1955, p. 16.*

PARRAKEETS (1953)

Careful pencil drawings by Larry Kettlekamp and Mr. Zim's clear, friendly way of imparting information give parrakeet owners and fanciers all they need to know to start raising their pets. Besides the birds' interesting Australian background and history of immigration to different countries and homes of the world, there are explicit instructions on raising, feeding, training (to talk) and the essentials of breeding. Simple enough for youngsters to follow, these are excellent directions and a directive for new pleasure in bird raising.

Virginia Kirkus' Bookshop Service, *August 1, 1953, p. 488.*

This simply presented information on the raising, training, and breeding of parrakeets . . . will be useful to those who already have these amusing pets and may well encourage others to become owners. Dr. Zim's explanation of color mutations according to the rules of genetics will interest serious young scientists. Plainly labeled drawings on every page are an important part of the book.

> *Virginia Haviland, in* The Horn Book Magazine *(copyright, 1953, by The Horn Book, Inc., Boston), October, 1953, pp. 363-64.*

OTHER CITATIONS

Bulletin of the Center for Children's Books, *November, 1953, p. 26.*

PIPES AND PLUMBING SYSTEMS (with James R. Skelly, 1974)

Zim and Skelly discuss informally the uses, manufacture and operation of plumbing systems, and their tendency to skim lightly over some puzzling matters (how does "the energy of the sun . . . raise water to high places" and what exactly happened when "the original lift pump . . . sucked air from a pipe"?) is balanced by the appeal of [Lee J.] Ames & [Mel] Erikson's precise diagrams of valves, fittings, meters and pipe systems. And those charts which distinguish a 45 degree street elbow from a reducing T and photos like that of a 20 foot high gate valve have a concrete fascination that will extend beyond the clear but generalized elementary level text.

> Kirkus Reviews *(copyright © 1974 The Kirkus Service, Inc.), March 15, 1974, p. 307.*

Superior to Urquehart's *Plumbing and How It Works* . . . the only other book available on this subject for the age group—this is a clear overview that covers water, sewer, and gas pipes and home heating systems. The authors then describe plumbing uses in industry; the history of plumbing; the manufacture and use of various valves, pipes, and pumps; the training procedure for plumbers and pipe fitters; and the jobs of inspectors, engineers, apprentices, journeymen, and master plumbers. The line illustrations of pipes, fittings, systems, and pumps are meticulously accurate and the many photographs show workers on the job (though no women are pictured).

> *Shirley Smith, in* School Library Journal *(reprinted from* School Library Journal, *September, 1974, published by R. R. Bowker Co., a Xerox company; copyright © 1974 by Xerox Corporation), September, 1974, p. 96.*

[*Pipes and Plumbing Systems*] is a delight to read, even by the technically trained adult. The authors show that the flow of fluids is a transportation problem. They then logically go through the steps in the supply of materials through pipelines, with a great deal of emphasis on the home water supply. Every aspect is covered—from the pipe layout, drains, vents, pumps and even valves which control the supply. Gas supply and heating systems are also detailed.

The mechanics of pipelines, their construction, and even the methods of making various types of pipes are presented. Illustrations are used to great benefit throughout. The whys of materials—i.e., why is copper best for water—are noted. The same attention is given to valves and fittings. Of most interest to the young reader are descriptions of the jobs of engineers, pipe fitters and plumbers. The author describes in detail how they are trained and what they will do. The only complaint is that some of the illustrations showing the layout of plumbing systems may be too technical to be comprehended by the young reader.

> *Robert E. Paaswell, in* Science Books & Films *(copyright 1975 by the American Association for the Advancement of Science), Vol. XI, No. 1 (May, 1975), p. 39.*

OTHER CITATIONS

The Booklist, *June 15, 1974, p. 1156.*

SHARKS (1966)

The style [in *Sharks*] is pedestrian and unoriginal. The material appears to have been paraphrased from other sources. The opening statement, "sharks are the largest, deadliest, and most feared creatures in the sea," overlooks the sperm and baleen whales. The author perhaps is unaware of the discovery of bone in the fossil sharks of the acanthodian group which raises a question as to whether the traditional view is correct that cartilage is more primitive than bone.

> Science Books *(copyright 1966 by the American Association for the Advancement of Science), Vol. 2, No. 2 (September, 1966), p. 131.*

The accuracy of [Zim's] opening statement that "Sharks are the largest . . . creatures in the sea," can be questioned; this distinction seems to belong to whales. Nevertheless, this is an interesting, informative, well-illustrated account of the shark's evolution, physical characteristics, feeding habits, and danger to man.

> *Alphoretta S. Fish, in* School Library Journal *(reprinted from* School Library Journal, *September, 1966, published by R. R. Bowker Co., a Xerox company; copyright © 1966 by Xerox Corporation), September, 1966, p. 256.*

SNAILS (with Lucretia Krantz, 1975)

[This book] packs lots of detail into a pared down text and informal drawings, beginning with curious facts (about flesh-eating and poisonous species, or in a comparative graph, snail's paces) and moving on to more specialized physiological information. . . . [Much] of the later material may prove bewildering; perhaps because snails seem so amorphous to begin with, the comparative sketches of opercula, balance organs, sexual differences, and foot shapes can be hard to interpret. At least the easiest material comes first, and while some youngsters may be frustrated later on, this will appeal to those who shy away from wordy explanations but don't mind puzzling over pictures.

Kirkus Reviews *(copyright © 1975 The Kirkus Service, Inc.), April 15, 1975, p. 463.*

[This] dry but thorough examination of snails covers many aspects including anatomy, location, reproduction, diet, and characteristics of different species. The numerous black-and-white drawings and diagrams [by René Martin] are for the most part useful and well labeled, although occasionally confusing. While the text is not divided into sections, it proceeds in an orderly fashion. [This is less] inspiring but more informative than [Lilo] Hess' *A Snail's Pace.* . . .

The Booklist *(reprinted by permission of the American Library Association; copyright 1975 by the American Library Association), June 15, 1975, p. 1078.*

[In *Snails* physical] characteristics of snails, including the interesting process of shell formation, are clearly described with scientific terms well defined. . . . Utilitarian in appearance (there are no color photographs though the beautiful hues of the shells are frequently mentioned) this is otherwise quite thorough and informative.

Margaret Bush, in School Library Journal *(reprinted from* School Library Journal, *September, 1975, published by R. R. Bowker Co., a Xerox company; copyright © 1975 by Xerox Corporation), September, 1975, p. 116.*

THE SUN (1953)

Mr. Zim presents a great deal of information about the sun [in this book]. . . . A few simple experiments are included which illustrate the power of the sun in respect to plant growth, light and heat. Unfortunately, in spite of interesting material, [*The Sun*] lacks some of the directness and simplicity which characterize the author's excellent books on animals.

Beatrice Davis Hurley, in The New York Times Book Review *(© 1953 by The New York Times Company; reprinted by permission), April 5, 1953, p. 20.*

[This is a] fascinating and solidly factual, though brief, study of the sun, easily read by younger children but of interest to a wider audience. Its text, in large print, explains the sun's temperature as that of an atomic furnace and discusses radiant energy and the mystery of sunspots. Suggestions, with diagrams, for simple experiments, give everyday significance to the subject. [Larry Kettelkamp's] sketches on each page are clear and well labeled.

Virginia Haviland, in The Horn Book Magazine *(copyright, 1953, by The Horn Book, Inc., Boston), June, 1953, pp. 225-26.*

OTHER CITATIONS

Kirkus Reviews, *January 15, 1953, pp. 115-16.*

Bulletin of the Center for Children's Books, *March, 1953, p. 55.*

TELEPHONE SYSTEMS (with James R. Skelly, 1971)

A broad view of the many human activities in the field of telephone communications is provided with the simplicity and clarity that characterizes many of Zim's books. The history and the uses of the system are sufficiently discussed and well-illustrated. The description of how a telephone works is excellent, but further discussion of the fundamentals of a telephone system is poor. For example, the description of a switchboard with plugs and jacks starts well and shows how a connection is made, but the complete circuit from one telephone to another is not shown. A better explanation and diagram of mechanical switching, so common now, should be offered; the illustration of it in the text is almost worthless. Classes investigating careers may profit from the pictures of operators, linemen, servicemen, and other employees on their jobs.

Science Books (copyright 1972 by the American Association for the Advancement of Science), Vol. VIII, No. 4 (March, 1972), p. 324.

OTHER CITATIONS

Kirkus Reviews, *September 1, 1971, p. 952.*

Shirley A. Smith, in School Library Journal, *February, 1972, p. 63.*

TRACTORS (with James R. Skelly, 1972)

In high gear after their similarly smooth treatises on *Trucks, Cargo Ships,* and *Machine Tools,* Zim and Skelly get good mileage from the impressive power and functional diversity of tractors and crawlers. . . . Easy, clear, and aimed straight at its likely audience—those kids who love being able to distinguish among a double grouser, triple grouser and semi-skeleton shoe.

Kirkus Reviews *(copyright © 1972 The Kirkus Service, Inc.), October 1, 1972, p. 1150.*

The title of this book probably suggests one well known and specific type of machine. At the very beginning, however, the authors explain the meaning of the word "traction", and thus from the start the reader is prepared to accept a much wider variety of information. By putting the subject into its rightful context the authors are able to give a very full account of the varieties of tractor, and of the diversity of work which they do—the initial all-embracing definition leading on to a host of detail, including the scientific—and even the completely ignorant and perhaps the initially uninterested will be intrigued by the facts given about diesel engines, hydraulic power, brakes, wheels, treads and tracks. The authors have the wisdom, too, to point out that the work of a tractor is not always executed for the common good. The book finishes with some information about career prospects in working with this type of machinery, and credit must be given for amassing so many facts in a short work. An index gives added value. There does seem to be some repetition here and there, and the writing itself is at times careless and clumsy. The diagrams are well defined and detailed but the photographs are not always sufficiently clear. A very useful book but not, unfortunately, particularly attractive in form or presentation.

The Junior Bookshelf, *December, 1974, pp. 375-76.*

OTHER CITATIONS

Marilyn Walker, in School Library Journal, *January, 1973, p. 73.*

The Booklist, *May 1, 1973, p. 862.*

TRUCKS **(with James R. Skelly, 1970)**

With *Trucks,* the partnership of Zim and Skelly performs with its usual efficiency and dispatch, supplying a pat on the "backbone of land transportation." And today trucking doesn't end at land's end: the impressive depiction of container shipping . . . gives this an edge on the competition. Also more thoroughgoing and graphic than in other books is the explanation of trucking operations in the terminal and on the road (including security measures and size and weight regulations). . . . [Stan Biernacki's] illustrations are integral and correspondingly clear.

> Kirkus Reviews *(copyright © 1970 The Kirkus Service, Inc.), October 1, 1970, p. 1103.*

[This is a] clear, concise presentation of the design, construction and operation of trucks. . . . The sound, basic information in 18 point type is accompanied by [Stan Biernacki's] competent black-and-white illustrations and diagrams. This provides more thorough coverage than Elting's *Trucks at Work* (. . . 1965), Stevens' *Trucks That Haul by Night* (. . . 1966) or Buehr's *Trucks and Trucking* (. . . 1956). School libraries will find it a useful companion to Behren's *Truck Cargo* (. . . 1970) for transportation units.

> *Evelyn F. Newlands, in* School Library Journal *(reprinted from* School Library Journal, *March, 1971, published by R. R. Bowker Co., a Xerox company; copyright © 1971 by Xerox Corporation), March, 1971, p. 133.*

OTHER CITATIONS

The Booklist, *December 1, 1970, p. 311.*

Zena Sutherland, in Bulletin of the Center for Children's Books, *April, 1971, p. 132.*

THE UNIVERSE **(1961; revised 1973)**

[Herbert Zim treats] young minds in his audience with respect, with no condescending tones·and no compromised facts. Stars, nebulae, and the tools for studying them are all here to contemplate, nicely complemented by Gustav Schrotter's artwork. In fact, the skillful blend of words and pictures is what makes the book stand out.

> *Henry W. Hubbard, in* The New York Times Book Review *(© 1961 by The New York Times Company; reprinted by permission), May 21, 1961, p. 36.*

Because of the nature of the material, the scope of subject,

and the lack of division in the text, [*The Universe*] seems heavy and turgid in presentation. There is, however, a great deal of accurate and interesting information given.

> *Zena Sutherland, in* Bulletin of the Center for Children's Books *(copyright 1962 by the University of Chicago; all rights reserved), May, 1962, p. 152.*

Zim surveys man's conception of the nature and size of the universe from ancient times to the present. He clearly and accurately discusses such topics as galaxies, clusters, variable stars, and how vast distances are measured. The first edition has been partially rewritten and revisions consist of the inclusion of an index, some new material on radio telescopes, reference to moon landings and interplanetary probes, updated figures, and a few new illustrations [by Gustav Schrotter and René Martin]. . . . [This is] the best book on the universe for the middle grade range.

> *René Jordan, in* School Library Journal *(reprinted from* School Library Journal, *April, 1974, published by R. R. Bowker Co., a Xerox company; copyright © 1974 by Xerox Corporation), April, 1974, p. 62.*

OTHER CITATIONS

Ethel Richard, in Junior Libraries, *May, 1961, p. 52.*

The Booklist and Subscription Books Bulletin, *June 1, 1961, p. 614.*

Alice Dalgliesh, in Saturday Review, *August 19, 1961, p. 22.*

WAVES **(1967)**

[*Waves*] was prepared for the use of elementary school students in their introduction to the oceans. It should serve that purpose well, being a highly readable discourse on a complex subject. If the book has a fault it lies in its brevity. The student may be left rather unchallenged by the matter-of-fact language, when the details of and exceptions to the fundamental information given will challenge scientific ingenuity for centuries.

> Science Books *(copyright © 1967 by the American Association for the Advancement of Science), Vol. 3, No. 3 (December, 1967), p. 219.*

[*Waves*] is intended for the "older junior pupil" and is a conscientious attempt to meet his needs; there is no contents page, but we have an index, the text is well spaced, there is an illustration on each page, the sentences are short. The subject chosen is a narrow one and the author covers it methodically, but in the end the weight of facts is too oppressive, and we yearn for some indication, in illustrations or text, of the excitement of the moving ocean.

> The Times Literary Supplement *(© Times Newspapers Ltd., 1968), October 3, 1968, p. 1128.*

YOUR BRAIN AND HOW IT WORKS **(1972)**

With no glossary or outright definitions, this comfortable-looking introduction to the structure, functions, and evolution of the brain is neither as easy as it looks or as straightforward as it reads. . . . Edith Weart's *The Story of Your Brain and Nerves* (1961), though less inviting in format, sticks closer to the basics, and Margaret O. Hyde's *Your Brain* (1964) offers older children a far more stimulating and clarifying survey of brain research.

> Kirkus Reviews *(copyright © 1972 The Kirkus Service, Inc.), March 15, 1972, p. 333.*

On the whole, Zim's . . . book is a simple, competent discussion of the evolution, physiology and functions of the human brain. However, the author's effort to differentiate between brain and mind may prove difficult for youngsters to grasp. Several terms treated at some length in the text, e.g., "myelin," "computers," "cerebral palsy," etc., are not listed in the index. The illustrations [by René Martin] are generally clear, though one depicts two native children apparently suffering from *kwashiorkor* (a protein deficiency) who seem to be nearly normal. Despite the above mentioned minor flaws, Zim's book will be useful for children not ready to tackle . . . more advanced and comprehensive works. . . .

> *Everett C. Sanborn, in* School Library Journal *(reprinted from* School Library Journal, *September, 1972, published by R. R. Bowker Co., a Xerox company; copyright © 1972 by Xerox Corporation), September, 1972, p. 87.*

OTHER CITATIONS

Zena Sutherland, in Bulletin of the Center for Children's Books, *October, 1972, p. 36.*

YOUR HEART AND HOW IT WORKS (1959)

In a straightforward fashion, Dr. Zim outlines [the heart's] capacity, structure, function, evolution, relationship to other organs, and the techniques with which science approaches it. Illustrated diagramatically by Gustav Schrotter, *Your Heart and How It Works*, like Herbert Zim's previous books, maintains a standard of clarity and factual generosity which recommends it as a valuable supplement to classroom study.

> Virginia Kirkus' Service, *August 15, 1959, p. 600.*

[*Your Heart and How It Works* is a] clearly written explanation of the anatomy and physiology of the human heart and the circulatory system. Although the title of the book does not indicate this, there is considerable attention devoted to the development of the heart as the organ that appears with increasing complexity in the lower species.

> *Zena Sutherland, in* Bulletin of the Center for Children's Books *(published by the University of Chicago), December, 1959, p. 71.*

YOUR STOMACH AND DIGESTIVE TRACT (1973)

[In *Your Stomach and Digestive Tract*, the] mechanical and chemical digestive processes that occur in the mouth, stomach, and small and large intestines are concisely explained in terms that are neatly geared to a child's understanding. . . . Zim also shows an awareness of what topics children are likely to wonder about—the mechanics of vomiting, the importance of "regularity," the source of the feces' color and odor, and the possible role in digestion of "good bacteria" from yogurt and buttermilk.

> Kirkus Reviews *(copyright © 1973 The Kirkus Service, Inc.), April 1, 1973, p. 394.*

[In *Your Stomach and Digestive Tract*, each] step of the process [of digestion] is described clearly, and the functions of the body organs involved are detailed. The digestive system in animals, vomiting, and effects of ulcers are also covered. This explanation of man's alimentary canal, accompanied by [René Martin's] black-and-white drawings, will complement the information found in the Silversteins' *The Digestive System: How Living Creatures Use Food.*

> *Marion F. Van Orsdale Gallivan, in* School Library Journal *(reprinted from* School Library Journal, *October, 1973, published by R. R. Bowker Co., a Xerox company; copyright © 1973 by Xerox Corporation), October, 1973, p. 122.*

OTHER CITATIONS

The Booklist, *November 1, 1973, p. 295.*

*   *   *

ZOLOTOW, Charlotte (Shapiro)   1915-

Charlotte Zolotow is an American editor, poet, and author of children's books. (See also *Contemporary Authors*, Vols. 5-8, rev. ed., and *Something About the Author*, Vol. 1.)

GENERAL COMMENTARY

Few writers for small children so empathize with them as does Charlotte Zolotow, whose books—with some exceptions—are really explorations of relationships cast in story form and given vitality by perfected simplicity of style and by the humor and tenderness of the stories. . . . [Her] understanding of children's emotional needs and problems, and her ability to express them with candor have made her one of the major contemporary writers of realistic books for small children.

> *May Hill Arbuthnot and Zena Sutherland, in their* Children and Books *(copyright © 1947, 1957, 1964, 1972 by Scott, Foresman and Co.), 4th edition, Scott, Foresman, 1972, p. 430.*

A FATHER LIKE THAT (1971)

A small boy whose father "went away before I was born" imagines—in variously sentimental and unlikely examples, with suitably washy-soft pictures [by Ben Schecter]—all the tender and supportive things his father, if he had one, would do. . . . It's a precocious child indeed who entertains such maudlin musings and a wise one who passes this by.

> Kirkus Reviews *(copyright © 1971 The Kirkus Service, Inc.), June 15, 1971, p. 640.*

The wistful catalog of perfection [presented in *A Father Like That*] is lightened by humor, and the soliloquy catches both a child's way of thinking and his way of expressing his thoughts. . . . The ending may not seem a solace to a child, and the phrase "in case he never comes" is rather ambiguous, since it isn't clear whether the real father may come back or a stepfather is being suggested, but the book in every other way has the same warmth and candor that has distinguished so many other small Zolotow gems.

> *Zena Sutherland, in* Bulletin of the Center for Children's Books (© *1971 by the University of Chicago; all rights reserved), September, 1971, p. 20.*

Charlotte Zolotow has written a book on a delicate subject seldom treated in children's books—the one-parent family. (That the ideal family includes both parents is stressed.) Though a gentle book, its impact on children is difficult to predict. Youngsters without fathers may become more aware of what they are missing while more fortunate children might complain that their fathers are still not "like that." Small, in format (6¾″ square), it's illustrated by Ben Schecter with soft colors to harmonize with the simple, childlike prose. It is best suited to reading aloud with small groups.

> *Patricia Vervoort, in* School Library Journal *(reprinted from* School Library Journal, *September, 1971, published by R. R. Bowker Co., a Xerox company; copyright © 1971 by Xerox Corporation), September, 1971, pp. 111-12.*

OTHER CITATIONS

Michael J. Bandler, in Book World, *November 7, 1971 (Part 2), p. 2.*

FLOCKS OF BIRDS (1965)

"Flocks of Birds," by Charlotte Zolotow, illustrated by Joan Berg . . ., becomes a lyrical bedtime story as a little girl's mother turns her thoughts to the birds flying south over people and mountains and rivers, as the sky itself wakes and sleeps. The simple, lulling poetry of the text conveys a sense of distance, time, and a soaring flight, while the illustrations are elegant and eloquent—and uneven.

> *Barbara Novak, in* The New York Times Book Review (© *1965 by The New York Times Company; reprinted by permission), November 7, 1965 (Part 2), p. 62.*

OTHER CITATIONS

Virginia Kirkus' Service, *August 1, 1965, p. 743.*

Gertrude B. Herman, in School Library Journal, *November, 1965, pp. 60-1.*

Priscilla L. Moulton, in The Horn Book Magazine, *December, 1965, p. 626.*

THE HATING BOOK (1969)

Although [*The Hating Book*] is a whit less smooth in style than most of the author's previous books, it has the same endearing quality of reflecting with fidelity the evanescent mood of a small child. The sprightly illustrations [by Ben Schecter] show a belligerent little girl who nurses her indignation with a catalog of her ex-friend's sins of commission.

> *Zena Sutherland, in* Bulletin of the Center for Children's Books (© *1970 by the University of Chicago; all rights reserved), September, 1970, p. 20.*

Very much a book for girls [*The Hating Book* is] about the kind of misunderstandings girls have and the ways they choose to demonstrate their animosity. It begins uncompromisingly, "I hate hate hated my friend", but in the end common sense prevails and friendship is restored. Ben Schecter's pen-and-wash drawings convey as sympathetically and effectively as Charlotte Zolotow's verse the attitudes and emotions of the characters.

> The Times Literary Supplement (© *Times Newspapers Ltd., 1972), November 3, 1972, p. 1333.*

OTHER CITATIONS

Jerome Beatty Jr., in The New York Times Book Review, *November 9, 1969, p. 68.*

IF IT WEREN'T FOR YOU (1966)

"If it weren't for you, I'd be the only child." So starts this book which then goes on to tell of all the advantages I would have, if I were an only child. The only mitigating circumstance comes on the last three pages: "But it's also true, I'd have to be alone with the grown-ups if it weren't for you." This weak ending certainly does not offset all the reasons given for the child preferring not to have a baby brother. [Russell] Hoban's *A Baby Sister for Frances* . . . and several others handle the sibling problem successfully where this picture book fails.

> School Library Journal *(reprinted from* School Library Journal, *September, 1966, published by R. R. Bowker Co., a Xerox company, copyright © 1966 by Xerox Corporation), September, 1966, p. 240.*

The loving X-ray Zolotow eye looks at dethronement [in *If It Weren't for You*]; a child ruefully lists the joys of life with no small brother. . . . The end isn't sugar-coated, but there is an admission that all is not gloom. [Ben Schecter's] illustrations are engaging; the text needs no plot, since it will probably awaken Instant Recognition Reflexes on every page. A percipient and charming book.

> *Zena Sutherland, in* Bulletin of the Center for Children's Books *(copyright 1966 by the University of Chicago; all rights reserved), October, 1966, p. 36.*

["If It Weren't for You"] makes me a little nervous. . . . [Its] purpose seems to be to incite fratricide. It is an illustrated enumeration of all the splendid things a boy could do and would have if it weren't for the existence of his little brother. Miss Zolotow has been commended by the Gesell Institute of Child Development, and maybe she and it know something we don't, but offhand "If It Weren't for You" seems to offer a dubious approach to the problem of sibling rivalry, and it makes one wonder whether our fears that a child may be "repressed" aren't founded on an exaggerated notion of his capacity for nastiness. One can be far from Wordsworthian about children and still give them a lot more credit for forbearance than this book of Miss Zolotow's does.

> *Janet Malcolm, in* The New Yorker (© *1966 by The New Yorker Magazine, Inc.), December 17, 1966, pp. 235-36.*

OTHER CITATIONS

Virginia Kirkus' Service, *May 15, 1966, p. 509.*

Zena Sutherland, in Saturday Review, *October 22, 1966, p. 61.*

IN MY GARDEN (1960)

[*In My Garden* is a] pleasant picture book in which a little girl describes what she likes best at different seasons of the year—especially what she likes best in her garden. . . . Limited in its appeal, it is not likely to be enjoyed by boys, and probably not by the child to whom the joys of a garden are unfamiliar. However, the appreciation of nature in its diversity, and the pattern of the seasons are told with relish and simplicity, and [Roger Duvoisin's] illustrations, both color and black and white, are attractive.

> *Zena Sutherland, in* Bulletin of the Center for Children's Books (*published by the University of Chicago; all rights reserved), November, 1960, p. 52.*

Children will like the details here in text and pictures showing a little girl's enjoyment of her garden through the seasons of a year. . . . Kindergarten teachers will find this an attractive and useful picture book to illustrate the changes of seasons. The drawings, half of them in full color, give strong impressions in a familiar Duvoisin manner.

> *Virginia Haviland, in* The Horn Book Magazine (*copyright, 1960, by the Horn Book, Inc., Boston), December, 1960, p. 507.*

OTHER CITATIONS

Saturday Review, *November 12, 1960, p. 96.*

JANEY (1973)

[Ronald Himler's pastel-colored] line drawings complement [Charlotte Zolotow's] simple text in a wistful evocation of a little girl's longing for her best friend who has moved away. . . . Although the lack of action or suspense will limit its appeal, it is, nevertheless, a book for sharing—and perhaps resolving—a common problem.

> *Mary M. Burns, in* The Horn Book Magazine (*copyright © 1973 by The Horn Book, Inc., Boston), October, 1973, p. 460.*

[*Janey* is a] gentle, wistful monologue by a child who

misses the best friend who has moved away. . . . Few writers see so clearly from the child's viewpoint, but this gentle liebeslied may not appeal to all children, since it has little humor or action; the appeal probably is to children old enough to have experienced a comparable situation rather than to the preschool child.

> *Zena Sutherland, in* Bulletin of the Center for Children's Books (© *1973 by the University of Chicago; all rights reserved), November, 1973, p. 56.*

There is certainly room for picture books aimed at children older than the pre-schoolers who are their usual recipients. But *Janey* is not a success. It is a tone poem, rather than a story, a soft-centred, very American celebration of the sadness of friends moving away. The whole text is fewer than 250 words. . . . The illustrations [by Ronald Himler] have a muted charm but faults too: the mother confuses by looking not a day over fifteen.

> The Times Literary Supplement (© *Times Newspapers Ltd., 1974), September 20, 1974, p. 1013.*

Beautifully written and beautifully illustrated [by Ronald Himler] this is in essence a very sad little book, full of a poignant expression of loss which makes it very moving. Perhaps a child does feel as intensely as this over the loss of a friend and suffers more through not being able to put into words what he is feeling, even to himself. This book, in crystallising the emotion, could help a child adjust to the loss of a friend, but it is such a very personal kind of story that it may be out of the emotional range of a lot of children. The gentle reflective style will possibly not involve children who prefer an action filled tale, but its poetic sensitivity makes it a book to remember long after reading it.

> *Sheila Pinder, in* Children's Book Review (© *1974 Five Owls Press Ltd.; all rights reserved), Autumn, 1974, p. 103.*

OTHER CITATIONS

Kirkus Reviews, *May 1, 1973, p. 513.*

Susanne Gilles, in School Library Journal, *September, 1973, p. 65.*

The Booklist, *October 1, 1973, p. 177.*

THE MAN WITH THE PURPLE EYES (1961)

There is an unusual combination here of reality and fancy that sometimes seems a bit strained, but is, nevertheless, haunting, and will probably have strong appeal to imaginative little girls. . . . Some of [Joe Lasker's] striking illustrations in black, white, and purple are sensitive and lovely.

> *Ruth Hill Viguers, in* The Horn Book Magazine (*copyright, 1961, by the Horn Book, Inc., Boston), August, 1961, p. 340.*

For the most part, the vocabulary in [*The Man with the Purple Eyes*] is not difficult, but the appeal would be greater to younger children; some of the passages are very long and the writing is slightly precious. A serious weakness in the story is that it makes too much of the drabness of the city.

Zena Sutherland, in Bulletin of the Center for Children's Books *(copyright 1962 by the University of Chicago; all rights reserved), May, 1962, p. 152.*

MY FRIEND JOHN (1968)

In *My Friend John* by Charlotte Zolotow, illustrated by Ben Schecter . . ., all the ramifications of friendship and what it means to two small boys are explored in a near-perfect picture book. Text and pictures are inseparable and together they show two personalities and how they complement each other. Their everyday life at home, at school, at the beach comes alive in pictures full of the warmth of understanding friendship and the fun of being a boy. The text, wisely sparse, uses only the words necessary for the mood.

Anne Izard, in Book World *(© The Washington Post), May 5, 1968 (Part 2), p. 6.*

OTHER CITATIONS

Kirkus Service, *February 1, 1968, p. 112.*

The Booklist and Subscription Books Bulletin, *May 15, 1968, p. 1097.*

Zena Sutherland, in Bulletin of the Center for Children's Books, *June, 1968, pp. 183-84.*

THE QUARRELING BOOK (1963)

[*The Quarreling Book* is a] small book, slight but appealing; the illustrations [by Arnold Lobel] are delightfully appropriate. . . . Children will enjoy the ravelling of the light plot and may be gratified at the admission that parents, like children, are affected by gloomy weather and gloomy behavior.

Zena Sutherland, in Bulletin of the Center for Children's Books *(copyright 1963 by the University of Chicago; all rights reserved), October, 1963, p. 36.*

OTHER CITATIONS

Carolyn H. Lavender, in The New York Times Book Review, *September 1, 1963, p. 12.*

Margaret Sherwood Libby, in Book Week, *October 13, 1963, p. 17.*

RIVER WINDING (1970)

[*River Winding* contains vapid] verses on nature, the seasons, some other things: 22 of them, trifles all, rhymed or unrhymed or awkwardly half-rhymed. They venture little, gain less: "Once we laughed together/ By the river side/ And watched the little waves/ Watched the waves.// Now I walk/ Along the bank/ The water's very blue/ And I am walking by the waves/ Walking by the waves/ Missing you." The book design lacks organization, unity; the poems just lack character.

Kirkus Reviews *(copyright © 1970 The Kirkus Service, Inc.), November 15, 1970, p. 1253.*

The quiet rhythmic flow of the [poems in *River Winding*] gently carries the reader with it through emotional areas many children only dimly perceive: the inevitability of living through memories in old age, the finality of death, estrangement from loved ones, and the knowledge of personal emotional change. . . . The pencil-gray, blue, or muted gold illustrations [by Regina Shekerjian] which accompany each poem are in perfect keeping with the tranquil tone of the book.

Sheryl B. Andrews, in The Horn Book Magazine *(copyright © 1971 by The Horn Book, Inc., Boston), February, 1971, p. 58.*

Autumn and the wind are recurring themes in these 22 short poems that are written in both rhyming and free verse styles. The accompanying illustrations [by Regina Shekerjian] are generally attractive, and, while some of the poems are imaginative and others are pedestrian, none are memorable.

Margaret Bush, in School Library Journal *(reprinted from* School Library Journal, *February, 1971, published by R. R. Bowker Co., a Xerox company; copyright © 1971 by Xerox Corporation), February, 1971, p. 78.*

Charlotte Zolotow . . . writes the kind of poetry that children write. She catches the fleeting moment as it passes and imprisons it in words. Her verses are frail and delicate. One readily acknowledges her sensitivity, and yet [*River Winding*] gives little pleasure. Like Regina Shekerjian's decorations the poems seem just a little over-refined, as if, in purging them of impurities, she has boiled out the goodness too.

Marcus Crouch, in The School Librarian, *September, 1971, p. 283.*

The poems [in *River Winding*] are short, simple; they have a Japanese quality in their imagery. Miss Zolotow does somehow catch a child's musing, and [Regina Shekerjian's] illustrations, though sometimes a trifle sentimental, complement the text admirably.

The Times Literary Supplement *(© Times Newspapers Ltd., 1971), October 22, 1971, pp. 1328-29.*

OTHER CITATIONS

Neil Millar, in The Christian Science Monitor, *May 6, 1971, p. B3.*

The Junior Bookshelf, *August, 1971, pp. 228-29.*

THE SKY WAS BLUE (1963)

"What was it like long ago? How did they feel?" The little girl in Charlotte Zolotow's "The Sky Was Blue" . . . asks these questions as she and her mother look in the family photograph album at pictures of mother, grandmother and great-grandmother. The answer is that important things never change. . . . Mrs. Zolotow ties the generations together in warm, affectionate and understandable fashion. The illustrations are appropriately soft and gentle, but they are not Garth Williams's best.

George A. Woods, in The New York Times Book Review (© *1963 by The New York Times Company; reprinted by permission), May 12, 1963 (Part 2), p. 5.*

Changes in styles of clothing, toys, and houses and in means of transportation through four generations are portrayed in a delightful manner as a little girl and her mother look through a photograph album. Children love to hear about what their parents did when they were children. They will be assured by the refrain that certain things, such as sky, grass, snow, sun, and feelings, do not change from one generation to another. Bright and cheerful illustrations [by Garth Williams] catch the mood of the story.

Dorothy M. King, in School Library Journal *(reprinted from* School Library Journal, *September, 1963, published by R. R. Bowker Co., a Xerox company; copyright © 1963 by Xerox Corporation), September, 1963, p. 159.*

OTHER CITATIONS

Margaret Sherwood Libby, in New York Herald Tribune Books, *May 12, 1968 (Sec. 12), p. 31.*

THE SUMMER NIGHT (1974)

[*The Summer Night* is a] revised edition of *The Night When Mother Was Away* (. . . 1958). The story of a father who patiently lulls his restless daughter to sleep now eliminates any mention of mother, inferring that this is a one-parent household. New illustrations by Ben Schecter depict a more equitable relationship—his father is younger and less self-assured than the one depicted by Reisie Lonnette, the little girl is older and more assertive than her cherubic predecessor—but the minor stylistic changes weaken Zolotow's original rhythmic prose. Those who cherished the first version for its luminous, dream-like illustrations and singing readability will find some of the magic missing from this "updated" remake of a pleasant bedtime tale.

Margaret Maxwell, in School Library Journal *(reprinted from* School Library Journal, *December, 1974, published by R. R. Bowker Co., a Xerox company; copyright © 1974 by Xerox Corporation), December, 1974, p. 159.*

Newly illustrated [by Ben Schecter], the book published in 1958 under the title *The Night Mother Was Away* now has softly tinted drawings that echo the gentle quality of the writing. . . . It isn't easy to establish mood in a book for children of the preschool group, but Zolotow achieves both a lulling sense of the night's still beauty and of the security of the relationship between father and child.

Zena Sutherland, in Bulletin of the Center for Children's Books (© *1975 by the University of Chicago; all rights reserved), February, 1975, p. 104.*

OTHER CITATIONS

Publishers' Weekly, September 30, 1974, p. 60.

Kirkus Reviews, October 15, 1974, p. 1101.

A TIGER CALLED THOMAS (1963)

A Hallowe'en picture book; pleasantly illustrated [by Kurt Werth], the story has a simple but satisfying plot, light writing style, and a gentle message. . . . [Zolotow] has handled mother's role very nicely: she is encouraging and patient, she doesn't force Thomas to make social overtures, and she doesn't hint at all at an I-told-you-so attitude when her child finds that Mother's prediction was right.

Zena Sutherland, in Bulletin of the Center for Children's Books *(copyright 1963 by the University of Chicago; all rights reserved), November, 1963, p. 52.*

OTHER CITATIONS

George A. Woods, in The New York Times Book Review, *October 27, 1963, p. 39.*

THE UNFRIENDLY BOOK (1975)

In this companion to *The Quarreling Book* (. . . 1963), Zolotow once again seizes on the real substance of children's social (and unsocial) relations. . . . Zolotow's message—what we see in other people depends on the bias of our own perceptions—is adroitly framed in [William] Péne du Bois' black-and-white illustrations which show each of Judy's friends through Bertha's critical eyes and then as Judy sees them. Unfortunately, Judy and Bertha with their purebred dogs look more like a pair of junior fashion mannequins than real-life, little girls.

Janet French, in School Library Journal *(reprinted from* School Library Journal, *April, 1975, published by R. R. Bowker Co., a Xerox company; copyright © 1975 by Xerox Corporation), April, 1975, p. 48.*

OTHER CITATIONS

Zena Sutherland, in Bulletin of the Center for Children's Books, *February, 1975, p. 104.*

Publishers' Weekly, February 24, 1975, p. 115.

WAKE UP AND GOODNIGHT (1971)

Leonard Weisgard's colorful illustrations effectively portray day and night scenes suggested by [Zolotow's] brief text. . . . The text, which is in the style of a chant, is uneven, however, and quite mediocre. Some of the lines are pleasantly poetic ("goodnight/ goodnight goodnight/ the golden sun is down/ the purple sky turns black/ the moon is pale"), but most are very ordinary ("wake up wake up wake up/ the trees are winging/ the birds are singing/ things are thinging").

Mary B. Mason, in School Library Journal *(reprinted from* School Library Journal, *May, 1971, published by R. R. Bowker Co., a Xerox company; copyright © 1971 by Xerox Corporation), May, 1971, p. 62.*

[*Wake Up and Goodnight*] shines with the delight and wonder of the world and living, and of the dreaminess of night, waiting for day to come again. Charlotte Zolotow's brief, poetic text is perfectly matched by Leonard Weisgard's sensitive paintings filled with brilliant sunshine, warm greens, and evening blues. This is a beautiful job of bookmaking.

> *Elizabeth Minot Graves, in* Commonweal *(copyright © 1971 Commonweal Publishing Co., Inc.), May 21, 1971, p. 263.*

Bright and clear in the morning light, [Leonard Weisgard's] pictures show a child greeting the new day. . . . The theme is expanded, then abruptly, with the turn of a page there are dark twilight colors. . . . The quiet pages of night scenes and cozy interiors are broken by a bright picture of a dream scene, and back to the purple still of the night. The text is evocative, simple, and deft, and the pictures very attractive but the shift in mood is often visually abrupt.

> *Zena Sutherland, in* Bulletin of the Center for Children's Books *(© 1971 by the University of Chicago; all rights reserved), September, 1971, p. 20.*

[This is an] ordinary book in the sense that [Weisgard's] simple pictures are of the day to day objects of a young child's life; a bed, a leaf, a bird, the moon. It is extraordinary only in that [Zolotow] has an astute perception of what the small child knows instinctively is important to him in that quickening moment when he awakens or at the end of the day when he slips into sleep and dreams. The poetry of the words and pictures will make any preschool child wriggle his toes with delight and wonder at this perfect mirror of domestic bliss.

> The Junior Bookshelf, *December, 1972, p. 372.*

OTHER CITATIONS

Kirkus Reviews, *April 1, 1971, p. 360.*

Selma G. Lanes, in Book World, *May 9, 1971 (Part 2), p. 6.*

The Booklist, *September 1, 1971, p. 61.*

WHEN I HAVE A LITTLE GIRL (1965)

In small books like this, the humor is often either all adult or all child. The blend in this one is perfect for shared laughter. These are the temptations and frustrations that girls have inherited. It staggers, while it delights, the imagination that all the way back to Neanderthal days, mothers were probably restraining their daughters from tickling the fox-faced furs of the imposing ladies in front of them.

> Virginia Kirkus' Service *(copyright © 1965 Virginia Kirkus' Service, Inc.), October 15, 1965, p. 1075.*

"When I have a little girl, she can wear party dresses to school. She can be fresh to unpleasant people." This little picture book details many more deliciously naughty things the small girl telling the story would, of course, love to do herself. The list is rather long, however, to hold the interest of preschoolers who may prefer to think up some of their own ideas before the story ends. "And I will never say to her, 'When you are a mother you will understand why all these rules are necessary.' My mother says her mother used to say it too" is something of a let-down as an ending.

> *Janet Hellerich, in* School Library Journal *(reprinted from* School Library Journal, *December, 1965, published by R. R. Bowker Co., a Xerox company; copyright © 1965 by Xerox Corporation), December, 1965, p. 68.*

OTHER CITATIONS

Zena Sutherland, in Bulletin of the Center for Children's Books, *January, 1966, p. 92.*

WHEN I HAVE A SON (1967)

Sort of a child's version of "Soliloquy" from *Carousel*, [*When I Have a Son*] genuinely captures a small boy's notion of freedom from bondage to the bothersome rituals of childhood—the narrator-lad promises that *his* son won't have to have *his* hair cut at regular intervals (or ever, perhaps)—and of the privileges that mark a fella's coming of age (like having a key all his own and being able to order triple malteds just before supper). Hilary Knight's pictures have a Norman Rockwell verisimilitude to them that is apt here.

> *Richard Kluger, in* Book World *(© The Washington Post), November 5, 1967 (Part 2), p. 6.*

[*When I Have a Son* is a] small book, very funny and often touching; the innocent ferocity of [Hilary Knight's] illustrations are (as they are in the author's companion piece, *When I Have a Little Girl*) an added pleasure. . . . The whole thing is so engagingly absurd it might even make a small boy see what's funny in his own behavior.

> *Zena Sutherland, in* Bulletin of the Center for Children's Books *(copyright 1968 by The University of Chicago; all rights reserved), March, 1968, p. 120.*

OTHER CITATIONS

Jean Pretorius, in School Library Journal, *October, 1967, pp. 168-69.*

Kirkus Service, *October 1, 1967, p. 1203.*

Patience M. Daltry, in The Christian Science Monitor, *November 2, 1967, p. B5.*

Ursula Nordstrom, in Saturday Review, *November 11, 1967, p. 41.*

WHEN THE WIND STOPS (1962)

This could almost be the transcript of any young child's day at that stage when the answer to any question is the immediate stimulus for a further inquiry. Why does the day end? Where does the sun go? What happens to the candle flame? Mrs. Zolotow handles her subjects with a tender lyricism, building a picture of the continuous change and re-forming through which the world passes. Her book presents very tellingly that sense of pantheism which is the beginning of religious experience.

Valerie Millington, in The School Librarian and School Library Review, *July, 1964, p. 223.*

[This] quietly reassuring book which will be a good bedtime story for young children. First published in 1962 with illustrations by Joe Lasker . . ., the minor changes tighten the author's prose and the original cartoon-like figures and bright colors seem harsh beside the muted tenderness of [Howard] Knotts' black-and-white pencil sketches.

Margaret Maxwell, in School Library Journal *(reprinted from* School Library Journal, *November, 1975, published by R. R. Bowker Co., a Xerox company; copyright © 1975 by Xerox Corporation), November, 1975, p. 68.*

This quiet story of a boy whose mother explains to him that the end of one thing is the beginning of another is a much improved update of the original edition first published in 1962. Serene pencil sketches [by Howard Knotts] replace the harsh scrawled crayon-pencil drawings of the original [by Joe Lasker], and some minor editing has improved the flow of the text.

The Booklist *(reprinted by permission of the American Library Association; copyright 1975 by the American Library Association), November 15, 1975, p. 459.*

OTHER CITATIONS

Kirkus Reviews, *November 1, 1975, pp. 1126-27.*

THE WHITE MARBLE (1963)

At first, ["The White Marble"] is thoroughly enchanting— but, imperceptibly, the magic wears thin. John Henry's lovely hour with Pamela was too ephemeral for so much artful scrutiny; it seems to shrivel like a wildflower between the pages. Perhaps, in the long run, there is something unpleasantly narcissistic about focusing a child reader's attention on the unselfconscious privacy of children.

[Lilian Obligado's] illustrations are quite as delightful initially and quite as exasperating in the end, from a similar excess of sentimentality. . . . "The White Marble" has all the charm of a groomed and cosseted lapdog; little of the inconvenient humanity of a child.

Mary Louise Birmingham, in The New York Times Book Review *(© 1963 by The New York Times Company; reprinted by permission), November 10, 1963 (Part 2), p. 49.*

[The White Marble *is an] unusual picture book in mood and treatment. . . . [This is a] fragile story that captures the charm of an evanescent moment, but one which will be less appreciated by children than by adults; only the unusually

sensitive child will enjoy the gentle mood rather than finding the book static.

Zena Sutherland, in Bulletin of the Center for Children's Books *(copyright 1964 by the University of Chicago; all rights reserved), January, 1964, p. 88.*

WILLIAM'S DOLL (1972)

[William's Doll *is an]* attempt to overcome sex stereotypes in a small picture book that seems as much a lecture for rigid parents as a reassurance for nonconforming boys. . . . William Pène Du Bois' pictures complement the gentle mood [of Zolotow's text] while softly emphasizing that William is quite a hand with the basketball too—and if you find Ms. Zolotow's tender affirmations substantial enough for girls, there's no reason to withhold them from little brother.

Kirkus Reviews *(copyright © 1972 The Kirkus Service, Inc.), May 1, 1972, p. 535.*

The warmth and humor of [William Pène du Bois'] illustrations, the clean look of the pages, and the simplicity and restraint of [Charlotte Zolotow's] writing style are in perfect agreement in a book that is as endearing for its tenderness as for the message it conveys: there is nothing, but nothing wrong with boys who play with dolls.

Zena Sutherland, in Bulletin of the Center for Children's Books *(© 1972 by the University of Chicago; all rights reserved), July-August, 1972, p. 180.*

Occasionally, the story line has been strained to make its point: William's wishing for a doll might be natural, but William's description of this doll . . . seems overdone. Yet, [Charlotte Zolotow's] story and [William Pène du Bois'] illustrations have been infused with a sweet and gentle air, and both illustrations and text remain as soft and wispy as the pastels used in the drawings. Consequently, whether one likes the message or not, little about the book offends the reader. In fact, by their placing of a contemporary issue in the packaging of such an absolutely old-fashioned, charming book, the author and illustrator have demonstrated their skill.

Anita Silvey, in The Horn Book Magazine *(copyright © 1972 by The Horn Book, Inc., Boston), December, 1972, p. 584.*

OTHER CITATIONS

Shirley Williams, in The New York Times Book Review, *May 7, 1972 (Part 2), p. 39.*

Publishers' Weekly, *May 22, 1972, p. 51.*

Zena Sutherland, in Saturday Review, *June 17, 1972, p. 72.*

Melinda Schroeder, in School Library Journal, *September, 1972, pp. 73-4.*

CUMULATIVE INDEX TO AUTHORS

CUMULATIVE INDEX TO TITLES

CUMULATIVE INDEX TO CRITICS